Local Customs and Common Laws

Legal History Library

VOLUME 67

The titles published in this series are listed at *brill.com/lhl*

Local Customs and Common Laws

Essays on the Law Governing Maritime Commerce in Sixteenth-Century Scotland

By

J.D. Ford

BRILL | NIJHOFF

LEIDEN | BOSTON

Cover illustration: *Beschrijvinge van een deel vann Schottlandt van Bambourg tot Aberdein*, Lucas Janszoon Waghenaer (1583). Reproduced by permission of the National Library of Scotland.

The Library of Congress Cataloging-in-Publication Data is available online at https://catalog.loc.gov
LC record available at https://lccn.loc.gov/2024015069

Typeface for the Latin, Greek, and Cyrillic scripts: "Brill". See and download: brill.com/brill-typeface.

ISSN 1874-1793
ISBN 978-90-04-69499-6 (hardback)
ISBN 978-90-04-69500-9 (e-book)
DOI 10.1163/9789004695009

This book is printed on acid-free paper and produced in a sustainable manner.

Contents

Preface

This collection of essays may be viewed to some extent as a companion volume to the same author's *The Emergence of Privateering*, published by Brill in 2023, since the writing of both books arose from his editing of *Alexander King's Treatise on Maritime Law*, published by the Stair Society in 2018. The writer of that sixteenth-century treatise devoted two chapters to discussion of the law governing the raiding of enemy shipping in wartime and the taking of reprisals in peacetime, and he planned to write a further chapter on illegal seizures by pirates, all topics dealt with in the 2023 book. King devoted several other chapters to discussion of the law governing maritime commerce in Scotland, examining topics dealt with in this book. However, whereas the 2023 book was designed to address a single question – how did privateering emerge as a new category of maritime raiding, distinct from the three categories that interested King? – and looked beyond sixteenth-century Scotland, this collection is designed to explore various aspects of the commercial law applied to shipping in that period and place, with different essays addressing different questions. Apart from the final essay, which attempts to draw conclusions from the preceding ten, each essay ought to make sense if read in isolation from the others. Nevertheless, the collection as a whole does have a unifying concern. If the contrast between the wartime raiding discussed by King and the wartime raiding later known as privateering demanded an explanation, there is also a significant difference between the commercial law discussed by King and the commercial law applied in the courts of the coastal towns of Scotland, which again demands an explanation. After an introductory essay concerned with discovering which courts tended to handle disputes over maritime trade, the first part of the collection contains essays on the law applied in the courts of the coastal towns, although the third essay in that part also considers the law applied in other courts. The second part of the collection contains essays on the writing of treatises by King and two of his contemporaries, and the third part contains essays on the relationship between the law of the towns and the law in the treatises. The conclusions drawn in the final essay are also concerned with this relationship, primarily between local customs and the *ius commune* taught in the European universities, although other types of common law are also considered.

Versions of four of the essays included in this collection have been published before. The second appeared in J.W. Armstrong and E.B.I. Frankot (eds), *Cultures of Law in Urban Northern Europe: Scotland and Its Neighbours, c. 1350-c. 1650* (London, 2021), the sixth in the *Journal of Legal History* in 2013, the ninth in

P. Hellwege and G. Rossi (eds), *Maritime Risk Management: Essays on the History of Marine Insurance, General Average and Sea Loan* (Berlin, 2021), and the tenth in A.R.C. Simpson and J.Ø. Sunde (eds), *Comparative Perspectives in Scottish and Norwegian Legal History, Trade and Seafaring, 1200–1800* (Edinburgh, 2023). Most were written in response to invitations to speak on specific topics at conferences, and the author is grateful both for those invitations and for permission to reprint the essays here, as well as for comments made by other participants in the conferences and by publishers' readers. Although the sixth essay was not written for a conference, instructive comments were again made when the topic was discussed at a meeting of the Scottish Legal History Group in 2013. Other essays owe something to papers presented at a 'Workshop on Practicks' in Aberdeen (the fifth) and at the British Legal History Conference in St Andrews (the fourth and seventh), and on these occasions too helpful comments were made. A few suggestions made in the final essay received an even more tentative airing at a conference held in Edinburgh shortly before the arrival of COVID-19. The essays previously published appear in a form closer to the versions originally written, and take more account of primary sources, but no attempt has been made to take further account of secondary sources published since their first appearance. Given the origins of most essays in a *pièce d'occasion*, there is inevitably a certain amount of repetition in the collection as a whole, as well as some revision of earlier thought, though not (it is believed) contradiction.

Especially when the restrictions imposed in response to the arrival of COVID-19 started to be relaxed, great assistance was received from archivists and librarians, some of whom had gone to some trouble to make sources available even while the restrictions were in place, and many of whom had already been very helpful before the restrictions were imposed. Further assistance has been received from Alessandra Giliberto, who as well as providing invaluable advice also arranged for a draft of the book to be read by anonymous experts, who suggested several improvements. The production process has been surprisingly painless for the author, thanks to the efforts of Petra Stiglmayer and David Aberra. It goes without saying that the author is deeply grateful to all these people for the help they have provided.

Abbreviations

Use is made of the following abbreviations in the citation of manuscript sources in footnotes to the essays, where a code is given for the archive or library holding the source, followed by a code for the source, which should be recognisable to the relevant archivists or librarians if readers request access to the source.

AYRSHIRE ARCHIVES (AA)

B6/11	court and council records of Ayr
B6/12	burgh court books of Ayr
B6/18	council minutes of Ayr

ABERDEEN CITY ARCHIVES (ACA)

CA1/1	council register of Aberdeen
CA2/1	register of sasines of Aberdeen
CA2/2	register of deeds of Aberdeen
CA5/1	bailie court books of Aberdeen

ABERDEEN UNIVERSITY LIBRARY (AUL)

MS 3070	papers of the Shipmasters Society of Aberdeen

BRITISH LIBRARY (BL)

Add. MS 12504	*De officio admiralitatis Angliae*
Add. MS 29439	*De officio admiralitatis Angliae*
Add. MS 48050	Latin digest of the 'auld lawes' of Scotland
Harley MS 2222	*De officio admiralitatis Angliae*
Lansdowne MS 142	papers relating to the English admiralty
Sloane MS 1605	*De officio admiralitatis Angliae*

CAMBRIDGE UNIVERSITY LIBRARY (CUL)

Ee.4.21	collection of the 'auld lawes' of Scotland
Kk.1.5(4)	collection of the 'auld lawes' of Scotland

DUMFRIES ARCHIVES CENTRE (DAC)

WC4	court and council records of Dumfries

DUNDEE CITY ARCHIVES (DCA)

BCMB	burgh court minute books of Dundee
GBD	guildry book of Dundee
MBBC	minute books of the burgh council of Dundee
PBD	protocol books of Dundee

DUMBARTONSHIRE HERITAGE CENTRE (DHC)

DB1/10	town clerk's records of Dumbarton (general series)
10/20/16	register of ship entries at Dumbarton

EDINBURGH CITY ARCHIVES (ECA)

SL1/1	council register of Edinburgh
SL144/1	dean of guild court books of Edinburgh
SL234/1	bailie court books of Edinburgh

ELGIN LIBRARY (EL)

BCBE	burgh court books of Elgin

EAST LOTHIAN ARCHIVE CENTRE (ELAC)

B30/9	burgh court books of Haddington
B30/10	burgh court books of Haddington
B30/13	council register of Haddington

EDINBURGH UNIVERSITY LIBRARY (EUL)

La. III 381a	Scots digest of the 'auld lawes' of Scotland
La. III 408	reorganisation of Balfour's practicks
La. III 741	King's treatise on maritime law

FIFE COUNCIL ARCHIVES (FCA)

B/CUL/1/1	council minutes of Culross
B/KDY/2/1	burgh court books of Kirkcaldy

FOLGER SHAKESPEARE LIBRARY (FSL)

V.a.379	King's treatise on maritime law

GLASGOW CITY ARCHIVES (GCA)

C1/1	council register of Glasgow

HIGHLAND ARCHIVE CENTRE (HAC)

B1/1	burgh court books of Inverness

HUNTER LIBRARY (HL)

A1/19	burgh court books of Arbroath

HARVARD LAW SCHOOL LIBRARY (HLSL)

MS 6026	King's treatise on maritime law

MAGDALENE COLLEGE LIBRARY (MCL)

PL2208	Welwod's abridgement of all sea laws

NATIONAL ARCHIVES AT KEW (NAK)

C66	patent rolls of the English chancery
SP12	letters and papers of the English secretaries of state
SP14	letters and papers of the English secretaries of state
SP16	transcripts of documents relating to the English admiralty
SP52	state papers (domestic) of the reign of Elizabeth

NATIONAL LIBRARY OF SCOTLAND (NLS)

Acc. 11218/5	collection of the 'auld lawes' of Scotland
Adv. MS 7.1.9	collection of the 'auld lawes' of Scotland
Adv. MS 7.1.10	collection of the 'auld lawes' of Scotland
Adv. MS 22.3.4	practicks (Colville and Haddington)

Adv. MS 24.1.5	practicks (Colville)
Adv. MS 24.2.4b	practicks (Balfour)
Adv. MS 25.2.5(1)	abridgement of the acts of sederunt of the lords of council and session
Adv. MS 25.2.7	abridgement of the acts of sederunt of the lords of council and session
Adv. MS 25.4.11	Latin digest of the 'auld lawes' of Scotland
Adv. MS 25.4.12	collection of the 'auld lawes' of Scotland
Adv. MS 25.5.6	collection of the 'auld lawes' of Scotland
Adv. MS 25.5.8	collection of the 'auld lawes' of Scotland
Adv. MS 25.5.9	collection of the 'auld lawes' of Scotland
Adv. MS 25.5.10	collection of the 'auld lawes' of Scotland
Adv. MS 25.9.7(1)	collection of the 'auld lawes' of Scotland
Adv. MS 28.4.7	King's treatise on maritime law
Adv. MS 31.4.9	notes on the council register of Edinburgh
MS 941	minute book of the society of mariners of Ayr
MS 1948	King's treatise on maritime law
MS 9931	miscellaneous correspondence
MS 16497	collection of the 'auld lawes' of Scotland

NATIONAL RECORDS OF SCOTLAND (NRS)

B6/1	protocol books of Ayr
B9/1	protocol books of Burntisland
B9/10	court and council records of Burntisland
B9/11	burgh court books of Burntisland
B19/1	notaries' minute books of Dundee
B20/10	burgh court books of Dunfermline
B21/1	protocol books of Dysart
B21/8	burgh court books of Dysart
B22/23	burgh court book of Edinburgh
B34/1/1	protocol book of Inverkeithing
B34/11/1	guildry minutes of Inverkeithing
B37/12	council records of Irvine
B48/7	council register of Linlithgow
B48/8	burgh court books of Linlithgow
B51/1	protocol books of Montrose
B51/10	burgh court books of Montrose
B72/5	court and council records of Wigtown
CC13/7	register of deeds of the commissariot of Kirkcudbright
CC20/11	register of deeds of the commissariot of St Andrews
CH2	kirk session records

CS1	books of sederunt of the lords of council and session
CS4	warrants of the books of sederunt of the lords of council and session
CS5	register of acts and decreets of the lords of council and session
CS6	register of acts and decreets of the lords of council and session
CS7	register of acts and decreets of the lords of council and session
GD1/47/1	documents relating to Montrose
GD1/413/15	notes on the court and council records of Dunbar
GD3/9/1	grant of admiralty jurisdiction over Cunningham
GD45/26/50	King's treatise on maritime law
GD63/37	foundation of bursary in memory of Martin Balfour
GD106/135	James Brown Craven bequest
GD111/3/8	receipt granted by Robert Douglas, servant of the duke of Lennox
GD112/71/5	Scots digest of the 'auld lawes' of Scotland
GD124/1/565	summons at the instance of Thomas Nudry, witnessed by John Nudry
GD150	Morton papers
GD220/1/F/8/4/1	charter granted to the duke of Lennox as admiral of Scotland
GD220/1/G/2/2/1	ratification of the duke of Lennox's infeftment as admiral
GD220/1/G/2/2/2	renunciation of admiralty rights by the duke of Lennox
NP1	protocol books of notaries public
NP2	admission register of notaries public
PA5/3	collection of the 'auld lawes' of Scotland
PC1	register of acts of the privy council
PS1	register of the privy seal
RD1	register of deeds of the lords of council and session
RH9	miscellaneous papers (foreign)

PERTH AND KINROSS COUNCIL ARCHIVES (PKCA)

B59/12	burgh court books of Perth
B59/13	burgh court register of decreets of Perth

ST ANDREWS UNIVERSITY LIBRARY (SAUL)

B10/8	burgh court books of Crail
B13/10	court and council records of Cupar
B65/8	burgh court books of St Andrews
msKF51.R4	collection of the 'auld lawes' of Scotland

STIRLING COUNCIL ARCHIVES (SCA)

SBC11/1	council minutes of Stirling
SBC37/1	burgh court books of Stirling

The following abbreviations are used in references to the basic sources of the civil and canon laws, which will be found in the *Corpus iuris civilis*, 3 vols, ed. T. Mommsen, P. Krüger, R. Schoell and G. Kroll (Berlin, 1872–7), and the *Corpus iuris canonici*, 2 vols, ed. A. Friedberg (Leipzig, 1879–81). Civil law sources are cited by book, title, text and section numbers, preceded by D. for *Digest*, J. for *Institutes*, C. for *Code* and N. for *Novels*. References to the *Decretum* are by *distinctio* (D.) and *capitulum* (c.), or – in the second part – by *causa* (C.), *quaestio* (q.) and *capitulum* (c.). References to the *Liber extra* are by book, title and chapter numbers, preceded by X.

Glossary

As some readers may struggle with quotations from sources written in early-modern Scots, the meanings of the more difficult terms are listed here, though generally a little reflection will reveal that the words quoted are variants of familiar English words, especially if it is remembered that 'quh' was equivalent to 'wh'. The meanings given below are those that the words appear to have had in the passages quoted. Fuller information may be found in W. Craigie, A.J. Aitken, J.A.C. Stevenson, H.D. Watson and M.G. Dareau (eds), *A Dictionary of the Older Scottish Tongue from the Twelfth Century to the End of the Seventeenth*, 12 vols (Chicago, London and Aberdeen, 1931–2002).

afor before
alanerlie only
anent about or concerning
astrickit bound
avail value or validity
ay always or continually
bludstouth violent theft
boist threat or to threaten
brokett drink made of ale and honey
brouke to have or enjoy something
by without
caution guarantee
childer crew
conduce to hire
cordell rope
coy cabin bed
cummer trouble or disturbance
dailisman charterer of ship
effer to belong or pertain to something
eik to add
equipage crew
feilzie failure or to fail
fure to carry or transport
graith equipment of ship
how hull
ilk each
kippage crew

lafe rest or remainder
leasum permissible or licit
ma more
mekill much or many
nor than
oncost overhead
or before
oupset to compensate
ourelop deck above hold of ship
outred to fit out or equip a ship
poind to distrain goods
prymgilt levy on loading or unloading of goods
quhilk which
quhill until
quhinzear short sword
raiff robbery
reidschip equipment of ship
replege to withdraw action to own court from another
ring to prevail
rive to tear, rip or rend something
roup aution or to auction
samekle as much or many
sic such
skaith harm or damage
sleuth sloth or negligence
spil to spoil or destroy, specifically to spill, something
stouth theft
syn then
tane the one of two
thir these
thole to permit or tolerate
thrang busy activity or overcrowding
till to
tinsale loss
toder the other of two
tow cable
tyne to lose
unlaw fine for misdemeanour
ward to distrain person
ware to expend money generally, to buy and sell goods particularly

warrandyse warranty
wathe hunting or fishing
werklum tool or implement
wier seaweed

Introduction

1

Overseas Trade and Maritime Jurisdiction in Sixteenth-Century Scotland

It was stated in the *Leges burgorum* that if a dispute arose after a ship from another country arrived at a Scottish port, it was to be dealt with there by officials referred to as the king's bailies (*ballivi domini regis*).[1] This particular provision, already part of the *Leges burgorum* when the earliest surviving collections of the 'auld lawes' of Scotland started to circulate towards the end of the thirteenth century, had been reinforced by an act of parliament passed in the fifteenth century.[2] The act required every contract for the carriage of goods by sea, wherever it was concluded, not only to be set down in writing in the form of a 'charter party', but also to contain an undertaking that, were a dispute to arise, the parties would 'undirly the jurisdiccioune and ordinance of the burghe quharto the schip is frachtit'.[3] Both this second requirement and the provision of the *Leges burgorum* behind it are perfectly intelligible given that another act passed on the same day reaffirmed the long-established rule that the king's subjects were not permitted to participate in overseas trade unless they were 'fremen, burges dwelland within burghe'.[4] That rule was bound up with a restriction on foreign mariners and merchants, who were forbidden from unloading goods anywhere in Scotland other than a burgh.[5] In fact, the monopoly over international commerce entailed by these rules was further limited to royal and ecclesiastical burghs, as opposed to burghs of barony

1 *The Acts of the Parliaments of Scotland*, 12 vols, ed. T. Thomson and C. Innes (Edinbrugh, 1814–75), vol. 1, p. 337; *The Ancient Laws and Customs of the Burghs of Scotland*, 2 vols, ed. C. Innes and R. Renwick (Edinburgh, 1868–1910), vol. 1, p. 13.

2 H.L. MacQueen and W.J. Windram, 'Law and Courts in the Burghs', in M. Lynch, M. Spearman and G. Stell (eds), *The Scottish Medieval Town* (Edinburgh, 1988), p. 208, at pp. 209–11; A. Taylor, *The Laws of Medieval Scotland: Legal Compilations from the Thirteenth and Fourteenth Centuries* (Edinburgh, 2019), pp. 8 and 37.

3 *Acts of the Parliaments of Scotland*, vol. 2, p. 87; Records of the Parliaments of Scotland, ed. K.M. Brown (www.rps.ac.uk), 1467/1/4.

4 *Acts of the Parliaments of Scotland*, vol. 2, p. 86; Records of the Parliaments of Scotland, 1467/1/1.

5 T. Keith, 'The Trading Privileges of the Royal Burghs of Scotland', (1913) 28 *English Historical Review* 454 and 678, at pp. 454–5; W.M. Mackenzie, *The Scottish Burghs* (Edinburgh, 1949), pp. 67–9; T.M. Devine, 'Scotland', in P. Clark (ed.), *The Cambridge Urban History of Britain, Volume II, 1540–1840* (Cambridge, 2000), p. 151, at p. 153.

 | DOI:10.1163/9789004695009_002

and regality.[6] In contrast to many other European countries, where comparable restrictions had been abandoned, the royal and ecclesiastical burghs of Scotland were still able to maintain their monopoly at the end of the sixteenth century.[7] If overseas trade was thus limited to royal and ecclesiastical burghs, it would make obvious sense for disputes arising from the transportation of goods to have continued to be dealt with by the bailies or other officials of those situated at the coasts. But is this what happened? The first section of this essay considers in more detail where overseas trade was actually conducted in sixteenth-century Scotland, before attention turns in the next three sections to where maritime jurisdiction was actually exercised. In the fifth and final section, after conclusions have been drawn about where disputes arising from overseas trade were resolved, consideration is given to where information about the law applied to these disputes may now be found.

1 Overseas Trade in the Coastal Burghs

In the absence of continuous records of the payment of customs duties on imports, which were not imposed generally until the end of the sixteenth century, the evidence of ships arriving in Scotland is fragmentary, though not insubstantial.[8] Continuous records of the payment of export duties on staple goods are available, however, and they show that after a prolonged slump in the fourteenth and fifteenth centuries, overseas trade was beginning to revive before the disruption of the Rough Wooings in the 1540s and the Reformation in the 1560s.[9] These records do not always identify the ports through which

6 I.H. Adams, *The Making of Urban Scotland* (London, 1978), pp. 40–1; R. Fox, 'Urban Development, 1100–1700', in G. Whittington and I.D. Whyte (eds), *An Historical Geography of Scotland* (London, 1983), p. 73, at p. 83; E.P. Dennison, *The Evolution of Scotland's Towns: Creation, Growth and Fragmentation* (Edinburgh, 2018), p. 113.

7 In the 1590s, for example, the authorities in Aberdeen were able to obstruct efforts to engage in overseas trade a few miles further north at Newburgh (*Extracts from the Council Register of the Burgh of Aberdeen*, 2 vols, ed. J. Stuart (Aberdeen, 1844–8), vol. 2, p. 81; ACA, CA1/1/38, p. 58, CA5/1/4, 13 August 1595, and CA5/1/5, 7 May 1597.).

8 It is evidence of this type that informs the older studies of maritime trade, including I.F. Grant, *The Social and Economic Development of Scotland before 1603* (Edinburgh, 1930), pp. 305–65; S.G.E. Lythe, *The Economy of Scotland in Its European Setting, 1550–1625* (Edinburgh, 1960), pp. 116–246; S.G.E. Lythe and J. Butt, *An Economic History of Scotland, 1100–1939* (Glasgow, 1975), pp. 54–64.

9 The pioneering study of these records was A.L. Murray, 'The Customs Accounts of Kirkcudbright, Wigtown and Dumfries, 1434–1560', (1961–2) 40 *Transactions of the Dumfries and Galloway Archaeological Society* 136, which was followed up in P.G.B. McNeill and H.L. MacQueen (eds), *Atlas of Scottish History to 1707* (Edinburgh, 1996), pp. 238–65.

goods passed out of the country, but they do indicate that traditional staples such as hides, wool, cloth and fish continued to be exported, together with newer products such as coal and salt, and that the volume of exports rose again in the last quarter of the sixteenth century, albeit never to a high level by European standards.[10] Ships returning from Norway tended to carry timber, which was no longer readily available in the more populous parts of Scotland.[11] Timber was also imported in smaller quantities from various places in the Baltic region, along with grain, hemp, iron, pitch and tar.[12] Manufactured items tended to be brought back from ports in the Netherlands and northern France, together with fruit and spices, and wine and salt were imported in surprisingly large quantities from southern France (the imported salt was more suitable for curing fish than the salt produced locally, while the amount of wine imported suggests that it was not only fish that got pickled).[13] Trade with Spain was starting to develop towards the end of the century, especially after markets there

For a more recent review of the records see M. Rorke, 'The Scottish Customs Books as a Source for 16th-Century Mercantile Studies', (2005) 11 *Scottish Archives* 90.

10 I. Guy, 'The Scottish Export Trade, 1460–1599', in T.C. Smout (ed.), *Scotland and Europe, 1200–1850* (Edinburgh, 1986), p. 62; I.D. Whyte, *Scotland before the Industrial Revolution: An Economic and Social History, c. 1050-c. 1750* (Harlow, 1995), pp. 271–4; D. Ditchburn, *Scotland and Europe: The Medieval Kingdom and Its Contacts with Christendom, 1214–1560* (East Linton, 2000), pp. 138–96; M. Rorke, 'Scottish Overseas Trade, 1275/86–1597', PhD dissertation, University of Edinburgh, 2001, 'The Scottish Herring Trade, 1470–1600', (2005) 84 *Scottish Historical Review* 149, and 'English and Scottish Overseas Trade, 1300–1600', (2006) 59 *Economic History Review* 265.

11 A. Lillehammer, 'The Scottish-Norwegian Timber Trade in the Stavanger Area in the Sixteenth and Seventeenth Centuries', in Smout (ed.), *Scotland and Europe*, p. 97; D. Ditchburn, 'Cargoes and Commodities: Aberdeen's Trade with Scandinavia and the Baltic, c. 1302-c. 1542', (1990) 27 *Northern Studies* 12; A. Crone and F. Watson, 'Sufficiency to Scarcity: Medieval Scotland, 500–1600', in T.C. Smout (ed.), *People and Woods in Scotland: A History* (Edinburgh, 2003), p. 60.

12 S.G.E. Lythe, 'Scottish Trade with the Baltic, 1550–1650', in J.K. Eastham (ed.), *Dundee Economic Essays in Commemoration of the Dundee School of Economics, 1931–55* (London, 1955), p. 63; J. Dow, 'Scottish Trade with Sweden, 1512–80', (1969) 48 *Scottish Historical Review* 64, and 'Scottish Trade with Sweden, 1580–1622', (1969) 48 *Scottish Historical Review* 124; D. Ditchburn, 'Trade with Northern Europe, 1297–1540', in Lynch, Spearman and Stell (eds), *Scottish Medieval Town*, p. 161; T. Riis, 'Long Distance Trade or Tramping: Scottish Ships in the Baltic, Sixteenth and Seventeenth Centuries', in T.C. Smout (ed.), *Scotland and the Sea* (Edinburgh, 1992), p. 59.

13 A.W.K. Stevenson, 'Trade between Scotland and the Low Countries in the Later Middle Ages', PhD dissertation, University of Aberdeen, 1982, and 'Trade with the South, 1070–1513', in Lynch, Spearman and Stell (eds), *Scottish Medieval Town*, p. 180.

were closed to English merchants in 1585.[14] At least one Scottish ship travelled as far as the Canary Islands, but voyages further afield were a novelty at the end of the century.[15] Trade with England and Ireland, where the same range of commodities tended to be produced as in Scotland, is perhaps best seen as an extension of a more local trade, which facilitated the redistribution of goods imported from abroad around the coasts, typically in smaller vessels referred to as 'boats' rather than 'ships'.[16]

Not all the burghs in which export duties were collected were located on the coast.[17] Well over half the revenues raised during the sixteenth century were collected in Edinburgh, which traded through its own port at Leith (mostly to the neglect of its other port at Newhaven).[18] Haddington and Linlithgow also had their own ports, at Aberlady and Blackness respectively, while further north merchants in Dunfermline traded out of a harbour at Limekilns and those in Cupar out of a harbour at Guardbridge, and still further north those in Elgin traded out of a harbour at Garmouth and those in Forres out of a harbour at Findhorn.[19] Export duties were also collected in Stirling and Perth, although

14 C. McLaughlin, 'An Evaluation of Scottish Trade with Iberia during the Anglo-Spanish War, 1585–1604', in R.J. Blakemore and J. Davey (eds), *The Maritime World of Early Modern Britain* (Amsterdam, 2020), p. 105.

15 DCA, BCMB, vol. 19, 24 March 1597, and vol. 20, 5 March 1599; T. Brochard, 'Scotland's First Transatlantic Crossing: The *William* of Aberdeen, 1593–1602', (2021) 109 *Scottish Local History Journal* 17.

16 N.J. Williams, *The Maritime Trade of the East Anglian Ports, 1550–90* (Oxford, 1988), pp. 80–5; S.G.E. Lythe, 'Early Modern Trade, c. 1550–1707', in G. Jackson and S.G.E. Lythe (eds), *The Port of Montrose: A History of Its Harbour, Trade and Shipping* (Tayport, 1993), p. 87, at pp. 98–100; E. Ewan, 'Living in the Late Medieval Town of St Andrews', in M. Brown and K. Stevenson (eds), *Medieval St Andrews* (Woodbridge, 2017), p. 117, at p. 122.

17 M. Lynch, 'The Social and Economic Structure of the Larger Towns, 1450–1600', in Lynch, Spearman and Stell (eds), *Scottish Medieval Town*, p. 261, at pp. 269–71; D.H. Sacks and M. Lynch, 'Ports, 1540–1700', in Clark (ed.), *Cambridge Urban History of Britain, Volume II*, p. 377, at pp. 410–14; M. Rorke, 'Edinburgh's Sixteenth-Century Exporting Community', (2008) 81 *Historical Research* 447, at pp. 458–9.

18 J. Russell, 'The Burgh of Leith', in D. Robertson (ed.), *Studies in the Development of Edinburgh* (London, 1939), pt 1, p. 41, at pp. 44–7; T. McGowran, *Newhaven-on-Forth: Port of Grace* (Edinburgh, 1985), pp. 99–101; J.S. Marshall, *The Life and Times of Leith* (Edinburgh, 1986), pp. 16–18.

19 W.F. Gray, *A Short History of Haddington* (Edinburgh, 1944), pp. 86–7; G. Stell, 'Urban Buildings', in Lynch, Spearman and Stell (eds), *Scottish Medieval Town*, p. 60, at pp. 62–3; W.F. Hendrie, *Linlithgow: Six Hundred Years a Royal Burgh* (Edinburgh, 1989), pp. 19–20; J.M. Webster and A.A.M. Duncan, 'Introduction', in *Regality of Dunfermline Court Book, 1531–8* (Dunfermline, 1953), p. 1, at pp. 12–25; D. Robertson, *The Bailies of Leith: A Miscellany of Historical Articles* (Leith, 1915), p. 109; P. Martin, *Cupar: The History of a Small Scottish Town* (Edinburgh, 2006), p. 2; *The Records of Elgin, 1234–1800*, 2 vols, ed. W. Crammond (Aberdeen, 1903–8), vol. 1, p. 80; *Charters and Writs Concerning the Royal Burgh of*

merchants there appear to have sent their goods by boat down the Forth or Tay to be loaded onto ships in other burghs (Perth in particular had come to be regarded as a 'craft' rather than a 'merchant' town).[20] Duties were not yet collected in Glasgow, from which only small boats could be sent down the Clyde to more accessible harbours.[21] Of the burghs located directly on the coast, Dundee had the largest share of overseas trade, followed by Aberdeen, and these two towns returned more revenue than any others apart from Edinburgh.[22] Some trade was also carried on to the south of Edinburgh in the established burghs of North Berwick and Dunbar, and on the north side of the Forth in the established burghs of Inverkeithing, Kinghorn and Crail, which were drawn into competition as the century progressed with Culross, Burntisland, Kirkcaldy, Dysart, Pittenweem and Anstruther.[23] Trade was carried on to the south of Dundee at St Andrews, and between Dundee and Aberdeen at Arbroath and Montrose, all long established as royal or ecclesiastical burghs. Further north, the main trading centre was Inverness, although customs accounts were also returned from Banff, and there was also some activity at Kirkwall.[24] In the

Haddington, 1318–1543, ed. J.G. Wallace-James (Haddington, n.d.), pp. 5–6; *Charters and Other Muniments Belonging to the Royal Burgh of Cupar*, ed. G. Home (Edinburgh, 1885), p. 6; *Registrum magni sigilli regum Scotorum: The Register of the Great Seal of Scotland*, 11 vols, ed. J. Balfour Paul, J.M. Thomson, J.H. Stevenson and W. K. Dickson (Edinburgh, 1984), vol. 2, pp. 492–3; ACA, CA1/1/34/1, pp. 239–40 and 254; EL, BCBE, vol. 2, pp. 72 and 278; ELAC, B30/13/1, ff. 42v, 73v and 110r, B30/13/2, ff. 9r, 20r, 38, 44v, 60r, 78r, 88r, 102r and 106r, and B30/9/2, ff. 78r and 217v-18r; NRS, B48/7/1, ff. 29v, 233v, 283r, 301r, 329v and 349r.

20 M. Verschuur, 'Merchants and Craftsmen in Sixteenth-Century Perth', in M. Lynch (ed.), *The Early Modern Town in Scotland* (London, 1987), p. 36, at pp. 36–7; E.P.D. Torrie, *Medieval Dundee: A Town and Its People* (Dundee, 1990), p. 35; D. Bowler and R. Cachart, 'Tay Street, Perth: The Excavation of an Early Harbour Site', (1994) 124 *Proceedings of the Society of Antiquaries of Scotland* 485, at pp. 486–7.

21 R. Renwick, J. Lindsay and G. Eyre-Todd, *History of Glasgow*, 2 vols (Glasgow, 1921–31), vol. 1, pp. 245–8; J.A. Dunn, *History of Renfrew* (Paisley, 1971), p. 105; E.P. Dennison and R. Coleman, *Historic Dumbarton: The Archaeological Implications of Development* (East Linton, 1999), p. 24; K.L. Moore, 'Maritime Trade', in J.R. Coull, A. Fenton and K. Veitch (eds), *Scottish Life and Society: A Compendium of Scottish Ethnology – Volume 4: Boats, Fishing and the Sea* (Edinburgh, 2008), p. 483, at pp. 484–5.

22 Some customs accounts are abridged in *Rotuli scaccarii regum Scotorum: The Exchequer Rolls of Scotland*, 23 vols, ed. J. Stuart, G. Burnett, A.J.G. Mackay and G.P. MacNeill (Edinburgh, 1878–1908), vols 11–23.

23 M. Lynch, 'Continuity and Change in Urban Society, 1500–1700', in R.A. Houston and I.D. Whyte (eds), *Scottish Society, 1500–1800* (Cambridge, 1989), p. 85, at p. 99. The establishment of royal and other burghs is catalogued in G.S. Pryde, *The Burghs of Scotland: A Critical List* (Oxford, 1965).

24 According to H.D. Smith, *Shetland Life and Trade, 1550–1914* (Edinburgh, 1984), pp. 10–11, Shetland remained 'a land of landowners and tenants', and benefited from trade only to the extent that the islands were visited by German merchants.

south west of the country a limited amount of overseas trade was carried on along the Solway coast at Dumfries, Kirkcudbright and Wigtown, and rather more on the firth of Clyde at Ayr, Irvine and Dumbarton.[25] While evidence exists of illicit trade being carried on elsewhere, it does appear to have been the royal or ecclesiastical burghs identified here to which merchants residing inland sent their goods for transportation overseas.[26]

The flow of traffic through each coastal burgh was obviously dependent on the adequacy of the facilities there. In a few places there was little more than a stretch of beach on which smaller vessels could be grounded safely.[27] Until the construction of a new harbour at Dunbar in the 1570s, for example, boats were beached there along a sheltered bay behind an island.[28] Indeed, one of the conditions attached to membership of the burgh was availability 'to help to draw ane grit boit to the se or fra the se in the havin'.[29] More often ships were moored in the sheltered pools formed where small rivers joined larger waterways.[30] In these places quays were constructed along the shore, and where space permitted jetties were projected into the water.[31] More substantial piers

---

25 DHC, DB1/10/6/7, 10–11 and 13, and 10/20/16; AA, B6/11/1/2, f. 270v, B6/11/3, ff. 25v and 41v, and B6/12/2, p. 82.

26 J.R. Turner, *Scotland's North Sea Gateway: Aberdeen Harbour, 1136–1986* (Aberdeen, 1986), p. 9; E.P.D. Torrie, 'The Guild in Fifteenth-Century Dunfermline', in Lynch, Spearman and Stell (eds), *Scottish Medieval Town*, p. 245, at p. 252; M. Ash, *This Noble Harbour: A History of the Cromarty Firth* (Edinburgh, 1991), pp. 143–4.

27 A. Graham and A.E. Truckell, 'Old Harbours in the Solway Firth', (1976–7) 52 *Transactions of the Dumfriesshire and Galloway Natural History and Antiquarian Society* 109, at p. 123; E.P. Dennison, 'Timothy Pont's Portrayal of Towns', in I.C. Cunningham (ed.), *The Nation Survey'd: Timothy Pont's Maps of Scotland* (East Linton, 2001), p. 125, at p. 134; D. Ditchburn, 'Maritime Ports and Transport, c. 1200–1560', in K. Veitch (ed.), *Scottish Life and Society: A Compendium of Scottish Ethnology – Volume 8: Transport and Communications* (Edinburgh, 2009), p. 24.

28 A. Graham, 'The Old Harbours of Dunbar', (1966–7) 99 *Proceedings of the Society of Antiquaries of Scotland* 173, at pp. 174–5; E.P. Dennison, S. Stronoch and R. Coleman, *Historic Dunbar: Archaeology and Development* (Edinburgh, 2006), p. 68; *Early Travellers in Scotland*, ed. P. Hume Brown (Edinburgh, 1978), p. 67.

29 NRS, GD1/413/15, pp. 81–2.

30 A. Jervise, *Memorials of Angus and the Mearns* (Edinburgh, 1861), pp. 64–5; D. Mitchell, *The History of Montrose* (Montrose, 1866), p. 154; A.D. Cameron, 'Communications: Water', in L. Maclean (ed.), *The Hub of the Highlands: The Book of Inverness and District* (Edinburgh, 1975), p. 232, at p. 232.

31 A. Graham, 'Archaeological Notes on Some Harbours in Eastern Scotland', (1968–9) 101 *Proceedings of the Society of Antiquaries of Scotland* 200, pp. 205–6; R. Gourlay and A. Turner, *Historic Ayr: The Archaeological Implications of Development* (Glasgow, 1977), p. 7, *Historic Kirkcudbright: The Archaeological Implications of Development* (Glasgow, 1978), p. 8, and *Historic Inverness: The Archaeological Implications of Development*

sometimes existed, made of timber or masonry, or of wooden frames filled with rubble, and a widespread development during the sixteenth century was the addition of bulwarks or breakwaters of similar construction.[32] At Leith the 'schoir, peir and bulwarkis' were fitted with 'beykins' to guide ships safely into the harbour, with 'ringis and makfastis' to tie them up, and with a 'cran' to assist in their unloading and reloading.[33] At Dundee regulations required merchants to remove unloaded cargo from the 'shoar' without delay, and mariners to move their ships away from the 'peir' as soon as they were reloaded, without then blocking the main passage around the 'bulwarkes'.[34] To limit congestion further 'in tyme of thrang', ships were forbidden from mooring with their 'braid syde' to the pier, yet some were still forced to ride at anchor 'in the reid', discharging their cargoes into lighters.[35] At Aberdeen it was always necessary for some cargoes to be discharged in this way, for the water around the shore and pier was too shallow for larger vessels to moor there.[36] When a crane was installed on the 'keyheid' in the 1580s – followed by new 'beakiningis

(Glasgow, 1977), p. 6; E.P.D. Torrie and R. Coleman, *Historic Kirkcaldy: The Archaeological Implications of Development* (Aberdeen, 1995), pp. 53–5.

32 G. Hay, *History of Arbroath to the Present Time* (Arbroath, 1876), pp. 314–17; A. Graham, 'Old Harbours and Landing Places on the East Coast of Scotland', (1976–7) 108 *Proceedings of the Society of Antiquaries of Scotland* 332, at pp. 363–4; A.T. Simpson and S. Stevenson, *Historic St Andrews: The Archaeological Implications of Development* (Glasgow, 1981), p. 7; S. Stevenson, *Anstruther: A History* (Edinburgh, 1989), p. 8; D.G. Adams, 'The Harbour: Its Early History', in Jackson and Lythe (eds), *Port of Montrose*, p. 27, at pp. 27–8; E.P. Dennison and R. Coleman, *Historic Dumbarton: The Archaeological Implications of Development* (East Linton, 1999), pp. 54–5; T. Smith, *Crail, History and Guide: The Story of an Ancient Scottish Burgh* (St Andrews, 2010), pp. 157–8.

33 S. Mowat, *The Port of Leith: Its History and Its People* (Edinburgh, 2003), pp. 116–17; *Extracts from the Records of the Burgh of Edinburgh*, 1st ser., 5 vols, ed. J.D. Marwick (Edinburgh, 1869–92), vol. 1, p. 99, and vol. 4, pp. 239 and 416; *Extracts from the Records of the Burgh of Edinburgh*, 2nd ser., 9 vols, ed. M. Wood and H. Armet (Edinburgh, 1927–67), vol. 1, p. 65.

34 A. Maxwell, *The History of Old Dundee, Narrated out of the Town Council Register* (Edinburgh, 1884), pp. 103–10; C. McKean, 'What Kind of Renaissance Town Was Dundee?', in C. McKean, B. Harris and C.A. Whatley (eds), *Dundee: Renaissance to Enlightenment* (Edinburgh, 2009), p. 1, at pp. 1–2; *Burgh Laws of Dundee, with the History, Statutes and Proceedings of the Guild of Merchants and Fraternities of Craftsmen*, ed. A.J. Warden (London, 1872), pp. 20–2.

35 DCA, BCMB, vol. 14, 22 April 1577, and MBBC, vol. 3, f. 5v.

36 J. Robertson, *The Book of Bon-Accord* (Aberdeen, 1839), p. 277; E.P. Dennison and J. Stones, *Historic Aberdeen: The Archaeological Implications of Development* (Edinburgh, 1997), p. 84; G. Jackson, 'The Economy: Aberdeen and the Sea', in E.P. Dennison, D. Ditchburn and M. Lynch (eds), *Aberdeen before 1800: A New History* (East Linton, 2002), p. 159, at pp. 163–4; K. Jillings, *An Urban History of the Plague: Socio-Economic, Political and Medical Impacts in a Scottish Community, 1500–1650* (Abingdon, 2018), pp. 4–6.

and feschningis' in the 1590s – it can only have helped with the loading and unloading of smaller vessels.[37] The maintenance of harbour facilities like these was a constant drain on burgh finances.[38] It may be that some authorities exaggerated the dilapidated state of their quays, piers and bulwarks when they sought to raise funds for their repair or renovation, but there is no doubt that weathering, silting and the dumping of ballast posed serious challenges to the prosperity of many towns.[39]

Having harbours attractive to foreign shipping might have been enough to enable Scottish merchants to participate in overseas trade, and there was in fact some anxiety that the wealth of the nation would be diminished by ships arriving with goods and departing with money.[40] The arrival of 'aventurers' with cargoes for sale was sufficiently common for regulations to be passed

---

37 ACA, CA1/1/30, pp. 645, 689 and 706–7, CA1/1/31, pp. 101, 331 and 423, CA1/1/32, pp. 1, 80 and 353, CA1/1/33/1, p. 480, CA1/1/35, p. 21, and CA5/1/2, 1 May and 17, 18 and 27 August 1582.

38 W. Stephen, *History of Inverkeithing and Rossyth* (Aberdeen, 1921), pp. 14–15; H. McGhee, 'The Harbour', in A.I. Dunlop (ed.), *The Royal Burgh of Ayr: Seven Hundred and Fifty Years of History* (Edinburgh, 1953), p. 197, at p. 207; J. Strawhorn, *The History of Irvine: Royal Burgh and New Town* (Edinburgh, 1985), pp. 13–15, and *The History of Ayr: Royal Burgh and County Town* (Edinburgh, 1989), p. 40; A.T. Simpson and S. Stevenson, *Historic Irvine: The Archaeological Implications of Development* (Glasgow, 1980), p. 6, *Historic Crail: The Archaeological Implications of Development* (Glasgow, 1981), p. 6, and *Historic Arbroath: The Archaeological Implications of Development* (Glasgow, 1982), pp. 7–8.

39 *Extracts from the Records of the Burgh of Edinburgh*, 1st ser., vol. 1, p. 113, vol. 2, pp. 209–12, 214–15, 218–19, 230, 241, 253, 291, 297–8 and 309–14, vol. 3, pp. 1, 7, 182, 245–6, 252, 262 and 279–81, and vol. 4, pp. 2–3, 12, 15, 47, 239, 285, 487–8 and 543; *Extracts from the Records of the Burgh of Edinburgh*, 2nd ser., vol. 1, pp. 65, 137, 179, 195, 247 and 249; *Burgh Laws of Dundee*, pp. 31–2 and 41; *Extracts from the Council Register of the Burgh of Aberdeen*, vol. 1, pp. 93–4, and vol. 2, pp. 77–8; *Aberdeen Council Letters*, 6 vols, ed. L.B. Taylor (London, 1942–61), vol. 1, pp. 5–7; *Records of the Convention of the Royal Burghs of Scotland*, 8 vols, ed. J.D. Marwick and T. Hunter (Edinburgh, 1870–1918), vol. 1, pp. 135 and 415–16, and vol. 2, pp. 2–3, 24–5, 36 and 57; *The Register of the Privy Council of Scotland*, 14 vols, ed. J.H. Burton and D. Masson (Edinburgh, 1877–98), vol. 2, pp. 417–18, 431 and 440, and vol. 4, pp. 104–5; ECA, SL1/1/4, pp. 478–9 and 485, SL1/1/5, f. 12v, SL1/1/9, pp. 190, 284, 304 and 343, and SL1/1/10, pp. 276, 306 and 492; DCA, BCMB, vol. 2, pp. 35, 46–7 and 67–8, and vol. 9, 20 February 1568, and MBBC, vol. 1, pp. 42, 89 and 119, and vol. 2, pp. 19 and 68; ACA, CA1/1/24, p. 172, CA1/1/27, pp. 327 and 595, CA1/1/32, pp. 229 and 617–18, CA1/1/33/1, pp. 490–1 and 523–5, CA1/1/34/2, p. 627, CA1/1/36, p. 195, CA1/1/37, p. 3, and CA5/1/1, f. 95r; FCA, B/KDY/2/1/3, ff. 81 and 86r, and B/KDY/2/1/4, ff. 106 and 135; SAUL, B10/8/7, p. 171; ELAC, B30/9/2, f. 65v; AA, B6/11/1/1, f. 169r, B6/11/1/2, f. 193, B6/11/1/3, ff. 387r, 423v-4r and 475v-6r, B6/11/2, ff. 9r, 41v, 87v, 108v, 153, 199r, 212r, 361v, 381v-2r, 444r, 490v, 509v-10r, 534r and 543r, and B6/11/3, ff. 33v, 88v, 151v-2r, 184r, 226, 230, 268r, 275v, 277v and 279r; NRS, B6/1/1, ff. 476–7r, and B51/1/2, f. 68r.

40 *Acts of the Parliaments of Scotland*, vol. 2, p. 306; Records of the Parliaments of Scotland, 1526/6/36; *Register of the Privy Council of Scotland*, vol. 1, pp. 103–4.

requiring them to offer their goods first to burgh representatives, for redistribution among the community, before they were offered to private parties.[41] Merchants sometimes hired space in these ships, however, and there is ample evidence of Scots acquiring ships of their own, either by buying them or by paying for their construction by local shipwrights.[42] One shipwright agreed to go and build a vessel in Norway, 'quhair best tymmer can be had', and essential equipment was sometimes hard to obtain in Scotland, yet ships frequently were fitted out there, not only by men.[43] That women were sometimes involved in trade is well known.[44] It is less well known that several owned ships and continued to send them to sea after the deaths of their husbands.[45] Before any

41 *Extracts from the Council Register of the Burgh of Aberdeen*, vol. 1, pp. 220–1, 229–30 and 334–5; *Records of Elgin*, vol. 1, pp. 60 and 80; *Kirkcudbright Town Council Records, 1576–1604*, ed. M.B. Johnston and C.M. Armet (Edinburgh, 1939), pp. 142, 159–61 and 297; *The Acts of the Lords of Council in Civil Causes, 1496–1501*, ed. G. Neilson and H. Paton (Edinburgh, 1918), pp. 358–9; *Acts of the Lords of Council, 1501–1503*, ed. A.B. Calderwood and A.L. Murray (Edinburgh, 1993), pp. 300, 312 and 334; ECA, SL1/1/2, f. 21r; DCA, PBD, vol. 1, f. 113r; ACA, CA1/1/8, p. 883, CA1/1/11, pp. 63 and 157–8, CA1/1/14, pp. 131, 147–8, 162, 195, 228, 248, 252–3 and 598, CA1/1/17, p. 220, CA1/1/21, p. 649, CA1/1/22, pp. 339, 350, 514–15 and 520–1, CA1/1/23, pp. 205, 207–8, 213 and 234–5, CA1/1/24, pp. 38, 43, 49, 88, 132, 197, 222, 260–1, 265, 270, 396, 425, 463 and 492, CA1/1/26, pp. 240, 426 and 432, CA1/1/27, p. 493, CA1/1/34/1, pp. 233–4, CA1/1/35, pp. 173 and 352, CA1/1/36, pp. 141–2, 207–8, 237, 243, 566–7, 571, 685 and 719, CA1/1/37, p. 511, CA1/1/38, pp. 21–2, 309, 372, 498, 733–4, 764 and 780, CA5/1/4, 4 February, 7 March, 3, 5 and 30 June and 21 July 1595, and CA5/1/5, 10 July and 3 December 1596, and 29 January, 23 March, 13 April and 3 and 16 September 1597; EL, BCBE, vol. 1, p. 41, and vol. 2, p. 158; DAC, WC4/8, f. 94r, and WC4/9/1, ff. 24v and 27v; AA, B6/11/1/1, f. 169r, B6/11/1/2, f. 270v, B6/11/1/3, ff. 361v-2r and 387r, B6/11/2, ff. 7, 74r and 355r, B6/11/3, ff. 12v-13r, 26r, 33v and 35v, B6/12/2, p. 220, and B6/12/3, 6 November 1559; NRS, B72/5, ff. 9, 186r, 244r and 272r.

42 *Extracts from the Records of the Burgh of Edinburgh*, 1st ser., vol. 2, p. 1; DCA, BCMB, vol. 14, 11 July 1576, 13 November 1577 and 18 September 1579; ACA, CA1/1/8, p. 495, CA1/1/12/2, p. 529, CA1/1/13, pp. 121, 159 and 456, and CA5/1/5, 31 January and 4 February 1597; FCA, B/KDY/2/1/2, f. 152r; SAUL, B10/8/5, pp. 907–8, and B65/8/1, f. 116r; HAC, B1/1/2(1), ff. 70v-1r and 75v; DAC, WC4/8, f. 94r; NRS, B9/11/2, f. 30v, B19/1/12, 17 March 1590. More is said about the acquisition of ships in the eighth essay in this collection.

43 *Extracts from the Records of the Burgh of Edinburgh*, 2nd ser., vol. 1, p. 164; ACA, CA1/1/16, pp. 104–5; NRS, B19/1/13, 12 and 28 January 1592.

44 S.G.E. Lythe, *Life and Labour in Dundee from the Reformation to the Civil War* (Dundee, 1958), p. 9; R.A. Houston, 'Women in the Economy and Society of Scotland, 1500–1800', in Houston and Whyte (eds), *Scottish Society*, p. 118, at p. 122; M. Rorke, 'Women Overseas Traders in Sixteenth-Century Scotland', (2005) 25 *Journal of Scottish Historical Studies* 81, p. 99. See now especially C. Spence, *Women, Credit and Debt in Early Modern Scotland* (Manchester, 2016), pp. 61–74.

45 The speculative observations made in F.E. Dyer, 'A Woman Shipowner', (1950) 36 *Mariner's Mirror* 134, can easily be substantiated (DCA, BCMB, vol. 9, 5 November 1565, vol. 10, 14 February 1569, vol. 12, 16 November 1571, vol. 14, 28 February, 14 March and 6 August 1578,

ship could be sent to sea safely it obviously needed to be put into the hands of competent navigators.[46] Masters were available for hire in most ports, along with steersmen or pilots who had special knowledge of dangerous stretches of coastline or the awkward entrances to some harbours.[47] The masters put in charge of ships were often burgesses themselves, unlike the ordinary mariners they employed, who were typically 'unfreemen'.[48] Although excluded from the membership of burghs and guilds, mariners tended to form fraternities, which by the end of the century were providing support for the families of those who were injured or killed at sea, or who managed to survive long enough to become too old and infirm to work there.[49] The duties of mariners extended in this period to the loading and unloading of cargoes, but in the larger ports there were 'warkmen upoun the schoir', 'pyoneris', 'polkmen', 'stingmen' or 'karteris', who carried goods to and from ships for fees fixed by the burgh authorities.[50]

---

vol. 15, 7 and 28 April 1581, vol. 18, 3 September, 31 October and 10 December 1595, vol. 20, 6 and 13 November 1598, and vol. 21, 5 December 1599; ACA, CA1/1/13, p. 336, and CA1/1/21, p. 743 and 745; FCA, B/KDY/2/1/2, ff. 40v, 44v and 70r, and B/KDY/2/1/3, ff. 133 and 154r; SAUL, B10/8/4, p. 373; NRS, B21/8/2, ff. 20r and 21r).

46 Ships were invariably crewed by men. No trace of female navigators has been found.

47 V.E. Clark, *The Port of Aberdeen: A History of its Trade and Shipping from the Twelfth Century to the Present day* (Aberdeen, 1921), pp. 22–4; *The Autobiography and Diary of Mr James Melvill*, ed. R. Pitcairn (Edinburgh, 1842), pp. 168–9, 251–3 and 280; 'Journey through England and Scotland made by Lupold von Wedel in the Years 1584 and 1585', ed. G. von Bülow (1895) 9 *Transactions of the Royal Historical Society* 223, at pp. 244–5; *Rentale Sancti Andree, 1538–46*, ed. R.K. Hannay (Edinburgh, 1913), pp. 122–4; *Extracts from the Council Register of the Burgh of Aberdeen*, vol. 2, pp. 158–9; ACA, CA1/1/37, p. 248; NRS, B9/11/1, f. 93v.

48 The observation in G. Jackson, 'Scottish Sailors', in P. van Boyen, J. Bruijn and J. Lucassen (eds), *'Those Emblems of Hell'? European Sailors and the Maritime Labour Market, 1570–1870* (St John's, Newfoundland, 1997), p. 119, at p. 120, that sailors tended to congregate during the eighteenth century in coastal (not inland) towns is as true of the period dealt with here.

49 J. Mason, *The History of the Trinity House of Leith* (Glasgow, 1957), pp. 1–6; F. Mudie, *The Fraternity of Masters and Seamen or Trinity House in Dundee* (Broughty Ferry, 1962), pp. 1–5; H. Robertson, *Mariners of Dundee: Their City, Their River, Their Fraternity* (Dundee, 2006), pp. 10–14; A. Clark, *A Short History of the Shipmaster Society or the Seamen's Box of Aberdeen* (Aberdeen, 1911), pp. 1–3; ECA, SL1/1/10, pp. 129, 131 and 186; DCA, MBBC, vol. 2, p. 87; ACA, CA1/1/37, p. 268, and CA1/1/38, pp. 323–8; AA, B6/11/3, f. 36r; NLS, MS 941, ff. 1–3r; AUL, MS 3070/8. If K. Davids, 'Seamen's Organizations and Social Protest in Europe, c. 1300–1825', (1994) 39 Supp. 2 *International Review of Social History* 145, at pp. 151–5, is correct, it must have been in Scotland that the use of insurance boxes was first adopted in northern Europe.

50 *Extracts from the Records of the Burgh of Edinburgh*, 1st ser., vol. 1, pp. 84, 134, 165 and 197–8, vol. 2, pp. 163–4, and vol. 4, pp. 302–4; *Extracts from the Records of the Burgh of Edinburgh*, 2nd ser., vol. 1, pp. 165 and 237–9; *Burgh Laws of Dundee*, p. 22; *Extracts from the Council Register of the Burgh of Aberdeen*, vol. 2, pp. 49–50; ECA, SL1/1/4, pp. 163 and 336, SL1/1/5,

Not surprisingly, these labourers also tended to be 'unfreemen', and some were actually women or children.[51]

2 Maritime Jurisdiction in the Coastal Burghs

Evidence of engagement in overseas trade can be found in the council register of Edinburgh, which survives almost without interruption from 1551 onwards, and from which excerpts had been transcribed into two manuscripts before earlier volumes in the series were lost.[52] If the customs accounts show that Edinburgh merchants sent far more goods abroad than those of all the other burghs combined, the register of tolls imposed on vessels passing into the Baltic shows that Edinburgh merchants were not sending much more in that direction than those in Dundee or Aberdeen, which strengthens the impression given by the council register that their trade was mostly conducted with the Netherlands and France.[53] Some of the entries in the register record the determination of disputes by the bailies, but very few of these disputes were of the kind envisaged in the provision of the *Leges burgorum* mentioned earlier, and it is even harder to find traces of the handling of disputes between merchants and mariners in the separate bailie court books that happen to have survived.[54] It is known that one dispute of this kind was dealt with in 1508 by the 'water bailie of the town and port of Leith, belonging to the jurisdiction of the burgh of Edinburgh', and it seems likely that similar cases would have come

f. 12, and SL1/1/7, ff. 32v and 34r; DCA, BCMB, vol. 2, pp. 17 and 53, vol. 13, 19 July 1574, and vol. 14, 19 September 1576, and MBBC, vol. 1, p. 129; ACA, CA1/1/8, pp. 980–1, CA1/1/20, p. 448, CA1/1/27, pp. 152 and 392, CA1/1/31, pp. 134 and 505, CA1/1/32, p. 408, CA1/1/35, p. 8, and CA1/1/36, pp. 340–1; SAUL, B10/8/6, p. 375, and B10/8/7, pp. 180–1; AA, B6/12/2, p. 266; NLS, Adv. MS 31.4.9, ff. 3v, 7r, 14v and 17r.

51 G. Gordon, *Prying with the Pynours, 1498–1978: An Intimate Look at the Aberdeen Shore Porters Society and Their Times* (Aberdeen, 1978), pp. 9–17, and *The Shore Porters Society of Aberdeen, 1498–1998* (Aberdeen, 1998), pp. 15–24.

52 D. Robertson and M. Wood (eds), *Castle and Town: Chapters in the History of the Royal Burgh of Edinburgh* (Edinburgh, 1928), pp. 277–301. The volumes covering the second half of the century are ECA, SL1/1/2–10. The two manuscripts referred to are SL1/1/1 and NLS, Adv. MS 31.4.9. Some entries have been printed in two series of *Extracts from the Records of the Burgh of Edinburgh*, cited in n. 33 above.

53 T. Riis, *Should Auld Acquaintance Be Forgot … Scottish-Danish Relations, c. 1450–1707*, 2 vols (Odense, 1988), vol. 2, pp. 29–51.

54 ECA, SL234/1/1, contains entries running from May to September 1507. SL234/1/2 is a modern index of the names found in SL234/1/3, which runs from 1581 to 1583. SL234/1/4 covers 1589 to 1592, and SL234/1/5 1598 to 1603. NRS, B22/23, catalogued as a burgh court book from 1500 to 1564, in fact consists of just a few pages, relating to 1500–13 and 1560–64.

to light if the records of the water bailie's activities had not been lost.[55] Holding a 'wattir court' at the 'schoir of Leith' was certainly one of the responsibilities imposed on him by the authorities in Edinburgh, their obvious intention being to provide swifter justice than would have been possible if litigants had been required to make their way to the tolbooth at St Giles' kirk.[56] The authorities in Linlithgow also appear to have appointed a bailie to deal with disputes arising at Blackness, and it may well be that similar arrangements were made by the other burghs with satellite ports.[57] Although records surviving from Linlithgow, Haddington, Dunfermline, Cupar and Elgin provide enough evidence of the engagement of merchants from those burghs in overseas trade to make it extremely likely that they became involved in disputes with mariners, records of such disputes are no easier to find there than in the records from Edinburgh.[58] Similarly, disputes between merchants and mariners are not easy to find in the records surviving from Stirling, Perth and Glasgow, which is scarcely surprising given that merchants there appear to have sent their wares abroad through other burghs, where any disputes arising from their dealings

55 J.C. Irons, *Leith and Its Antiquities from the Earliest Times to the Close of the Nineteenth Century*, 2 vols (Edinburgh, 1898), vol. 1, pp. 137–8.

56 *Extracts from the Records of the Burgh of Edinburgh*, 1st ser., vol. 1, p. 220, vol. 2, pp. 238–9, 241–2 and 243–7, vol. 3, p. 172, and vol. 4, pp. 403–4; *Extracts from the Records of the Burgh of Edinburgh*, 2nd ser., vol. 1, pp. 237–9; *Register of the Privy Council of Scotland*, vol. 4, pp. 79–80; *Protocol Book of John Foular, 1500–34*, 4 vols, ed. W. MacLeod, M. Wood and J. Durkan (Edinburgh, 1930–85), vol. 1, p. 28; ECA, SL1/1/1, ff. 3v, 29 and 37r, SL1/1/2, ff. 75, 76v and 77v-8r, SL1/1/4, pp. 163 and 173, SL1/1/5, ff. 80r, 179v, 188v, 192v and 196v, SL1/1/7, ff. 155v-8r, 200v and 217v, and SL1/1/10, pp. 307, 365–6 and 425–9; NLS, Adv. MS 31.4.9, ff. 9 and 14v.

57 G. Waldie, *A History of the Town and Palace of Linlithgow* (Linlithgow, 1868), pp. 96–7.

58 NRS, B48/7/1, is a volume of the council register of Linlithgow, running from 1528 to 1565, and B48/8/1–5 are volumes of its burgh court book, running from 1581 until the end of the century. ELAC, B30/13/1–2, are volumes of council register of Haddington, running from 1554 until the end of the century, B30/9/2 is a volume of its burgh court book, covering 1530 to 1545 and 1552 to 1555, and B30/10/1–7 continues the court book from 1555 until the end of the century. NRS, B20/10/1, begins with a court book from Dunfermline, covering 1488 to 1528, which has been printed in *The Burgh Records of Dunfermline, 1488–1584*, ed. E. Beveridge (Edinburgh, 1917), while B20/10/2 is another court book, running from 1573 to 1575, from which selected entries have been printed in *Extracts from the Burgh Records of Dunfermline in the 16th and 17th Centuries*, ed. A. Shearer (Dunfermline, 1951). At least for present purposes, the most interesting records from this burgh are printed as *The Gild Court Book of Dunfermline, 1433–1597*, ed. E.P.D. Torrie (Edinburgh, 1986). SAUL, B13/10/1, is a volume of the court and council records of Cupar, covering 1549 to 1555. EL, BCBE, vols 1–2, are burgh court books of Elgin, running from 1540 to 1554 and 1570 to 1585, from which some entries have been printed in the *Records of Elgin*, cited in n. 19 above. No relevant records appear to have survived from Forres, the other burgh with a satellite port.

with mariners are more likely to have been resolved.[59] It may be expected that merchants from other inland burghs who sent their wares abroad would also have expected any disputes they had with mariners to be settled in the port towns, for it was probably not in Edinburgh alone that the need for swift adjudication was recognised.[60]

That disputes between merchants and mariners were sometimes settled in the courts of the coastal burghs is confirmed by the extensive records preserved in Dundee.[61] The involvement of burgesses there in overseas trade is evident from records of both the burgh council and the bailie court, covering most of the second half of the century, supplemented with shipping lists compiled in the 1580s.[62] Vessels did arrive quite frequently from the far side of the Øresund, having departed with cargoes loaded in Stralsund, Danzig,

---

59 SCA, SBC11/1/1, contains council minutes from Stirling, running from 1597 until the end of the century, and SBC37/1/1–6 are volumes of the Stirling burgh court books, running from 1519 to 1530 and then from 1544 until the end of the century, though with several gaps and overlaps. Some entries have been printed in *Extracts from the Records of the Royal Burgh of Stirling, 1519–1752*, 2 vols, ed. R. Renwick (Glasgow, 1887–9), and in *The Stirling Guildry Book: Extracts from the Records of the Merchant Guild of Stirling, 1592–1846*, ed. W.R. Cook and D.B. Morris (Stirling, 1916). PKCA, B59/12/1–9, are burgh court books of Perth, running from 1507 until 1587, and B59/13/1–2 are volumes of a register of decreets of the same court, running from 1577 to 1600. Evidence of engagement in overseas trade can also be found in *The Perth Guildry Book, 1452–1601*, ed. M.L. Stavert (Edinburgh, 1993). GCA, C1/1/1–5, are volumes of the council register of Glasgow, running from 1573 until the end of the century, with a few gaps. Some entries have been printed in *Burgh Records of the City of Glasgow, 1573–81*, ed. J. Smith (Edinburgh, 1832), *Memorabilia of the City of Glasgow, Selected from the Minute Books of the Burgh, 1588 to 1750*, ed. J. Hill (Glasgow, 1835), *Memorabilia of the City of Glasgow, Selected from the Minute Books of the Burgh, 1588 to 1750*, ed. W. Watson (Glasgow, 1868), and *Extracts from the Records of the Burgh of Glasgow*, 6 vols, ed. J.D. Marwick and R. Renwick (Glasgow, 1876–1911).

60 *Cf.* F.R. Sanborn, *Origins of the Early English Maritime and Commercial Law* (New York, 1930), pp. 192–3.

61 A. Maxwell, *Old Dundee, Eccelsiastical, Burghal and Social, Prior to the Reformation* (Edinburgh, 1891), pp. 303–21.

62 DCA, MBBC, vols 1–3, cover the period from 1553 until the end of the century, though not in a sequence, and these volumes need to be examined along with BCMB, vol. 2, which contains legislation enacted by the council, sometimes before 1553. The legislation recorded in these four volumes has mostly been printed in *Burgh Laws of Dundee*, cited in n. 34 above. BCMB, vol. 1, records proceedings of the bailie court between 1520 and 1524, and vols. 3–21 record proceedings of that court between 1550 and the end of the century, except that the volume covering 1586 to 1589 has been lost. Ship entries were often included in the court records, but the separate lists referred to have been printed in *The Compt Buik of David Wedderburne, Merchant of Dundee, 1587–1630*, ed. A.H. Millar (Edinburgh, 1898), pp. 195–228.

Königsberg, Stockholm and other places around the Baltic.[63] Vessels also arrived from Copenhagen, Nylöse, Bergen, Tønsberg, Hamburg and other northern places on the near side of the sound.[64] Most vessels arriving from the Netherlands had been loaded at Veere, the Scottish staple port, but others came from Flushing, Middelburg, Antwerp and Enkhuizen, and considerable amounts of business were also conducted in Dieppe, Le Havre and Rouen, or in La Rochelle and Bordeaux.[65] The cargoes unloaded in Dundee often belonged to merchants there, or to merchants from Perth, to which they were transferred by boat, and goods were also redistributed as far north as Orkney and Shetland, or even around the north to the Hebrides.[66] It was probably the transfer of goods as far south as Scarborough, Yarmouth, Harwich, London and even Southampton that enabled connections to be formed that would eventually facilitate an expansion of trade with Cadiz, Malaga and other 'pairtis of Spane'.[67] Inevitably, disputes did arise after vessels arrived in Dundee, and the crucial point for present purposes is that many of these disputes were dealt with in the bailie court. Merchants complained that their goods had not been delivered safely, and mariners that freight had not been paid for the delivery of goods as agreed. Masters also complained that services were not being provided by the ordinary mariners they had taken on, and ordinary mariners that they were not being paid the wages they were promised. As other essays in this collection show, the details of these actions varied a great deal, and there were other types of action heard after the arrival of ships, but the point that needs to be made here is that there are records of almost three hundred disputes of the types outlined being heard in the bailie court. Some are mentioned in single entries in the court books, and some entries are brief and perfunctory, but other disputes are mentioned in several entries, some of which are quite elaborate. Since the records mostly survive from the second half of the century, most of the cases found were heard between 1550 and 1600, and more have been found in the records covering the last quarter of the century than the third, which seems consistent with the broad increase in overseas trade revealed by the customs records.[68]

---

63 Stralsund appears in Scottish records as Trailsound, Danzig as Danskin and Königsberg as Queenisburg.

64 Nylöse appears as Newluidhouse, Bergen as Birrum and Tønsberg as Townisberrie.

65 Enkhuizen appears as Incusen.

66 C.A. Whatley, D.B. Swinfen and A.M. Smith, *The Life and Times of Dundee* (Edinburgh, 1993), p. 31.

67 *An Itinerary Written by Fynes Moryson, Gent.* (London, 1617), p. 155.

68 That fewer were found from the 1580s (just twenty) than the 1570s (over seventy) and 1590s (over eighty) is partly attributable to the gap in the records between 1586 and 1589,

The most complete records of any Scottish burgh are those preserved in Aberdeen, which include a council register running continuously throughout the sixteenth century, along with bailie court books covering parts of its last three decades, and also accounts covering its last few years, which note the arrival of ships and boats.[69] Ships frequently arrived in Aberdeen from Norway (Bergen, Tønsberg, Stavanger and Trondheim are all named), and sometimes from Denmark (normally Copenhagen). Of the much larger number of ships arriving from the Baltic, most had come from Danzig, though a few came from Lübeck, Rostock or Stralsund. Vessels from Hamburg appear to have visited Aberdeen more often than Dundee.[70] Vessels arriving in Aberdeen from the Netherlands had almost invariably been in Veere, and those from France had usually been in Dieppe. Voyages from further south were less frequent, but trade with La Rochelle and Bordeaux seems to have increased towards the end of the century. Ships as well as boats travelled between Aberdeen, Leith and Dundee, sometimes carrying goods belonging to merchants residing in other Scottish towns, and goods were commonly transferred to Banff and Inverness. Ships occasionally sailed from Aberdeen to Scarborough, Hull or Yarmouth, which may again have facilitated the development of trade with Spain in the 1590s. As in Dundee, disputes arising after the arrival of ships were often dealt with in the bailie court of Aberdeen, the proceedings of which were recorded in the council register, sometimes at surprising length.[71] In the first half of the century, over three hundred and thirty complaints concerning the delivery of goods, the payment of freight, the provision of services or the payment of wages were dealt with by the bailie court, with the number of actions raised increasing gradually during the first four decades of the century, before declining in

---

and partly to the fact that the cases were not spread evenly across any decade. In the 1550s and 1560s around a hundred cases were heard altogether, roughly fifty in each decade.

69 The relevant volumes of the council register are ACA, CA1/1/7–38. CA5/1/1 is the bailie court book for 1571 to 1572 and 1575 to 1576. CA5/1/2 runs from 1581 to 1582, CA5/1/3 from 1585 to 1587, CA5/1/4 from 1594 to 1595, and CA5/1/5 from 1596 to 1597. Some entries from these records have been printed in *Extracts from the Council Register of the Burgh of Aberdeen*, cited in n. 7 above, and in a 'Collection of Decisions of the Borough Court of Aberdeen, 1399–1561', in W. Kennedy, *Annals of Aberdeen, from the Reign of King William the Lion to the End of the Year 1818*, 2 vols (London, 1818), vol. 2, p. 471. The arrival of ships is noted in the *Aberdeen Shore Work Accounts, 1596–1670*, ed. L.B. Taylor (Aberdeen, 1972), pp. 24–42.

70 Some of those arriving from Danzig had sailed previously from Hamburg.

71 More will be said about the relationship between the council register and the bailie court books below. On the council register see W. Hepburn and G. Small, 'Common Books in Aberdeen, c. 1398-c. 1511', in J.W. Armstrong and E.B.I. Frankot (eds), *Cultures of Law in Urban Northern Europe: Scotland and Its Neighbours, c. 1350-c. 1650* (London, 2021), p. 41.

the fifth. In the second half of the century, fewer than one hundred and twenty complaints of the same types were handled, a significantly small number in comparison both with the number heard in the first half of the century and with the number heard in the second half of the century in Dundee. If the decline in the 1540s seems consistent with the broad decline of Scottish trade at that time, it has to be wondered why the number of cases handled did not increase again in the last quarter of the century, as it did in Dundee. Concerns were raised in early 1590 about merchants 'passing to Edinburgh, Dundie, Perth and utheris pairtis besouth this burght', and purchasing there 'all soirtis of Frenche, Flanderis and uther forrane wairis', which threatened to make Aberdeen, 'as it war, ane dry poirt, na schipping thairin nor salling to pairtis beyound sie'.[72] Yet the concern arose from the behaviour of 'ane few number of privat personis', and trade in Aberdeen does not appear to have declined relative to trade in Dundee, where export duties were collected in broadly similar amounts. Moreover, it is clear from other entries in the Aberdeen council register – acknowledgements of obligations, registrations of contracts, disputes between merchants, and so on – that a great deal of overseas trade continued to be conducted through Aberdeen in the second half of the century. An explanation for the decline in the level of litigation between merchants and mariners or masters and mariners will have to be looked for elsewhere.

Before the enquiry is taken any further, it needs to be added that 'seafaring causes' of the types enumerated were also heard by bailie courts in other coastal burghs. Some evidence has survived from Dunbar and North Berwick, though it is disappointing for present purposes.[73] More informative records survive from the north side of the Forth: there are council records from Culross (1588–1600), court and council records from Burntisland (1582–1600), court books from Kirkcaldy (1567–71 and 1586–97), court and council records from Dysart (1534–1600), court and council records from Crail (1553–92), and a court book from St Andrews (1588–92).[74] Beyond Dundee court books survive from

72 ACA, CA1/1/32, pp. 622–3 and 637–40.

73 NRS, GD1/413/15, consists of notes taken from a volume of the council register of Dunbar, running from 1537 to 1566, but while the original is supposed to be held by the East Lothian Archive Centre, it could not be found there. NRS, GD110/546 is catalogued as a burgh court book of North Berwick, running from 1543 to 1583, but it actually consists of a single sheet of paper, folded over to form four pages of a lost book.

74 FCA, B/CUL/1/1/1; NRS, B9/10/1 and B9/11/1–2; FCA, B/KDY/2/1/1–4; NRS, B21/8/1–6; SAUL, B10/8/1–8, and B65/8/1. Some entries from these records have been printed in *Memorabilia of the City of Glasgow*, ed. J. Hill, app., pp. 21–33; *The Kirkcaldy Burgh Records*, ed. L. Macbean (Kirkcaldy, 1908); *Notices from the Local Records of Dysart*, ed. W. Muir (Glasgow, 1853). See too *Annals of Pittenweem, Being Notes and Extracts from the Ancient Records of that Burgh, 1526–1793*, ed. D. Cook (Anstruther, 1867).

both Arbroath (1550–55 and 1563–75) and Montrose (1586–7), and beyond Aberdeen from Inverness (1556–86).[75] From the west coast there are court books from Dumfries (1506–37, 1561–64 and 1569–89), council records from Kirkcudbright (1576–1600), court and council records from Wigtown (1512–35), court and council records from Ayr (1547–60 and 1580–1600), and council records from Irvine (1593–1600).[76] It is apparent from these records that ships arrived at the smaller burghs on the east coast from roughly the same range of places as those arriving at Dundee and Aberdeen, again with a more northerly bias the further north the burgh was situated.[77] Merchants on the west coast appear to have traded primarily with England and Ireland, but they also travelled as far as Brittany, and were not slow to enter the new Spanish market.[78] As well as providing evidence of engagement in overseas trade, the records listed also show that at least forty actions relating to the delivery of goods, the payment of freight, the provision of services or the payment of wages were dealt with by the bailie courts of the smaller coastal burghs. In view of the volume of material available, the number of actions found is not high, and seems more comparable to the figure calculated for Aberdeen in the second half of the century than to the figures calculated for Aberdeen in the first half

75 HL, A1/19/1–2; NRS, B51/10/2; HAC, B1/1/1–2. Some entries from the Inverness records have been printed in *Records of Inverness*, 2 vols, ed. W. Mackay, H.C. Boyd and G.S Laing (Aberdeen, 1911–24). Use was made of a court book from Banff, running from 1546–53, in the compilation of *The Annals of Banff*, 2 vols, ed. W. Cramond (Aberdeen, 1891–93), but where it is now is a mystery. See too *The Annals of Cullen, 961–1904*, ed. W. Cramond (Buckie, 1904), and *Charters and Other Records of the City and Royal Burgh of Kirkwall*, ed. J. Mooney (Aberdeen, 1952).

76 DAC, WC4/8–11; *Kirkcudbright Town Council Records*, cited in n. 41 above; NRS, B72/5; AA, B6/11/1–3, B6/12/2–3 and B6/18/1; NRS, B37/12/1. Some entries from these records have been printed in *Memorabilia of the City of Glasgow*, ed. J. Hill, app., pp. 1–21; A.E. Truckell, 'Early Shipping References in the Dumfries Burgh Records', (1954–5) 33 *Transactions of the Dumfriesshire and Galloway Natural History and Antiquarian Society* 132, 'Wigtown Burgh Court Book, 1512–35', (1987) 62 *Transactions of the Dumfriesshire and Galloway Natural History and Antiquarian Society* 66, and 'Dumfries Burgh Court Books in the 16th Century', (1999) 73 *Transactions of the Dumfriesshire and Galloway Natural History and Antiquarian Society* 183, and (2000) 74 *Transactions of the Dumfriesshire and Galloway Natural History and Antiquarian Society* 77. See too *Records of the Burgh of Prestwick in the Sheriffdom of Ayr, 1470–1782*, ed. J. Fullarton (Glasgow, 1834).

77 On trade north of Inverness see T. Brochard, 'The Socio-Economic Relations between Scotland's Northern Territories and Scandinavia and the Baltic in the Sixteenth and Seventeenth Centuries', (2014) 26 *International Journal of Maritime History* 210.

78 For a particularly interesting example of trade with Spain see AA, B6/11/1/3, f. 465v-6, which illustrates the advantage being taken of the restrictions imposed on English merchants.

of the century or Dundee in the second half of the century. Especially when the extent of the individual records is taken into account, it is notable that most of the material available from the smaller burghs was produced in the second half of the century. Further enquiry follows, but to sum up the findings presented so far, it is clear from the evidence that happens to have survived that the burgh courts of sixteenth-century Scotland dealt with nearly eight hundred disputes of the types envisaged when the provision quoted from the *Leges burgorum* at the start of this essay was written, and the actual total must have been much higher.

3 Maritime Jurisdiction in the Admiralty Courts

Admirals had been appointed in Scotland since the early fifteenth century and had been exercising some sort of jurisdiction by the start of the sixteenth century.[79] An admiralty court sat in Edinburgh or Leith, usually presided over by 'deputes' appointed by the 'great admiral of Scotland'.[80] Beyond the Forth another court was held by an 'admirale depute within the boundis of Fyfe and Angus', sometimes in Dundee, but in principle anywhere 'within the boundis foirsaidis'.[81] Another admiral depute was authorised to hold courts 'in the north partis of Scotland, fra the north watter of Esk to Ross inclusive', and he sat in Aberdeen or elsewhere in that area.[82] Whether another depute was given jurisdiction over the far north of the mainland is unknown, but reference was

79 A.R.G. McMillan, 'The Admiral of Scotland', (1923) 20 *Scottish Historical Review* 11, at pp. 11–13; J. Goodare, *The Government of Scotland, 1560–1625* (Oxford, 2004), pp. 165–6; E.B.I. Frankot, 'Maritime Law and Practice in Late Medieval Aberdeen', (2010) 89 *Scottish Historical Review* 136, at pp. 143–4, and *'Of Laws of Ships and Shipmen': Medieval Maritime Law and Its Practice in Urban Northern Europe* (Edinburgh, 2012), pp. 56–7.

80 *Acta curiae admirallatus Scotiae, 1557–62*, ed. T.C. Wade (Edinburgh, 1937); *Protocol Book of James Young, 1485–1515*, ed. G. Donaldson (Edinburgh, 1952), pp. 375–6; *Register of the Privy Council of Scotland*, vol. 2, pp. 630 and 632, vol. 3, pp. 123–4, and vol. 4, p. 357; *Acts of the Lords of Council in Public Affairs, 1501–54*, ed. R.K. Hannay (Edinburgh, 1932), p. 243; DCA, BCMB, vol. 11, 16 February 1571; ACA, CA1/1/33/1, pp. 235 and 246, and CA5/1/5, 5 March and 21 September 1597; NRS, CS5/36, f. 17r, and CS7/115, ff. 109–10r, and CS7/116, ff. 46v-7r; NLS, MS 9931, ff. 10–11.

81 *Acta curiae admirallatus Scotiae*, pp. 44, 50, 154–8 and 162; *The Scottish Correspondence of Mary of Lorraine*, ed. A.I. Cameron (Edinburgh, 1927), p. 446; DCA, BCMB, vol. 3, 11 November 1546 (*sic*), and 5 August 1551, and vol. 5, 20 June and 5 July 1558, and PBD, vol. 11, f. 46; HAC, B1/1/2, f. 420v; NRS, B9/11/1, ff. 89–90r and 92r, and B21/8/2, f. 31v.

82 *Extracts from the Council Register of the Burgh of Aberdeen*, vol. 1, p. 297; ACA, CA1/1/22, p. 504, CA1/1/24, pp. 435–6, CA1/1/37, p. 390, CA1/1/38, pp. 80–2, 328–8 and 349–50, and CA2/2/3, ff. 79–81r.

also made to an 'admirall depute within the boundis of Orknay and Zeitland'.[83] On the other side of the country there was an 'admirall depute of the west partis of this realme', who exercised jurisdiction in the Solway ports and as far north as Ayr, beyond which there was another 'admiral depute within the bounds of Cuninghame'.[84] North of the Clyde jurisdiction was exercised by the earl of Argyll, who did not originally serve the great admiral but appointed his own deputes as 'admirale of the west seyis', although eventually the supremacy of the great admiral was recognised.[85] One court book has survived, providing evidence of how justice was administered in Edinburgh or Leith between 1557 and 1562.[86] Most of the cases recorded related to the seizure of prizes during a war with England, and in one case it was argued that the admiral's jurisdiction was limited to disputes arising from 'weirfair'.[87] The argument was unsuccessful, however, and other cases are included in the court book that related to the delivery of goods, the payment of freight, the provision of services or the payment of wages. Jurisdiction was assumed in commercial cases provided they had a seafaring dimension and were contested between parties who had arrived by sea at a Scottish port, regardless of where any agreement between them had been made.[88] When the activities of the admiral deputes sitting outside Edinburgh and Leith are mentioned, it is sometimes disclosed that they were assisted by clerks, and that the clerks kept records of the proceedings of their courts, but unfortunately no other court books have survived apart from the one mentioned. How representative it was is hard to tell, yet it is clear that not all the cases heard elsewhere related to warfare, which was in fact avoided during the last few decades of the century.[89]

---

83 *Register of the Privy Council of Scotland*, vol. 2, p. 595.

84 *Register of the Privy Council of Scotland*, vol. 1, pp. 179–82, 195–6, 207–8 and 229–32; *Registrum secreti sigilli regum Scotorum: The Register of the Privy Seal of Scotland*, 7 vols, ed. M. Livingston, G. Donaldson, J. Beveridge and D.H. Fleming (Edinburgh, 1908–66), vol. 8, p. 79; *Memorials of the Montgomeries, Earls of Eglinton*, 2 vols, ed. W. Fraser (Edinburgh, 1859), vol. 2, pp. 120–1; AA, B6/11/1/1, f. 76, B6/11/2, ff. 80v-1, and B6/11/3, ff. 149v and 150v; NRS, GD3/9/1.

85 *Acts of the Lords of Council in Public Affairs*, p. 633; *Acta curiae admirallatus Scotiae*, pp. 56–8; *Fourth Report of the Royal Commission on Historical Manuscripts* (London, 1874), p. 481; DHC, DB1/10/12/1; NRS, CS6/3, f. 58r. An attempt to assert admiralty jurisdiction in the north east by the earl of Huntly came to nothing (ACA, CA1/1/34/2, p. 637).

86 This book was printed as *Acta curiae admirallatus Scotiae*, cited in n. 80 above.

87 *Acta curiae admirallatus Scotiae*, pp. 191–4.

88 *Acta curiae admirallatus Scotiae*, pp. 64, 153–4 and 214–15.

89 James VI (1567–1625), who took great pride in his status as a *rex pacificus*, kept Scotland out of external conflicts throughout his reign, although foreign forces were involved in a civil war during his minority.

In 1529, in a dispute between a master and merchants relating to the delivery of goods, the bailie court of Aberdeen was informed that the master 'desirit ane almirell court to decide the debatis betwix the said merchandis and skipar, and the merchandis elikwiss desirit the same', yet the court proceeded to deal with the dispute itself.[90] Five years later, in another case of the same type, the defender objected that it 'was ane see mater, and pertenit nocht to the provest and bailzeis, bot pertenit to the almarell court', calling upon the admiral depute 'to defend his privelege and replege' the action to his court.[91] The provost and bailies responded angrily that the admiral depute was bound by an oath he had sworn at his admission as a burgess 'to stand witht the towne, and nocht to stand incontrar the towne in nay thingis that the towne hes bene in auld use of', and the court again proceeded to deal with the dispute itself. Three years later, in a third case of the same type, a suggestion that it should be 'remittit' to the admiralty court was simply ignored.[92] By the late 1540s, however, attitudes appear to have been changing. In one case the bailies agreed to assist the admiral by gathering evidence of the seizure of a ship and goods in enemy action, and in another they recognised that prize cases concerned 'onlie the jurisdictioune of the admiralitie'.[93] More significantly, in 1547 the bailies agreed to gather evidence for the admiral in a case that appears to have had no connection with warfare, and a few years later they acceded to his request that they record his appointment of a new admiral depute.[94] Further north, the bailies of Inverness agreed to hear a commercial case only on the understanding that the litigants would exonerate them, if the need arose, at 'the greit almerall and his deputis handis'.[95] Further south, it was found by a bailie court in Crail that an offence had been 'committit within the seyflude, sua that the cognitioun theroff iustlie belangit to my lord admirall and his deputtis', to whom the case was remitted, while in Dysart it was found that an action was 'siefarin' and must therefore 'be remitit to the admirrall and his deputis'.[96] The bailies in Edinburgh were forbidden by the privy council from hearing a case relating to

90 ACA, CA1/1/12/2, pp. 689–90, 697–701, 703, 705–6, 710–12 and 773.

91 ACA, CA1/1/13, pp. 412–13, 417–18, 421–6, 428, 430, 434 and 441.

92 ACA, CA1/1/15, pp. 19, 26–8, 30, 48, 52 and 108–10.

93 *Extracts from the Council Register of the Burgh of Aberdeen*, vol. 1, pp. 225–8 and 304–6; ACA, CA1/1/19, pp. 290–1 and 299–300, and CA1/1/22, pp. 590–2. In another case it was similarly recognised that the admiral of England had jurisdiction over piracy cases (ACA, CA1/1/33/1, pp. 237–8, 240–5, 248–52, 254–6 and 265).

94 *Extracts from the Council Register of the Burgh of Aberdeen*, vol. 1, p. 297; ACA, CA1/1/19, pp. 322, 324–5 and 327, and CA1/1/22, p. 504. See too ACA, CA1/1/33/2, p. 1037.

95 *Records of Inverness*, vol. 1, pp. 254–5; HAC, B1/1/2, ff. 402v-3r.

96 SAUL, B10/8/8, p. 135; NRS, B21/8/6, f. 20r.

shipwreck since it 'appertenis properlie to the judgement and determinatioun of the admirall and his deputis'.[97] The admiral sought to repledge a case to his court from the bailie court of Perth on the basis that it related to 'seyfair', and while the outcome of this case is not known, a similar 'replegiatioun' was successful in Kirkcaldy.[98] Lawyers writing in the second half of the century had no doubt that the admiralty courts had acquired an exclusive jurisdiction over seafaring causes.[99] When one reproduced in translation the provision of the *Leges burgorum* cited earlier, he replaced the phrase 'the king's bailies' with the phrase 'the king's admiral or his deputis'.[100]

As the figures presented in the previous section of this essay show, seafaring causes did continue to be heard in the bailie courts throughout the second half of the century. In most of these cases the explanation appears to be that if an action was raised before a court, if the defender did not oppose its hearing, and if the admiral's officers did not intervene, the bailies would simply proceed to deal with it without thinking about whether their court was the appropriate forum. Nevertheless, there are other cases in which the bailies made a deliberate decision to proceed with the handling of an action despite concerns being raised about their competence. These cases fall into three categories. In the first place, if defenders did not raise objections at an early stage in the proceedings, the bailies would rule that it was too late for the action to be discontinued.[101] In 1566, for instance, when a defender argued in a case raised in Dysart that the bailies 'on no wayis can be juges in respect the clame, as it is persewit, concernis fraucht betwix marcheantis and marinalis, and sua aucht to be remittit to the admiral and his deputis, only proper juges thairto', the bailies held that he could not challenge their jurisdiction when he had already submitted 'his defensis declinatouris of befor in wrytte', without mentioning any such concern.[102] In the second place, the bailies would proceed to hear a case if they did not agree that it was of a seafaring nature.[103] In 1580,

---

97 *Register of the Privy Council of Scotland*, vol. 3, pp. 242–3.

98 PKCA, B59/13/1, pp. 508 and 512–13; FCA, B/KDY/2/1/3, f. 55r. On the rather surprising Perth case see too n. 103 below.

99 David Chalmers of Ormond, *La recerche tant des singularitez plus remarquables concernant l'estat d'Escosse* (Paris, 1579), f. 19v; *Alexander King's Treatise on Maritime Law*, ed. J.D. Ford (Edinburgh, 2018), pp. 20–3, 28–9, 32–5 and 353; William Welwod, *An Abridgement of All Sea-Lawes* (London, 1613), p. 10.

100 *The Practicks of Sir James Balfour of Pittendreich*, 2 vols, ed. P.G.B. McNeill (Edinburgh, 1962–3), vol. 2, p. 627.

101 ACA, CA1/1/26, pp. 56, 60, 64, 76, 78–9, 84, 107, 110–11, 151 and 154; SAUL, B10/8/5, p. 199.

102 NRS, B21/8/2, ff. 36v-7r.

103 ACA, CA1/1/27, pp. 301, 305, 315, 318, 326, 328, 331–2, 335, 338, 340–1, 346–7, 351, 353, 355, 375, 378–9, 399, 414, 419, 422–3, 425, 428–9, 437, 443–4, 446–8, 450, 452–3, 458, 484, 494–5,

for instance, when an officer dispatched by the admiral appeared before the bailies of Dundee and sought to have an action 'remittit to the said admirall as juge competent therto', they accepted the pursuer's answer that 'the said repledgiatioune aught nocht to be obeyit, be reasone the actioune dependis betwix merchand and merchand'.[104] In the third place, the bailies might refuse to acknowledge that the admiral had an exclusive jurisdiction over seafaring causes.[105] In 1562, for instance, when the master of a ship raised an action against cargo owners in Dundee for contributions to losses he had sustained in an effort to preserve their goods, the merchants objected that the bailies 'culd on na wyse be jugeis competent to tham in the said actioun, be ressoun that the same wes seyfarand', and an admiralty officer sought to have the action 'repledgit' to his court, yet the bailies decided that they could proceed since 'all sic actiouns as concernis skaith hes bene evir decydit befoir the bailleis of this burght in tymes bypast, and thai in use and possessioun of the judgment thairof, as diverse decretis gevin be thame thairintill can testifie, for evading of grit expensis maid in persute befoir the admirall or his deputs'.[106] In fact, the examples in this third category have all been found in the records of the bailie court of Dundee, which helps to explain why more cases of a seafaring nature have been found there than in the records of other bailie courts surviving from the second half of the century.[107] In 1581 the burgh council of Dundee tried to revive the fifteenth-century act of parliament requiring charter parties to commit their signatories to the litigation of any disputes arising between them by a bailie court, 'renuncand all other judgments'.[108]

As is explained more fully in the ninth essay in this collection, at about this time the burgh authorities in Dundee were supporting a more widespread campaign to regain control from the admiralty courts over the liability of

---

530, 549–51, 568–9, 650 and 762–4, and CA1/1/28, pp. 8–10, 12, 24, 91, 272 and 277–8; AA, B6/11/2, ff. 80v-1, and B6/11/3, f. 150v. It may be that the Perth case cited at n. 98 above was continued on the same basis, since the admiral's claim that it had a seafaring dimension seems rather contrived.

104 DCA, BCMB, vol. 15, 2, 7 and 11 May 1580.

105 DCA, BCMB, vol. 3, 20–1 June 1552, vol. 6, 21 June and 1 and 3 July 1562, and vol. 14, 18, 23–4 and 27 November, and 2, 11, 16 and 18 December 1579, and 13 January 1580.

106 DCA, BCMB, vol. 6, 14, 21 and 26 January 1562. The 'diverse decretis' that might have been, and possibly were, produced in testimony must mostly have been delivered in the first half of the century. For an earlier case from that period see BCMB, vol. 1, ff. 119v-20r, 121r and 139r.

107 On the other hand, in 1588 the council sent a messenger to the admiral to 'declair the townis gude will to his lordschipis furtherance and service' (DCA, MBBC, vol. 2, p. 15).

108 *Burgh Laws of Dundee*, p. 41; DCA, BCMB, vol. 2, p. 68, MBBC, vol. 1, p. 119, and GBD, f. 17r.

merchants to contribute to losses sustained at sea.[109] Ten years later complaints about the admiral's imposition of 'new exactiounis' on the burghs were supplemented with complaints about his 'usurping of judicatour of caussis of burgessis', and in 1592 an act of parliament was passed, declaring that in future the admiral ought not to 'exerce nor usurp na jurisdictioun, nather yit exact nor crave ony kynd of dewtie, eschaet nor casualitie, bot according to that quhilk wes usit to be exercesit or takin be the admirall for the tyme befoir the deceiss of King James the Fyft of noble memorie'.[110] The intention was thus to restore the arrangements in place at the beginning of the 1540s. Another act of parliament was passed in 1593, declaring that the dean of guild in each burgh ought to exercise the same jurisdiction as the dean of guild in Edinburgh, which was understood to cover 'all materis and actionis concerning merchandis, betwix merchand and merchand, and betwix merchand and mariner'.[111] Since the guild of each burgh comprised the burgesses who were merchants, as opposed to craftsmen, it is hardly surprising that the surviving records of some dean of guild courts recount the handling of disputes 'betwix merchand and merchand'.[112] In 1564 it was argued before the bailie court of Perth that an action was 'betwix merchand and merchand, intentit upoun ane merchand bill and actioun of merchandis of furth waring and hame waring, and sua aucht and suld be remittit to the dene of gild and to the merchands of the said burght as jugis compitent thairto allanerlie, conforme to the dalie practik and use of burrowis withtin this realme'.[113] Strangely enough, the dean of

109 *Records of the Convention of the Royal Burghs of Scotland*, vol. 1, pp. 44–5, 99–100 and 117–18; *Register of the Privy Council of Scotland*, vol. 3, pp. 308–9; *Burgh Laws of Dundee*, p. 121; DCA, BCMB, vol. 2, p. 72.

110 *Extracts from the Records of the Burgh of Edinburgh*, 1st ser., vol. 4, pp. 528 and 530–1; *Extracts from the Records of the Burgh of Edinburgh*, 2nd ser., vol. 1, p. 13; *Records of the Convention of the Royal Burghs of Scotland*, vol. 1, pp. 339–41; *Acts of the Parliaments of Scotland*, vol. 3, p. 580; Records of the Parliaments of Scotland, 1592/4/101.

111 *Acts of the Parliaments of Scotland*, vol. 4, p. 30; Records of the Parliaments of Scotland, 1593/4/57.

112 W.C. Dickinson, 'Introduction', in *Early Records of the Burgh of Aberdeen* (Edinburgh, 1957), p. xvii, at pp. cix–xiv; C. Gross, *The Gild Merchant: A Contribution to British Municipal History*, 2 vols (Oxford, 1964), vol. 1, pp. 199–240; I. Gray, *Guide to Dean of Guild Court Records* (Glasgow, 1994), p. 3; A.M. Smith, *The Guildry of Dundee: A History of the Merchant Guild of Dundee up to the 19th Century* (Dundee, 2005), pp. 41–2 and 48–9.

113 PKCA, B59/12/5, pp. 189–91. The argument was unsuccessful, and it would be a mistake to suppose that in all the Scottish burghs a clear distinction was drawn between the jurisdiction of the dean of guild and the bailies. In Dundee, for instance, a 'guildry book' was kept from 1570 onwards, but no records of court proceedings were entered in it before the end of the century. Instead, the dean of guild and his council were sometimes involved in the decision of cases raised before the bailies (e.g. DCA, BCMB, vol. 15, 10 February

guild's court in Edinburgh seems to have dealt with cases of a different type.[114] Two volumes of its proceedings have survived and they only record disputes relating to boundaries between properties, the maintenance of gable walls and other existing structures, or the erection of new structures, all aptly described as 'questiounis of nichtbourheid'.[115] In 1585 the burgh council had decided that the dean of guild should also deal with 'all questiouns of compt and rekning anent merchandice quhilk may happin to fall out betwix twa gild brether and burgessis', and should make sure that commercial regulations were complied with by 'skipperis and merchants of schips', but this does not appear to have affected the actual business of the court.[116] Moreover, it was not even proposed that the dean of guild should deal with actions 'betwix merchand and mariner', which was an innovation in the act passed by parliament in 1593.[117] No evidence has been found that deans of guild did begin to hear seafaring causes in the later 1590s, nor has a marked increase been found in the hearing of these cases by the bailie courts in that period.[118] There is reason to believe that an admiral was justified in claiming in 1628 that his courts had continued, despite

and 15 September 1581), and sometimes decisions made in cases raised before the dean and his assessors were recorded in the bailie court books (e.g. DCA, BCMB, vol. 14, 26 February 1580).

114 J. Colston, *The Guildry of Edinburgh: Is It an Incorporation?* (Edinburgh, 1887), pp. 37–41; J.C. Irons, *Manual of the Law and Practice of the Dean of Guild Court* (Edinburgh, 1895), pp. 34–6; R. Miller, *The Edinburgh Dean of Guild Court: A Manual of History and Procedure* (Edinburgh, 1896), pp. 22–4; R.G. Rodger, 'The Evolution of Scottish Town Planning', in G. Gordon and B. Dicks (eds), *Scottish Urban History* (Aberdeen, 1983), p. 71, at pp. 76–7; A.M. Jackson, *Glasgow Dean of Guild Court: A History* (Glasgow, 1983), pp. 12–14; I. Gray, 'Dean of Guild Court Records: A Unique Resource for Scottish Urban History', (1999) 5 *Scottish Archives* 41, at pp. 41–2.

115 ECA, SL144/1/1 runs from 1529 to 1557, and SL144/1/2 from 1566 to 1607. One part of the first volume is primarily a collection of legislation, but it too contains notes of decisions by the court.

116 *Extracts from the Records of the Burgh of Edinburgh*, 1st ser., vol. 4, pp. 395–8.

117 If there is any basis for the assertion in William Welwod, *The Sea-Law of Scotland* (Edinburgh, 1590), sig. C6r, that maritime jurisdiction pertained 'according to the common custome' to 'the deane of gyld, a judge of many hundred yeirs auld in this lande', it must reside in the practice of the courts before the sixteenth century.

118 On Dundee, see again n. 68 above. In Aberdeen nearly thirty cases were found from the 1590s, as compared with fewer than twenty-five from each of the preceding four decades. Of course, as in the Perth case cited at n. 113 above, some accounting actions did relate to maritime commerce. See too R. Edgar, *An Introduction to the History of Dumfries* (Dumfries, 1915), p. 169; D.B. Morris, *The Stirling Merchant Gild and the Life of John Cowane* (Stirling, 1919), pp. 119–21; H. Whitbread, *The Guildry of Stirling, Being the Story of the Gild Brether and Town Counsellors of Stirline* (Stirling, 1966), pp. 48–9; D.B. Thoms, *The Guildry of Brechin* (Brechin, 1968), pp. 12–13; NRS, B34/11/1, p. 1 (originally p. 590).

the acts of 1592 and 1593, to hear 'civill actiouns'.[119] It is understandable that in 1595 the bailies of Aberdeen had not dismissed out of hand an objection by an admiral depute that a civil action between mariners 'properlie belongis to his jurisdictioun'.[120]

4 Maritime Jurisdiction in the Central Courts

'Of procuratouris and advocattis', the members of parliament were reminded in 1567, 'gretast plentie ar at Edinburgh, being the cheif sait and justice place of the realme', since it was there that disputes were handled by 'the privie counsale, the college of justice, the justice criminall, the consistoriall judgement, the constable court, the admirale court, the schiref court, and the jurisdictioune of the towne'.[121] Although there were consistorial, admiralty, sheriff and burgh courts in other towns too, where litigants were sometimes represented by notaries public and other procurators with expertise in judicial procedure, there were more lawyers in Edinburgh than elsewhere, and it was rare for litigants to be represented outside Edinburgh by advocates with an academic training in law, who became members of the College of Justice after it was established in 1532.[122] In fact, the admiralty court that often sat in Edinburgh instead of Leith was also viewed as a central court, with jurisdiction over the whole country, like the College of Justice, the privy council and the justiciary court.[123] In two cases recorded in its surviving court book, when the admiral depute of Fife and Angus argued that its jurisdiction extended only as far north as the Forth, it was said to be the '*ordinarius ordinariorum* of the admirallis jurisdictioun within this realme', so that, 'lik as na sheref within this realme may replege fra the lordis of counsale, becaus thai ar the supreme sait, siclik na inferiour admirale depute may replege fra the saidis jugeis of the principale admiralatie'.[124] It was apparently for this reason that the court also rejected the argument (in the second case) that 'the tolbuith of Edinburgh is nocht place competent nor lauchfull to fens ane admirale court, for of the law municipale,

119 *Extracts from the Records of the Burgh of Edinburgh*, 2nd ser., vol. 3, pp. 297–8.
120 ACA, CA5/1/4, 4 August 1595.
121 *Acts of the Parliaments of Scotland*, vol. 3, p. 41; Records of the Parliaments of Scotland, 1567/12/62.
122 J. Finlay, *Men of Law in Pre-Reformation Scotland* (East Linton, 2000).
123 The central courts did not invariably remain in Edinburgh in this period, but they were based there.
124 *Acta curiae admirallatus Scotiae*, pp. 44, 50, 154–8 and 162.

at the leist of the practik of this realme, all admirale courtis aucht to be fensit and haldin within the sey mark, quhair the samyn fillis and flowis'.[125] In dealing with disputes relating to ships that had not arrived in Leith, the deputes in the Edinburgh court were no different from the 'lords of council', who became the judges in the College of Justice, and who dealt during the first half of the century with a large number of disputes relating to ships plundered on the high seas or wrecked anywhere on the coasts of Scotland.[126] After separate records began to be kept of the proceedings of the privy council in the middle of the 1540s, the jurisdiction of the College of Justice was more sharply focused on claims to compensation for the 'spuilzie' of ships or goods, though the division between the two conciliar courts was never exact.[127] In 1561, for instance, the privy council rejected an argument that it could not deal with an action concerning a 'spulyeit' ship because the 'lordis of sessioun' (as the lords of council were also called when they sat in the College of Justice) had been 'appointit and ordanit supreme jugeis to discuss upoun all civile caussis within this realme'.[128] Civil actions for spuilzie continued to be heard by both courts, much as criminal actions for piracy were heard both by the privy council and by the justiciary court.[129]

It has been appreciated for a long time that jurisdiction over disputes arising from seizures of ships and goods in wars – either in public wars declared between rulers or in more limited wars of reprisal – was contested in the first half of the sixteenth century.[130] In 1517, when the admiral, the third earl of Bothwell, remained a minor, his tutor was instructed by the lords of council

---

125 *Cf. Alexander King's Treatise on Maritime Law*, pp. 408–9.

126 These cases are calendared in *Acts of the Lords of Council in Public Affairs*, and some are discussed in J.D. Ford, *The Emergence of Privateering* (Leiden, 2023), pp. 8–101.

127 A.M. Godfrey, 'The Constitutional Accountability of the Court of Session in Scotland, 1532–1625', in I. Czeguhn, J.A. López Nevot and A. Sánchez Aranda (eds), *Control of Supreme Courts in Early-Modern Europe* (Berlin, 2018), p. 117, and 'The College of Justice, Court of Session and Privy Council in Sixteenth-Century Scotland, 1532–1603', in A.M. Godfrey and C.H. van Rhee (eds), *Central Courts in Early-Modern Europe and the Americas* (Berlin, 2020), p. 151.

128 *Register of the Privy Council of Scotland*, vol. 1, pp. 165–7, 171–82, 187–91, 195–8, 207–14 220, 224–7, 229–32 and 234.

129 Some of the records of piracy cases are reproduced in *Ancient Criminal Trials in Scotland*, 3 vols, ed. R. Pitcairn (Edinburgh, 1833), and some of these cases too are discussed in Ford, *Emergence of Privateering*, pp. 8–101.

130 A.R.G. McMillan, 'The Scottish Court of Admiralty: A Retrospect', (1922) 34 *Juridical Review* 38 and 164, pp. 40–1 and 164–5; W.C. Dickinson, 'Courts of Special Jurisdiction', in G.C.H. Paton (ed.), *An Introduction to Scottish Legal History* (Edinburgh, 1958), p. 396, at pp. 398–9; S. Murdoch, *The Terror of the Seas? Scottish Maritime Warfare, 1513–1713* (Leiden, 2010), pp. 10–11.

'to fens ane court within the flud mark' at which they would themselves sit alongside an admiral depute as assessors in determining the legitimacy of a seizure made during a war with Flanders.[131] When the lords of council failed to attend a sitting of the court, the admiral depute proceeded to deliver a decision on his own, but it was then subjected to review by the council. In 1542, when a master from Gelderland complained about his ship and goods being seized by Frenchmen when there was 'na weir betuix France and Gilleris', an admiral depute appeared before the lords of council to object that 'this actioun pertenit to the admiralite, and thairfor desirit the said mater to be referrit to him as juge ordinar'.[132] The council remitted the case to the admiralty court, but nominated some of its own members to assist in its hearing as assessors.[133] In 1544, after the earl of Bothwell reached the age of majority and returned from the Continent to assume responsibility for the administration of justice in maritime cases, one of his officers objected to the hearing of another prize case by the lords of council.[134] One of the lords reported that they had accepted the response by counsel for the pursuers that, 'albeit thair be divers utheris ordinarie judges, as schireffis and lordis of regalitie, yit thai may nocht repledge from the lordis of the sessione any caus or actione intendit betwix pairties duelland within thair jurisdictione fra the lordis, becaus the lordis ar judges ordinar in civill caussis to all the haill contrey'.[135] Seven months later Bothwell complained to parliament that while he was abroad he had been 'scharplie done to be my lordis of counsale and sessioune, quha hes tane, and takis dailie as occurris, diverse materis befoir thame that principallie concernis his office of admiralite', protesting that he was the 'principale ordinar and competent juge' in all cases relating to navigation.[136] It was decided that the admiral should deal with the 1544 case with assistance from members of the council

131 *Acts of the Lords of Council in Public Affairs*, pp. 76 and 82; *Practicks of Sir James Balfour of Pittendreich*, vol. 2, p. 630; W.S. Reid, *Skipper from Leith: The History of Robert Barton of Over Barton* (Philadelphia, 1962), p. 132.

132 *Acts of the Lords of Council in Public Affairs*, pp. 521 and 530; *Registrum secreti sigilli regum Scotorum*, vol. 2, pp. xiv–xx and 762–3, and vol. 3, pp. 50–2; *Practicks of Sir James Balfour of Pittendreich*, vol. 2, p. 634.

133 In 1523 the council had accepted a complaint from merchants in Leith against the hearing of a prize dispute by the provost and bailies of Edinburgh when 'thai materis pertenit ay to the admirall and na uthir juge' (*Acts of the Lords of Council in Public Affairs*, p. 162).

134 NRS, CS6/28, f. 9r; R. Gore-Browne, *Lord Bothwell* (London, 1937), pp. 28–31.

135 Sinclair's Practicks (http://home.uni-leipzig.de/jurarom/scotland/dat/sinclair.html), n. 367. See too Godfrey, 'College of Justice, Court of Session and Privy Council in Sixteenth-Century Scotland', pp. 170 and 173.

136 *Acts of the Parliaments of Scotland*, vol. 2, p. 449–50; Records of the Parliaments of Scotland, 1544/11/28–9.

as assessors, but due to delays in the hearing of the action it was called back for determination before the lords of council.[137] While it goes too far to conclude (as was done in the nineteenth century) that the lords of council emerge from these cases as the judges ordinary of prize litigation, they certainly did exercise supervision over the admiral's proceedings.[138]

The supervision was not confined to cases arising from conflicts at sea. In a case heard in 1533 the lords of council and session held that an action for the payment of a debt should be remitted from the admiralty court of Fife and Angus to the bailie court of Montrose because the admiral and his deputes were 'na competent jugis in the said mater'.[139] It was in essence an action of debt between merchant and merchant, not a seafaring cause. In 1584 the lords of council and session were asked to assume jurisdiction in a case pending before the admiral depute in the south west because the defender had never arrived there by sea, but had simply been summoned to appear at the market cross of Ayr, while he remained in Bordeaux.[140] The lords held that it was too late for an action to be 'advocated' to them when the admiral depute had already passed an act of litiscontestation, but other actions were advocated to the lords of council and session, and it was also possible for actions to be brought before them by way of 'reclamation' after a final decision had been delivered.[141] The intervention of the same judges was possible when actions were pending before bailie courts. While a case was being heard in Aberdeen, for instance, the bailies were informed that the defenders were being summoned to appear in Edinburgh, and that the bailies should 'decist and ceise fra all calling' of the action and leave it to be discussed 'afore the lordis of our soverane lordis consale, thair to be decidit as the law requiris'.[142] In other cases heard in Aberdeen disgruntled litigants announced their intentions to have actions 'advocattit' or 'reclamet and appelit' to the session.[143] No trace of any

137 *Acts of the Lords of Council in Public Affairs*, pp. 538–40; NLS, Adv. MS 25.2.7, ff. 19r, 21v and 27v, and Adv. MS 25.2.5(1), ff. 32r, 34v and 39v.

138 J. Riddell, *Inquiry into the Law and Practice in Scottish Peeragages*, 2 vols (Edinburgh, 1842), vol. 1, pp. 325–31; *Acts of the Lords of Council in Public Affairs*, pp. 608 and 626; *The Acts of Sederunt of the Lords of Council and Session*, 2 vols (Edinburgh, 1790–1811), vol. 1, p.1.

139 *Acts of the Lords of Council in Public Affairs*, p. 404; *Practicks of Sir James Balfour of Pittendreich*, vol. 2, p. 635; NRS, CS6/2, f. 779.

140 NRS, CS7/98, ff. 37r-9r.

141 A.M. Godfrey, *Civil Justice in Renaissance Scotland: The Origins of a Central Court* (Leiden, 2009), pp. 192–200.

142 ACA, CA1/1/14, pp. 254, 256–7, 259–62, 264–5, 268, 282 and 295. The bailies did not desist and cease from calling the case as desired.

143 ACA, CA1/1/20, pp. 121, 126, 129, 131–48, 150–6, 158–68, 170–3, 175–7 and 370, and CA1/1/28, p. 281.

of these three actions could actually be found in the records of the session, nor of several other actions in which similar moves were made, and the suspicion has to be that the litigants were merely manoeuvring for advantage in their debates before the bailies, as they frequently did when, in response to decisions they disliked, they vaguely 'protestit for remeid of law'. It must still be true, however, that these manoeuvres were effective because the intervention of the lords of council and session was a real possibility. Occasionally actions were transferred in the opposite direction, as when an action was remittted from the session to the bailie court of Dundee, or when the same court was instructed to implement a decreet of the session.[144]

It has been suggested that the lords of council and session, who had inherited from their predecessors a special responsibility to protect the interests of 'strangers', almost invariably assumed jurisdiction over actions with a foreign dimension.[145] This suggestion has met with understandable scepticism.[146] The evidence adduced in its support consists entirely of cases heard in the first half of the sixteenth century in relation to plundered ships or wrecks, and it is clear that not every case of these types was remitted to the session.[147] Attention was paid to some of the spuilzie cases by judges who reported memorable decisions of the court, yet they never reported seafaring causes of a commercial character.[148] Moreover, though not all of the two hundred and fifty-three volumes of the register of acts and decreets of the lords of session written in the sixteenth century have been searched through thoroughly for traces of maritime litigation, seventy volumes have been examined and barely a handful of relevant entries have been found, which contrasts sharply with the results of the survey of the burgh records.[149] As over three hundred and thirty cases of the types

144 DCA, BCMB, vol. 17, 18 August 1593; NRS, CS7/53, f. 288.

145 J. Finlay, 'Foreign Litigants before the College of Justice in the Sixteenth Century', in H.L. MacQueen (ed.), *Stair Society: Miscellany Four* (Edinburgh, 2002), p. 37, at p. 39.

146 E.B.I. Frankot, 'Aberdeen and the East Coast of Scotland: Autonomy on the Periphery', in W. Blockmans, M. Krom and J. Wubs-Mrozewicz (eds), *The Routledge Handbook of Maritime Trade around Europe, 1300–1600* (Abingdon, 2017), p. 411, at pp. 421–3.

147 The hearings recorded in the *Acta curiae admirallatus Scotiae* are sufficient to substantiate the point.

148 The *Practicks of Sir James Balfour of Pittendreich* and 'Sinclair's Practicks' have already been referred to. Other reports from the sixteenth century can be found in *The Practiques of Sir Richard Maitland of Lethington*, ed. R.S. Sutherland (Edinburgh, 2007), NLS, Adv. MS 22.3.4, pp. 417–599, and Adv. MS 24.1.5, ff. 134r-247v (Sir Alexander Colville), and Adv. MS 22.3.4, pp. 635–82 (Thomas Hamilton, later earl of Haddington).

149 It may be added that extracts taken from the register of acts and decreets by a seventeenth century lawyer, in NLS, Adv. MS 25.2.7, ff. 1–30r, and copied into Adv. MS 25.2.5(1), ff. 12v-41, do not include seafaring causes of a commercial character either.

under consideration were found in the council register of Aberdeen covering the first half of the century (the only record covering the whole period), and as roughly twelve per cent of the export revenues of the country were then being collected there, a crude extrapolation would appear to indicate that as many as three thousand eight hundred seafaring causes may have been handled in other burgh courts at this time, with other actions probably being raised in the admiralty courts. As the export revenues of the country increased during the second half of the century, the number of seafaring causes raised is also likely to have increased, though apparently in the admiralty courts more than the bailie courts, after the admirals began to assert an exclusive jurisdiction over such causes.[150] While not every seafaring cause found in the burgh records involved a foreign litigant, and while the selected volumes of the register of acts and decreets of the lords of session are not necessarily representative of the rest, it does seem unlikely – to put it mildly – that all cases involving a foreign litigant were advocated to the session. That seafaring causes were determined locally is readily intelligible. As well as providing that disputes arising after the arrival of a ship at a Scottish port should be handled by the king's bailies, the *Leges burgorum* had also provided that disputes of a commercial nature should be 'endyt wythin the thrid flud of the see'.[151] By the sixteenth century this rule had degenerated into a requirement that court orders should be fulfilled within three tides, however long it took for the court to reach the point of issuing an order, but the original purpose of the rule had not been forgotten.[152] It was taken to explain, for example, the entitlement of successful litigants to the payment of expenses by those who had contested their claims and forced them to remain in a port when there was profitable business to be conducted elsewhere.[153]

150 It is surely no coincidence that the number of seafaring causes heard by the bailies of Aberdeen began to fall in the 1540s, that it was in 1544 that the third earl of Bothwell sought to exclude the lords of council and session from the hearing of prize litigation, and that parliament tried in 1592 to turn the clock back to 1542. In 1544 the claim was made that Bothwell ought to 'brouke his heretage of admiralite as in utheris realms, and as hes bene the consuetude and use in this realme in tymes bigane', but Scottish practice appears previously to have differed from practice in France, England and other neighbouring nations.

151 *Acts of the Parliaments of Scotland*, vol. 1, p. 334; *Ancient Laws and Customs of the Burghs of Scotland*, vol. 1, p. 6.

152 Cases could drag on for several months, especially if parties or witnesses returned to sea before they were concluded, but swift adjudication remained a priority. It also needs to be remembered that the lords of council and session only sat for half of each year, and not in the summer months, the busiest time for maritime trade.

153 ACA, CA1/1/27, p. 293.

5 Court Records in Historical Enquiry

It will by now be obvious that there are major obstacles in the way of any attempt to study the law governing maritime commerce in sixteenth-century Scotland. The first is that the records of the courts in which law was applied to maritime disputes have mostly been lost. If there is reason to suppose that these disputes were still being dealt with in bailie courts in the first half of the century, it is a problem that very little evidence of their handling has survived from burghs other than Aberdeen. In particular, as the customs returns suggest that over half the goods exported from Scotland passed through Leith, where seafaring causes appear to have been dealt with in the court of the water bailie, the loss of the records of this court leave a gaping chasm in the evidence required for a reliable view to be formed of how these causes were determined. Likewise, if there is reason to suppose that most seafaring causes were dealt with in the admiralty courts during the second half of the century, it is a problem that a single court book has survived from the central court sitting in Edinburgh or Leith, which may not have been typical of the court books kept elsewhere, given the concentration in Edinburgh of lawyers educated at continental universities. While the records of maritime cases found in the surviving book can be added to the records of almost eight hundred cases found in the court and council books of the burghs, and while a few more cases can be added from the records of the session, the total falls far short of the many thousands of actions that were probably raised after ships arrived in Scottish ports. It needs to be remembered too that no account is being taken here of the determination of disputes involving Scottish merchants and mariners in other countries, although even the local records reveal that Scots often were involved in litigation elsewhere.[154] When disputes were raised between Scottish merchants and mariners in Veere, they were handled by the court of the conservator of their privileges in the Netherlands, in accordance with their own law.[155]

---

154 *Register of the Privy Council of Scotland*, vol. 5, pp. 175–6; *Records of the Convention of the Royal Burghs of Scotland*, vol. 1, pp. 178–9; *Extracts from the Council Register of the Burgh of Aberdeen*, vol. 1, pp. 333–4; *Aberdeen Council Letters*, vol. 1, p. 4; DCA, BCMB, vol. 14, 29 July and 5 October 1579; ACA, CA1/1/10, pp. 251, 253 and 255, CA1/1/16, p. 855, CA1/1/20, p. 363, CA1/1/24, pp. 186–7, CA1/1/25, pp. 152–3, CA1/1/27, pp. 250, 256, 258–9, 300 and 303, CA1/1/29, pp. 20–1, CA1/1/37, pp. 269–70, and CA5/1/5, 4 April 1597; AA, B6/12/2, p. 75.

155 J. Davidson and A. Gray, *The Scottish Staple at Veere: A Study in the Economic History of Scotland* (London, 1909), pp. 363–7 and 377; M.P. Rosseboom, *The Scottish Staple in the Netherlands* (The Hague, 1910), pp. 33, 49–50 and 84; A.D. Gibb, *International Private Law in Scotland in the Sixteenth and Seventeenth Centuries* (Edinburgh, 1928), pp. 11–12. See too V. Enthoven, 'The Last Straw: Trade Contacts along the North Sea Coast – The Scottish

Towards the end of the century the king appointed a conservator of the privileges of Scots trading in Spain, and attempted to appoint a similar officer in England, although the actual or intended effect of these appointments on the handling of litigation is unclear.[156] Were account to be taken of the cases heard overseas in which Scots law may have been applied, the number of cases of which no record has been found would need to be increased further.

Some compensation for the loss of crucial court records – especially those of the admiralty courts – is provided by the survival of a surprising number of surveys of maritime law written during the 1580s. Although only fragments remain of a treatise written by David Kintor (if, as has been suggested, the author was the admiral depute of that name who features in the court book covering the late 1550s and early 1560s), a 'collection of sea laws' was written by Sir James Balfour of Pittendreich, a former president of the session, an 'abridgement of all sea laws' was written by William Welwod, a professor of law at St Andrews, and a 'tractatus legum et consuetudinum navalium' was written by Alexander King, an advocate and admiral depute in the central court.[157] It may be imagined that there is no need to search court records for evidence of maritime law when the subject had already been scrutinised by contemporary experts. Indeed, much that has been written about the maritime law of early-modern Scotland in the past rests on the assumption that the treatises can be read as reliable accounts of the law applied in the courts. This assumption, however, is itself unreliable. Two of the treatises, for example, cite the fifteenth-century act of parliament requiring contracts for the transportation of goods by sea to be set down in the form of charter parties as if it remained in full force and effect, yet the admiralty courts could not have taken over responsibility for the determination of seafaring causes from the bailie courts, as both authors believed had happened, if that had been true.[158] All three authors

---

Staple at Veere', in J. Roding and L.H. van Voss (eds), *The North Sea and Culture, 1550–1800* (Hilversum, 1996), p. 209.

156 *Records of the Convention of Royal Burghs*, vol. 2, pp. 48–9 and 62; *Extracts from the Records of the Burgh of Edinburgh*, 2nd ser., vol. 1, pp. 253–4; *Extracts from the Council Register of the Burgh of Aberdeen*, vol. 1, pp. 189–92; ECA, SL1/1/10, p. 491; ACA, CA1/1/38, pp. 702–3 and 708–11; McLoughlin, 'Scottish Commercial Contacts with the Iberian World', pp. 66–8, and 'The Control of Trade in Scotland during the Reigns of James VI and Charles I', (2013) 45 *Northern Studies* 46, at p. 57.

157 *Practicks of Sir James Balfour of Pittendreich*, vol. 2, pp. 614–44; *Alexander King's Treatise on Maritime Law*, pp. 1–208 and 352–72. The relationship between Welwod's 'abridgement' and his *Sea-Law of Scotland*, is examined in the sixth essay in this collection.

158 *Practicks of Sir James Balfour of Pittendreich*, vol. 2, p. 618; *Alexander King's Treatise on Maritime Law*, p. 357. See again nn. 99–100 above. It has also been seen that the 1592 act of parliament was not entirely effective.

wrote as if the provisions of the 'Schiplawis', a version of the *Rôles d'Oléron* included in several collections of the 'auld lawes' of Scotland, were binding laws, yet it has been seen that the provisions of the *Leges burgorum*, more often included in these collections, were not adhered to religiously.[159] It cannot be assumed from the fact that written laws existed, or even that they were cited by lawyers, that they formed part of the law followed in practice. As with any texts written in the past, the treatises on maritime law need to be read in the light of their authors' presuppositions, intentions and methodology, which need to be recovered from the contexts in which they worked. Far from careful investigation of court records being superfluous, it is essential if the treatises are not to be misinterpreted.

Unfortunately, there are further problems with the court records, highlighted by a series of entries made in the council register of Aberdeen towards the end of the century. The provost, bailies and other members of the council observed that 'the cheiff burrowis of this realme hes housis belanging to the burght, callit the townis housis, quhilkis servis for a wreting buyth to thair commoun clerk, and a hous for keping of thair buikis and registeris, and advysing of the processis dependand betwixt nichtbour and nichtbour befoir the provest and bailleis'.[160] The lease of a room in a house close to the tolbooth of Aberdeen was about to expire, and it had in any case proved to be so small that their clerk had been 'compellit to keip the saidis registeris and buikis in his awin dwelling hous'. It was decided that a new room should be added to the tolbooth 'to keip the saidis registeris, buikis and proces, with ane studie in the end theirof for the clerk himselff'.[161] What exactly the clerk was expected to do in his study is not explained in these entries, but by the time they were made he was compiling not only a council register but also the separate bailie court books mentioned earlier, which contained drafts of some of the entries in the register dealing with the proceedings of the bailie court, along with accounts of

159 E.B.I. Frankot, 'The Scottish Translations of the *Rôles d'Oléron*: Edition and Commentary', in A.M. Godfrey (ed.), *Stair Society: Miscellany Eight* (Edinburgh, 2020), p. 13.

160 *Extracts from the Records of the Burgh of Aberdeen*, vol. 2, pp. 152–3 and 157–8; ACA, CA1/1/36, pp. 419–20 and 717–18, CA1/1/37, pp. 221, and CA5/1/5, 4 May 1597.

161 The addition of a clerk's office in Aberdeen is noted in *Tolbooths and Town-Houses: Civic Architecture in Scotland to 1833* (Edinburgh, 1996), produced under the auspices of the Royal Commission on the Ancient and Historical Monuments of Scotland, but nothing is said about where clerks worked elsewhere, though there was an 'over clarkis chalmer' in Edinburgh (ECA, SL1/1/5, f. 182, an entry that sheds light on the review of earlier records mentioned at n. 52 above). The clerk's office in Edinburgh seems to have been above the room in which actions were heard, and it may be that the bailies sometimes withdrew there to 'advise' or deliberate on cases in the same way as was described in Aberdeen.

cases that do not also appear in the register. It thus transpires that the council register does not provide a complete record of the proceedings of the court.[162] Calculations of the numbers of types of case heard like those presented earlier must accordingly be viewed with considerable caution. George Kitson Clark famously exhorted his fellow historians: 'Do not guess, try to count, and if you cannot count, admit that you are guessing'.[163] A more insidious tendency than guessing without acknowledgement is counting without acknowledgement that the figures are less than accurate, which is why only rough figures were presented earlier in this essay, and in words rather than in numerals, which can give a false impression of precision.[164] The figures presented previously, and also in some later essays in this collection, must be regarded as approximations, not exact computations, and as a basis for broad generalisations, not statistical analysis.

Another implication of the entries in the Aberdeen council register is that the accounts of cases composed by the clerk, while possibly closer to contemporaneous records than both the reports written by judges and the recollections of treatise writers, are not as contemporaneous as might have been thought. The clerk apparently wrote up his accounts of cases after he had withdrawn from the court room in which they were heard, and in which they were heard quite literally. A few pages ago it was noted in passing that allegations could be presented to courts 'in wrytte', and sometimes clerks reproduced written submissions at length in their records, instead of rephrasing them in their own words.[165] Yet defenders were summoned before the courts 'to sie and heir' decisions given against them, unless they could show why a pursuer's complaint should be dismissed, and even when written allegations were submitted, they were the subject of oral debate. As has often been pointed out, court records are not repositories of objective facts as much as rhetorical reconstructions of events, and they require to be read as critically and contextually as the treatises composed by lawyers.[166] They are often formulaic,

162 In fact, entries in the register sometimes refer to earlier proceedings and decisions that cannot be found there, and the same is true of entries in the records of other burghs.

163 G.K. Clark, *The Making of Victorian England* (London, 1972), p. 14.

164 Of course, the realisation that even the most comprehensive records are incomplete means that the figures presented are likely to be on the low side, although it should also be acknowledged that distinguishing between different cases is not always easy.

165 Even the allegations reproduced at length could have been written by professional scribes in their own styles.

166 E. Ketelaar, 'Records Out and Archives In: Early-Modern Cities as Creators of Records and as Communities of Archives', (2010) 10 *Archival Science* 201, at p. 207; M. Friedrich, *The Birth of the Archive: A History of Knowledge*, tr. J.N. Dillon (Ann Arbor, 2018), pp. 10–11.

and for the voices of the parties or their procurators to be heard, some effort must be made to discover where a clerk's preconceptions of style gave way to the substance of the allegations advanced.[167] Some effort must also be made to discover connections between the allegations advanced and the decisions delivered, and these need to be connections that might have been discerned by those involved, who may not have included lawyers. The expectations of trained lawyers are likely to have differed from those of any merchants or mariners they represented, and the expectations of modern lawyers are likely to differ even more. For the applicable law to be identified, attention must be paid to where those involved in court proceedings believed the law could be found. None of this is easy, and in view of the problems identified, it would be unrealistic to aim at producing anything like a definitive restatement of the law governing maritime commerce in sixteenth-century Scotland. What seems more realistic is to approach the subject from different angles by writing essays in the original sense of attempts to explore diverse themes and test out what can be achieved.[168] Despite the difficulties that need to be overcome, so much rich material has been found in the court records and legal treatises that it simply cannot be ignored. The burgh records, it may be worth repeating, provide information about the involvement of merchants and mariners in overseas trade not only in the entries relating to the seafaring causes focused on in this introductory essay, but also in many other entries.[169] These too shed helpful light on the law regulating their activities, as other essays in this collection show.

---

167 A. Butcher, 'The Functions of Script in the Speech Community of a Late-Medieval Town, c. 1300–1550', in J. Crick and A. Walsham (eds), *The Uses of Script and Print, 1300–1700* (Cambridge, 2004), p. 157; E.S. Cohen, 'She Said, He Said: Situated Oralities in Judicial Records from Early-Modern Rome', (2012) 16 *Journal of Early Modern History* 403. See too A. Brendecke, '*Arca, Archivillo, Archive*: The Keeping, Use and Status of Historical Documents about the Spanish *Conquista*', (2010) 10 *Archival Science* 267, at p. 268.

168 R.A. Sayce, *The Essays of Montaigne: A Critical Exploration* (London, 1972), pp. 19–22.

169 As well as records of litigation, both burgh and central courts often kept separate books in which contracts or other documents were registered, some of which related to overseas trade. Although some documents identified commissary courts as another place where registration might happen (*e.g.* ACA, CA2/2/2, 29 August 1584, and CA2/2/3, ff. 57–8), no relevant examples have been found in the commissary court books examined (*e.g.* NRS, CC13/7/1 and CC20/11/1–2).

PART 1

Legal Customs

2

Telling Tales

Maritime Law in Aberdeen in the Early Sixteenth Century

Edda Frankot has shown that the burgh records of Aberdeen provide a rich repository of information about maritime trade and its legal regulation in the fifteenth century.[1] In fact, many hundreds of entries relating to the same subject can also be found in the records surviving from the first half of the sixteenth century, until they start to thin out in the later 1540s, after the Scottish admiral began to assert an exclusive jurisdiction over seafaring causes.[2] These entries are not merely of great interest for historians intent on tracing the development of maritime law, but actually constitute the single most significant source available for the period. Relevant entries can be found in other burgh records, and seafaring causes were occasionally heard in the central courts, but no other source is as richly informative as the council registers of Aberdeen.[3] However, for scholars used to working on the records of the central courts (as legal historians tend to be) the burgh records are awkward to handle.[4] They are bound to seem both familiar and unfamiliar, and the temptation to focus on the familiar features, while attributing the unfamiliar to curiosities of the recording process, needs to be resisted. The aim of this essay is not to engage in the task of tracing the development of maritime law in Scotland, which will be attempted elsewhere, but is to consider how such a task might safely be undertaken, which requires examination of the character of the records and

---

1 'Maritime Law and Practice in Late Medieval Aberdeen', (2010) 89 *Scottish Historical Review* 136, and *'Of Laws of Ships and Shipmen': Medieval maritime law and its practice in urban northern Europe* (Edinburgh, 2012).

2 On the change in jurisdiction reference was originally made here to J.D. Ford, 'Introduction', in *Alexander King's Treatise on Maritime Law* (Edinburgh, 2018), p. ix, at pp. lxxi–vii, but see now the preceding essay in this collection.

3 ACA, CA1/1/7–20. As is explained in W. Hepburn and G. Small, 'Common Books in Aberdeen, c. 1398-c. 1511', in J.W. Armstrong and E. Frankot (eds), *Cultures of Law in Urban Northern Europe: Scotland and Its Neighbours, c. 1350-c. 1650* (Abingdon, 2021), p. 41, 'council register' may be a misleading description of these varied records.

4 This essay was written for the benefit of 'legal historians' in the broad sense of scholars committed to tracing the development of law and thinking about law. There is of course much in the records examined that should be of interest to social, economic and other historians as well, but these aspects are only touched on in passing.

 | DOI:10.1163/9789004695009_003

of the law found in them.[5] After a preliminary overview is provided of the types of entry examined (in which a change in the procedure followed by litigants comes to light), three possible approaches to the study of the records are considered in turn. It will be seen that the choice between these approaches, which to some extent build upon each other, hinges on the nature of the law referred to in the records, and on the sense in which there was a 'culture of law' in Aberdeen in the early sixteenth century.[6]

1 Court Actions and Legal Remedies

The entries in the records relating to maritime trade are of various types, but they can mostly be divided into three categories.[7] In the first place, many entries simply state that something has happened, such as the delivery of goods from a ship or the payment of freight for the carriage of goods. Although some of these entries may conceivably have been made in the course of disputes that were otherwise unrecorded, they appear usually to have been attempts to have it put on record that something has happened in the way it should have. In the second place, and in sharp contrast, many entries record protestations that something has not happened in the way it should have, for instance (to take the same examples) that goods have not been delivered or that freight has not been paid. Although these entries too may sometimes have been made in the course of disputes, they appear usually to have been made by or at the behest of merchants or mariners who wished to put it on record not only that something had not been done properly, but also that any loss resulting should be borne by another party. In the third place, many entries more clearly record the stages of disputes between parties.[8] They record the making of complaints by merchants and mariners against one another, the summoning of parties to respond to complaints, the setting of dates for hearings, the receipt

5 When originally written, this essay was very much a first faltering attempt to make sense of the subject. A further attempt is now made in the essay that follows this one, where some of the themes opened up here are explored further.

6 This essay was originally written as a contribution to a project on 'Cultures of Law in Urban Northern Europe', part of a broader project on the Aberdeen burgh records. Although less is said about the cultural nature of the law found in the burgh records in the essay following this one, that is not because doubts have arisen on this point.

7 Only the entries in the third category were included in the figures presented in the preceding essay.

8 As well as thinning out generally in the later 1540s, the entries relating to maritime trade by then fall mainly into the first two categories.

of arguments or evidence, and the delivery of decisions by the bailie court.[9] When decisions were delivered, parties were ordered to deliver goods, to pay freight, to contribute towards losses sustained by others, or something similar.

To some extent the entries in the third category resemble those found in the earliest surviving records of the burgh, which date back to the fourteenth century.[10] At the beginning of the sixteenth century defenders were still summoned to answer a 'borgh', of which they were given a copy, and of which a copy was sometimes entered in the records.[11] These documents typically opened with an assertion – in the first person – that the pursuer had 'found ane borgh' on the defender, went on to explain that something had happened because of which the defender ought to do something else, 'and wrangis and he do it nocht', and closed with the formula, 'and tharto my borgh and ane borgh to follow my borgh'.[12] Although the term 'borgh' was applied to the documents used to initiate actions, it applied more precisely to the security parties were required to provide for their appearance before the court. Borghs were a form of the *attachiamenta* referred to in the opening words of a famous procedural manual that formed part of the 'auld lawes' of Scotland.[13] In accordance with a process widely used in previous centuries, defenders were given four opportunities to appear before the court.[14] If they failed to appear at the fourth hearing, a penalty or 'amerciament' was imposed upon them and the court proceeded to give judgment in their absence. If they did appear, pleas and proofs were received from either party, usually at further hearings, before the court proceeded to deliver its decision.

In the early 1530s actions started to be initiated in a different way. On 23 February 1531 the bailies assigned further dates to a defender to appear and answer two 'petitions' submitted against him.[15] These petitions were like borghs in complaining that something had been done because of which the

9 In most of the relevant entries in the council register parties were generally said to have appeared before the *curia ballivorum burgi*, though sometimes the provost sat along with the bailies in this court, and sometimes maritime matters were considered elsewhere.

10 *Early Records of the Burgh of Aberdeen, 1317 and 1398–1407*, ed. W.C. Dickinson (Edinburgh, 1957).

11 ACA, CA1/1/9, p. 543, CA1/1/10, p. 211, and CA1/1/12/2, p. 520.

12 ACA, CA1/1/8, p. 1036, CA1/1/11, p. 636, CA1/1/12/1, pp. 16, 164, 278 and 286, and CA1/1/12/2, pp. 520, 701, 753 and 773.

13 *Quoniam attachiamenta*, ed. T.D. Fergus (Edinburgh, 1996), pp. 116–17. See too *The Ancient Laws and Customs of the Burghs of Scotland*, 2 vols, ed. C. Innes and R. Renwick (Edinburgh, 1868–1910), vol. 1, pp. 27, 36–7, 54 and 57.

14 *Habakkuk Bisset's Rolment of Courtis*, 3 vols, ed. P.J. Hamilton-Grierson (Edinburgh, 1920–6), vol. 3, pp. 29–84.

15 ACA, CA1/1/13, p. 95.

defender ought to do something else, 'and wrangs that he dois it nocht', but instead of being addressed to the officer of the court to whom security was given, they begged the judges directly to provide 'remeid of lawe'.[16] For the next fifteen years defenders were often summoned to answer 'petitions' submitted against them.[17] Those copied into the records followed the style of the 1531 petitions, except that they typically opened with a formal address to the court, contained a standardised statement that the defender was acting 'wranguslie and aganes the law', and ended by saying something like, 'and this my complent and petitioun to haf the strynth of ane borgh gif neid beis'.[18] As the phrases added at the end indicate, some effort was made to reconcile the use of petitions with the established procedure, although other changes were also made at the same time.[19] In the first petition submitted in 1531 the judges were actually asked to provide remeid of law 'conforme to our soverane lords letteris direktat to you', which probably meant letters issued in response to a petition presented to the king.[20] Around the same time the bailies received letters from the king concerning a ship wrecked on the coast nearby, in relation to which a 'summonds of spulzie' was being raised before 'the lords of counsall'.[21] When a summons was raised before this central court it was in response to a bill of complaint or supplication of a type similar to the petitions coming into use in Aberdeen.[22] Within a decade local courts throughout the country would be

16 ACA, CA1/1/13, pp. 96–7.

17 Although it is possible that petitions were already in use in other types of case, a more comprehensive search through the two parts of ACA, CA1/1/12, has revealed that they contain as many as forty borghs but not a single petition. Similarly, in the first ninety-five pages of CA1/1/13, five borghs have been found but no petitions.

18 ACA, CA1/1/13, p. 303, CA1/1/14, pp. 256–7, 260 and 587–8, CA1/1/15, pp. 286, 298, 334–5, 368–9, 445, 653–5, 662, 665, 682–3 and 736–7, CA1/1/16, pp. 90–1, 122, 189, 452, 454, 467, 521–2, 561–2, 611, 711–12, 741, 760, 794 and 855, CA1/1/17, pp. 440–1, CA1/1/18, p. 248, and CA1/1/19, pp. 4, 98 and 123–4.

19 Instead of court officers receiving borghs from defenders, for example, defenders were increasingly required to provide the bailies themselves with security in the form of 'caution', which could be both *de iudicio sisti et iudicatum solvi* (that is, a guarantee both that they would appear before the court to hear sentence given and that any award of damages the court made would be satisfied).

20 The study of petitions as a direct link between rulers and ruled has of course become a growth industry in recent years (see, for example, K. Bowie, 'From Customary to Constitutional Right: The Right to Petition in Scotland before the 1707 Act of Union', (2018) 38 *Parliaments, Estates and Representation* 279). The essential element in the 1531 case is that those in authority were being begged to intervene in a dispute.

21 ACA, CA1/1/13, pp. 15–23, 103, 115–17, 134–9 and 143–4.

22 *Acts of the Lords of Council, 1501–1503*, ed. A.B. Calderwood (Edinburgh, 1993), p. xxv.

instructed to imitate the procedure favoured by the lords of council.[23] It may be that awareness of how cases were raised in Edinburgh was already encouraging the bailie court of Aberdeen to imitate the example of the central court.

Whatever the reason for the move from borghs to petitions may have been, it clarified the purpose of raising actions. Many petitions – resembling again the documents used before the lords of council – spelled out the pursuer's concern that the defender would not do as he should 'without he be compellit be the law'.[24] Of course, whichever form of process was used, all pursuers must have wanted defenders to be subjected to legal compulsion, as is borne out by the recurrence throughout the records of statements that defenders should 'underly the lawe' or 'answer as law will'.[25] The adoption of the standard phrase 'wranguslie and aganes the law' similarly served to clarify the significance of the phrase 'wrangis and he do it nocht' found in the earlier borghs. Both phrases are reminiscent of the technical expression 'wrang et unlaw', which appears in the fourteenth century records. Historians studying these and other records have observed that lawyers in late medieval Scotland had an opportunity to develop the law by teasing out the meaning of this expression in relation to the cases they handled.[26] Whether or not that actually happened, lawyers appearing before the lords of council certainly did something similar in refining their understanding of various species of wrong like 'spuilzie'.[27] It happens that when spuilzie was mentioned in the entries examined here, it was always in connection with the practice of the lords of council, yet it may be wondered whether a comparable process of legal abstraction was under way in the bailie

23 *The Acts of the Parliaments of Scotland*, 12 vols, ed. T. Thomson and C. Innes (Edinbrugh, 1814–75), vol. 2, p. 358; Records of the Parliaments of Scotland, ed. K.M. Brown (www.rps .ac.uk), 1540/12/14.

24 ACA, CA1/1/14, pp. 587–8, CA1/1/15, pp. 286, 298, 334–5, 368–9, 445, 655, 662, 665 and 736–7, CA1/1/16, pp. 90–1, 122, 452, 454, 467, 521–2, 561–2, 611, 627–8, 760 and 855, and CA1/1/19, pp. 123–4.

25 ACA, CA1/1/8, p. 798 and 830, CA1/1/10, pp. 29, 115, 167, 169, 277 and 366, CA1/1/11, pp. 521 and 636, CA1/1/12/1, pp. 126 and 261–3, CA1/1/12/2, pp. 522, 666, 700–1, 710–11, and 753–4, CA1/1/13, pp. 172, 180, 506 and 508, CA1/1/14, pp. 254, 256, 259, 264–5, 266–7, 536, 545 and 620, CA1/1/15, pp. 33–5, 48, 55, 108, 110, 167, 204, 294, 387, 445 and 448, CA1/1/16, pp. 104–5, 131, 155 and 375, CA1/1/18, p. 243, and CA1/1/19, pp. 310, 316–17 and 394.

26 A. Harding, 'Rights, Wrongs and Remedies in Late-Medieval English and Scots Law', in H.L. MacQueen (ed.), *Stair Society: Miscellany Four* (Edinburgh, 2002), p. 1; H.L. MacQueen, 'Some Notes on Wrang and Unlaw', in H.L. MacQueen (ed.), *Stair Society: Miscellany Five* (Edinburgh, 2006), p. 13.

27 A.M. Godfrey, *Civil Justice in Renaissance Scotland: The Origins of a Central Court* (Leiden, 2009), pp. 239–47.

court of Aberdeen.[28] Since merchants and mariners complained there about 'wrangis' done to them, it may be wondered whether different categories of wrong were carefully distinguished, and conditions of liability for each type of wrong painstakingly specified.

2 Written Pleadings and Legal Reasoning

On 13 April 1543 an 'obligatioun' was produced before the bailie court by a creditor.[29] A date was set for the debtors named in the document to respond, but their procurator – a university graduate who may possibly have studied law – argued that they need not answer as 'the balze ma nocht decerne bot on wrangis, and thair is na wrang done specifiit in the obligatioun', adding that the debtors 'sould nocht be decernytt to gyf ony answer thairto withtout formaill petitioun and liball war maid thairupoun'.[30] The creditor was informed that he would need to present a petition if he wished to proceed, but whether any need was sensed for a wrong like 'breach of contract' to be specified is doubtful. No petition was presented for the creditor, perhaps because the debtors' procurator had meanwhile presented a successful petition on their behalf, alleging that the creditor had removed their goods from a ship and was refusing to return them, 'wrangously and aganes the law'.[31] The wrong was not specified here either, nor was a wrong identified precisely in any of the other petitions entered in the records. There is one petition, however, that does go further than the rest. On 9 August 1538 it was alleged that certain merchants were refusing to contribute towards losses sustained by others when a ship they shared was plundered of some of its cargo by pirates.[32] What makes the petition exceptional is that it declared their refusal to contribute to be inconsistent with a rule of law established by the 'ald lovabill use lang observit withtin this nobill burght'. This petition at least went beyond alleging vaguely that the merchants were acting wrongfully and against the law by making some attempt to identify the law they were contravening. The court agreed that the

28 ACA, CA1/1/14, pp. 566–8 and 570–2, ACA, CA1/1/15, pp. 485–6, and ACA, CA1/1/18, p. 241. Actions for spuilzie can be found in *Records of the Sheriff Court of Aberdeenshire*, 3 vols, ed. D. Littlejohn (Aberdeen, 1904–7), vol. 1, pp. 47–63, 149–63 and 255–6, and they may well be found elsewhere in the burgh records.

29 ACA, CA1/1/17, pp. 434–6.

30 ACA, CA1/1/17, p. 440.

31 ACA, CA1/1/17, pp. 441, 446, 450, 453, 463 and 571.

32 ACA, CA1/1/15, pp. 711–12.

merchants were obliged to contribute, 'conforme to the ald lovabill consuetud of this burght'.

If this exceptional petition may be taken to contain a syllogism, in which averments of fact were connected as a minor premiss with a proposition of law as a major premiss, leading to the conclusion that a legal remedy must be granted, the other petitions and borghs may perhaps be regarded as enthymemes, in which the major premiss of the argument was left unstated.[33] There are several reasons why it could have been considered appropriate for the law underpinning pleadings to remain implicit.[34] The applicable law could have been considered too uncontentious to be in need of statement, especially if the dispute centred on the accuracy of factual averments, as it clearly did in many cases. Conversely, where the law did seem contentious, the writers of petitions and borghs could have been reluctant to commit parties to defined positions before argument was engaged in before the court. That legal argument was sometimes expected is suggested by entries recording the willingness of defenders to do whatever 'happennit to be decernit and fundin, other be law or prettike', or to make payments 'gif it wer fundin of law that thai aucht to'.[35] Entries like these are unusual, however, and when they do occur there is rarely any indication of a finding being made, still less of how it was made. It is possible that the clerks who compiled the records preferred not to set down in writing all the oral exchanges they heard in the court, in which case the task of the legal historian might be to fill in the gaps in the records by identifying propositions of law that would have rendered the reasoning in the pleadings coherent. But before this is assumed, the traces of legal argument that do exist need to be examined carefully.

When parties petitioned the court for 'remeid of law', seeking to have their opponents 'compellit be the law' to do something, and when it was stated that their opponents should appear before the court to 'underly the lawe' or 'answer as law will', the word 'law' was used primarily to signal a desire for disputes to be determined by way of a coercive process.[36] The first of these expressions recurs quite frequently in statements that a party objected to how a case was

33 For the later use of this Aristotelian distinction by Scots lawyers see J.D. Ford, *Law and Opinion in Scotland during the Seventeenth Century* (Oxford, 2007), pp. 513–15.

34 J.G.H. Hudson, 'Court Cases and Legal Arguments in England, c. 1066–1166', (2000) 10 *Transactions of the Royal Historical Society* 91, explains why this may have happened and how historians may respond in dealing with truncated pleadings.

35 ACA, CA1/1/9, p. 399, and CA1/1/11, p. 535.

36 The process was backed up with recurring threats of seizure of property (poinding) or person (warding), and occasionally with other threats too.

being handled and 'protestit for remeid of law', meaning that he intended to take any steps he could to challenge the court's ruling.[37] When a party in one case asked for copies of depositions received from witnesses, the other party's procurator 'protestit that he gett nocht the same, becaus it is aganis the pratik and styill of court, and for remeid of law gif the bailzeis dois in the contrar'.[38] As parties who protested for 'remeid of law' were making a procedural move, the likelihood is that parties who petitioned for 'remeid of law' were doing the same, and were asking not so much to have their opponents compelled to fulfil their obligations under substantive law as to have them subjected to a process governed by procedural law. It was apparently the procurator who referred to 'the pratik and styill of court' who also complained in the case mentioned earlier about parties being summoned to answer an 'obligatioun'.[39] Given that types of wrong never were specified in petitions, his concern was presumably less with the lack of specification than with the attempt to initiate an action with an obligation instead of a petition. Another common use of the word 'law' was in court orders requiring payments to be made 'within terme of law', which meant that payments were to be made within the period prescribed by procedural law.[40] Accordingly, the point of saying that parties would make payments 'gif it wer fundin of law that thai aucht to' may simply have been that they were prepared to make payments if they were ordered to do so in a court process governed by law, not that they were prepared to make payments if required to do so by substantive law. But what about parties who undertook to do whatever 'happennit to be decernit and fundin, other be law or prettike'? Were they referring to rules directly regulating the activities of merchants and mariners?

A few entries in the records from the 1530s and 1540s are indicative of inquiry into law of a more substantive variety. In one case it was found to be 'the law of the sey' that someone employed as an ordinary sailor on one ship could accept appointment as 'ane bottisman' on another.[41] What exactly was meant by 'the law of the sey' is not apparent, but the idea that sailors should be free to assume more responsible positions on other vessels was broadly consistent with a provision of the maritime code known as the laws of Wisby.[42] In other cases equally vague reference was made to 'the ammarrellis lawis',

37 A particularly instructive example can be found at ACA, CA1/1/16, pp. 632 and 637.

38 ACA, CA1/1/16, p. 617.

39 See again the quotations at n. 30 above.

40 This expression is equated with the equally common 'within thre tydis' in ACA, CA1/1/12/2, p. 672.

41 ACA, CA1/1/14, p. 413.

42 *The Black Book of the Admiralty*, 4 vols, ed. T. Twiss (London, 1871–6), vol. 4, p. 283.

'the commont law', or simply 'the law'.[43] When the question was raised 'quhidder gold and silver cumand hayme in ane schip to this realme suld scot and lote witht uther gudis or nocht', the court found that 'all kind of mony, baitht gold and silver, cunzeit and uncunzeit, and als rings, being in ane schip, suld lott and scott witht the uther guds of the said schip'.[44] It is unclear where this answer was found, but it could have been in Justinian's *Digest*, where the same question had been answered in the same way by a Roman jurist.[45] The issue remained controversial in Aberdeen, yet the court's ruling seems to have been remembered by the draftsman of the exceptional petition in which a proposition of law was enunciated, for his complaint related to merchants who carried goods alone, yet the proposition was that if goods were lost, everyone else with 'gudds and money' aboard a ship had to contribute towards the loss sustained.[46] Another exceptional entry contains a protestation that merchants whose goods were stowed in the hold of a ship should not contribute towards losses sustained by those whose goods were stacked above deck, 'conform to the act of parliament maid thairupoune'.[47] Protestations in similar terms were actually quite frequent, but on no other occasion was support drawn from an act of parliament, or for that matter from an ordinance of the burgh council on the same subject.[48]

3 Maritime Practice and Legal Customs

If an obvious question to ask is why so little interest seems to have been shown in the origins of the rules occasionally applied, there are two equally obvious answers, neither of which is reassuring if the aim is to confirm that more legal reasoning went on than the records reveal. The first is that authoritative sources were not cited in the way they often were by lawyers for the simple reason that lawyers were seldom involved in the handling of cases. As has been seen, procurators with university degrees did occasionally represent parties. Their critical comments on the court's procedure are recorded, but there is

43 ACA, CA1/1/13, pp. 403–4, and CA1/1/12/2, pp. 675 and 689–90.

44 ACA, CA1/1/13, pp. 410 and 425.

45 D.14.2.2.2.

46 ACA, CA1/1/13, pp. 465, 506–9 and 511–13, CA1/1/14, pp. 139–40, and CA1/1/15, pp. 711–12.

47 ACA, CA1/1/16, p. 784.

48 For the protestations see ACA, CA1/1/8, pp. 1029–30, CA1/1/9, p. 732, CA1/1/12/1, pp. 407–8, CA1/1/12/2, p. 529, CA1/1/15, pp. 89–90, 94, 96, 118 and 278; for the legislation see *Acts of the Parliaments of Scotland*, vol. 2, pp. 87 and 178; Records of the Parliaments of Scotland, 1467/1/4 and 1487/10/19; ACA, CA1/1/9, p. 398.

no indication that they were prone to rehearsing rules, citing authorities or analysing the terms in which borghs and petitions were expressed.[49] As for the bailies who presided over hearings, they were burgesses who appeared at other times as parties to actions of a mercantile or maritime nature. In many cases the bailies assembled assizes from among the suitors of the court, whose findings were delivered as the court's decisions, yet the suitors were also merchants and mariners, who appeared at other times as litigants.[50] The clerks of the court are identified in one entry as 'notars', and the draftsmen of the borghs and petitions may have been notaries public as well.[51] As has been seen, however, the documents used to initiate actions generally failed to enunciate propositions of law, and while the clerks may be suspected of omitting to record all the arguments advanced orally before the court, it can scarcely be supposed that it was normal for a clerk to prompt parties with arguments they were unable to articulate on their own. Assuming – as we surely must – that the clerks performed a more passive role, the bailie court emerges as a forum in which the affairs of merchants and mariners were subjected to regulation by merchants and mariners themselves.

The second obvious explanation for the absence from the records of references to authoritative sources of law – the laws of Wisby, Justinian's *Digest*, acts of parliament and so on – is that the law was not conceived of in the fashion familiar to lawyers. The exceptional petition already mentioned may have owed something in its composition to written sources, but the rule of law it contained was said to have been established by the 'ald lovable use lang observit withtin this nobill burght'. Similar language is encountered elsewhere. In one case merchants were required to make payments 'eftir the forme of the auld ryte and lovable consuetude usit in this towne a lang tyme bigane'.[52] In several other cases parties were required to make payments in accordance with 'use and wont', 'as use is', or 'as use and wont is amang marineris'.[53] A mariner claimed in one of these cases that, 'be use and custum amang marineris', a master ought to reimburse him for expense he had incurred while recovering from an illness contracted on a voyage. Support for this claim could have been

49 For a persuasive explanation of the involvement of lawyers in an unusual episode see A.R.C. Simpson, 'Spuilzie and Shipwreck in the Burgh Records', (2018) 9 *Journal of Irish and Scottish Studies* 70.

50 *Cf. Early Records of the Burgh of Aberdeen*, pp. cxxviii–ix.

51 ACA, CA/1/13, p. 18.

52 ACA, CA1/1/13, pp. 157–8. Another entry in which similar language is used will be returned to below.

53 ACA, CA1/1/13, p. 502, CA1/1/15, p. 230, CA1/1/16, p. 205, CA1/1/17, pp. 573–4 and 579–80, and CA1/1/19, p. 4.

drawn from an article in the laws of Wisby, although it is not mentioned in the record.[54] Another article in that code could have been cited to support a claim that a master ought to pay for the hire of a lighter required to transfer goods from his ship into an inaccessible harbour, though reference is again made to 'use and custum' alone.[55] Similarly, mariners who wished to terminate their employment on a ship were told that they must first help to complete its unloading, 'conforme to the use of marenellis', although here too reference might have been made to the laws of Wisby.[56] It is of course possible that the clerks failed to record references that were actually made to these articles, but it is also possible, and indeed more likely, that no copy of the code was consulted, that reliance was at most placed on distant recollections of its provisions, and that mariners were largely unconscious of any influence the code had exerted on the shaping of their practices.[57] In any case, whether or not the code was cited, and however accurately its provisions may or may not have been remembered, the crucial point is that it would not have contained directly applicable rules if what made behaviour obligatory was its customary observance.

When it was found that 'the law of the sey' permitted an ordinary mariner to withdraw from service on one ship to become an officer on another, the rule was said to have been 'sufficientlie provyne' before the court by 'certane famouse skipperis'.[58] Even if the relevant provision of the laws of Wisby had been cited, what clearly mattered here was the testimony of recognised experts that the practice was known to them.[59] Testimony was taken because to ask what was lawful among mariners was to ask what was normal. As normative behaviour was thus identified with normal behaviour, there was no sharp distinction, as lawyers would have expected, between questions of law and questions of fact. An assize found in one case that a ship had 'come saifly

54 *Black Book of the Admiralty*, vol. 4, p. 270. The corresponding article in the laws of Oleron (*Black Book of the Admiralty*, vol. 1, pp. 94–7) was less supportive.

55 ACA, CA1/1/12/2, p. 672; *Black Book of the Admiralty*, vol. 4, p. 281.

56 ACA, CA1/1/19, p. 401; *Black Book of the Admiralty*, vol. 4, p. 280.

57 None of the findings listed matches the terms of the code exactly. Frankot, *'Of Laws of Ships and Shipmen'*, pp. 154–7 and 195, found not only that the code was unknown in the fifteenth century, but also that rulings then were influenced in the same vague and probably indirect way by the laws of Oleron. She is presumably correct in suggesting that legislation informing the laws of Wisby is more likely to have been known about earlier in the sixteenth century than the code itself. Essentially, though, mariners and merchants in Scotland are less likely to have consulted written statements of the law at any stage than to have remembered conversations they had with merchants and mariners from overseas. This point is now returned to in later essays in this collection.

58 ACA, CA1/1/14, p. 413.

59 Again, the practice was not covered exactly by the terms of the provision in the code.

in the havin of Abirdene and thair was maid fast witht hir anchoris and towis, efter the use and custum as maisteris and marenellis usis to lay thair schip'.[60] In another case a master claimed to have moored his ship in 'the souerast fassoun, be the avyse and sycht of marinaris', and asked the bailies to 'sand men of knawlege to se and considder gif the said schipe was soueralie fastnyt'.[61] After a leaking ship was brought into Aberdeen on an earlier occasion, the master had asked the court 'to send downe certane schipmen to se and consider the same'.[62] In these cases, confirmation that standard practice had been adhered to would have amounted to confirmation that obligations had been discharged. There was a normative dimension to an otherwise factual inquiry, and it is not easy to distinguish cases like these from others in which, for example, the issue was whether goods were dry when loaded onto a ship, 'it beand considerit be famous merchand men'.[63] The recourse to renowned experts in some of these cases is revealing, but it was not typical. The court was generally able to rely on the expertise of the merchants and mariners present to discover how their affairs were normally conducted.

Even if the more numerous entries in which reference is made to 'use and custum' are added to the handful of entries in which substantive 'law' is mentioned, they still amount to a small proportion of all the entries relating to maritime trade. There are other entries, however, in which questions of law appear to have been brought into focus, albeit without answers being provided. For instance, when evidence presented in one case showed that lint had been wet while being taken in a lighter from a ship into a harbour, the question was raised 'quhidder the awnaris of the schip or merchandis aucht to pay the skaytht done to the lynt in the forsaid lychtaris defalt'.[64] Furthermore, even when no questions were asked, entries often have a repetitive quality that enables regularities of behaviour to be identified with such confidence that it has to be wondered whether things happened as a rule (descriptively) because governed by a rule (prescriptively). If it would be misleading for legal historians to reconstruct the reasoning that might have gone on in the bailie court had lawyers been involved, perhaps it would be possible for them to discover customary norms that offer answers to the questions sometimes raised, or that seem to be implicit in regularities of behaviour discernible elsewhere. As commissions of enquiry were established in many parts of Europe, both before and during the

---

60 ACA, CA1/1/20, p. 24.
61 ACA, CA1/1/12/2, p. 865.
62 ACA, CA1/1/12/1, p. 245.
63 ACA, CA1/ 1/12/1, p. 293.
64 ACA, CA1/1/16, p. 389.

sixteenth century, to investigate and redact the usages and customs considered normative by lay people, and as lawyers (who tended to feature prominently on these commissions) sometimes endeavoured to describe popular customs in books they wrote, there may be some warrant for historians attempting to perform a similar task.[65] Perhaps they could try to identify customary norms in the way contemporary lawyers might have done. Perhaps, although they would need to bear in mind the lessons learned by both historians and anthropologists from study of the codification of legal customs, for what has repeatedly been found is that customary norms tend to change in character when reduced to writing by lawyers.[66] Indeed, even to talk of customary norms may be misleading.[67] For this second approach to be adopted, some way would need to be found of preserving the character of the usages and customs considered normative by merchants and mariners.

4 Local Knowledge and Legal Cultures

The position reached so far is that although there is some evidence of an ability to think like lawyers among those involved in court cases in Aberdeen in the early sixteenth century, the evidence is too slight to justify an attempt to reconstruct other cases in a way that would make them satisfy the expectations of lawyers. The merchants and mariners who adjudicated on their own affairs would no doubt have agreed with any suggestion put to them that the law consisted of rules, for they did occasionally express their thinking in such terms. For the most part, however, they do not seem to have thought in terms of legal abstractions that could have been applied to the facts of cases. The entries in the records in which some semblance of legal reasoning can be found are vastly outnumbered by those in which normative thinking is embedded in factual observations, which is understandable given that the normative

65 D. Heirbaut, 'Exploring the Law in Medieval Minds: The Duty of the Legal Historian to Write the Books of Non-Written Law', in A. Musson and C. Stebbings (eds), *Making Legal History: Approaches and Methodologies* (Cambridge, 2012), p. 118, recommends such an approach.

66 See, for instance, E. Kadens, 'Custom's Past', in C.A. Bradley (ed.), *Custom's Future: International Law in a Changing World* (Cambridge, 2016), p. 11.

67 As Heirbaut points out, German historians distinguish between legal customs of the kind found in Aberdeen (*Rechtsgewohnheiten*), and the customary laws reconstructed from them by lawyers (*Gewohnheitsrechten*). The precise significance of these terms is apt to vary from one historian to another, but the crucial point is that lay people and trained lawyers tended to view customs in different ways.

appears to have been identified with the normal. The only justification for treating the rare cases in which those involved may have reasoned like lawyers as paradigms for the many in which such reasoning could only be read into the records would be if the records of the majority of cases are unintelligible otherwise. Yet the entries relating to maritime trade can be understood in a different way. A feature common to entries in all three of the categories distinguished earlier is that merchants and mariners were reporting each other's actions to the court, often in the expectation that something would be done about them.[68] They reported one another to the court in much the same way as children tell tales on each other to their parents or teachers. This should not be taken to mean that the merchants and mariners were engaging in some form of puerile behaviour, as if they lacked the sophistication of the trained lawyers who were appearing around the same time in other courts. Just as smart children appreciate that for the tales they tell to be effective they need to resonate with the presuppositions of their parents or teachers, so merchants and mariners must have appreciated that reporting one another to the court would only have produced the results they wanted if the court shared their understanding of how things were meant to be done.[69] The tales told had to be tellable tales, and in principle an accumulation of tellable tales may be as effective, extensive and elaborate as an assemblage of applicable rules. If the task of the legal historian is seen as the recovery of tellable tales, or as the investigation of the presuppositions shared by those involved in the court process, then there may be some prospect of an account of the maritime law adhered to in courts like the bailie court of Aberdeen remaining true to the character of the source material available.

Some readers may be reminded of the account of *adat* adjudication in Indonesia originally presented in the Storrs Lectures delivered by Clifford Geertz in 1981.[70] Noting that *adat* was generally perceived to be a kind of custom, Geertz warned that the confusion caused by the concept of custom among anthropologists was exceeded only by the confusion it caused among lawyers. Among anthropologists, custom tended to be reduced to the level of practice, habit or a way of doing things – in other words, to a matter of

68 Even when the aim was to record satisfaction with something that had been done, the expectation generally was that the person responsible would be released from an obligation.

69 This is not a round-about way of saying that children need to know the rules of the game, although some of them may think in these terms. On this point much can of course be learned from the later Wittgenstein.

70 *Local Knowledge: Further Essays in Interpretive Anthropology* (London, 1993), pp. 167–234.

fact – whereas among lawyers it tended to be turned into abstract generalisations or written rules – in other words, into a kind of law.[71] *Adat*, Geertz insisted, was bound to be misconceived by anyone who thought in terms of a binary opposition between fact and law. As he saw it, *adat* consisted of acceptable representations of reality, or ways of describing the world that were believed to be appropriate. The purpose of adjudication, he believed, was to work towards a consensus on how far something that had happened could be described as something that ought to have happened. Viewed in this way, the legal process was not merely 'functional' but deeply 'cultural', in the sense that it was a means not merely of determining disputes but also of generating social awareness. Geertz famously described people as animals suspended in webs of significance that they themselves had spun, and maintained that the task of the cultural anthropologist was to explain the significance of the webs spun by social groups, not by 'translating' them into supposedly corresponding terms, concepts and symbols drawn from other cultures, but by engaging in a necessarily hermeneutic process of 'interpretation'.[72] Law, he argued in his Storrs Lectures, was one of the types of web people spin, and it needed, if it was to be properly understood, to be interpreted in ways that rendered the thinking of its users intelligible, not simply restated or reworked in keeping with the thinking of external observers.[73] Properly understood, law was intrinsically cultural. The point was not just that the development of a culture could be affected by law, or even that a developed culture could involve expectations of law, but that law was itself a cultural development. As Geertz put it, law needed to be perceived as 'a species of social imagination'.[74]

Geertz also envisaged law as a species of 'local knowledge', by which he appears to have meant two things. The first is that law in a form like *adat* does not consist of abstract generalisations that can be applied logically to separately discovered facts, but is bound up with the facts of circumstantial cases.[75] Knowledge of this type of law is unavoidably localised because it cannot be abstracted from the cases in which it is found without being turned

---

71 On the reworking of *adat* by legal scholars see, for instance, Z.Z. Mutaqin, 'Indonesian Customary Law and European Colonialism: A Comparative Analysis on *Adat* Law', (2011) 4 *Journal of East Asia and International Law* 351.

72 *The Interpretation of Cultures: Selected Essays* (New York, 1973), pp. 3–30.

73 Whether all law may be viewed in the same way, as Geertz suggested, need not be considered here. The important point for present purposes is that the law referred to in the Aberdeen records does appear to have had this cultural significance.

74 *Local Knowledge*, p. 232.

75 See too Geertz, *Available Light: Anthropological Reflections on Philosophical Topics* (Princeton, 2000), pp. 133–40.

into something it is not. A natural response for some lawyers to make is that 'case law' is a category with which they are all too familiar, and that extracting general rules from particular decisions is what they do best. But could the merchants and mariners who raised cases, served as bailies and sat on assizes in Aberdeen have made the same response? To have been able to extract transferable rules from earlier rulings they would at the very least have required access to those rulings. Written records were obviously being made, and parties frequently asked to be provided with copies of entries affecting them.[76] The existence of these records could have changed the character of the law mentioned, so long as they were used as a source of reference.[77] The reality is, however, that while there were occasions on which earlier rulings were drawn to the court's attention, this only occurred when the rulings had been made at previous stages in the same proceedings.[78] Earlier rulings do not feature anywhere in the entries examined here as what lawyers call 'judicial precedents'. The most that may be suggested is that people involved in litigation sometimes remembered previous cases, which would have given any rules they formulated the fluidity commonly taken to typify the operation of an oral tradition of usage and custom.[79] It has been seen that when a proposition of law was enunciated in one petition, it appeared to build on a decision delivered in a previous case, and it is proposed here to treat regularities found in other entries as evidence of legal customs.[80] Different entries related to different cases, distinct from each other in their factual circumstances, yet the entries were often expressed in strikingly similar language. However, the proposal is not to restate these similarities as abstract generalisations of a kind that could be used to supplement

76 ACA, CA1/1/12/1, pp. 170, 173, 216 and 351, CA1/1/12/2, pp. 477, 480–1, 526, 674, 697–701 and 711, CA1/1/13, pp. 15–23, 134–9, 143–4, 406, 410–13, 415–18, 421–5, 495–8 and 513, CA1/1/14, pp. 141, 191, 215, 429, 546–7 and 589, CA1/1/15, pp. 20, 36, 47, 70, 87, 167, 408 and 485, CA1/1/16, pp. 67, 83, 175, 195, 256, 271, 316, 391, 452, 462, 465, 474, 487, 604, 612, 632, 653 and 744, CA1/1/17, pp. 573–4, CA1/1/18, pp. 235, 251, 364, 373, 512, 529 and 579, and CA1/1/19, pp. 104, 291, 301, 303, 310, 324, 412 and 418.

77 Interesting questions are raised in S. Teuscher, 'Document Collections, Mobilized Regulations and the Making of Customary Law at the End of the Middle Ages', (2010) 10 *Archival Science* 211.

78 ACA, CA1/1/12/1, pp. 216–17 and 228, CA1/1/14, p. 360, CA1/1/17, p. 575, and CA1/1/18, p. 415.

79 The relevant literature is reviewed with characteristic insight in J. Goody, *The Logic of Writing and the Organisation of Society* (Cambridge, 1986), pp. 127–70.

80 To be clear, it has been seen that the draftsman of a petition may have remembered a previous ruling, which is not the same thing as citing a previous ruling as if it provided some sort of authority for a rule. There is evidence in the records of other burghs during the sixteenth century that court decisions were sometimes expected to have an effect on legal development, but not as what lawyers would now call precedents.

the small number of propositions of law found in the records, but is rather to identify certain broad forms of narrative that came to be considered acceptable, and to examine the presuppositions that made them acceptable.

In seeking to examine the presuppositions that made tales tellable, less may perhaps be learned from the methodology of legal historians than from the methodology of intellectual historians, who are used to investigating the linguistic or ideological conventions behind the particular modes of discourse they study.[81] The modes of discourse studied are particular not simply in the sense that intellectual historians tend to concentrate on specific kinds of thought, but in the crucial sense that they take thought to be constrained by conventions shared among members of particular linguisitic communities.[82] To this extent they are in agreement with the second thing Geertz appears to have had in mind when he remarked that legal knowledge must be local, which is that anything resembling *adat* has to be particular to the community in which it is generated.[83] Law, as a species of social imagination, must be particular to the social group responsible for its development, and it therefore needs to be asked how the group responsible for developing the maritime law adhered to in Aberdeen was defined. In one case it was argued that the crew of a foreign ship should not be required to make a payment, 'becaus it is nocht the use of thair cuntra', but the court concluded that they ought to pay, 'conforme to the auld use observit withtin this guid towne past memour of man'.[84] As has been seen already, reference was made in other cases to the custom 'usit in this towne' or 'withtin this nobill burght'.[85] When the latter phrase was used in the exceptional petition in which a proposition of law was enunciated, reference was initially made to the custom of the 'realm', possibly because account was being taken of a ruling in an earlier case, for in that case advice had been sought from 'the towne of Edinburgh'.[86] However, the court insisted

81 Something could perhaps be learned from the varied contributions made in recent years to 'legal narratology' (see, for example, G. van Niekerk, 'Indigenous Law and Narrative: Rethinking Methodology', (1999) 32 *Comparative and International Law Journal of South Africa* 208), but there is a difference between attending to the stories people sometimes tell about the law and recognising that some law sometimes consists in the stories people tell.

82 See, for example, A. Brett, 'What Is Intellectual History Now?', in D. Cannadine (ed.), *What Is History Now?* (Basingstoke, 2003), p. 113.

83 The connection is formed by a shared debt to linguistic philosophy.

84 ACA, CA1/1/15, pp. 167–8. For what may have been a different view of the law applicable to prize taking, a matter generally left to the admiralty courts, see ACA, CA1/1/20, p. 120.

85 ACA, CA1/1/13, pp. 157–8, and CA1/1/15, p. 716.

86 ACA, CA1/1/13, p. 425.

on the petition being 'correctit' and 'reformit', and the word 'realm' was excised and replaced with 'burght', a firm indication that the court believed its concern to be with its local law.[87] Adherence to its own law – to the development of a shared understanding of how maritime trade should be regulated, or to the generation of a culture of law – was one of the ways in which the urban community defined itself.[88] It may be illuminating to search for the origins of the burgh's law, which may reveal the extent to which it was open to external influences, but however cosmopolitan these influences may turn out to have been, it was ultimately the usages and customs of the burgh that were given effect.[89]

5 Conclusion: Urban Discourse and Legal Constraints

It now seems clear that the study of language must be central to any attempt to trace the development of maritime law in the early sixteenth century, not just for the obvious reason that knowledge of the subject has to be drawn from what is said about it in written records, but also because lawful behaviour appears to have been conceived of as behaviour susceptible to acceptable description.[90] As intellectual historians have shown, linguistic conventions constrain both the ways in which behaviour can be justified and the range of behaviour people can indulge in when they may need to provide justifications for their actions.[91] Aware that they might have to appear before the bailie court to defend themselves, mariners and merchants had to be mindful of the tales that might be told there and to act accordingly. On the one hand, these tales described established practices, yet on the other hand, the practices had come to be established because there were tales that could be told about them. It was

87 The entries involving maritime law may be compared with ACA, CA1/1/19, pp. 341–2, where a case about customs dues was taken to be governed by the 'use and prattik of the burrowis of the realme'. Whether the attitudes encountered in Aberdeen in the early sixteenth century were widespread throughout the country and century needs further investigation.

88 *Cf.* C. Hawes, 'The Urban Community in Fifteenth-Century Scotland: Language, Law and Political Practice', (2017) 44 *Urban History* 365.

89 T. Johnson, 'Law, Space and Local Knowledge in Late-Medieval England', PhD dissertation, Birkbeck, University of London, 2014, deals with law as local knowledge in this sense.

90 The fundamental importance to work in this area of J. Kopaczyk, *The Legal Language of Scottish Burghs: Standardization and Lexical Bundles, 1380–1560* (Oxford, 2013), will be apparent.

91 The classic study remains Q. Skinner, 'The Principles and Practice of Opposition: The Case of Bolingbroke versus Walpole', in N. McKendrick (ed.), *Historical Perspectives: Studies in English Thought and Society in Honour of J. H. Plumb* (London, 1974), p. 93.

the approbatory description of standard ways of doing things, or more accurately the availability of approbatory descriptions, that gave normal practice its normative dimension. Sometimes, inevitably, practices were raised for discussion before they were fully established, and it was on these occasions that resort was taken to what looks more like the reasoning of lawyers. Propositions of law were remembered – and the possibility remains that they were recited from written sources – yet even then the law does not appear to have been regarded as something distinct from the factual situations to which it might be applied.[92] However clearly propositions of law may have been recalled, what made them binding was not their origin in authoritative sources but their absorption into the usage and custom of the burgh. Recalling propositions of law formed part of the process of negotiating acceptance of new tales. These moments of uncertainty, when a degree of innovation occurred, are especially interesting for historians intent on tracing the development of the law, but they should not be allowed to give a false impression of the nature of the law that was being developed.

92 The likelihood that written sources were actually produced will be seen to diminish in later essays.

3

Regulated Trade

Legislation and Litigation Relating to Charter Parties in Scotland during the Sixteenth Century

Merchants who wished to send goods to overseas markets might in principle have done so in various ways: they might have acquired ships and hired mariners of their own; they might instead have hired ships owned by other people, on the understanding either that crews would be provided with the ships, or that they would hire mariners as well; or they might have paid other people to transport goods in ships they owned and operated, on the understanding either that access would be granted to space on board the ships, or that the crews would accept responsibility for the handling of the goods.[1] Which approach was adopted would presumably have depended to a large extent on how much business the merchants hoped to conduct in the overseas markets, but possibly also on the preferences of shipowners in the towns from which the goods were being sent.[2] It might also have depended to some extent on how the carriage of goods by sea was regulated by the law in force in the places where agreements were made, or to which ships were heading, or perhaps in other places. In Scotland, for instance, several acts of parliament had been passed to regulate the engagement of merchants in overseas trade.[3] In particular, an act passed in the fifteenth century had required every agreement for the carriage of goods by sea to be set down in writing in the form of a 'charter party', and had required all charter parties to contain certain prescribed conditions.[4] It

1 Further complications would arise if agreements were not simply made between merchants and shipowners, for instance if merchants dealt with masters who acted on behalf of owners, or if one owner acted on behalf of other owners, or if one merchant acted on behalf of other merchants. These complications are mostly reserved for discussion in the eighth essay in this collection, the only exception being the first.

2 I. Leimus and A. Mänd, 'Reval (Tallinn): A City Emerging from Maritime Trade', in W. Blockmans, M. Krom and J. Wubs-Mrozewicz (eds), *The Routledge Handbook of Maritime Trade around Europe, 1300–1600* (Abingdon, 2017), p. 273, at p. 284.

3 *The Practicks of Sir James Balfour of Pittendreich*, 2 vols, ed. P.G.B. McNeill (Edinburgh, 1962–3), vol. 2, p. 621.

4 J. Kopaczyk, *The Legal Language of Scottish Burghs: Standardization and Lexical Bundles, 1380–1560* (Oxford, 2013), p. 284, points out that this expression came into relatively early use in Scotland.

 | DOI:10.1163/9789004695009_004

was found in the first essay in this collection, however, that at least one of these conditions came to be ignored in the practice of the courts, so that it cannot safely be assumed that goods were invariably (or even normally) transported overseas in accordance with the terms of the legislation. The aim of this essay is not to discover how goods were actually transported – though light is shed on that topic in passing – but is to discover how the transportation of goods by sea was actually regulated. The legislation relating to charter parties is first examined, then evidence of the use of charter parties, then records of litigation in relation to charter parties in the ports through which goods passed on their way to or from foreign markets.[5] An attempt is made to identify rules governing the carriage of goods by sea, and to explain further the nature of the legal customs that were found in the preceding essay to govern engagement in overseas trade.[6]

1 Legislation

It was in 1467 that one of James III's parliaments declared that no ship was to be 'frachtyt' by any of his subjects, 'without our realm nor within', unless the agreement was made in the form of 'a charter party, contenand thir poyntis under writtin'.[7] A 'charter party' or 'carta partita' was a document written in duplicate, one half of which was given to each of its signatories, with the halves cut apart for additional security along a jagged line resembling teeth which could be matched up against each other (hence the alternative name 'indenture').[8] Of the six points prescribed, the first was that 'the master of the schip' was obliged to employ 'sufficiand stermane, tymmerman and schipmen convenient for the schip', and to supply 'the merchandis' throughout the voyage with 'fyre, watter and salt, on his cost'.[9] It was thus envisaged that a

5 The focus, in other words, is on the understanding of the law among merchants and mariners themselves. The views of the lawyers trained in continental universities are largely ignored for the time being, but are returned to in later essays.

6 As will be apparent from a reading of the previous essay, the word 'rules' is being used quite loosely here.

7 *The Acts of the Parliaments of Scotland*, 12 vols, ed. T. Thomson and C. Innes (Edinbrugh, 1814–75), vol. 2, p. 87; Records of the Parliaments of Scotland, ed. K.M. Brown (www.rps.ac.uk), 1567/1/4.

8 In the sixteenth century the expression 'charter partie or indentour' was not used only in relation to contracts of affreightment (*e.g.* DCA, BCMB, vol. 13, 24 February 1574).

9 As is explained further in later essays in this collection, while the 'stermane' was obviously someone expert in navigation, and the 'tymmerman' in carpentry, the 'schipmen' were not expected to have any special expertise.

shipowner would agree to provide a crewed ship to merchants who would be present during the voyage. The second point was the one mentioned in the introductory essay in this collection, namely that 'gif their hapnis ony contencioune or debate betwix the maister or the merchandis, that thai sal undirly the jurisdiccioune and ordinance of the burghe quharto the schip is frachtit'.[10] The third point was an undertaking that 'na merchandis gudis be revin nor spilt with unresonable stollin as with spakis, nor that na gudis be schorne nor strikin up in na wise, into the maisteris defalt or his servandis, under the pane of tinsale of the said fraucht and amending of the skaith to the merchandis'. The verbs used in this provision were mostly related to the noun 'skaith', meaning harm or damage.[11] The words 'revin' and 'schorne' bore the connotations 'ripped' and 'cut', and were presumably being used with reference to cloth or hides, while the words 'spilt' and 'strikin up' bore the connotations 'spilled' and 'broken open', and were presumably being used with reference to containers of wine or oil. The phrase 'unresonable stollin as with spakis' is at first sight more difficult to construe, since 'stollin' seems to have meant no more than the English word 'stolen', which sits uneasily with the words 'revin' and 'spilt', and also with the implication that either might be 'resonable'.[12] However, 'stollin' was a variant spelling of the word 'stowin', so that the unreasonable loading of goods, for instance with the use of pointed implements, was being contrasted with harm or damage that was not in 'the maisteris defalt or his servandis'.[13] The fourth point, touched on briefly in the second essay above and examined at greater length in the eighth essay below, was an undertaking that the master would 'fure na gudis upone his ourelop, the quhilk and he do, tha gudis sal pay na fraucht, nor na gudis under the ourlop to scot nor lot with tha gudis in case thai be castin'. Basically, the master was only to transport goods in the hold of his ship, was to receive no freight for goods loaded elsewhere, and was

10 As was remarked in the first essay above, this point seems to have owed something to a provision in the *Leges burgorum*, a component in collections of the medieval laws of Scotland that circulated in manuscript.

11 The crucial guide to the meaning of the language used is of course W. Craigie, A.J. Aitken, J.A.C. Stevenson, H.D. Watson and M.G. Dareau (eds), *A Dictionary of the Older Scottish Tongue from the Twelfth Century to the End of the Seventeenth*, 12 vols (Chicago, London and Aberdeen, 1931–2002).

12 As will be seen shortly, and again later in this essay, a distinction came to be drawn between the theft of wine or other comestibles by mariners and their reasonable appropriation if provision could not otherwise be made for a ship's company during a voyage. This does not seem to have been the point in 1467, however.

13 This is how the statement is read in the *Dictionary of the Older Scottish Tongue*, vol. 9, p. 651.

not to claim contributions towards losses sustained by merchants whose goods were carried elsewhere from those whose goods were properly stowed in the hold. The fifth point was an undertaking that payments would be made on every voyage to 'the chaplane of the natione', and the sixth that the master would claim 'na drynk silver', but would make a payment 'to the kirk werk of the toune'. Support was therefore to be given to the church of the staple port in the Netherlands (the particular destination envisaged), and to the church of the port where the loading of the ship took place, the completion of which was not to be celebrated by the crew in a local tavern. In 1487 another parliament declared that the 1467 act should be 'put to executioune efter the tenour of the samyn', and added a financial penalty for breach of the third or fourth points, payable for the king's benefit to 'the hede frauchtismen of the schip'.[14]

The draftsman of the 1467 act seems to have been following the example of an act passed by the town council of Edinburgh in 1438.[15] According to that act, 'quhat men frauchtis ony schippis of Edinburgh to cum hamewart or furthwart', whether the contract was made 'on this syde the see or beyound', were to provide in a 'chartour pairtie that thair be na gude, woll nor skynnis, spakit no schorne', so that any master who 'dois or tholes the contrer to be done sall tyne the fraucht of tha gudis, and emend the skayth to the merchant'.[16] Merchants who failed to have this provision included in a charter party were to pay a fine to 'the kirk wark', and the act added more generally that for every voyage payments were to be made to 'Sanct Rynanes Ile in Brugis' and 'St Geillis wark' at home.[17] In an act passed in 1494 the payments to 'St Ninianes altare in Bruges' and 'St Gelis wark' in Edinburgh were said to be required by 'our soverane lordis actis of parliament', as was the more basic requirement to enter into a charter party, which was to be done in the presence of 'the commoun clerk' of the burgh.[18] In another act, passed five years later, it was instead ordered that all ships be freighted in the presence of one of the bailies, before whom

14 *Acts of the Parliaments of Scotland*, vol. 2, p. 178; Records of the Parliaments of Scotland, 1587/10/19.

15 E.B.I. Frankot, 'Aberdeen and the East Coast of Scotland: Autonomy on the Periphery', in Blockmans, Krom and Wubs-Mrozewicz (eds), *Routledge Handbook of Maritime Trade around Europe*, p. 411, at p. 421.

16 *Extracts from the Records of the Burgh of Edinburgh*, 1st ser., 5 vols, ed. J.D. Marwick (Edinburgh, 1869–92), vol. 1, pp. 5–6. Although continuous records of the town council's proceedings only survive from 1551 onwards, earlier legislation was preserved in ECA, SL1/1/1, and NLS, Adv. MS 31.4.9.

17 Veere did not replace Bruges as the Scottish staple in the Netherlands until the sixteenth century.

18 *Extracts from the Records of the Burgh of Edinburgh*, 1st ser., vol. 1, pp. 56–7.

'the clerk sal mak ane charter partie under his signe manuell, the merchandis haiffand the ane half, the skipper the uther half'.[19] The charter party drawn up by the clerk was to include all 'the pointtis contenit in our soverane lordis act of parliament of frauchting of schippis', the water bailie of Leith was not to allow any ships to depart from the port unless he was shown a 'charter pairtie under the clerkis hand', and merchants were not to pay freight, in Scotland or elsewhere, 'quhill the chartour pairtie be schawin'. It was ordered again in 1501 that ships be freighted, 'efter forme of the act of parliament', in the presence of burgh officials, not 'in taverns or ony uther place, bot in the tolbuith alanerlie'.[20] Although the 1501 act was only intended to remain in force for one year, many later acts reiterated the opposition to 'privie frauchting', eventually transferring responsibility for the supervision of contracting to the dean of guild.[21] Further legislation required the masters of ships to provide the council or dean of guild with guarantees that they would not receive passengers onto their ships without authorisation, would not charge freight at higher rates than those specified from time to time by the council, would receive goods from local merchants before others, would receive goods from merchants only if custom duties had been paid, and would not unpack or break into the goods they received.[22] An attempt was made to codify all this legislation in an act passed in 1579, which referred to the guarantees required from masters as 'conditionis' to be included in charter parties.[23]

---

19 *Extracts from the Records of the Burgh of Edinburgh*, 1st ser., vol. 1, pp. 78–9.

20 *Extracts from the Records of the Burgh of Edinburgh*, 1st ser., vol. 1, p. 89. Scotland lacked the exchanges or bourses found in other countries (D. Calabi, 'Trading Spaces in European Port Cities: The Architectural Models of Bourses, Lonjas and Exchanges', in Blockmans, Krom and Wubs-Mrozewicz (eds), *Routledge Handbook of Maritime Trade around Europe*, p. 57), but its tolbooths or town houses provided a public alternative to private venues for business such as homes or taverns (E.B.I. Frankot, 'Legal Business outside the Courts: Private and Public Houses as Spaces of Law in the Fifteenth Century', in J.W. Armstrong and E. Frankot (eds), *Cultures of Law in Urban Northern Europe: Scotland and Its Neighbours, c. 1350-c. 1650* (Abingdon, 2021), p. 173).

21 *Extracts from the Records of the Burgh of Edinburgh*, 1st ser., vol. 1, pp. 95 and 222, and vol. 4, pp. 27, 35–6 and 395–7; ECA, SL1/1/1, f. 29r, and SL1/1/4, pp. 238, 254 and 494; NLS, Adv. MS 31.4.9, ff. 140v and 141v-2r.

22 *Extracts from the Records of the Burgh of Edinburgh*, 1st ser., vol. 1, pp. 221–2, vol. 2, pp. 119, 184 and 216, and vol. 4, pp. 27–9 and 35–7; ECA, SL1/1/2, ff. 54v, 110r and 112r, SL1/1/4, pp. 361–2 and 525, SL1/1/5, ff. 65v, 72r and 193r, and SL1/1/7, f. 80v; NLS, Adv. MS 31.4.9, ff. 140v and 142v. Authorisation for transporting passengers had also been required by acts of parliament, which may again have been inspired by the example of Edinburgh (*Acts of the Parliaments of Scotland*, vol. 2, p. 348, and vol. 3, p. 42; Records of the Parliaments of Scotland, 1535/41 and 1567/12/71).

23 *Extracts from the Records of the Burgh of Edinburgh*, 1st ser., vol. 4, pp. 133–4.

As early as 1526 the town council of Dundee had ordered that 'na schip be frachted within this brugh without the advice of the deane of gild'.[24] The order was opposed by the merchants of the town, who insisted that it should be 'leasum to any neighbour, brother of gild, to fracht frielie, as use and wont was, without ony restriction'.[25] In 1550, however, it was ordered that 'no ship be fraughted be privat persones but openly in presence of provest or baillies, or than befor the dean of gild, to pas in merchandice in France, Flanders, Denmark, Danskine or any free port without this realme'.[26] Three years later it was ordered that when any agreement was made, the dean of guild was to 'subscryve the samen charter partie', the 'principall headis' of which were to be 'registrat in his buikis, and this to avoid process, question and debait, quhilkis commonlie are used betwixt awners of schippis and merchandis daylie in the tolbuith of this brugh'.[27] On the same day it was also declared that because it was 'notarlie knowen that the merchandis are heavilie hurt, defrauded and damnaged in drinking and drawing of thair wines coming furth at Buordeous', the masters of ships, if it could be proved that wine had been taken by mariners, were to pay for the losses sustained. In 1570 and 1576 it was reaffirmed that the dean of guild was to supervise the making of every contract, 'and the haile contentes of the charter partie to remaine with the said deane of gild', who was to ensure that only people 'qualified in using of merchandise' sent goods abroad.[28] An act passed in 1581 required charter parties to contain an undertaking that 'all matters questionable falling out betwix the merchand and maister, the owner and the mariner, be only decyded and judged be the provest and baillies of this brugh, renuncand all other judgments, and this conforme to the act of parliament'.[29] On the same day the problem of lost wine was revisited. Mariners were to swear under oath that they had done no wrong, 'with certification and thai faillie, the samen sall be holden precontest, and the maister sall be decerned to pay the skaithe'.[30] In the 1580s and 1590s the town

24 *Burgh Laws of Dundee, with the History, Statutes and Proceedings of the Guild of Merchants and Fraternities of Craftsmen*, ed. A.J. Warden (London, 1872), p. 95. It is not clear where Warden found this act or some of the others cited below.

25 *Burgh Laws of Dundee*, p. 99.

26 *Burgh Laws of Dundee*, p. 13; DCA, BCMB, vol. 2, p. 1, and GBD, f. 15v; *Mariners of Dundee: Their City, Their River, Their Fraternity*, ed. H. Robertson (Dundee, 2006), p. 9.

27 *Burgh Laws of Dundee*, pp. 16–17; DCA, BCMB, vol. 2, p. 13, and GBD, f. 16r (the act is also in MBBC, vol. 1, pp. 57–8, but with the date 18 January 1567, when it may perhaps have been reissued).

28 *Burgh Laws of Dundee*, pp. 114 and 118–19.

29 *Burgh Laws of Dundee*, p. 41; DCA, BCMB, vol. 2, p. 68, and GBD, f. 17r.

30 As the previous act had explained, liability could arise both from loss of wine and from damage to wine left in containers.

councils of Ayr and Kirkcudbright addressed the problem of ships arriving and selling their cargoes to merchants who claimed to have ordered them in advance, thus evading regulations requiring 'adventurers' to offer their cargoes to the burgh authorities before anyone else.[31] The act passed in Ayr warned that no such contract would receive effect 'except the same be past be charter pairtie befoir the clerk of this town', who was to record its terms 'in the townis buik'.[32] The implication seems to be that charter parties were expected to be made in similar ways when merchants bought goods overseas and arranged for them to be brought home.[33] At different times, the town council of Aberdeen, the convention of the royal burghs and the king's council passed acts reinforcing the requirements that goods be stowed in the holds of ships and that passengers be authorised to travel.[34]

A significant amount of legislation was therefore enacted in relation to charter parties both before and during the sixteenth century, and even more might well have come to light had the surviving records of the coastal burghs been less fragmentary.[35] The primary purpose of most of these statutes was apparently to avoid the 'process, question and debait' complained about in the act passed by the council of Dundee in 1553. A tried and tested method of limiting the scope for controversy was to insist on agreements not only being reduced to writing, but also being written in a form that made sure both parties had corresponding statements of the terms they had agreed.[36] Another tried and tested method was to insist on agreements being made in public, which usually meant having them drafted and authenticated by 'notaries public', who were scribes entrusted by the authorities with the task of producing reliable documents.[37] The town clerks mentioned in the Scottish legislation often were notaries public, although the acts did not stipulate that those involved in the

31 The regulation of trading with 'adventurers' is touched on briefly in the first essay in this collection.

32 AA, B6/11/1/3, ff. 361v-2r (also copied at B6/11/2, f. 7); *Kirkcudbright Town Council Records, 1576–1604*, ed. M.B. Johnston and C.M. Armet (Edinburgh, 1939), pp. 370–1.

33 The act had in fact added that 'gif the bargane sal happin to be maid beyond sey, in that caise the same to be past be charter pairtie in presens of the clerk of that town quhair the same sal happin to be maid'.

34 *Records of the Convention of the Royal Burghs of Scotland*, 8 vols, ed. J.D. Marwick and T. Hunter (Edinburgh, 1870–1918), vol. 1, pp. 10–12 and 105; *Practicks of Sir James Balfour of Pittendreich*, vol. 2, pp. 619–20; *Acts of the Lords of Council in Public Affairs, 1501–54*, ed. R.K. Hannay (Edinburgh, 1932), p. lxiii; ACA, CA1/1/9, p. 398; NRS, CS5/19, f. 170.

35 The relevant records are reviewed in the second section of the first essay above.

36 M.T. Clanchy, *From Memory to Written Record: England, 1066–1307* (Oxford, 1993), pp. 87–8.

37 R.C. Head, *Making Archives in Early-Modern Europe: Proof, Information and Political Record Keeping, 1400–1700* (Cambridge, 2019), pp. 47–53.

production of charter parties had to be.[38] Emphasis was instead placed on the supervision of other officials, on the making of contracts in public places, and on the registration of contracts in the common records of the burghs. These measures would all have prevented parties from alleging that they had agreed terms of which there could be no evidence beyond their own recollections, as would the prescription of terms to be included in every contract of affreightment. Much of the legislation passed in the burghs during the sixteenth century was designed to reinforce the prescription of terms by the acts of parliament passed during the fifteenth century, with the addition of some new conditions. The standardisation of contractual terms would have been sufficient in itself to reduce the risk of disruptive litigation, and attention seems to have been focused on points that might otherwise have been controversial. It is notable that the legislation did not cover obvious points such as the need for the master to return goods at an agreed destination or for merchants to pay for their transportation. Presumably no one would have disputed that obligations to deliver goods and to pay freight were bound to arise from any contract of affreightment. On the other hand, it is also notable that the terms prescribed related mostly to the obligations of the master, and did not require merchants to provide promised cargoes promptly, or anything of the sort. The legislation seems to have been framed in the interests of the merchants, which is unsurprising in view of their prominence in the coastal communities.[39] Yet it has to be wondered whether masters – or more importantly the shipowners who employed them – would have been eager to comply with the legislation. Indeed, it has to be wondered whether it was only in Dundee, and in the later 1520s, that merchants themselves objected to having their freedom of contract restricted by legislation.[40]

2 Charter Parties

In 1548 a master from Saint Valery at the mouth of the Somme produced before the bailies of Aberdeen his half of an 'indentour' made there six months earlier

38 J. Durkan, 'The Early Scottish Notary', in I.B. Cowan and D. Shaw (eds), *The Renaissance and Reformation in Scotland: Essays in Honour of Gordon Donaldson* (Edinburgh, 1983), p. 22, at p. 34.

39 Although shipowners and masters also tended to be burgesses, and were sometimes themselves merchants or former merchants, they were greatly outnumbered by those who dealt only in the buying and selling of goods in foreign markets.

40 The fragmentary survival of the burgh records again needs to be borne in mind.

with ten local merchants.[41] Unusually, the contract was entered in its entirety into the court's records. It began by stating that 'the said maister and skipar hes lattin his said schip to fraucht to the said merchandis and thair complices fra the port and havin of Abirdene to the frow port of Danskin'.[42] The freight due for the voyage was then specified, 'this fraucht to be pait withtin tene dais efter the said schip cumis to Danskin'.[43] The merchants were to have 'xviii lying dais heir in Abirdene efter the dait of this writ' in which to provide a cargo, and were to pay a specified sum to the master 'for every day he lyis langar' while waiting for the cargo. Conversely, if the departure of the ship was delayed because the master was 'nocht rady to saill witht the said merchandis at the said terme, wind and wedder servand', he was to pay the same amounts to them. The cargo of iron, pitch, tar and potash that the merchants were expected to provide for a return voyage from Danzig to Aberdeen, each in proportion to his share of the outward cargo, was then outlined. This time the merchants were to have 'xx lying dais efter the said schip cumis to Danskin to lay in the said lastage', but with the same penalties due for delay on either side. In addition to the agreed cargo, the merchants were allowed to offer the master further goods, failing which he was to be at liberty 'to tak his avantage of utheris'. The freight the merchants were to pay, within six days of their goods being 'laid fre one the key heid of Abirdene', was then specified, before it was finally promised that the master would provide 'ane thicht schip, sufficient witht anchors, cabillis, fresche water, fyre and salt, witht ane sufficient steirman out and in, and all uther necessars pertening to ane schip to have, witht ane condigne nummer of marenellis'. To confirm their commitment to 'observing and keiping' the agreed terms, the merchants had 'sett thair merks usit in merchandeis to this half of this wreat, remaning witht the said skipar'. The existence of the charter party had not prevented disputes from arising in Aberdeen after the return of the ship, nor did its production hasten their determination.[44] The litigation resulting from the voyage in fact dragged on for fifteenth months.

---

41 ACA, CA1/1/20, pp. 133–4. Here, as elsewhere, adjustments are silently made to complete abbreviations.

42 The relationship between merchants and their 'complices' is examined in the eighth essay in this collection. It appears that the intended destination of the voyage was the Nowy Port at the mouth of the Mottlau, not the older port further upstream (A. Januszajtis, '1000 Years of the Harbour of Gdansk' (1999) 3 *Task Quarterly* 141).

43 The freight was due mostly in Prussian currency but also in items of clothing to be bought in Danzig. Later in the document, as will be mentioned shortly, freight was also specified for a return journey, but in 'crownis of the sone', not 'merkis Spruiss', which were presumably to be obtained by selling the goods shipped to Danzig.

44 ACA, CA1/1/20, pp. 121, 126, 129, 131–48, 150–6, 158–68, 170–3, 175–7 and 370.

Another charter party had already been transcribed into the records of the Aberdeen court in 1532, three more examples were transcribed into the records of the bailie court in Dundee in the last few decades of the century, and two more were transcribed into the books kept by the lords of council and session in Edinburgh.[45] All six of these further examples followed much the same pattern as the charter party recorded in Aberdeen in 1548, except that the clauses did not always appear in the same order, and that the contracts did not always begin by spelling out the basic point that the master was 'lattine the said schip to fraucht'.[46] When that point was made, it was sometimes added that the master was acting 'with consent and assent of the awneris and delismen of the said schip', who were sometimes more directly involved in making the contract.[47] When the point was not made, the intended destination of the voyage was still identified somewhere, more or less precisely – for instance, one contract specified a voyage 'to the port and havin of Hamburgh', while another required a cargo to be transported to 'Deip or Feir, quhar sche sall happin to be frauchtit to'.[48] This last phrase was used because the cargo was to be transported 'apon ane competent fraucht, as sall be aggreit', although generally the freight to be paid was agreed before the contract was concluded. All of the examples found specified the periods within which cargoes had to be provided, both at the port of departure and, if there was to be a return voyage, at the port of arrival. Penalties were imposed for the late delivery of goods to the ship, though one contract carefully described the sum due as the 'liquidat pryce for feilzie, or costis, skethis and expensis'. Conversely, if (as one contract put it) 'the merchandis tareis our the lying dais in the skipar, schipis, steirsman or marenellis defaltis, the schip and skipar sall pay the merchandis expensis'. It was usually a matter of some importance to the master that 'the haill merchandis havand gudis furthtwart in the said schip sall gif hir hir full laiding haymewart agane', and for each merchant to provide goods for a return voyage 'corisponden to his gudis furthtwart'. As in the 1548 charter party, the types of goods merchants were expected to purchase abroad were sometimes specified. At one place or another all six contracts stated that the master was to provide a ship 'weill

45 ACA, CA1/1/13, p. 452; DCA, BCMB, vol. 10, 8 June 1569, vol. 16, 14 September 1584, and vol. 20, 30 July 1599; NRS, CS6/5, ff. 183v-4r, and RD1/48, ff. 151–2.

46 Charter parties have also been found making provision for voyages that were not of a commercial character (DCA, BCMB, vol. 12, 17 June 1573; NRS, RD1/2, ff. 125v-6, RD1/34, ff. 380v-2r, and RD1/41, ff. 199–200), but these are understandably different in style from those discussed here.

47 The relationship between shipowners and 'dalismen' is also examined in the eighth essay in this collection.

48 'Deip' was of course Dieppe, and 'Feir' was Veere.

and sufficientlie furnesit with sallis, kabells, anchors and utheris furnesing and necesseris usit and frequentit to ane guid schip'. One contract, entered into at the end of the century, stated a little more exactly that the ship provided was to be 'weill furnisit witht ankeris, saillis, towis, marineris, fier, water and salt, according to the the act of parliament'. None of these contracts added clauses omitted from the one recorded in 1548.[49]

One of the charter parties just examined was written in Norway, and entries in the records of Aberdeen and Dundee refer to many others written in foreign countries.[50] Although none of these other charter parties was copied into the court records, studies of contracts written in other countries have tended to identify similar patterns of composition.[51] Examples of charter parties involving Scottish merchants can be found in printed extracts from the protocol books of notaries public practising in La Rochelle. The Scots involved in these or other transactions recorded in the books either had a working knowledge of French or were assisted by someone 'qui entend les langues francoyse et d'Escosse'.[52] The four 'chartes parties' of special interest here were written by three different notaries yet were similar in their contents.[53] All four started with a statement that a master (*maistre du navire*) had let and freighted his ship (*avoyr loué et frecté ledict navire*) or part of it to certain merchants (*marchans*), promising them that it would be sufficiently tight and furnished, equipped and provided with everything necessary for the voyage about which they were agreeing (*bien estanche, muny, equippé et garny de toutes choses necessaires pour bien et deuhement faire le voyage cy apres declairé*). The merchants promised to provide within a specified period a cargo, normally of salt or wine, which the master promised to transport to a specified destination as soon as it was possible to

49 One did mention in passing that goods were to be stowed below deck without hinderance to the ship's pump.

50 ACA, CA1/1/12/1, p. 121, CA1/1/13, pp. 497–8, CA1/1/19, p. 284, CA1/1/20, p. 88, CA1/1/27, p. 652, CA1/1/34/2, p. 802, CA1/1/36, p. 249, CA1/1/37, pp. 33–4, 241–3 and 530–1, and CA5/1/5, 21 September 1596 and 11 September 1597; DCA, BCMB, vol. 3, 10 October 1550, and vol. 16, 14 September 1584.

51 E. Trocmé and M. Delafosse, *Le commerce rochelais de la fin du XVe siècle au début du XVIIe*, (Paris, 1952), pp. 18–19; M. Mollat, *Le commerce maritime normand à la fin du Moyen Âge: Étude d'histoire économique et sociale* (Paris, 1952), pp. 409–10; N.J. Williams, *The Maritime Trade of the East Anglian Ports, 1550–90* (Oxford, 1988), pp. 207–14; R. Ward, *The World of the Medieval Shipmaster: Law, Business and the Sea, c. 1350–1450* (Woodbridge, 2009), pp. 78–93.

52 *Documents pour server à l'histoire du commerce des Pays-Bas avec la France jusqu'à 1585*, 2 vols, ed. M.A. Drost (The Hague, 1984–9), vol. 1, pp. 277–8 and 282–4.

53 *Documents pour server à l'histoire du commerce des Pays-Bas avec la France jusqu'à 1585*, vol. 1, pp. 305–7, 327–8, 400–1 and 436–7.

do so (*Dieu aydant, du premier bon temps sans sejour*). After their goods were returned there, the merchants were to pay the master his freight (*frect*) within a specified period, along with any other charges required by custom (*aux us et coustume de la mer*).[54] Provision was made in some contracts for the loading of a cargo for a return voyage within a specified period, and invariably, if the departure of the ship was delayed through the fault (*negligence et deffault*) of either party, for the reimbursement of the other party's losses (*despens, dommages et interestz*). All four contracts also provided that if a merchant's goods were damaged through the fault of the master, his crew or ship (*par la faulte et coulpe dudict maistre, de ses gens ou mariniers, a cause dudict navyre quy ne seroyt bien estang et autrement par leur deffault*), he was to be compensated for the damage by the master. An abbreviated entry included at the end of some of the charter parties appears to have committed the parties to submission of any disputes that might arise between them to the jurisdiction of a court in the port to which they were headed (*Renonçant etc. Jugé et condampné etc.*).

As one of the charter parties copied into the court books of Dundee had been written by a notary public, and as further evidence has come to light of the involvement of notaries in the drafting of these contracts, it might be expected that further examples would be found in the protocol books written by Scottish notaries.[55] The fact is, however, that while over a hundred protocol books written in the coastal burghs of Scotland have been searched through, and while these books do occasionally contain documents connected with the carriage of goods by sea, not a single example of a charter party has been found there.[56] Perhaps this is not so surprising given the emphasis in the Scottish legislation on the making of charter parties in the presence of burgh officials, in public spaces, and in terms registered in records kept by each town. When some of the legislation enacted in Edinburgh was gathered together in one volume, the compiler inserted a note on 'the manner of frauchting of schips of auld', briefly summarising from 'louse leffis' the terms agreed in contracts made in 1519, 1533 and 1534.[57] Yet none of the surviving records of the burgh contain

54 One of the charter parties found in the Scottish records also referred to charges being paid 'use and wont'.

55 ACA, CA1/1/19, pp. 123–4 and 134; NRS, B19/1/9, 11 September 1578, B19/1/12, 7 March 1590, and B19/1/13, 10 April 1591.

56 NRS, B6/1/1/2, ff. 526v-7, contains a document referring to a charter party made in Brittany, but it is not itself a charter party, nor does it reproduce the terms agreed.

57 NLS, Adv. MS 31.4.9, ff. 136–7r. These summaries are presented in chronological order in the *Extracts from the Records of the Burgh of Edinburgh*, 1st ser., vol. 1, pp. 186–7, and vol. 2, pp. 60–1 and 66, which gives the misleading impression that they were entries made when ships were freighted.

similar entries made when ships were freighted, notwithstanding the imposition of penalties on masters and others when vessels were 'nocht frauchtit be the dene of gild'.[58] In Dundee a 'Guildrie Book' was kept from 1570 until the end of the century, recording the enactment of statutes, the election of deans and their councils, the submission of accounts and various other matters, but never the freighting of ships, even though the acts requiring charter parties to be made in the dean's presence had ordered that 'the principall headis heirof be registrat in his buikis'.[59] An entry in the burgh court book of Dundee refers to a charter party being made in the 'hous' of one of the merchants, and the charter party copied into the council register of Aberdeen in 1548 was not the only one to have been made there in a merchant's home.[60] Sometimes charter parties appear to have been written by one of the merchants or by the clerk of a ship.[61] If some entries in the court books reveal anxiety that it would be impossible to pursue a claim without the warrant of a charter party, and if charter parties often were 'producit for instructioun of the clame', these entries also reveal that sometimes duplicate copies of the contract had not actually been written.[62] Moreover, there is evidence that contracts of affreightment could be given effect by the burgh courts even if they had not been reduced to any form of writing.[63] Indeed, when the authorities in Edinburgh sought to reinforce the statutory requirement that ships be hired in writing, they referred to 'sic as ar

58 *Extracts from the Records of the Burgh of Edinburgh*, 1st ser., vol. 2, p. 169; ECA, SL1/1/2, ff. 13r and 92r, SL1/1/3, ff. 69v-70r, and SL1/1/5, f. 199v. No charter parties have been found in the records of Ayr either.

59 DCA, GBD, f. 5r. It may not have been coincidental that the guildry book was opened at around the time that a new act was passed on the freighting of ships.

60 DCA, BCMB, vol. 6, 12 and 31 August 1562; ACA, CA1/1/12/2, p. 480.

61 DCA, BCMB, vol. 3, 20 June 1552; ACA, CA1/1/15, p. 668. A charter party written in Aberdeen 'in Dutche' was presumably drafted by the clerk of the German ship (ACA, CA1/1/36, p. 612, and CA5/1/5, 14 September 1596). *The Register of the Privy Council of Scotland*, 14 vols, ed. J.H. Burton and D. Masson (Edinburgh, 1877–98), vol. 1, pp. 179–82, seems to equate a charter party with 'the clerkis buke'.

62 ACA, CA1/1/13, pp. 417–18 and 497–8, CA1/1/15, p. 27, CA1/1/27, p. 496, CA1/1/33/1, pp. 592–4, CA1/1/34/1, pp. 244–6, 448 and 455–7, and CA1/1/38, pp. 217–18 and 500–1; DCA, BCMB, vol. 13, 13 July 1575, and vol. 16, 11 February 1583.

63 ACA, CA1/1/8, p. 857, CA1/1/9, p. 282, CA1/1/15, p. 425, CA1/1/16, pp. 58, 104–5, 155 and 157, and CA1/1/36, p. 512; DCA, BCMB, vol. 1, f. 32r, vol. 3, 2 June 1552, vol. 9, 22 January 1567, vol. 19, 23 June and 15 September 1596, and vol. 20, 11 October 1597; SAUL, B10/8/6, p. 618; NRS, B9/11/1, f. 98; *Extracts from the Records of the Royal Burgh of Stirling, 1519–1752*, 2 vols, ed. R. Renwick (Glasgow, 1887–9), vol. 1, p. 9.

frauchtit be chairter pairty', and to the recording of a 'charter pairtie gif ony be', which would seem to have allowed for other possibilities.[64]

3 Language Games

Although there is evidence that contracts of affreightment were not always reduced to writing in the way stipulated in the legislation, there is a great deal more evidence that charter parties often were drawn up and authenticated, for entries in the surviving records of the burgh courts make frequent reference to them, and more particularly to clauses of the types found in the examples that happen to have been copied into court books in their entirety.[65] Litigants referred to written agreements that ships would sail to, and sometimes back from, named destinations, that merchants would provide cargoes within specified periods, that they would pay specified rates of freight after their goods were returned to them, that parties responsible for delays would make additional payments to the others, and that masters would supply sufficient ships and crews, together with sustenance for merchants who travelled with their goods.[66] The language in which this last point was expressed was often reminiscent of the language used in the act of parliament passed in 1467, to which (it has been seen) one of the recorded charter parties drew attention expressly. Nevertheless, while regularities can be identified in the terms typically included in charter parties, it cannot be concluded that they were drawn up in accordance with the rules laid down by parliament. Most of the clauses included in charter parties were not mentioned either in the 1467 act or in the other legislation found.[67] More importantly, most of the clauses prescribed in the legislation appear to have been omitted from most of the charter parties subscribed by merchants, masters and shipowners.[68] No evidence has been

64 *Extracts from the Records of the Burgh of Edinburgh*, 1st ser., vol. 4, pp. 133–4; ECA, SL1/1/4, pp. 238 and 361–2.

65 These entries are examined in detail later in this essay.

66 Even when a round trip was envisaged, the voyages were not always as simple as 'there and back again', but sometimes followed more triangular routes. Merchants sold goods at the initial destination, bought goods there to be sold at a second destination, and returned home with goods bought at the second port.

67 As was noted earlier, their inclusion may have seemed too obvious for legislators to have felt any need to prescribe them.

68 The word 'subscribed' is used here rather loosely. The Aberdeen charter party of 1548 was not the only one in which merchants' marks were added instead of signatures, and others were either signed by writers on behalf of merchants, or were signed by merchants with manual assistance from writers.

found that the charter parties drafted in Scotland commited their signatories to litigation before the courts of the burghs at which ships arrived, and what was found in the first essay in this collection was that the statutory requirement did not prevent the jurisdiction of the burgh courts in 'seafaring causes' from being supplanted by admiralty courts in the second half of the sixteenth century, which would surely have been difficult if the prescribed clause had been included in most contracts. Similarly, in contrast to the charter parties drafted in La Rochelle, those drafted in Scotland do not appear to have contained a standard clause about damage to goods. Nor do they appear to have contained clauses about goods being stowed in the holds of ships, or about payments being made to churches, or not being made so that mariners could obtain refreshments after loading ships. Furthermore, the prescription of additional clauses by the burgh authorities appears to have been no more successful than their opposition to 'privie frauchting'. If the legislation examined in the first section of this essay was not simply ignored in practice, it was not closely adhered to either.

As the clauses found in the surviving examples of charter parties written in Scotland have also been found in the examples of charter parties written in La Rochelle, it may be wondered whether their inclusion was dictated by a different body of rules, common to at least some parts of Europe. A version of the *Rôles d'Oléron*, originally compiled during the thirteenth century on an island close to La Rochelle to regulate the wine trade with Scotland as well as England, Brittany, Normandy and Flanders, was reproduced in many manuscript collections of the medieval laws of Scotland.[69] In other versions of the laws of Oleron (as the code was also known) there is an article referring to a ship being 'frette' under a 'partie chartre', but no article required all contracts of affreightment to be made in this way.[70] Another article required merchants to compensate masters if they delayed the departure of a ship for 'xv days or mar', which may have helped to encourage the inclusion of clauses about 'lying days' in later charter parties.[71] At most, however, broad influence may be suggested, since no trace of the fifteen-day rule has been found in later sources. It

69 E.B.I. Frankot, *'Of Laws of Ships and Shipmen': Medieval Maritime Law and Its Practice in Urban Northern Europe* (Edinburgh, 2012), pp. 11–12, and 'The Scottish Translations of the *Rôles d'Oléron*: Edition and Commentary', in A.M. Godfrey (ed.), *Stair Society: Miscellany Eight* (Edinburgh, 2020), p. 13.

70 *Collection de lois maritimes antérieures au XVIIIe siècle*, 6 vols, ed. J.M. Pardessus (Paris, 1828–45), vol. 1, pp. 332–3; *The Black Book of the Admiralty*, 4 vols, ed. T. Twiss (London, 1871–76), vol. 1, pp. 104–7.

71 Frankot, 'Scottish Translations of the *Rôles d'Oléron*', p. 53.

certainly cannot be concluded that charter parties were drafted during the sixteenth century in accordance with rules prescribed in the laws of Oleron. It has been pointed out that the Scottish copies of these laws were often written by notaries public.[72] When one scribe was admitted to practice as a notary in the later sixteenth century he was described as having 'guid literature, knawleage and conversatioun', which could conceivably have meant that he had some acquaintance with the learned laws studied in the universities.[73] Several handbooks had been composed elsewhere in Europe for the benefit of notaries, and although they did not deal with charter parties in particular, they did encourage their readers to think of hire more generally in terms of the contract of *locatio conductio* discussed in the sources of Roman law.[74] Yet it is even harder to trace connections between the clauses found in the charter parties and the provisions of Roman law than it is to trace connections with the laws of Oleron. The 'guid literature' studied by notaries is in any case more likely to have been the 'humanitie' mentioned when another scribe was admitted to practice, the point being that he was familiar with 'the prettik of wreting alse weill in our langage as utheris'.[75] The normal requirement for admission was simply that the candidate had served an apprenticeship with another scribe and was 'sufficientlie instructit and exerceisit in the formes and styllis of writting concerning ane notar publict'.[76] If notaries and other scribes learned to include standard clauses in charter parties, it was probably by imitating exemplars they were shown, which may sometimes have been written in other countries.

Must it therefore be concluded that the regularities encountered in charter parties were purely accidental, or were merely a consequence of the tendency of draftsmen to follow the style of other documents they had seen? If the notaries and others who wrote charter parties were not adhering to rules laid down in local legislation, the laws of Oleron or the learned laws, is it possible that

72 R.J. Lyall, 'Vernacular Prose before the Reformation', in R.D.S. Jack (ed.), *The History of Scottish Literature: Volume 1, Origins to 1660* (Aberdeen, 1988), p. 163, at pp. 164–6.

73 NRS, NP1/33, f. 1. See more generally Durkan, 'Early Scottish Notary', pp. 23 and 28–31.

74 Rolandinus de Passaggeriis, *Summa totius artis notariae* (Venice, 1546), pt 1, ff. 115–128r; *Artis notariatus, hoc est de officio exercitioque tabellionum, tomi duo* (Frankfurt, 1539), pp. 284–8; Stephanus Marcilletus, *Doctrinale florum artis notariae sive formularium instrumentorum* (Venice, 1518), ff. 31v-4; Leo Speluncanus, *Artis notariae tempestatis huius speculum* (Venice, 1574), 211–15r.

75 NRS, NP1/36, f. 1.

76 NRS, NP1/44, f. 1, NP1/49, f. 1, and B34/1/1, f. 1. As the purpose of opening the register of admissions now preserved as NP2/1–2 was to renew the existing appointment of apostolic notaries before the lords of council and session (*Acts of the Parliaments of Scotland*, vol. 2, pp. 541–2; Records of the Parliaments of Scotland, 1563/6/16), the register is less informative than might have been hoped.

they were following rules of some other kind? It may help to begin by reflecting at a more basic level on what these draftsmen were doing. The obvious reason for asking notaries or other literate people to draft contracts would have been a belief that they could be relied upon to write correctly.[77] But what does it mean when we talk about writing correctly? For example, readers of a certain age may feel uncomfortable with a prediction that 'the writer of this essay will likely clarify the issue', if not because they fear that he is apt to get in a muddle then because they sense that the word 'likely' is being misused. So what does it mean for words to be misused? As everyone ought to know, Ludwig Wittgenstein maintained in his later years that the proper use of language depends not on its correspondence to some external reality (as he had once supposed), or on an appreciation of its intrinsic significance (as others still supposed), but on its consistency with norms formed in social settings – the use of private languages, he famously insisted, was impossible.[78] Wittgenstein envisaged the development of these social norms as analogous to the playing of a game, in which people tried statements out on each other until they reached agreements about how words should be used.[79] Their agreements could be reached more or less firmly. In seeking to explain how the word 'likely' ought to be used, for instance, Sir Henry Fowler observed that 'in educated speech and writing in England the adverb is never used without *very*, *most* or *more*'.[80] Of course, Fowler was not in a position to legislate on the use of language.[81] He could not require people to write in a particular way, and is best seen as making a move in a game of language formation, encouraging a particular use of the adverb by disdainfully distinguishing its usage in England from its usage in Scotland and Ireland, where it was often heard 'in speech' without qualification, and in the United States of America, where it was even seen 'in print' in the same way.[82] This was not Fowler's most successful move in the game.

77 Even in the case of notaries, this was not necessarily a reliable belief (J. Finlay, 'The History of the Notary in Scotland', in M. Schmoeckel and W. Schubert (eds), *Handbuch zur Geschichte des Notariats der europäischen Traditionen* (Baden-Baden, 2009), p. 393, at pp. 396–9 and 414–15).

78 S. Kripke, *Wittgenstein on Rules and Private Language* (Oxford, 1982). In this sense, 'privie frauchting' was never a possibility.

79 For a sixteenth-century example of the sort of game he first envisaged see *The Complete Essays of Montaigne*, tr. D.M. Frame (Stanford, 1971), p. 129.

80 H.W. Fowler, *A Dictionary of Modern English Usage* (Oxford, 1983), p. 337.

81 R. Burchfield, *The English Language* (Oxford, 1985), pp. 54 and 91.

82 On Fowler's resistance to what he saw as the 'Scotticising' tendencies of Sir James Murray and Sir William Craigie see J. McMorris, *The Warden of English: The Life of H.W. Fowler, Author of Fowler's Modern English Usage* (Oxford, 2001), pp. 95–6.

Through a lack of either education, or commitment to the ideal of sounding English, or any sense of linguistic propriety, writers throughout the United Kingdom now make frequent adverbial use of 'likely' without any qualification. Does it follow that they are no longer misusing the word? Indeed, could they ever have been misusing the word? Are words properly used in whichever way people choose to use them? Wittgenstein's point was not that language use is an unregulated activity, but that its rules – if they can be called that – are inseparable from the contexts in which they are used.[83] The rules of language are not abstract entities, existing independently of how people express themselves, but are explanations of how expressions are employed when people communicate with each other successfully.[84] As the rules of language are embedded in their usage, the boundary between the normal and the normative, or between the descriptive and the prescriptive, is bound to remain fluid and negotiable.[85] Fowler may have explained how the adverb 'likely' was used by educated writers in Britain in the early twentieth century, but whether his explanation remains valid in the early twenty-first century is open to doubt.[86]

Wittgenstein's later philosophy has been so influential that the points just made may seem too obvious to be worth making, yet they are of great significance for the present enquiry. To turn to a more relevant example, the statement 'the master will provide a sufficient ship' could have made sense in sixteenth-century Scotland only because the words used had agreed meanings in the context of overseas trade – the sort of thing Wittgenstein referred to as 'a form of life'.[87] This is not to say that those involved in overseas trade must have reached an agreement about the meaning of the words in the same way that legislators reach agreements when enacting statutes, or that parties do when concluding contracts, though there could occasionally have been attempts to settle meanings in this way.[88] Rather, the words 'master' and 'ship' would have

83 G. Baker, 'Following Wittgenstein: Some Signposts for *Philosophical Investigations*, §§. 143–242', in S.H. Holzman and C.M. Leich (eds), *Wittgenstein: To Follow a Rule* (London, 1981), p. 31, at pp. 59–64.

84 O. Hanfling, *Wittgenstein and the Human Form of Life* (London, 2002), pp. 51–65.

85 H.F. Pitkin, *Wittgenstein and Justice: On the Significance of Ludwig Wittgenstein for Social and Political Thought* (Berkeley, 1993), pp. 18–19.

86 Nevertheless, those who wish to be recognised as educated and competent users of the English language by all readers in Britain may need to adhere to the older usage.

87 *Philosophical Investigations*, tr. G.E.M. Anscombe, P.M.S. Hacker and J. Schulte (Chichester, 2009), §§. 23 and 241.

88 B. Stroud, 'Mind, Meaning and Practice', in H. Sluga and D.G. Stern (eds), *The Cambridge Companion to Wittgenstein* (Cambridge, 1996), p. 296, at pp. 302–4; E. Minar, 'The Life of the Sign: Rule-Following, Practice and Agreement', in O. Kuusela and M. McGinn (eds), *The Oxford Handbook of Wittgenstein* (Oxford, 2011), p. 276, at pp. 288–91.

had agreed meanings because they were widely used with reference to certain persons and things, and the word 'sufficient' would have had an agreed meaning because some ships were judged to be 'sufficient' but not others. As Wittgenstein put it, the meaning of words tends to depend less on decisions about their proper usage than on consistency in their usage – on 'agreement in judgment'.[89] Meaning tends to be a matter of consensus or shared opinion more than of convention or a meeting of minds (though the word convention remains a useful label for this type of agreement). The statement 'the master will provide a sufficient ship' would have been meaningful insofar as there was consistency in its usage. In contrast, the statement 'the master will provide a nuclear submarine' could have had no meaning in the sixteenth century since the words 'nuclear' and 'submarine' had no agreed meanings then, nor could they have acquired agreed meanings until practices developed with reference to which they could have been used. But what about the statement 'the cooper will provide reliable advice'? The problem here is not that the words 'cooper', 'reliable' and 'advice' had no agreed meanings in the sixteenth century, but that the statement did not tend to be made in relation to overseas trade. It might have been made in relation to a specific voyage, on which a cooper agreed to accompany a cargo stored in barrels and to advise on their handling, but it would only have been meaningful in that context. Had it been carelessly copied into a charter party for another voyage it would have been meaningless, and it could not have become a standard term in charter parties unless the practice of coopers advising on the handling of barrels became widespread.[90] Accordingly, while the clauses the draftsmen of charter parties tended to compose may not have been governed by legislation or other written sources of law, they must to some extent have been governed by the linguistic conventions constraining the proper description of the form of life in which merchants and mariners were involved. It was not only normal for certain commitments to be made but was also normative for them to be made in certain ways. Another question thus arises: if the writing of charter parties was constrained by the linguistic conventions governing the description of overseas trade, was the practice of overseas trade itself constrained by the same linguistic conventions? As the use of language was described by Wittgenstein

89 *Philosophical Investigations*, §. 242.

90 *Philosophical Investigations*, §. 199. See again n. 49 above for an actual example of a statement that might have been, but does not in fact appear to have been, standardised. As usual, though, it needs to be remembered that the records are incomplete.

as a 'custom' or 'institution', it has to be asked whether it could have formed the basis of other customs or institutions.[91]

4 Protestations

There can be little doubt that merchants and mariners did attribute normative significance to statements of the types typically included in charter parties. This often became apparent soon after a contract was made. On 22 January 1529, for example, a Norwegian master appeared before the bailie court in Aberdeen and declared that although his ship had been freighted by several merchants of the burgh, who had undertaken in a charter party written in one of their homes to provide a cargo before Candlemas, that date (2 February) was approaching and the hold of his ship remained almost empty.[92] He was therefore 'protestand' that if they failed to provide the cargo, they would be 'indettit to oupset him all costis, skaithtis and expensis he or his childer makis or sustenis in his lying heir langar thane his said lying dais in thair defaltis'. Having made this declaration, the master asked for an 'instrument' to be issued, witnessed by 'the haill court'. Other masters made similar declarations, sometimes adding that they should receive 'waist fraucht' for any space left empty in the holds of their ships.[93] When the owner of a ship complained on another occasion that his freightsmen had failed to load their goods, and 'protestit solemptlie for coistis, skaitht, dampnage, interes and expensis sustenit and to be sustenit be him', the merchants responded that he had failed to provide 'ane sufficient schip', protesting in turn that he should reimburse them for the 'coists, skaithts, dampnages and expensis' they had incurred in loading and unloading their goods.[94] It was more common for merchants to complain that despite 'wynd and wedder beyng fair', the master had failed to depart with their goods, and here too they protested for their costs.[95] In 1553, for example, merchants in Aberdeen complained that while their goods

91 D. Bloor, *Wittgenstein, Rules and Institutions* (London, 1997), pp. 27–42.

92 ACA, CA1/1/12/2, p. 480.

93 ACA, CA1/1/8, p. 971, CA1/1/10, p. 390, CA1/1/15, p. 318, CA1/1/16, p. 219, CA1/1/18, p. 419, 497–8 and 529, CA1/1/21, p. 323, and CA1/1/22, p. 573; DCA, BCMB, vol. 5, 3 August 1558 and 21 May 1560, and vol. 7, 26 March 1563.

94 ACA, CA1/1/24, pp. 16–18. On an earlier occasion it was the merchants who took the initiative in protesting that a master had failed to provide a sufficient ship (ACA, CA1/1/12/1, p. 407).

95 ACA, CA1/1/8, p. 604, CA1/1/16, pp. 98 and 880–1, CA1/1/21, pp. 472–3, CA1/1/22, pp. 261–2, CA1/1/27, p. 200, and CA5/1/1, f. 19r; DCA, BCMB, vol. 12, 8 and 28 August 1573.

were ‘all schippit, and thameselffis reddy in all behalffs’, the master had failed to depart, protesting ‘for ane crowne of the sone evere day thai ly heir in his defalt eftir thair lying daise’, and for compensation for whatever ‘dampnage or skaitht thai incur throw spilling of thair skynnis and merchandris in schipburd, tynsell of tham be sey, or tynsell of thair mercat’.[96] The master explained that he lacked the funds to prepare the ship for sea because he had still not received the freight due to him for a voyage into Aberdeen, ‘and protestit quhat beis obtenit or recoverit upoune him be the saidis merchandis’ should be reimbursed by those who had failed to pay for the previous voyage. In other cases masters responded by protesting that if they were forced to sail before their ships were ready, the merchants ought to cover any costs incurred.[97] Before ships departed masters and merchants made protestations against each other on various other grounds, such as failure to pay custom duties or other charges, and failure to appear as passengers.[98] A frequent cause of complaints was the loading of goods onto a ship when its hold was already full.[99]

Protestations were also made after the arrival of ships. Several masters complained that merchants were refusing to receive their goods promptly, protesting that they should not be liable for any ‘skaith’ suffered through deterioration of the goods in the holds of their ships, or that they should be reimbursed for ‘sellar maill’ they had been forced to pay to have the goods ‘housit’ on dry land.[100] Conversely, merchants might complain about slow delivery.[101] One merchant, for instance, professing himself ‘rady to pay all fraucht and oncostis maid one his guds’, protested that the master ought to compensate him for any ‘skatht’ the goods suffered, ‘togidder witht the hiest price sic gudis gaf in

96 ACA, CA1/1/21, p. 469.

97 ACA, CA1/1/16, p. 517, and CA1/1/17, p. 460.

98 ACA, CA1/1/9, p. 635, CA1/1/12/1, pp. 126, 351 and 407, CA1/1/12/2, p. 532, CA1/1/13, p. 270, CA1/1/14, pp. 12–13 and 512, CA1/1/15, pp. 550–1, CA1/1/16, pp. 23, 184, 462, 465, 641, 653, 707 and 784–5, CA1/1/17, pp. 131 and 459, CA1/1/18, pp. 279, 359 and 364, and CA1/1/22, p. 654; DCA, BCMB, vol. 1, f. 153r, vol. 7, 11 January 1563, vol. 12, 16 July 1573 and 13 January 1574, vol. 13, 22 March, 21 April, 9 August and 20 October 1574, and 14 January 1575, vol. 15, 22 September 1581, and vol. 17, 19 January 1592.

99 ACA, CA1/1/8, pp. 1029–30, CA1/1/9, p. 732, CA1/1/12/1, pp. 407–8, CA1/1/12/2, p. 529, CA1/1/15, pp. 89–90, 94, 96, 188 and 278, and CA1/1/16, p. 784. See too ACA, CA1/1/14, pp. 12–13 (reproduced in ‘Collection of Decisions of the Borough Court of Aberdeen, 1399–1561’, in W. Kennedy, *Annals of Aberdeen, from the Reign of King William the Lion to the End of the Year 1818*, 2 vols (London, 1818), vol. 2, p. 471, at pp. 477–8).

100 ACA, CA1/1/8, p. 255, CA1/1/11, pp. 146–7, CA1/1/12/1, p. 279, CA1/1/12/2, p. 494, and CA1/1/16, p. 391.

101 ACA, CA1/1/12/1, p. 170, CA1/1/13, pp. 172 and 495–6, and CA1/1/20, p. 156; DCA, BCMB, vol. 1, f. 154v.

Scotland in ony tyme he withtheld the samyn, witht all maner of expensis maid be him thairupone'.[102] After goods had been delivered or at least offered to merchants, masters complained about delays in the payment of freight.[103] One complained that he had been forced to prolong his visit from Germany 'in defalt of pament of his fraucht, and had maid grit costis and expensis throght his said lying, and as yit culd nocht get pament of his fraucht, protestand solemplie for costis, skaithtis, dampnis and expensis he maid and sustenit thairthrow, als weill as the principall fraucht'.[104] Another recurring problem was the failure of merchants to provide cargoes promised for return voyages.[105] Merchants were warned by a master that if the cargo was not produced within the agreed lying days, 'the schip and marenellis suld lie one thair expensis, and at tha suld be indettit to refund him his dampnage, interess and expensis'.[106] Ocasionally ships arrived in ports unexpectedly, driven in by storms and the need for urgent repairs, and masters might then urge merchants to receive their goods from the hold, both to protect them from harm and to facilitate the repairs, 'protestand solemplie that quhat skaitht the said gudis sustenit on the schipis boddum, or the said schip hirself, that it suld cum on the frauchtismen and merchandis and thair gudis, and at tha suld be indettit to oupset the samyn'.[107] Merchants might protest in response that the real problem was the insufficiency of the ship supplied, or might insist that the ship was still capable of sailing to the agreed destination.[108] Protestations were also made for various other reasons after ships arrived.[109] A Flemish master who had received a guarantee against liability to several merchants protested after the litigation dragged on that the guarantor ought to reimburse him for any 'costis, skaithtis, dampnis and expensis he maks or sustenis throught his tareing and

102 ACA, CA1/1/12/1, p. 138.

103 ACA, CA1/1/8, pp. 1042–3, CA1/1/9, pp. 280 and 769, CA1/1/10, pp. 171 and 349, CA1/1/11, p. 609, CA1/1/12/1, p. 259, CA1/1/13, pp. 305–6, 315, 332, 413, 504, 508 and 510, CA1/1/14, p. 156, CA1/1/15, pp. 17–18, 36, 434 and 540, CA1/1/16, p. 28, CA1/1/18, p. 309, CA1/1/20, pp. 138, 146, 156, 160 and 175–6, CA1/1/21, pp. 6–7, 151 and 849, CA1/1/26, p. 164, and CA1/1/34/1, pp. 239–40; DCA, BCMB, vol. 3, 30 October 1551; GCA, C1/1/1, f. 128r.

104 ACA, CA1/1/13, p. 329.

105 ACA, CA1/1/10, p. 213, CA1/1/12/1, p. 309, CA1/1/14, pp. 537 and 589, CA1/1/16, pp. 332 and 775, and CA1/1/18, p. 386. Some of the complaints listed at n. 93 above may possibly have related to return voyages.

106 ACA, CA1/1/12/2, pp. 496–7.

107 ACA, CA1/1/11, p. 521, CA1/1/12/1, p. 245, CA1/1/13, p. 495, and CA1/1/18, pp. 235 and 245.

108 ACA, CA1/1/12/2, pp. 689–90, 697–8 and 700–1, CA1/1/13, p. 403, CA1/1/20, p. 269, CA1/1/25, p. 301, and CA1/1/37, pp. 244–6.

109 ACA, CA1/1/8, pp. 363 and 730, CA1/1/12/1, p. 214, CA1/1/12/2, pp. 481 and 865, CA1/1/16, pp. 710–12; DCA, BCMB, vol. 3, 10 October 1550, and vol. 5, 3 February 1559.

postponing of his vaege', and a French master whose ship had been arrested for a debt owed by one of his freightsmen protested that the debtor should cover 'the hail costis, skaithis, dampnage and interes quhilk he suld sustene or mak heirefter'.[110]

Almost two hundred examples of protestations have been found in the records of the burgh courts, though how representative they are of practice across Scotland is impossible to tell.[111] Most of those found were made during the first half of the century and in Aberdeen, which happens to be the only burgh from which extensive records covering that period have survived.[112] As the Aberdeen records in fact cover the whole century, and as they provide far fewer examples dated after 1550 than before, it may be suspected that it became more usual in the second half of the century for protestations of the varieties outlined to be made in the admiralty courts.[113] It also appears to have become more common then for protestations to be made in the presence of notaries public rather than judges, and to be recorded in their protocol books rather than in court books.[114] The number of examples found there is not large, but they are almost all dated after 1550.[115] These protestations were made in Edinburgh, Dundee, Dysart, Montrose and Ayr, where they were recorded in similar styles to those found in the court books. A notary in Dundee, for instance, recorded that he had accompanied a merchant 'to the schoir off the said burght', where it had been pointed out that a master was failing to prepare his ship for a voyage within the time stipulated in a charter party made between them, in view of which the merchant had protested 'that quhat expenses, cost, skaith, damnage and intres that he is to sustene throw the non radynes off the said schip, and tynsell off his vayege, he mycht obtene the samyn aganis the

110 ACA, CA1/1/13, pp. 518–19; DCA, BCMB, vol. 6, 8 December 1561.

111 Protestations made in response to protestations are included in this rough figure, but not those of a procedural character (for 'remeid of law' and so on).

112 Over a hundred and fifty examples dated between 1500 and 1550 were found in the Aberdeen records, along with another twenty or so dated after 1550. Almost all the other examples were found in the records of Dundee, most of which are dated after 1550.

113 Examples cannot be found in *Acta curiae admirallatus Scotiae, 1557–62*, ed. T.C. Wade (Edinburgh, 1937), but protestations may still have been made in other periods or in other admiralty courts, the availability of which is considered in the first essay above.

114 *Protocol Book of Mr Gilbert Grote, 1552–73*, ed. W. Angus (Edinburgh, 1914), p. 27; DCA, PBD, vol. 11, f. 65r, and vol. 18, f. 51v; NRS, B6/1/1/1, ff. 366v-7r and 463, B19/1/1, 2 February 1573, B19/1/9, 11 September 1578 and 20 February 1579, B19/1/12, 20 January 1589 and 7 May 1590, B21/1/1, ff. 14v and 51r, and B51/1/1, pt 2, f. 17r.

115 D. Murray, *Legal Practice in Ayr and the West of Scotland in the Fifteenth and Sixteenth Centuries: A Study in Economic History* (Glasgow, 1910), p. 61, pointed out that it remained common for notaries to record protests by merchants and mariners in his own time.

said skipper'. As this entry was written by a notary who sometimes helped to record court proceedings, and others were written by notaries who acted more regularly as clerks of courts, it may be that protestations were usually recorded by notaries, in one place or another.[116] That protestations all shared the same basic structure – a report of a factual state of affairs followed by a normative inference that something ought to happen – probably resulted from the use of related exemplars in the training of notaries throughout the country.[117] Much of the recurring phraseology in the examples that have come to light may also have resulted from the same practice.[118] Apart from anything else, it is unlikely that merchants and mariners would have peppered their speech with 'the said', or have cautiously referred to 'expenses, cost, skaith, damnage and intres' when one or two words would surely have seemed sufficient to lay people. Yet the voices of merchants and mariners can to some extent be made out behind the protestations.[119] The words used may often have been provided by the scribes, but not the complaints being put into words. Merchants and mariners must have had some sense of what was troubling them. Furthermore, not only the factual statements but also the normative inferences drawn could be quite circumstantial, and could not always have been lifted with slight adjustments from style books. When a clerk in Aberdeen recorded the complaint that a master, who had undertaken to provide a ship with 'sufficient marenaris and all uther necessaris according to ane sufficient schip', was not ready to depart on an agreed date, 'wynd and wedder beyng fair', he may have been using familiar language, but it is more likely to have been the merchants who talked about loading the ship with 'thair gudis, that is to say, salmond for the maist part', about asking the master 'to put hir in the reid to bygyn hir viage', about his inability to do so 'in falt of towis and salis', and about their desire to receive compensation not simply for 'quhat skaytht thai sustenit at the mercat', but specifically for the loss of profit they sustained 'throw nocht cumyng of the said fyschis in dew tym thairto'.[120]

The crucial point for present purposes is that merchants and mariners are unlikely to have expressed concerns before clerks or other notaries unless they

116 Strictly speaking, NRS, B19/1/1–18, were notaries' minute books rather than protocol books, and they appear to have been compiled in connection with the practice of the burgh court.

117 Robert Weddderburn, the clerk referred to above, had served an apprenticeship with the burgh clerks of both Dundee and Edinburgh (NRS, NP2/2, ff. 43v-4r; DCA, PBD, vol. 15, f. 1).

118 *Cf.* J. Bailey, 'Voices in Court: Lawyers' or Litigants'?', (2001) 74 *Historical Research* 392.

119 *Cf.* E.S. Cohen, 'She Said, He Said: Situated Oralities in Judicial Records from Early-Modern Rome', (2012) 16 *Journal of Early Modern History* 403.

120 ACA, CA1/1/16, p. 98.

believed that something was happening which ought not to be happening, or that something was not happening which ought to be happening. The normative components in protestations were often supported with statements that parties ought to behave 'conforme to thair chartour party', or more generally that they ought to behave 'conform to thair promeis' or 'conform to thair conditioun'. Charter parties were only mentioned in a quarter of the known examples, however, and often then for the detail they provided about the length of lying days, the amounts of freight to be paid, or the 'painis' to be endured for failing to fulfil obligations promptly. Indeed, in some instances, as when it was complained that goods were being loaded onto ships after their holds had been filled up, reference was being made to obligations that do not appear to have been specified in charter parties. The normative component in protestations clearly cannot have been founded in every instance on the promises parties made to each other, however significant promises may have been in some situations. In one of the protestations relating to the loading of goods 'aboun the ourloft', reference was made to 'the act of parliament maid thairupoune', but other references to written sources of law have not been found.[121] In the vast majority of protestations parties simply asserted that they were entitled to redress for misbehaviour without explaining why. The most striking feature of the protestations is how rarely their normative components were challenged. When one master protested for his 'coistis, skaythis and expenses' if a merchant did not 'lay and input in his schip the geir and marchandreis, as he is obleist in his chartour party, witht all diligence, because his lying daise ar bipast', the merchant protested in response that he was not bound to do so unless the master found 'sufficient cautioun and souerte for having of his said schip to the portis contenit in the chartour party and na others'.[122] In another case, when a merchant protested for 'quhat skaytht cumis to himself or his guids' as a result of the ship failing to leave on an agreed date, the master protested in response that he should 'obsett na skaytht to hym, becaus it is nocht his defalt his heir tareing'.[123] It is not clear whether there was a disagreement about the need for the delay to be the master's fault.[124] Usually, when one party responded to a protestation, it was not by challenging its normative component but was by making another factual statement and protesting that it

121 ACA, CA1/1/16, p. 784.

122 ACA, CA1/1/21, p. 323.

123 ACA, CA1/1/17, p. 459.

124 Other cases in which there may possibly have been disagreement about obligations owed can be found in ACA, CA1/1/12/2, pp. 689–90 and 700–1, CA1/1/17, pp. 573–4, and CA1/1/18, pp. 502–3. All these cases are discussed in the eighth essay in this collection.

shifted responsibility onto the other party or onto a third party. Subject to an exception is mentioned below, the impression given by the examples found is that care was mostly taken to draw inferences with which the other parties would agree. So what exactly was going on here?

5 Speech Acts

It may be observed to begin with that the written laws mentioned in the last paragraph are examples of what the philosopher J.L. Austin once called 'performative' as opposed to 'constative' utterances.[125] The legislators who enacted laws in Scotland or elsewhere were not simply making statements of fact, which might be shown to be true or false, but were also laying down the law, either successfully or unsuccessfully. They were doing something with the words they pronounced, or were attempting to do something with them. If this observation leaves us with the problem of knowing whether the legislation discussed in the first section of this essay was successful – we have reason, it has been suggested, to be doubtful – another problem is that these manifest acts of legislation do not seem so different from the protestations discussed in the last section.[126] When a master protested that merchants who failed to provide a cargo should compensate him for any loss he sustained, he was attempting to identify (to put the point tentatively) an applicable norm. He too was trying to do something with his words, or was engaging in a 'speech act', requiring assessment in terms of its success more than its accuracy. In fact, at around the time that Wittgenstein realised that 'words are also deeds', Austin moved away from his distinction between performative and constative utterances and distinguished instead between the 'locutionary meaning', the 'illocutionary force' and the 'perlocutionary effect' of all utterances.[127] To grasp the locutionary meaning of an utterance like 'tha salbe indettit to oupset him all costs, skaithts and expensis', we need to know that the word 'oupset' was used in the 'sense' that compensation was to be paid, and that the expression 'costis, skaithtis and expensis' was used with 'reference' to payments that a master might have

125 *Philosophical Papers*, ed. J.O. Urmson and G.J. Warnock (Oxford, 1979), pp. 233–52.

126 Of course, unlike the legislative statements discussed in the first section, the protestations discussed in the last section were in origin 'utterances' in a literal sense, even though they were recorded in writing.

127 Wittgenstein, *Philosophical Investigations*, §. 546; Austin, *How to Do Things with Words* (Oxford, 1975).

to make or might not receive.[128] Some attention was paid to the locutionary meaning of the protestations found in the burgh records in the last section of this essay, but the question now is whether we can clarify the nature of the norms implicit in these statements. It may be thought that the solution will lie in attending to their perlocutionary effect. We may wonder whether a statement like the one quoted would have had the effect of relieving a master of the costs he incurred, and we may suppose that if he received compensation it was an effective norm. A practical problem is that we rarely have enough information to know what effect protestations actually had. Fortunately, Austin realised that the key to understanding speech acts was to investigate their illocutionary force, which he believed to be dependent on the contexts in which they were uttered, and often on the existence of some sort of convention.[129] Regardless of its effectiveness, a statement would have had the force of legislation if it was made by someone recognised as a legislator and in a manner recognised as a legislative process.[130] Similarly, though also differently, a statement would have had the force of a protestation if it was made in a way that enabled other people (including the clerk of a court) to recognise it as a formal act of protesting.[131] Whether the protestation was effective would again have been another matter.

A further advance was made by one of Austin's pupils, J.R. Searle, who found that all speech acts belong to one of five basic types.[132] Some are 'representative', as when a master alleged that goods had not yet been placed in the hold of his ship. Others are 'directive', as would have been the case if a court had ordered a merchant to cover a master's costs.[133] Others are 'declarative', as would have been the case if a court had ruled more generally that merchants who failed to load goods promptly were obliged to cover any costs incurred by a master. Others again are 'commissive', as when merchants promised to load goods by a certain date, and finally some are 'expressive', as when masters

128 ACA, CA1/1/12/2, p. 480; *Dictionary of the Older Scottish Tongue*, vol. 8, pp. 217–23, and vol. 11, p. 392.

129 Austin himself believed that speech acts were always dependent on conventions, but philosophers of language have not always been convinced by this. For present purposes the point does not matter especially.

130 For an example of analysis of legislation in these terms see N. Allott and B. Shaer, 'The Illocutionary Force of Laws', (2018) 61 *Inquiry* 351.

131 Compare the discussion of warnings in P.F. Strawson, 'Austin and "Locutionary Meaning"', in G.W. Warnock (ed.), *Essays on J.L. Austin* (Oxford, 1973), p. 46.

132 'A Classification of Illocutionary Acts', (1976) 5 *Language in Society* 1.

133 Examples of court orders will be considered in the next section of this essay.

thanked merchants for loading goods promptly.[134] For present purposes, the crucial distinctions are between the first three types of act. When a representation is made, the aim is to say something that maps onto reality (Searle talked about 'word-to-world fit'). The master's allegation would have been successful if he could have proved that the hold of his ship was still empty.[135] In contrast, when a direction is given, the aim is to make reality map onto what is said ('world-to-word fit'). The court's order would have been successful if the merchant had proceeded to pay the master.[136] In the case of a declaration, however, something unique and remarkable is happening. The ruling that merchants should cover the master's costs would have been designed to bring it about that merchants compensated masters for the costs they incurred ('world-to-word fit' again), yet if the ruling was successful it would also have been an accurate statement of the merchants' obligation to compensate the master ('word-to-world fit'). As Searle explained, when he moved on to use the philosophy of language as a foundation for his development of a new philosophy of society, declarative speech acts are the means by which people construct social reality.[137] Whereas language may merely be used to describe 'brute facts', such as the presence of some objects (goods) in another (the hold of a ship), it may also be used both to describe and to create 'social facts', such as an obligation to cover a master's costs. If it is declared that merchants should cover the master's costs, and if it is accepted that the declaration is accurate, then merchants are obliged to cover the master's costs. A combination of the use of language and acceptance that it is being used correctly brings social facts like obligations into existence, and there is no other way in which they can be brought into existence.[138] The language recorded in the sources studied by historians is therefore of fundamental importance, not simply because we have few other

---

134 Commissive statements have of course been exemplified by the charter parties examined in the second section of this essay. Expressive statements, in which parties acknowledged the payment of freight, delivery of goods and so on, can also be found in the court records but are not examined here.

135 In this instance, recovering the illocutionary force of the allegation would have coincided to a large extent with recovering its locutionary meaning, since its success would have been dependent on its accuracy.

136 Here, recovering the illocutionary force of the order would have coincided with recovering its perlocutionary effect to the extent that the court's intention was grasped by someone who recognised its authority.

137 *The Construction of Social Reality* (London, 1995), and *Making the Social World: The Structure of Human Civilization* (Oxford, 2010).

138 Even if a merchant had recognised that he should cover a master's costs, there would have been no obligation to do so as a social fact until there was acceptance of the accuracy of a statement made between at least two people that someone in his position should do so.

representations of social worlds to rely on, but because the language recorded was constitutive of those worlds, and enables us to observe their creation.[139] Searle explained further that declarative speech acts are used both to bring social worlds into existence and to maintain them in existence. To keep social facts alive, people continually elicit support for them by declaring that one thing counts as another – that a failure to load goods, for instance, was a situation in which merchants were bound to compensate masters.[140]

If obligations may thus be created and maintained as social facts, an obvious question to ask is how legal obligations may be differentiated from those belonging to fields like ethics or etiquette.[141] An answer proposed by Searle is that declarations may be made at one level to give a special status to declarations made at another level.[142] If it were declared and accepted that a declaration made by a particular person or body in a particular way 'counted as law', then every declaration made by that person or body in that way would count as law, without itself requiring further acceptance.[143] Had it been accepted, for example, that the acts passed by the Scottish parliament, a burgh council or the convention of royal burghs must have the force of law, then every act passed by one of these bodies would have counted as law, whether or not it was accepted as binding by the people whose behaviour it was intended to regulate. The problem that has emerged here is that while the legislation passed in Scotland in relation to charter parties clearly was regarded as a source of law, it was not adhered to closely enough for it to be clear that it became binding without further acceptance by those to whom it applied. The impression given is that legislation was regarded less as a definitive mechanism for creating law

139 It is suggested in R. D'Andrade, 'Commentary on Searle's "Social Ontology": Some Basic Principles', (2006) 6 *Anthropological Theory* 30, that the process of developing a social world is what anthropologists have in mind when they use the word 'culture'.

140 H. Rakoczy and M. Tomasello, 'The Ontogeny of Social Ontology: Steps to Shared Intentionality and Status Functions', in S.L. Tsohatzidis (ed.), *Intentional Acts and Institutional Facts: Essays on John Searle's Social Ontology* (Dordrecht, 2007), p. 113, point out that children acquire the basic capacity to declare that one thing counts as another at an early age (as in playing games like 'you be Batman and I'll be Robin').

141 For a discussion of this issue see D.N. MacCormick, 'Law as Institutional Fact', (1974) 90 *Law Quarterly Review* 102. The present concern, it must be emphasised, is not with the soundness of the philosophy outlined, but with the assistance it may provide in making sense of a historical phenomenon.

142 See too G.P. Fletcher, 'Law', in B. Smith (ed.), *John Searle* (Cambridge, 2003), p. 85.

143 The word 'declaration' is perhaps a little misleading here, for although a declaration that other declarations should count as law might be made explicit in a constitutional document or something of the sort, it might instead be implicit in the way people behaved (another example of what Wittgenstein meant by 'agreement in judgment').

than as a more or less influential contribution to a process of norm formation, which continued outside the parliament, council or convention that had intervened in the process. Another possibility raised in the previous paragraph is that a court might have been recognised as having the authority to make a binding pronouncement of the law. As far as the parties to a particular action were concerned, a court would indeed have had this authority as soon as the parties submitted to its jurisdiction. Any declaration of the applicable law made by the court would have been binding on the parties because they had declared in advance that they would accept it as a binding ruling.[144] However, for a declaration of the applicable law to have been binding on other parties in other actions, it would have been necessary for people to accept more broadly that courts had the authority to lay down the law in their rulings, as if they too had the status of legislators. Nothing in the evidence examined so far in this essay suggests that the masters and merchants who entered into charter parties and made protestations before the burgh courts did attribute this broader authority to the courts.[145] While there is very limited evidence that an act of parliament could be cited in support of the normative component of a protestation, no evidence at all has been found that court decisions were cited to the same effect.[146]

There is another possibility. Searle also pointed out that law could come into existence without any person or body being declared to have the authority to lay it down. People could have told each other that there was a proper way of behaving – perhaps that merchants who failed to load goods promptly onto ships should cover any costs incurred by their masters – and their statements could have come to be accepted as correct, at least through a gradual process of repetition.[147] Had it been further accepted, at a different level, that people were legally obliged to behave properly, then what was accepted as proper would also have been legally obligatory.[148] Law might thus have been created

144 The records of the burgh courts often stated explicitly that litigants had accepted the court's jurisdiction. Many cases were submitted in a similar way to arbitration.

145 As is explained in other essays in this collection, some evidence of such a belief can be found elsewhere, in particular in the thinking of lawyers.

146 As always, it needs to be remembered that the evidence available is far from complete.

147 One master who protested for the costs he was incurring long after the expiry of his lying days observed that the merchants ought to pay 'conforme to his utheris protestations maid divers tymes afore' (ACA, CA1/1/13, p. 329). The reality appears to have been that parties almost invariably relied on the similarity between the claims they were making and those made on previous occasions, without direct contradiction.

148 If it would have been natural for the binding force of written laws to be declared in writing, it would have been less natural for the binding force of proper behaviour to be

by a process of declaration and acceptance, at two different levels, but it would have been a different process from the creation of laws by legislators or courts. Of course, legal historians and philosophers are familiar with the idea that law could have been created by custom as well as by legislation. Usually they identify custom with established practice, as if (to take the current example) an established practice of compensating masters for costs they incurred after the expiry of lying days could have given rise to a legal obligation to compensate them.[149] Yet explaining what was happening in this way is problematic. Not only does it involve attributing to masters and merchants the erroneous belief that an 'ought' can be derived from an 'is', but it also means that we cannot know whether merchants were obliged to compensate masters unless we have evidence that they actually did so.[150] The great attraction of Searle's social philosophy is that it both provides a plausible explanation of how legal norms could have been brought into existence without forceful legislation, and enables us to interpret protestations as an exercise in norm formation and preservation.[151] We do not need to know whether merchants actually compensated masters for their losses as long as we know that masters regularly protested for compensation without being contradicted by merchants. From the positive evidence of the protestations recorded in court and protocol books we know that declarative statements were frequently made, and from the negative evidence of the absence of contradiction, despite the fact that protestations could elicit responses in other protestations, we have reason to believe that the declarations were accepted. The obligation to compensate masters for costs incurred through delays was brought into existence and kept in existence by the protestations masters made, coupled with their acceptance by merchants. This is not to say that the actual practice of compensating masters is irrelevant – Wittgenstein's insistence that the use of language is embedded in social life remains important – but it is to say that the survival of court records enables historians to observe the process of norm creation and preservation. The surviving records provide evidence of how masters and mariners generated norms to regulate their engagement in maritime trade. These could have been

declared in the same way. The acceptance of its binding force is more likely to have been implicit in the way people spoke to each other about their behaviour.

149 For an interesting exception, which seems more consistent with Searle's theory than most discussions of the subject, see G.J. Postema, 'Custom, Normative Practice and the Law', (2021) 62 *Duke Law Journal* 707.

150 As already mentioned, such evidence is lacking.

151 See too J.R. Searle, *Speech Acts: An Essay in the Philosophy of Language* (Cambridge, 1969), pp. 175–98.

legal norms, though the protestations themselves do not actually make it clear that they were seen in this way. To confirm that the norms expressed in protestations were regarded as legal norms the enquiry has to be widened.

6 Litigation

Confirmation is available from the entries recorded in the court books of the coastal burghs after parties moved beyond warning each other about the consequences of failure to fulfil obligations and sought to have their fulfilment enforced judicially. On 21 July 1553 a master from Antwerp informed the bailie court of Aberdeen that two local merchants had promised to pay him freight within twelve days of the delivery of their goods, that he had 'honestlie and trewlie compleittit and fulfillit' his side of the bargain 'contenit in the chartour party maid betwix us', but that they 'wrangouslie, wilfullie and aganis the law and use and consuetude of frauchtismen and trew merchandis' refused to pay the freight.[152] He therefore asked the court 'to decerne, caus and compell be justice' the payment of the freight owed, along with compensation for further 'skaitht, coistis and dampnage' he had sustained. When claims like this one were made before a court, its officers were instructed to summon the merchants to attend a hearing, warning them that if they persistently failed to appear the court might order payment in their absence.[153] If defenders appeared, they might seek to avoid liability in various ways. Obviously, proving that payment had already been made would defeat an action, as would proving that goods had not actually been received, or even that goods had been shipped without a merchant's instructions.[154] The allegations made on either side could be proved in several ways. Usually a master would produce a 'chartour pairtie' to show how much freight had been promised for specified quantities of goods, and his 'clerkis buik' so show the quantities that had in fact been carried, but occasionally it was left to an assize to determine how much was owed 'conforme to use and custome', and the return of goods or the

152 ACA, CA1/1/21, pp. 462–3 (similar examples can be found in CA1/1/12/1, pp. 164 and 214, CA1/1/15, p. 31, CA1/1/16, pp. 561–2, CA1/1/19, p. 123, CA1/1/20, p. 140, CA1/1/34/1, pp. 258–9, and CA5/1/5, 11 September 1597).

153 ACA, CA1/1/8, p. 447, CA1/1/12/2, p. 659, CA1/1/26, pp. 669 and 692, CA1/1/27, p. 300, and CA1/1/32, p. 597; DCA, BCMB, vol. 3, 29 March 1552; AA, B6/11/2, ff. 497v-8r.

154 ACA, CA1/1/11, p. 42, CA1/1/12/1, pp. 144–5, CA1/1/26, pp. 402–3 and 442, and CA1/1/38, pp. 217–18; DCA, BCMB, vol. 4, 18 September 1556, and 27 January and 12 March 1557, vol. 5, 16 September 1558, vol. 6, 8, 20 and 24 July 1562, vol. 14, 30 March and 17 July 1579, and vol. 15, 19 July 1581; SAUL, B10/8/7, p. 224; NRS, B9/11/1, ff. 72v-3r.

payment of freight was normally established by the 'aytht *de veritate*' of one of the parties or the testimony of 'witnessis'.[155] In many entries in the court books merchants were simply ordered to pay a master 'as use is of payment of fraucht', or 'conforme to use and wont', without any indication that they had contested his claim or that he had needed to lead evidence, sometimes with the addition of a warning that if they failed to make payment within the customary term, they would also be made to cover any 'costs, skaithtis, dampnis and expensis he sustenit throught the want of the samyn'.[156] In these and some

155 ACA, CA1/1/8, pp. 546 and 560, CA1/1/10, p. 212, CA1/1/12/1, pp. 20, 192–3 and 198, CA1/1/14, p. 241, CA1/1/15, pp. 510, 519, 528, 530 and 540, CA1/1/16, pp. 487, 501 and 617, CA1/1/27, pp. 584, 649 and 652, CA1/1/30, p. 144, CA1/1/31, p. 569, CA1/1/32, pp. 29, 610 and 613, CA1/1/33/1, pp. 263–4, CA1/1/33/2, pp. 1141 and 1200, CA1/1/36, p. 304, CA1/1/37, p. 37, and CA5/1/1, ff. 126v and 246r; DCA, BCMB, vol. 3, 29 -30 October 1551, 29 January 1552, and 14 December 1554, vol. 4, 27 January and 5 February 1556, vol. 5, 7 September 1558, 10 February 1559, and 13 September and 21 October 1560, vol. 6, 16 October 1561, 15 and 23 January, 25 February and 11 March 1562, vol. 7, 20, 25 and 27 November 1562, vol. 9, 5 November 1565, and 15 March 1568, vol. 10, 6 and 8 October 1568, and 13 June 1569, vol. 11, 10 November 1569, 7 and 14 April, 9 and 16 June, 7 July and 13 December 1570, and 24 and 31 January, 9 February and 13 July 1571, vol. 12, 5 March, 13 October and 5 November 1572, 16 December 1573, and 20 January 1574, vol. 14, 19 June 1577, 4 July 1578, and 25 March and 15 July 1579, vol. 15, 5 April 1581, vol. 16, 6 and 15 February 1583, vol. 17, 9 October 1590, vol. 18, 16 September 1594, and 14 and 17 September 1595, vol. 19, 9 and 14 April, 23 June, 15 September and 23 October 1596, vol. 20, 6, 8 and 27 July, and 11 October 1597, 10 July and 4 August 1598, and 12 May 1599, and vol. 21, 5 December 1599; SAUL, B13/10/1, 20 November 1551; AA, B6/12/2, pp. 110, 115–17 and 185, B6/11/1/3, f. 349r, and B6/11/2, f. 353v; GCA, C1/1/4, ff. 83r and 122v.

156 ACA, CA1/1/7, p. 1012, CA1/1/8, pp. 173, 856 and 928, CA1/1/9, pp. 17, 134, 303, 349 and 768–9, CA1/1/10, pp. 40, 95, 120, 345 and 348, CA1/1/11, p. 64, CA1/1/12/1, pp. 77, 82–3, 97, 169, 216–17, 228, 258–9 and 309, CA1/1/12/2, pp. 609–10, 654, 666 and 668, CA1/1/13, pp. 180, 253, 343, 480 and 482, CA1/1/14, pp. 310, 317, 399, 544, 620, 622 and 626, CA1/1/15, pp. 62, 65, 79, 358 and 486, CA1/1/16, pp. 54, 124, 297, 312, 361, 387, 503, 506 and 539, CA1/1/18, pp. 308 and 497, CA1/1/19, pp. 11, 35 and 380, CA1/1/20, pp. 152, 160, 168, 172, 446–7, 450–1 and 488, CA1/1/21, pp. 105 and 108, CA1/1/22, pp. 606 and 699, CA1/1/23, p. 191, CA1/1/24, pp. 164, 303–4, 355, 501, 570, 597 and 605, CA1/1/25, pp. 160, 303 and 308, CA1/1/26, p. 699, CA1/1/27, pp. 166, 200, 300, 326, 433, 547, 551, 563–4, 655 and 789, CA1/1/28, p. 409, CA1/1/29, p. 346, CA1/1/30, pp. 263, 699 and 712, CA1/1/31, pp. 55, 335 and 425, CA1/1/32, pp. 62 and 267, CA1/1/33/2, p. 1072, CA1/1/34/2, pp. 589–90, CA1/1/35, pp. 40–1 and 47, CA1/1/37, pp. 246–7, 378 and 664, CA1/1/38, pp. 109, 305, 418, 769 and 938, CA5/1/1, f. 146v, CA5/1/2, 18 August 1581, and 10 January, 24 August and 7 September 1582, CA5/1/3, 13 June 1586, CA5/1/4, 22 August and 12 September 1595, and CA5/1/5, 28 February and 1 April 1597; DCA, BCMB, vol. 1, f. 119v, vol. 3, 12 November 1550, 19 July 1552, 26 October 1553, and 3 September, 30 October, and 10 and 17 December 1554, vol. 4, 27 January, 18 May, 5 June and 29 July 1556, and 4 August 1557, vol. 5, 1 July 1558, 23 and 27 August, and 12 September 1560, vol. 6, 13–14 January 1562, vol. 8, 14 January 1564, vol. 11, 1 June 1571, vol. 12, 2 November 1571 and 17 June 1572, vol. 13, 1 July 1575, vol. 14, 27 January 1576, 19 June 1577, 8 October 1578, 7 and 23 March, and 29 July 1579, and 24 January 1580, vol. 15, 5 April and 8 May 1581, vol. 16, 31 January and 12 April 1583,

other entries merchants were often required to pay further charges 'use and wont', such as 'steirmanfee', 'prymgilt' or 'keilhire'.[157] If there was any doubt about a merchant's ability or willingness to pay the sum ordered, he might be required to provide security before he left the tolbooth, or to remain there until payment was made by someone else.[158] Otherwise the merchant would be threatened with the 'poyndyng of his rediest guidis and geir, or wardyng of his persoun', and goods sometimes were seized (poindit) and sold by auction (roupit) to recover the sum due.[159]

Essentially the same coercive process was followed whenever a merchant complained that a master who owed him an obligation would not provide satisfaction 'except he be compellit thairto be the law', for example if he complained that goods he had 'schippit' had not been 'deliverit' to him after their arrival at an agreed destination.[160] The merchant would petition the court to force the master to return the goods or pay him their value, 'according to justice' or 'according to the consuetude of merchandis', to which the master might reply that he had never received the goods in the first place, or that he had in fact returned them already.[161] In some cases the complaint was that the master

vol. 17, 12 October 1590, 3 and 11 September, and 1 and 26 November 1591, vol. 19, 5, 20 and 23 October 1596, and 21 January 1597, vol. 20, 1, 27 and 30 June, 5 and 26 August, 7, 11 and 17 October, and 18 and 24 November 1597, 15 February, 19 June, 4 August and 7 September 1598, and 12 February and 18 September 1599; SAUL, B10/8/4, p. 304, B13/10/1, 22 October 1550, and B65/8/1, f. 123; *Kirkcudbright Town Council Records*, p. 169.

157 ACA, CA1/1/9, p. 722, CA1/1/10, p. 126, and CA1/1/13, pp. 502, 504 and 508; DCA, BCMB, vol. 3, 22 November 1553, and vol. 5, 1 July 1558.

158 ACA, CA1/1/11, pp. 610–11, CA1/1/12/1, pp. 157, 262–3 and 272, CA1/1/14, p. 38, CA1/1/14, p. 544, CA1/1/15, pp. 27 and 165, and CA1/1/19, p. 265; DCA, BCMB, vol. 1, f. 104r.

159 ACA, CA1/1/12/1, pp. 141 and 150, CA1/1/12/2, pp. 658 and 677, CA1/1/13, p. 425, CA1/1/14, pp. 139–40, CA1/1/16, pp. 375 and 520, CA1/1/21, pp. 107 and 482, and CA1/1/25, p. 68; DCA, BCMB, vol. 3, 19 October 1552, vol. 6, 15 January 1562, vol. 8, 14 January 1564, vol. 13, 1 and 3 September 1574, vol. 14, 30 August 1576, vol. 15, 7 April and 15 September 1581, vol. 20, 20 April 1599, and PBD, vol. 11, f. 130r; SAUL, B10/8/5, p. 441, B10/8/6, pp. 132 and 618, and B65/8/1, 3 December 1591.

160 Fairly complete processes can be pieced together from the Aberdeen records as follows: (1) ACA, CA1/1/15, pp. 286–7, 294, 301–2, 438 and 444–5; (2) CA1/1/15, pp. 363, 366–9, 375–6, 380 and 387; (3) CA1/1/15, pp. 662, 666, 669–70, 689, 692, 701–2, 704, 715 and 720; (4) CA1/1/16, pp. 122, 124, 131, 136, 140, 157 and 172; (5) CA1/1/16, pp. 452, 457, 463–4, 467–8, 472, 474, 476, 482, 486 and 474; (6) CA1/1/20, pp. 121, 126, 129, 131–48, 150–6, 158–68, 170–3, 175–7 and 370; and (7) CA1/1/20, pp. 131–2, 134–5, 137–8, 147–8 and 165. The sixth example was the case mentioned at n. 44 above.

161 ACA, CA1/1/7, p. 1016, CA1/1/8, pp. 393 and 1017, ACA, CA1/1/9, p. 177, CA1/1/10, pp. 141–2 and 381, CA1/1/12/1, p. 264, CA1/1/13, pp. 413, 422, 425, 428, 434, 441, 502 and 510, CA1/1/14, pp. 134, 137, 536, 539, 556–60 and 606, CA1/1/15, pp. 18, 28–9, 54, 75, 204, 298, 334–5, 362–3, 549, 655, 685, 690, 693–4 and 698–9, CA1/1/16, pp. 67, 157, 540, 655, 736 and 742, CA1/1/18, pp. 282

had refused to receive goods or transport them to an agreed destination, 'conforme to the chartour party maid thairupoune'.[162] Whether goods had been received or returned was proved by the oaths of litigants, the testimony of witnesses or documentary evidence, especially the production of the 'buik' kept on most large ships by the clerk.[163] Although bills of lading were in use elsewhere in Europe, no evidence has been found of their use in the burgh courts of Scotland.[164] Whichever mode of proof was adopted, what precisely needed to be proved depended on the meaning attached to the words 'schippit' and 'deliverit', which in turn depended on the practices described, or more accurately on agreements about how appropriate practices could be described. When a merchant claimed to have 'schippit' a barrel of goods in Crail to be transported to Dieppe, the master denied 'the ressait off the said barrell', or that he knew of 'the schipping or inputting off the samin', to which the merchant answered that he had 'obtenit licence' from the master 'to schippe the said barrell', and that in any case the master had 'intromettit thairwitht' later in the voyage.[165] Other entries show that merchants often were permitted to load

and 529, CA1/1/20, pp. 144 and 452, CA1/1/21, p. 619, CA1/1/23, p. 189, CA1/1/27, p. 204, CA1/1/28, p. 173, CA1/1/31, pp. 333 and 335, CA1/1/34/1, pp. 480–1, CA1/1/37, pp. 186 and 260–1, and CA5/1/2, 16 January 1582; DCA, BCMB, vol. 1, f. 112r, vol. 3, 12 November 1550, and 29 May and 3 July 1551, vol. 4, 5 November 1555 and 22 April 1556, vol. 10, 11 June 1568, vol. 12, 17 June and 5 November 1572, vol. 13, 6 September 1574 and 20 June 1575, vol. 14, 22 October 1576, 3 March 1578 and 20 February 1579 (misplaced in a sequence of entries after 5 February 1580), vol. 17, 23 September 1590, and 31 May and 6 September 1592, and vol. 18, 27 May and 10 June 1594; SAUL, B10/8/4, p. 159, and B65/8/1, ff. 105v-6r; AA, B6/11/1/1, f. 91v, and B6/11/1/3, f. 368; NRS, B9/11/1, f. 98.

162 ACA, CA1/1/20, pp. 131, 135, 137, 139, 142, 151–2 and 160, CA1/1/21, pp. 70–1, 78, 107, 393–4, 412, 448–9, 456–9, 461–3, 465, 468–9, 472–3, 477, 479 and 482, CA1/1/22, p. 608, CA1/1/26, pp. 306, 318, 321, 326 and 329, CA1/1/34/1, pp. 448 and 455–7, and CA1/1/37, pp. 31–2; DCA, BCMB, vol. 1, f. 32r, and vol. 17, 23 April 1591; AA, B6/11/2, ff. 310v-11, 472v-3r, 494 and 497v-8r.

163 ACA, CA1/1/8, p. 1002, CA1/1/9, pp. 278–9, CA1/1/10, pp. 251, 253 and 255, CA1/1/12/1, pp. 153, 262–3, 349 and 352, CA1/1/13, pp. 203, 206 and 215, CA1/1/14, pp. 153–4, 546–7 and 584, CA1/1/15, pp. 457, 510, 519, 528, 530, 540 and 711, CA1/1/16, pp. 23 and 187, CA1/1/20, pp. 68, 145, 152, 159, 166–7, 448 and 450, CA1/1/32, pp. 342, 365–6 and 477, CA1/1/33/1, pp. 118–19, CA1/1/33/2, pp. 927–8, and CA5/1/5, 4 April and 4 September 1597; DCA, BCMB, vol. 3, 23 August 1553, vol. 4, 17 December 1555 and 4 August 1557, vol. 6, 13 January 1562, vol. 7, 29 April and 8 July 1563, vol. 11, 19 December 1569, vol. 12, 21 January 1572, and vol. 13, 19 March 1574, 17 June 1575 and 13 July 1575.

164 S.F. Du Toit, 'The Evolution of the Bill of Lading', (2005) 11–12 *Fundamina* 12. The suggestion in M.H.B. Sanderson, *Mary Stewart's People: Life in Mary Stewart's Scotland* (Edinburgh, 1987), p. 122, that a master did issue a bill of lading is not supported by the source cited (NRS, RH9/1/5).

165 SAUL, B10/8/6, pp. 219–20. For a similar entry see ACA, CA1/1/14, p. 408.

goods onto ships themselves.[166] Indeed, when a master protested in Dundee that he would not be obliged 'to ony man that schippis gere withtout thai mak adverteisment to him or his clerk', the dean of guild insisted on behalf of the merchants of the burgh that the master should continue to be responsible for all the goods loaded, 'conforme to auld use and wount'.[167] The alternative of presenting goods to the master 'upoun the schoir', so that they could be 'input in his schip' or 'schipit in his schip' by the mariners, was especially important when it was not possible for a ship to tie up at a quay.[168] When a merchant expressed concern about a statement in a charter party that he should 'lay the laiding and tymber to the schippis syd', he was reassured by two masters that he would be 'na forder astrictit thairto nor use and wount is'.[169] The merchant's anxiety is understandable, for other entries in the court books indicate that a master was not normally obliged to return goods unless they had been 'tane in and schippit', or had been put into a lighter 'to haif bene furit and put in the said schip'.[170] On the other hand, goods appear to have been considered 'deliverit' when they were returned to merchants on the shore or the quay, 'as use is of skiparis'.[171] In 1545 an assize in Aberdeen tried to establish a new rule by announcing that a master was 'nocht indettit to his merchandis further thane to deliver thame thair gudis at his schip in the havin fre furtht of takkall, and the merchandis to cause ressave thame thair and fuir thame to the key heid as tha think expedient'.[172] No further trace of this rule has been found, however,

166 ACA, CA1/1/8, pp. 952 and 1072, CA1/1/9, pp. 224–5, 281, 441–2, 543, 545, 635, 703 and 729, CA1/1/10, pp. 169–70, 172, 215 and 221–2, CA1/1/11, pp. 460 and 610, CA1/1/13, pp. 265 and 270, CA1/1/15, p. 588, and CA1/1/21, pp. 757–8; DCA, BCMB, vol. 4, 11 October 1557, vol. 11, 13 and 17 March 1570, vol. 14, 13 November 1577, vol. 19, 3 June 1597, and vol. 20, 4 August 1598; DAC, WC4/8, f. 184v; HAC, B1/1/2, ff. 470–1r (reproduced partly in *Records of Inverness*, 2 vols, ed. W. Mackay, H.C. Boyd and G.S. Laing (Aberdeen, 1911–24), vol. 1, p. 267).

167 DCA, BCMB, vol. 15, 22 September 1581. No other example has been found of a protestation being used as an attempt to modify practice.

168 ACA, CA1/1/8, p. 989, CA1/1/9, pp. 282, 288 and 725, CA1/1/13, pp. 421–4, 426, 428 and 430, CA1/1/14, pp. 256–7, 260 and 587–8, CA1/1/17, p. 128 and 131, CA1/1/20, p. 445, CA1/1/28, p. 629, CA1/1/32, pp. 394–5, and CA1/1/33/2, pp. 1035–6; DCA, BCMB, vol. 3, 18 September 1551, and vol. 11, 10, 13 and 15 March and 15 April 1570.

169 NRS, B19/1/3, 30 July 1576.

170 ACA, CA1/1/8, pp. 958, 961–4, 973–4, 980, 982 and 985–6, CA1/1/10, p. 140, CA1/1/11, p. 110, CA1/1/12/2, p. 583, CA1/1/15, pp. 30, 32–3 and 52, CA1/1/16, pp. 604–6 and 610, CA1/1/19, pp. 87, 90, 96, 141, 148 and 157, CA1/1/20, pp. 137, 141–3, 147 and 160–2, CA1/1/34/1, pp. 455–7, and CA1/1/37, pp. 31–2; DCA, BCMB, vol. 6, 19 December 1561.

171 ACA, CA1/1/8, p. 857, CA1/1/9, pp. 362 and 369, CA1/1/10, p. 141, CA1/1/12/1, pp. 272 and 279, CA1/1/12/2, p. 531, CA1/1/15, p. 48, and CA1/1/16, pp. 391 and 760.

172 ACA, CA1/1/18, p. 512.

and litigants in Aberdeen and elsewhere continued to tell each other that the proper place to return goods was 'one the key heid' or 'upoun the schoir'.[173]

In other cases merchants complained that although their goods had been returned to them, they had been damaged in transit.[174] Often the question put to the court was whether goods that were 'wet and spilt' at the end of a voyage had been 'dry, without skaitht', when loaded onto a ship.[175] In one case the question was put more precisely whether the goods had been damaged 'withtin the said schip and in hir defalt, or upoun the key heyd of Aberdene or the imputting thairof in the sayd schip', and in other cases too reference was made to the master's promise to provide 'ane sufficient thycht schip, wytht all necessaris efferand thairto'.[176] An alternative line of argument was hinted at by a merchant who complained about hides being 'spilt and rottin in the said schip for the tyme in hir defalt throw hir insufficientnes, or at lest in defalt of the said skipper'.[177] Another merchant who complained about hides being 'rottin and spilt' in a ship submitted a revised petition to the court in which the only change was the insertion of a statement that the damage had been done in the master and crew's 'defalt'.[178] It seems to have been considered essential for that word to be used, either in relation to the ship or in relation to the mariners. The fault of mariners certainly was often alleged, and one way for masters to avoid liability was to prove that damage had been done by other merchants, or had been caused by the development of a leak through nobody's fault after a ship departed.[179] When merchants complained after the arrival of a ship in

173 ACA, CA1/1/20, pp. 145–6 and 152, and CA1/1/27, p. 650; DCA, BCMB, vol. 7, 25 November 1562.

174 ACA, CA1/1/8, pp. 318 and 445, CA1/1/10, p. 215, CA1/1/13, p. 419, CA1/1/15, pp. 93 and 723, CA1/1/16, pp. 51, 61, 71, 86, 90–1, 96, 453 and 778, and CA1/1/20, pp. 126 and 155; DCA, BCMB, vol. 9, 22 and 24 October 1567.

175 ACA, CA1/1/12/1, pp. 293, 295–6, 298, 308 and 310, CA1/1/14, pp. 567 and 572, CA1/1/15, pp. 18, 21–2, 27–9, 34–5, 44, 49–50 and 52, and CA1/1/20, pp. 140–1, 145, 147, 153, 155–6, 161 and 170; DCA, BCMB, vol. 4, 26 November and 9 December 1555; AA, B6/12/2, p. 7; *Extracts from the Council Register of the Burgh of Aberdeen*, 2 vols, ed. J. Stuart (Aberdeen, 1844–8), vol. 1, pp. 310–11.

176 ACA, CA1/1/8, pp. 493, 496 and 552–3, CA1/1/10, pp. 390–1, CA1/1/12/2, pp. 496–7, 499, 503–4, 508, 512, 516 and 522–5, CA1/1/14, p. 126, ACA, CA1/1/15, pp. 698–9, 703 and 717, CA1/1/16, pp. 840, 845 and 855, CA1/1/18, p. 373, and CA1/1/21, pp. 195, 200, 204, 210, 321, 323A, 330, 332, 338, 351, 363, 366, 382 and 384; DCA, BCMB, vol. 12, 18 January 1572.

177 ACA, CA1/1/21, pp. 190–1.

178 ACA, CA1/1/16, pp. 454–5, 520–2, 527, 534, 539–40, 600, 617, 630, 632, 637 and 647.

179 ACA, CA1/1/8, pp. 83–5, 117, 917 and 1077, CA1/1/9, pp. 289–90, 728–9 and 732–3, CA1/1/12/1, p. 314, CA1/1/12/2, pp. 443, 462 and 465, CA1/1/15, p. 204, CA1/1/16, pp. 175, 387 and 389, CA1/1/20, pp. 121, 147, 154–5 and 161, CA1/1/21, p. 13, CA1/1/27, p. 303, and CA1/1/38, p. 769; DCA, BCMB, vol. 1, f. 21v, vol. 4, 5 and 21 May and 23 July 1557, vol. 11, 5 March 1571, vol. 14, 29 July and 11 September 1579, and 22 January 1580, vol. 18, 19 June 1594, and vol. 20, 8 July 1597.

Aberdeen that malt had been 'watt and spilt in the schipp within the havin in the defalt of the said skipper and his marenellis', no compensation was awarded after it was found that the crew had behaved perfectly properly in 'the fasining, laing and keiping of his schip'.[180] Some cases related to the problem of goods being 'strukyne up' from containers in which they had been loaded onto a ship.[181] When a merchant in Ayr complained about the appropriation of 'wyne, brokett and aquavyte' from the hold of a ship, seeking an award of the amount of money the 'guidis and gayre wald haif gevyn hym' had he been able to sell them in the market they were heading towards, the master 'denyit the hale libell afoyr writtyn except sax quartis of wyne, the quhilk he grantit that he tuk fra hym allanerlie and na mayre'.[182] If comestibles were taken from the hold and, 'in defalt of the victuallis, wer usit to the furnising of the equipage of the said schip', or if goods were 'sellit for vittaling of the said maranars of the said schipe', the master would again be required to reimburse the merchants, but none of the examples found in the court books involves an allegation of fault, nor is it ever suggested that a master should compensate merchants for the loss of profits they hoped to make through the sale of the goods.[183]

The language used in the cases concerned with damage to goods was strikingly similar to the language used in the legislation reviewed in the opening section of this essay, yet none of that legislation was explicitly cited in any of the records of litigation reviewed in this closing section.[184] In a case heard in Dundee in 1581 merchants pursued for failing to provide a cargo alleged that there was 'ane act and statut maid within this burght' requiring masters who were waiting for goods to draw the issue to the attention of the dean of guild, so that a master who had neglected to do so should not be able to raise an action before the bailies.[185] The pursuer disputed this interpretation of 'the pretendit act and ordinance, gif ony be', and no trace of the statute has in fact been found anywhere else in the records of the burgh. The most significant

180 ACA, CA1/1/10, pp. 114–17, 120, 123 and 127.

181 ACA, CA1/1/12/1, pp. 16, 20 and 221, CA1/1/13, p. 406, CA1/1/14, p. 532, and CA1/1/15, p. 665; DCA, BCMB, vol. 3, 15 December 1550, vol. 4, 3 February 1557, and vol. 7, 8 July 1563; AA, B6/12/2, p. 204; NRS, B21/8/2, ff. 20r and 21r.

182 AA, B6/12/2, pp. 43–4.

183 ACA, CA1/1/13, pp. 27–8; DCA, BCMB, vol. 13, 17 June 1575, and vol. 14, 14 October 1575.

184 The explanation cannot simply be that the people involved in litigation before the burgh courts knew nothing about legislation, for other statutes were sometimes cited in cases concerned with other matters. In disputes over the payment of custom duties, for instance, reference was sometimes made to 'the actis of parliament' governing the subject (*e.g.* ACA, CA1/1/37, p. 873, and CA1/1/38, pp. 51, 55–6, 415 and 817–18).

185 DCA, BCMB, vol. 15, 10 February 1581.

aspect of the case may be the defenders' further allegation that 'the said act hes tane effect in the maist pairt of schippis arryving at this port wanting of thar laidning', which would appear to suggest that statutes were considered binding only if they were received into usage. In a case heard in Aberdeen in 1553 a merchant complained that a master from Hamburg had left the safety of the harbour and run his ship aground on the treacherous Buchan coast, where the goods he had on board had been damaged in the master's 'sleuthtfulnes, and in his defalt'.[186] The master replied that the merchant had only himself to blame as he had failed to provide a 'sufficient steirman'. The merchant might in turn have replied that it was the master's duty under the act of parliament passed in 1467 to provide a steersman, but instead of doing so he 'producit twa buikis, *viz.* ane almanak and ane callit the *Seyricht*', along with three witnesses. The first book may have contained relevant tide tables, and the second was probably the code of maritime law known as the *Waterrecht*, the laws of Wisby or the Gotland sea law, which had reproduced from the laws of Oleron an article requiring masters to seek the advice of their crews before sailing.[187] Perhaps the witnesses were asked to confirm that no discussion had taken place. Whatever happened, the master acknowledged a month later that he had reached a settlement with the merchant, agreeing to compensate him for the damage sustained 'in the said skipper and his childeris defalt, and in thair sleucht and neglegens'. No other reference to the laws of Oleron or Wisby has been found.[188] If the clerks who rephrased pleadings in the court books had learned about these laws from collections of the medieval laws of Scotland, they did not take the opportunity to import references to them into the records, nor did they make use of any knowledge they may have acquired of the laws

---

186 ACA, CA1/1/21, pp. 313–117, 323, 323A and 355.

187 E.B.I. Frankot, '*Der Ehrbaren Hanse-Städte See-Recht*: Diversity and Unity in Hanseatic Maritime Law', in J. Wubs-Mrozewicz and S. Jenks (eds), *The Hanse in Medieval and Early-Modern Europe* (Leiden, 2013), p. 109, at pp. 116–17; *Black Book of the Admiralty*, vol. 4, pp. 66–9. That the production of the *Seyricht* was noted suggests that the production of written codes in other cases would also have been noted. The use of the phrase 'ane callit the' suggests that it was not well known already.

188 For instance, one provision (in Frankot, 'Scottish Translations of the *Rôles d'Oléron*', pp. 38–40) might have been found instructive in disputes over the sufficiency of tackle used to unload cargoes (ACA, CA1/1/12/1, pp. 293 and 295; DCA, BCMB, vol. 14, 2 March 1580 – in a sequence of entries misplaced after 5 February 1580). As is explained in the final essay below, a couple of provisions were eventually copied into the 'guildry buik' of Dundee, but no evidence has been found that they had any effect on the handling of cases there.

taught in the universities.[189] In any case, the substance of the pleadings they recorded must to a large extent have reflected the arguments advanced by merchants and masters.[190] These litigants submitted their disputes to (as one of them put it) 'the reull of the law', but they scarcely ever looked for the law in written sources.[191] Indeed, they did not even regard the written contracts they had subscribed as the foundations of all the obligations they owed each other. Although almost six hundred and fifty cases concerned with the payment of freight or the safe delivery of goods have been found in the court books, charter parties are only mentioned in about one hundred of them, and some disputes – including those over the negligent damage of goods by mariners – hinged on points that do not appear to have been spelled out in the charter parties written in Scotland.[192] The applicable law was generally referred to as 'use and custum', 'use and consuetud' or 'use and wount'. As well as constantly reminding each other of how they were expected to conduct themselves, merchants and mariners also reminded each other that their expectations were a kind of law. They agreed at one level that agreements they made at another level were legally binding. At both levels the agreements were rarely about anything – they were unlike the agreements reached in contracting – but were mostly examples of what Wittgenstein called agreement in judgment.[193] It was through their consistent use of language that a consensus gradually emerged and was sustained on how overseas trade was regulated.

189 Although litigants were sometimes represented by procurators with university degrees, they do not appear to have made explicit references to written sources of law either.

190 *Cf.* K.L. Doty and R. Hiltunen, 'Formulaic Discourse and Speech Acts in the Witchcraft Trial Records of Salem, 1692', (2009) 41 *Journal of Pragmatics* 458.

191 ACA, CA1/1/34/1, pp. 244–6.

192 Vaguer references were often made to promises, contracts or conditions. Yet again it needs to be remembered that the records are incomplete. In particular, the court books of Edinburgh, where learned lawyers were present, might well have given a different impression had more survived.

193 As the rules governing overseas trade were comparable to the rules governing language use, they were bound to be dynamic and indeterminate, so that it would have been impossible to restate them reliably here, even if the records of the burgh courts had survived more comprehensively. Nevertheless, some impression may have been given of the rules merchants and mariners adhered to in dealing with one another.

Legal Customs and Customary Laws

The Employment of Mariners in Scotland during the Sixteenth Century

In the Clarendon Lectures he delivered at the University of Oxford in 1999, Sir John Baker urged historians of English law to extend their enquiries beyond the large body of cases and statutes that they usually study.[1] The law of England, he explained, had 'two bodies', one consisting of the 'formal' sources that continue to drive legal development today, the other of 'informal' sources, most notably the 'common erudition' of the legal profession, which had played an important role in legal development before the modern period.[2] Although derived in part from the examination of cases and statutes, this body of learning also took account of other sources, including popular usages and customs, which are also relevant to the study of legal history insofar as they came 'within the understanding and contemplation of lawyers'.[3] But why, it might be asked, should these sources only be relevant to the extent that – and in the way that – they were understood by lawyers? Even if a compelling answer can be given in relation to the history of English law, can it be assumed that legal history always needs to be investigated from the point of view of lawyers?[4] If lay people believed that their activities were regulated by usages and customs, and if their disputes were settled in courts that compelled them to adhere to usages and customs, is there any reason to doubt that usages and customs were a kind of law, even if lawyers were not involved in their discussion?[5] In the first of its two sections, this essay begins by investigating the handling of disputes about the employment of mariners in the burgh courts of sixteenth-century Scotland, where masters and mariners were occasionally represented by procurators, but

1 J.H. Baker, *The Law's Two Bodies: Some Evidential Problems in English Legal History* (Oxford, 2001).

2 The distinction between formal and informal sources owed something to S.F.C. Milsom, *Studies in the History of the Common Law* (London, 1985), pp. 171–90.

3 Baker, *Law's Two Bodies*, pp. 2 and 60–3.

4 Further questions are raised about the history of English law in T. Johnson, *Law in Common: Legal Cultures in Late-Medieval England* (Oxford, 2020).

5 The previous two essays in this collection found that all three of these conditions – popular belief that usages and customs were laws, judicial compulsion to comply with usages and customs, and minimal involvement of lawyers in forensic debates – were satisfied in the burgh courts of sixteenth-century Scotland.

 | DOI:10.1163/9789004695009_005

where disputes were normally settled without the involvement of people who earned a living by providing expert advice on the law.[6] In the second section, comparison is made with the handling of similar disputes in the same century and the same country in courts in which lawyers were present. Although these lawyers were not expert in the common law of England, they were expert in another species of common erudition. Conclusions are eventually drawn about the difference it made when the usages and customs known to masters and mariners came within the understanding and contemplation of learned lawyers. In other words, this essay aims not only to shed light on the employment of mariners in Scotland during the sixteenth century, but also to clarify the relationship between the legal customs discussed in local courts and the customary laws discussed in central courts.[7]

1 Litigation between Masters and Mariners in the Burgh Courts

Sometimes a mariner appeared before the bailies of a burgh at which a ship had arrived and complained that after being 'promest' payment for service in the ship, which he had duly provided, he 'was nocht as yit payit of his hyre', in response to which 'he protestit for coistis, skaitht, dampnage and expensis, ay and quhill he be pait of his said hyr'.[8] More often the court books of the coastal burghs record actions raised by mariners 'anent thair hyris and wages', typically against the master of a ship, though sometimes against its owners, and even in one instance against merchants whose goods had been transported

6 While the procurators who occasionally appeared sometimes had university degrees, certainly knew something about court procedure, and were probably paid in some cases for their services, they do not appear to have been expert in the same way as the advocates who were members of the College of Justice in Edinburgh. More is said about the legal education that appears to have been available in Scotland in essays included in the second part of this collection.

7 What is meant here by 'local' and 'central' courts is explained in the opening essay in this collection, where it is also emphasised that caution is required in drawing conclusions from partial evidence. In particular, while no trace has been found of the involvement of learned lawyers in the proceedings of courts in many burghs around the coasts of Scotland, they may have been involved in proceedings before the court of the water bailie in Leith, of which records have not survived. Of course, even if that were true, it would not diminish the contrast between what happened in courts where lawyers were absent and in courts where they were present.

8 ACA, CA1/1/12/2, pp. 638 and 649, CA1/1/15, p. 347, and CA1/1/21, pp. 464 and 467; DCA, BCMB, vol. 5, 24 May 1560.

in a ship.[9] In 1582, for example, three French mariners presented a petition to the bailie court of Ayr, alleging that the master of a vessel they had recently arrived in from Brittany had 'hyrit' them 'to serve as mariners', that they had actually 'servit in the said bark the veyage foirsaid', but that the master would not pay them their wages 'withtout he be compellit'.[10] In this, and many other similar cases, the master was ordered to pay the promised wages, together with expenses the mariners had incurred while awaiting payment, 'in respect of sufficient verificatioun', which was provided by the production of documentary evidence, the testimony of witnesses or the swearing of oaths of verity by the parties.[11] In another action raised by mariners in Ayr the owner of the ship 'grantit thair hyring, and referit the quantitie of thair hyres to thair awin aythis, quha, being sworne, maid faytht upoun the quantitis'.[12] He was ordered to pay the sums specified, subject to deduction of 'the expenssis sustenit in bringing of the said schip fra the Fairlie raid to the port of the said burght of Air', which the mariners 'war haldin of dewitie to do and failzeit thairintill'. When mariners were taken on for a voyage to another country and back again, the normal understanding was that they would receive 'half hyre' for each leg of the trip (sometimes referred to as 'out and hayme hyris').[13] In 1598 a controversy arose in Ayr 'betwix the awneris and maisteris of schippis, on the ane pairt, and the marineris and company thairof, sailleris of the same schippis, on the uther pairt', over how wages ought to be paid if, in the course of a voyage to La Rochelle or Bordeaux, a ship put into a port in England or Ireland instead.[14] The society of mariners in the town hoped to have it agreed that

---

9 ACA, CA1/1/11, p. 686, and CA1/1/19, p. 215; DCA, BCMB, vol. 12, 23 January 1573, and vol. 14, 5, 7 and 12 August 1579.

10 AA, B6/11/1/1, ff. 84v-5r.

11 ACA, CA1/1/11, pp. 52 and 64, CA1/1/12/1, pp. 313–14, CA1/1/12/2, pp. 443 and 462, CA1/1/15, p. 734, CA1/1/21, p. 8, CA1/1/28, p. 154, and CA1/1/36, p. 393; DCA, BCMB, vol. 1, f. 65r, vol. 3, 20 September 1554, vol. 8, 14 and 24 January 1564, vol. 9, 1 December 1567, vol. 11, 17 October 1569, vol. 14, 4 November 1575 and 28 February 1578, vol. 18, 13 September and 18 October 1594, 3 September 1595 and 8 April 1579, vol. 19, 15 January and 23 March 1596, vol. 20, 5 October 1597 and 4 August 1598, and vol. 21, 19 December 1599; AA, B6/11/2, f. 492; *Kirkcudbright Town Council Records, 1576–1604*, ed. M.B. Johnston and C.M. Armet (Edinburgh, 1939), p. 195.

12 AA, B6/11/1/3, ff. 426v and 428r.

13 ACA, CA1/1/16, pp. 487–8, CA1/1/28, p. 63, CA1/1/29, p. 693, and CA1/1/37, p. 522; DCA, BCMB, vol. 10, 21 January 1569, vol. 12, 8 August and 15 December 1573, vol. 13, 26 June 1575, vol. 14, 8 April, 29 July and 7 August 1579, vol. 16, 17 April 1583, vol. 17, 14 July 1590 and 23 July 1593, vol. 18, 6 and 11 September 1594, and 30 May and 24 September 1595, vol. 19, 6 and 11 February 1596, vol. 20, 23 October 1598, and vol. 21, 7 November 1599.

14 NLS, MS 941, ff. 5v-6r.

when this happened, 'the marineris and company sall haif thair Frenche half hyre thair, at the port of dischairging be the way foirsaid, notwithstanding the schip or bark pas not forward to France, and at thair hame cuming fra that port of discharge agane to this port sall resave thair Scottis half hyre elykmaner'. The assumption, here and elsewhere, appears to have been that mariners were employed for particular voyages, but there are exceptional entries in the court books referring to employment 'during this symmer sessoun', 'unto the feist of Pasche cum ane yeir', or 'for ane yeir to cum, for twa *s.* the day'.[15]

In 1562 the bailies of Dundee were informed by the mariners of a ship lately returned from Harwich that its master and owners had 'conditionat and promittit to the saids marineris at the said port of Harwiche as mony grottis for thair half of hyir as ony uther marineris gat saling furth of Scotland to ony port of Ingland this present yeir'.[16] The judges sent a commission to the 'bailleis of Leithe' for the examination of witnesses familiar with voyages to England, instructed the mariners to travel south 'to heir and se the saids witnesses sworne and ressevit', and appointed a day for the mariners 'to report agane the said commissioun'. When they returned, the master and owners argued that they were not obliged to reimburse the mariners for the expenses 'sustenit be thame in thair actioun', since it was an inevitable consequence of the agreement they had made that the mariners would have 'to preve be the prattik of utheris skipparis the liquidatioun of thair hyris'.[17] In reaching a decision in the case the bailies took pains to insist that 'this present decreitt be nane preparative law nor prattik to hurt ony mannis privilege, be ressoun the same hes proceidit upoun ane conditioun maid betwix the saids pairties'.[18] In ordering payment to be made in accordance with another 'conditioun' ten years later, the bailies similarly did so 'under protestatioun that this be nocht prejudiciall to na lovable actis, use or consuetud of this burght'.[19] It was implicit in both these declarations, however, that the 'prattik' of the courts might otherwise have contributed, along with the 'prattik' of masters and mariners, to identifying

15 ACA, CA1/1/8, pp. 551, 599 and 892, and CA1/1/12/1, p. 214; DCA, BCMB, vol. 3, 10 October 1550, vol. 14, 20 September 1577, and vol. 15, 13 September 1581; SAUL, B65/8/1, 26 March 1591.

16 DCA, BCMB, vol. 7, 2, 16, 18, 20 and 22 November 1562.

17 This was not the only case in which wages were fixed by reference to what others received (DCA, BCMB, vol. 9, 29 January 1567 and 16 January 1568).

18 No trace has been found in the Scottish records of anything comparable to the document reproduced in F.W. Brooks, 'A Wage Scale for Seamen, 1546', (1945) 60 *English Historical Review* 234.

19 DCA, BCMB, vol. 12, 13 October 1573.

obligations that were not stipulated in contracts.[20] Masters sometimes promised to pay mariners 'according to the use of payment of hyris', which does not seem to have meant that they would receive customary amounts of pay but that they would receive agreed amounts at customary times.[21] Yet in one case the bailies of Dundee accepted advice from 'the skipperis of this burght' that when a master had put into an English port instead of sailing to Flanders as planned, he remained bound to pay the wages agreed since he had received as much freight for the voyage as originally expected.[22] Several cases heard in Dundee towards the end of the century related to the overpayment of wages.[23] In one the master complained about a miscalculation of the exchange rate in Flanders, to which the mariners replied that they had received only what was due to them 'conforme to auld use and wont'.[24] In another the master complained that the mariners had insisted on receiving the 'half hyre' due to them in Danzig, despite being offered instead 'the thrid of the fraucht of the said schip the said vayage, conforme to use', which meant (he argued and the bailies agreed) that the wages due to the mariners were limited to a third of the amount of freight the master eventually received from the merchants.[25]

The master's argument is reminiscent of an article of the *Rôles d'Oléron*, of which a version was included in many manuscript collections of the medieval laws of Scotland.[26] The article, which had also been incorporated into codes of maritime law circulating in the Netherlands and the Baltic region, required masters to give mariners a choice between 'freighting for themselves' or participating in 'the freight of the ship' (*voulez-vous freter vostre ordinaire en particulier, ou bien voulez à vous le prendre sur l'entier fret de la nef*).[27] It referred to a practice, which may have originated in the Mediterranean, of giving

20 *Cf.* C.A. Fury, *Tides in the Affairs of Men: The Social History of Elizabethan Seamen, 1580–1603* (Westport, CT, 2001), pp. 99–100.

21 DCA, BCMB, vol. 3, 24 February, 4 and 7 March and 4 April 1552, vol. 4, 27 January and 19 March 1556, vol. 8, 14 January 1564, and vol. 14, 18 November 1579. *Cf.* R. Davis, *The Rise of the English Shipping Industry in the Seventeenth and Eighteenth Centuries* (London, 1962), pp. 127 and 134.

22 DCA, BCMB, vol. 5, 30 April 1560.

23 For an earlier case on the same point see DCA, BCMB, vol. 14, 17 June 1578.

24 DCA, BCMB, vol. 19, 15 and 29 April and 2 May 1597.

25 DCA, BCMB, vol. 20, 11 October 1597. The same line of argument was advanced at BCMB, vol. 20, 15 July 1597.

26 E.B.I. Frankot, 'The Scottish Translations of the *Rôles d'Oléron*: Edition and Commentary', in A.M. Godfrey (ed.), *Stair Society: Miscellany Eight* (Edinburgh, 2020), p. 13, at p. 48.

27 *Collection de lois maritimes antérieures au XVIIIe siècle*, 6 vols, ed. J.M. Pardessus (Paris, 1828–45), vol. 1, pp. 336–7; *The Black Book of the Admiralty*, 4 vols, ed. T. Twiss (London, 1871–76), vol. 4, pp. 90–3, 274 and 438–41.

mariners the use of space in the hold of a ship to carry goods on their own account.[28] Evidence that Scottish mariners were granted such rights – known as 'portage' – throughout the sixteenth century has been found in sources from Kirkcaldy, Burntisland, St Andrews, Crail, Dundee and Aberdeen on the east coast, and from Kirkcudbright, Ayr and even Glasgow on the west coast.[29] Indeed, it seems that the main purpose of paying half hire to mariners at the end of the outward leg of a return journey was to enable them to buy cargo for the homeward leg. When a master who appeared before the bailies of Dundee in 1552 confirmed his willingness to pay his mariners half of their wages in Bordeaux or La Rochelle, 'conform till utheris awnaris and maisteris', one mariner talked about 'ane puncioun of wyne quhilk wes bocht in the Rochell with his half hyre'.[30] A few years earlier a mariner had complained in Aberdeen that although he had been promised portage before a voyage to Veere, 'as use and wont is amang marinars', and ought therefore 'to have had my half hire in my hand thair, and to have warit it upoun sic smale geir as suld have bene best for me for the tyme, and till have put it in the said schip als my portage as utheris did', he had been deprived of the opportunity to buy goods by being refused his half hire.[31] The right to bring goods home for sale usually enabled 'sic puir marineris as wes nocht habill to by thair fredom' to participate in the overseas trade that was otherwise restricted to members of royal or ecclesiastical burghs.[32] In view of this widespread practice, it appears that in offering his mariners a choice between receiving half their wages in Danzig or receiving a third of the freight earned on the return trip after they got back to Dundee,

---

28 R.P. Jackson, 'From Profit-Sailing to Wage Sailing: Mediterranean Owner-Captains and Their Crews during the Medieval Commercial Revolution', (1987) 16 *Journal of European Economic History* 605; R.J. Blakemore, 'Pieces of Eight, Pieces of Eight: Seamen's Earnings and the Venture Economy of Early-Modern Seafaring', (2017) 70 *Economic History Review* 1153. For a Mediterranean example see *Consulate of the Sea and Related Documents*, tr. S.S. Jados (University, AL, 1975), pp. 71–3; *Collection de lois maritimes*, vol. 2, pp. 125–8.

29 ACA, CA1/1/11, pp. 263, 307, 309 and 686, CA1/1/16, p. 21, CA1/1/20, pp. 450–1, and CA1/1/35, p. 128; DCA, BCMB, vol. 3, 18 September 1551, vol. 13, 21 January and 11 May 1575, vol. 14, 5 October 1579, vol. 15, 7 April 1581, vol. 16, 6 February 1583, vol. 17, 30 March 1590, vol. 18, 18 October 1594, and vol. 20, 8 October 1597, and 18 March and 28 August 1598; FCA, B/KDY/2/1/1, p. 30; SAUL, B10/8/5, pp. 600–1, and B65/8/1, f. 17v; AA, B6/11/1/2, f. 266v, B6/11/2, f. 353v, and B6/11/3, ff. 45, 46v-7r and 50–1r; NRS, B9/11/1, f. 159v, B9/11/2, ff. 15 and 154v-5r, and RH9/1/5, ff. 5r, 12r, 18v and 53v; GCA, C1/1/5, f. 20r; *Kirkcudbright Town Council Records*, p. 195; *The Compt Buik of David Wedderburne, Merchant of Dundee, 1587–1630*, ed. A.H. Millar (Edinburgh, 1898), pp. 213, 217, 219–20, 222–3 and 225–8.

30 DCA, BCMB, vol. 3, 31 March 1552.

31 ACA, CA1/1/19, pp. 4 and 12.

32 DCA, BCMB, vol. 12, 12 January 1574, and vol. 15, 28 June 1581, and PBD, vol. 11, f. 65v.

the master mentioned at the end of the last paragraph was inviting them to choose between exercising their rights of portage and permitting him to use their space in the hold to carry further cargo on the ship's account. The choice may have owed something to the codes of maritime law, but none of them was explicitly mentioned in the record of the case, and the rule that offering mariners a third of the freight would limit the amount of hire they could claim did not originate there. That rule, if it was widely accepted, or other rules like it, would help to explain why it sometimes transpired that mariners had been paid too much, and why there was often a need for a ship's accounts to be adjusted at the end of a voyage.[33] It complicated the calculations further that mariners also laid claim to 'prymgelt' and other duties 'usit and wountit'.[34] The actions raised by mariners against masters were not always for the payment of specific sums of money promised to them as wages, but were often claims for money or goods due to them after account was taken of their customary rights.

In the cases concerned with the overpayment of wages, it was usually the master who was pursuing the mariners. Sometimes masters sought complete reimbursement of wages because the services promised by mariners were not provided.[35] In a case raised in Aberdeen in 1531, for example, a master recovered the half hire he had paid in Danzig to a mariner who 'passit nocht witht him the said vaege', so that it could be 'alowit to him in his compt of the awnar of the said schip'.[36] More often masters sought to have mariners compelled to provide the services promised.[37] In 1573 the bailies of Dundee ordered two mariners to embark on a ship 'conforme to thair conditioun and resaving of thair half hyre', threatening them with 'warding of thair persones' if they failed to comply.[38] In 1593, on the other hand, when a master pursued a mariner 'as ane hyrit man to serve in his schip for the veyage to cum', the bailies of Ayr dismissed the claim after the mariner swore under oath that the master 'gaif him his leif to serve quhair he plesit'.[39] Occasionally mariners who were unwilling

33 ACA, CA1/1/11, p. 686, CA1/1/15, pp. 428–9, and CA1/1/17, p. 18; DCA, BCMB, vol. 20, 27 July and 7 October 1597, and 20 September 1598.

34 DCA, BCMB, vol. 6, 21 June, and 1 and 3 July 1562, vol. 10, 4 July 1569, vol. 12, 9 February 1573, and vol. 13, 24 February 1574.

35 ACA, CA1/1/20, pp. 184 and 187; DCA, BCMB, vol. 14, 2 December 1577, and vol. 20, 18 November 1597.

36 ACA, CA1/1/13, p. 236.

37 ACA, CA1/1/8, p. 882, CA1/1/16, p. 205, CA1/1/19, p. 14, CA1/1/20, p. 532, CA1/1/27, pp. 573–4 and 582, and CA1/1/34/1, pp. 435–6 and 476; DCA, BCMB, vol. 9, 14 February 1567, vol. 12, 6 August 1572, vol. 13, 21 February 1575, vol. 14, 20 September 1577, and vol. 15, 13 September 1581, and PBD, vol. 1, f. 73r; SAUL, B65/8/1, 26 March 1591.

38 DCA, BCMB, vol. 12, 24 August 1573.

39 AA, B6/11/2, f. 311v.

to sail were ordered to find suitable replacements, or else to pay for them to be found.[40] In 1523 a master informed the bailies of Aberdeen that although he had 'hyrit and conducit' a mariner, and had 'pait him his hir and portage' when the ship reached its destination, he had then refused to return home again, 'protestand solemply that quhat skatht come apone thair said schip or gudis' as a result of the mariner's absence should be recompensed by him.[41] Claims to compensation for 'costs, skaythtis, dampnis and expensis' resulting from the withdrawal of services were often made in the course of actions for the return of wages.[42] An alternative was to seek compensation from anyone who had lured a mariner into service on another ship, or had prevented the performance of a contract of employment in another way.[43] In an exceptional entry in the Aberdeen records a master was ordered to deliver to 'his sterisman his kist and werklumyis within his schip, and he to wyrk at he may wyrk, and the said skipper to pay him his hyr'.[44] There was an article in the maritime codes circulating in Scotland, the Netherlands, the Baltic region and elsewhere that hinted at a right to retain a mariner's 'kyst' until he fulfilled his obligations.[45] Other articles required mariners who failed to fulfil their obligations to repay the master one and a half times the wages promised, raised the possibility of absconding mariners being executed, and permitted masters to refrain from paying mariners who had tried to obtain employment on other ships.[46] If these articles had any effect on Scottish practice, it can only have been at the level of broad influence.[47]

The maritime code circulating in the Baltic region also provided that 'if a pilot or mariner buys a ship, or is made master of one, he shall be discharged

40 ACA, CA1/1/20, pp. 25–6; *Protocol Book of Gavin Ros, 1512–32*, ed. F.J. Grant (Edinburgh, 1908), pp. 216–17.

41 ACA, CA1/1/11, p. 263.

42 ACA, CA1/1/11, pp. 532–3, CA1/1/15, pp. 735–8, CA1/1/16, pp. 15, 19 and 271, and CA1/1/19, p. 15; DCA, BCMB, vol. 14, 13 November 1577 and 12 November 1578; NRS, B21/8/3, f. 25v.

43 ACA, CA1/1/8, p. 892, CA1/1/14, p. 616, CA1/1/16, pp. 606, 611–13 and 619, CA1/1/20, pp. 279–80, and CA1/1/37, p. 262; *Protocol Book of Gavin Ros*, p. 157.

44 ACA, CA1/1/9, p. 592.

45 Frankot, 'Scottish Translations of the *Rôles d'Oléron*', p. 49; *Collection de lois maritimes*, vol. 1, pp. 337 and 485; *Black Book of the Admiralty*, vol. 4, pp. 92–3, 274 and 440–1.

46 *Collection de lois maritimes*, vol. 1, pp. 463–4 and 500; *Black Book of the Admiralty*, vol. 4, pp. 54–7, 122–3 and 282.

47 Again, the codes were never actually cited. Not surprisingly, there is even less reason to suppose that the laws developed in the Mediterranean were influential (*e.g. Consulate of the Sea and Related Documents*, pp. 69–71, 74–7, 80–90, 97–8, 137–8, 151–5 and 181–2; *Collection de lois maritimes*, vol. 2, pp. 122–5, 129–33, 137–54, 164, 222–3, 241–8 and 287–9).

from his own master, paying him back what he received of him'.[48] In 1577 a mariner who was pursued in Aberdeen 'to saill as ane hyrit marenar to France this present veage' explained that he had been 'desyrit and conducit to be steirman to ane uther schip, and thairby may haff grytar proffeit, be resone of promotioune to ane grytar office and cuir', arguing that he ought to be released from his current employment 'according to the commoune practik in seafer causis'.[49] If he was aware of the written rule he did not mention it but instead 'referit the practik to the said skipperis awyn aitht and declaratioune of his conscience'. It was replied that the mariner, 'be practik, as he hes said, may remove fra his first conductioune, being promotit to ane hyer office, with licence of the skipper, putting ane sufficient man in his place, and na utherwayis'. The master's reply was not entirely consistent with the written rule, although it did receive some support form an ordinance issued by the burgh council in 1506 to the effect that 'nay mane sale conduce nor fee na uther man as boytman withtout speciale licence of the master witht the quhilks he dwellis, askit and optenit'.[50] The ordinance does not appear to have been remembered in 1534 when the bailies of Aberdeen found that a mariner 'mycht of his awin will pass, but conschente of the man that had conducit him afore as ane marinall, and be ane bottsman or stirsman' on another ship.[51] They enunciated this rule 'because it wes sufficientlie provyne afore thame be certane famouse skipparis that it wes the law of the sey', yet in referring to promotion as a 'bottsman or stirsman' it too was not entirely consistent with the written rule. Even ordinary mariners were expected to have a certain degree of expertise. Apprenticeship contracts registered or described in the records of the courts reveal that it could take as much as seven years for a mariner to learn enough to be fully qualified for service on a ship.[52] An experienced mariner would undertake to instruct a novice in 'the airt of navigatioun' in exchange for a 'prenteis fee', and eventually the apprentice would start to receive payment for services he rendered, not just training, food, clothing and shelter. One of the registered contracts

48 *Collection de lois maritimes*, vol. 1, p. 501; *Black Book of the Admiralty*, vol. 4, pp. 124–5 and 283.

49 ACA, CA1/1/29, p. 105.

50 ACA, CA1/1/8, p. 598.

51 ACA, CA1/1/14, p. 413.

52 ACA, CA1/1/37, p. 262, and CA5/1/5, 4 May 1597; DCA, BCMB, vol. 11, 31 December 1569, and PBD, vol. 1, f. 173r; SAUL, B10/8/4, p. 437, and B65/8/1, f. 159; AA, B6/11/3, ff. 62–4r and 65v-8r; NRS, B19/1/12, 30 April 1589. Two of the registered contracts are reproduced in T. Riis, 'Navigation et formation des marins en Ecosse vers 1600', in H. Dubois, J.-C. Hocquet and A. Vauchez (eds), *Horizons marins, itinéraires spirituels, ve–XVIIIe siècles*, 2 vols (Paris, 1987), vol. 2, p. 295.

provided for instruction in 'the see crayft and boitwret schip crayft', and distinctions were drawn elsewhere between 'tymmermen' and other mariners.[53] A master who undertook the 'mending of tymmer wark' on a ship during a voyage, because 'the tymmermen thairof wes deidlie seik', later claimed additional payment from the owners who had hired him.[54] While masters were expected to direct the navigation of their ships, specialist steersmen might be taken on in addition, either to take charge of the steering of the ship for the whole voyage, or to pilot it along a difficult stretch of coast or into an awkward harbour.[55] The word 'boatsman' was used with reference to someone who sailed a boat rather than a ship, but it may also have signified the officer known in England as the 'boatswain' or 'bosun', which would certainly help to make sense of the ordinance passed in 1506 and the ruling delivered in 1534.[56]

The appointment of a mariner to a promoted post on another ship was not the only way in which a contract of employment could be terminated before it had run its course. A master was ordered in one case to pay the 'hyr promittit' to a mariner who had died during a voyage to his widow.[57] No mention is made in the record of an article in the maritime codes requiring masters to arrange treatment for sick sailors, which stated that if a sailor survived, he ought to receive his pay, 'and gif he deis, his wyf or his next frendis aw till haf it for him'.[58] Nor was that article cited in the record of a case in which a mariner who had not received his pay told a court that, 'suppois I had bene seik, as I was ane certane tyme efter my hiring, I aucht to have had the same, be use and custum amang marinaris'.[59] In another case a master swore under oath that he 'promittit nocht' his mariners 'thair expensis to hef tham hame, by thair feis and hyirs, in case that the said schip brak, perisit or hapnytt to be sald'.[60] If the mariners drew attention to an article in the maritime codes dealing with the master's duty to bring his crew home after a shipwreck – no easy task when

53 ACA, CA1/1/8, p. 551, and CA1/1/37, p. 262; *Protocol Book of Gavin Ros*, p. 157.

54 *Extracts from the Council Register of the Burgh of Aberdeen*, 2 vols, ed. J. Stuart (Aberdeen, 1844–8), vol. 1, pp. 331–3; ACA, CA1/1/24, pp. 177–8.

55 ACA, CA1/1/9, pp. 450 and 452, CA1/1/16, p. 760, CA1/1/21, pp. 3, 6, 17 and 25, CA1/1/27, p. 560, and CA1/1/31, pp. 465–6; DCA, BCMB, vol. 5, 4 August 1559 and 20 July 1560, vol. 12, 8 August 1573, and vol. 19, 24 March 1597; NRS, B9/11/2, f. 125.

56 ACA, CA1/1/8, pp. 599, 617 and 619. *Cf.* G.V. Scammell, 'Manning the English Merchant Service in the Sixteenth Century', (1970) 56 *Mariner's Mirror* 131, at pp. 149–50.

57 DCA, BCMB, vol. 18, 29 July 1594.

58 Frankot, 'Scottish Translations of the *Rôles d'Oléron*', pp. 33–4; *Collection de lois maritimes*, vol. 1, pp. 327–8 and 474–5; *Black Book of the Admiralty*, vol. 4, pp. 72–5, 270 and 422–3.

59 ACA, CA1/1/19, p. 4.

60 ACA, CA1/1/17, p. 88. This was the case in which the same mariner complained about being unable to buy goods to send home for sale.

he was forbidden to sell the remains of the ship without express permission from its owners – the clerk of the court omitted it from the record.[61] When the mariners on another ship testified that one of their colleagues had used 'impertinat langage' to the master, a court found that the master should give the offender 'his half hyir within iii tydis, and gif him liberte to pas quhar he pleisis and discharg him of his service, or ellis ressave him thankfullie agane to service within iii tidis, and pay him his haill hyir'.[62] No mention is made in the record of an article in the maritime codes on how a master ought to deal with mariners who 'rebel again hym', or of an additional article in the code circulating in the Baltic region (in fact derived from Dutch legislation) which stated that a master who dismissed a mariner was to give him half his wages.[63] When the master of a ship moored in Aberdeen feared that it was in danger from 'ankeris plessit of uthar schippis in the herbrie', he asked the steersman and mariners 'to provyd and forsee the remeid thairof, quhilk thai wald nocht obey, bot obstinatlie refusit to do the same, be ressone thai war efter drunkines and stryff amang thameselffis'.[64] Although the ship had since been 'dryvin upoun ane anker in thair sleutht and defalt, quhairthrow scho is abill to wraik', the master did not want to dismiss the steersman and mariners from his service but to have them forced to obey his orders. The record of this case is less formulaic than many, and is full of circumstantial details that must have been reported to the court by the master, yet there is no mention again of articles in the maritime codes dealing with the dropping of anchors close to other ships, and with mariners going ashore to get drunk and fight.[65] The crew had remained in service because the ship had put in temporarily at Aberdeen on its way to Leith. In a case in which Aberdeen was the final destination of a voyage it was found that the crew were 'fre at this tyme to pas and serve quhar tha pleis', provided they first helped the master to unload the ship, 'conforme to the use of marenellis'.[66] That assistance with unloading was required by a written rule was not mentioned in the record.[67] Other cases reported in the

---

61 Frankot, 'Scottish Translations of the *Rôles d'Oléron*', p. 29; *Collection de lois maritimes*, vol. 1, pp. 324–5 and 471–2; *Black Book of the Admiralty*, vol. 4, pp. 68–9, 269 and 418–19.

62 ACA, CA1/1/12/2, p. 501.

63 Frankot, 'Scottish Translations of the *Rôles d'Oléron*', pp. 43–4; *Collection de lois maritimes*, vol. 1, pp. 333–4, 481 and 494–5, and vol. 4, p. 33; *Black Book of the Admiralty*, vol. 4, pp. 84–7, 110–13, 272 and 432–5.

64 ACA, CA1/1/31, pp. 465–6.

65 Frankot, 'Scottish Translations of the *Rôles d'Oléron*', pp. 32–3 and 46; *Collection de lois maritimes*, vol. 1, pp. 327, 334–5 and 482–3; *Black Book of the Admiralty*, vol. 4, pp. 70–3, 88–91, 270, 273, 420–3 and 436–7.

66 ACA, CA1/1/19, p. 401. See too ACA, CA1/1/27, pp. 573–4 and 582, and CA1/1/34/1, pp. 435–6.

67 *Collection de lois maritimes*, vol. 1, p. 498; *Black Book of the Admiralty*, vol. 4, p. 280.

court books raised questions about the effect on employment of the sale of a ship to new owners, and of a delay in departing on a voyage, on which answers were sought from 'merchandis, schiparis and marenaris'.[68]

Despite the relevance of the written codes of maritime law to many of the questions raised in litigation before the burgh courts in connection with the employment of mariners, they are never referred to in any of the records that happen to have survived.[69] Perhaps the clerks who compiled the records saw little point in mentioning references that were actually made to the codes in pleadings, but that seems rather less likely than that they were not cited by litigants at all. It is significant that although distant echoes of some articles can be heard in the arguments recorded, those arguments tended to deviate in detail from the texts of the codes.[70] Distant echoes can also be heard of the Roman law texts studied in the universities, as when a contract of employment was described as a 'conductioune', or when mariners were said to have received an 'arle penny' on agreeing to serve.[71] Here again, though, the written sources do not appear to have been followed precisely. Clerks could write, for instance, that mariners had 'conducit thameselffis' to masters when, strictly speaking, they could only have 'locatit' their services to them, and it was in relation to the contract of sale (*emptio venditio*) rather than hire (*locatio conductio*) that the Roman jurists had talked about the payment of *arra* in token of the conclusion of a bargain.[72] A clearer indication of the character of the law that was understood to govern the employment of mariners is provided by the frequent references made to 'use or consuetud', 'auld use and wont', 'the commoune practik in seafer causis', the 'use and custum amang marinaris' or the 'use of marenellis'. Even when reference was made to 'the law of the sey', reliance seems to have been placed on the advice of 'certane famouse skipparis' rather than on a written code of law. The practices of masters and mariners in Scotland were probably influenced by the practices of the masters and mariners they encountered in their travels, and those practices may in turn have been influenced

---

68 ACA, CA1/1/16, p. 205, and CA1/1/20, p. 280. Nothing has been found in the maritime codes touching on these final questions.

69 Of course, it needs to be remembered that the records are far from complete.

70 *Cf.* R.J. Blakemore, 'The Legal World of English Sailors, c. 1575–1729', in M. Fusaro, B. Allaire, R. Blakemore and T. Vanneste (eds), *Law, Labour and Empire: Comparative Perspectives on Seafarers, c. 1500–1800* (Basingstoke, 2015), p. 100.

71 ACA, CA1/1/8, p. 617, CA1/1/11, p. 263, CA1/1/16, p. 760, CA1/1/19, p. 14, CA1/1/20, pp. 184 and 187, CA1/1/27, pp. 573–4, and CA1/1/29, p. 105; DCA, BCMB, vol. 5, 20 July 1560, and vol. 20, 8 October 1597 and 18 March 1598.

72 W.W. Buckland, *A Text-Book of Roman Law from Augustus to Justinian* (Cambridge, 1963), pp. 481–2 and 504–5.

(or maybe even dictated) by the written codes of maritime law, but it was as practices that they came to be regarded as a kind of law in the burgh courts. Evidence was not normally taken of how masters and mariners behaved. The exception was the case heard in Dundee in 1562, when evidence was obtained from Leith of the wages paid to mariners travelling to English ports, and in that case the bailies emphasised that they were interpreting a particular contract made between the parties, not recognising a rule applicable in other cases. Rules were recognised not by receiving evidence of practice as such, but by accepting the accuracy of descriptions of sound practice by litigants or expert advisers. It was the consensus of everyone involved in litigation that formed 'the commoune practik in seafer causis', and it was this law that regulated the relationship between masters and mariners in the burgh courts.[73]

2 Litigation between Masters and Mariners in the Central Courts

There is some evidence that actions relating to the employment of mariners were heard in the admiralty courts sitting in coastal towns around Scotland, but the records of those courts have not survived.[74] One court book has survived, however, from the central admiralty court sitting in Leith or Edinburgh.[75] Most of the entries it contains were concerned with prize litigation resulting from the renewal of Scottish involvement in the Habsburg-Valois conflict at the end of the 1550s, but some were concerned with actions relating to the employment of mariners, either on warships or on ships transporting goods to and from overseas markets.[76] In one case a mariner pursued a master for 'hyre promittit to him' for service on his ship during 'the last viage maid be hir furth of this realme to Burdeaulx and frathin hame agane'.[77] The court ordered payment after the mariner 'referrit the haill punctis of his clame' to the master's oath *de veritate* and the master ignored a summons to appear, 'with certificatioun to him and he failzeit thairintill it wald be haldin *pro confesso* aganis him'.

73 The way in which a 'decreitt' could function as a 'preparative law' or 'prattik' for later cases is returned to below.

74 *The Register of the Privy Council of Scotland*, 14 vols, ed. J.H. Burton and D. Masson (Edinburgh, 1877–98), vol. 2, pp. 630 and 632; ACA, CA1/1/33/1, pp. 235 and 246.

75 The status of this admiralty court as a central court, in contrast to the local courts sitting elsewhere, is looked at in the first essay in this collection.

76 Some of the prize cases are discussed in J.D. Ford, *The Emergence of Privateering* (Leiden, 2023), pp. 24–39.

77 *Acta curiae admirallatus Scotiae, 6th Sept. 1557-11th March 1561–2*, ed. T.C. Wade (Edinburgh, 1937), p. 126.

In another case a mariner 'grantit' that he had already received money from one of the owners of a ship 'for his half hyre to have servit thairin to Burdeaulx the viage now making thairto'.[78] Proof that wages were still due could also be provided by the testimony of witnesses, and in one case the court sent a commission to 'the mair and baillies of the town of Dovar, to exeme the witnes to be producit befoir thame'.[79] Occasionally it was masters who pursued mariners for 'wrangus departing' from their service. When one complained about the absence of a mariner who was 'oblisit and conducit to mak him thankfull service quhill the feist of Mertimes nixt heirefter following', the court ordered the mariner 'to enter in service incontinent', but also warned the master that he was obliged to protect the mariner against 'bodelie harme' by another member of his crew, who was issuing daily 'boistis and mannissis' against him.[80] The basic procedure followed in handling these cases was similar to the procedure followed in the burgh courts: submission of a written claim by the pursuer; admission or denial of the facts alleged by the defender, or submission of defences based on further allegations of fact; consideration of the legal relevance of the allegations made, perhaps leading to interlocutors specifying dates for proof to be presented, in the form of documentary evidence, the testimony of witnesses or the swearing of oaths; finally, if an action was pursued all the way to a conclusion, pronunciation of a decreet by the court.[81] The use of a broadly similar procedure throughout the country was probably due to the widespread availability of notaries public, whose training equipped them to offer advice on the handling of litigation, or even to represent parties at hearings, and who usually acted as the clerks who kept orderly records of a court's proceedings.[82] The training they had received was in settled ways of conducting business, in accordance with established styles and routines, though some knowledge may also have been acquired of the legal theory taught in the universities.[83] When the notary who kept the court book of the central admiralty

78 *Acta curiae admirallatus Scotiae*, p. 71.

79 *Acta curiae admirallatus Scotiae*, pp. 63–5 and 128; and see too p. 148.

80 *Acta curiae admirallatus Scotiae*, p. 40.

81 For more detail see T.C. Wade, 'Introduction', in *Acta curiae admirallatus Scotiae*, p. xi, at pp. xxi–vi.

82 In one of the cases mentioned in the first section of this essay (AA, B6/11/3, ff. 45, 46v-7r and 50-1r), one of the parties was represented by a procurator who was specifically designated a 'notar', and the procurators named without designation in other cases may sometimes have been qualified in the same way too.

83 J. Durkan, 'The Early Scottish Notary', in I.B. Cowan and D. Shaw (eds), *The Renaissance and Reformation in Scotland: Essays in Honour of Gordon Donaldson* (Edinburgh, 1983), p. 22, at pp. 29–32.

court composed one entry in Latin, he used vocabulary familiar from Roman law sources in writing about a mariner (*nauta*) pursuing a skipper (*nauclerus*) for payment of hire (*merces*) he had been promised for service on a voyage from Scotland to Norway and back again, yet he proceeded to write that the skipper had given the mariner leave 'to conduce himself' with any other skipper (*facultatem dedit sese conducere cum quovis alio nauclero*).[84] The question that needs to be addressed now is what difference it made if lawyers with a better knowledge of Roman law became involved in litigation.

Several other cases recorded by the clerk were concerned with the termination of contracts of employment. In the first a member of a crew alleged that he was so 'seik and evill disposit that he mycht nocht saill nor travell and mak service with thame the viage libellat'.[85] Before receiving proof of the illness from the mariner, the court 'referrit to the knawlege of certane honest seyferand men' the question whether 'this marinar suld rander the hyre or half hyre ressavit or nocht'. Their answer was not recorded, but it could not simply have been drawn from the written codes of maritime law since the problem dealt with there was what ought to happen if a mariner fell ill during a voyage, not what ought to happen if he fell ill 'or that thai mak viage'. In a second case a mariner complained about a master 'brekking up of the lok of his coy within the havin of Burdeaulx', confiscating his belongings and 'boisting of him with his quhinzear, and putting of him furth of the schip to his awin expenssis, quhair necessitie constrynit him to pas to the Rochell raid, quhair he remanit out of service xx dayis'.[86] The court instructed the master to return the belongings he confessed to having taken, and appointed a date to receive proof of the expenses incurred by the mariner, though why his allegations were considered relevant was not made clear. In a third case a shipowner complained that a master had sold tackle recovered from the wreck of his ship, without his 'licence, commissioun, command or tollerance'.[87] In support of his complaint he made reference to 'the common law', which may have meant the article in the written codes requiring masters to provide mariners with assistance in returning home after a shipwreck, while adding that the remains of ships could not be sold unless the owners consented.[88] There are certainly entries in the court book, relating to other types of complaint, in which a litigant is

---

84 *Acta curiae admirallatus Scotiae*, pp. 202, 210 and 135.
85 *Acta curiae admirallatus Scotiae*, p. 81.
86 *Acta curiae admirallatus Scotiae*, pp. 208–9.
87 *Acta curiae admirallatus Scotiae*, pp. 7, 10, 12, 29 and 72.
88 Frankot, 'Scottish Translations of the *Rôles d'Oléron*', p. 29; *Collection de lois maritimes*, vol. 1, pp. 324–5 and 471–2; *Black Book of the Admiralty*, vol. 4, pp. 68–9, 269 and 418–19.

said to have 'repetit the dispositioun of the buk of Olrinis, togidder with the use and prettik of the seyfair', and in which an advocate – a university graduate admitted to practice before the lords of council and session – is said to have 'repetit the law of the buik of Olouris, safer as thai ar ressavit in this realme'.[89] In a fourth case relating to the termination of a contract of employment, when another advocate representing a master argued that a mariner who had been 'conducit' to sail on his ship should be compelled to do so, an advocate representing the mariner pointed out that 'the use and consuetude of seyfair usit and observit in sik caissis' permitted a mariner to withdraw from service if he was 'promovit to ane gretar office'.[90] No mention is made of the relevant article of the written codes, perhaps because it was not part of the laws of Oleron, or perhaps because it referred more precisely to promotion to the office of master.[91] Although the advocate representing the master then 'allegit the foirsaid practick to be express aganis baith law, equitie and gude conscience', and argued that it 'suld nocht be admittit', it was accepted that the mariner could withdraw from service.

Alexander Skene, the advocate who criticised the rule about promotion to a higher office, appears to have studied in France – at the University of Paris in particular – before he became a lawyer in Scotland, where he set an example, according to his younger brother, of how academic learning (*iuris scientia*) could be combined with practical experience (*rerum usus*).[92] In France he would have learned that the Romans had recognised custom as a kind of law.[93] The *Digest*, *Code* and *Institutes* all contained texts making it clear that in the absence of written laws, recourse ought to be taken to *usus* or *consuetudo*, on the understanding that it rested upon the tacit agreement of the people who conformed to it.[94] In the schools of civil law students were taught to use the term *consuetudo* both as a *nomen facti*, signifying the type of behaviour that might give rise to law (*ex quo resultat ius*), and as a *nomen iuris*, signifying a binding rule that was believed to be inherent in behaviour (*quod sit ius*).[95] In

89 *Acta curiae admirallatus Scotiae*, pp. 31 and 164–5.

90 *Acta curiae admirallatus Scotiae*, pp. 86 and 98–9.

91 Some variants were more specific still in talking about a mariner becoming master of a ship he had bought.

92 John Vaus, *Rudimenta puerorum in artem grammaticam* (Edinburgh, 1566), sig. O3r; *Regiam maiestatem: Scotiae veteres leges et constitutiones*, ed. Sir John Skene of Curriehill (Edinburgh, 1609), sig. A2; *Memorials of the Family of Skene of Skene*, ed. W.F. Skene (Aberdeen, 1887), pp. 93–5.

93 P.G. Stein, 'Custom in Roman and Medieval Civil Law', (1995) 10 *Continuity and Change* 337.

94 D.1.3.33 and 35, C.8.52(53).1 and 3, and J.1.2.9.

95 Cinus de Pistoria, *In Codicem et aliquot titulos primi Pandectorum tomi, id est Digesti veteris, doctissima commentaria* (Frankfurt, 1578), f. 523r (ad C.8.52(53).2); Bartolus de

studying canon law, the primary focus of attention at Paris, Skene would have learned similar lessons.[96] There were texts in the *Decretum* indicating that custom should be adhered to in the absence of statute or scripture.[97] Other canon law texts, however, declared that customs should never receive effect if they were contrary to religion, reason or law.[98] One of these texts, which stated that custom should not be shown so much respect that it overcame either reason (*ratio*) or statute (*lex*), had actually been borrowed from the Roman law sources.[99] As one influential commentator concluded, custom lacked binding authority if it conflicted with *lex rationabilis*, which meant legislation 'that has intrinsic equity, or just motivation from its legislator'.[100] Customs were appraised in the light of their consistency with reason or equity, and if they were found wanting they could be denied effect, especially if they were privileges or exceptions from general rules.[101] When Skene argued that the 'practick' permitting mariners to accept promotion to higher offices on other vessels was 'express aganis baith law, equitie and gude conscience, and suld nocht be admittit', he may have meant that the practice of withdrawing labour (a *consuetudo* only as a *nomen facti*) could not be recognised as a legal privilege (a *consuetudo* as a *nomen iuris*) since it was contrary to natural equity.[102] Moreover, he may actually have meant – and the words 'express aganis baith law' support this reading – that the custom was invalid since it was contrary to the civil law, conceived of as *ratio scripta* or *aequitas constituta*.[103] He may have been mindful of a *Digest* text that required anyone who had promised his services to two employers at the same time to fulfil his contract with the employer he had promised first.[104]

Sassoferrato, *Opera quae nunc extant omnia*, 10 vols (Basel, 1588–9), vol. 9, pp. 168–75 (ad J.1.2.9); Baldus de Ubaldis, *Super Institutionibus commentaria* (Lyons, 1543), f. 4v (ad J.1.2.9).

96 D. Bauer, 'Custom in Canon Law and the Expansion of Legal Reality', in P. Andersen and M. Münster-Swendson (eds), *Custom: The Development and Use of a Legal Concept in the Middle Ages* (Copenhagen, 2009), p. 107.

97 D. 1 c. 5, D. 11 cc. 5 and 7, and D. 12 cc. 3–9.

98 D. 11 cc. 1, 4 and 6.

99 C.8.52(53).2.

100 Baldus de Ubaldis, *Super Codice commentaria*, 4 vols (Lyons, 1539), vol. 4, f. 188r (ad C.8.52(53).2).

101 J. Krynen, 'Entre science juridique et dirigisme: Le glas medieval de la coutume', (2000) 7 *Cahiers de recherches médiévales* 170.

102 Bartolus, *Opera omnia*, vol. 1, pp. 57–8 (ad D.1.3.32.pr.).

103 Albericus de Rosate, *Lectura subtilis et aurea super Codicem*, 2 vols (Venice, 1518), vol. 2, f. 171 (ad C.52(53).2).

104 D.19.2.26. When commenting on this text, Paulus de Castro, *Commentaria in Digesto vetere*, 2 vols (Lyons, 1535), vol. 2, f. 132v, insisted that the rule would remain the same

The customary rights of mariners came within the contemplation of lawyers again in 1579. After returning to Leith from Bordeaux, a mariner removed wine he had transported in a ship and took it across the bridge to his home on the north side of the Water of Leith, within the regality of Holyroodhouse and outwith the jurisdiction of the water bailie appointed in Edinburgh.[105] When the mariner went up the hill to Edinburgh later that day, he was brought before the bailie court there and incarcerated in the tolbooth until he arranged for the wine to be placed in a cellar on the south side of the bridge.[106] A complaint was then presented on the mariner's behalf, with support from 'the haill remanent maisteris, skipparis and marineris' living in Leith, to the privy council.[107] It was claimed that mariners had been 'in use and consuetude, past memorie of man, of portage, as ane part of thair fie and hyir', and that they had always carried their portage goods 'to thair awin dwelling houssis and sellaris on the said north side, without stop, truble, or impediment'. The Edinburgh authorities were summoned to respond, and appointed the advocate John Sharp to represent them.[108] The mariners had difficulty in finding counsel to represent them, since most advocates were involved in the town's business in some way, but eventually they appointed both Edmund Hay and Thomas Craig.[109] Sharp argued on behalf of the burgh authorities that they were within their rights to imprison a mariner who had contravened legislation, citing an act of parliament requiring goods imported from abroad to be unloaded 'at fre portis alanerly', and two more acts requiring wine imported from abroad to be offered for sale to the authorities of the burgh at which it was unloaded.[110] An attempt to have the first act reinforced with a penalty by a convention of the royal burghs at Dundee a year earlier had provoked a protest from the mariners there that having to unload goods at the ports of royal or ecclesiastical burghs should not be taken to diminish in any way the portage rights they had enjoyed 'past

even if the employee reinforced the second contract with an oath. The text was certainly regarded as a *lex rationabilis*, expressing an intrinsically equitable rule.

105 Rights of portage had also been mentioned in passing in *Acta curiae admirallatus Scotiae*, p. 137, where the owners of a ship claimed freight from a mariner for woad and wine carried in excess of his allowance.

106 ECA, SL1/1/5, ff. 184r and 185v-6r.

107 *Register of the Privy Council of Scotland*, vol. 3, pp. 246–8; NRS, PC1/10, pp. 384–7.

108 M.H.B. Sanderson, *Mary Stewart's People: Life in Mary Stewart's Scotland* (Edinburgh, 1987), pp. 22–33.

109 F.J. Grant, *The Faculty of Advocates in Scotland, 1532–1943* (Edinburgh, 1944), pp. 43 and 98; J. Finlay, 'The Early Career of Thomas Craig, Advocate', (2004) 8 *Edinburgh Law Review* 298.

110 *The Acts of the Parliaments of Scotland*, 12 vols, ed. T. Thomson and C. Innes (Edinbrugh, 1814–75), vol. 2, pp. 373–4 and 499, and vol. 3, p. 42; Records of the Parliaments of Scotland, ed. K.M. Brown (www.rps.ac.uk), 1540/12/17, 1555/6/36 and 1567/12/69.

memor of man, conform to the auld lovabill use and wont of this burgh'.[111] Hay similarly replied on behalf of the mariners of Leith that their customary rights should be respected despite the acts of parliament, but the privy councillors took the narrow view that the only question they had to address was whether it was lawful for a burgh to imprison a man until a court order was fulfilled, which they believed it was. They therefore declined to consider the relative authority of statutes and customs, remitting the 'remanent pointis' of the complaint 'to be decidit befoir the judges competent thairto'. While there might have been some discussion of the effect of legislation on customary rights if the case had returned to the bailie court of Edinburgh or had been drawn to the attention of the lords of session, no further trace of it has been found. That the mariner was involved in a new voyage to Bordeaux a couple of months later suggests that he had accepted defeat and transferred his wine to south Leith.[112]

Had there been further discussion of the case, Sharp might have adopted Skene's approach and have argued that the alleged portage rights should not be viewed as legal privileges since they were contrary to *aequitas naturalis* or *aequitas constituta*, although it is by no means obvious how this line of argument could have been substantiated. On their side, Hay and Craig might have argued more plausibly that the acts of parliament cited were contrary to the natural freedom protected by the civil law, which – according to the theory of statutory interpretation taught in the law schools – would not have rendered the acts invalid but would have required a court to construe them strictly – so that, for instance, 'to loise or laid' could not have been taken to encompass the storage of goods after their removal from ships.[113] The arguments that were advanced before the privy council, however, suggest that the advocates were inclined to think less about the relationship between the local law (*ius proprium*) and learned law (*ius commune*) than about the relationship between *propria statuta* and *propriae consuetudines* as components of the local law.[114] Students learned from a text in the *Digest* to examine laws set down in writing (*scriptae leges*) before they turned their attention to laws introduced by usage and custom (*quod moribus et consuetudine inductum est*).[115] It was on the

111 *Records of the Convention of the Royal Burghs of Scotland*, 8 vols, ed. J.D. Marwick and T. Hunter (Edinburgh, 1870–1918), vol. 1, pp. 68–9; DCA, PBD, vol. 11, f. 65v.

112 ECA, SL1/1/6, ff. 86–7r. An interesting dispute arising from the new voyage is returned to in the ninth essay in this collection.

113 W.P. Müller, 'Signorolus de Homodeis and the Medieval Interpretation of Statutory Law', (1995) 6 *Rivista internazionale di diritto commune* 217.

114 Baldus de Ubaldis, *In Digestum veterem commentaria*, 2 vols (Venice, 1577), vol. 1, f. 13r (ad D.1.1.9).

115 D.1.3.32.

basis of this text that Craig was to discuss the sources of Scots law in a treatise he wrote at the end of the sixteenth century, and it goes some way towards explaining the tendency in the central courts, unlike the burgh courts, for written sources to be expressly 'repetit' before the judges.[116] Yet the same text had gone on to explain that because statutes and customs both derived their force from the will of the people (*populi voluntas*), statutes could be deprived of effect not only through abrogation in later enactments but also through falling into disuse (*in desuetudine*).[117] The doctors of civil law had explained further that a statute could be deprived of effect either through being neglected (*desuetudo* in the strict sense) or through the emergence of an inconsistent custom (*contraria consuetudo*).[118] Had the discussion of the perceived conflict between the acts of parliament cited by Sharp and the custom defended by Hay and Craig been resumed in another forum, it might therefore have been argued that a customary law would prevail over enacted legislation on the strength of the general principle enunciated by the doctors that *consuetudo vincit legem*.[119] As the exercise of portage rights was long established, and extended in Leith to mariners putting their goods into storage at their own homes, the acts of parliament could have been denied effect to the extent that they prevented mariners from removing their goods from the port of a free burgh until they gave the authorities there an opportunity to buy the goods. So at least it might have been argued by advocates who had studied the civil law at continental universities, as long as the consistency of the mariners' privileges with reason and equity was not called into question.

The portage rights of mariners were returned to in the central courts in 1592, when several masters in Leith raised an action against mariners before the central admiralty court, claiming that since they carried goods on portage they ought to be involved in the distribution of losses sustained during voyages among masters and merchants.[120] The mariners tried to have the action transferred for decision to the lords of session, before whom they were represented

116 Thomas Craig of Riccarton, *Jus feudale tribus libris comprehensum, Book 1*, tr. L. Dodd (Edinburgh, 2017), pp. 172–81.

117 Indeed, another text (D.1.3.36) stated that customs were arguably of greater authority (*magnae auctoritatis*) than statutes since they received so much popular approval that they did not need to be set down in writing.

118 Albericus de Rosate, *Lectura subtilis et aurea super Codicem*, 2 vols (Venice, 1518), vol. 2, ff. 175v-6 (ad C.8.52(53).2); De Castro, *Commentaria in Digesto vetere*, vol. 1, f. 13 (ad D.1.3.32).

119 Albericus de Rosate, *Singularis ac perutilis tractatus in materia statutorum* (Milan, 1511), sig. A2v.

120 The issue raised is discussed more fully in the ninth essay in this collection.

by the advocate Umphra Blindseil.[121] Observing that there was 'na act of parliament, as positive law of this realme, maid at ony tyme of befoir in sik caisis', he argued that there was in fact a 'continewall consuetude, to wit, that the mariners contributs not in thair fie and portage witht the merchand'.[122] This negative custom was consistent with 'equitie', for whereas a merchant might hope to make 'greit gaine and commoditie be the aventour of his guids', a mariner who participated in a voyage could expect to receive 'na thing bot his simple fie and hyre, and hes na libertie to imput ony forder in the schip except the pure fie and wareing therof in portage', even though all mariners were required 'be nycht and day to hasart ther lyf'. Addressing the procedural point, Blindseil argued that 'sik noveltie' as was proposed by the masters 'cannot be jugeit bot be the lords of counsall as suppreme juges of the realme, quha hes onelie power to juge and decyde in the said like maters of novelitie as this is, to the effect the same may remane as ane commoun practike fra thynce furth to all inferiour jugis'. There were a number of texts in the *Corpus iuris civilis* that he may have had in mind in advancing this argument. According to one *Digest* text, usually read in conjunction with two others, if a party alleged a custom of a particular place (*civitas vel provincia*), the first question that needed to be asked was whether it had ever been confirmed by a court order delivered in contentious proceedings (*contradictum iudicium*).[123] This was not taken to mean that a custom had to be confirmed by a judicial decision before it could amount to a customary law, given that other texts indicated that the tacit consent of the people could be identified from recurring practice (*frequens usus*) over a long period of time (*diuturnus tempus*), but it was taken to mean that if a custom was confirmed in contentious proceedings, no further proof of inveterate practice was needed for the custom to be applied in future cases.[124] As one leading commentator explained, 'while a custom is introduced by tacit consent, and in a court decision is imposed on someone who is unwilling, or while the consent of the loser is not implicit in the sentence, the consent of wise men in favour of sentences concurs nonetheless with the same, as well as the consent of other citizens providing assistance and agreeing with such sentences, from which the consent of the people, or the greater part of them,

121 A.M. Godfrey, *Civil Justice in Renaissance Scotland: The Origins of a Central Court* (Leiden, 2009), pp. 192–6.

122 NRS, CS7/139, ff. 1–2.

123 D.1.3.34 and 37–8.

124 Cinus de Pistoria, *In Codicem et aliquot titulos primi Pandectorum tomi, id est Digesti veteris, doctissima commentaria*, f. 522r (ad C.8.52(53).2).

can be gathered'.[125] The recognition of customs in courts staffed with learned lawyers was thus a shortcut to establishing them as customary laws.[126]

Blindseil may also have been thinking of a pair of texts in Justinian's *Code*, which began by stating that if a doubt arose about a new law (*novum ius*) which had not yet been clarified by prolonged usage (*inveteratus usus*), the proposal of a judge (*suggestio iudicantis*) was as necessary to its resolution as the sovereign authority of a sentence (*sententiae principalis auctoritas*), before adding that when the emperor delivered a sentence in a case referred to him, it was to be taken by other judges to apply to similar cases as well (*sciant hoc esse legem non solum illi causae, pro qua producta est, sed omnibus similibus*).[127] These texts were traditionally understood to relate to recently enacted statutes, and were connected with another *Code* text requiring any doubts about legislation to be referred to the legislator, but Blindseil may have assumed from the reference to *ius* (as opposed to *lex*) that the concern was with law more generally, and may have regarded the session, which had after all originated in the *curia regis*, as a body with the *principalis auctoritas* to lay down *sententiae* binding on lower courts.[128] No evidence has been found that the courts in which actions between masters and mariners were typically initiated did pay attention to the decisions of the lords of session, who were persuaded in the 1592 case by Alexander King, an advocate representing the Leith masters, to remit the case for decision to the admiralty court, albeit with assistance from expert assessors. It has been seen that the bailies of Dundee mentioned the possibility of one of their decisions forming a 'preparative law' for other cases, but no evidence has been found of decisions of the bailie courts being cited as precedents in later cases either. The preparative law or 'prattik' envisaged appears to have been at most a rule proposed for acceptance – not imposed by anything approximating to legislative authority – to the community of masters and mariners – not expert lawyers.[129] If the binding force of legal

125 Albericus, *Lectura subtilis et aurea super Codicem*, vol. 2, f. 172 (ad C.8.52(53).2).

126 Bartolus, *Opera omnia*, vol. 1, pp. 26–7 (ad D.1.1.9), 57–61 (ad D.1.3.32.pr.) and 61–70 (ad D.1.3.32.1), and vol. 8, pp. 324–33 (ad C.8.52(53)2).

127 C.1.14.11–12. See too C.1.14.2 and 7.62.34.

128 *Codex imperatoris Iustiniani* (Lyons, 1527), f. 29v (gl. 'Cum de novo' ad C.1.14.11); Cinus, *In Codicem et aliquot titulos primi Pandectorum tomi, id est Digesti veteris, doctissima commentaria*, f. 27v (ad C.1.14.11); Baldus, *Super Codice commentaria*, f. 66v (ad C.1.14.11); Raphael Fulgosius, *In D. Iustiniani Codicem commentarii*, 3 vols (Lyons, 1547), vol. 1, ff. 30v–1r (ad C.1.14.11). See too A. Alibrandi, *La maîtrise de l'interprétation de la loi: L'apport doctrinal de la Sacrée Congrégation du Concile au XVIIe siècle* (Rome, 2022), p. 57.

129 Even the use of the word 'rule' here may be misleading (P. Bourdieu, *Outline of a Theory of Practice*, tr. R. Nice (Cambridge, 1977), pp. 16–17).

customs derived ultimately from the tacit consent of those affected by it, their consent was not implicit in their behaviour so much as in their acceptance of the accuracy of descriptions of sound behaviour.[130] These descriptions would presumably have been acceptable to masters and mariners only if the behaviour seemed reasonable, but again there is no evidence that a distinction was drawn in the burgh courts between recognising customs as a matter of fact and as a matter of law, or that settled practices were appraised by comparison with any external standard of rationality, let alone the written reason of the learned laws. Legal customs were not accommodated as customary laws within the common erudition of lawyers unless they were alleged in pleadings presented to central courts.

3 Conclusion

While only a few cases have been found in which advocates were involved in discussion of the employment of mariners, it is clear that they viewed the applicable law in a different way from the people to whom it applied. The lawyers educated in the civil and canon laws gave priority to written sources, and even though one of these sources taught them that statutes would lose force if they fell into desuetude, they took this to mean that written laws would be binding only if they remained in use, which was different from believing that written laws were relevant (if at all) only to the extent that they had been influential in practice.[131] It follows that it would be seriously misleading to view the legal customs recognised in the burgh courts through the lens of the learned theory of customary law studied in the schools of law.[132] The masters and mariners who regulated their own affairs in proceedings before the burgh courts showed little interest in written sources and took the law to consist instead in descriptions of sound behaviour that were agreed to be accurate. The legal customs they recognised would not have lost significance, or have survived only to the extent that they came within the contemplation of lawyers as customary

130 As the philosophy of society adopted in the previous essay makes clear, while the acceptance of the accuracy of descriptions may have been tacit, behaviour had to be vocalised in descriptions for it to stand any chance of becoming obligatory.

131 It may be worth emphasising again that any influence the written codes of maritime law may have had seems more likely to have resulted indirectly from contact with foreign masters and mariners than directly from study of the codes.

132 E. Kadens, 'Myth of the Customary Law Merchant', (2012) 90 *Texas Law Review* 1153, needs to be read in the light of the same author's 'Custom's Past', in C.A. Bradley (ed.), *Custom's Future: International Law in a Changing World* (Cambridge, 2016), p. 11.

laws, unless it had been accepted that the employment of mariners was governed by the law known to the lawyers who appeared in cases raised before the central courts. Whatever may have happened in England, it seems clear that for much of the sixteenth century the employment of mariners continued to be governed in Scotland by the law known to masters and mariners.[133]

133 Whether it is always appropriate to look at custom in England from the perspective of the common lawyers (as is done, for example, in A. Fox, *Oral and Literate Culture in England, 1500–1700* (Oxford, 2000), pp. 259–98) is for historians of English law to decide, but doubts may certainly be raised. Obviously, comparison could also be made with developments in other countries, but for reasons explained in the final essay in this collection, comparison with England seems especially instructive.

PART 2

Legal Treatises

5

James Balfour's Collection of Sea Laws

As first printed in 1754, and reprinted by the Stair Society in 1962–3, the book now known as *The Practicks of Sir James Balfour of Pittendreich* contains near its end material entitled: 'The sea lawis, collectit furth of the actis of parliament, the practiques, the lawis of Oleron and the lawis of Wisbie, and the constitutiounis of Francois, king of France, *annis* 1543, 1557'.[1] That Balfour was responsible for the compilation of the *Practicks* was demonstrated convincingly by Hector McKechnie in an article published over ninety years ago.[2] In his introduction to the Stair Society's edition Peter McNeill endorsed McKechnie's conclusions, but he was far less confident about the authorship of the collection of 'sea lawis'.[3] He pointed out that maritime law was one of four subjects that did not fit into the general arrangement of the book, that the passages dealing with these subjects appeared to have been written after the completion of the book, and that to some extent at least they must have been written after Balfour died in 1583, since they made use of sources of a later date. The central aim of this essay is to find out who wrote the collection of 'sea lawis' appended to the *Practicks*, or more precisely whether there is good reason to suppose that it was someone other than Balfour himself. This will of course involve consideration of the relationship between the *Practicks* and the appendix on maritime law. Two sections are focused on the *Practicks* and two on the appendix. The first section is concerned with how the compiling of the *Practicks* came to be conceived of as a project, and the second with how the project was carried out. The third section is concerned with how the materials on sea law were collected together, and the fourth with how this collection came to be conceived of as an appendix to the practicks. There will necessarily be some reflection on the purposes behind the writing of the *Practicks* and the appendix, but it needs to be borne in mind that the aim of the essay is to discover who wrote the appendix, not why either it or the *Practicks* was written.[4] It will be seen that asking why

1 *The Practicks of Sir James Balfour of Pittendreich*, 2 vols, ed. P.G.B. McNeill (Edinburgh, 1962–3), vol. 2, p. 614. Quotations from this and other primary sources are faithful to the orthography of the original texts but not to the punctuation, capitalisation and italicisation.

2 H. McKechnie, 'Balfour's *Practicks*', (1931) 43 *Juridical Review* 179.

3 P.G.B. McNeill, 'Introduction', in *Practicks of Sir James Balfour of Pittendreich*, vol. 1, p. xi, at pp. xxxii and lxiii.

4 The purposes behind the writing of both the *Practicks* and the appendix are returned to in the seventh essay in this collection.

 DOI:10.1163/9789004695009_006

the *Practicks* and the appendix were written sheds less light on the question of authorship than asking how they were written, and that on this question a significant advance has been made since the early 1960s. A subsidiary aim of the essay is to review the gradual progress made over the past hundred years towards a better understanding of how Balfour's *Practicks* was composed.

1 The Conception of Balfour's *Practicks*

If McKechnie felt obliged to argue in 1931 that Balfour was responsible for the production of the *Practicks*, he was able to report that there was general agreement about the occasion on which the book was put into shape.[5] On 5 March 1575 a parliamentary commission had been appointed 'anent the sichting, collectioun and reformatioun of the lawis of this realme', in the following terms.[6]

> My lord regentis grace and estaittis presentlie convenit, understanding the harme quhilk this commoune weill sustenis throw want of a perfyte writtin law, quhairupoun all jugeis may knaw how to proceid and decerne, thairfoir it is thocht convenient and concludit that thir personis following, thay ar to say, Johnne, Lord Glammis, chancellair, Williame, Lord Ruthvene, thesaurare, Robert, Lord Boyd, Johnne, Lord Hereis, James, commendatare of Pettinweme, Maister Williame Baillie, lord provand, president of the College of Justice, Maister James Haliburtoun, provest of Dunde, Maister Michaell Cheisholme, burges of Edinburgh, and Johnne Patersoun, provest of Cowper, sall convene togidder in Edinburgh upoun the tent day of Apryle nixtocum, and thair, calling unto thame sic utheris of the lordis of the sessioun or advocattis as thay sall think expedient, sall begin and visite the bukis of the law, actis of parliament and decisionis befoir the sessioun and draw the forme of the body of oure lawis, alsweill of that quhilk is alreddy statute as thay thingis that wer meit and convenient to be statute, that the same, being reportit agane to the estaittis, it or samekill thairof as salbe found gude and allowabill may be ratifiit and establissit in parliament, quhairthrow thair may be ane certain writtin

5 'Balfour's *Practicks*', pp. 181–2.
6 The new year is taken here to have commenced on 1 January.

> law to all oure soverane lordis jugeis and ministeris of law to juge and decyde be.[7]

Balfour was at the time the commendator of Pittenweem, and the obvious point is that in the *Practicks* extracts from 'the bukis of the law' were gathered together with citations from the 'actis of parliament' and summaries of 'decisionis befoir the sessioun', in what might easily have been regarded as 'the forme of the body of oure lawis'.[8] Since McKechnie's time greater hesitancy has been expressed about the origins of the project, partly because Balfour was also appointed to a commission established by Mary I in 1566, the renewal of which appears to have been proposed in 1567, following the accession of James VI to the throne.[9] Indeed, it has been suggested that the *Practicks* should be regarded as a response to the 1567 commission rather than the 1575 commission.[10] Comparison thus needs to be made of the terms in which all these commissions were established, together with those of several others already established in the fifteenth century or to be established later in the sixteenth century. In fact, similar commissions were to go on being established until the parliamentary union of 1707.[11]

The instructions issued to the reform commissioners during the fifteenth and sixteenth centuries differed from each other in three main ways, starting with the range of sources the commissioners were meant to consult. In 1426 six representatives of each of the three estates, 'the quhilkis knawis the lawys', were directed to 'examyn the bukis of law of this realme, that is to say, *Regiam majestatem*, *Quoniam attachiamenta*'.[12] In 1469 four representatives of each estate were directed to examine 'the kingis lawis, *Regiam majestatem*, actis, statutis and uthir

7 *The Acts of the Parliaments of Scotland*, 12 vols, ed. T. Thomson and C. Innes (Edinburgh, 1814–75), vol. 3, p. 89; Records of the Parliaments of Scotland, ed. K.M. Brown (www.rps.ac.uk), A1575/3/7.

8 J. Goodare, *The Government of Scotland, 1560–1625* (Oxford, 2004), p. 78. The meaning of all the expressions quoted will be returned to shortly.

9 *The Actis and Constitutiounis of the Realme of Scotland* (Edinburgh, 1566), sig. 2; *Acts of the Parliaments of Scotland*, vol. 3, p. 40; Records of the Parliaments of Scotland, 1567/12/54; McNeill, 'Introduction', pp. xvii and lviii; J.W. Cairns, T.D. Fergus and H.L. MacQueen, 'Legal Humanism and the History of Scots Law: John Skene and Thomas Craig', in J. MacQueen (ed.), *Humanism in Renaissance Scotland* (Edinburgh, 1990), p. 48, at pp. 50–1.

10 R. Sutherland, *Lord Stair and the Laws of Scotland* (Glasgow, 1981), pp. 23–4.

11 J.D. Ford, 'Paradigms of Authority in the College of Justice in Scotland', in G. Rossi (ed.), *Authorities in Early-Modern Law Courts* (Edinburgh, 2021), p. 29, at pp. 45–7.

12 *Acts of the Parliaments of Scotland*, vol. 2, p. 10; Records of the Parliaments of Scotland, 1426/13.

bukis'.[13] While this could have been a more elaborate description of the contents of 'the bukis of law' referred to forty-three years earlier, in the meantime another commission comprising 'xii persounis of the thre estatis' had been established with instructions to 'examyn al actis of parliamentis and general consallis haldyn in oure soverane lordis tym and in his fadiris tym', meaning the legislation of the reigns of James I and James II.[14] It could therefore be that the intention in 1469 was to extend scrutiny beyond the old books of law to include more recent acts of parliament.[15] These sources were certainly brought together in the instructions issued by Mary I in 1566, which directed the eighteen commissioners appointed to examine 'the lawis of this our realme, maid be us and our maist nobill progenitouris, be the avise of the thre estatis in parliament haldin be thame, beginnand at the buikis of the law callit *Regiam maiestatem* and *Quoniam attachiamenta*, and sua consequentlie following be progres of tyme unto the dait of this our commissioun'.[16] The efforts made a hundred years earlier to have 'the bukis of the law' examined by 'certane leirnit, wyse and expert men' were recalled in the commission, where the legislation of the fifteenth and sixteenth centuries was explicitly treated as an addition to the written law already accumulated in the old books. The 'sufficient personis' of an unspecified number who were mentioned in the following year – there is no record of a commission being established then, but only of a proposal that 'ane commissioun be gevin' – were intended to bring together 'the civile and municipale lawis', of which the latter would surely have been taken to encompass both the old books and the more recent acts.[17] Accordingly, there was nothing novel about the direction given to the 1575 commissioners to examine 'the bukis of the law' and 'actis of parliament', although it is notable that these two sources were more clearly distinguished in 1575 than in 1566. The novel feature of the 1575 commission was the direction to examine the 'decisionis befoir

13 *Acts of the Parliaments of Scotland*, vol. 2, p. 97; Records of the Parliaments of Scotland, 1469/34.

14 *Acts of the Parliaments of Scotland*, vol. 2, p. 36; Records of the Parliaments of Scotland, 1450/1/21.

15 The 1469 commission is linked with the 1450 commission in J.J. Robertson, 'The Development of the Law', in J.M. Brown (ed.), *Scottish Society in the Fifteenth Century* (London, 1977), p. 136, at p. 143. It may be that the appointment of twelve commissioners was meant to bring to mind the compilation of Justinian's *Code*. The eighteen appointed on other occasions seem more reminiscent of the seventeen appointed to compile Justinian's *Digest*.

16 *Actis and Constitutiounis of the Realme of Scotland*, sig. 2.

17 *Acts of the Parliaments of Scotland*, vol. 3, p. 40; Records of the Parliaments of Scotland, 1567/12/54.

the sessioun', which had never been referred to in any previous commission. The 'municipale lawis' referred to in 1567 could conceivably have been taken to include the decisions of the highest civil court, but Balfour certainly did not follow those instructions in compiling his *Practicks*, for he made no use of material derived from the books of the civil law. As far as the range of sources examined is concerned, Balfour's *Practicks* does appear to be more consistent with the instructions issued to the 1575 commissioners than with those issued to any others. The least likely inspiration for the compilation, from this point of view, is the 1567 proposal.

The second way in which the instructions issued to the various reform commissions differed from each other is in the problems they were meant to tackle. The concern expressed in 1426 was with litigants or their representatives committing 'fraude of the law' by pleading 'frivolus' defences to actions.[18] The concern behind the 1469 commission was not identified, nor had it been explained in 1450 why it was felt necessary to have the legislation of James II and his immediate predecessor examined. Just four years after the 1469 commissioners were appointed, however, the establishment of another commission was proposed, perhaps because the existing commissioners were disappointing expectations. If so, it may be significant that the 1473 proposal expressed concern over 'the gret diverseite now fundin in diverse bukis put in be diverse persones that ar callit men of law', as well as over 'diverse obscure materis that ar now in our lawis and that daily occuris'.[19] It may be that the 1469 commissioners were also expected to deal with the problem of inconsistencies between the circulating manuscripts of the old books, and with the problem of obscurities in more recent acts of parliament. In 1566 the concern expressed was with 'misknawlege and ignorance' of the law, which was feared as a source of 'misordour, inobedience, tumult and troubling of the commounweill'.[20] It was not explained in 1567 why the establishment of another commission was being proposed so soon after the last, but if the aim was to renew the deposed queen's instructions – albeit in far from identical terms – under the authority of the new king, then it may be assumed that the concern was still with ignorance of the law. More particularly, the concern would still have been with the

18 *Acts of the Parliaments of Scotland*, vol. 2, p. 10; Records of the Parliaments of Scotland, 1426/13.

19 *Acts of the Parliaments of Scotland*, vol. 2, p. 105; Records of the Parliaments of Scotland, 1473/7/17.

20 *Actis and Constitutiounis of the Realme of Scotland*, sig. 2r. *Cf.* A.R.C. Simpson, 'Legislation and Authority in Early-Modern Scotland', in A.M. Godfrey (ed.), *Law and Authority in British Legal History, 1200–1900* (Cambridge, 2016), p. 85, at pp. 85–9.

popular ignorance that was in danger of fostering rebellion, which is different from the ignorance hinted at in the 1575 commission. The concern expressed there with the 'want of a perfyte writtin law, quhairupoun all jugeis may knaw how to proceid and decerne', was with the judicial ignorance that might result in a failure to provide justice or in the making of arbitrary decisions. Although the obvious problem was imperfect knowledge among the judiciary of the old books, acts of parliament and decisions of the session, a further problem was the treatment of one of the sources listed in the courts. Three years later another commission was established to address the difficulty that not all acts of parliament were 'throuchlie consultit and avisit upoun, sua that the samin at this tyme cannot be declarit be our soverane lord and estaitis of parliament to be establischit as lawis'.[21] One member of this 1578 commission was the humanist George Buchanan, who was working at the time on a book in which he complained about the transient quality of many acts passed by the Scottish parliaments (*non in perpetuum, sed in tempus facta*), and about the arbitrary quality of many decisions delivered by the lords of session (*arbitria sola sunt pro legibus*).[22] He was troubled, it seems, by the learned doctrine that statutes could lose authority by falling into desuetude, in response to which it was suggested in 1578 that the unanimous ratification of acts by the estates would serve to 'estableis the same as perpetuall lawes'.[23] It seems likely that the 'certain writtin law' envisaged in 1575 was expected to have a similar permanence.

The solutions proposed to the problems raised is the last way in which the instructions issued to the reform commissioners differed from each other. The 1426 commissioners were invited to advise on which defences to actions were 'lauchefull', and the 1450 commissioners on which acts of parliament were 'gud and concordand'.[24] It is possible that advice given by the 1426 commissioners informed several acts passed in the intervening period in relation to defences.[25] The suggestion in 1469 was that the written laws circulating in manuscript copies ought 'to be put in a volum and to be autoriyit, and the laif to be distroyit', and in 1473 that 'thare be a buke maid contenand al the lawis of this realme,

21 *Acts of the Parliaments of Scotland*, vol. 3, p. 105; Records of the Parliaments of Scotland, 1578/7/18.

22 *Rerum Scoticarum historia* (Edinburgh, 1582), f. 147v; *The History of Scotland*, 2 vols, tr. J. Aikman (Glasgow, 1827), vol. 2, p. 306.

23 J.D. Ford, 'Conciliar Authority and Equitable Jurisdiction in Early-Modern Scotland', in Godfrey, *Law and Authority in British Legal History*, p. 140, at pp. 141–50.

24 *Acts of the Parliaments of Scotland*, vol. 2, pp. 10 and 36; Records of the Parliaments of Scotland, 1426/13 and 1450/1/21.

25 H.L. MacQueen, 'Pleadable Brieves, Pleading and the Development of Scots law', (1986) 4 *Law and History Review* 403, at p. 414.

that sall remain at a place quhare the lafe may have copy, and nane uthir bukis be usit bot of the copy of it'.[26] It is possible that a collection of the old books produced in the later fifteenth century represents the work of the 1469 commission.[27] Not surprisingly, however, manuscript copies with inconsistent readings remained in circulation, and in 1566 the plan was to have a volume 'imprentit', which would become the only version with 'autoritie to be allegeit and reheirsit'.[28] Contrary to the terms of their instructions, the commissioners – of whom Balfour was especially active in his capacity as clerk register – began by preparing an edition of the acts of parliament passed since James I's time for the press.[29] Their promise to proceed to a printed edition of the old books was not fulfilled, perhaps because a rather different suggestion was then made.[30] The proposal in 1567 was that commissioners should be appointed 'to mak ane body of the civile and municipale lawis, devidit in heidis, conforme to the fassone of the law Romane'.[31] To reduce the written law *in uno volumine* or *in unum corpus* would itself have been in keeping with the emperor Justinian's approach to law reform, but the proposal now was to reorganise the law under subject headings, in the way that material had been reorganised in the *Digest* and *Code*, maybe following the order of the *Institutes*.[32] Although the proposal was 'apprevit nocht' – Balfour was certainly not issued with instructions in 1567 – the idea that the Scots might form their own *corpus iuris* resurfaced

26 *Acts of the Parliaments of Scotland*, vol. 2, pp. 97 and 105; Records of the Parliaments of Scotland, 1469/34 and 1473/7/17.

27 A. Taylor, *The Laws of Medieval Scotland: Legal Compilations from the Thirteenth and Fourteenth Centuries* (Edinburgh, 2019), pp. 117 and 388–9. If it is correct that the 1469 commissioners were supposed to reduce both the old books and more recent acts into a single volume then the point of the 1473 proposal – it appears, like the 1567 proposal, to have been no more than that – may have been to insist on consideration being given to the acts as well as the old books.

28 *Actis and Constitutiounis of the Realme of Scotland*, sig. 2v.

29 *Actis and Constitutiounis of the Realme of Scotland*, sig. 3v. The separate treatment of the acts of parliament and old laws in 1566 helps to explain why they were more clearly distinguished in the 1575 instructions.

30 An updated edition of parliamentary legislation would be produced, in response to other reform commissions (*Acts of the Parliaments of Scotland*, vol. 3, pp. 520 and 564; Records of the Parliaments of Scotland, 1587/7/156 and 1592/4/67), before an edition of the old books finally appeared in the following century.

31 *Acts of the Parliaments of Scotland*, vol. 3, p. 40; Records of the Parliaments of Scotland, 1567/12/54.

32 *Constitutio Deo auctore*, 1–2, prefaced to the *Digest*, and *Constitutiones Haec*, pr., *Summa*, 1, and *Cordi*, pr., prefaced to the *Code*. These texts also make it clear that the *Digest*, *Code* and *Institutes*, in their enacted forms, were to be the only sources that could be cited authoritatively before the emperor's judges. See too n. 16 above.

in the instruction issued to the 1575 commissioners to 'draw the forme of the body of oure lawis'. In 1567 the thinking appears to have been that Scots law consisted partly of the civil law (*ius commune*) and partly of the municipal law (*ius proprium*), and that both elements would have to be brought together in any comprehensive restatement of the existing law. By 1575 the thinking was that a 'perfyte writtin law' could be produced by reorganising material found in the old books of law, acts of parliament and decisions of the session.[33] The commissioners were also invited to advise on 'thay thingis that wer meit and convenient to be statute', and the expectation may have been that in doing so they would draw upon their knowledge of the civil law, but there is an obvious difference between regarding the civil law as an integral part of the law of Scotland and regarding it as an extraneous source from which rules and concepts might be borrowed in the framing of legislation. The failure to mention the civil law in the 1575 instructions would have pleased Buchanan.[34]

2 The Compilation of Balfour's *Practicks*

It would appear, then, that the consensus obtaining in 1931 that the composition of Balfour's *Practicks* was inspired by the author's membership of the 1575 commission has a great deal to recommend it, and that there is much less reason to associate his work either with the 1566 commission, which was meant to result in the printing of definitive editions of the old books and later legislation, or with the commission proposed in 1567, which was meant to integrate the local sources of Scots law with the sources studied in the continental law schools. In an article published in 1937 John Buchanan drew attention to some striking similarities between the printed *Practicks* and a 'digest' of the old books of law, in which excerpts were organised under subject headings.[35] Two manuscript copies of the digest are known to have survived.[36] Buchanan

33 On the use of the word 'perfyte' to signify completeness see W. Craigie, A.J. Aitken, J.A.C. Stevenson, H.D. Watson, and M.G. Dareau (eds), *A Dictionary of the Older Scottish Tongue from the Twelfth Century to the End of the Seventeenth*, 12 vols (Chicago, London and Aberdeen, 1931–2002), vol. 5, pp. 420–2.

34 Ford, 'Conciliar Authority and Equitable Jurisdiction in Early-Modern Scotland', pp. 154–5. It may seem odd for Buchanan, generally seen as a proponent of popular sovereignty, to have insisted that law should be imposed by a legislator, but the legal concept of sovereignty is not the same thing as the political concept, and Buchanan had some notion of popular involvement in the legislative process, which is considered in the essay cited.

35 'The MSS of *Regiam maiestatem*', (1937) 49 *Juridical Review* 217, at pp. 220–1.

36 NLS, Adv. MS 25.4.11, ff. 10r-92v, and BL, Add. MS 48050, ff. 1–106.

pointed out that the Latin excerpts of which the digest mostly consists are similar in content to excerpts found in the *Practicks*, that the vernacular excerpts the digest also contains are mostly identical with those found in the *Practicks*, and that the books from which the excerpts were taken are cited in the same way in the digest as in the *Practicks*. He also observed that several excerpts in the digest could not be found in similar terms in any other manuscript copy of the old books, yet could be found in similar terms in the first printed edition, seen through the press in 1609 by Sir John Skene of Curriehill.[37] In the early seventeenth century it was believed that the task of drafting a 'perfyte writtin law' had been assigned in 1575 not only to Balfour especially, but also to Skene.[38] Although Skene was not a member of the commission, a pension was granted to him in 1577 to compensate for his loss of earnings as an advocate while engaged in the commission's business.[39] He had been admitted to the bar on 19 March 1575, a fortnight after the commission was appointed, and on 14 June 1575 he had embarked on a careful reading of a copy of the old books acquired from one of his brothers.[40] It was feared in 1577 that Skene might continue to be absorbed in the work of the commission for 'ane lairge space heirefter', and his pension was renewed in 1578 and 1579, though never again afterwards.[41] It could be that the digest discovered by Buchanan was written during the period of Skene's involvement with the commission, between 1575 and 1579, but it could have been written before then, since the latest date it contains is 9 March 1556, and its composition could possibly have been connected with the idea circulating in 1567 that the law of Scotland should be digested along Roman lines.[42] Whenever it was composed, the digest did not simply contain the material from the old books found in the *Practicks*. For example, a section about procurators reorganised excerpts from a series of titles in *Regiam maiestatem*, which was not specifically identified, and interspersed among

37 In McNeill, 'Introduction', p. lviii, NLS, Adv. MS 25.4.11 is said to incorporate material 'a *Skeen* collectis', and BL, Add. MS 48050 to have been found 'among the papers of Skene', but why is not immediately apparent from examination of the manuscripts themselves, nor from anything said about the latter copy in W. Nicholson, *The English, Scotch and Irish Historical Libraries* (London, 1736), pt 2, p. 99, cited by McNeill.

38 David Hume of Godscroft, *The History of the Houses of Douglas and Angus* (Edinburgh, 1644), p. 358; David Calderwood, *The History of the Kirk of Scotland*, 8 vols, ed. D. Laing (Edinburgh, 1842–9), vol. 3, pp. 575–6.

39 *Registrum secreti sigilli regum Scotorum: The Register of the Privy Seal of Scotland*, 7 vols, ed. M. Livingston, G. Donaldson, J. Beveridge and D.H. Fleming (Edinburgh, 1908–66), vol. 7, pp. 159–60.

40 NRS, CS1/2/2, f. 4r; Taylor, *Laws of Medieval Scotland*, pp. 52–3.

41 *Registrum secreti sigilli regum Scotorum*, vol. 7, pp. 243–4 and 291–2.

42 NLS, Adv. MS 25.4.11, f. 67, and BL, Add. MS 48050, ff. 72v-3r.

them excerpts from (or references to) four other sources, which were specifically identified – it seems clear that *Regiam maiestatem* was used as the basis of the compilation.[43] In the corresponding title of the *Practicks*, although it has some striking similarities with the section of the digest, not all the excerpts from *Regiam maiestatem* were included, and excerpts from (or references to) three further sources were added.[44]

Three sources of information were used in the compilation of the *Practicks*. It is scarcely surprising that in turning to the acts of parliament passed since James I's accession to the throne, Balfour – and anyone who was assisting him – relied on the edition printed in 1566. For example, a paragraph headed 'Procuratouris sould be gevin to puir folk' begins with a reference to '*Jac.* 1. *fol.* 8. *act.* 49. 12 *Mart.* 1424. *in fine*', inserting the number of the folio on which the passage cited was printed into a conventional statement of the act's numerical identifier and the date on which it was passed.[45] As McNeill remarked in 1962, in the first hundred and thirty pages of the printed version of the *Practicks* the acts of parliament cited are reproduced fully, not merely referred to in their already printed form.[46] At one place an act is reproduced in an abbreviated form, with a note added at the end reading: '*Vid. latius in lib. impresso*'.[47] An almost identical phrase appears shortly after the last passage in which an act is reproduced fully, although it makes less sense here:

> Divers ordinances maid anent beggaris. *Vide in libro impresso. Ja.* VI. *fol.* 5. *act.* 7. 20 *Octob.* 1579. *Ja.* VI. *parl.* 10. *c.* 16. 10 *Decemb.* 1585. *Ja.* VI. *parl.* 12. *c.* 147. 5 *Junii*, 1592. *Ja.* VI. *parl.* 15. *c.* 288. 19 *Decemb.* 1597.[48]

Unless attention was being drawn to acts omitted from the list provided, the instruction to see the printed book was misleading, for all the acts listed were passed after 1566, and most after Balfour had died. To some extent at least, this passage must have been written by somebody else. In fact, while a move from the full reproduction to the mere citation of acts can be found in the surviving manuscripts of the 'Practicks' as well, it occurs at different places in different copies.[49]

---

43 NLS, Adv. MS 25.4.11, f. 48, and BL, Add. MS 48050, ff. 47v-8r.

44 *Practicks of Sir James Balfour of Pittendreich*, vol. 2, pp. 297–301.

45 *Practicks of Sir James Balfour of Pittendreich*, vol. 2, p. 299; *Actis and Constitutiounis of the Realme of Scotland*, ff. 7v-8r.

46 McNeill, 'Introduction', pp. xxxiii and lx–lxi.

47 *Practicks of Sir James Balfour of Pittendreich*, vol. 1, p. 64.

48 *Practicks of Sir James Balfour of Pittendreich*, vol. 1, pp. 131–2.

49 Something will be said about the earliest manuscripts shortly.

If a decision not to waste further time and effort in copying acts already available in print was made by copyists, it may not always have been at the same point in the transcription process. Another possibility is that Balfour himself decided not to turn back into manuscript form material that had been stabilised in print, but this would not explain why some acts are reproduced fully in all the known versions of his book, or why the transition to bare citations is made at different places in different versions. There was, of course, no printed version of the old books to which reference could have been made in a similar style, and instead specific copies were cited, as they eventually would be in Skene's edition.[50] No printed reports of the decisions of the session were available either, instead of which use was made of a manuscript compendium referred to as the *Registrum*, which no longer survives. It evidently consisted of two volumes, one containing cases decided between 1469 and 1570, the other cases decided between 1540 and 1577. Although it was once supposed that the arrangement was thematic, as in the digest of the old books, William Gordon argued in two important essays that it was primarily chronological, like the printed edition of the acts of parliament.[51] Some use seems to have been made in the composition of the *Registrum* of reports written by judges, but most of the cases covered could only have been found in the records of the court. In the title of the *Practicks* on procurators, for example, ten decisions are noted, one of which was reported by John Sinclair, and another by Sir Richard Maitland of Lethington, but most of which were in fact decided before Sinclair started to compose the earliest collection of reports.[52] One of the earlier decisions was summed up in the following statement: 'ane procuratorie or mandate is of nane avail gif the constituent happinis to deceis *re integra*, for in that cais the mandate and powar expyris and endis be deceis of the maker thairof'.[53] It is quite clear from the record of the case in the register of acts and decreets of the lords of council and session that it had been decided on the basis of the civil law rule that *mandatum morte mandatoris revocatur*, yet the statement of

50 The manuscripts tended to be labelled in the same way in Balfour's book and Skene's edition, and also in the digest discovered by John Buchanan, who provided as an example the frequent references in all three sources to the mysterious *Liber Sconensis*.

51 W.M. Gordon, *Roman Law, Scots Law and Legal History: Selected Essays* (Edinburgh, 2007), pp. 267–96.

52 *Practicks of Sir James Balfour of Pittendreich*, vol. 2, pp. 298–301; Sinclair's Practicks, ed. A. Murray and G. Dolezalek (www.home.uni-leipzig.de/jurarom/scotland/dat/sinclair.html), n. 189; *The Practiques of Sir Richard Maitland of Lethington*, ed. R. Sutherland (Edinburgh, 2007), pp. 33–4.

53 *Practicks of Sir James Balfour of Pittendreich*, vol. 2, p. 301.

the decision was typical in giving the impression that the authority for the rule in Scots law was the decision of the court.[54]

While the use made of the digest of the old books, the edition of the acts of parliament and the *Registrum* of decisions was familiar by the time the Stair Society published its edition of the *Practicks*, a significant breakthrough in understanding has been achieved since then in another of the society's publications. In his monumental census of Scottish legal manuscripts Gero Dolezalek has drawn attention to two copies of a digest of the old books written entirely in the vernacular.[55] Both copies appear to have been made during the sixteenth century.[56] The wording of the excerpts in this Scots digest is almost identical with the wording found in the *Practicks*, and, unlike the Latin digest, the Scots digest contains most of the excerpts found in the *Practicks*, arranged in much the same order. One of the manuscripts contains two further items. The first is a list of legal topics, arranged alphabetically, and headed 'Ane conformitie of the titillis of *Regiam maiestatem*, actis of parliament and of the practisie'.[57] Underneath the letter 'P', for example, the following entry appears: 'Procuratoures M 4.5. *Vid.* procuratouris A. *Vid.* advocatis'.[58] The fifth title of the fourth of six books into which the Scots digest was divided is headed 'Of procuratouris'. If 'M' represented the digest of *Regiam maiestatem* and the rest of the old books, 'A' presumably represented an index or (less probably) a rearrangement of the acts of parliament.[59] To judge from other entries in the list, the example reproduced ought to have ended with 'P', presumably representing the 'practicks' noted in the *Registrum* or – if its arrangement was mostly chronological – an index or (again less probably) a rearrangement of the decisions under subject headings. Dolezalek's suggestion that the list served as a guide to the amalgamation of the three sorts of material eventually

54 NRS, CS6/2, f. 228; D.2.1.6 and 17.2.26.pr; C.4.35.15; J.3.26.10; *Regulae iuris tam civilis quam canonici* (Lyons, 1565), p. 463. Although authority was also provided here by a reference to one of the old books, the other summaries of decisions gave the same impression of laying down binding rules.

55 *Scotland under Jus Commune: Census of Manuscripts of Legal Literature in Scotland, Mainly between 1500 and 1660*, 3 vols (Edinburgh, 2010), vol. 3, pp. 86–104 and 207–8; see too p. 258.

56 NRS, GD112/71/5, ff. 5–129r, and EUL, La. III 381a, pp. 1–283.

57 NRS, GD112/71/5, ff. 1–3r.

58 NRS, GD112/71/5, f. 2v.

59 The old books were sometimes known as the 'law of the majestie', and the Scots digest is headed 'The lawis of *Regiam maiestatem*, proffitable for the commounweill of this realme, selectit and gadderit in ane competent methode and faithfullie translatit in Inglische'. An index was not included in the *Actis and Constitutiounis of the Realme of Scotland*.

combined in the *Practicks* seems more than plausible. The other item in one of the manuscripts is a scheme for the organisation of the titles of a legal work into six books.[60] The scheme is not identical with the arrangement of the Scots digest, and is closer to the arrangement of the *Practicks*, except that the *Practicks* in its printed form lacks a division into books.[61] For example, the first ten titles of the fourth book of the new scheme may be compared as follows with titles found in the other versions – including the Latin digest, which was arranged in seven books.

Latin digest	Scots digest	New scheme	Practicks
4.1 judgments	4.1 judgments	4.1 parliament	70 parliament
4.2 judges	4.2 courts	4.2 session	71 session
4.3 courts	4.3 pursuer	4.3 courts	72 courts
4.4 defender	4.4 defender	4.4 judges	73 judges
4.5 bail	4.5 procurators	4.5 assise	74 ambassadors
4.6 procurators	4.6 judges	4.6 pursuer	75 assise
4.7 judge	4.7 assise	4.7 defender	76 regality
4.8 attachments	4.8 summons	4.8 procurators	77 pursuer
4.9 summons	4.9 assoilzie	4.9 attachments	78 defender
4.10 excuses	4.10 libel	4.10 summons	79 procurators

It takes no excess of imagination to detect a gradual movement from the Latin digest through the Scots digest and the new scheme proposed towards the arrangement finally adopted in the *Practicks*. The manuscripts discovered by Dolezalek tend to confirm that the old books were treated as a foundation for the compilation, that their contents were reorganised thematically (with *Regiam maiestatem* treated as the most basic text), and that material drawn from the acts of parliament and decisions of the session was later added to the excerpts already taken from the old books.

The Scots digest of the old books opens with a preface found in *Regiam maiestatem* – the source, of course, of that book's title – but instead of crediting

60 NRS, GD112/71/5, ff. 3r-4.

61 There are in fact some manuscripts of the 'Practicks' in which the titles are divided into books. Whether this resulted from the later intervention of copyists hardly matters for present purposes.

David I with responsibility for the book's composition, it contains the following passage.[62]

> As concerning the lawis off this realme, it is verray difficle in thir our dayis to comprehend and put thame all in wreit, pairtlie throw the ignorance off the writaris thairof, and pairtlie throw the confusit multitude off the lawis thameselff. Nevirtheles, thair is sum statutis and ordinanceis commounlie usit and observit in judgment, and yit oft tymis abusit throw ignorance, the quhilk, as appeiris to me withtout arrogancie or obsurdite, may be collectit and put in wreit. And thairfoir, for the helpe off the reidaris memorie, at command and charge off ane maist excellent, reverint prince and oure soverane, King James the sext, witht advyse off the richt mychtie lord James, erle off Mortoun, lord off Dalkeithe, regent for the tyme to his hienes, his realme and leigis, I have collectit, gadderit togidder and put in wreit all and sindrie the godlie and profitable lawis and constitutionis maid, usit and practisit in tyme off the regne off our soverane lord and off his predecessouris kingis off Scotland, in ane commodius and guid forme off method, and in vulgar and popular language, using sumtymes willinglie sic termis and wordis as is commounlie usit in judgment, to the effect the same may be thairby mair familiar and the bettar knawin to all oure soverane lordis liegis and pepill off his realme.[63]

In some ways this passage may seem more reminiscent of the instructions drafted in 1566 or 1567 than those issued in 1575, yet the earl of Morton had not become regent until 1572, and it was the 1575 commission for which he was given credit.[64] He is not mentioned in versions of the preface included in the Latin digest and some manuscript copies of the 'Practicks', nor is any preface included in the printed edition.[65] As Morton is said to have been regent 'for the tyme', the passage appears to have been written after his removal from that office on 8 March 1578, for although he recovered control of the royal administration a few months later, he did not regain the title 'regent'.[66] In May

62 The opening words 'Imperatoriam maiestatem' were replaced with 'Regiam maiestatem'. Only later were the kings of Scotland declared to be emperors in their own realm.

63 NRS, GD112/71/5, f. 5r.

64 Morton's responsibility for the 1575 commission was recognised in the historical works cited in n. 39 above, and receives support from the sources cited in nn. 8, 40 and 42.

65 The preface in the Latin digest simply omits the passage about David I, while some manuscript copies have a preface, but making an incoherent reference to David I.

66 G.R. Hewitt, *Scotland under Morton, 1572–80* (Edinburgh, 1982), pp. 44–51 and 59–60.

1579 Morton turned against Balfour, forcing him into exile in France, and they remained implacable foes until Morton's execution in 1581.[67] It has long been supposed that work on the *Practicks* was suspended while Balfour was abroad, and the failure to renew Skene's pension after 26 January 1579 supports this.[68] By the end of 1580 Balfour had returned quietly to Scotland, where he was expected to assist in engineering Morton's final downfall.[69] Until his death in the second half of 1583 Balfour remained at Burleigh Castle, near Loch Leven, where work was evidently resumed on the *Practicks*.[70] In the early seventeenth century Habakkuk Bisset recalled that he and another scribe had assisted Balfour there in 1582 and 1583, and made reference to

> Balfouris Practikis, quhereof there is sum copies writtin be me in my Lord Curriehill or his brother Mr Johnis handis. Bot gif the principall writtin be me mycht be had, the samin is maist correct, quhilk is reported to have bene in the Erle Ergyle or Lord Burlies handis in keiping, quhairof the maist pairt is of the handwreit of me, the authoure heirof.[71]

It seems clear that by the end of Balfour's life a 'principall' copy existed of the work already known as 'Balfouris Practikis', mostly written by Bisset during his period of employment at Burleigh. While an earlier version could have existed, the better reconstruction of events may be that work on the project had reached the stage evidenced in the manuscripts discovered by Dolezalek when Balfour departed for France, and that the materials he and his assistants had been gathering and organising were not assembled together into the 'Practicks' until after his return.[72] Other copies were also made by Bisset, and that some of these were in the hands of Skene's descendants suggests that he may also have become involved in the project again. In fact, the only surviving copy that is

67 McNeill, 'Introduction', pp. xxvii–viii.

68 However, Gordon, *Roman Law, Scots Law and Legal History*, p. 286, points out that it is probably an error to believe that the latest cases cited from the *Registrum* were dated in the same year.

69 *Calendar of State Papers Relating to Scotland and Mary, Queen of Scots, 1547–1603*, 13 vols, ed. J. Bain, W.K. Boyd, H.W. Meikle, A.I. Cameron, M.S. Giuseppi and J.D. Mackie (Edinburgh, 1898–1969), vol. 5, pp. 387 and 586–7.

70 McNeill, 'Introduction', pp. xxx–i.

71 *Habakkuk Bisset's Rolment of Courtis*, 3 vols, ed. P.J. Hamilton-Grierson (Edinburgh, 1922–6), vol. 2, p. 275.

72 If the preface in the Scots digest, crediting the former regent with the project, is unlikely to have been written before March 1578, it is also unlikely to have been written after May 1579.

known with certainty to have been written before the end of the sixteenth century concludes with an early version of Skene's legal dictionary, *De verborum significatione*.[73] The manuscript was written between 1589 and 1593 by Thomas Newbie, 'pro Alexandro Hay', perhaps the Alexander Hay who was the clerk register and a lord of session between 1579 and 1594.[74]

3 The Compilation of Balfour's 'Sea Lawis'

By the time the principal copy was written during the last year and a half of Balfour's life, he had gone some way towards fulfilling the instructions issued to the 1575 commissioners. He and Skene (and possibly other assistants) had examined the old books, acts of parliament and decisions of the session, had organised excerpts from, references to and notes of these sources under subject headings, and had formed the materials assembled into a body based on *Regiam maiestatem*, which had itself followed the broad pattern of Justinian's *Institutes* by dealing in order with persons, things and actions.[75] That a book attributed to Balfour was not presented to parliament to be 'ratifiit and establissit' is scarcely surprising, for he was *persona non grata* with the king, who believed – with good reason – that he had been complicit in the murder of Lord Darnley.[76] Furthermore, the instructions issued in 1575 had not been fulfilled fully, for although the book dealt with 'that quhilk is alreddy statute', it did not deal with 'thay thingis that wer meit and convenient to be statute'. A possible explanation for the shortcoming is the natural scepticism of an experienced judge about the possibility of producing a code of law so perfect that it would

73 NLS, Adv. MS 24.2.4b, ff. 279–90. For other copies that could possibly have been written during the sixteenth century see Dolezalek, *Scotland under Jus Commune*, vol. 2, pp. 212–13, and vol. 3, pp. 248–9 and 250–1. NLS, Adv. MS 24.2.4b, cannot have been the principal copy, as suggested in McNeill, 'Introduction', pp. xxxv, since it contains references to sources dated after Balfour's death, including those listed at n. 49 above.

74 A.J.G. Mackay, 'Who Wrote *Balfour's Practicks*?', (1899) 13 *Scottish Antiquary* 1, at pp. 2–3, pointed out correctly that it is mistaken to assume that the copy was made in 1593, which may have been the date on which someone else acquired the manuscript from Hay. For the *terminus a quo* see Dolezalek, *Scotland under Jus Commune*, vol. 2, pp. 214–15.

75 A. Watson, *Legal Transplants: An Approach to Comparative Law* (Athens, GA, 1993), pp. 36–7. While it may be possible to discern a closer parallel between the arrangement of the *Institutes* and the *Practicks*, it was clearly in *Regiam maiestatem* that 'the forme of the body of our lawis' was found, and no great effort was made to have material arranged under the 'heidis' familiar from 'the law Romane', as might have assisted amalgamation.

76 *Acts of the Parliaments of Scotland*, vol. 3, p. 89; Records of the Parliaments of Scotland, A1575/3/7; *Calendar of State Papers Relating to Scotland*, vol. 5, pp. 587, 610 and 618.

dictate the decision of every future case. The prospect that has beguiled many legislators may also have beguiled scholars like George Buchanan, but it is less likely to have taken in a former commissary and president of the session. Another explanation may be that the instructions issued in 1575 delivered a mixed message. While the aim may have been to prevent the decisions of the judges from being regarded as the only laws available (*arbitria sola sunt pro legibus*) – in other words, to prevent judges from being a law unto themselves – it might well have been concluded from the mention of the 'decisionis befoir the sessioun' as something comparable to the 'bukis of the law' and 'actis of parliament' that they were to be regarded as a kind of *leges* or 'writtin law'.[77] Since the experience in the late 1570s had been that the lords of session were continuing to deliver significant decisions, worthy of inclusion in the *Registrum*, the expectation in the early 1580s may well have been that the decisions of the lords of session would remain a dynamic source of legal development in the future.[78] That the more innovative decisions might have seemed arbitrary to lay people like Buchanan need not have bothered Balfour, who had clearly moved away from the concern with educating the judiciary, and reverted to the earlier concern with educating the people of Scotland generally, by the time the preface to the Scots digest was written.[79] Why he had moved in this direction must be left aside for further consideration elsewhere.[80] The question to be answered here is whether there is good reason to suppose that the

77 When Skene appended 'Ane admonition to the reader tuiching the buikes conteinand the lawes of this realme' to the enlarged version of his *De verborum significatione* (Edinburgh, 1597), sig. S6r, he included not only the old books and acts of parliament but also the 'decreetes given be the lords of the session and councell'.

78 The moment at which Balfour decided not to produce a perfect statement of the law for enactment might have been an obvious time for him to decide not to reproduce the acts of parliament fully, but it would still need to be explained why some acts are reproduced fully in all versions of his book, and not the same acts in every version.

79 Alternatives to Buchanan's perspective are identified in Ford, 'Conciliar Authority and Equitable Jurisdiction in Early-Modern Scotland', though Balfour may at least have shared Buchanan's concern about acts falling into desuetude. The decision to translate the Latin excerpts from the old books into Scots could have been connected with this move – Skene was to produce a Scots edition of the old books for lay readers, as well as a Latin edition for lawyers – although it may always have been expected that a draft code would be produced in the vernacular.

80 It is suggested in the seventh essay in this collection that Balfour's own education may have inclined him to move in this direction. Ironically, his inclinations also derived ultimately from the study of the humanities.

collection of 'sea lawis' was made after the 'Practicks' was completed, and not by Balfour himself.[81]

To start with, it is important to note that material on maritime law is included in what has been called the Latin digest, although in one of the exceptional passages written mostly in the vernacular.[82] The first of the seven books into which that digest was divided ended with a long series of titles based on the *Leges burgorum*, followed by two more based on the *Statuta gildae* and *Iter camerarii*, and finally a title headed 'Leges navium'. This final title consisted mostly of material drawn from a source cited as 'Schiplawis', meaning the *Rôles d'Oléron*, as translated in many collections of the old books.[83] The material in the digest may be compared with the edition of the 'Schiplawis' prepared for the Stair Society by Edda Frankot.

Article number in Frankot's edition	Citation in the Latin digest	Paragraph number in the Latin digest
1	c. 16 et c. 26	3
2	c. 17 et 27	4
3	c. 18 et c. 28	16
4	c. 19	17
5	c. 20 et c. 30	7
6	c. 21 et c. 31	8
7	c. 22 et c. 33	9
8	c. 23 et c. 34	18
9	c. 24 et c. 35	19
10	c. 25 et c. 36	21
11	c. 4 et c. 37	20
12	c. 5	10
13	c. 6	unnumbered

81 There is certainly no good reason to suppose that the main body of the *Practicks* was anything other than the final version of the book Balfour had been working on. That it contains references to specific copies of the old books need not mean that it was only ever intended 'to circulate within a small group of persons who had access to these particular volumes' (Dolezalek, *Scotland under Jus Commune*, vol. 3, p. 94). Skene, after all, referred to specific copies in the same way in his printed edition of the old books. Also, that it contains references to acts of parliament and other sources dated after 1583 tells us something about the practices of copyists, not the author's intentions.

82 NLS, Adv. MS 25.4.11, ff. 32v-34, and BL, Add. MS 48050, ff. 28–30v.

83 E.B.I. Frankot, 'The Scottish Translations of the *Rôles d'Oléron*: Edition and Commentary', in A.M. Godfrey (ed.), *Stair Society: Miscellany Eight* (Edinburgh, 2020), p. 13.

Article number in Frankot's edition	Citation in the Latin digest	Paragraph number in the Latin digest
14	c. 12 et c. 39	1
15	c. 25 in fine et c. 38	22
16	c. 13 et c. 40	23
17	c. 2 et 41	5
18	c. 8 et c. 42	12
19	c. 9	14
20	c. 10 prior eius pars	15
21	c. iv parte post et c. 44	6
22	c. 14 et c. 47	13
23	c. 14 et c. 45	2
24	c. 11 et c. 46	11

The copy of the *Rôles d'Oléron* used in the compilation of the digest apparently ran through the twenty-four articles of the original version twice, which was not unusual, with the articles sometimes rearranged, which again was not unusual, although no surviving copy has exactly the same arrangement. The second run followed the pattern of the original version, subject to a few adjustments, while the first presented the last fourteen articles before the first ten, and jumbled up the last fourteen.[84] All twenty-four articles were reproduced in the digest, but in another rearrangement, and with three excerpts added in Latin from other sources. One was attributed to the *Leges forestarum*, another both to the *Leges forestarum* and to the *Liber de iudicibus*, and the third to the *Leges burgorum*, and all three passages can indeed be found in these three sources in at least one collection of the old books.[85] The provision extracted from the *Leges burgorum* was concerned with the jurisdiction of the bailie courts over cases arising from shipping. It was placed at the end of the title and provides an explanation for the placing of the title on maritime law after the other titles relating to the law administered in the burghs.

A title headed 'Schiplawis' appears at the same place in the Scots digest.[86] Moreover, the excerpts found in the Latin digest all appear again in the

84 The arrangement seems to have been: c. 1 blank – *art. 17* – c. 3 blank – *arts 11–13* – c. 7 blank – *arts 18–20, 24, 14, 16, 22* – c. 15 blank – *arts. 1–10, arts 1–3* – c. 29 blank – *arts 5–6* – c. 32 blank – *arts 7–9* – c. 35 blank – *arts 10–18* – c. 43 blank – *arts 21, 23–4 and 22.*

85 NLS, Adv. MS 25.4.12, ff. 135v, 181v, 242v and 250v–1r.

86 NRS, GD112/71/5, ff. 38v-42r, and EUL, La. III 381a, pp. 74–83. While the heading 'Liber secundus' appears in the former copy before the titles based on the *Leges burgorum*,

Scots digest, and in basically the same order. Obviously, the excerpts in Latin were translated into Scots, but two less obvious alterations were also made. First, the vernacular excerpts were reworded, in a way that tended to render them more intelligible. Secondly, use was made of a new source, cited as the *Liber Kyntoris*. At two places a reference to the new source was added before the existing reference to the 'Schiplawis', and at two more a reference to the new source took the place of an earlier reference to the 'Schiplawis'. In all these places the wording of the excerpt differed markedly from the wording of the corresponding excerpts in the Latin digest. At three further places the *Liber Kyntoris* was cited at the end of excerpts that do not appear in the Latin digest.[87] These three excerpts do not correspond to articles in the original version of the *Rôles d'Oléron*, but they do correspond to articles added to the original twenty-four in a version that circulated in France.[88] The seven citations can be compared with a modern edition of this version as follows.[89]

Citation in the Scots digest	Article number in the French version	Citation in the Latin digest
Kyntor. c. 5	5	c. 20 et c. 30
Kyntor. c. 14	12	c. 12 et c. 39
Kyntor. c. 22	22	[c. 14 et c. 47]
Kyntor. c. 24	25	
Kyntor. c. 25	27	
Kyntor. c. 25	26	
Kyntor. c. 45	4	[c. 18 et c. 28]

As the editor of the French version notes, the arrangement of its articles varied to some extent from copy to copy. The repetition of 'c. 25' in the Scots digest

Dolezalek, *Scotland under Jus Commune*, vol. 3, pp. 95–6, is probably correct in suggesting that this was an error. For present purposes, what matters is that the title on maritime law is placed at the end of the sequence of titles on the law administered in the burghs.

87 In addition, at the end of the title, after the excerpt from the *Leges burgorum*, there is a note about, rather than an excerpt of, a provision relating to 'cap. 6', ending: '*vid.* Schipl. c. 6 et *Lib. Kyntor.* c. 13'. The significance of the note is far from clear.

88 *Collection de lois maritimes antérieures au XVIIIe siècle*, 6 vols, ed. J.M. Pardessus (Paris, 1828–45), vol. 1, pp. 340–2.

89 The citations in square brackets are those omitted from the Scots digest.

was clearly an error, and there seem to have been others.[90] Nevertheless, the broad correspondence between the figures in the first two columns above (in contrast to those in the third) can leave little room for doubt that the compilers of the Scots digest found in the *Liber Kyntoris* either the longer French version of the *Rôles d'Oléron*, or a translation of that version into Scots.[91] They incorporated into the new digest three provisions that had not appeared in the Latin digest since they were not part of the version of the *Rôles d'Oléron* included in collections of the old books.[92] They replaced two provisions already found in the old books with the corresponding provisions found in the *Liber Kyntoris*. They also added references to the provisions found in that book in amending the wording of two other excerpts from the original version. If it was a translation they found then it is possible that they adopted its readings for all their excerpts from the *Rôles d'Oléron*, retaining the references to the 'Schiplawis' found in the Latin digest unless the new wording differed markedly from the old.

The following entry appears in 'Ane conformitie of the titillis of *Regiam maiestatem*, actis of parliament and of the practisie', found in one of the manuscripts containing the Scots digest.

> Schiplawis M 1, *tit. ult. Vid.* ferriares A. *Vid.* lettir off mark A. *Vid.* schippis A. *Vid.* schiplawis P. flud mark P.[93]

All the excerpts included in the title headed 'Schiplawis' in the Scots digest can also be found in the appendix on 'sea lawis' attached to the printed edition of the *Practicks*, and in virtually identical terms.[94] The same appendix contains citations of acts of parliament, listed under the subheadings 'Anent ferriaris', 'Anent letter of mark' and 'Of the makand of shippis', together with summaries

90 In the corresponding paragraphs of the *Practicks*, the second 'c. 25' reference is replaced with 'c. 26', and the reference to 'c. 45' is replaced with 'c. 4'. On the other hand, 'c. 14' stays the same. The explanation appears to be that art. 12 in Pardessus' edition was not actually the provision cited. Although it deals with the same subject as the excerpt labelled 'Kyntor. c. 14' in the Scots digest and the *Practicks*, it differs in substance, and resembles a separate paragraph also included in other copies of the French version (*Alexander King's Treatise on Maritime Law*, ed. J.D. Ford (Edinburgh, 2018), pp. 378–81).

91 Whether more than the first twenty-six or twenty-seven articles of the French version were included is by no means certain.

92 Although variable in their contents, these collections always focused on the original twenty-four articles.

93 NRS, GD112/71/5, f. 2v. That 'Schiplawis M' is identified as the last title of the first book of the Scots digest supports the suggestion mentioned in n. 87 above.

94 *Practicks of Sir James Balfour of Pittendreich*, vol. 2, pp. 614–29.

of two decisions of the session relating to topics covered in excerpts from the 'Schiplawis', and three more presented under the subheading 'Anent the flude mark'.[95] All of this is equally true of the appendix attached to the copy of the 'Practicks' written by Thomas Newbie, which is very similar to the printed version, except that its lists of statutes often omit items included in the printed lists, or add items not included in those lists, and do not always appear under the same subheadings.[96] The scheme for the new organisation of the titles found in one copy of the Scots digest still proposed a sequence of titles on the laws administered in the burghs, but it no longer proposed the inclusion of a title on maritime law at the end of the sequence.[97] Actually, a title on maritime law appeared nowhere in the scheme. Instead, a note was added at the end reading as follows.

> *Postremum memorandum*: off the forrest lawis, sea lawis and bordoure lawis, *item*, off beggaris, off hostellaris and off regalletie, in quhat buik and title thai salbe placet.[98]

As far as the new organisation was concerned, McNeill was quite correct that the material on maritime law 'did not fit into the scheme', yet it does not follow that the 'sea lawis' appendix must have been 'added after the completion of the bulk of the work'.[99] It is evident both from the Latin and Scots digests and from the 'conformitie of the titillis' that the treatment of maritime law eventually presented as an appendix first took shape as an integral part of the 'Practicks'. By the time the new organisation was proposed, doubts were emerging about where it should be fitted into the scheme, although it was still expected that it would be fitted in somewhere. At some point it was decided to move it to the end of the 'Practicks' as an appendix, which is not the same thing as fashioning

95 There is a sixth case summary in the passage just cited, which takes up the first half of the appendix. It relates to the use of letters of marque, and follows the reference to an act of parliament on that subject.

96 NLS, Adv. MS 24.2.4b, ff. 258-64r. The variations in the lists of statutes alone add weight to the impression that it was the copyists who decided to replace full transcriptions of acts of parliament with bare citations of the edition printed in 1566.

97 NRS, GD112/71/5, f. 3r.

98 NRS, GD112/71/5, f. 4v.

99 McNeill, 'Introduction', p. lxiii. Nor, for that matter, does the appendix on 'sea lawis' contain material drawn from sources dated after 1583. The example given by McNeill was 'the injunctions to commissaries of 1610'. In Newbie's manuscript there is an appendix concerned with the commissaries, but it contains only the instructions issued in 1563. The same is true, incidentally, of NLS, Adv. MS 24.2.4b, which is not identical with the printed edition, as has been suggested.

material left over into an entirely new appendix. This final move remains to be considered.

4 The Conception of Balfour's 'Sea Lawis'

Doubts about the best place to include the treatment of maritime law may have arisen initially from a perusal of the *Liber Kyntoris*. It is notable that the heading given to the appendix begins by talking about materials being 'collected furth of the actis of parliament, the practiques, the lawis of Oleron', making no mention of 'the bukis of the law'.[100] The discovery of the origins of the 'Schiplawis' – which would be omitted from Skene's editions of the old books – seems to have raised doubts about their authenticity, and it could have been from the *Liber Kyntoris* that Balfour and his assistants made the discovery.[101] If their continuing expectation that their title on maritime law could be fitted into the proposed reorganisation suggests rather that they had not yet made the discovery when that scheme was worked out, the *Liber Kyntoris* must at least have made it clear that the 'Schiplawis' was connected with a larger body of material on maritime law, some of which was not of local origin. In the appendix another reference to the *Liber Kyntoris* was added to an excerpt already taken from the 'Schiplawis'.[102] Two paragraphs absent from the Latin and Scots digests were introduced, closing with references to 'Kintor. pag. 31. art. 6' and 'Kintor. pag. 31. art. 9'.[103] Alternative translations or paraphrases of the provisions excerpted here appeared in a collection of materials on maritime law assembled in the early seventeenth century by Habakkuk Bisset, who attributed them to an edict registered at the *parlement* of Rouen in 1557.[104] As the edict was in fact issued by Francis I in 1555, it is revealing that the heading given to the 'sea lawis' appendix also refers to an edict of 1557. At a later

100 *Practicks of Sir James Balfour of Pittendreich*, vol. 2, p. 614; *Acts of the Parliaments of Scotland*, vol. 3, p. 89; Records of the Parliaments of Scotland, A1575/3/7.

101 The 'Schiplawis' was also omitted from the list of sources of written law at the end of Skene's *De verborum significatione*.

102 The excerpt ended in the appendix with 'Shiplawis c. 5. Kintor. c. 12', which confirms that the twelfth article in the *Liber Kyntoris* corresponded to the twelfth article in the French version (*cf.* n. 91 above).

103 *Practicks of Sir James Balfour of Pittendreich*, vol. 2, pp. 636 and 638.

104 *Habakkuk Bisset's Rolment of Courtis*, vol. 2, pp. 235–9. The edict is not reproduced in the major collections of French legislation, presumably because its provisions were incorporated into a major restatement of maritime law issued by Henry III in 1584 (*Collection de lois maritimes antérieures au XVIIIe siècle*, vol. 4, pp. 312–13).

stage in the appendix a third provision was excerpted from the same edict, this time with the citation 'Const. c. 6, *anno* 1557', and a fourth provision was actually included as well, with the erroneous citation 'Wisbie c. 8'.[105] Two further paragraphs introduced in the appendix close with references to 'Kintor. fol. 29. c. 3' and 'fol. 29. c. 2'.[106] The provisions excerpted again reappeared in Bisset's collection, where they were linked with 'the admirallis ordinances'.[107] What this meant is unclear. The arrangement of Bisset's material suggests that the admiral in question may have been French, but it could instead be that material of more local origin was being incorporated at this point, for there is another reference to the *Liber Kyntoris* in the title of the *Practicks* on custom duties, and here there can be little doubt that Scottish practice was being dealt with.[108] The only other use that is known to have been made of the *Liber Kyntoris* is by William Welwod, who backed up a statement in his treatise on maritime law about one of the provisions from the 1555 edict with a reference to 'l'admiral de France, et Kintor, c. 6', and referred at another place to 'Oleron, Denmark, Kintor'.[109] The latter reference is peculiar, for the provision outlined at this place can only be located in the source cited in the *Practicks* as 'the lawis of Wisbie'.[110] While the *Liber Kyntoris* may have included provisions from this source as well, it could have done so without making their origins clear, just as it could have included a version of 'the lawis of Oleron' without labelling it distinctly, or explaining how it related to the 'Schiplawis' known in Scotland. Whatever it may have done, reading the *Liber Kyntoris* must have been an unsettling experience for Balfour and his assistants. If everything collected together there was relevant to the handling of maritime litigation in Scotland then a treatment of that area of law could not be fitted into a compilation restricted to the old books, acts of parliament and decisions of the session.

To some extent this difficulty might have been circumvented by concentrating on the law governing maritime commerce. To borrow a phrase to which

105 *Practicks of Sir James Balfour of Pittendreich*, vol. 2, pp. 627–8; *Collection de lois maritimes antérieures au XVIIIe siècle*, vol. 4, pp. 313 and 315. Another, more accurate, reference to 'Wisbie c. 8' appears elsewhere. The use made of this source will be returned to shortly. The citation 'Const. c. 6, *anno* 1557', was not attached to the same provision as 'Kintor. pag. 31. art. 6'. In Bisset's collection the first provision appears as art. 2, the other as art. 6, and in the edict itself they were also numbered 2 and 6. The first citation thus appears to be a mistake.

106 *Practicks of Sir James Balfour of Pittendreich*, vol. 2, pp. 628 and 640–1.

107 *Habakkuk Bisset's Rolment of Courtis*, vol. 2, pp. 258–60.

108 *Practicks of Sir James Balfour of Pittendreich*, vol. 1, pp. 87–8.

109 *Alexander King's Treatise on Maritime Law*, pp. 363 and 372.

110 *The Black Book of the Admiralty*, 4 vols, ed. T. Twiss (London, 1871–6), vol. 4, pp. 58–9.

pundits of a particular breed are prone, the 'sea lawis' appendix was a game of two halves, of which the first – nearly over when the Scots digest was written – was dominated by that variety of law, while the second – still to 'kick off' when plans were made for the amalgamation of materials and reorganisation of titles – was dominated by the law governing maritime warfare.[111] It was in the second half of the appendix that the provisions originating in the 1555 edict and the admiral's ordinances would mostly appear, together with a much larger number of provisions derived from an edict issued by Francis I in 1544, the summaries of ten decisions derived from the *Registrum*, and a lengthy excerpt taken from the terms of a truce agreed on the border with England in 1549.[112] Like the provisions from the 1555 edict and the admiral's ordinances, the provisions from the 1544 edict were to reappear in Bisset's collection, despite the enactment in the year following Balfour's death of a comprehensive restatement of maritime law, in which the previous edicts were superseded.[113] The decisions of the session relating to maritime warfare do not appear to have been taken into account when the plan was devised for the amalgamation of the excerpts from the old books with the other materials assembled, yet it did contain the following entry.

> Weirfair M. *Vid.* hoistis A. *Vid.* wappinschawing A. *Vid.* bordour lawis M. *Vid.* assurance A. *Vid.* bordoure lawis P. *Vid.* weir A.[114]

The Latin digest had ended with a seventh book, 'De re militari', comprising seven titles, the last of which was concerned with the *Leges marchiarum*, and the Scots digest had ended with an unnumbered title on the 'Border lawis

111 Although 'letters of marque' were dealt with in the first half, during Balfour's lifetime they were not granted against enemies in wars but against peaceful mariners and merchants, and as a means of securing redress for the disruption of trade by compatriots of those mariners and merchants. This subject is examined in J.D. Ford, *The Emergence of Privateering* (Leiden, 2023).

112 *Practicks of Sir James Balfour of Pittendreich*, vol. 2, pp. 629–44; *Recueil général des anciennes lois françaises*, 29 vols, ed. F.-A. Isambert, M. Jourdan and M. Decrusy (Paris, 1822–33), vol. 12, pp. 854–69; *Leges marchiarum*, ed. W. Nicholson (London, 1747), pp. 65–70. The provisions of the 1544 edict are cited simply by an article number, or in one instance (surely erroneously) as 'Act 41'.

113 *Habakkuk Bisset's Rolment of Courtis*, vol. 2, pp. 216–27. Since the first edict was enacted before 25 March 1544, Balfour and Bisset referred to it as an edict of 1543.

114 NRS, GD112/71/5, f. 3r. Insofar as the decisions on maritime warfare had been left out of the plan, McNeill was correct that the appendix had to deal with material left over after the rest of the *Practicks* was compiled.

concerning weirfair.[115] Some consideration appears to have been given to connecting the material on maritime warfare with the other material on warfare, for just as finishing the original version of the title about maritime law with the article from the *Leges burgorum* helped to connect it with the preceding sequence of titles about the burghs, so finishing the expanded treatment of maritime law with the terms of the truce would have helped to connect it with a sequence of titles about warfare and the border laws.[116] The *postremum memorandum* had indeed mentioned the 'sea lawis and bordoure lawis' together.

If a solution to the problem posed there might have been to separate the two halves of the appendix, linking the first on maritime commerce with the burgh laws and the second on maritime warfare with the border laws, it is not hard to see why an alternative solution was preferred. One of the summaries of decisions of the session found in the *Registrum* stated that 'the admiral and his deputis are judges competent to all contraversies and debaitis betwix Scottismen and Scottismen and betwix strangeris and Scottismen anent all shippis, gudis, geir and merchandice takin upon the sea'.[117] Another summary of a prize decision went further in stating that 'the lordis of counsal are not competent judges to this mater, bot the samin sould be decidit befoir the admiral and his deputis, because the samin is ane actioun of weirfare'.[118] The first article added to the appendix from the 1544 edict went further still in stating that the admiral had jurisdiction over actions arising 'als weill in time of weir and be the occasioun of the samin as alswa for the effairis of merchandice and fishing', and that no other judges could 'exerce or use the said jurisdictioun bot the admiral or his deputis allanerlie'.[119] At least since 1544 it had been asserted by the admirals of Scotland that they enjoyed an exclusive jurisdiction over all seafaring causes, and this assertion appears to have been accepted when the appendix was being compiled.[120] Admittedly, in the second half of the appendix another decision was noted in which it had been found that when a foreigner pursued a burgess for debt, 'the admiral nor his deputis ar na wayis

115 NLS, Adv. MS 25.4.11, f. 92-incomplete, and BL, Add. MS 48050, ff. 89v-100; NRS, GD112/71/5, f. 129r, and EUL, La. III 381a, p. 283.

116 EUL, La. III 408, which could have been written in the late sixteenth century (Dolezalek, *Scotland under Jus Commune*, vol. 3, pp. 241–5), is an attempt to reorganise the 'Practicks', and here the treatment of maritime law was inserted after the treatment of the border laws. The copy used was divided into seven books, the last headed 'De legibus nautarum', and like Newbie's copy it ended with the early version of Skene's legal dictionary.

117 *Practicks of Sir James Balfour of Pittendreich*, vol. 2, p. 630.

118 *Practicks of Sir James Balfour of Pittendreich*, vol. 2, p. 634.

119 *Practicks of Sir James Balfour of Pittendreich*, vol. 2, pp. 629–30.

120 J.D. Ford, 'Introduction', in *Alexander King's Treatise on Maritime Law*, p. ix, at pp. lxxi–vii.

judges competent thairintill, bot the samin sould be decidit befoir the provest and baillies of the burgh quhair the debtour dwellis'.[121] Furthermore, the provision on jurisdiction from the *Leges burgorum* was still included in the first half of the appendix.[122] By the time the appendix was written, however, a crucial change of mind had occurred. Whereas both the Latin and Scots digests had reproduced the provision from the *Leges burgorum* in its original form, with a statement that maritime controversies were to be handled by 'the kingis bailzeis', the provision was adjusted in the appendix to say that these cases should be handled by 'the kingis admiral or his deputis'.[123] The provision did not appear at the close of the first half of the appendix, and the second half, which opened with the article from the 1544 edict, continued under the heading 'Anent the admiral, his office and jurisdiction', until the excerpt from the 1549 truce was provided with a new heading at the end. A decision had clearly been made to keep all the material on maritime law together, and one reason for the decision seems to have been an acceptance that the appendix did not deal with part of the law administered in the bailie courts, but dealt instead with the law administered in the admiralty courts.[124] While the admiralty courts did not deal with prize cases alone, ending the appendix with provisions from the 1549 truce may still have been meant to connect it with the titles on the border laws, which are separated from the appendix in the *Practicks* only by a brief title about taxation.[125]

It is possible that the move towards acceptance that the appendix was concerned with the law administered in the admiralty courts was also stimulated by Balfour's encounter with the *Liber Kyntoris*. Thomas Callander Wade suggested persuasively in 1937 that the compiler of that volume was David Kintor, one of the admiral deputes who dealt with the cases recorded in a court book published by the Stair Society in that year.[126] In the same way that

121 *Practicks of Sir James Balfour of Pittendreich*, vol. 2, p. 635.

122 *Practicks of Sir James Balfour of Pittendreich*, vol. 2, p. 627.

123 NLS, Adv. MS 25.4.11, f. 34v, and BL, Add. MS 48050, f. 30v; NRS, GD112/71/5, f. 42r, and EUL, La. III 381a, pp. 82–3. The change also appears in NLS, Adv. MS 24.2.4b, f. 263r, and EUL, La. III 408, f. 105r.

124 An account of the law administered in the admiralty courts would have been especially helpful to the earl of Bothwell when he was called home from his studies on the Continent to replace Morton as admiral in 1581.

125 If it is wondered whether the collection of sea laws really was conceived of as an appendix, distinct from the main body of the *Practicks*, the convincing evidence is the heading given to the collection, which seems to have been designed to set it off from everything that had preceded it.

126 'Introduction', in *Acta curiae admirallatus Scotiae, 1557–62*, ed. T.C. Wade (Edinburgh, 1937), p. xi, at p. xv.

the *Liber Kyntoris* may or may not have clarified the relationship between the 'Schiplawis' and 'lawis of Oleron', it may or may not have clarified the relationship between the various materials it gathered together and the practice of the admiralty courts. As already mentioned, it may also have been where provisions of the 'lawes of Wisbie' were first discovered, although it seems to have been elsewhere that the version used in the appendix was actually found.[127] There are twelve explicit references to 'Wisbie' in the appendix, one of which has been found to be an error. Two were added to existing paragraphs that ended with references to the 'Schiplawis' – the laws of Wisby had incorporated many articles from the laws of Oleron – but the remaining nine were all attached to new paragraphs added in the first half of the appendix. The numbers assigned to the provisions do not tie in exactly with any known version of the laws of Wisby, and the wording of the provisions can be quite distantly related to any known version. In both respects, however, the provisions attributed to 'Wisbie' in the *Practicks* are strikingly similar to provisions included in Bisset's collection. After presenting material drawn from the French edicts, Bisset presented material drawn from the laws of Oleron in two stages, beginning with the original twenty-four articles, and dealing later with additional articles found in the longer French version.[128] Between these two series he inserted some 'reulis of sea lawes quhilkis ar nocht contened in the majestie and lawes of the realme of Scotland, nor in the buik of Oleron, bot ar called the auld lawes of Visbie'.[129] Not only are the rules rehearsed by Bisset similar to the paragraphs of the *Practicks* attributed to the laws of Wisby, but a provision was included here which cannot be traced to the laws of Wisby yet can be found in the *Practicks*, without a citation.[130] Bisset's rules end with two legal opinions that have nothing to do with the laws of Wisby. The second related to a case in which 'A.B. in Deip' entrusted 'R.D'. with a sum of money to be delivered to 'C.D. in Edinburghe, his merchand', only for the whole sum to be lost in a storm at sea.[131] In the 1580s a ship called the *Fleur de lis* belonged jointly to 'Andro Balfour and Johne Maill', of whom the latter was certainly a member

127 No references to the laws of Wisby can be found in the Scots digest.

128 *Habakkuk Bisset's Rolment of Courtis*, vol. 2, pp. 241–58.

129 Unlike Balfour and Skene, Bisset evidently adhered to the view that the 'Schiplawis' were an authentic part of the old books of law, distinguishing it from the version of the laws of Oleron found in the *Liber Kyntoris*.

130 *Practicks of Sir James Balfour of Pittendreich*, vol. 2, p. 625. The similarities with the *Practicks* were noted in the first volume of Hamilton-Grierson's edition of Bisset's book.

131 *Habakkuk Bisset's Rolment of Courtis*, vol. 2, pp. 255–6.

of the community of Scottish factors operating in Dieppe, and probably also the former.[132] As James Balfour's youngest brother was called Andrew, the possibility arises that it was from him that he acquired a copy of the selection of provisions from the laws of Wisby that was used in the compilation of both the *Practicks* and Bisset's collection.[133] It was reported at the time that Balfour had 'long lingered at Dieppe' on his way home to Scotland in 1580.[134] While he was there he may also have read a book by a local judge in which the 1555 edict was said to have supplemented the 1544 edict.[135] All this may be unduly speculative, but it would be consistent with the impression formed earlier that the *Practicks* was finally pieced together after Balfour returned from France if it was in Dieppe that he had first come across the laws of Wisby and the 1544 edict. What seems clear in any case is that Bisset retained among his papers several sources that were only made use of in the *Practicks* at a fairly late stage in its development. There is no reason to suppose that the person responsible for the compilation of the 'sea lawis' appendix was anyone other than the person responsible for the compilation of the rest of the work, who was identified without hesitation by Bisset, the scribe of the principal copy, as Sir James Balfour of Pittendreich.[136]

---

132 NRS, B19/12/1, 17 March 1590, and RD1/32, ff. 201–2r; ACA, CA1/1/27, pp. 459, 469 and 477, CA1/1/29, p. 808, CA1/1/31, pp. 328–9, and CA5/1/2, 14 and 17 June 1581; DCA, BCMB, vol. 14, 26 February 1580.

133 NRS, CS7/42, ff. 329v-31r. The Andrew Balfour who served as a 'bailie of Leyth' in 1557 – possibly as the water bailie – may have been the same person (*Acta curiae admirallatus Scotiae*, p. 25). Of course, 'A.B'. and 'C.D'. could simply have been abstractions, rather than the initials of actual people, but the reference to 'R.D'. makes this less likely.

134 *Calendar of State Papers Relating to Scotland*, vol. 5, p. 474; *Calendar of State Papers, Foreign Series, of the Reign of Elizabeth*, 23 vols, ed. J. Stevenson, A.J. Crosby, A.J. Butler, S.C. Lomas, A.B. Hinds and R.B. Wernham (London, 1863–1950), vol. 14, pp. 295 and 476; *Extracts from the Records of the Burgh of Edinburgh*, 5 vols, ed. J.D. Marwick (Edinburgh, 1869–92), vol. 5, pp. 220–1.

135 Guillaume Terrien, *Commentaires du droict civil tant public que privé, observé au pays et duché de Normandie* (Paris, 1574), pp. 558–81.

136 The importance of Bisset's book as confirmation of Balfour's authorship of the *Practicks* was pointed out in McNeill, 'Introduction', p. xxxii. What was not appreciated, and could not have been appreciated properly until Dolezalek made his momentous discovery, was the importance of Bisset's book as a guide to the compilation of the 'sea lawis' appendix.

6

William Welwod's Treatises on Maritime Law

William Welwod is generally believed to have two claims to fame: as the writer of the first treatise about maritime law to be printed in Britain, and as the only critic of Hugo Grotius' *Mare liberum* to elicit a direct response from its author.[1] The treatise with which he made publishing history was *The Sea-Law of Scotland*, printed by Robert Waldegrave of Edinburgh in 1590.[2] The critique with which he stung Grotius into action was published as a chapter of another treatise, printed by Humfrey Lownes of London in 1613, under the title *An Abridgement of All Sea-Lawes*. Three years later Welwod had a third treatise about maritime law printed, under the title *De dominio maris*.[3] This 1616 treatise was apparently an expanded version of his earlier critique, made accessible to a wider audience by being turned from English into Latin, much as the 1613 treatise appears to have been expanded from his 1590 treatise and adapted to the needs of a wider audience by being written in English rather than Scots. In fact, Welwod wrote a further treatise on maritime law, which was never printed and has previously received no attention. The aims of this essay are to provide a fresh examination of all four of Welwod's treatises on maritime law, to reconsider the ways in which the printed treatises were related to each other in the light of the evidence provided by the manuscript treatise, and to identify at least some of the contexts in which the various texts will need to be

1 T.W. Fulton, *The Sovereignty of the Sea* (Edinburgh, 1911), pp. 352–4; W. Senior, 'Early Writers on Maritime Law', (1921) 37 *Law Quarterly Review* 323, at pp. 323 and 335–6; A.R.G. McMillan, 'Admiralty and Maritime Law', in H. McKechnie (ed.), *An Introductory Survey of the Sources and Literature of Scots Law* (Edinburgh, 1936), p. 325, at pp. 329–30; D. Armitage, *The Ideological Origins of the British Empire* (Cambridge, 2000), pp. 110–11; M.J. Van Ittersum, '*Mare liberum* versus the Propriety of the Seas? The Debate between Hugo Grotius (1583–1645) and William Welwood (1552–1624) and Its Impact on Anglo-Scotto-Dutch Fishery Disputes in the Second Decade of the Seventeenth Century', (2006) 10 *Edinburgh Law Review* 239, at pp. 244–5.

2 As is noted in P.G. Stein, *The Character and Influence of the Roman Civil Law: Historical Essays* (London, 1988), p. 316, this was also the first treatise on any branch of law to be printed in Scotland.

3 The title page reads: 'Cosmopoli, *Excudebat G. Fonti-silvius* 16. *Calend. Ianuar*. 1615'. The book thus appears to have been printed at London in 1616, though G. Fonti-silvius was obviously William Welwod himself. According to A.W. Pollard and G.R. Redgrave, *A Short-Title Catalogue of Books Printed in England, Scotland and Ireland and of English Books Printed abroad, 1475–1640*, 3 vols (London, 1976–91), vol. 2, p. 447, and vol. 3, p. 47, the book was actually printed by Thomas Creede.

 | DOI:10.1163/9789004695009_007

located if they are not to be misconstrued by modern readers. While the aim is not to develop contextual readings of the texts here but to enable that to be done elsewhere, some indication is given of the direction in which such readings may be expected to move. The three aims outlined are each pursued in a separate section below, after which some brief conclusions are drawn about how Welwod's treatises should be approached in the future.

1 Analysis of the Four Treatises on Maritime Law

If the ultimate aim is to identify the contexts in which Welwod's treatises ought to be located, the first task must be to examine carefully the texts that need to be placed in context. Bibliographical information about each treatise is followed below by fairly basic analysis of its structure, style and sources, and where possible comparison is made with the structure, style and sources of the other treatises.

1.1 *The Sea-Law of Scotland*

Very few copies of the 1590 treatise are known to have survived.[4] There is one copy in each of the university libraries of Oxford and Cambridge and another in the library of the New York Historical Society, but no other copy has been traced.[5] A facsimile reprint of the Oxford copy is available in the series called 'The English Experience', and a digital reproduction of the Cambridge copy is available on the site called 'Early English Books Online'.[6] A new edition of the treatise was published by the Scottish Text Society in 1933, providing an exact transcription of the original text faced by an unreliable and sometimes comical attempt by an early reader to translate the treatise into English.[7]

The full name that appeared on the title page of the treatise, followed by a quotation from Psalm 107, was *The Sea-Law of Scotland, Shortly Gathered and Plainly Dressit for the Reddy Use of All Seafairingmen*. After a table of contents, a dedicatory epistle addressed to the king, and a 'Proheme, Bearand the

4 R. Dickson and J.P. Edmond, *Annals of Scottish Printing* (Cambridge, 1890), pp. 414–15; H.G. Aldis, *A List of Books Printed in Scotland before 1700* (Edinburgh, 1970), n. 220; Pollard and Redgrave, *Short-Title Catalogue of Books Printed in England, Scotland and Ireland*, vol. 2, p. 447.

5 There is, however, a photocopy in the National Library of Scotland.

6 William Welwod, *The Sea-Law of Scotland* (Amsterdam, 1969); http://eebo.chadwyck.com.

7 'The Sea Law of Scotland', ed. T.C. Wade, in Scottish Text Society, *Miscellany Volume* (Edinburgh, 1933), p. 38.

Origin of the Sea Law, the Ground of this Treatie and the Occasions Theroff', the treatise itself opened with a chapter ('Title 1') explaining its 'Summe and Ordour'.[8] The dedication and *prooemium* will be returned to later, but what is of immediate interest is the statement at the end of the first chapter that the book would deal 'summarly bot orderly' with the whole law affecting seafarers, 'beginning at the fraughting of schips, as a thing concerning the chiefe use and end of schipping, syn the persons, thair duties, powers and priviledges, thirdly the manifolde chaunces, with the maner of judgement thairin, and last of the judges ordinair to all seafair debaits and causes'. The second chapter was indeed concerned with the freighting or hiring of ships, after which three chapters examined the duties owed by the master of a ship to its owners, to the merchants and passengers he contracted with, and to the mariners he employed.[9] The part of the treatise about 'the persons, thair duties, powers and priviledges', continued with chapters on the duties and privileges of mariners, the responsibilities of pilots, and the liability of an 'outredder' or *exercitor* of a ship.[10] The next six chapters (Titles 9–14) were concerned with such 'manifold chaunces' as the jettisoning of cargo in a storm, the depredations of pirates and the loss of goods by shipwreck, and one chapter was devoted to explaining the means by which contributions towards the reimbursement of losses suffered by some of those involved in a maritime enterprise might be claimed from others.[11] The final chapter was about 'the judge ordinair to seafair causes'.[12] The suggestion in the first chapter that the discussion of 'the judges ordinair' would follow on appropriately from discussion of 'the maner of judgement' was rather misleading, for the chapter on shipwreck intervened after the chapter on how contributions might be claimed, and that chapter was concerned with how amounts due should be assessed and masters should arrange for payments to be made, not with how disputes might be determined by judges.

In style the final chapter was more like the first – and the preliminary matter preceding it – than the twelve central chapters, where the substantive law affecting seafarers was dealt with. The opening passage of the second chapter is as good an example as any of the style of these chapters. It is presented

8 *Sea-Law of Scotland*, sigg. A1v-B2r. In quotations from this and the other treatises, the original orthography is preserved, subject to standardisation of certain letters and modernisation of symbols, but greater liberties have been taken with punctuation and capitalisation.

9 *Sea-Law of Scotland*, sigg. B2r-6r.

10 *Sea-Law of Scotland*, sigg. B6v-C1r.

11 *Sea-Law of Scotland*, sigg. C1r-6r.

12 *Sea-Law of Scotland*, sig. C6r.

here with references found in the margins of the text inserted between square brackets at the places they are cited.

> Na schip suld be fraughtit without ane charterparty, beirand that the maister sall provide an sufficient steirseman, timberman and schipmen convenient for the schip, with fyre, water and salt on his awin cost, and gif any debate sall happen betwixt the master and merchant, thay sall underly the jurisdictioun of the brough quhairunto the ship is fraughtit, without any exemption, and that na drinke silver bee tane fra the merchandis under the paine of the tinsell of the fraught and ane tunnes fraught to the kirk warke of the town to the quhilk thay are fraughted [c. 17 et 130, actor. Iacob. 3]. Gif a schip be nocht reddy at the day appointed in the charterparty to go to the sea, the merchant may not onlie quyte himselfe of her [per l. item 13, §. si lege, loc.], except hee had his peace and discharge hir not at the day, for then he appearis againe be silence to consent againe of new [d. l. item, §. fin.], bot also obtein all costs, skaiths and interest [c. 16, Olon], except the master schaw sum excuse of a notorious necessitie, or of a chaunce quhilk could nocht ben eschewed, and than he lossis only his fraught, becaus he hes not servit thairfoir [per l. ex conducto, in pr., l. si item fundus, l. et haec distinctio, et l. si in lege, §. colonus, locat.].[13]

The first sentence in this passage summarises accurately most of the provisions of an act of parliament issued in 1467 and ratified in 1487.[14] The next sentence begins with two pairs of clauses, relating to a merchant's right to resile from a contract, which share the dogmatic style of the first sentence but are in fact more loosely based on two texts cited from the *Digest*.[15] The first text relates to the failure of someone commissioned to perform a task to complete it within a specified time, and the other to the tacit renewal of tenancies of land. If the texts were understood to reflect more general principles of the Roman law of hire, and if the charter parties referred to in the Scottish statutes

13 *Sea-Law of Scotland*, sig. B2.

14 *The Actis and Constitutiounis of the Realme of Scotland* (Edinburgh, 1566), ff. 48r and 78r; *The Acts of the Parliaments of Scotland*, 12 vols, ed. T. Thomson and C. Innes (Edinburgh, 1814–75), vol. 2, pp. 87 and 178; Records of the Parliaments of Scotland, ed. K.M. Brown (www.rps.ac.uk), 1467/1/4 and 1487/10/19. It is of course the first source cited, known as the 'Black Acts', that would have been available to Welwod, whose numbering of the acts is consistent with its usage.

15 D.19.2.13.10–11.

were understood to be governed by that law, the texts could have been thought to have some bearing on the rights of merchants when masters failed to depart on the dates specified in their charter parties. The next clause of the second sentence is based on a provision found in the maritime code known as the laws of Oleron, which states that if a master fails to depart on a specified date, the merchant may not only withdraw from the contract but may also claim compensation for any loss he suffers as a result of the delay.[16] In the last part of the passage quoted, this right to compensation is said to be limited to cases in which the master has no excuse for his failure. The texts cited from the *Digest* indicate that a landlord would be liable to compensate a tenant for loss suffered through the early termination of a lease only if something could have been done to prevent it.[17] The dogmatic style of this last part of the passage is again typical of the central chapters of the treatise, where statements of the type quoted, generally in the form of rules of law, are strung together in a more or less coherent fashion.

The passage quoted is also typical of the range of sources cited in the treatise. The second chapter ends as it begins with a statement backed up by reference to an act of parliament, and further use of Scottish legislation is made elsewhere, though on no more than eight occasions in the central chapters, and with reference to no more than four different statutes.[18] More frequent use is made of the source cited as 'Olon', on which almost forty statements are based. These statements, like those based on acts of parliament, tend to be fairly straightforward summaries of the provisions referred to, though tracing the relevant provisions is not always easy. Copies of the laws of Oleron differ widely, but in the sixteenth century there were three main versions available.[19] In the first place, there were copies in both manuscript and print of a collection of around twenty-four 'rules' or 'judgments' concerning seafaring that were believed to have been issued on the island of Oleron in the late thirteenth

---

16 *The Black Book of the Admiralty*, 4 vols, ed. T. Twiss (London, 1871–6), vol. 1, pp. 118–19 (or maybe 120–3).

17 D.19.2.15.pr., 19.2.33, 19.2.25 and 19.2.24.4. The relevance of the first text cited is not entirely clear.

18 *Actis and Constitutiounis of the Realme of Scotland*, ff. 21, 48r, 78r and 122; *Acts of the Parliaments of Scotland*, vol. 2, pp. 19, 87, 178 and 348; Records of the Parliaments of Scotland, 1430/19, 1467/1/4, 1487/10/19 and 1535/41.

19 P. Studer, 'Introduction', in *The Oak Book of Southampton*, 2 vols (Southampton, 1910–11), vol. 2, p. v, at pp. xlii–lxiii; D. Burwash, *English Merchant Shipping, 1460–1540* (Toronto, 1947), pp. 171–4; M. Deniel, 'Les Rôles d'Oléron du Moyen Age au XVIIe siècle', MA dissertation, University of Brest, 1971, pp. 14–28.

century.[20] As the provisions in this collection are found in all the other versions too and can be traced back to the earliest surviving exemplars, it is usually referred to as the original version. Variants of this version had often been included in compilations of the old books and acts of Scots law made during the fifteenth century, and the same variants continued to be included in copies of these compilations produced during the sixteenth century.[21] In the second place, manuscript copies were also in circulation of a version of the laws of Oleron that began like the original version but then added another eleven articles.[22] As these copies were almost invariably made in England and include provisions that were first issued there, this collection of around thirty-five articles is usually referred to as the English version.[23] In the third place, a printed edition of the laws of Oleron was available in which the original version was followed by twenty additional provisions.[24] As this collection of forty-seven articles was published at Poitiers and derived from manuscripts circulating in Brittany, it is usually referred to as the French version.[25]

The numbering of the citations in Welwod's treatise does not correspond to the numbering of the provisions in any known variant of any version of the laws of Oleron. Sometimes, indeed, more than one number is used with reference to the same provision, and sometimes the same number is used with

20 *The Rutter of the See* (London, 1536), sigg. D5r-E7v; *La grand coustumier du pays et duche de Normendie* (Rouen, 1539), ff. 61v-3r; D.W. Waters, *The Rutters of the Sea* (New Haven, 1967), pp. 157–66 and 103–24. A new edition of the original version, with translation and commentary, is available in R. Ward, *The World of the Medieval Shipmaster: Law, Business and the Sea, c. 1350–1450* (Woodbridge, 2009), pp. 183–205.

21 E.B.I. Frankot, 'Maritime Law and Practice in Late Medieval Aberdeen', (2010) 89 *Scottish Historical Review* 136, at pp. 136–8, and *'Of Laws of Ships and Shipmen': Medieval Maritime Law and Its Practice in Urban Northern Europe* (Edinburgh, 2012), pp. 81–5, describe most of the Scottish manuscripts, though see too CUL, Kk.1.5(4), ff. 2–4, and NLS, Acc. 11218/5, ff. 297r-309r. This last copy was produced during the sixteenth century, as were CUL, Ee.4.21, ff. 306–12, and NLS, Adv. MS 7.1.9, ff. 100–5, and Adv. MS 25.5.9, ff. 143v-50. See now E.B.I. Frankot, 'The Scottish Translations of the *Rôles d'Oléron*: Edition and Commentary', in A.M. Godfrey (ed.), *Stair Society: Miscellany Eight* (Edinburgh, 2020), p. 13.

22 *Black Book of the Admiralty*, vol. 1, pp. 88–127.

23 Ward, *World of the Medieval Shipmaster*, pp. 22–3.

24 *La grant routtier et pyllotage et encrage de la mer* (Poitiers, 1520), sigg. L4v-M5r; Waters, *Rutters of the Sea*, pp. 376–93; *Black Book of the Admiralty*, vol. 2, pp. 432–81.

25 M.A. Pawlowski, 'Pierre Garcie, dit Ferrande, et ses imitateurs', (1900) 1 *Bulletin de géographie historique et descriptive* 135, as well as providing bibliographical and biographical information about the editor, also notes that Thomas Petyt, who printed the first of the sources listed in n. 20 above, belonged to a family of booksellers in France. Petyt's English translation, often reprinted, was of an edition of the original version included in Garcie's *Le routier de la mer* (Rouen, n.d.), sigg. C5v-D5v.

reference to more than one provision. However, it can usually be worked out which provision was supposed to underpin the statement made in the text. Not surprisingly, some of the provisions relied on form part of the original version, long familiar in Scotland. More surprisingly, at least one of the other provisions relied on forms part of the additional run of articles found only in the English version.[26] More surprisingly still, some of the statements in the treatise backed up by reference to 'Olon' are not supported by any provision found in any copy of the laws of Oleron yet are clearly supported by provisions of the code known as the laws of Wisby.[27] The obvious source of confusion was that the code believed to have been issued at Wisby included many provisions adopted from the laws of Oleron, some of them more than once, but the point is that as well as relying on provisions common to both codes, Welwod also relied on provisions unique to one or other.[28] Despite the inconsistency in the numbering of his citations, if those that can be taken with confidence to refer to a particular provision are placed in numerical order, a broad pattern does emerge.[29]

c. 1 (sig. B3v)	O. 1 (*Black Book of the Admiralty*, vol. 1, pp. 88–9)
c. 2 (sig. B4r)	O. 2 (*Black Book of the Admiralty*, vol. 1, pp. 88–91)
c. 3 (sig. B6v)	O. 3 (*Black Book of the Admiralty*, vol. 1, pp. 90–1)
c. 4 (sig. B2v)	O. 4 (*Black Book of the Admiralty*, vol. 1, pp. 92–3)
c. 5 (sig. B6v)	O. 5 (*Black Book of the Admiralty*, vol. 1, pp. 92–5)
c. 6 (sig. B5v)	O. 6 (*Black Book of the Admiralty*, vol. 1, pp. 94–5)
c. 6 (sig. B6r)	O. 7 (*Black Book of the Admiralty*, vol. 1, pp. 94–7)
c. 7 (sig. B5r)	O. 11 (*Black Book of the Admiralty*, vol. 1, pp. 102–3)
c. 8 (sig. B5v)	O. 12 (*Black Book of the Admiralty*, vol. 1, pp. 104–5)

26 *Sea-Law of Scotland*, sig. C1v; *Black Book of the Admiralty*, vol. 1, pp. 126–7; see too n. 16 above.

27 On the confused awareness of this source in early modern Scotland see too Frankot, '*Of Laws of Ships and Shipmen*', p. 87.

28 The laws of Wisby were first printed as *Dyt ys dat högeste unde öldeste water recht* (Copenhagen, 1505). Later editions include *Collection de lois maritimes antérieures au XVIIIe siècle*, 6 vols, ed. J.M. Pardessus (Paris, 1828–45), vol. 1, pp. 463–502, and *Black Book of the Admiralty*, vol. 4, pp. 264–84.

29 For convenience, since reference has to be made here to a copy of the English version of the laws of Oleron, reference is made throughout to editions of the laws printed in the *Black Book of the Admiralty*. Obviously, O. is short for Oleron and W. for Wisby. In the edition referred to, the original version ends at O. 24. In the first column, only one example is given of each citation, though some provisions were cited more than once.

c. 9 (sig. B6v)	O. 12 (*Black Book of the Admiralty*, vol. 1, pp. 104–5)
c. 9 (sig. C2r)	O. 9 (*Black Book of the Admiralty*, vol. 1, pp. 98–101)
c. 10 (sig. B6v)	O. 14 (*Black Book of the Admiralty*, vol. 1, pp. 106–7)
c. 12 (sig. B4r)	O. 16 (*Black Book of the Admiralty*, vol. 1, pp. 110–11)
c. 15 (sig. B7r)	O. 21 (*Black Book of the Admiralty*, vol. 1, pp. 116–17)
c. 16 (sig. B7r)	O. 18 (*Black Book of the Admiralty*, vol. 1, pp. 112–13)
c. 16 (sig. B2v)	O. 23 (*Black Book of the Admiralty*, vol. 1, pp. 120–3)
c. 17 (sig. B7v)	O. 24 (*Black Book of the Admiralty*, vol. 1, pp. 120–1)
c. 19 (sig. C1v)	O. 32 (*Black Book of the Admiralty*, vol. 1, pp. 126–7)
c. 20 (sig. C1v)	O. 32 (*Black Book of the Admiralty*, vol. 1, pp. 126–7)
c. 20 (sig. C1r)	W. 20 (*Black Book of the Admiralty*, vol. 4, p. 270–1)*
c. 22 (sig. B4r)	W. 45 (*Black Book of the Admiralty*, vol. 4, p. 278)*
c. 23 (sig. B3r)	W. 46 (*Black Book of the Admiralty*, vol. 4, pp. 278–9)
c. 24 (sig. B6r)	W. 18 (*Black Book of the Admiralty*, vol. 4, p. 270)*
c. 25 (sig. B4v)	W. 49 (*Black Book of the Admiralty*, vol. 4, p. 279)*
c. 25 (sig. B6v)	W. 54 (*Black Book of the Admiralty*, vol. 4, p. 280)
c. 28 (sig. B3r)	W. 53 (*Black Book of the Admiralty*, vol. 4, p. 280)
c. 30 (sig. C3v)	W. 55 (*Black Book of the Admiralty*, vol. 4, p. 281)
c. 31 (sig. C3v)	W. 59 (*Black Book of the Admiralty*, vol. 4, p. 282)
c. 35 (sig. B6v)	W. 25 (*Black Book of the Admiralty*, vol. 4, p. 272)*
c. 35 (sig. B7r)	W. 61 (*Black Book of the Admiralty*, vol. 4, p. 282)
c. 36 (sig, B7r)	W. 63 (*Black Book of the Admiralty*, vol. 4, p. 283)
c. 37 (sig. B7r)	W. 63 (*Black Book of the Admiralty*, vol. 4, p. 283)
c. 41 (sig. B4r)	W. 68 (*Black Book of the Admiralty*, vol. 4, p. 284)

What Welwod seems to have had before him was a collection of sea laws that started with provisions from the original version of the laws of Oleron, moved on to at least one of the provisions found only in the English version of the same code, and ended with provisions drawn from the laws of Wisby, some of which (those marked with an asterisk) might instead have been found in the laws of Oleron.[30] That Welwod was confused about the relationship between the two

30 An example occurs at *Sea-Law of Scotland*, sig. B4v-5r, where reference is made first to art. 10 of the laws of Oleron (as numbered in the edition cited here) and then to art. 11, yet the notes read '25, Olon' and 'c. 7, eod'., perhaps because the first reference was actually to the former provision as it appeared in the laws of Wisby. In fact, the wording in the laws of Wisby, art. 49, provides marginally clearer support to the point made than the wording in the laws of Oleron. Comparison may usefully be made here with *Habakkuk Bisset's Rolment of Courtis*, 3 vols, ed. P.J. Hamilton-Grierson (Edinburgh, 1920–6), vol. 2,

codes is clear from his 1613 treatise, in which he remarked rather strangely that the 'lawes of *Oleron* were afterward translated into Dutch by them of *Wisby*, for the sea use of the Dutch coast'.[31]

The opening of the second chapter of the 1590 treatise is again representative of the remainder of the central chapters in its preponderance of citations from the *Digest*. If eight statements may be taken to have been backed up with references to acts of the Scottish parliaments, and almost forty with references to the laws of Oleron or Wisby, over eighty may be taken to have been backed up with references to civilian sources.[32] In the notes attached to these statements, nearly a hundred references were made to the *Digest*, a dozen to the *Code*, a couple to the *Institutes*, and eight to constitutions of the later emperors, the ordinary gloss and the works of Bartolus and Baldus.[33] Where the opening of the second chapter is less representative is in its citation of texts concerned with tenancy agreements, for all but twenty-five of the civilian sources cited in these chapters were concerned directly with seafaring. The civilian references mostly back up statements summarising the texts cited in much the same way as other statements summarise the provisions of acts of parliament and the laws of Oleron or Wisby. It is nevertheless a distinctive feature of the civilian references that they are not invariably used in the same way.[34] It can at times be difficult to understand why a civil law source was cited, just as the significance of references to the laws of Oleron is not always easy to discern.

1.2 *An Abridgement of All Sea-Lawes*

Copies of the 1613 treatise have survived in greater numbers than copies of the 1590 treatise, partly no doubt because it was more successful commercially. A new edition was printed in 1636 by Thomas Harper of London, and in 1686

pp. 241–58, where a copy of 'the buik of Oleron' is followed by a copy of provisions from 'the auld lawes of Visbie', though in this instance the copyist understood perfectly well that he was turning from one code to another.

31 *Abridgement of All Sea-Lawes*, p. 3. As is well explained in Frankot, *'Of Laws of Ships and Shipmen'*, pp. 6–26, the laws of Oleron had been translated into Dutch as the *Vonesse van Damme* in the late thirteenth or early fourteenth century, a few decades before the code seems to have been translated into Scots. It was a combination of the *Vonesse van Damme*, legislation from the Netherlands and further legislation from Lübeck that came to be known as the laws of Wisby.

32 The individuation of statements is of course quite artificial, so the figures provided must be regarded as a rough guide only. Three statements were backed up with references to both the *Digest* and 'Olon'.

33 Bartolus was cited four times, Baldus and the ordinary gloss just once each, and reference was made to two *authenticae*.

34 This point will be returned to below.

the treatise reappeared as an appendix to a new edition of Gerard Malynes' *Consuetudo vel lex mercatoria*.[35] A facsimile reprint of the 1613 edition was published in 1972, and digital versions are now available at several places.[36]

The full title of the treatise was *An Abridgement of All Sea-Lawes, Gathered Forth of All Writings and Monuments which Are To Be Found among Any People or Nation, upon the Coasts of the Great Ocean and Mediterranean Sea, and Specially Ordered and Disposed for the Use and Benefit of All Benevolent Sea-Farers within His Majesties Dominions of Great Britanne, Ireland and the Adjacent Isles Therof.* The order or disposition of the treatise was similar to the arrangement of the 1590 treatise save for three variations. In the first place, between the *prooemium* and the opening chapter – explaining the origin, objective and organisation of the treatise – and the chapter on the freighting of ships – beginning the discussion of the substantive law of seafaring – the 1613 treatise included five chapters identifying the judge ordinary for maritime causes and other officers of his court, outlining the procedure followed there, and introducing the types of person typically involved in seafaring.[37] In the second place, although the discussion of the substantive law of seafaring followed the pattern of the discussion in the 1590 treatise, at four stages a further chapter was inserted, dealing with the functions of the clerk of a ship, with the granting of maritime loans, with partnerships formed for maritime enterprises, and with the privileges granted to certain ships and their owners.[38] In the third place, instead of the chapter on the judge ordinary with which the 1590 treatise finished, the 1613 treatise had a series of seven chapters at the end, concerned mostly with the international law of the sea rather than the law of maritime commerce, and dealing with things found or taken at sea, with the fishing trade, with the dominion of the seas, and with the commanders and crews of warships, watermen and shipwrights.[39]

The central chapters of the 1613 treatise were written in the same style as the central chapters of the 1590 treatise. By and large the 1613 treatise simply restated in English the propositions made in Scots in the 1590 treatise, and even in the four central chapters that were absent from the 1590 treatise, or in passages that can be found in other central chapters of the 1613 treatise

35 William Welwod, *An Abridgement of All Sea-Lawes* (London, 1636); 'A Collection of All Sea-Laws', in Gerard Malynes, *Consuetudo vel lex mercatoria* (London, 1686), pt 2, pp. 43–78.

36 William Welwod, *An Abridgement of All Sea-Lawes* (Amsterdam, 1972); http://gallica.bnf.fr; http://eebo.chadwyck.com; http://archive.org.

37 *Abridgement of All Sea-Lawes*, pp. 8–22.

38 *Abridgement of All Sea-Lawes*, pp. 35–8, 40–1 and 48–9.

39 *Abridgement of All Sea-Lawes*, pp. 51–77.

alone, the same style was used. Both treatises thus consist for the most part of dogmatic statements backed up by marginal references to sources. On the other hand, both treatises started and finished with material that was often presented in a more descriptive or deliberative style, and this material was a great deal more extensive in the 1613 treatise. Furnished with a new dedicatory epistle to the king, and with a further address to the admirals of Scotland, England and the Cinque Ports, the 1613 treatise also appeared with a different and longer 'Proheme', which will again be returned to later. The first chapter, explaining 'The Order of this Treatise', was like the first chapter of the 1590 version, except that it took into account the two series of chapters included at the start and finish of the 1613 treatise alone. The chapters included at the start of the treatise, particularly the chapter on court procedure, do contain some statements made in the familiar style, but space is also devoted there to consideration of the history of institutions and the diversity of vocabulary. For example, the chapter introducing the 'Persons Ordinary in Ships' reads at one point as follows:

> he who beares charge over all the ship and kippage, is commonly called by us, and most part of nations, both now and of olde, and specially by the Romane lawes, *Navicularius*, or *Magister Navis*: that is, as we speake, Master of the ship; by the Dutches, Skipper; and by the Grecians, *Navarchus* or *Nauclerus*; by the Italians, *Patrono*. But if the ship be a warfaring ship, the principall person is commonly called Capitaine by us and other neere nations.[40]

The aim here was clearly to describe rather than prescribe linguistic usage, as well no doubt as to impress the reader with the author's erudition, and even the discussion of court practice was couched more in terms of what was 'found needful' than of what had to be done.[41] Similarly, although the seven chapters at the end of the 1613 treatise were written to a large extent in the familiar style of dogmatic statements backed up by references to sources, more descriptive passages, with minimal support from sources, can also be found there, and sometimes there is engagement in argument, as when it is claimed that the practice of authorising reprisals against people from foreign countries where

40 *Abridgement of All Sea-Lawes*, p. 20.

41 There were marginal references beside the passage quoted not only to the *Digest* and *Code* but also to Vegetius' *Epitoma rei militaris*.

justice has been denied could still be resorted to in Scotland, notwithstanding that it had fallen into disuse there.[42]

This more argumentative style is much more prominent in the chapter devoted to discussion 'Of the Communitie and Proprietie of the Seas'.[43] More than twice the length of any other chapter, the critique of Grotius' *Mare liberum* was written in a style that contrasts sharply with the accumulation of authoritative propositions mostly indulged in elsewhere. For instance, Welwod wrote at one point as follows:

> His next conclusion is this; *Est igitur mare in numero eorum quae in commercio non sunt, hoc est, quae proprii iuris fieri non possunt*: that is, The Sea to be of that order of things, which cannot bee appropriate to any man. His warrants for his conclusion also are the Roman Lawyers, whom I said to be wrested by *Mare liberum*; and therefore must shew the same, contrary to his purpose indeed. *Martianus*, as the Author of *Mare liberum* largely graunts, saith, that if any private man have himselfe alone, by any lawfull space of time sufficient for a prescription, kept and exercised fishing in any creeke or nooke of Sea, which they call *Diverticulum*; hee may forbid all others to fish therin: which *Papinianus* also confirmeth. The which, as I accept, so I would further demand of him, By what reason should a private man, who hath no other care nor respect but to himselfe alone, be thus priviledged and preferred to a Prince?[44]

The direct engagement in argument with the author of *Mare liberum* (whose identity was unknown to Welwod), the complaint that the author had misconstrued the texts he cited from the *Digest*, and the claim that these texts should actually be understood to sanction the appropriation of fishing rights in coastal waters, were all typical of this chapter of the treatise.[45] The direct engagement in argument with an author, and the discussion of how sources should be read, was equally atypical of the other chapters of the treatise, and especially of the central chapters. The references in the margins of the chapter

42 *Abridgement of All Sea-Lawes*, p. 56. The Scottish position in relation to reprisals is examined in some detail in J.D. Ford, *The Emergence of Privateering* (Leiden, 2023), pp. 54–70.

43 *Abridgement of All Sea-Lawes*, pp. 61–72.

44 *Abridgement of All Sea-Lawes*, pp. 70–1, citing Hugo Grotius, *The Freedom of the Seas*, ed. J.B. Scott and tr. R.V. Magoffin (New York, 1916), pp. 32–4, and D.44.3.7 and 41.3.45.

45 On Welwod's similar complaint about Grotius' use of the Bible see M. Somos, 'Secularisation in *De iure praedae*: From Bible Criticism to International Law', in H.W. Blom (ed.), *Property, Piracy and Punishment: Hugo Grotius on War and Booty in De iure praedae* (Leiden, 2009), p. 147.

on the dominion of the seas served mostly to identify the sources under discussion in the text itself, whereas in the central chapters the text was constructed from statements summarising the sources cited, and in a way that neither engaged in nor encouraged discussion of their significance. If the chapters at the beginning and end of the 1613 treatise at times came a little closer to the style of the long chapter on the dominion of the seas, it nevertheless has a distinctive character that sets it apart from the rest of the book.

A further difference between the chapter on the dominion of the seas and the other chapters is that it concentrates mostly on discussion of civil law sources, supplemented with occasional comments on passages from the Bible and from the works of Plautus, Cicero and Virgil. The other chapters, as well as referring frequently to civil law sources, also refer regularly to acts of the Scottish parliaments and to the laws of Oleron or Wisby. The citations are often less precise than those in the 1590 treatise – Roman law texts are specified but seldom sentences within texts, and vague reference is made to 'Oleron' or 'la Roole d'Oleron', never to numbered articles – though mostly the same sources were being summarised again.[46] In addition to summarising the same three sources as the 1590 treatise, the 1613 treatise also dealt in a similar way with several others. The first was the Rhodian sea law, as published in 1561 by Simon Schard.[47] In his *prooemium* Welwod explained that he understood the law reduced to writing in this Byzantine collection to have been adopted by the Romans as the basis of their law of maritime commerce.[48] It

46 There is an exceptional reference, at *Abridgement of All Sea-Lawes*, p. 49, to 'Wisbie, c. 10', but quite apart from the mention of both 'Wisbie' and 'c. 10' being exceptional, no article in any known version of the laws of Wisby seems at all relevant to the point being made.

47 *De varia temporum in iure civili observatione, Eustathii olim Constantinopolitani antecessoris libellus; item, Leges Rhodiorum navales, militares et georgicae Iustiniani*, ed. Simon Schard (Basle, 1561), pp. 212–69. Not only do Welwod's references conform to this edition, specifically mentioned in his *prooemium*, but sometimes he clearly made use of Schard's annotations in writing his own book (for instance, compare his *Abridgement of All Sea-Lawes*, pp. 20–1, with *De varia temporum in iure civili observatione*, pp. 273–5). The edition normally used today is *The Rhodian Sea Law*, ed. W. Ashburner (Oxford, 1909).

48 *Abridgement of All Sea-Lawes*, pp. 1–2. For modern discussions see R.D. Benedict, 'The Historical Position of the Rhodian Law', (1909) 18 *Yale Law Journal* 223; C.S. Lobingier, 'The Maritime Law of Rome', (1935) 47 *Juridical Review* 1; W.P. Gormley, 'The Development of the Rhodian-Roman Maritime Law to 1681, with Special Emphasis on the Problem of Collision', (1961) 3 *Inter-American Law Review* 317; K.M.T. Atkinson, 'Rome and the Rhodian Sea-Law', (1974) 25 *IURA* 46; H.S. Khalilieh, *Admiralty and Maritime Law in the Mediterranean Sea, ca. 800–1050* (Leiden, 2006), pp. 10–13; M.T.G. Humphreys, 'Law, Power and Imperial Ideology in the Iconoclast Era', PhD dissertation, University of Cambridge, 2012, pp. 154–66.

was the neglect of the Rhodian and Roman law, he went on to explain, that had resulted in the introduction of new codes of maritime law by leading cities on the Mediterranean, culminating in the *Consolato del mare*, many provisions of which were also summarised in the 1613 treatise.[49] A third source treated in much the same way was the legislation of several northern nations. Welwod mentioned the code of maritime law enacted by Henry III of France in 1584 in his *prooemium*, and almost all his references to 'L'Admirall de France' can be traced without difficulty to provisions of this code, though the fuller reference he makes at one point to 'that Booke called *L'Admirall de France*' suggests that he may actually have been using the work of that name by Lancelot du Voisin, sieur de la Popelinière, in which provisions of the code were reorganised and connected with other sources.[50] Welwod also mentioned a code enacted in 1561 by Frederick II of Denmark, which he believed to be 'for most part all one with *La Roole d'Oleron*', though it was actually based more directly on the laws of Wisby, together with a code enacted ten years earlier in the Netherlands, which in turn was heavily influenced by the legislation of Francis I of France.[51] Almost all the references to 'Denmark' in the 1613 treatise can be traced without difficulty to provisions of the 1561 code. Finally, Welwod also indicated in his *prooemium* that the kings of England had legislated on maritime matters, referring vaguely in the margin to *Statuta Angliae*, and suggesting misleadingly in the body of the text that the work known as *De officio admiralitatis Angliae* derived from a legislative initiative.[52] A few equally vague references were made to *Statuta Angliae* elsewhere, but it was sections of the *De officio admiralitatis Angliae* that were summarised in the familiar way in several passages. Along with the civil law sources, acts of the Scottish parliaments and laws of Oleron or Wisby, it was the Rhodian sea law, *Consolato del mare* and the legislation (or supposed legislation) of France, Denmark and England that formed the major sources of the 1613 treatise, though from time to time, and especially

49 *Abridgement of All Sea-Lawes*, p. 3. Several editions of the *Consolato del mare* were printed during the sixteenth century, and it was presumably one of these that Welwod used. Later editions include *Collection de lois maritimes*, vol. 2, pp. 49–368; *Black Book of the Admiralty*, vol. 3, pp. 449–95; *Consulate of the Sea and Related Documents*, tr. S.S. Jados (University, AL, 1975), pp. 3–262.

50 *Abridgement of All Sea-Lawes*, pp. 4 and 74; *Collection de lois maritimes*, vol. 4, pp. 295–324; Lancelot du Voisin, sieur de la Popelinière, *L'amiral de France, et par occasion de celuy des autres nations, tant vieiles que nouvelles* (Paris, 1584).

51 *Collection de lois maritimes*, vol. 3, pp. 241–68.

52 *Black Book of the Admiralty*, vol. 1, pp. 221–45; BL, Add. MS 29439, ff. 160–5, Harley MS 2222, ff. 20–9, and Sloane MS 1605, ff. 3–15. What was meant by 'Statut. Ang'. is hinted at in the last line of Title 26: '*Vid. statuta Angliae, tit.* of fishing, in the Abridgements'.

in the chapters at the beginning and end of the treatise, passing reference was also made to other sources, including two works on Scots law that have since been lost, charter evidence from both Scotland and England, a few canon law sources, and various classical authors.[53]

1.3 *De dominio maris*

The distinctive chapter of the 1613 treatise on the dominion of the seas has recently been reprinted, in conjunction with a translation of Grotius' response, in an English edition of *Mare liberum*.[54] Grotius was not himself aware of the longer treatment of the subject published by Welwod in 1616, but it did eventually provoke a response from Dirk Graswinkel, after a new edition was published in the Netherlands in 1653.[55] Copies of both editions survive in reasonable numbers, and digital reproductions are now available online.[56]

The full title of the 1616 treatise was *De dominio maris iuribusque ad dominium praecipue spectantibus assertio brevis et methodica*. After a dedicatory epistle to the queen and a short preface addressed to the reader, the treatise itself was divided into four chapters, asserting in turn that there were distinct *dominia* in the sea, that *ius navigandi* was not unlimited, that *ius piscandi* was subject to appropriation, and that the sea was *vectigale*, so that taxation could be imposed legitimately on those sailing or fishing in coastal waters. Whereas the chapter on the dominion of the seas in the 1613 treatise had consisted of refutations of claims made in the fifth chapter of Grotius' *Mare liberum*, the 1616 treatise dealt with a wider range of issues in a more coherent order. Grotius' treatise was mentioned in passing, and arguments advanced in the 1613 chapter were sometimes advanced again, but the 1616 treatise did not take

53 One of the lost sources Welwod used was the *Registrum Scotiae*, cited at *Abridgement of All Sea-Lawes*, pp. 10 and 55, on which see W.M. Gordon, *Roman Law, Scots Law and Legal History: Selected Essays* (Edinburgh, 2007), pp. 273–4. The other lost source was the treatise about maritime law written by David Kintor, cited at *Abridgement of All Sea-Lawes*, p. 15.

54 Hugo Grotius, *The Free Sea*, ed. D. Armitage (Indianapolis, 2004), pp. 63–130. The translation of Grotius' response was first published in H.F. Wright, 'Some Less Known Works of Hugo Grotius', (1928) 7 *Bibliotheca Visseriana* 154, and the Latin original in S. Muller, *Mare clausum: Bijdrage tot de Geschiedenis der Rivaliteit van Engeland en Nederland in de Zeventiende Eeuw* (Amsterdam, 1872), p. 331.

55 William Welwod, *De dominio maris* (The Hague, 1653); Dirk Graswinkel, *Maris liberi vindiciae adversus Gulielmum Welwodum, Britannici maritimi dominii assertorem* (The Hague, 1653). Fulton, *Sovereignty of the Sea*, p. 412, suggests that Welwod's book was reprinted merely to provide Graswinkel with 'a theme and target'.

56 The first edition is available at http://eebo.chadwyck.com., the second at http://gallica.bnf.fr.

the form of a direct response to someone else's arguments. For instance, the passage quoted above from the 1613 chapter gave way to the following passage in the 1616 treatise:

> Denique, ut per viam interrogationis, concludam, ius piscandi non omnibus ubique gentibus commune esse; iam non quaero cum *Paulo* Si maris proprium ius quisquam habeat, aut an ad aliquem id pertineat. Sed cum *Marciano, Papinianoque*, dico, affirmoque, *quia privatus quispiam in diverticulo Maris pluribus annis solus Piscatus fuerit, id quod certe et Princeps concedere potest, illud ideo quasi proprium sibi asserere aliosque prohibere potest*; atque hinc planissime infero, licere Principi, homini, nec privato, nec privata curanti, sed publica, Populoque suo universaliter prospicienti, ratione multo fortiori maris partem Provinciae suae obiectam, communique idcirco prudentum consensu, quasi eius Dominio adiudicatam, sic pro suo possidere, ut exteros omnes inde ab omni Piscatione iure optimo prohibere possit. Adeo ut quamvis Ius istud sponte negligat, Dominium tamen illud apud ipsum manet: secundum illud *Ulpiani, Differentia inter Dominium et possessionem haec est, quod Dominium nihilominus eius manet, qui Dominus esse non vult.*[57]

The argument remained that since the civil law permits private citizens to acquire exclusive fishing rights, princes must surely be able to acquire the same rights in the public interest.[58] However, instead of being presented as a response to a point made by Grotius, the argument was now connected with

57 *De dominio maris*, p. 19: 'Let me finally conclude, as a logical inference, that the right of fishing is not common to all nations everywhere. I am not now asking with Paul if anyone may have a proper right in the sea, or whether it may pertain to anyone, but am stating and affirming with Marcian and Papinian that since any private person who may have fished alone for several years in an inlet of the sea can thence assert that the fishing is in effect proper to him and exclude others, that can certainly be allowed to the prince also. And from this I deduce very plainly, by far more forceful reasoning, and accordingly by the common consent of prudent people, that it is permissible for the prince, a man not caring about himself or his private affairs but constantly providing for public affairs and his people, to bring part of the sea within his province, as if allocated to his ownership, in such a way that he can possess it as his own and so exclude all foreigners from all fishing by sovereign right, to the extent that even if he were willingly to neglect that right, the ownership still remains his, in accordance with Ulpian's remark that "the difference between ownership and possession is this, that ownership still remains with somebody who does not wish to be owner"'.

58 The argument rested on an imprecise reading of D.41.3.7 and 44.3.7, in which Papinian and Marcian had talked about fishing 'in fluminis publici deverticulo', not 'in diverticulo

two other Roman law texts, in one of which Paul had considered what would happen 'si maris proprium ius ad aliquem pertineat', and in the other of which Ulpian had explained the difference between the right of ownership, which Welwod associated with the right of fishing, and the factual state of being in possession.[59] In comparison with the 1590 treatise and most of the 1613 treatise, the 1616 treatise was generally written in a more deliberative style, and if still argumentative it was less polemical than the chapter in the 1613 treatise on the dominion of the seas. One advantage of moving away from immediate engagement with Grotius was that the focus could more easily be kept on fishing rights, without the necessity of insisting that Grotius' ostensible concern with navigation on the high seas was designed to disguise an attempt to challenge the Scottish king's right to exclude foreign fishermen from coastal waters.

The range of sources cited in the 1616 treatise was broadly similar to the range of sources cited in the 1613 chapter. There were about ninety references to texts from the *Corpus iuris civilis* (over seventy of which were from the *Digest*), and there were about twenty-five further references to the works of later writers on the civil law, the majority of whom were medieval commentators (Bartolus was cited seven times and Baldus three), though one innovation was the inclusion of references to a few writers who worked during Welwod's own lifetime (including Wesenbecius and Tholosanus). Another innovation was the inclusion of a handful of references to canon law sources, which had been mentioned in some chapters of the 1613 treatise but not in the one on the dominion of the seas. There was also a large increase in the number of references to the Bible (about twenty-five) and classical writers (about fifteen), which is disproportionate to the increase in length of the 1616 treatise over the 1613 chapter. Attention was devoted at one stage to an agreement previously observed by the Scots and Dutch, but no more interest was shown in the 1616 treatise than the 1613 chapter in the Rhodian sea law, the *Consolato del mare*, the laws of Oleron and Wisby, or the legislation of Scotland, England, France and Denmark.

Maris'. Welwod's crucial claim was that the sea was viewed by the Roman jurists as a *res communis* in the sense of a *res publica*, which meant that navigable rivers were to be regarded as the same type of thing as the sea.

59 D.47.10.14 and 41.2.17.1 Other texts from the *Digest* and *Code* were cited in the margin here, along with the *Glossa ordinaria*.

1.4 *MCL, PL2208*

Welwod's other treatise on maritime law is preserved in a manuscript volume forming part of the Pepys Library at Magdalene College, Cambridge.[60] Most of the volume is occupied by a transcription of the practicks of James Balfour of Pittendreich, to which a treatise on maritime law was appended, but towards the end there is another treatise on the maritime law of Scotland, followed by a copy of the work known as *De officio admiralitatis Angliae*.[61] The second treatise on the maritime law of Scotland has an explicit reading 'Finis amen me Robertum Douglas 1611', which is repeated without any date after the copy of the *De officio admiralitatis Angliae*.[62] An inscription at the front of the volume reads: 'Presented to the Duke of Lauderdale by his graces humble servant Geo. Mackenzie, 14 Nov. 1676'. Samuel Pepys acquired the volume in 1692 when the manuscript collection previously belonging to Lauderdale was auctioned at Tom's Coffee House in London.[63] The relevant item was described in the sale catalogue as 'Balfour's Practiques and Old Sea-Laws (on Paper) Fol'., which is essentially how the volume was described in Pepys' own catalogue.[64]

The second treatise on the maritime law of Scotland has no title but opens with a sheet of paper marked only with a heading: 'The Proheme, Bearing the Origin of the Sea Law, the Grund of this Treatie and Occasioun Thairof'.[65] To judge from the size of the paper and handwriting, too much space was left for a *prooemium* of the length found in the 1590 treatise to be added but about enough for a *prooemium* like the one found in the 1613 treatise. After this, the arrangement of the manuscript treatise is similar in some respects to the arrangement of the 1613 treatise, as indicated below.

---

60 MCL, PL2208. The author gratefully acknowledges his indebtedness to Richard Luckett for authorising his use of the manuscript, and to Phillipa Grimstone for making the conditions in which it was examined more agreeable than could reasonably have been expected.

61 J.R. Tanner, *Bibliotheca Pepysiana: A Descriptive Catalogue of the Library of Samuel Pepys*, vol. 1, '"Sea" Manuscripts' (London, 1914), p. 10; *Catalogue of the Pepys Library at Magdalene College, Cambridge*, 7 vols, ed. R. Latham (Woodbridge, 1978–92), vol. 5, pt 2, p. 36; G. Dolezalek, *Scotland under Ius Commune: Census of Manuscripts of Legal Literature in Scotland, Mainly between 1500 and 1660*, 3 vols (Edinburgh, 2010), vol. 3, pp. 31–2.

62 MCL, PL2208, ff. 481v and 487r.

63 *Particular Friends: The Correspondence of Samuel Pepys and John Evelyn*, ed. G. de la Bédoyère (Woodbridge, 2005), p. 201; *The Bannatyne Miscellany*, 3 vols, ed. D. Laing (Edinburgh, 1827–55), vol. 2, pp. 152 and 154; *Catalogi librorum manuscriptorum Angliae et Hiberniae*, 2 vols, ed. Edward Bernard and Humphrey Wanley (Oxford, 1697), vol. 2, p. 209.

64 *Catalogue of the Pepys Library*, vol. 7, pt 1, p. 216.

65 MCL, PL2208, f. 472.

1590 Treatise	1611 Manuscript	1613 Treatise
Proeme	Proheme	Proheme
1. Ordour of this treatie	1. Ordour of this treatise	1. Order of this treatise
	2. Judge ordinar	2. Judge ordinary
	3. Admirall clerk	3. Admirall clerke
	4. Advocattis	4. Advocates
	5. Maner of proceidingis	5. Manner of proceeding
	6. Persones in schippis	6. Persons in ships
2. Fraughting of schips	7. Frauchting of schipis	7. Fraughting of ships
3. Maister of the schip	8. Maister of the schip	8. Master of the ship
4. Duetie to marchant	9. Dewtie to merchand	9. Duety to merchant
5. Duetie to mariners	10. Dewtie to marineris	10. Duety to mariners
6. Mariners thair duetie	11. Marineris thair dewtie	11. Dueties of mariners
	12. Clerk of ane schip	12. Clerke of a ship
7. Pilote or steirseman	13. Pylot or steirsman	13. Pilot or steirsman
	14. Money lent to sea	14. Money lent to sea
8. Outredder of ane schip	15. Outredderis of schippis and [thair] discords	15. Outreaders of ships
		16. Sundry partners
9. Gudis cassin	16. Guidis cassin	17. Casting of goods
10. Pirats	17. Pyratis	18. Pirats
11. Spilt gear	18. Spilt geir	19. Spoyled goods
12. Lichtning	19. Lighting	20. Disburdening
13. Contributioun	20. Contributioun	21. Contribution
	21. Priviledgit schippis	22. Priviledged ships
14. Shipwracke	22. Shipwrak	23. Shipwracke
15. Judge ordinair	23. Things found or taken on sea	24. Things found on sea
		25. Things taken on sea
		26. Fishers and fishing
		27. Propriety of seas
		28. Warships
		29. Watermen
		30. Shipwrights

Most of the titles listed have been abbreviated to facilitate comparison, from which it will be apparent that the manuscript treatise follows the same the pattern as the 1613 treatise by including the series of chapters at the start about the judge ordinary and his court, and about the types of person typically involved in navigation. It also includes the chapters about the clerk of a ship, maritime loans and the privileges accorded to some ship owners, and while it does not include separate chapters about partnerships and things taken at sea, it does in fact contain discussions of these topics towards the end of the preceding chapters about outredders and things found at sea. However, the manuscript treatise includes neither the chapter on the judge ordinary with which the 1590 treatise ended nor the five chapters on the fishing trade, the dominion of the seas and the personnel of warships, watermen and shipwrights with which the 1613 treatise ended.

In substance the manuscript treatise is similar to the treatises printed in 1590 and 1613. It consists for the most part of the same dogmatic statements backed up by references to sources that are found in the printed treatises, though with some more descriptive and deliberative passages in its first six chapters. In these chapters, as well as those about the clerk of a ship, maritime loans and the privileges accorded to ship owners, the manuscript treatise is naturally more similar to the 1613 than the 1590 treatise, but even in these chapters it is more like the 1590 treatise in being written in Scots rather than English. Even in the chapters absent from the 1590 treatise the focus is on Scottish practice, and statements about English practice found in the 1613 treatise are often omitted. An example is a sentence found in the chapter about court procedure in the 1613 treatise alone, which reads: 'The like is to be observed also in causes of spoyle; where, by the lawes of England, it is sufficient for the spoyler to prove his goods by his marke, &c.[mm]'.[66] The note labelled '[mm]' reads 'Vide statut. Ang'. and is situated between notes labelled 'm' and 'n', both of which can be found in the manuscript treatise, beside the statements they support.[67] In fact, citations from *Statuta Angliae* are entirely lacking from the manuscript treatise, though it does contain statements based on the source called *De officio admiralitatis Angliae*, together with statements based on the Rhodian sea law, *Consolato del mare* and French and Danish legislation. For instance, the title 'Anent Persones Ordinar in Schippis' is based partly on civil law sources but mostly on the Rhodian sea law and *Consolato del mare*, while the title 'Off the Admirall Clerk' is based partly on an act of a Scottish parliament but mostly

66 *Abridgement of All Sea-Lawes*, p. 18.
67 MCL, PL2208, f. 475v.

on the source cited as 'l'Admirall de France'.[68] In the chapters common to the manuscript treatise and both the printed treatises, the manuscript treatise tends to contain the statements based on the Rhodian sea law, *Consolato del mare* and French and Danish legislation that are absent from the 1590 treatise. In the chapter about the hiring of ships, for example, after the first few lines quoted earlier, the 1590 treatise continues:

> Bot gif the fault be in the merchant, he sall pay the skipper and schips skaith [d. l. ex conducto, §. item quum quidam], and in case the merchant hald not out his veyage, he sal pay the haile fraught [l. pen., §. tamen, loc., facit d. l. si in lege, l. si domus, et l. domus horreor., §. fin., eod.], for it was aneuch that the maister was reddy at the day appointit [per l. sed adde, §. fin., eod.].[69]

As in the first few lines, the statements made here were more or less loosely based on the texts cited from the *Digest*. In contrast, the manuscript treatise reads at this point, in broad agreement with the 1613 treatise:

> Bot if the falt be in the merchand, he sall pay the skipper and schippis skayth [d. l. ex conducto]. Bot efter the Rhodian law, he sall enterteine the ecquippage ten dayis and, gif he stay longer, sall pay fraucht for all accoirdinglie [art. 25, legum na. selectar], and quhat farder hurt happinis than to the schip salbe upset be the merchandis, quhidder fyre or wrak efter the terme appointit [art. 29, eod.]. And in cais the merchand hald not his voyage, he sall pay the haill fraucht [d. l. si in lege, et l. ult. ad l. Rhod, et d. l. ex conducto], accoirding to the Romane lawis, bot accoirding to the Rhodian lawis onelie the half fraucht, and the skipper the haill, gif he faill [art. 24, legum select].[70]

The references to the *Digest* are less precise and numerous here, but the more striking difference is the inclusion of statements based on provisions of the Rhodian sea law, which are shown to be inconsistent with the Roman law texts.

---

68 MCL, PL2208, ff. 474v and 476r. Reference was also made in the former title to Plautus, and in general the manuscript treatise contains many of the isolated references to other sources found in the 1613 treatise.

69 *Sea-Law of Scotland*, sig. B2v, citing D.19.2.15.6, 19.2.61.1, 19.2.24, 19.2.45, 19.2.55.2 and 19.2.19.10.

70 MCL, PL2208, f. 476v, citing D.19.2.15, 19.2.24, 14.2.10 and 19.2.15 again, and *Rhodian Sea-Law*, 26, 28, 103 and 107. *Cf. Abridgement of All Sea-Lawes*, p. 23.

No attempt is made to reconcile the contrasting statements. It is as typical of the manuscript as the printed treatises that statements summarising sources are accumulated without discussion.

2 Reconsideration of the Relationship between the Treatises

The obvious way to explain the relationship between the manuscript treatise and the printed treatises of 1590 and 1613 is by supposing that it was written around 1611 as an expanded version of the 1590 treatise, before being translated two years later into English and expanded further, particularly by the inclusion of new references to English sources. By and large, the manuscript treatise does look as if it may have been composed by inserting statements backed up by references to the Rhodian sea law, the *Consolato del mare* and the legislation of France, Denmark and England into the text printed in 1590, and it would help to explain why some of the chapters printed for the first time in 1613 retain a peculiarly Scottish flavour if they were first written before the decision was made to prepare the treatise for republication in England. However, the passages that look as if they were composed by the insertion of additional statements into the 1590 text could just as easily have been abbreviated for publication in 1590 by the excision of those statements, and there are a few passages that make it seem more likely that this is what happened. None of these passages can be taken on its own to show that the manuscript treatise was written first, but taken together they give an increasingly firm impression that the text copied in 1611 was the earliest of Welwod's treatises on maritime law, and that in 1613 he reverted to this treatise instead of developing the 1590 treatise further.

To begin with, the account Welwod gave of the structure of his 1590 treatise – quoted above – may be compared with a parallel passage in the manuscript treatise, which reads:

> Off quhilk thingis ordourlie and summerlie this abridgement sall mak schaw, beginning at the judge ordinar of seafair causes, the memberis of his court, and maner of proceiding thair, syne to the frauchting of schippis, as almaist concerning the cheif end and uses of schippis, thridlie anent all the persounis abovementionat, thair poweris, dewties and priviledges, ferdlie the manifest chances of seafairing, with the maner of doing tharintill, and last of priviledgit schippis, schipwrakis and thingis found on sea.[71]

71 MCL, PL2208, f. 473r. *Cf.* the passage quoted from the *Sea-Law of Scotland* above between nn. 8 and 9.

It was remarked earlier that the account given in the 1590 treatise was misleading in suggesting that its closing chapter on 'the judges ordinair to all seafair debaits' would follow on from discussion of 'the maner of judgment' in cases of contribution. The manuscript passage seems less contrived, more accurate and in general more coherent, its only weakness being the omission of any mention of the title about people found on ships. In other words, the manuscript passage reads like a fairly straightforward description of the contents of the book, whereas the printed passage reads as if its author was struggling to justify the inclusion of a chapter about the handling of maritime litigation at the end of his book. It is worth noting too that in these passages Welwod described his treatise as an 'abridgement'. He certainly did not decide in 1613 to replace a treatise on the sea law of Scotland with an abridgement of a wider range of sea laws. An abridgement of all relevant sea laws was what he had always been intent on producing.

A more significant passage appears in the chapter about the responsibilities of a ship's master towards his mariners. In the manuscript treatise it runs as follows:

> Seing the maister is the ordinar rewler to his ecquippage, he aucht thairfoir be a speciall authoritie to hald thame in peace sa lang as thay eat his bread [Oleron], and gif ony mariner[ ] be hurt in ony service to quhilk he is commandit, or gif he be unable to flie out of the schip, [or] happin to be hurt throw the falt of ane uther mariner, the master sall heal him, as quha is haldin to answere for all deidis schipbuird [per l. 1, de excer. act., et l. fin, nau. caup.], and be the same authoritie caus the uther mariner restoir that he hes payit for his healing his coistis, and quhat ever he hes loist thairby [art. 5, leg. select.], except that he that is hurt or slane haif bene provoked be the evident invasioun and straikis from the uther [art. 6, eod.].[72]

The statement preceding the reference to the laws of Oleron is clearly supported by a provision of that code, as indeed is the statement immediately afterwards.[73] It is only the explanation that the master 'is haldin to answere for all deidis schipbuird' that receives support from the *Digest* texts referred to, one of which actually indicates that liability will not extend to a case where one mariner injures another.[74] The last two statements summarise accurately

72 MCL, PL2208, f. 477v.

73 *Black Book of the Admiralty*, vol. 1, pp. 94–5 and 104–5.

74 D.14.1.1 and 4.9.7. The texts concern the *exercitor*'s liability, but that was parasitic on the master's.

the articles cited from the Rhodian sea law.[75] In the 1590 treatise the corresponding passage runs as follows:

> Seeing the master is the ordinair ruler to his kippage, he aught thairfoir be an special authority to hald tham in peace sa lang as they eat his bread [c. 8, Olon], and giff any mariner be hurt in any service of the ship, commandit therto be the maister [c. 6, eod.], or gif he be unable to flee out of the schip, happnis to be hurt through the fault of an uther mariner quhilk might haif bene eschewit, the master sal heale him [per l. 1, §. 3, de excer., et l. fin, naut., caup.], as he quha is haldin to answere for the deid of al within his schip [l. 1, §. fin., eod.], namly his mariners, bot in this last caise may rather bee his awne authority garre the uther mariner heale him, or els repete the samin coast fra him [arg., l. 7, eod.]. Bot ther is a farder considerationn yit, giff the fault proceede of evident wilfulnes.[76]

That two provisions of the laws of Oleron were being relied on is at least made clearer here. However, as already indicated, the *Digest* texts cited next support the statement that now comes after the reference, not the preceding statement, and the statement for which they do provide support is instead backed up here by reference to a text that provides less clear support.[77] Whereas the first two texts cited indicate clearly that the master is responsible for the actions of the crew, the third indicates that he is also responsible for the actions of any passengers (which sits strangely with the phrase 'namly his mariners'). The final reference indicates that it is arguable from one of the texts already cited that a mariner who injures another may be required to cover the costs of his cure.[78] Presumably the argument was that since a master is said in the text not to be liable where one mariner injures another, the mariner must himself be liable, though it seems less likely that Welwod was actually drawing this inference than that he was reworking the statement found in the manuscript treatise. Most revealing of all is the final statement in the passage from the 1590 treatise, which is exceptional in not having any support provided, and which still looks like a summary of the second article cited in the manuscript treatise from the Rhodian sea law. It is hard to believe that this passage was not originally written with reference to the Rhodian sea law.

75 *Rhodian Sea Law*, pp. 13–14 and 83–4.
76 *Sea-Law of Scotland*, sig. B5v-6r.
77 D.4.9.1.8.
78 D.4.9.7.

In the next chapter of the manuscript treatise there is another passage worth comparing with the parallel passage in the 1590 treatise. In the manuscript treatise it runs as follows:

> Ane mariner aucht all dew obedience to the maister, evin in suffering, bot against ma nor ane straik may defend himself, for in cais of rebellioun, quhilk is than thocht to be committit quhan the maister hes thryst liftit the towell fra befoir him, and yit he offeris na mendis, then may he nocht onelie be commandit of the schip at the first [land], bot also, if he mak oppin stryft and plane debait with the maister, he tynes his half hyre, and that quhilk he hes aschipbuird [la rool d'Oleron]. And gif he tak up airmour, and with ane wapin invaid the maister, then sould the marineris bind him, prisone him and put him to justice, and quha amang the marineris refuises to lay to his hand and assist sall tyne his hyre and that quhilk he haith aschipbuird [il consolato, c. 16]. Yea, gif ony marineris band and conspyre against the skipper, and force him to go to ane uther harberie and port nor he wes frauchtit to, thay may be puneischit as for a deidlie cryme [Denmark]. Bot if the rebellious mariner tymouslie offer amendis and submit himself to his fellowis, he may follow the schip and obtene his hyre in cais the skipper refuis his offer and submission [Oleron].[79]

Here the reference to 'la rool d'Oleron' signifies two articles on which the preceding statements are firmly based, though at the end use was clearly made of a provision of the *Consolato del mare* as well, which also provided firm support for the statement that then followed.[80] The next statement is equally firmly supported by an article in the Danish code of 1561, and the last statement by one of the articles already cited from the laws of Oleron.[81] In the 1590 treatise the parallel passage reads more briefly:

> A marriner aught all dew obedience to the maister, evin in suffering, bot in ane straike onelye, for against ma straikes he may defend himselfe [c. 9, Olon], for utherwaies, in caise of rebellioun, he may be commandit furth of the schip at the first land [c. 35, eod.], except he offer ane mendis for his fault, submitting himself to the judgement of his fellowes, in quhilk

79 MCL, PL2208, f. 478r.

80 *Black Book of the Admiralty*, vol. 1, pp. 104–7; *Consulate of the Sea*, p. 85.

81 *Collection de lois maritimes*, vol. 3, p. 247; *Black Book of the Admiralty*, vol. 1, pp. 106–7.

> caise, giff the maister refuse him, he may follow the schip and notwithstanding obteine his hyre as he had servit [c. 10, eod.].[82]

This passage is more typical of the 1590 treatise in simply omitting the statements that can be found in the manuscript treatise backed up with references to the Rhodian sea law, the *Consolato del mare* or the legislation of France, Denmark or England. What seems strange, however, is the reference to 'c. 35, eod'. Everything preceding the first reference (to 'c. 9, Olon') is clearly based on the first of the two articles from the laws of Oleron relied on in the manuscript treatise, and everything afterwards (as far as the reference to 'c. 10, eod'.) is clearly based on the second article.[83] So why was a reference included to 'c. 35, eod'.? Part of the explanation may be that Welwod was using what he thought was a copy of the laws of Oleron but was in reality an amalgam of the laws of Oleron and Wisby, and that 'c. 35' in that copy was the same provision as 'c. 10', as it had reappeared in the laws of Wisby.[84] But why would he trouble to mention the repetition of this particular provision, unlike the one just cited or many others that were replicated, and why would he mention it towards the middle of the statement based on the provision? The vital clue may be that 'c. 35, eod'. is cited at precisely the point at which material from other sources was included in the manuscript treatise. As the inclusion of this material broke the statement based on 'c. 10' into two parts, it could be that in revising the manuscript treatise Welwod felt the need to find a new reference to support the first part of the statement.

Another strange passage in the 1590 treatise appears in one of the chapters about contribution. In the manuscript treatise Welwod commented that a general rule would not apply if contradicted by the terms of a charter party, 'for then conditioun makis law', which he took to be supported by a *Digest* text declaring that *contractus legem ex conventione accipiunt*.[85] A little later in the same chapter he stated that a general rule would apply 'except thair be sum uther conditioun, quhilk in all thingis makis lawe, as said', again referring to the *Digest*. Both these statements appear in the 1590 treatise, with the *Digest* references attached again, but the first ends 'for thair condicioun makis law, as said is', and the second 'except thair be ane uther speciall condicioun, quhilke

82 *Sea-Law of Scotland*, sig. B6v.

83 In some editions of the laws of Oleron, unlike the one cited, these articles appear successively.

84 *Black Book of the Admiralty*, vol. 4, p. 272.

85 MCL, PL2208, f. 480, citing D.16.3.1.6.

in all things makis lawe'.[86] When he wrote 'as said is' Welwod must already have said somewhere that 'condicioun makis law', but it was not in the 1590 treatise itself.

In this instance, the manuscript treatise makes better sense than the 1590 treatise, but it can also be revealing when the opposite happens. The preceding chapter of the manuscript treatise reads in its entirety:

> Gif through the lousing of ony geir cassin, or be any sic neidfull occasioun, ather geir in the schip restand be spilt with water or utherwayis, in that cais contributioun salbe maid for geir castin, becaus the awner thairof is also hurt as he quhais guids ar cassin, and alwayis that consideratioun to be had in setting skat, sua that gif it fell ony certane guids to pay ten pound skat, and in the meanetyme it wer fortie schillingis wore be lousing thairof, the xl schillingis sould be deducit [l. navis, 4, ad l. Rhod.] of the ten pound.[87]

This chapter involves a rather unsuccessful attempt to condense the terms of the text cited from the *Digest*, in which Callistratus considered what would happen where the jettisoning of goods in a storm resulted in damage to some of the goods left on board a ship.[88] Distinguishing between the case where goods on board a ship happened to have been damaged and the case where it was the jettisoning of other goods that had exposed them to the elements, he explained that a person whose goods were damaged as a result of jettison should be taken to have suffered loss for the common good like a person whose goods were thrown overboard. As contributions to the reimbursement of a person whose goods were thrown overboard would be calculated in proportion to the value of the goods left on board, the obvious solution was to base the calculation of the contribution due from a person whose goods were damaged on their value after the damage was inflicted. In the 1590 treatise the corresponding chapter reads:

> Giff it happins throw the lowsing of the gear cassin, or be any sick neidfull occasioun, that any uther gear in the schip be spilt with water or otherwaies, in that caise contributioun sall be made thairfoir, even as for the gudis cassin, because the awner of the spilt gear is hurt as well as he

86 *Sea-Law of Scotland*, sigg. C3r and C4r.

87 MCL, PL2208, f. 480r.

88 D.14.2.4.

> quhais gudis are cassin, for it is alyke to loose ten crownes and gear to be made ten crownes worse. Yea, suppois the skaith be bot meane, yit consideratioun suld be had thairof in setting the skatt for the guds cassin, that ane kinde of gear suffer nocht twa skaithes. And thairfoir, giffe for example it fell to any certain gear to pay ten pound skatt, and in the meane time it were fourty shillings worse through the lowsing of the gear cassin, the fourty shillings suld be deducit [l. navis, 4, §. 2, ad l. Rhod.]. Bot giff the skaith cum otherwaies, thair is na sic regarde to be had thairof [arg. d. §. 2].[89]

While still not entirely transparent in its meaning, this more expansive discussion is easier to follow than the chapter in the manuscript treatise. It seems more likely that the discussion was improved in 1590 than that it was rendered less intelligible at a later stage, though that could of course have happened.[90]

Another notable feature of the manuscript treatise is the relative imprecision of its references to the *Digest* and laws of Oleron, a feature shared with the 1613 treatise. It would seem odd for Welwod to have made his references less precise in revising his treatise, and it cannot be that he had made a policy decision (however odd) to be more vague since he did provide article numbers for the Rhodian sea law and *Consolato del mare*. It seems more likely that the 1590 references were a refinement of those in the manuscript treatise than vice versa. Moreover, something else worth noting is that the sources on which the manuscript treatise was based were all available before 1590. That Welwod made use of Simon Schard's 1561 edition of the Rhodian sea law rather than the new edition that appeared in 1596 need not in itself be terribly significant, and his reliance on a manuscript version of the *De officio admiralitatis Angliae* instead of the extended version printed in 1591 may easily be attributed to ignorance, but the same explanation cannot so easily be given for his use of an important Scottish source.[91] The manuscript treatise ends with the following passage:

---

89 *Sea-Law of Scotland*, sigg. C2v-3r.

90 Welwod appears to have given up the struggle by 1613, for the parallel passage in his *Abridgement of All Sea-Lawes*, p. 44, simply reads: 'Yf through the losing of any cast goods, or upon any needfull occasion, the remaining goods be spoyled either with wette, or otherwayes; a contribution shalbe made, proportionable for so much as they are made worse'. Presumably he did not look at the 1590 version.

91 *Rhodian Sea Law*, pp. xli–ii; *Articles Concerning the Admiralty of England and the Jurisdiction Thereof* (London, 1591); BL, Add. MS 12504, f. 143. The version Welwod used was believed to be a sixteenth century translation into Latin of an original written in French during the fourteenth century.

> Bot quhair admiralities ar constitut and allowit, gif schipis or boatis be found upon the sea or at the coistis without ony levand creatour in the same [vide statut. Alexa. 2], and na man clameand the same for yeir and day, or gif a dead man be found with jewellis on him, or iron, timber or great fisches in sum countries, the half belangis to the admirall, the rest to the finder [de offi. admir. Angli.]. And agane in uther countries, a third to the king, a thrid to the admirall, and a thrid to the finder, as in France [l'admirall de France]. And becaus in Scotland the prince hes quatt his thrid to the admirall, thairfoir is it that the admirall drawis twa pairtis of all fand geir [vide diploma admiralli de Scotland]. Evin sua is it anent pyratis and the guids and schip tane with thame, the twa pairt fallis to the admirall of Scotland and the third pairt to the taker [Denmark et l'admirall de France]. Bot anent pryses, the tent pairt onelie and na mair fallis to the admirall of Scotland, as lykwayis of France, &c. [vide diplom. admir.] And alwayis the prissoneris of all pryses sould be presented unto the admirall dirrectlie, nor yit may ony schip clame ony pairt of a pryse except scho sett saill and fecht with the rest [l'admiral de France, et Kintor, c. 6].[92]

English, French and Danish sources are cited here, as elsewhere, not only for purposes of comparison but also to support statements made about the rights of the Scottish admiral.[93] An old Scottish statute and the lost treatise by David Kintor are cited to provide local authority, but the crucial source cited is the 'diploma' or royal charter granted to Francis Stewart, fifth earl of Bothwell, in 1587, the terms of which were reiterated in 1591 when Ludovic Stewart, second duke of Lennox, replaced Bothwell as admiral.[94] As well as stating clearly that the Scottish admiral was entitled to two thirds of any ships found adrift at sea and to a tenth of any prizes taken in wartime, the charter had stated more generally that he was to exercise his office 'as freely as any admirals of the kingdoms of France, Spain, England, Denmark or other foreign nations', and was 'to follow, imitate, assimilate and cause to be applied and put into practice' the

92 MCL, PL2208, f. 481v.

93 *Black Book of the Admiralty*, vol. 1, p. 241; *Collection de lois maritimes*, vol. 4, pp. 300, 303 and 312–13. The reference to 'Denmark et l'admirall de France' here is the only one in the book that cannot be traced.

94 *Regiam maiestatem Scotiae, veteres leges et constitutiones*, ed. Sir John Skene of Curriehill (Edinburgh, 1609), pt 2, pp. 28–9; *Registrum magni sigilli regum Scotorum: The Register of the Great Seal of Scotland*, 11 vols, ed. J. Balfour Paul, J.M. Thomson, J.H. Stevenson and W.K. Dickson (Edinburgh, 1984), vol. 5, pp. 449–50 and 638.

laws of all these nations.[95] However, in 1592 an act of parliament was passed restricting the admiral's rights to those established before the middle of the century, 'nochwtstanding ony greitar specialitie contenit in any of the saidis admirallis infeftmentis bygane or to cum'.[96] As a consequence of this act, when Lennox became embroiled in an argument about his rights and privileges in 1600 he was unable to rely directly on the 1591 charter and had instead to refer more loosely to his infeftment in the admiralty and to the continual exercise of the rights and privileges since then by his deputies, 'without ony impediment or molestatioun maid to them thairin in ony time bigane'.[97] In 1603 Lennox was granted a new charter and was reinvested in office as admiral, but without his rights being specified in the way they were in the 1587 and 1591 charters.[98] As Welwod must surely have been aware, it was not possible after the 1592 act was passed to rely on any 'diploma admiralli de Scotland' as an authoritative statement of the admiral's rights. That act – and another confirming the dean of guild's jurisdiction – is ignored in the manuscript treatise.[99]

3 Contexts in Which the Treatises May Be Located

Further evidence remains to be considered of the early production of the manuscript treatise, but mention of the admiral's charter has moved discussion in the direction of consideration of the contexts in which Welwod was working, and it may be as well at this point to move more deliberately in the same direction. In pursuing this line of enquiry, the aim is not to identify all the contexts in which the different texts may be located, but to identify three that seem

95 *Registrum magni sigilli regum Scotorum*, vol. 5, p. 450: 'adeo libere quam quicunque admiralli regnorum Gallie, Hispanie, Anglie, Danie aut aliarum extranearum nationum exercebant dictum officium, secundum iura regni sui et dictarum nationum, que iura rex ordinavit suum admirallum, viceadmirallum et deputatos sequi, imitari, colligere, et imprimi facere ut practicarentur in futurum'.

96 *Acts of the Parliaments of Scotland*, vol. 3, p. 580; Records of the Parliaments of Scotland, 1592/4/101. One of the *Journal of Legal History*'s readers drew attention to A.R. MacDonald, 'The Parliament of 1592: A Crisis Averted?', in K.M. Brown and A.J. Mann (eds), *Parliament and Politics in Scotland, 1567–1707* (Edinburgh, 2005), p. 57.

97 *The Register of the Privy Council of Scotland*, 14 vols, ed. J.H. Burton and D. Masson (Edinburgh, 1877–98), vol. 6, pp. 177–8; B. Seton, 'The Vice Admiral and the Quest of the "Golden Pennie"', (1923) 20 *Scottish Historical Review* 122, at p. 125.

98 *Registrum magni sigilli regum Scotorum*, vol. 6, pp. 501–2; NRS, GD220/1/F/8/4/1.

99 *Acts of the Parliaments of Scotland*, vol. 4, p. 30; Records of the Parliaments of Scotland, 1593/4/57.

particularly significant. An important point to bear in mind is that although a few passages have been found in which the editing of the 1590 treatise appears to have been executed clumsily, for the most part traces of the editing process are difficult to detect. If it is to be believed that Welwod prepared his 1590 treatise for the press by excising from the manuscript treatise statements based on sources other than the acts of the Scottish parliaments, the laws of Oleron and Wisby and the texts and commentaries of the civil law, it will need to be explained why he felt the need to take such care in carrying out the task.

3.1 *'A Reformation of the Justice within This Land'*

In dedicating his 1590 treatise to the king, Welwod announced that he was writing 'in this common expectation and great hoip of all peiple for a reformatioun of the Justice within this land'.[100] It has been suggested that the expectation of reform had begun in 1587, when a concerted effort had been made to improve the administration of justice in Scotland, and that the grant of a new charter to the admiral in that year had formed part of the same programme.[101] The instruction issued to the admiral and his deputies to follow the example of the admiralty laws of France, Spain, England, Denmark and other nations 'in futurum' clearly suggests that a degree of innovation was intended, although turning to the example of foreign laws was far from novel. As early as 1544 it had been argued that the Scottish admiral must be taken to enjoy the same jurisdiction as his counterparts 'in utheris realmes'.[102] Just months earlier a code of maritime law had been introduced in France, many provisions of which were incorporated into the collection of 'sea lawis' attached to Sir James Balfour's practicks, which also indicated that use had been made of French legislation in David Kintor's lost treatise.[103] Kintor appears to have been a judge in the central admiralty court in the late 1550s and early 1560s, the period covered by the only court book surviving from the sixteenth century, which reveals that

---

100 *Sea-Law of Scotland*, sig. A2r.

101 M. Lee, *John Maitland of Thirlestane and the Foundations of the Stewart Despotism in Scotland* (Princeton, 1959), pp. 120 and 157–8; D.H. Willson, *King James VI and I* (London, 1963), p. 97; J.W. Cairns, 'Academic Feud, Bloodfeud and William Welwood: Legal Education in St Andrews, 1560–1611', (1998) 2 *Edinburgh Law Review* 158 and 255, at pp. 158–9; J. Goodare, *State and Society in Early Modern Scotland* (Oxford, 1999), p. 74, and *The Government of Scotland, 1560–1625* (Oxford, 2004), pp. 53 and 279.

102 *Acts of the Parliaments of Scotland*, vol. 2, p. 449; Records of the Parliaments of Scotland, 1544/11/28.

103 *The Practicks of Sir James Balfour of Pittendreich*, 2 vols, ed. P.G.B. McNeill (Edinburgh, 1962–3), vol. 2, pp. 614–44.

use was sometimes made of foreign laws in forensic debates.[104] The 1587 charter thus endorsed an existing trend, yet the perception was that its terms had served as a pretext for the extension of the admiral's powers in a way that was damaging to the interests of the coastal burghs.[105] It was the complaints of these burghs about 'sindry new exactiounis' and the 'usurping of judicatour of caussis of burgessis' that resulted in the restriction of the admiral's powers by parliament in 1592.[106] The dispute with the burghs was at its height when the king returned with his new bride from Denmark in 1590, amid rumours that a fresh wave of reforms was intended.[107] A convention of the estates was asked to consider 'the reformation of the council, sessions and inferior courts', and it advised in June that the judges ought to decide for themselves how best to improve the practice of their tribunals.[108] It was at the end of the same month that Welwod wrote his dedicatory epistle to the king.[109]

As noted already, the 1590 treatise differed significantly in its structure from the manuscript treatise, for it ended with a chapter on 'the judges ordinair to all seafair debaits' and omitted the chapters at the beginning of the manuscript treatise about the admiral and his court. Drawing frequently in these early chapters from French, Danish and English sources, and describing how

104 *Acta curiae admirallatus Scotiae, 1557–62*, ed. T.C. Wade (Edinburgh, 1937), pp. 15 and 73. That the book cited by Balfour as the *Liber Kyntoris* was written by this David Kintor is not certain but does seem highly likely. There are also places in Welwod's treatise at which foreign laws seem to have been relied on without being explicitly cited.

105 A.R.G. McMillan, 'The Scottish Court of Admiralty: A Retrospect', (1922) 34 *Juridical Review* 38 and 164, at pp. 42–3, and 'The Admiral of Scotland', (1923) 20 *Scottish Historical Review* 11, at pp. 15–16; L.B. Taylor, 'Introduction', in *Aberdeen Council Letters*, 6 vols (London, 1942), vol. 1, p. ix, at pp. liv–v; Goodare, *Government of Scotland*, pp. 165–7; A.R. MacDonald, *The Burghs and Parliament in Scotland, c. 1550–1651* (Aldershot, 2007), pp. 67–8.

106 *Records of the Convention of the Royal Burghs of Scotland*, 8 vols, ed. J.D. Marwick and T. Hunter (Edinburgh, 1870–1918), vol. 1, pp. 339–41; *Extracts from the Records of the Burgh of Edinburgh*, 1st ser., 5 vols, ed. J.D. Marwick (Edinburgh, 1869–92), vol. 4, pp. 528 and 530–1; *Extracts from the Records of the Burgh of Edinburgh*, 2nd ser., 9 vols, ed. M. Wood and H. Armet (Edinburgh, 1927–67), vol. 1, p. 13.

107 Lee, *John Maitland of Thirlestane*, pp. 215–21; Willson, *King James VI and I*, pp. 97–8; Goodare, *State and Society in Early Modern Scotland*, pp. 74–5; D. Stevenson, *Scotland's Last Royal Wedding: The Marriage of James VI and Anne of Denmark* (East Linton, 1997), pp. 55–6.

108 *Calendar of State Papers Relating to Scotland and Mary, Queen of Scots, 1547–1603*, 13 vols, ed. J. Bain, W.K. Boyd, H.W. Meikle, A.I. Cameron, M.S. Giuseppi and J.D. Mackie (Edinburgh, 1898–1969), vol. 10, pp. 306, 322, 325, 330 and 416; Sir James Melville of Halhill, *Memoirs of His Own Life*, ed. T. Thomson (Edinburgh, 1827), pp. 376–7; David Moysie, *Memoirs of the Affairs of Scotland, 1577–1603*, ed. J. Dennistoun (Edinburgh, 1830), p. 84.

109 *Sea-Law of Scotland*, sig. A2v: 'At Edinburgh, the 30 of Iunii 1590'.

admiralty courts had been established throughout Europe 'be commoun consent of nationis', Welwod had observed:

> It is trew that in Scotland, befoir the erectioun of ane admirall, the denes of gild wer judges in civile debaitis betwix mercheand and mariner, as the water bailzie betwein mariner and mariner, lyk as the hie justice wes judge in thair criminallis, quhilk actiounis of all sortis falling furth now betwixt the personis seafairing foirsaid, of rycht perteinis to the jurisdictioun of the admirall since his erectioun.[110]

In explaining his purpose and method in his opening chapter Welwod had already declared that jurisdiction in seafaring causes did not 'pertene to ilk judge and court, bot onelie to the great judge of the sea, quha is admirall'.[111] In the 1590 treatise, on the other hand, it was declared in the opening chapter that jurisdiction in seafaring causes did not 'pertein to ilk Judge and place, but quhylis to the great Judge of the Sea onely, quha is Admirall, and quhylis to the Deanes of Gild also, not without soume entres in soume thinges to uther judges and persons, according to the provision of lawe and use of the land'.[112] In sharp contrast to the boldness and clarity of the statement in the manuscript treatise, this statement begins with a suggestion that admiralty jurisdiction is exclusive, then dilutes its effect by indicating that jurisdiction is shared between the admiral, deans of guild and other judges and persons. In the final chapter of the 1590 treatise Welwod returned to the theme:

> Lyk as al actions amang men ar chiefly ather civil or criminal, evin sa ar the seafayr causis. As for the civill debaits, namly, sic as fallis out betwixt merchand and skipper, it wes ordain of auld that they suld be without excemption decydit be the judge of the brough quhairunto the schip is frauchtit, quha is according to the common custome the Deane of Gyld, a judge of many hundred yeirs auld in this lande. As for the criminalls of bludstouth, raiff etc., done within the sea-flud, the admiral senn his erection amang us is judge propir and ordinair thairto, as also, be the custome

110 MCL, PL2208, ff. 473v-4r. Welwod also made reference in these chapters to the *Consolato del mare*, but whether he regarded it as a Spanish source is far from clear. As a devout Protestant, he may have found the example of Spain less agreeable than the examples of Denmark and England, or even of France, where there was still some prospect of a Protestant regime emerging.

111 MCL, PL2208, f. 473r.

112 *Sea-Law of Scotland*, sig. B1v.

> of uther nations quhom we follow in that erectioun, judge to the civill causis, bot without prejudice of the lawis and consuetud foresaid. The place ordinair for this jurisdiction is not as yit constitute, quhilk wald be at the lest ane certain in ilk seaward shire, quhilk thing I hope my lord Admiral will consider in the reformation of this jurisdictioun.[113]

In the last sentence of this passage – the last sentence of the treatise – Welwod offered advice to the admiral on how the reform of his court might be carried forward through the appointment of deputies in coastal towns, yet what jurisdiction the deputies were expected to enjoy is not made clear. Around the beginning of the fourteenth century, jurisdiction in seafaring causes had been assigned to the 'kyngis bailzeis' by the *Leges quatuor burgorum*, but by the time Balfour came to extract this provision for his 'sea lawis' treatise he thought it appropriate to replace the phrase 'kyngis bailzeis' with 'King's Admiral'.[114] In his manuscript treatise Welwod agreed that the admiral had acquired an exclusive jurisdiction in seafaring causes, yet in his 1590 treatise he stated that any jurisdiction the admiral enjoyed was without prejudice to the ancient rights of the burghs to determine civil disputes between merchants and mariners. He referred again here to the 1467 act of parliament with which he had opened his pivotal chapter on the hiring of ships, where he had strayed from the subject by rehearsing the rule that 'gif any debate sall happen betwixt the master and merchant, thay sall underly the jurisdictioun of the brough quhairunto the ship is fraughtit, without any exemption'.[115] This statement was omitted from the manuscript treatise, which was more focused on the subject under discussion, and which elsewhere contained half a dozen statements asserting the admiral's rights, all of which were omitted from the 1590 treatise.[116]

By now it should be clear both that Welwod was taking sides in a debate about the future of the admiralty and that he took different sides in his manuscript and 1590 treatises.[117] The impression given by a comparison of the two treatises is that to begin with, in his manuscript treatise, he accepted the admiral's claim to an exclusive jurisdiction, and that he later became more

113 *Sea-Law of Scotland*, sig. C6r.

114 *Acts of the Parliaments of Scotland*, vol. 1, p. 25; *The Ancient Laws and Customs of the Burghs of Scotland*, 2 vols, ed. C. Innes and R. Renwick (Edinburgh, 1868–1910), vol. 1, p. 13; *Collection de lois maritimes*, vol. 4, pp. 219–20; *Practicks of Sir James Balfour*, vol. 2, p. 627.

115 *Sea-Law of Scotland*, sig. B2.

116 MCL, PL2208, ff. 476, 477r, 478 and 481.

117 *Cf.* McMillan, 'Scottish Court of Admiralty', p. 166, and 'Admiralty and Maritime Law', pp. 328–9; W.A. McNeill, 'Papers of a Dundee Shipping Dispute, 1600–1604', in *Miscellany*

sympathetic towards the burghs' interests when he wrote his 1590 treatise, in which his discussion of the jurisdiction issue became more convoluted, if not downright contradictory. In moving in this direction he would have been moving with the times, and it is certainly hard to see how the manuscript treatise – particularly the passage relying on the admiral's charter – could have been written after the burghs succeeded in having the 1592 act passed. It is in contrast quite easy to see how the manuscript treatise could have been written before 1590. In the *prooemium* to the 1590 treatise Welwod claimed that

> a 13 yeirs since, out of all the wrets authorizit be our nation, I collectit briefly not onely the remains of the Rhodian lawe, as it is left interpret to us be the Romaine lawers, with the reulis of Olon receavit be our cuntrey men, bot also the acts of parliament, with uthers rests of the Romain law concernand the Seafairing, and hes now, I trow, in a convenient tyme, at the earnest desire of sundrie, orderlie digest and publishit the samin, for the reddier usage to all Seafairing men.[118]

Given that the 1590 treatise only runs to about seven thousand words, it seems less likely that Welwod had been engaged in writing it for thirteen years than that he had, as he indicates here, first collected materials relating to maritime law together and only later digested them in an orderly treatise. In 1577 he was employed as a teacher of mathematics at St Andrews University, though he appears to have studied law at Wittenberg a few years earlier, and may already have been developing an interest in maritime law.[119] In 1577 he was one of two recipients of a patent for a water pump, and when he later published a treatise about the invention he dedicated it to the earl of Bothwell as admiral of

of the Scottish History Society x (Edinburgh, 1965), p. 53, at p. 65; A.M. Jackson, *Glasgow Dean of Guild Court: A History* (Glasgow, 1983), p. 12; D.M. Walker, *A Legal History of Scotland*, 7 vols (Edinburgh, 1988–2004), vol. 3, pp. 48, 337 and 583.

118 *Sea-Law of Scotland*, sig A3v.

119 J.H. Baxter, 'William Welwood of St Mary's College', in *Ecclesia: Een Bundel Opstellen aangeboden aan Prof. dr J.N. Bakhuizen van den Brink* (The Hague, 1959), p. 241, at pp. 246–51; D.M. Walker, *The Scottish Jurists* (Edinburgh, 1985), pp. 84–6; H.C.G. Matthew and B.H. Harrison (eds), *Oxford Dictionary of National Biography*, 61 vols (Oxford, 2004), vol. 58, pp. 96–8. On the Wittenberg connection see too Cairns, 'Academic Feud, Bloodfeud and William Welwood', p. 173. When Welwod matriculated at Wittenberg on 25 October 1573 the presiding officer was Matthaeus Wesenbecius, though this does not necessarily mean that Welwod was one of his pupils (*Album academiae Vitebergensis*, 3 vols, ed. E.W. Förstemann, O. Hartwig and K. Gerhard (Leipzig, 1841–1905), vol. 2, p. 241). The Wittenberg connection is now explored further in the seventh essay in this collection.

Scotland.[120] It was in 1587, the year in which Bothwell received his new charter, that Welwod received appointment to the chair of law at St Andrews, and it would obviously have made sense for him to have determined at this moment to digest his notes on maritime law into a treatise consistent with the terms of the admiral's charter.[121] Another significant feature of the passage quoted above is that Welwod not only claimed there to have gathered his materials out of Roman law texts as well as acts of parliament and the laws of Oleron, but also claimed that in working on the Roman law texts he had examined 'the remains of the Rhodian lawe'. In the *prooemium* attached to his 1613 treatise he acknowledged that '*Simon Shardius, anno* 1561, promised this same compend and collect of sea lawes forth of all lawes (which presently by Gods grace I intend) but by death prevented, could not performe it'.[122] Schard had died in 1573, the year in which Welwod had gone to Wittenberg, before he could accomplish the task he set himself in his edition of the Rhodian sea laws of forming a compendium of all the major codes of maritime law.[123] Welwod's claim to have assumed the task seems plausible enough, and the likelihood is that he assumed it when he began to gather his materials together in 1577. Ten years later a digest of all the codes used in the admiralty courts of Europe was precisely what the admiral's new charter appeared to be inviting.

If the thesis that Welwod wrote – or at least revised – his manuscript treatise around 1587 is to be sustained, it will need to be explained why he shifted his ground before he published his 1590 treatise. A possible explanation may be that he lost faith in Bothwell between these two dates. After his return to Scotland from the Continent in 1582, the year in which Welwod dedicated his first treatise to him, Bothwell was regarded as a promising leader of the Protestant cause.[124] However, his hospitable treatment of survivors of the Spanish Armada in 1588, and his involvement in the rebellion of the Catholic

120 *De aqua in altum per fistulas plumbeas facile exprimenda apologia demonstrativa* (Edinburgh, 1582), sig. A2r.

121 Welwod may have felt under particular pressure to establish his credentials for the chair because of opposition he was facing within the university. For a succinct summary see S.J. Reid, *Humanism and Calvinism: Andrew Melville and the Universities of Scotland, 1560–1625* (Farnham, 2011), pp. 115–17.

122 *Abridgement of All Sea-Lawes*, p. 6.

123 *De varia temporum in iure civili observatione*, p. 271. Although he was from Saxony, Schard neither studied nor taught at Wittenberg. When he died he was a judge in the *Reichskammergericht*, and he had been living in Basel when his edition of the Rhodian sea law was printed there.

124 R.G. Macpherson, 'Francis Stewart, 5th Earl Bothwell, c. 1562–1612: Lordship and Politics in Jacobean Scotland', PhD dissertation, University of Edinburgh, 1998.

earls of Huntly and Errol in 1589, raised doubts about the sincerity of his commitments, which may have troubled the devoutly Protestant Welwod in 1590. Four years later, when Welwod was believed to be promoting Andrew Melville's plea for a union of the crowns of Scotland and England as a means of humbling Spain and Rome, he was also believed to be acting as a spokesman for 'sum of this realme who hated Bothwell, and wissed his majesties prosperitie', but who also wanted the king 'to reconcile with Bothwell, for strenthening him self'.[125] The mixture of disillusion and persistence in the belief that Bothwell might yet be of service, which typified attitudes among the presbyterian ministers at this time, may perhaps be detected behind the advice Welwod offered the admiral in 1590. But whether or not this is so, there is a more plausible explanation for his change of stance. After acknowledging his debt to Schard in the *prooemium* to his 1613 treatise, Welwod explained that in publishing his new book he meant to confront two problems:

> [First], whereas the most civill, wise, and politick nations have even most carefully distinguished the Jurisdiction of the sea from the Jurisdiction of the land in all respects, yet neverthelesse some men prease alwayes, upon what intent I wot not, to confound the same. And [secondly], the multitude of these who doe acknowledge the foresaid distinction, as specially the Mariners, through ignorance contemne all other lawe but the rule of *Oleron*.[126]

It has been shown with meticulous care that Welwod, the son of a merchant burgess of St Andrews, was as much a member of the burghal as of the academic community there.[127] Having written a treatise that he hoped would be of interest 'to all Seafairing men', he would in all probability have shown it to mariners in the town, and they would almost certainly have responded by raising the very objections he sought to confront in 1613. The campaign to have the admiral's powers retrenched got under way in the autumn of 1588, after which mariners consulted on the east coast are likely to have questioned Welwod's assertion of the admiralty court's exclusive jurisdiction in seafaring causes. That part of the basis for that and other assertions was the example of

125 *Original Letters of Mr John Colville, 1582–1603*, ed. D. Laing (Edinburgh, 1858), pp. 120–1 and 125; *Calendar of State Papers Relating to Scotland*, vol. 11, pp. 284, 424, 427 and 430–1; David Calderwood, *The History of the Kirk of Scotland*, 8 vols, ed. D. Laing (Edinburgh, 1842–9), vol. 5, pp. 294–5 and 307.

126 *Abridgement of All Sea-Lawes*, pp. 6–7.

127 Cairns, 'Academic Feud, Bloodfeud and William Welwood'.

foreign laws would in itself have been a reason for objecting to the wide range of sources cited in the manuscript treatise, and for Welwod's careful excision of references to these laws from his manuscript treatise. A more obvious reason would simply have been that use was not openly made of the Rhodian sea law or *Consolato del mare* in Scotland. At about the time Welwod was preparing his 1590 treatise for the press, another treatise on the law of the sea was being written by the advocate and admiralty judge Alexander King.[128] Beholden for his judicial office to Bothwell, to whom he dedicated his treatise, and himself involved at the time in Catholic intrigues, King made use of several foreign sources in writing his book, yet like Balfour before him, he never made any explicit reference to the Mediterranean sources used by Welwod.[129] Although it is possible that these sources had influenced the development of some of the rules of law commonly recognised by mariners, it seems fairly clear that they would not have been considered directly applicable to the navigation in which Scottish mariners were engaged.[130] It also seems fairly clear that the 1590 treatise would have been a great deal more acceptable to east coast mariners than the manuscript treatise.

3.2 *'Even for All the Coasts of Your Highnes Dominions'*

Another question in need of an answer is why Welwod's manuscript treatise, if it was written before 1590 and radically altered then, resurfaced in 1611. It should be remembered to begin with that 1611 marked a turning point in Welwod's career, for in that year he was forced out of his chair at St Andrews and moved to England, in search of new patronage.[131] It should also be remembered that the person who made a copy of the manuscript treatise in 1611 was called Robert Douglas. In view of the trouble he had in transcribing several technical terms in the treatise, it is no great surprise that it has proved impossible to identify a lawyer with that name, common enough as it was. A document exists, however, that acknowledges the payment of a debt due to the duke of Lennox and was written by 'Robert Douglas, servand to my lord duikis

128 NLS, Adv. MS 28.4.7 and MS 1948; NRS, GD45/26/50; EUL, La. III 741; FSL, V.a.379; HLSL, MS 6026.

129 Information about King is now provided in the introduction to *Alexander King's Treatise on Maritime Law*, ed. J.D. Ford (Edinburgh, 2018).

130 The possible relevance of these sources, and King's possible use of them, is now returned to in the source just cited. The extent of Scottish navigation in the sixteenth century is now considered in the first essay in this collection.

131 The fundamental study of this transition remains the second part of Cairns, 'Academic Feud, Bloodfeud and William Welwood', though see too Reid, *Humanism and Calvinism*, pp. 242–3.

grace'.[132] Since the document is written in a very similar hand to the copy of Welwod's treatise, the possibility is raised that the treatise was made available to Lennox, who remained the admiral of Scotland, though he had moved south with the king in 1603. As previously noted, when Welwod's *Abridgement of All Sea-Lawes* appeared in London two years later, the dedicatory epistle to the king was followed by a further address to Lennox as admiral of Scotland, together with the earl of Nottingham as admiral of England and Ireland, and the earl of Northampton as admiral or warden of the Cinque Ports.[133] It may be that Welwod, detached from the burghal setting in which he had worked until 1611, and probably disgruntled with his treatment there, hoped to secure patronage by reviving his earlier advocacy of the admiral's rights. The recognition by parliament in 1609 that the admiralty court was 'a soverane judicatorie', with previous doubts being attributed to 'the insufficiencie, corruptioun and defectis whilkis wer in the deputtis and memberis of these courtis in former tymes', may also have inclined Welwod to believe that the admiral's rights were ripe for revival.[134] Yet the act of 1592 had not been repealed, and not even in 1612, when parliament ratified the terms of Lennox's 1603 infeftment in the admiralty, was a new charter granted.[135] By 1613, however, Welwod had devised a new line of argument, which involved moving from a Scottish to a British context. In that year he told the king that in publishing his new treatise he was 'offring service to your M. even for all the coasts of your Highnes dominions'.[136]

As well as remarking in his *prooemium* that 'the most civill, wise, and politick nations' tended to maintain a distinct jurisdiction over maritime causes, Welwod also expressed the wish in addressing the three admirals that

> as you bee every other way Noble, your nobilitie may be crowned with a carefull attention to the speciall parts of the Admiraltie requiring the same, to a memoriall surpassing all ancesters: I meane the conservacie, jurisdiction and priviledges therof. The jurisdiction, albeit it be most faithfully and diligently exercised, and namely in England by Sir *Daniel Dunn*, and Dr *Trevor*, most learned, sincere, and woorthy collegues, Judges in the high court there: yet the daily thwarting and curbing of the processe

132 NRS, GD111/3/8.

133 *Abridgement of All Sea-Lawes*, sig. A3.

134 *Acts of the Parliaments of Scotland*, vol. 4, p. 440; Records of the Parliaments of Scotland, 1609/4/34.

135 *Acts of the Parliaments of Scotland*, vol. 4, p. 497; Records of the Parliaments of Scotland, 1612/10/46; NRS, GD 220/1/G/2/2/1.

136 *Abridgement of All Sea-Lawes*, sig. A2r.

> of the Judicature, urges a clearing or designing of the limits and marches, to a better distinguishing thereof from all other jurisdictions ordinarie; without which, due justice can neither bee administered, concerning the sea customes (of which no court else can take knowledge) for strangers traffiquing here (importing no small staine to the king his justice) nor yet for his M. lieges traffiquers on sea, whose contracts and charter-parties ordinarily beare the clause of ruling by law of *Oleron*; a forraine law, as all the other laws of the Admirall court commonly are, whereof no other Judicature here can take cognissance.[137]

Initially addressing all three admirals, Welwod first narrowed his discussion down to the admiralty court of England, commenting on how cases were handled 'there', then widened the focus again, commenting on how maritime trade was conducted 'here'. In commenting on the handling of cases in the admiralty court of England he was no doubt mindful of the use of writs of prohibition in the common law courts as a means of drawing commercial litigation away from the admiralty court.[138] An attempt had been made in 1611 to end the dispute between the common law and admiralty judges, and Welwod may perhaps have seen some of the papers circulated by Daniel Dunn and others.[139] He certainly appears to have expected the three admirals and his wider audience to be impressed with the arguments advanced on behalf of the English court, and his strategy appears to have been to strengthen the position of the Scottish admiral by associating him with the admirals serving elsewhere in Britain.[140] In reworking the chapters in his manuscript treatise about the admiral and

137 *Abridgement of All Sea-Lawes*, sig. A3v.

138 B.P. Levack, *The Civil Lawyers in England, 1603–41: A Political Study* (Oxford, 1973), pp. 77–9; L.M. Hill, *Bench and Bureaucracy: The Public career of Sir Julius Caesar, 1580–1636* (Stanford, 1988), pp. 32–45; M.J. Prichard and D.E.C. Yale, 'Introduction', in *Hale and Fleetwood on Admiralty Jurisdiction* (London, 1993), p. xvii, at pp. xlvii–xcix.

139 Sir Edward Coke, *The Fourth Part of the Institutes of the Laws of England* (London, 1648), pp. 134–6; *Hale and Fleetwood on Admiralty Jurisdiction*, pp. 300–10; L.A. Knafla, *Law and Politics in Jacobean England: The Tracts of Lord Chancellor Ellesmere* (Cambridge, 1977), pp. 282–96; BL, Lansdowne MS 142, ff. 424–40; NAK, SP16/208, ff. 306–17.

140 Whether Welwod was aware of the enquiries made in England at about this time into the admiral's administration of the navy is less evident. See R.W. Kenny, *Elizabeth's Admiral: The Political Career of Charles Howard, Earl of Nottingham, 1536–1624* (Baltimore, MD, 1970), pp. 301–18; A.P. McGowan, 'Introduction', in *The Jacobean Commissions of Enquiry 1608 and 1618* (London, 1971), p. xiii, at pp. xiii–xvii; L.L. Peck, *Northampton: Patronage and Policy at the Court of James I* (London, 1982), pp. 152–6.

his court, Welwod added one or two additional references to English sources, but attention continued to be centred on the Scottish admiral. In reworking the statements at the end of the treatise that were backed up with references to the Scottish admiral's charter, Welwod referred instead to what he called the 'diplomata admiraliorum in utroque regno', though the statements now made were closely based on the terms of the English admiral's appointment and had no basis in any Scottish charter.[141] The same source was used and cited in the same way at two other places in the 1613 treatise, where the aim may in part have been to appeal to an English audience, but seems mostly to have been to reinforce the claims made in the manuscript treatise for the Scottish admiral.[142]

After reminding the three admirals how important it was for their jurisdiction to be 'vindicat from all sort of encroching and usurping', Welwod proceeded to stress the importance of another responsibility of any well established admiralty:

> the conservacie (as the chiefe point of that office) requires security and safety in common for all loyall subjects, traders on Sea: specially, for Fishers and others, happily disposed to adventure and exercise the trade of fishing; to the end, that not onely a peaceable, but also a full and a plentifull fishing may be enjoyed by the inhabitants of his M. kingdoms, even according to that which God so freely and bountifully offers into their verie doores. For which cause, the barbaritie of the Ilanders would be repressed, and strangers stayed from scarring, scattring, and breaking the shoals of our fishes; namely, upon our coasts of Scotland. There could be no better employment for some (at least) of his M. ships and companies, *Ne vel illi usque turbent, aut isti intercipiant, quod nos capere oportet.*[143]

In making these remarks Welwod was probably aware of two other issues being debated in England. In the first place, proposals for the construction of a fishing fleet to rival the Dutch in the North Sea, though in circulation since the sixteenth century, were the subject of particularly close scrutiny between 1611 and 1613.[144] James I's interest in the English proposals has been seen as

141 *Abridgement of All Sea-Lawes*, p. 53; NAK, C66/1263; BL, Add. MS 29439, ff. 180–3. The terms of Northampton's appointment were more vague – see NAK, SP12/264, pp. 261–3, and Peck, *Northampton*, p. 42.

142 *Abridgement of All Sea-Lawes*, pp. 12 and 76.

143 *Abridgement of All Sea-Lawes*, sig. A3v.

144 J. Cramsie, 'Commercial Projects and the Fiscal Policy of James VI and I', (2000) 43 *Historical Journal* 345.

a continuation of his earlier support for the fishing industry in Scotland, but actually the construction of a fishing fleet was not a popular idea there. When proposed to the burghs in 1605 it elicited the response that 'the maist profitabill and easie fisching att all tymeis is to be had in the ileis and lochis', for which sufficient vessels were already available, and from which the burghs were being held back by 'the violence and barbarous crueltie, abusis and extortiounis of the hielandis and cuntre men'.[145] This was the concern Welwod echoed when he urged that 'the barbaritie of the Ilanders would be repressed'. In the second place, at the same time as the construction of a fishing fleet was being considered in England, a more novel proposal was circulating that the king should assert his dominion over coastal waters and impose a tax on both local and foreign fishermen who operated there.[146] This idea is believed to have been inspired by the traditional levying of a tax known as the 'assize herring' on Scottish fisherman, and at least one Scottish lawyer wrote in defence of the proposed extension of the tax to foreign fishermen.[147] But the complaint heard from the Scottish burghs between 1609 and 1613 was that the abundance of fish previously available at 'thair awn dooris' was being diminished by the breaking up of shoals of fish by 'Fleamings' operating further out from the coast.[148] This was the concern Welwod echoed when he wrote about the plentiful fishing offered to the Scots 'into their verie doores', and urged that strangers be 'stayed from scarring, scattring, and breaking the shoals of our fishes'. Neither here nor in his chapters on fishing and the dominion of the seas did he say anything about the taxation of foreigners, his point instead being that the king had the right to exclude foreign fishermen from 'our coasts of Scotland'.

As in writing about the admiral's jurisdiction, so in writing about the fisheries Welwod was touching on topical issues in England as a means of approaching issues of concern in Scotland from a novel angle. No doubt some of what he had to say, in particular in his chapter about the dominion of the seas, would have been of interest to English readers, and efforts were certainly made to render his treatise accessible to an English audience. Yet Welwod's aim was not so much to engage in English debates as to reinvigorate Scottish debates by placing them in a British – not English – setting.[149] In 1607 the 'act anent the

145 *Records of the Convention of the Royal Burghs of Scotland*, vol. 2, pp. 202–4.

146 Fulton, *Sovereignty of the Sea*, pp. 138–208.

147 *Calendar of State Papers, Domestic Series, of the Reign of James I*, 4 vols, ed. M.A.E. Green (London, 1857–9), vol. 1, p. 426; NAK, SP14/32, ff. 51–2.

148 *Records of the Convention of the Royal Burghs of Scotland*, vol. 2, pp. 323, 350, 374 and 405; *Extracts from the Records of the Burgh of Edinburgh*, 2nd ser., vol. 2, pp. 58–9.

149 A.D. Nicholls, *The Jacobean Union: A Reconsideration of British Civil Policies under the Early Stuarts* (Westport, CT, 1999), pp. 152–5.

unioun of Scotland and England' had expressly reserved to 'Scottishmen thair trade of fisheing, within thair loches, firthis and bayis within land, and in the seas within fourtene mylis of the costis of the realme of Scotland, wheir nather Englishmen nor ony stranger or forinaris have use to fishe'.[150] Nevertheless, it was argued in 1609 that by raising revenue from the fishing trade the king would be 'maintayning thereby navigacion and marrinors, and setting of an infinite nomber of subjectts on worke within the realme of Ingland and Scottland, to strengthen his majestes dominions by sea and land, as the cheif point of the most commendable union'.[151] It was understood that despite the rejection of his schemes for a closer union, James had determined to treat his navy at least as a British institution.[152] When the imposition of a tax on all fishermen was announced in 1609 it was by way of a royal proclamation affecting all 'our Coasts and Seas of Great Britaine, Ireland and the rest of the Isles adjacent'.[153] A year earlier Nottingham had placed naval vessels at the disposal of the Scottish privy council to assist in an attempt to impose obedience on the 'Yllismen', as Welwod may have remembered when he observed that 'there could be no better employment for some (at least) of his M. ships and companies' than the suppression of the islanders and exclusion of the foreigners who were disrupting the inshore fishing trade.[154] What he certainly had in mind was the intervention of the royal navy as a means of accomplishing the admiral's duty to protect the fisheries. He may also have been aware that in 1612 an English vessel had been sent to Orkney and Shetland to assist the Scottish admiral in collecting the assize herring there.[155] The extension of the tax to these northern waters was proving controversial, and would involve the admiral in disputes with the burghs for several years to come.[156] It was discovered long ago that Welwod was commissioned to develop his arguments in

150 *Acts of the Parliaments of Scotland*, vol. 4, pp. 366–71, at p. 369; Records of the Parliaments of Scotland, 1607/3/12.

151 BL, Lansdowne MS 142, f. 371.

152 J. Grant, 'General Introduction', in *The Old Scots Navy from 1689 to 1710* (London, 1914), p. vii, at pp. xvi–xvii; Goodare, *State and Society in Early Modern Scotland*, pp. 249–50; S. Murdoch, *The Terror of the Seas? Scottish Maritime Warfare, 1513–1713* (Leiden, 2010), pp. 127–8.

153 *Stuart Royal Proclamations*, 2 vols, ed. J.F. Larkin and P.L. Hughes (Oxford, 1973–83), vol. 1, pp. 217–19.

154 *Register of the Privy Council*, vol. 8, pp. 514–16.

155 *Records of the Convention of the Royal Burghs of Scotland*, vol. 2, p. 540; *Register of the Privy Council*, vol. 9, pp. 531–2, and vol. 10, pp. 231–2 and 239; *State Papers, and Miscellaneous Correspondence of Thomas, Earl of Melros*, 2 vols, ed. J. Maidment (Edinburgh, 1837), vol. 1, pp. 129–31.

156 Fulton, *Sovereignty of the Sea*, pp. 165–75.

his 1616 treatise – where he wrote for the first time about the king's right to tax fishermen – by the queen, to whom an interest in the assize herring had been granted.[157] Another interested party, who was involved in further negotiations with the queen over rights of admiralty, was the duke of Lennox.[158] Whether it had been his intention to do so or not, Welwod was not only providing renewed support for the admiral but was also opposing once more the interests of the coastal burghs of Scotland.

3.3 *'Upon the Conscience of My Profession of the Civill Lawe'*

In the *prooemium* to his 1613 treatise Welwod was himself eager to situate his text in a particular setting. After writing about the origins of maritime law, he remarked that 'albeit there hath bin, and yet remaines, a great number of professors and doctors of the Roman civill lawe who have written largely therupon, yet few or none hath taken in hand to write pertinently or expressly upon the lawes concerning Sea-faring, the traffique on Sea and by Sea, with the dueties requisit of every Sea-faring person, of all sorts and degrees'.[159] He acknowledged that Giulio Ferretti had written 'a discourse for the addressing of Navies with convenient and expert Governours, and all sorts of necessaries for hostilitie on the sea', that Petrus Peckius had 'learnedly commented upon the titles of the civill lawe, touching the sea-lawes', and that Benvenuto Stracca had included some chapters relating to 'sea matters' in his book on mercantile law.[160] In the new chapters at the end of his own book Welwod made reference to the treatise by Ferretti, but he never mentioned the works of Peckius and Stracca elsewhere, and he insisted that no one before him had come close to fulfilling Schard's aim of writing a comprehensive compendium of all maritime laws.[161] He was now publishing his book, he proceeded to make clear, 'upon the conscience of my profession of the civill lawe, having no employment or part in any Admiraltie'.[162] In addressing the three admirals he

157 J.D. Alsop, 'William Welwood, Anne of Denmark and the Sovereignty of the Sea', (1980) 59 *Scottish Historical Review* 171.

158 *Registrum magni sigilli regum Scotorum*, vol. 7, p. 527; NRS, GD220/1/G/2/2/2.

159 *Abridgement of All Sea-Lawes*, p. 5.

160 Giulio Ferretti, *De iure et re navali, et de ipsius rei navalis et belli aquatici praeceptis legitimis liber* (Venice, 1579); Petrus Peckius, *Commentaria in omnes pene iuris civilis titulos ad rem nauticam pertinentes* (Louvain, 1556); Benvenuto Stracca, *Tractatus de mercatura seu mercatore* (Cologne, 1576).

161 This is not to say that he never made use of these books in writing his own treatises. For instance, in MCL, PL2208, f. 481v, there is a reference that may have been lifted from Peckius, *Commentaria in omnes pene iuris civilis titulos ad rem nauticam pertinentes*, p. 212.

162 *Abridgement of All Sea-Lawes*, p. 6.

had claimed that his main purpose in publishing was 'to serve your Honours in my calling', and on the title page of the treatise he had been designated a 'professor of the Civill Lawe'.[163] Although the word 'professor' could at this time have meant nothing more than 'professional', Welwod was taking care to maintain that he had written not as a practitioner but as an academic expert, and if, as suggested here, he had written his manuscript treatise in 1587 then he had in fact written the original version of his 1613 treatise while holding a university chair.[164] Immediately before claiming to have sent his book to the press in exercise of his 'profession of the civill lawe', he claimed that having examined all the sea laws available he had decided 'to mend a weake piece of labour, which I intended many yeares since, intituled the Sea-lawe of Scotland, and to frame the same in a very harmonicall collection of all sea-lawes'.[165] Welwod's aim in making this statement, which does give the impression that his 1613 treatise was an enlarged version of his 1590 treatise, may have been to connect his 1613 treatise with the treatise he had published while he held his chair. The statement needs to be read with care, however, for Welwod does not say that he has framed or relocated his 1590 treatise within a collection of all sea laws, but that he has framed or fashioned the sea laws he has examined into a harmonious collection. Moreover, he does not say that he published his 'Sea-lawe of Scotland' many years since, but that he 'intended' some such publication, by which he could have meant his manuscript treatise.[166] Perhaps the ambiguity was deliberate, but in any case what Welwod was eager to maintain in all these passages was that despite writing in the vernacular and in a style accessible to laymen, who would perhaps have expected the law to consist of nothing more than lists of rules, he had written as an expert in the civil law.

His method is illustrated by the opening of his chapter about the hire of ships. As was noted earlier, he began this chapter in his 1590 treatise by rehearsing the terms of two acts of parliament requiring the use of charter

163 *Abridgement of All Sea-Lawes*, sigg. A1r and A3v.

164 *Cf.* H.L. MacQueen, '*Glanvill* Resarcinate: Sir John Skene and *Regiam maiestatem*', in A.A. MacDonald, M. Lynch and I.B. Cowan (eds), *The Renaissance in Scotland* (Leiden, 1994), p. 385, at p. 389.

165 *Abridgement of All Sea-Lawes*, p. 6.

166 In dedicating his *Abridgement* to the king he reminded him of his readiness 'some yeeres past, most graciously to accept of this birth, in the great weaknes and infancie thereof', adding that 'now beeing strong, and by all warrants inarmed, it most thankefully returnes' (sig. A2r). The *Abridgement* was presented here as a mature version of the *Sea-Law of Scotland.* In addressing the admirals, however, he explained that he also felt the need to present his *Abridgement* to them, 'having intended a painfull and new labour', which would be of interest to them as well as all seafaring men (sig. A3r). If he was being

parties.[167] In his manuscript and 1613 treatises he began instead by citing an article of the Rhodian sea law to back up the proposition that 'no schip sould be fraucht without a chartour pairtie written and subscrivit', after which he took the acts of parliament to specify the terms required in charter parties.[168] As was also noted earlier, he proceeded to consider the liabilities of masters and merchants described in the *Digest* and laws of Oleron (and, in the case of the manuscript and 1613 treatises, the Rhodian sea law). Observing at one point that if a ship were not ready to depart on a day appointed in a charter party, the master would forfeit his fee under Roman law, and would also have to compensate the merchant for any loss he suffered under the laws of Oleron, Welwod added that no compensation would be due unless the master could have avoided the delay, citing the *Digest* again in support of this qualification. The significant point about this discussion for present purposes is its illustration of the way in which Welwod not only interpreted the acts of parliament and laws of Oleron in the light of the Roman law sources (and the Rhodian sea law), but also interpreted them narrowly in the light of those sources. Thus he not only took the acts of parliament and laws of Oleron to be laying down particular rules in relation to the Roman contract of *locatio conductio*, but where one of the rules was not entirely consistent with the Roman texts, he restricted its application to situations in which it was not flatly contradictory to those texts. In writing like this, here and elsewhere, he was conforming to the well known precepts of the *mos Italicus*, as his predilection for authors like Bartolus and Baldus would have led his readers to expect.[169] His dismissive treatment of Peckius as an author 'more busied about the exposition of words then of the matter' suggests a degree of impatience with the *mos Gallicus*, though it has been noted that in his manuscript and 1613 treatises he did himself show some interest in the philological and historical aspects of his subject, and in doing so he referred to Guillaume Budé's *Annotationes in Pandectas*.[170] When he complained that Stracca 'holds straightly within the compasse of the civill lawe', paying insufficient attention to 'the sea customes, which is our principal

---

consistent in these two passages – which of course he need not have been – then the labour pains referred to must have been those endured when he was giving birth to the treatise 'intended' before 1590.

167 See again the passage quoted at n. 13 above.

168 MCL, PL2208, f. 476r; *Abridgement of All Sea-Lawes*, p. 22; *Rhodian Sea Law*, pp. 23–4 and 98.

169 W. Ullmann, 'Bartolus and English Jurisprudence', in D. Segoloni (ed.), *Bartolo da Sassoferrato*, 2 vols (Milan, 1962), vol. 1, p. 49, at p. 64.

170 MCL, PL2208, f. 476r; *Abridgement of All Sea-Lawes*, p. 22; Guillaume Budé, *Annotationes in xxiiii Pandectarum libros* (Lyons, 1541), pp. 384–6.

argument', Welwod revealed again that he was not a strict adherent of the *mos Italicus*. That he may be better associated with early exponents of what eventually became known as the *usus modernus Pandectarum* is suggested by his determination to gather together texts relating to maritime law and present his findings in treatises arranged according to their subject matter.[171]

Further evidence of this tendency is provided by his explanation of 'the force and authority of the Civill Romane Lawe amongst all Nations Christian', in which he observed that just as the Romans themselves, 'who alwaies excelled all other Nations in devising of humane lawes', had submitted 'to the *Rhodians* in the sea lawes', so the law found in the *Corpus iuris*, 'as it were by common consent of Nations, obtaines the prerogative throughout all *Europe*, as in *Great Britaine*, *Germany*, *France*, *Italie* and *Spaine*'.[172] It was the civil law that Welwod most often had in mind when he used the expression 'common law' in his treatises, though at one place he used the expression 'the common lawis of the sea' to encompass both the civil law and the laws of Oleron, and at another he seems to have meant by the 'common lawe' something distinct from the civil law.[173] In the *prooemium* to his 1590 treatise be opened the passage already considered above as follows:

> The daily traffike on the sea constrainit the Rhodians of auld to dytte lawis in the Mediterrane Sea, and not very lang since the Olonois to set furth thair lawis in the Ocean, quhilks lawis the singular skill of baith peiple sa commendit, and equitie sa approvit, that not only hes the Rhodian law, be a speciall ordinance, bin imbraced throghout the Romaine dominion, and sicklike a great part of the reulis of Olon fellowit in our quarter of the Ocean, bot are also baith receavit in the maist part of the quarter foresaid, at lest sa far as they are commonly knawin be peiple. Quhilk

171 G.C.J.J. van den Bergh, *The Life and Work of Gerard Noodt, 1647–1725: Dutch Legal Scholarship between Humanism and Enlightenment* (Oxford, 1988), pp. 263–4; A.A. Wijffels, 'Early-Modern Literature on International Law and the *Usus modernus*', (1995–6) 16–17 *Grotiana* 35, at pp. 35–8; R.C.H. Lesaffer, *European Legal History: A Cultural and Political Perspective* (Cambridge, 2009), pp. 358–9.

172 *Abridgement of All Sea-Lawes*, pp. 1–5. The civil law is envisaged here as a law common to the whole of Europe, but its authority is attributed to its common reception, not to its promulgation by an emperor or its status as *ratio scripta*, although its intrinsic rationality is apparently taken to explain its reception.

173 MCL, PL2208, ff. 475v, 476v-7r and 479r; *Sea-Law of Scotland*, sigg. B3v-4r and B8v-C1r; *Abridgement of All Sea-Lawes*, pp. 17–18, 25–6 and 39; *De dominio maris*, p. 13 (although the expression *ius commune* is also used at p. 2 of this last work, it signifies there a common right to the sea).

> knawledge, becaus I haife commonly found [it] to be very litle in this cuntry, notwithstanding that all men be bound to ken the law, namely, thair awne common lawe; notwithstanding also the worthines and daily neide thairof in this great increnesse of traffick, quhilke evin of auld was ay haulden to tende till a great commonwealth; therfoir, a 13 yeirs since, out of all the wrets authorizit be our nation, I collectit briefly not onely the remains of the Rhodian lawe, as it is left interpret to us be the Romaine lawers, with the reulis of Olon receavit be our cuntrey men, bot also the acts of parliament, with uthers rests of the Romain law concernand the Seafairing.[174]

Welwod supported his statement that all men were bound to know their own common law by citing civil law sources on the rule that *ignorantia iuris neminem excusat*, but what he seems to have been thinking of here was a view articulated by the king a few months later.[175] After taking advice from the advocate John Russell in the witchcraft trial that resulted in Bothwell's downfall, the king declared that the laymen assembled in inquests were required 'to knowe onely the comon lawes of this realme', while 'the knowledge of the civill lawe apperteyneth to the lords of the session and such like'.[176] In his manuscript treatise Welwod himself observed at one point that 'the debaitis of seafaireris and seafairing actiounes aucht to be decydit accoirding to the receaved customes and statutes of the sea, quhilkis failzeand then the voitis and opiniounis of honest men skillit in seafairing ar to be soucht and followit'.[177] The seamen who formed the inquests he had in mind, which can be found reporting in the surviving records of the admiralty court, were not expected to be expert in the civil law.[178] Welwod wondered in his 1590 treatise how expert they really were in their own common law, perhaps because he was by this point dismayed to find that the only foreign source they were prepared to recognise as relevant to their practice was the laws of Oleron, or perhaps because he wondered how familiar they were even with that source. If this might have raised doubts about how far the laws of Oleron had actually been received in Scotland, Welwod was able to claim that he had worked from 'the wrets authorizit be our nation'.[179]

---

174 *Sea-Law of Scotland*, sig. A3.

175 C.1.14.9; Bartolus de Sassoferrato, *Opera omnia*, 5 vols (Lyons, 1523), vol. 2(1), ff. 128–9r (ad D.42.2.2); *Digestum vetus* (Lyons, 1552), col. 349 (gl. 'Non iuris' ad D.3.2.11).

176 *Calendar of State Papers Relating to Scotland*, vol. 10, pp. 521–5.

177 MCL, PL2208, f. 475r.

178 *Acta curiae admirallatus Scotiae*, pp. 4–5 and 15–16.

179 Whether in making this statement Welwod was 'alluding to a contemporary notion of sovereignty', as suggested in Cairns, 'Academic Feud, Bloodfeud and William Welwood',

The inclusion of the laws of Oleron in some collections of the old books of law meant that they might arguably be regarded as part of what was referred to by Bartolus as the *ius municipale scriptum*.[180] It has been suggested that Sir John Skene's efforts around the end of the sixteenth century to have the old books of law printed may have been influenced by his experience as a student at Wittenberg in the 1570s, his aim being to reduce the need for recourse to the civil law by building up the resources of the *lex municipalis*.[181] His contemporary at Wittenberg may have had a similar aim in relation to maritime law, believing that the laws of Oleron should be regarded by the Scots as their own common law, and hoping in some periods of his life that these laws could be augmented with others.

However, while this may have been Welwod's line of thought when he wrote his manuscript and 1590 treatises, in 1613 it was turned on its head. Lamenting that many mariners 'through ignorance contemne all other lawe but the rule of *Oleron*', he wrote in another passage quoted already that without jurisdiction at sea being clearly distinguished from jurisdiction on land,

> due justice can neither bee administered, concerning the sea customes (of which no court else can take knowledge) for strangers traffiquing here (importing no small staine to the king his justice) nor yet for his M. lieges traffiquers on sea, whose contracts and charter-parties ordinarily beare the clause of ruling by law of *Oleron*; a forraine law, as all the other laws of the Admirall court commonly are, whereof no other Judicature here can take cognissance.[182]

Referring at this point to the dispute over jurisdiction in England, Welwod's argument was that the common law courts were not equipped to handle maritime cases since the law applicable was often foreign. By now contending that

p. 161, is open to question. Although he was associating the laws of Oleron with the *Corpus iuris civilis* on the one hand and with the acts of the Scottish parliaments on the other, and although his aim here may have been to connect the laws of Oleron with the old books of law, which were traditionally attributed to royal legislators, what he was arguing was that the intrinsic equity of the laws of Oleron had earned them approval among the expert mariners of Europe in much the same way as the intrinsic equity of the *Corpus iuris* had earned it approval among the learned lawyers of Europe.

180 Bartolus, *Opera omnia*, vol. 2(1), f. 129r (ad D.42.2.2).

181 J.D. Ford, *Law and opinion in Scotland during the Seventeenth Century* (Oxford, 2007), pp. 129–30 (and see too pp. 56–8 and 398 for further similarities between Welwod and Skene, who was also ambiguous about the authority he attributed to the old books).

182 *Abridgement of All Sea-Lawes*, sig. A3v and pp. 7 and 22.

the laws of Oleron needed to be mastered because they were often adopted as the laws regulating a contract, he implied that other sea laws would also need to be mastered because they too might be adopted by the parties to a contract. Yet if this enabled him to revert to the full range of sources cited in his manuscript treatise, any attempt to augment the common law of Scotland had to be abandoned, for the argument now was that maritime cases must be left to the jurisdiction of a specialised court precisely because they were not normally governed by the common law, at least in the sense of 'thair awne common lawe'.[183] It was the civil law alone that retained its status as common law, not only in the chapters dealing with the law of maritime commerce but also in the new chapters dealing with the international law of the sea. Another suggestion made elsewhere is that in their exchange of views about the dominion of the seas Welwod and Grotius were arguing at cross-purposes, with Welwod assuming that they were engaging in a disputation as expert civilians while Grotius was consciously steering the discipline of international law in a different direction.[184] In his chapter on prize law Welwod again displayed a lack of awareness of the changes under way in the study of international law, for his discussion could have been written at any time before the late sixteenth century and makes no reference to the emerging concept of privateering.[185]

4 Conclusions

As was warned at the outset, the aim of the present essay has not been to develop a new reading of Welwod's treatises but to enable that to be done elsewhere. Nothing has been found to cast doubt on the reliability of existing scholarship on the 1616 treatise, which does appear to have been a reworking of a chapter first written for inclusion in the 1613 treatise. It was in the 1616 treatise that Welwod wrote for the first time about the possibility of imposing

183 Welwod's decision to abandon his earlier line of argument may have been encouraged by Skene's decision not to include the laws of Oleron in the editions of the old books he published in 1609.

184 J.D. Ford, 'The Law of the Sea and the Two Unions', (2005) 127 *Proceedings of the British Academy* 127, at pp. 132–3. For a particularly lucid account of the transition from the view that international relations were governed by the civil law to the view that a distinct body of international law could and should be developed, see R.C.H. Lesaffer, 'Alberico Gentili's *Ius post bellum* and Early-Modern Peace Treaties', in B. Kingsbury and B. Straumann (eds), *The Roman Foundations of the Law of Nations: Alberico Gentili and the Justice of Empire* (Oxford, 2010), p. 210, at pp. 214–20.

185 See now J.D. Ford, *The Emergence of Privateering* (Leiden, 2023).

a tax on foreign fishermen operating in waters over which the king could claim dominion, and nothing previously published on this aspect of his work is undermined by the discovery of the treatise copied in 1611. However, if the argument advanced in this essay is found convincing, several points will need to be borne in mind when Welwod's other treatises are examined in future. In the first place, the starting point of any investigation will need to be the manuscript treatise, which seems to have been composed around 1587, when Welwod became a professor of law at St Andrews, and when the Scottish admiral was issued with a new charter encouraging reference to the full range of sources Welwod had been exploring since 1577.[186] In the second place, the 1590 treatise will need to be read as a deliberate attempt to promote the model of maritime law and jurisdiction favoured by the coastal burghs, not as an uncontentious description of a prevailing state of affairs.[187] In the third place, the 1613 treatise will need to be read not as an attempt to expand and repackage the 1590 treatise for an English audience, but as an attempt to revitalise the manuscript treatise in a British context.

186 An edition of the manuscript treatise has now been published as an appendix to the edition of Alexander King's treatise cited at n. 129 above.

187 It cannot, for instance, be assumed without investigation that the deans of guild had been exercising jurisdiction in maritime cases in the way Welwod described. This point is now dealt with in the first essay in this collection.

7

Legal Education and Legal Writing in Sixteenth-Century Scotland

Two remarkable facts may conceivably have had some bearing on each other. The first is that no fewer than three treatises on maritime law appear to have been written in Scotland during the 1580s, at a time when relatively little was being written about any branch of the law in Scotland, or for that matter about maritime law anywhere else.[1] The second is that most of the lawyers involved in the production of these treatises had studied at the same universities. Of course, it is not in the least surprising that James Balfour, William Welwod and Alexander King had all graduated as masters of arts from St Andrews, given that it was the university nearest to their family homes in Fife and Edinburgh, nor is it surprising that King had gone abroad to continue his studies at universities in the southern Netherlands and northern France, which was a common preparation for admission to practice as an advocate in the College of Justice.[2] What is surprising is that both Balfour and Welwod, and also Balfour's assistant John Skene, had not only taken the unusual course of pursuing further education in northern Germany, but had actually gone to the same university there.[3] In the entire course of the sixteenth century fewer than twenty Scottish graduates continued their studies at the University of Wittenberg, and of them fewer than ten pursued any sort of legal career after returning to Scotland.[4]

1 James Balfour and William Welwod began to gather materials on maritime law together in the later 1570s, and Alexander King was still working on his treatise at the start of the 1590s, but it seems to have been in the 1580s that their treatises were put into shape. There was an earlier treatise too, apparently written by David Kintor, but it has not survived. The writing of the surviving treatises is explored in the previous two essays in this collection and in the introduction to *Alexander King's Treatise on Maritime Law*, ed. J.D. Ford (Edinburgh, 2018).

2 *Acta facultatis artium universitatis Sanctiandree, 1413–1588*, 2 vols, ed. A.I. Dunlop (Edinburgh, 1964), vol. 2, pp. 396, 399, 429, 434, 438 and 441; *Early Records of the University of St Andrews*, ed. J.M. Anderson (Edinburgh, 1926), pp. 145, 147, 163, 165, 167, 169, 245, 273 and 277; J. Durkan, 'The French Connection in the Sixteenth and Early Seventeenth Centuries', in T.C. Smout (ed.), *Scotland and Europe, 1200–1850* (Edinburgh, 1986), p. 19, at pp. 25–7.

3 *Album academiae Vitebergensis*, 3 vols, ed. E.W. Försterman, O. Hartwig and K. Gerhard (Leipzig, 1841–1905), vol. 1, p. 216, and vol. 2, pp. 170 and 241.

4 More will be said about these students below. Although J. Durkan, 'The Cultural Background in Sixteenth-Century Scotland', in D. McRoberts (ed.), *Essays on the Scottish Reformation, 1513–1625* (Glasgow, 1962), p. 274, at p. 320, has suggested that two students

 DOI:10.1163/9789004695009_008

Yet three of these students were involved in the production of treatises on maritime law. Was this a pure coincidence, or was there perhaps a connection between the education on offer at Wittenberg and the treatises produced in Scotland? A possible link between Skene and Welwod could have been the former's brother William, who held the chair of civil law at St Andrews while both of them – and also King – studied there. Although there were no students enrolled to study law at the time, William Skene taught a basic course for the benefit of arts students intent on legal careers, also taking them on visits to the local commissary court where he patiently answered any questions they raised.[5] It seems likely enough that he would have provided advice on suitable destinations for further study, and have told Welwod about his younger brother's experience at Wittenberg. But why had his younger brother gone there in the first place, why had Balfour done the same thing fifteen years earlier, and why did King, who probably attended the civil law classes on offer at St Andrews, go to other continental universities? More to the point, what possible bearing could any of this have had on the books these men produced after they came home? While it may prove impossible to answer these questions, the fact that Balfour, Skene and Welwod all went to Wittenberg is sufficiently intriguing in itself to merit closer investigation, and some light may be shed by the investigation on the writing of treatises on maritime law in Scotland during the 1580s.

1 Topical Invention of Sea Laws

Hardly anything is known about the first two students to matriculate at Wittenberg in the sixteenth century, but the suggestion that they helped to spread reformed ideas in Scotland after their return seems fairly plausible.[6] The 'Ioannes Nutrisen Scotus dioc. Sancti Andree' enrolled in 1518 may possibly have been a relative of the prominent ecclesiastical lawyer Thomas Nudry.[7]

---

who matriculated 'ex Hybernia' should be added to the number of the Scots at Wittenberg, the evidence that they came from the Western Isles is so thin as to be invisible.

5 *The Autobiography and Diary of Mr James Melville*, ed. R. Pitcairn (Edinburgh, 1842), pp. 28–9.

6 W.S. Reid, 'Lutheranism in the Scottish Reformation', (1945) 7 *Westminster Theological Journal* 91, at p. 94.

7 *Album academiae Vitebergensis*, vol. 1, p. 86; *Acts of the Lords of Council in Public Affairs, 1501–54*, ed. R.K. Hannay (Edinburgh, 1932), pp. 56, 100, 215–16 and 310; *St Andrews Formulare, 1514–46*, 2 vols, ed. G. Donaldson and C. Macrae (Edinburgh, 1942–4), vol. 1, pp. 46–9, 77 and 321–3; *The Letters of James the Fourth, 1505–13*, ed. R.K. Hannay (Edinburgh, 1953), pp. 121, 169, 210–11, 219, 229–30, 265–7, 300–1, 306–7, 434–6 and 518–20; *Registrum*

The 'Nicolaus Botwynni Scotus' who enrolled ten years later has been identified as a brother of Sir John Borthwick, whose trial for heresy in 1540 – the year in which Balfour matriculated at St Andrews – was designed to send a signal to other Scots with evangelical leanings.[8] Sir John Borthwick escaped from Scotland before his trial and entered the service of the English government, as Nicholas Borthwick may also have done, although the evidence that he went to England is slight.[9] In the next two decades several Scots sought refuge in Wittenberg itself.[10] When Alexander Allan (Latinised as Alesius) matriculated there in 1533 the letter 'D' was placed before his name, perhaps to indicate that he was not a recent graduate who had come to continue his studies in the normal way, for he had not received a doctorate at this stage in his distinguished career.[11] Before moving on to teach theology at Cambridge, Frankfurt on Oder

magni sigilli regum Scotorum: The Register of the Great Seal of Scotland, 11 vols, ed. J. Balfour Paul, J.M. Thomson, J.H. Stevenson and W. K. Dickson (Edinburgh, 1984), vol. 2, pp. 666–7; *Diocesan Registers of Glasgow*, 2 vols, ed. J. Bain and C. Rogers (London, 1875), vol. 1, pp. 373–4, 391–3 and 397–400, and vol. 2, pp. 185–6, 213–16 and 221–5; *Protocol Book of John Foular, 1514–28*, ed. M. Wood (Edinburgh, 1953), pp. 252–3; *Protocol Book of John Foular, 1528–34*, ed. J. Durkan (Edinburgh, 1985), p. 43; *Fasti ecclesiae Scoticanae Medii Aevi ad annum 1638*, ed. D.E.R. Watt and A.L. Murray (Edinburgh, 2003), pp. 71, 179, 206, 215, 314 and 358; J. Herkless and R.K. Hannay, *The Archbishops of St Andrews*, 5 vols (Edinburgh, 1907–15), vol. 2, pp. 195–6; *The Heads of Religious Houses in Scotland from Twelfth to Sixteenth Centuries*, ed. D.E.R. Watt and N.F. Shead (Edinburgh, 2001), pp. 39, 52–3, 85, 99–100 and 185; NRS, GD124/1/565.

8 *Album academiae Vitebergensis*, vol. 1, p. 133; M.H.B. Sanderson, *Cardinal of Scotland: David Beaton, c. 1494–1546* (Edinburgh, 1986), pp. 82–4, 91–2 and 306, and *Biographical List of Early Scottish Protestants, Heretics and Other Religious Dissidents, 1407–1560* (Edinburgh, 2010), p. 46; D. McKay, 'Parish Life in Scotland, 1500–60', in McRoberts (ed.), *Essays on the Scottish Reformation*, p. 85, at p. 114. The trial of Sir John Borthwick will be returned to below.

9 *Letters and Papers, Foreign and Domestic, of the Reign of Henry VIII, 1509–47*, 21 vols, ed. J.S. Brewer, J. Gairdner and R.H. Brodie (London, 1862–1910), vol. 17, p. 479, and vol. 19(2), p. 126; *Calendar of State Papers Relating to Scotland and Mary, Queen of Scots, 1547–1603*, 13 vols, ed. J. Bain, W.K. Boyd, H.W. Meikle, A.I. Cameron, M.S. Giuseppi and J.D. Mackie (Edinburgh, 1898–1969), vol. 1, p. 6; *The Hamilton Papers*, 2 vols, ed. J. Bain (Edinburgh, 1890–2), vol. 1, pp. 245, 279–80, 319, 323, 395 and 397; Durkan, 'Cultural Background in Sixteenth-Century Scotland', pp. 300–1.

10 *Album academiae Vitebergensis*, vol. 1, p. 213, and vol. 2, pp. 151 and 186.

11 J.H. Baxter, 'Alesius and other Reformed Refugees in Germany', (1934) 5 *Records of the Scottish Church History Society* 93; A.F.S. Pearson, 'Alesius and the English Reformation', (1950) 10 *Records of the Scottish Church History Society* 57; J.T. McNeill, 'Alexander Alesius, Scottish Lutheran, 1500–65', (1964) 55 *Archiv für Reformationsgeschichte* 161; R.J. Lyall, 'Alexander Allan (Alesius) and the Development of a Protestant Aesthetics', in G. Caie, R.J. Lyall, S. Mapstone and K. Simpson (eds), *The European Sun: Proceedings of the Seventh International Conference on Medieval and Renaissance Scottish Language and Literature* (East Linton, 2002), p. 388; R.J. Dickie, 'Alexander Alesius: Scotland's First International Reformer', in D. Somerset (ed.), *Scotland's Debt to Martin Luther* (Edinburgh, 2018), p. 72.

and Leipzig, he taught in the arts faculty at Wittenberg, at the same time participating in disputations 'de fide, de ecclesia et de traditionibus humanis', along with Martin Luther, Philip Melanchthon and several other professors of theology.[12] The common belief that the 'Ioannes Scotus' who arrived six years later was John Wedderburn, the compiler of *The Gude and Godlie Ballatis*, is probably mistaken, as 'Ioannes Scotus' was one of four students who arrived that year 'ex Plawen', yet it did come to be believed that Wedderburn visited Wittenberg, 'where he heard Luther and Melancton, and became verie fervent and zealous'.[13] In 1540 the letter 'D' was again placed in front of the name of a more advanced visitor from Scotland.[14] John Macalpine (Latinised as Maccabeus), who already held a theology degree from Cologne, received his doctorate two years later, after defending a series of theses 'de ecclesia' under Luther's supervision.[15] He then moved on to a chair at Copenhagen, where he remained for the rest of his life, sending his son back to Wittenberg as a student in 1555.[16] In the meantime, in May 1544, just four months before Balfour arrived in Wittenberg, the names of two schoolmasters from Dundee were entered together there in the *album studiosorum*.[17] John Fethy (Latinised as Fidelis) went on to succeed Allan in his theology chair at Frankfurt on Oder,

12 *Die Baccalaurei und Magistri der Wittenberger philosophischen Fakultät, 1503–60*, 4 vols, ed. D.J. Köstlin (Halle, 1887–91), vol. 2, pp. 15, 21 and 25; *Liber decanorum facultatis theologicae academiae Vitebergensis*, ed. C.E. Förstemann (Leipzig, 1838), p. 29; *Album academiae Vitebergensis*, vol. 2, p. 131; Iacobus Thomasius, *Orationes* (Leipzig, 1683), pp. 300–22.

13 David Calderwood, *The History of the Kirk of Scotland*, 8 vols, ed. D. Laing (Edinburgh, 1842–9), vol. 1, pp. 142–3; J. Durkan, 'Heresy in Scotland: The Second Phase, 1546–58', (1992) 24 *Records of the Scottish Church History Society* 320, at pp. 330–1; A.A. Macdonald, 'Introduction', in *The Gude and Godlie Ballatis* (Edinburgh, 2015), p. 1, at pp. 31–6. The 'Ioannes Scotus' who matriculated in 1539 may well have belonged to a family that originated in Scotland or Ireland.

14 F.B. Petersen, 'Dr Johannes Macchabeus, John MacAlpin: Scotland's Contribution to the Reformation in Denmark', PhD dissertation, University of Edinburgh, 1935, pp. 85–123; J. Durkan, 'Scottish "Evangelicals" in the Patronage of Thomas Cromwell', (1982) 21 *Records of the Scottish Church History Society* 127, at pp. 139–40 and 151–2; E.L. Tapscott, 'Propaganda and Persuasion in the Early Scottish Reformation, c. 1527–57', PhD dissertation, University of St Andrews, 2013, pp. 41–3.

15 *D. Martin Luthers Werke: kritische Gesamtausgabe*, 120 vols, ed. J.K.F. Knaake, R. Hermann, G. Ebeling et al. (Weimar, 1883–2009), vol. 39(2), pp. 145–84; *Liber decanorum facultatis theologicae academiae Vitebergensis*, pp. 32 and 84.

16 Macalpine's son Christian, apparently named after the king of Denmark, was not designated a 'Scotus' in the *Album academiae Vitebergensis*, vol. 2, p. 309.

17 T.A. Fischer, *The Scots in Germany* (Edinburgh, 1902), pp. 167–9; Durkan, 'Heresy in Scotland: The Second Phase', pp. 327–8 and 347–9; *cf.* B. Bradshaw, 'George Browne, First Reformation Archbishop of Dublin, 1536–54', (1970) 21 *Journal of Ecclesiastical History* 301, at pp. 318–19.

and Walter Spalding may have followed the Borthwicks into English service, on Melanchthon's recommendation.[18] In September 1544 Balfour's own name was entered in the *album studiosorum* alongside that of William Ramsay, as it had been when he was enrolled at St Andrews as an arts student, in November 1540, and as a master of arts, in March 1544.[19] That summer the two graduates travelled to Germany together, pausing in Denmark to visit Macalpine, who was impressed with their piety.[20] Ramsay has been identified as the *Scotus* who participated in theological disputations in December 1544 and July 1545, but it could be that Balfour was also involved.[21] He appears to have been the Scot named only as 'Iacobus' who was encouraged by Melanchthon to travel to Leipzig to observe his compatriot Alexander Allan in a disputation.[22] As for Ramsay, after teaching philosophy in Bordeaux and delivering public lectures on the arts in Glasgow and Edinburgh, he became a regent in the arts at St Andrews in 1560.[23] At the end of that year he was identified by the general

18 *Corpus reformatorum*, 101 vols, ed. K.G. Bretschneider, H.E. Bindseil, A.E. Caunitz, J.W. Baum, E. Egli, G. Finsler and W. Köhler (Halle, 1834–1959), vol. 6, cols 780–1; *Original Letters Relative to the English Reformation*, 2 vols, ed. H. Robinson (Cambridge, 1847), vol. 2, p. 428; *Original Letters and Papers in Illustration of the History of the Church in Ireland*, ed. E.P. Shirley (London, 1851), pp. 19–21.

19 *Album academiae Vitebergensis*, vol. 1, p. 216; *Acta facultatis artium universitatis Sanctiandree*, vol. 2, pp. 396 and 399; *Early Records of the University of St Andrews*, pp. 145–7 and 245.

20 H. Ilsøe, 'Christian og Johannes Machabaeus', (1963–5) 5 *Kirkehistoriske Samlinger* 454, at pp. 468–9.

21 *D. Martin Luthers Werke*, vol. 39(2), pp. 302, 348, 352 and 371.

22 *Corpus reformatorum*, vol. 4, col. 793. Although this letter is assigned the date 'March 1542', it contains an obvious reference to Macalpine's recommendation (n. 20). It was not until 1544 that Allan moved to Leipzig, which is closer to Wittenberg than Edinburgh is to Glasgow. On the other hand, the 'Schotte Jakob' referred to in a letter written in 1540 (*Melanchthons Briefwechsel: kritische und kommentierte Gesamtausgabe*, 25 vols, ed. W. Thüringer, R. Wetzel, J. Loehr, C. Mundhenk, M. Dall'Asta and H. Schneible (Stuttgart, 1977–2019), vol. 3, p. 106) was clearly someone else. Durkan, 'Heresy in Scotland: The Second Phase', pp. 325–6, got in a muddle on this point, and has misled M. Fink-Jensen, 'Reformation across the North Sea: Early Protestant Connections between Denmark, England and Scotland', in J.E. Kelly, H. Laugerd and S. Ryan (eds), *Northern European Reformations: Transnational Perspectives* (Cham, 2020), p. 115, at p. 124. The strange idea that Ramsay went to Wittenberg as Balfour's tutor was introduced by J. Kirk, '"Melvillian" Reform in the Scottish Universities', in A.A. MacDonald, M. Lynch and I.B. Cowan (eds), *The Renaissance in Scotland: Studies in Literature, Religion, History and Culture Offered to John Durkan* (Leiden, 1994), p. 276, at p. 284.

23 J. Durkan, 'The Royal Lectureships under Mary of Lorraine', (1983) 62 *Scottish Historical Review* 73, at pp. 74–6; J.K. Cameron, 'Aspects of the Lutheran Contribution to the Scottish Reformation, 1528–52', (1984) 22 *Records of the Scottish Church History Society* 1, at p. 2.

assembly of the newly reformed kirk – along with William Skene – as one of the few men resident in the city who was suitably qualified 'for ministering and teaching', and he had become a kirk minister by the time of his death in 1570.[24] Fifteen years earlier John Lyne had become the last Scot to matriculate at Wittenberg before the 1560s.[25] He is last heard of as a courier passing between Philip Melanchthon in Wittenberg, John Fethy in Frankfurt on Oder, Heinrich Bullinger in Zurich and John Calvin in Geneva.[26]

It seems fairly clear that Balfour would have been the odd man out among the Scots who studied at Wittenberg in the decades leading up to the Scottish Reformation if he had been drawn there by anything other than an interest in Protestant theology. He was back in Scotland by the summer of 1546, when he joined three of his brothers in the defence of the castle in St Andrews, following the assassination of David Beaton, the archbishop.[27] Despite assistance from England, which was facilitated by local agents including Andrew Balfour of Montquhanny, the father of the four brothers in the castle, the siege ended a year later.[28] The former student at Wittenberg was one of those forced into penal servitude on a French galley, where he rowed alongside John Knox, with whom he became intimately familiar.[29] Several decades later Knox would complain about Balfour's refusal to celebrate communion with the Calvinists on the pretext that he had been raised as a Lutheran, insisting that he had shown no such scruples during the siege, but it could be that Knox was exaggerating the consistency of his own commitments before and after he studied at Geneva in the later 1550s.[30] In any case, his firm impression, which he had been in a good position to form accurately, was that during the later 1540s Balfour had been 'the chief and principal Protestant that then was to be found in this realm', and that he was only lured away from devotion to the true faith by the offer of appointment as the official of Lothian in the early

24 *The Acts and Proceedings of the General Assemblies of the Church of Scotland, 1560–1618*, 3 vols, ed. D. Shaw (Edinburgh, 2004), vol. 1, p. 3; S.J. Reid, *Humanism and Calvinism: Andrew Melville and the Universities of Scotland, 1560–1625* (Farnham, 2011), p. 36.

25 *Album academiae Vitebergensis*, vol. 1, p. 312; Durkan, 'Heresy in Scotland: The Second Phase', pp. 329–30.

26 *Corpus reformatorum*, vol. 8, cols 815–16.

27 W.S. Reid, *Trumpeter of God: A Biography of John Knox* (New York, 1974), pp. 32–53.

28 M.H. Merriman, 'The Assured Scots: Scottish Collaborators with England during the Rough Wooing', (1968) 47 *Scottish Historical Review* 10, at pp. 18–19.

29 J. Dawson, *John Knox* (New Haven, 2015), pp. 56–7.

30 *John Knox's History of the Reformation in Scotland*, 2 vols, ed. W.C. Dickinson (New York, 1950), vol. 1, pp. 93–4 and 108.

1550s.[31] This last observation casts doubt on the supposition often made – by the editors of the *Practicks* among others – that Balfour's intention when he went abroad in 1544 was to study the canon law in preparation for a career in the church courts.[32] Admittedly, the university of St Andrews was closely associated with the local official's court.[33] Indeed, the official of St Andrews was not only a senior figure in the academic establishment but was also related to Balfour, who was to become his executor in the early 1550s.[34] Had Balfour been contemplating a career as a church lawyer, he might well have sought advice on where to study from the official, who was formally designated in the court records a 'iuris pontificii bachalarius'.[35] It seems unlikely, however, that the advice would have been to go to Wittenberg. Having already been involved in the trial for heresy of one individual with Lutheran sympathies in 1537, Martin Balfour had been a member of the court that convicted Sir John Borthwick of the same crime in 1540, when one of the charges against him was that he denied the authority of the canon law.[36] On hearing about the charge, Borthwick responded that he did 'condempne those lawes which the bishoppes of Rome have made accordinge to theyr owne wil and minde', denouncing

31 Balfour was not well qualified for the appointment. Having only studied abroad for two years, he could not possibly have acquired a law degree, nor did he have any forensic experience at the time.

32 W. Goodal, 'The Publisher to the Reader', in Sir James Balfour of Pittendreich, *Practicks, or a System of the More Ancient Law of Scotland* (Edinburgh, 1754), p. i; P.G.B. McNeill, 'Introduction', in *The Practicks of Sir James Balfour of Pittendreich*, 2 vols (Edinburgh, 1962–3), vol. 1, p. xi, at p. xii.

33 Dunlop, 'Introduction', in *Acta facultatis artium universitatis Sanctiandree*, vol. 1, p. xi, at pp. lvi–ix; S. Olivant, *The Court of the Official in Pre-Reformation Scotland* (Edinburgh, 1982), pp. 50–2 and 174; Sanderson, *Cardinal of Scotland*, pp. 98–100 and 119–20.

34 NRS, GD63/37. Though sometimes referred to as James Balfour's uncle, Martin Balfour appears to have been the brother of his grandfather, Michael Balfour, who is often confused with his father, Andrew Balfour. The true identity of the father is entirely clear from NRS, CS7/42, ff. 329v-31r.

35 *Liber officialis Sancti Andree*, ed. J.H. Forbes (Edinburgh, 1845), pp. 81, 86 and 141. Elsewhere the official is said to have been 'in sacris literis et decretis bacchalarius' (*Registrum magni sigilli regum Scotorum*, vol. 3, pp. 614 and 646). W.F. Leith, *Pre-Reformation Scholars in Scotland in the XVIth Century* (Glasgow, 1915), p. 100, refers to 'M. Martin Balfour, in utroque iure bac., in sacris literis doc'., but no source is cited, nor has any been found, to support this. On his ownership of a book relating to canon law see J. Durkan and A. Ross, *Early Scottish Libraries* (Glasgow, 1961), p. 74, and C.P. Finlayson, *Clement Litill and His Library: The Origins of Edinburgh University Library* (Edinburgh, 1980), pp. 2 and 54.

36 *Register of the Minister, Elders and Deacons of the Christian Congregation of St Andrews, 1559–1600*, 2 vols, ed. D.H. Fleming (Edinburgh, 1889–90), vol. 1, pp. 90–104; *St Andrews Formulare*, vol. 2, pp. 72–5 and 225–7; Herkless and Hannay, *Archbishops of St Andrews*, vol. 3, pp. 210–12.

as 'plaine rebelles agaynste the woorde of God' any clerics who would presume 'to appoynte or set anye new lawes uppon the people of God'.[37] Nevertheless, while James Balfour probably travelled to Wittenberg to study theology, with the encouragement of his closest relations, he could also have learned something about the canon law during his relatively brief sojourn there.[38]

In 1520 Luther had marked his decisive break with Rome by consigning to a bonfire lit by his students not only a papal bull threatening him with excommunication, but also the core texts taught in the schools of canon law.[39] Sir John Borthwick's antipathy to the subject could have been informed by what he learned from his brother about attitudes at Wittenberg, where it certainly had been maintained that the usurpation of legislative authority by popes and bishops was contrary to scripture, although by the time of Nicholas Borthwick's arrival there in 1528 a reappraisal was getting under way.[40] During the later 1520s the belief that Christians who received the gospel were freed from the law had become confused with the belief that they should withdraw from the established structures of church and state, or should dispense with institutions like marriage, property and contracts, or should engage in violent resistance to both spiritual and secular authorities.[41] In a confession presented to the imperial diet at Augsburg in 1530 the Lutherans repudiated the more radical beliefs attributed to sects of 'anabaptists', declaring that 'the gospel does not overthrow civil authority, the state and marriage, but requires that all these be kept as true orders of God'.[42] Others had been equally mistaken, Melanchthon added in a commentary on the confession, 'in imposing upon us the judicial laws of Moses'.[43] It was suggested in the confession itself that it was the example of Moses that had misled the bishops into exercising authority that did not belong to them.[44] The proper role of the clergy, it was insisted there, was 'to preach the gospel and administer the sacraments', and while the church, like other organisations, might need to issue regulations as a means of preserving

37 John Foxe, *Actes and Monuments of These Latter and Perillous Dayes Touching Matters of the Church* (London, 1563), pp. 581–3.

38 It is of course possible that Balfour intended to return to Wittenberg after the summer of 1546.

39 H.A. Oberman, *Luther: Man between God and the Devil* (New York, 1992), p. 186.

40 J. Witte, *Law and Protestantism: The Legal Teachings of the Lutheran Reformation* (Cambridge, 2002), pp. 53–85.

41 O. Chadwick, *The Early Reformation on the Continent* (Oxford, 2001), pp. 351–82.

42 *Confessions and Catechisms of the Reformation*, ed. M.A. Noll (Leicester, 1991), pp. 91–2.

43 *The Apology for the Augsburg Confession*, tr. F. Bente and W.H.T. Dau (Ithaca, NY, 2020), p. 170.

44 *Confessions and Catechisms of the Reformation*, pp. 113–20.

order, only the state could enact laws that were susceptible to coercive enforcement. In his defence of the confession Melanchthon made it clear that the Lutherans were hostile not so much to the canon law as to its mishandling, and that they were willing to comply with ecclesiastical ordinances 'for the sake of utility and tranquillity', as long as they were not inconsistent with the gospel.[45] As the 1530s progressed, it was recognised within the University of Wittenberg that it would be of assistance to the secular authorities if graduates were produced who had expertise not only in the civil law, which became the primary focus of attention in the law schools, but also in the canon law, which had for centuries regulated important areas of life, such as marriage.[46] In the year before Balfour arrived in Wittenberg a former professor of law there published a book about that subject in which extensive use was made of canon law sources.[47] In a dedicatory epistle attached to the book the author explained that it was impossible to rely solely on the New Testament, which contained only a couple of texts touching on marriage, or on the Old Testament, which had sanctioned unsound practices like marriage to half-sisters, or on the civil law, which had failed to eradicate pagan practices like concubinage, so that the best guide to the subject available was still the canon law of the medieval church, provided it was used with appropriate circumspection.[48]

There was certainly awareness among evangelical Scots of the more accommodating attitudes towards the canon law adopted after the 1520s. Henry Balnaves of Halhill, a lord of session until he joined the defenders of the castle in St Andrews, was imprisoned after its fall in Rouen, where he responded to the reproaches of his captors by drafting his own confession of faith.[49] He complained that against the convictions he had acquired from a careful reading of the scriptures, 'the adversaries of faith and veritie crye the canon lawe, the aucthoritie of the church, the long consuetude, the example of the fathers, the bishop of Romes aucthoritie, the generall counsels', all of which he regarded

45 *Apology for the Augsburg Confession*, pp. 154–66 and 256–61.

46 G. Strauss, *Law, Resistance and the State: The Opposition to Roman Law in Reformation Germany* (Princeton, 1986), pp. 191–239.

47 K. Pennington, 'Protestant Ecclesiastical Law and the *Ius commune*', (2015) 26 *Rivista internazionale di diritto comune* 9, at pp. 17–18.

48 Melchior Kling, *Matrimonialium causarum tractatus methodico ordine scriptus* (Frankfurt, 1543), sigg. ¶2–3.

49 H. Watt, 'Henry Balnaves and the Scottish Reformation', (1935) 5 *Records of the Scottish Church History Society* 23; M.H. Dotterwich, 'The Emergence of Evangelical Theology in Scotland to 1550', PhD dissertation, University of Edinburgh, 2002, pp. 220–67; J.W. Keddie, 'Henry Balnaves and the Doctrine of Justification', in Somerset (ed.), *Scotland's Debt to Martin Luther*, p. 138.

as 'heresie'.[50] Yet he went on to acknowledge not only the need for 'politike or civill justice', without which 'no commonweale might bee conserved and kept in rule and order', but also the benefits of 'ceremoniall justice', achieved through conformity to 'the statutes, ordinances and traditions of man, made by the bishop of Rome and other bishops'. Ecclesiastical regulations were to be obeyed when 'not repugnant to the law of God', which provided 'a perfite rule' for human life. Balnaves managed to send the draft of his confession to Knox, who forwarded it with his approval (and some additions) to Scotland.[51] It took a further forty years for the confession to appear in print, but whether or not Balfour was familiar with it, he must surely have known the Augsburg Confession, which became the definitive statement of Lutheran doctrine.[52] Moreover, whether or not he attended classes in law at Wittenberg, he must surely have recalled the Lutheran theologians' attitudes towards law when papal jurisdiction was rejected in Scotland in the 1560s.[53] At the beginning of that decade the courts of the Catholic church, which persisted in adhering to the canon law, competed in their handling of matrimonial disputes with the courts of the reformed church of Scotland, which sought to rely exclusively on the law of God elucidated in the scriptures, and to complicate matters further new commissary courts were set up, which used both the canon law and the law of God, along with other sources, in developing their own consistorial law.[54] It has been suggested that what made Balfour an appropriate person to lead the establishment of the commissary courts was not only his experience as the last official of Lothian, but also his acquaintance with the approach to the handling of matrimonial disputes that had gradually taken shape in Lutheran Germany.[55] All the same, it has also been pointed out that it was not until the 1570s that the secular character of the consistorial law developed in the commissary courts was fully recognised, and that Balfour took care in compiling his *Practicks* to preserve the possibility of the reinstatement of bishops' courts to administer ecclesiastical law.[56] His approach was not straightforwardly

---

50 *The Confession of Faith* (Edinburgh, 1584), pp. 50 and 54–6.

51 Knox, *History of the Reformation in Scotland*, vol. 1, p. 92.

52 As is explained in Dawson, *John Knox*, pp. 57–8, Balfour was no longer with Knox when his galley docked in Rouen.

53 T.M. Green, 'The Sources of Early Scots Consistorial Law: Reflections on Law, Authority and Jurisdiction during the Scottish Reformation', in A.M. Godfrey (ed.), *Law and Authority in British Legal History, 1200–1900* (Cambridge, 2016), p. 120, at p. 126.

54 T.M. Green, *The Spiritual Jurisdiction in Reformation Scotland: A Legal History* (Edinburgh, 2019).

55 T.M. Green, 'Introduction', in *The Consistorial Decisions of the Commissaries of Edinburgh, 1564 to 1576/7* (Edinburgh, 2014), p. xvii, at pp. xxxi–iii.

56 Green, *Spiritual Jurisdiction in Reformation Scotland*, pp. 65 and 175.

Lutheran, though it would have been even less consistent with the presbyterian reorganisation of the church that came to be borrowed from Geneva.

If there is thus some reason to suppose that Balfour's contribution to the early work of the commissary courts in Scotland was coloured by his experience as a student at Wittenberg, there is also some reason to suppose that his contribution to the work of the commissions set up to reform the law in Scotland was coloured by the same experience. When Balfour studied at Wittenberg, instruction in the university was informed by a coalescence of evangelical and humanist commitments.[57] The belief that human beings, in their fallen state, lacked the ability to understand let alone follow the perfect rule of divine law had cast doubt on the Aristotelian assumption that the essential feature of human beings was their ability to grasp the truth when they encountered it.[58] Of course, it had always been recognised that there were limitations to the capacities of individual scholars, but it had been believed in the medieval universities that by working collectively within traditions of enquiry, in strict conformity with the precepts of logic, scholars were able to refine and augment their understanding of philosophy, theology, law and medicine.[59] To Luther it seemed that devotion to Aristotle's philosophy encouraged the erroneous belief that people could contribute in some way to their own salvation.[60] But if coherent bodies of knowledge could not be fashioned through the unaided exercise of reason, was there any form of enquiry worth pursuing apart from close study of the revealed word of God? The answer offered by Melanchthon was that study of the humanities, quite apart from supplying the linguistic

57 L.W. Spitz, 'The Importance of the Reformation for Universities: Culture and Confession in the Critical Years', in J.M. Kittelson and P.J. Transue (eds), *Rebirth, Reform and Resilience: Universities in Transition, 1300–1700* (Columbus, OH, 1984), p. 42.

58 While Luther's 'Disputatio contra scholasticam theologiam' (*Luther's Works*, 55 vols, ed. J. Pelikan and H.T. Lehmann (St Louis, MO, and Philadelphia, PA, 1955–86), vol. 31, pp. 9–16), which was published eight weeks before his famous theses against indulgences (A. Pettegree, *Brand Luther: 1517, Printing and the Making of the Reformation* (New York, 2015), pp. 50–2), dealt primarily with soteriological issues, it also contained a series of theses attacking adherence to Aristotle (J.H. Overfield, *Humanism and Scholasticism in Late Medieval Germany* (Princeton, 1984), pp. 300–1). For Luther's views on scholasticism see too L. Grane, 'Luther and Scholasticism', in M.J. Harran (ed.), *Luther and Learning: The Wittenberg University Luther Symposium* (Cranbury, NJ, 1985), p. 52, and C. Augustijn, '*Wittenberga contra scholasticos*', in W.J. van Asselt and E. Dekker (eds), *Reformation and Scholasticism: An Ecumenical Enterprise* (Grand Rapids, 2001), p. 65.

59 E. Grant, *God and Reason in the Middle Ages* (Cambridge, 2001).

60 D. Janz, *Luther and Late Medieval Thomism: A Study in Theological Anthropology* (Waterloo, ON, 1983); N. Slenczka, 'Luther's Anthropology', in R. Kolb, I. Dingel and L. Batka (eds), *The Oxford Handbook of Luther's Theology* (Oxford, 2014), p. 212.

skills required for a reliable reading of the scriptures and the effective preaching of the gospel, also offered a method of organising information that would facilitate its recollection and deployment in argument.[61] In his *Loci communes rerum theologicarum* he adopted techniques taught by the Roman rhetoricians in order to catalogue sources that might prove useful in handling standard topics of debate such as 'law' or 'gospel'.[62] In dealing with 'law', for example, he assembled biblical and other texts under subheadings, such as 'Divine Law' and 'Natural Law'.[63] Along with the law revealed in the Old Testament, he explained, a few basic rules had been imprinted by God on human minds (*impressas mentibus humanis*), though these rules too were known by a kind of divine revelation, not discovered through the exercise of human intellects (*non inventam a nostris ingeniis*). Melanchthon persuaded the professors of law at Wittenberg that the best way to approach their discipline would also be by reorganising the material in the books they studied under topical headings.[64] In treatises published in the ten years preceding Balfour's arrival there, Johann Apel, Conrad Lagus and Melchior Kling saw an opportunity to revive Cicero's project of *ius civile ad artem redigere*, finding reassurance in the recognition in Justinian's *Institutes* of the need to present the civil law methodically to novices (though easing students into a discipline gradually was not quite the same thing as reorganising a discipline in the only way that might give it coherence).[65] Lagus went so far as to assemble texts from the civil and canon laws together under common headings, and to deal in a similar way with the written sources of Saxon law (albeit in a book that would only be published later).[66]

Even though Balfour may not have had direct experience of the teaching of the civil and canon laws at Wittenberg, he cannot have studied there without

---

61 E. Rummel, *The Humanist-Scholastic Debate in the Renaissance and Reformation* (Cambridge, MA, 1995), pp. 140–7.

62 Q. Breen, 'The Terms *Loci communes* and *Loci* in Melanchthon', (1947) 16 *Church History* 197.

63 *Corpus reformatorum*, vol. 21, col. 117; *Commonplaces: Loci communes 1521*, tr. C. Preus (St Louis, MO, 2014), p. 62.

64 H.J. Berman and C.J. Reid, 'Roman Law in Europe and the *Ius commune*: A Historical Overview with Emphasis on the New Legal Science of the Sixteenth Century', (1994) 20 *Syracuse Journal of International Law and Commerce* 1, at pp. 13–25.

65 Johann Apel, *Methodica dialectices ratio ad iurisprudentiam adcommodata* (Nuremberg, 1535), sigg. A2 and A3v-4r, and *Isagoge per dialogum in quatuor libros Institutionum divi Iustiniani imperatoris* (Bratislava, 1540), sig. A3r; Conrad Lagus, *Protestatio adversus improbam suorum commentariorum de doctrina iuris editionem ab Egenolpho factam* (Dantzig, 1544), sigg. A4 and B3–4; Melchior Kling, *In quatuor Institutionum iuris civilis principis Iustiniani libros enarrationes* (Frankfurt, 1542), sig. ¶3 and f. 1.

66 *Iuris utriusque traditio methodica* (Frankfurt, 1543), and *Compendium iuris civilis et Saxonici* (Magdeburg, 1597).

becoming familiar with the idea that topical arrangement was the only satisfactory means of rendering large bodies of diffuse material intelligible.[67] It would be surprising if he was not reminded of this when the reform of Scots law returned to the political agenda around the time of the Reformation, after a gap of almost a century.[68] He was a member of a commission instructed by Mary I in 1566 'to visite, sycht and correct the lawis of this our realme', beginning at 'the buikis of the law callit *Regiam maiestatem* and *Quoniam attachiamenta*', before working forwards through all the legislation enacted 'be the avise of the thre estatis in parliament'.[69] As an active member of that commission he would probably have been appointed to a new commission proposed in 1567, following the deposition of the queen, had the estates then accepted the proposal that they 'mak ane body of the civil and municipal lawis, devidit in heidis conforme to the fassone of the law Romane'.[70] When a commission 'anent the sichting, collectioun and reformatioun of the lawis of this realme' was established eight years later, Balfour was not only among its members, but appears to have started work on his *Practicks* as a result of his appointment.[71] The new commission was instructed to examine 'the bukis of the law, actis of parliament and decisionis befoir the sessioun, and draw the forme of the body of oure lawis, alsweill of that quhilk is alreddy statute as thay thingis that wer meit and convenient to be statute', reporting their findings to the estates in order for them to enact 'a perfyte writtin law, quhairupoun all jugeis may knaw how to proceid and decerne'.[72] Whereas the 1566 commission had resulted in the production of an edition of legislation, arranged in chronological order, the *Practicks* contained material found in the three sources drawn to the attention of the 1575 commission, arranged under headings such as 'Of the law' and 'Of the trew and halie kirk'.[73] Once it had become apparent that a wider range of written sources would need to be used in the treatment 'Of schip lawis',

67 By 1544 Melanchthon's *Loci communes rerum theologicarum* had replaced Peter Lombard's *Sententiarum libri quatuor* as the basic textbook used by theology students at Wittenberg.

68 A.R.C. Simpson, 'Legislation and Authority in Early-Modern Scotland', in Godfrey (ed.), *Law and Authority in British Legal History*, p. 85, at pp. 85–9.

69 *The Actis and Constitutiounis of the Realme of Scotland* (Edinburgh, 1566), sig. 2.

70 *The Acts of the Parliaments of Scotland*, 12 vols, ed. T. Thomson and C. Innes (Edinburgh, 1814–75), vol. 3, p. 40; Records of the Parliaments of Scotland, ed. K.M. Brown (www.rps.ac.uk), 1567/12/54. Balfour was singled out for praise as a particularly active member of the 1566 commission in Edward Henryson's preface to the *Actis and Constitutiounis of the Realme of Scotland*, sig. 3v.

71 H. McKechnie, 'Balfour's *Practicks*', (1931) 43 *Juridical Review* 179, at pp. 181–2.

72 *Acts of the Parliaments of Scotland*, vol. 3, p. 89; Records of the Parliaments of Scotland, A1575/3/7.

73 *Practicks of Sir James Balfour of Pittendreich*, vol. 1, pp. 1 and 20.

that subject was moved to the end of the *Practicks* as an appendix, in which material was arranged under subheadings that would enable readers to locate sources 'Anent frauchting of shippis', 'Anent letter of mark', and so on.[74] An apt title for Balfour's collection of sea laws might have been *Loci communes legum nauticarum*, since it amounted to a topical compendium of all the sources he had examined. While there is no reason to suppose that the draftsmen of the instructions issued to the 1575 commissioners were influenced by Lutheran ideology, there is reason to suppose that Balfour's reading of the instructions was coloured by his educational experience at Wittenberg.[75]

In envisaging the enactment of a *Corpus iuris Scoticani*, the draftsmen may have been mindful of the reference in the 1567 proposal to a body of laws 'devidit in heidis conforme to the fassone of the law Romane', but what they did not revive was the proposal to combine in a single body 'the civil and municipal lawis'. It has been suggested that there was considered to be no need for the civil and canon laws to be incorporated into surveys of the law of early-modern Scotland since that part of the law was amply dealt with in writing elsewhere and was well known to local lawyers.[76] As far as the instructions issued in 1575 are concerned, this is not easy to square with the plan to produce 'a perfyte writtin law, quhairupoun all jugeis may knaw how to proceid and decerne'. The intention was clearly for all the applicable law to be contained in a code enacted by the estates.[77] Balfour, however, did not try to produce a code capable of dictating every judicial decision in the future, for while he dealt with 'that quhilk is alreddy statute', he refrained from advising on 'thay thingis that wer meit and convenient to be statute'. Indeed, he included rulings in his *Practicks* that 'gif any questioun sall happin to aryse before any jugeis of this realme quhilk cannot be decydit be no cleir writtin law, the decisioun and declaratioun thairof aucht and sould be referrit and continewit unto the nixt parliament', and similarly that 'gif ony actioun or cause intentit or persewit befoir the lordis of sessioun be of swa greit difficultie that thay may not

74 The relationship between the appendix and the main body of the *Practicks* is examined in the fifth essay in this collection.

75 Of course, this is not to suggest that only someone who had studied at Wittenberg would have written in the way that Balfour did. *Cf.* David Chalmers of Ormond, *Compendium of the Laws of Scotland*, ed. W. Coutts, J. Goodare and A.R.C. Simpson (Edinburgh, 2023).

76 G. Dolezalek, *Scotland under Jus Commune: Census of Manuscripts of Legal Literature in Scotland, Mainly between 1500 and 1660*, 3 vols (Edinburgh, 2010), vol. 1, pp. 3–7.

77 On the use of the word 'perfyte' to signify completeness see W. Craigie, A.J. Aitken, J.A.C. Stevenson, H.D. Watson, and M.G. Dareau (eds), *A Dictionary of the Older Scottish Tongue from the Twelfth Century to the End of the Seventeenth*, 12 vols (Chicago, London and Aberdeen, 1931–2002), vol. 5, pp. 420–2.

decide nor declare the samin, thay sould refer it to be decidit be the estatis in parliament'.[78] It is possible that the lord of session were only expected to remit cases to parliament if questions could be answered neither from the *lex municipalis* surveyed by Balfour nor from the *ius commune* studied in the universities, yet trouble appears to have been taken in framing the summaries of decisions included in the *Practicks* to disguise the learned origins of some of the answers provided, and to give a firm impression that it was the rulings of the lords of session that made the answers authoritative.[79] The decisions of the session had after all been identified as one of the sources to be examined by the commissioners, along with the old books of law and the acts of parliament. Moreover, even in his collection of sea laws, where he moved beyond assembling together extracts from the old books, references to the acts of parliament, and summaries of decisions of the session, Balfour continued to eschew even passing allusions to the learned laws. His determined focus on local sources may have been connected with the move he appears to have made in the late 1570s away from instructing judges in how to decide the actions brought before them towards making the law 'bettar knawin to all oure soverane lordis liegis and pepill'.[80] Since this move was itself connected with the translation of the extracts taken from the old books out of Latin into Scots, it may be wondered whether he remembered the efforts made at Wittenberg to free theology from clerical control, and to involve lay people in its study, by translating the Bible into German and publishing pamphlets for a popular audience.[81] Balfour wanted lay people as well as lawyers to know about the law of Scotland, but he did not think it appropriate to draw their attention to the texts studied in the continental law schools, nor did he show any interest in the legal customs by which lay people believed their activities to be regulated. It may shed further light on his thinking if attention is turned now to the Scots who studied at Wittenberg after 1560, for in the late 1570s Balfour was receiving assistance with his work on law reform from John Skene.[82]

78 *Practicks of Sir James Balfour of Pittendreich*, vol. 1, pp. 1–2 and 268.

79 J.D. Ford, *Law and Opinion in Scotland during the Seventeenth Century* (Oxford, 2007), p. 203.

80 NRS, GD112/71/5, f. 5r.

81 A.G. Dickens, *The German Nation and Martin Luther* (London, 1974), pp. 107–9; M.U. Edwards, *Printing, Propaganda and Martin Luther* (Berkeley, 1994), pp. 37–40.

82 *Registrum secreti sigilli regum Scotorum: The Register of the Privy Seal of Scotland*, 7 vols, ed. M. Livingston, G. Donaldson, J. Beveridge and D.H. Fleming (Edinburgh, 1908–66), vol. 7, pp. 159–60; David Hume of Godscroft, *The History of the Houses of Douglas and Angus* (Edinburgh, 1644), p. 358; Calderwood, *History of the Kirk of Scotland*, vol. 3, pp. 575–6.

2 Comparative History of Sea Laws

To the extent that their later careers can be traced, the Scots who studied at Wittenberg during the last four decades of the sixteenth century seem to have had more varied ambitions than those who studied there before the Reformation.[83] Some did have kirk connections.[84] Philip Hislop became the minister of the parish of Inveresk in 1595, after returning from two years of study in Germany to resume a teaching post in the liberal arts at the recently founded University of Edinburgh.[85] It may have been as a step in the same direction that William Strang, who seems to have spent some time as a schoolteacher after returning from Germany, became a reader in Leith.[86] William Lowe appears to have belonged to a group of Aberdeen graduates who were encouraged to continue their studies in Germany by Alexander Arbuthnot, the minister of Old Machar and principal of King's College, who may also have been the uncle of a student with the same name who went to Wittenberg in 1590, after visiting Rostock and before moving on to Helmstedt and Heidelberg.[87]

83 *Album academiae Vitebergensis*, vol. 2, pp. 48, 170, 182, 241–2, 280, 323, 362, 369, 376–8 and 383.

84 As no trace has been found of a graduate called Andrew Black, it may be wondered whether the exceptionally named 'Andreas Schwartz Scotus' who matriculated in 1562 was in fact the composer Andrew Blackhall, whose equally exceptional transition from monastic life to the charge of a parish in 1567 would be more explicable if a period of study at a Protestant university had intervened (C.H. Haws, *Scottish Parish Clergy at the Reformation, 1540–74* (Edinburgh, 1972), pp. 50, 113, 190 and 194; K. Elliott, '*Some Helpes for Young Schollers*: A New Source of Early Scottish Psalmody', in MacDonald, Lynch and Cowan (eds), *Renaissance in Scotland*, p. 264, at pp. 267–8; J. Reid-Baxter, M. Lynch and E.P. Dennison, *Jhone Angus, Monk of Dunfermline, and Scottish Reformation Music* (Dunfermline, 2011), p. 50). The 'Andreas Niger Britannus' who matriculated in 1573 must have been a different person (*Album academiae Vitebergensis*, vol. 2, p. 240).

85 Thomas Craufurd, *History of the University of Edinburgh from 1580 to 1646* (Edinburgh, 1808), pp. 31–2, 34 and 37–8; *A Catalogue of the Graduates in the Faculties of Arts, Divinity and Law of the University of Edinburgh since Its Foundation* (Edinburgh, 1858), pp. xi, 7 and 10; *Fasti ecclesiae Scoticanae: The Succession of Ministers in the Church of Scotland from the Reformation*, 11 vols, ed. H. Scott, J.A. Lamb, D.F.M. Macdonald and F.A.J. Macdonald (Edinburgh, 1915–2000), vol. 1, p. 325; *The Commissariot Record of Edinburgh: Register of Testaments, 1514–1800*, 3 vols, ed. F.J. Grant (Edinburgh, 1897–9), vol. 1, p. 132.

86 J. Durkan and J. Reid-Baxter, *Scottish Schools and Schoolmasters, 1560–1633* (Woodbridge, 2006), p. 259; *South Leith Records*, ed. D. Robertson (Edinburgh, 1911), pp. 4–5 and 7–8; NRS, CH2/716/1, pp. 28, 36 and 50. Why it is stated in M. Todd, *The Culture of Protestantism in Early Modern Scotland* (New Haven, 2002), p. 70, that Strang became a minister in Leith is unclear, though serving as a reader often was a step towards ordination as a minister.

87 Fischer, *Scots in Germany*, pp. 313–14; W.C. Taylor, 'Scottish Students in Heidelberg, 1386–1662', (1908) 5 *Scottish Historical Review* 67, at p. 68; P.S.-M. Arbuthnot, *Memories of the Arbuthnots of Kincardinshire and Aberdeenshire* (London, 1920), pp. 43–8; J.K. Cameron,

What became of these two students, and of the James Turner who travelled to Wittenberg from St Andrews in 1579, or the Archibald Anderson who seems to have gone there from Aberdeen in 1588, is unknown.[88] In contrast, there is no doubt about the future destination of John Craig, a brother of the advocate Thomas Craig, for he moved on to teach philosophy at Frankfurt on Oder, before eventually becoming the king's personal physician.[89] The 'M. Iacobus Bannazinus Scotus Angusianus' who matriculated in 1589, if he was the chaplain of Brechin and rector of Rothes referred to in several later documents as 'Mr James Bannatyne, writer', became a kind of lawyer.[90] Similarly, Robert Wedderburn, a close kinsman of the writer of *The Gude and Godly Ballatis*, spent a short time at Wittenberg prior to his admission to practice as a notary public in 1575, after which he recorded transactions in a protocol book brought home from Wittenberg.[91] Apart from John Skene and William Welwod, however, the most prominent lawyer to have studied at Wittenberg in the closing decades of the century was Thomas Nicolson, a future advocate of whom more will be said at the start of the next section of this essay, together with John

'Introduction', in *Letters of John Johnston and Robert Howie* (Edinburgh, 1963), p. xii, at pp. xviii–xix; I.D. McFarlane, *Buchanan* (London, 1981), pp. 365–6; C. Bing, *The Lairds of Arbuthnott* (Edzell, 1993), pp. 49–52; P. Dukes, *The Universities of Aberdeen and Europe: The First Three Centuries* (Aberdeen, 1995), pp. 58–60.

88 *Acta facultatis artium Universitatis Sancti Andree*, vol. 2, pp. 444 and 460; *Early Records of the University of St Andrews*, pp. 172, 176 and 282. Matriculation and graduation records for the sixteenth century have not survived from Aberdeen, but since Archibald Anderson (like William Lowe and Alexander Arbuthnot) does not appear in the records surviving from the other Scottish universities, it is likely that he studied in Aberdeen.

89 A. Keller, 'The Physical Nature of Man: Science, Medicine, Mathematics', in J. MacQueen (ed.), *Humanism in Renaissance Scotland* (Edinburgh, 1990), p. 97, at pp. 109–10; D. McOmish, 'Not Just a Lawyer: Thomas Craig and Humanist Edinburgh', (2016) 67 *Innes Review* 93, at pp. 94–6.

90 *Registrum episcopatus Brechinensis, cui accedunt cartae quamplurimae originales*, 2 vols, ed. P. Chalmers and C. Innes (Aberdeen, 1856), vol. 2, pp. 222 and 365; *Inquisitionum ad capellam domini regis retornatarum, quae in publicis archivis Scotiae adhuc servantur, abbreviatio*, 3 vols, ed. T. Thomson (Edinburgh, 1811–16), vol. 1, Haddington 211; *Registrum magni sigilli regum Scotorum*, vol. 5, pp. 642–3, and vol. 6, p. 11. William Lowe may also have returned to Brechin (*Registrum secreti sigilli regum Scotorum*, vol. 8, p. 249; *Registrum magni sigilli regum Scotorum*, vol. 5, p. 185).

91 A. Wedderburn, *The Wedderburn Book: A History of the Wedderburns in the Counties of Berwick and Forfar*, 2 vols (n.p., 1898), vol. 1, pp. xlviii–ix and 99–101; W.B. Menzies, 'Robert Wedderburn, Notary and Poet, 1546–1611', in *Scottish Text Society: Miscellany Volume* (Edinburgh, 1933), p. 181, at pp. 181–2; C. McKean, 'What Kind of Renaissance Town Was Dundee?', in C. McKean, B. Harris and C.A. Whatley (eds), *Dundee: Renaissance to Enlightenment* (Dundee, 2009), p.1, at pp. 20–2; NRS, NP2/2, ff. 43v-4r; DCA, PBD, vol. 15, f. 1.

Murdison, another future advocate, who matriculated at Wittenberg a few months after Nicolson.[92] Given that Wittenberg became an inhospitable place for Calvinists to study towards the end of the sixteenth century, it is tempting to suppose that the Scots who chose to travel there were less than comfortable in the reformed kirk, but this does not appear to have been true.[93] It is more significant that hostility to Aristotle had diminished between the deaths of Luther in 1546 and Melanchthon in 1560, and that during the next four decades teaching at Wittenberg gradually became less distinctively evangelical and humanist in character.[94]

When John Skene travelled to Wittenberg in the 1560s, however, he may have expected to experience the same style of teaching as James Balfour and William Ramsay had over twenty years earlier. That he later recalled returning to Scotland in 1575, 'imbued with some sort of learning in the civil law', after spending seven years in 'the seat and home of *bonae litterae*', does indeed suggest that he had gone to Germany in search of a humanist education in the law.[95] He had previously matriculated at St Andrews at the same time as his elder brother, 'Magister Gulielmus Skene, in utroque iure licentiatus', and after 1560 he had joined his brother on the teaching staff there.[96] William Skene seems to have acquired his law degree at the University of Bourges, where the professors of law were known to enhance their teaching with insights drawn

92 NRS, CS1/4/1, f. 151, and CS1/4/2, f. 364v.

93 A.L. Drummond, *The Kirk and the Continent* (Edinburgh, 1956), pp. 53–4. For a less than convincing attempt to trace Lutheran commitments among these students see E.L. Lindseth, 'The Evolution of Protestant Ideas and the Humanist Academic Tradition in Scotland: With Special reference to Scandinavian/Lutheran Influences', PhD dissertation, University of Edinburgh, 1991, pp. 324–7.

94 J.E. McGoldrick, *Luther's Scottish Connection* (Cranbury, NJ, 1989), pp. 59–61; P.F. Grendler, 'The Universities of the Renaissance and Reformation', (2004) 57 *Renaissance Quarterly* 1, pp. 20–2. On 'Lutheran Scholasticism' see generally L.C. Green, 'Melanchthon's Relation to Scholasticism', in C.R. Trueman and R.S. Clark (eds), *Protestant Scholasticism: Essays in Reassessment* (Carlisle, 1999), p. 273; R. Preus, *The Inspiration of Scripture: A Study of the Theology of the Seventeenth Century Lutheran Dogmaticians* (Edinburgh, 1955).

95 *Regiam maiestatem: Scotiae veteres leges et constitutiones*, ed. Sir John Skene of Curriehill (Edinburgh, 1609), sig. A2r. He travelled widely in northern Europe, and must have studied somewhere else for two years before he reached Wittenberg in 1570 (*The Lawes and Actes of Parliament*, ed. Sir John Skene of Curriehill (Edinburgh, 1597), sig. P2v; Thomas Dempster, *Historia ecclesiastica gentis Scotorum*, 2 vols, ed. D. Irving (Edinburgh, 1829), vol. 2, p. 600).

96 *Acta facultatis artium Universitatis Sancti Andree*, vol. 2, pp. 423–4; *Early Records of the University of St Andrews*, p. 264; W.F. Skene, *Memorials of the Family of Skene of Skene* (Aberdeen, 1887), p. 107. Graduation records are lacking for 1559 and 1560, the years in which John Skene probably became a bachelor and master of arts.

from the humanities.[97] In 1563, when George Buchanan devised a scheme for the reorganisation of teaching at St Andrews, he planned to teach the humanities himself in one college, to have philosophy taught by other humanists in a second college, and to assign the teaching of law to William Skene in a third college, the central purpose of which would have been the teaching of theology by William Ramsay.[98] Although the scheme came to nothing, it sheds light on the inclinations of those teaching in St Andrews at that time, when the Skene brothers seem likely to have heard from Ramsay about the style of teaching he and Balfour had experienced when they went to Wittenberg in the 1540s.[99] They could also have read Melanchthon's *De legibus oratio*, first delivered in 1524, but frequently printed since, in France as well as Germany.[100] Drawing on classical authors to whom Buchanan would turn in writing about law in the late 1570s, Melanchthon had stressed the importance in every human society of written laws, insisting that it was better for disputes to be settled according to fixed laws (*certae leges*) than left to the discretion (*arbitrium*) of judges, who might lack the ability to discriminate accurately between equity and iniquity.[101] The great civilisations of antiquity had all discovered this, but it was the Romans who had become the masters of jurisprudence. 'As the Romans have already taught us literature and the other arts', Melanchthon asked, 'for what reason have we not been imitating their laws as well, since there was no commonwealth that could have provided us with either more numerous or more renowned examples of virtue and humanity, or with more humane laws?'[102] Like other aspects of classical civilisation, the laws that Cicero had considered to be ideal in his *De legibus* deserved to be studied, imitated (*imitatae*) and used as a basis for the critical reappraisal of the local legislation (*municipalia*

---

97 Durkan, 'French Connection in the Sixteenth and Early Seventeenth Centuries', pp. 25–6; M.-C. Tucker, *Maîtres et étudiants écossais à la Faculté de droit de l'Université de Bourges, 1480–1703* (Paris, 2001), pp. 221–3 and 255; see too pp. 224–5 on Alexander Arbuthnot, the principal of King's College, Aberdeen, who also appears to have studied law at Bourges.

98 *The Bannatyne Miscellany, Containing Original Papers and Tracts, Chiefly Relating to the History and Literature of Scotland*, 3 vols, ed. W. Scott and D. Laing (Edinburgh, 1827–55), vol. 2, pp. 87–100; J. Durkan, 'Education: The Laying of Fresh Foundations', in MacQueen (ed.), *Humanism in Renaissance Scotland*, p. 123, at p. 155.

99 On William Skene's interest in humanistic jurisprudence see too J.W. Cairns, *Law, Lawyers and Humanism: Selected Essays on the History of Scots Law* (Edinburgh, 2015), pp. 75–8.

100 J.Q. Whitman, *The Legacy of Roman Law in the German Romantic Era: Historical Vision and Legal Change* (Princeton, 1990), pp. 19–21.

101 On Buchanan see J.D. Ford, 'Conciliar Authority and Equitable Jurisdiction in Early-Modern Scotland', in Godfrey (ed.), *Law and Authority in British Legal History*, p. 140, at pp. 141–50.

102 *De legibus oratio* (Paris, 1534), p. 27–9.

statuta) already in use.[103] Melanchthon had found nothing to recommend in his oration from over four hundred years of scholarship in the schools of civil and canon law.

For the modern expression 'legal humanism' to be used with any precision it probably needs to be confined to thinking of the type exemplified by Melanchthon.[104] Yet the fact is that while some humanists turned their attention to legal texts, and some lawyers paid attention to the *litterae humaniores*, teachers of law who favoured the excavation and imitation of ancient Roman law, as opposed to the continued study of the civil law, were few and far between.[105] John Skene acknowledged a lasting debt to Mattheus Wesenbeck (*praeceptor meus*), who had been appointed to a chair of law at Wittenberg a year before his own arrival there in 1570.[106] He made particular reference to Wesenbeck's *Paratitla in Pandectas iuris civilis*, to which a 'Prolegomena de studio iuris recte instituendo' had been attached.[107] Meaning to contribute to a new genre of guidance on 'how to study law', from which a scheme devised by François le Duaren at Bourges was singled out for praise, Wesenbeck likened himself to a mariner who, on returning to port after confronting constant challenges while navigating a 'vast ocean', was in a position to advise those 'casting off' on the best 'course' to follow, and on the 'shoals and rocks' to avoid.[108] The first step students of law needed to take was a careful reading of Justinian's *Institutes*, which they had to pour over 'night and day' until they had it 'committed to memory'.[109] They were then to deal in the same way with the last two titles of the *Digest*, on the meaning of words and settled rules of law. After this

---

103 Although Cicero had written about the laws of an ideal state, not Rome, Melanchthon was correct that he had found many of his examples in Roman law (J. Harries, *Cicero and the Jurists: From Citizens' Law to the Lawful State* (London, 2006), pp. 51–3). The basic texts for William Skene's course on law at St Andrews were 'Cicero, *De legibus*, and divers partes of the *Institutiones* of Justinian' (*Autobiography and Diary of Mr James Melville*, pp. 28–9).

104 While the word 'humanist' was used during the sixteenth century, to signify a scholar of the humanities, the word 'humanism' is often used to signify an ideology, identified by modern historians.

105 For a recent collection of essays on the subject see P.J. du Plessis and J.W. Cairns (eds), *Reassessing Legal Humanism and Its Claims: Petere Fontes?* (Edinburgh, 2016).

106 *Lawes and Actes of Parliament*, sig. H2v; *Album academiae Vitebergensis*, vol. 2, p. 162.

107 *Paratitla in Pandectas iuris civilis* (Basel, 1566), pp. 25–40.

108 As Wesenbeck pointed out, the new genre built on the programmatic statements attached to the *Institutes* and *Digest*.

109 He also encouraged use of commentaries on the *Institutes*, of which he published an annotated edition of his own, entitled *Institutionum divi Iustiniani sacratissimi principis libri quatuor, aediti, et argumentis ac scholiis explicati, a Matthaeo Wesenbecio*, 2 vols (Jena, 1566).

rudimentary material had all been memorised, 'it would be fitting to advance maturely to the reading of the *Digest*, because the whole science of law, as the name itself indicates, is contained within it'. Since it was at this point, when students embarked on the profound 'meditation' required for mastery of the material in earlier titles of the *Digest*, that they would find themselves at sea, it was at this point that Wesenbeck offered to come to their aid with his *Paratitla*, another contribution to a new genre of literature, which had been pioneered at Bourges by Jacques Cujas. The idea was to prepare students for engagement with the denser detail of the assembled texts by providing them with overviews of entire titles, identifying the parts of the praetor's edict with which the jurists had been concerned, and examining the subject matter in terms of standard topics, such as the efficient, final, material and formal causes of laws.[110] While Wesenbeck promised that relating subjects to the 'topics of dialectical method' would render them more memorable, he understood topics not so much in the Ciceronian sense of *sedes argumentorum* – a method of storing and recovering data – as in the Aristotelian sense of *argumenti communes* – a method of reviewing and analysing data.[111] Moreover, while he was critical of the style in which the medieval doctors of law had written, he did not agree with those who wished to revert 'to the praetorian edict, as if to the era and courts of the ancient Romans', pointing out that students destined for forensic practice would be hopelessly lost without the glosses and commentaries added to the texts of the *Digest*, *Code* and *Novels* by the doctors.[112] Apart from anything else, it was in the medieval literature that students would learn about the forms of process used in contemporary litigation, and it was there too that they were most likely to find answers to the questions raised in litigation.[113]

If the expectation was that students would themselves set sail on the vast ocean of the law, following their gradual introduction to the art of navigation,

---

110 In his *Oeconomia iuris* (Basel, 1574) Wesenbeck dealt in a similar way with the books rather than the titles of the works comprised in both the *Corpus iuris civilis* and the *Corpus iuris canonici*.

111 Melanchthon himself had moved towards a more Aristotelian view of the subject in successive editions of his *Loci communes*, and other Lutheran theologians had also moved in the same direction. See further A.N. Burnett, 'The Educational Roots of Reformed Scholasticism: Dialectic and Scriptural Exegesis in the Sixteenth Century', (2004) 84 *Nederlands Archief voor Kerkgeschiedenis* 299.

112 Wesenbeck recommended in particular the *Glossa ordinaria* of Francesco Accorso – 'a man equipped with a very sharp mind and a divine memory' – the *Speculum iudiciale* of Guillaume Durand, and the *Commentaria* of Bartolo da Sassoferrato and Giasone del Maino.

113 As Whitman, *Legacy of Roman Law in the German Romantic Era*, pp. 21–8, explains, Melanchthon had also become more sympathetic towards the teaching of the civil law.

the humanities did not serve a purely propaedeutic purpose for a teacher like Wesenbeck. He believed that it was because of their background in the humanities that a new breed of jurists were not only writing about their discipline with refreshing elegance, 'in imitation of the ancients', but were also restoring 'the laws of the ancients to their purity and pristine clarity'.[114] 'Without knowledge of Roman history', he maintained, 'the whole discipline of jurisprudence would be blind'. The humanist slogan *sine historia caecam esse iurisprudentiam* had been coined shortly before Wesenbeck published his *Paratitla* by François Baudouin, whose own *De institutione historiae universae et eius cum iurisprudentia coniunctione prolegomenon* had originated in lectures he delivered at Heidelberg.[115] The slogan had both a negative and a positive aspect. On the one hand, the realisation that Roman law, however impressive, belonged to a particular civilisation, located in its own time, raised doubts about its reliability as a guide to universal truth, to be followed blindly in preference to every other law.[116] The story had been recounted in the *Digest* of the orator Servius Sulpicius being stung into legal study by Quintus Mucius' remark that it was shameful for somebody involved in court actions to be ignorant of the law around which they revolved.[117] 'But it is far more shameful', Baudouin commented, 'for us to seem like foreigners in our fatherland and home', explaining that 'if we are Frenchmen, or Britons or Germans or Spaniards or Italians, then to be able to talk about ourselves it is essential for us to be familiar with the history of the Franks, Angles, Saxons, Goths and Lombards'.[118] On the other hand, it seemed to Baudouin and some other French jurists that the comparative study of legal history would enable them to discern the truly universal elements of jurisprudence.[119] With the aid of history they would be able to transform

114 *Paratitla in Pandectas iuris civilis*, pp. 25–6 and 38.

115 The *Paratitla* had been published for the first time in 1563. Passages have been cited from the 1566 edition, which differed here and at many other points from the first edition, because it is the 1566 edition – reprinted in 1568 – that Skene is most likely to have known.

116 This negative lesson of history received its most vigorous exposition in François Hotman's *Antitribonianus, sive dissertatio de studio legum*, written in 1567, in which it was pointed out that Roman law had itself changed significantly in different periods of time. See G. Huppert, *The Idea of Perfect History: Historical Erudition and Historical Philosophy in Renaissance France* (Urbana, 1970), pp. 152–4. Hotman was also the author of one of the commentaries on the *Institutes* recommended by Wesenbeck to his students.

117 D.1.2.2.43.

118 *De institutione historiae universae et eius cum iurisprudentia coniunctione prolegomenon* (Paris, 1561), pp. 35 and 37.

119 J. Moreau-Reibel, *Jean Bodin et le droit public comparé dans ces rapports avec la philosophie de l'histoire* (Paris, 1933), pp. 34–68; J.L. Brown, *The Methodus ad facilem historiarum cognitionem of Jean Bodin: A Critical Study* (Washington, 1939), pp. 29–45; J.H. Franklin,

their discipline into a genuine science, would be able to advise princes on the reform of their laws, and would be able to restore a degree of order to a fragmented world of knowledge and belief.[120] Although it is not clear how far Wesenbeck was in sympathy with this programme, he did urge his students to read learned studies of the codified customs of various parts of Europe, and he published an edition of a commentary on Justinian's *Institutes* by his former colleague Johann Schneidewin in which comparison was often made between Roman law and German law, especially the *ius Saxonicum*.[121] Statutory reform of the law had been attempted in Germany as well as in France and Scotland since the fifteenth century, and when Skene was in the middle of his studies there a new code of Saxon law had been framed by members of the law faculties at Leipzig and Wittenberg, in response to complaints about inconsistencies in court rulings.[122] Whereas codification in other parts of Germany had often strengthened the influence of the civil law, the customary law of Saxony had proved more resilient, largely because of its earlier redaction in a treatise written during the thirteenth century, which had since been reinforced with a myth of official authorisation, had been subjected to learned commentary, and had become the basis of a 'common law' for the whole region.[123]

When Skene later reflected on his return to Scotland from Germany, in a dedicatory epistle attached to his Latin edition of the old books of law, he recalled his determination not to follow the example of most other advocates who had gone abroad to study, 'for they spend days and nights in mastering the civil law of the Romans, and put all their effort into meditating on it, and (their national laws having been neglected) are possessed of no passion for the law of Scotland, which should be their principal concern'.[124] His complaint was obviously not about the civil law being studied by way of pernoctation

---

Jean Bodin and the Sixteenth-Century Revolution in the Methodology of Law and History (New York, 1963), pp. 7–79.

120 D.R. Kelley, *Foundations of Modern Historical Scholarship: Language, Law and History in the French Renaissance* (New York, 1970), pp. 116–48.

121 *Paratitla in Pandectas iuris civilis*, p. 39. Schneidewin's *In quatuor Institutionum imperialium D. Iustiniani libros commentarii*, 2 vols (Strasbourg, 1571), published posthumously, was reissued in 1575 with a preface by Wesenbeck.

122 Witte, *Law and Protestantism*, pp. 177–96; Strauss, *Law, Resistance and the State*, p. 87.

123 C.C. Turpin, 'The Reception of Roman Law', (1968) 3 *Irish Jurist* 162, at p. 171; W. Kunkel, 'The Reception of Roman Law in Germany: An Interpretation', in G. Strauss (ed.), *Pre-Reformation Germany* (London, 1972), p. 263, at pp. 277–9; M. Dobozy, 'Introduction', in *The Saxon Mirror* (Philadelphia, 1999), p. 1, at pp. 28–32; T. Duve, 'Some News on the Making of the *Sachsenspiegel* and Its Medieval Glosses', (2008) 19 *Patristica et Mediaevalia* 63, at p. 65.

124 *Regiam maiestatem: Scotiae veteres leges et constitutiones*, sigg. A2–3.

and meditation, which is how he had been told it should be studied, but was about Scots lawyers studying only the civil law in this way. 'They do not follow the example of the jurist Servius', he added, although Mucius' complaint that advocates should know some law was rather different from the complaint that advocates should know their own law above all. That Skene was aware of the argument advanced by Baudouin is shown by his recurring remarks that 'it would be shameful, as well as unavailing for the handling of cases in court, if one were domesticated in foreign matters and foreign in the domestic', that advocates were frequently 'guests in their own commonwealth, citizens in someone else's', and that he 'believed it preferable to be of little worth among foreigners than foreign at home'. In his edition of the old books, 'clarified with emendations, and restored to their early splendour', they were compared (*collatae*) with foreign laws, partly as a means of identifying the best readings of texts, partly as a means of tracing the origins of Scots law and partly as a means of confirming the consistency of provisions with other laws.[125] His editing of the Latin texts of the old books, together with his work on a vernacular version published at the same time, and on a new edition of the acts of parliament published previously in 1597, appears to have resulted from his membership of commissions appointed in 1587 and 1592 to advise on the publication of all the 'municipall lawes and actis of parliament bygane quhairof thair is registeris or autentik monumentis extant'.[126] However, he had started to study the old laws as soon as he came home from Germany in 1575, when he was employed as an assistant to James Balfour and was given a manuscript copy of the sources by William Skene.[127] It was evidently in relation to the work of the 1575 commission, charged with the task of combining in a single volume the old books, acts of parliament and decisions of the lords of session, that he first wrote a dictionary of legal vocabulary, which he called 'De verborum significatione' in imitation of the penultimate title of the *Digest*. Although the dictionary was printed in conjunction with the edition of parliamentary legislation he finished in 1597, an early version was already in circulation in conjunction with

125 *Regiam maiestatem: Scotiae veteres leges et constitutiones*, sigg. A1r and A5–6r.

126 *Acts of the Parliaments of Scotland*, vol. 3, pp. 520 and 564; Records of the Parliaments of Scotland, 1587/7/156 and 1592/4/67. These commissions revived the project of publishing editions of the old books as well as the acts of parliament, which had been only partially fulfilled in 1566.

127 See again the sources cited in n. 82 above. A. Taylor, *The Laws of Medieval Scotland: Legal Compilations from the Thirteenth and Fourteenth Centuries* (Edinburgh, 2019), pp. 52–3, deals with the manuscript received from William Skene. It is of some interest for present purposes that collections of the old laws were also owned by Alexander Arbuthnot and Thomas Nicolson.

Balfour's *Practicks*.[128] The dictionary contained references to some of the copies of the old books cited in the *Practicks*, and to both the earlier edition of the acts of parliament and some of the decisions of the session cited there. In what often amounted to short essays in comparative legal history, Skene used the full range of reading recommended by Wesenbeck, and here, and in annotations included in his Latin edition of the old books, he drew comparisons with treatises on the laws of England and Normandy that had been written around the same time as some of the old books and the early treatise on the law of Saxony.[129] In a preface attached to his vernacular edition, he defended the belief that the old books had been publicly authorised, if not when they were written then by later legislators.[130]

At one place in his dictionary Skene referred to a source called the 'Leges navium', as transcribed in the copy of the old books he had received from his brother, yet this source was not included in either of his editions of the old books.[131] It could have been omitted from the Latin edition simply because it was, despite its title, a Scots translation of the *Rôles d'Oléron*, which had originally been written in French.[132] This would not explain its omission from the vernacular edition, however, or from a list of 'the buikes conteinand the lawes of this realme' that was attached to his dictionary when it was printed in 1597.[133] Skene clearly doubted the authenticity of the 'Leges navium' as a component of the municipal law on which he wanted his colleagues to concentrate their attention, and similar doubts may have affected Balfour's decision to move his treatment of maritime law to an appendix at the end of his *Practicks*.[134] Although provisions from the 'Schiplawis' continued to form

128 NLS, Adv. MS 24.2.4b, ff. 279–90, a copy of Balfour's book that was written before 1593. When a different early copy was reorganised in EUL, La. III 408, it seems to have been thought that the dictionary formed part of Balfour's book. On the printed edition see R. Donaldson, 'A "Mixed Edition" of *De verborum significatione*', (1959–62) 3 *Bibliotheck* 219.

129 On the relationship between the English and Norman treatises see A.-M. Kuskowski, 'The Development of Written Custom in England and in France: A Comparative Perspective', in R.W. Kaeuper (ed.), *Law, Governance and Justice: New Views on Medieval Constitutionalism* (Leiden, 2013), p. 101.

130 *Regiam maiestatem: The Auld Lawes and Constitutions of Scotland*, ed. Sir John Skene of Curriehill (Edinburgh, 1609), sigg. A3v-5r.

131 *Lawes and Actes of Parliament*, sig. K2v.

132 E.B.I. Frankot, 'The Scottish Translations of the *Rôles d'Oléron*: Edition and Commentary', in A.M. Godfrey (ed.), *Stair Society: Miscellany Eight* (Edinburgh, 2020), p. 13.

133 *Lawes and Actes of Parliament*, sig. S6r. The 'Leges navium' was also omitted from NLS, Adv. MS 7.1.10, a version of the collection Skene was compiling that was written in 1601 to 1602, which contained both Latin and vernacular texts.

134 See again the fifth essay in this collection.

the basis of Balfour's account of the law regulating maritime commerce, he appears to have come to regard 'the lawis of Oleron' as a foreign source, not one of the old books of Scots law. In contrast, William Welwod had no doubt that 'the reulis of Olon, receavit be our cuntrey men', belonged among 'the wrets authorizit be our nation'.[135] Following his graduation from St Andrews in 1570, Welwod was enrolled at Wittenberg in 1573, under Wesenbeck's supervision, and while Skene was still in residence.[136] It is uncertain, but probable, that Welwod studied law in Germany, for although he was appointed to a teaching post in mathematics when he returned to Scotland in 1577, it was also then that he started to gather material together for his treatise on maritime law.[137] As he later recalled, he had decided to pursue a plan proposed by the Saxon jurist Simon Schard to publish a comprehensive 'edition of the maritime laws observed in the German Ocean and Mediterranean Sea'.[138] Welwod had been reading an edition of the *Nomos Rhodion nautikos* published by Schard in 1561, and was aware that he had died in 1573 before he could fulfil his broader plan. Welwod had been persuaded that the maritime laws devised on the island of Rhodes had been taken by the Romans to govern all disputes about navigation in the ancient Mediterranean, and he maintained that the maritime laws devised on the island of Oleron had been taken in a similar way to govern all seafaring causes arising 'on the great ocean, which is our sea'.[139] It was on these foundations, he insisted, that later legislators had frequently built, in Scotland and elsewhere.[140] Schard might have agreed with all this, but presumably his plan had been to reproduce his sources *in extenso*, as he had done with the Rhodian laws, whereas Welwod produced what he described perfectly accurately as an 'abridgement' of his sources, in which provisions were paraphrased 'summerlie' under headings arranged in an 'ordourlie' fashion. When a shortened version of the treatise was printed in 1590, he announced that his aim was

135 *The Sea-Law of Scotland* (Edinburgh, 1590), sig. A2v.

136 It is possible that Welwod, like Skene, studied somewhere else on the Continent before going to Wittenberg.

137 The two subjects were not entirely divorced from each other, as Skene discovered when he found it necessary in writing his dictionary to obtain advice from John Napier of Merchiston, 'ane gentleman of singuler judgement and learning, specially in mathematicque science' (*Lawes and Actes of Parliament*, sig. P1v).

138 Schard, *De varia temporum in iure civili observatione* (Basel, 1561), p. 271; Welwod, *An Abridgement of All Sea-Lawes* (London, 1613), p. 6.

139 Welwod was of course alluding to the Roman perception of the Mediterranean as *mare nostrum*.

140 The 'proheme' to Welwod's *Abridgement of All Sea-Lawes*, in which these comments appear, may have been drafted for the original version of his treatise, printed in *Alexander King's Treatise on Maritime Law*, p. 351.

to make his sources accessible and intelligible to 'all seafairing men', complaining that familiarity with the laws of the sea was 'very litle in this cuntry', while warning that 'all men be bound to ken the law, namely, thair awne common lawe'.[141]

Welwod's plea for a better understanding of maritime law is quite perplexing. For one thing, he insisted that mariners ought to be familiar with the laws of Oleron since they formed part of the common law, yet he also stated that they formed part of that law 'sa far as they are commonly knawin be peiple'. Paradoxically, people were at fault for not knowing a common law which existed as such only to the extent that it was known to them. Furthermore, while it was 'thair awne common lawe' that people were expected to know, Welwod included among 'the wrets authorizit be our nation' not only 'the reulis of Olon' and 'the acts of parliament' but also 'the Romain law', which had acquired 'force and authority' throughout Europe 'by common consent of nations'.[142] It was also paradoxical that the law taught in the universities had become the *ius commune* of Europe by being received into the *ius proprium* of each nation, in much the same way as the Rhodian law had become common to the whole Roman empire by being received into the *ius proprium* of the Romans themselves, 'who always excelled all other nations in devising of humane lawes'.[143] Some light is shed on Welwod's complex thinking by another book he published during his tenure of the civil law chair at St Andrews.[144] His *Iuris divini Iudaeorum ac iuris civilis Romanorum parallela* was written for the benefit of theology students, and encouraged these 'iuris divini studiosi' to compare the laws prescribed in the Old Testament with those preserved in the *Corpus iuris civilis*.[145] On the one hand, by comparing texts from these sources with each other he hoped to demonstrate the consistency of much of Roman law, 'easily the best among all human laws', with the laws of God, which was not so surprising, he explained, as the Romans had borrowed their laws from the Greeks, who had in turn borrowed their laws from the Egyptians, who had been taught to legislate by Hermes Trismegistus, who had in turn learned the

141 *Sea-Law of Scotland*, sig. A2. It is assumed here that the argument advanced in the preceding essay is sound.

142 *Abridgement of All Sea-Lawes*, pp. 4–5. *Cf. Calendar of State Papers Relating to Scotland*, vol. 10, pp. 521–5.

143 D.1.1.9, and J.1.2.1. The point is that 'thair awne common lawe' was a contradiction in terms.

144 J.W. Cairns, 'Academic Feud, Bloodfeud and William Welwood: Legal Education in St Andrews, 1560–1611', (1998) 2 *Edinburgh Law Review* 158 and 255, at p. 162.

145 *Iuris divini Iudaeorum ac iuris civilis Romanorum parallela* (Leiden, 1594), sigg. *2–3.

craft from Moses.[146] On the other hand, by juxtaposing texts – or paraphrases of them – from his two sources under headings that would have been familiar to law students, he hoped to persuade theology students that their grasp of divine law would be enhanced by study of the more elaborate, yet essentially consistent, rules of Roman law.[147] His aim in writing about maritime law appears to have been broadly similar. Like Balfour – who had moved from involvement in the production of editions of texts to the composition of a methodical compendium – he aimed to make the law accessible by organising its provisions under topical headings.[148] Like Skene – who had moved from involvement in the composition of a methodical compendium to the production of editions of texts – he aimed to augment the law that was 'commonly knawin' by encouraging its comparison with other laws of historical significance. He hoped that the seafaring men he was addressing would recognise in the laws of Oleron the written origins of the rules with which they were familiar, that they would then recognise connections between the laws of Oleron and the other written laws he summarised, and that they would embrace the rules found in these laws as part of an enhanced appreciation of the law applicable to their activities. In his treatises on maritime law he wove restatements of his sources together to form a tapestry that his readers would have struggled to unpick.[149]

---

146 Although a similar line of argument was advanced in Melanchthon's *De legibus oratio*, at pp. 22–6, there is a difference between arguing (as Melanchthon did) that the ancient world should be imitated since imitation was practised in the ancient world itself, and arguing (as Welwod and other civil lawyers did) that the truth should be looked for in Roman law since its origins could ultimately be traced back to a moment of divine intervention. *Cf.* G. Hamza, 'Comparative Law and Antiquity in the Trends of Legal Humanism and Natural Law', (2007) 47 *Acta Antiqua Academiae Scientiarum Hungaricae* 279, at p. 282.

147 The sources paraphrased were cited in the margins of the treatise in the same way as the sources summarised in the sea law treatise. François Rageau, *Leges politicae ex sacris iurisprudentiae fontibus haustae collectaeque, et ob commodiorem usum ad formam Iustinianei Codicis digestae* (Frankfurt, 1577), also gathered biblical texts together under headings taken from Roman law, but no reference was made to Roman law texts, and the biblical texts tended to be reproduced more fully than in Welwod's treatise.

148 Although Balfour reproduced excerpts from some of his sources, he summarised the decisions of the session in statements comparable to Welwod's summaries of his sources. It should perhaps be made clear that Welwod adhered to his sources more closely in his treatise for theology students than in his treatise for mariners.

149 That Welwod himself unpicked the tapestry to some extent in his *Sea-Law of Scotland* does not mean that his readers would have found it easy to perform the same task.

3 Traditional Enquiry into Sea Laws

The last Scot to continue his studies at Wittenberg before the end of the sixteenth century was 'M. Ioannes Murdisonus', who arrived there in 1591, just after the shorter version of William Welwod's treatise on maritime law was published, and at about the time that Alexander King abandoned work on his treatment of the subject.[150] John Murdison had graduated as a master of arts at Edinburgh four years earlier.[151] As it happens, he graduated alongside Philip Hislop, and he went on like him to become a teacher of the arts, although he did not proceed like him to become a kirk minister.[152] Murdison had gone to Helmstedt in 1588, and a year after moving to Wittenberg he went to Middelburg, where he began teaching in the Latin school. In 1599 he matriculated as a law student at Leiden, where he eventually received a doctorate, earning a living in the meantime as a professor of physics.[153] He remained at Leiden until 1605, when he was admitted to the bar in Edinburgh.[154] Twelve years later Robert Boyd of Trochrigg, the principal of the University of Glasgow, recorded the death of a 'Mr Murisoun, doctor of laws, which he taught at Edinburgh, long known to me at Saumur'.[155] Boyd had occupied a chair of theology at the Protestant academy at Saumur from 1608 until 1614, and his name appears towards the end of records of the academy that have survived from a

150 *Album academiae Vitebergensis*, vol. 2, p. 383; Ford, 'Introduction', pp. lxii–iii.

151 *Catalogue of the Graduates in the Faculties of Arts, Divinity and Law of the University of Edinburgh*, p. 7.

152 J.K. Cameron, 'Some Scottish Students and Teachers at the University of Leiden in the Late Sixteenth and Early Seventeenth Centuries', in G.G. Simpson (ed.), *Scotland and the Low Countries, 1124–1994* (East Linton, 1996), p. 122, at pp. 126–7; *Dictionary of Seventeenth- and Eighteenth-Century Dutch Philosophers*, 2 vols, ed. W. van Bunge, H. Krop, B. Leeuwenburgh, H. van Ruler, P. Schuurman and M. Wielema (Bristol, 2003), vol. 2, pp. 716–17.

153 *Album scholasticum academiae Lugduno-Batavae, 1575–1940*, ed. C.A. Siegenbeek van Heukelom-Lamme (Leiden, 1941), pp. 108 and 193; *Album studiosorum academiae Lugduno-Batavae, 1575–1875*, ed. W.N. Du Rieu (The Hague, 1875), p. xxxix and col. 57.

154 The assumption that Murdison had died by this time is rightly challenged in Durkan, 'French Connection in the Sixteenth and Early Seventeenth Centuries', p. 27, and R. Feenstra, 'Scottish-Dutch Legal Relations in the Seventeenth and Eighteenth Centuries', in Smout (ed.), *Scotland and Europe*, p. 128, at p. 137.

155 *Bannatyne Miscellany*, vol. 1, p. 289; R. Wodrow, *Collections upon the Lives of the Reformers and Most Eminent Ministers of the Church of Scotland*, 2 vols, ed. W.J. Duncan (Edinburgh, 1834–48), vol. 2, p. 261; F. Michel, *Les Écossais en France, les Français en Écosse*, 2 vols (London, 1862), vol. 2, pp. 249–50.

period after 1613, along with those of many other Scots.[156] Murdison is never mentioned, nor does his name appear in various catalogues of teaching staff that historians have compiled, yet there is no reason to doubt the accuracy of Boyd's recollection that a doctor of laws with a name like Murdison was at Saumur for a long time between 1608 and 1614.[157] As there is independent evidence that Murdison died around 1617, and it is unlikely that two doctors of laws with similar names died in the same place at the same time, the implication would seem to be that Murdison had returned to the Continent to resume his teaching career.[158] If so, he must once again have been providing instruction in the arts, for at Saumur, in keeping with many other institutions modelled more or less directly on the Academy of Geneva, teaching was provided, at three distinct levels, in the humanities, philosophy and theology.[159] At some places allowance was also made for a professor of law to offer basic teaching in association with theology – much as Buchanan had proposed for St Andrews – but not at Saumur.[160] Assuming again that Boyd was correct, Murdison did go on to offer some sort of instruction in law during his last few years in Edinburgh. Presumably he provided private tuition, though there could conceivably have been a connection between his death and a decision apparently made by the

156 H.M.B. Reid, *The Divinity Principals in the University of Glasgow, 1545–1654* (Glasgow, 1917), pp. 128–37. The records have been made readily available at http://archives.ville-saumur.fr.

157 L.J. Méteyer, *L'Académie protestante de Saumur* (Paris, 1933), pp. 19 and 145–50; D. Bourchenin, *Étude sur les académies protestantes en France au XVIe au XVIIe siècle* (Geneva, 1969), pp. 463–4; M.-C. Tucker, *Professeurs et régents écossais dans les académies protestantes en France, de l'Édit de Nantes à la Révocation* (Paris, 2020), p. 220, and 'Scottish Philosophy Teachers at the French Protestant Academies in the Seventeenth Century', in A. Broadie (ed.), *Scottish Philosophy in the Seventeenth Century* (Oxford, 2020), p. 50, at p. 54. It may be as well to note too that Murdison is never mentioned in J. Pannier, 'Scots in Saumur in the Seventeenth Century', (1934) 5 *Records of the Scottish Church History Society* 140, or for that matter in M. Guignet, 'Mark Duncan, Professor at Saumur, 1606–40', (1933) 5 *Records of the Scottish Church History Society* 73.

158 *Inquisitionum ad capellam domini regis retornatarum, quae in publicis archivis Scotiae adhuc servantur, abbreviatio*, vol. 2, Inquisitiones generales 747.

159 J.P. Dray, 'The Protestant Academy of Saumur and Its Relations with the Oratorians of *Les Ardilliers*', (1988) 9 *History of European Ideas* 465, at p. 468; D. Boisson, 'Le collège et l'académie de Saumur, un même établissement?', in Y. Krumenacker and B. Noguès (eds), *Protestantisme et éducation dans la France moderne* (Lyons, 2014), p. 109.

160 S. Deyon, 'Les académies protestantes en France', (1989) 135 *Bulletin de la Société de l'histoire du protestantisme français* 77, at p. 82; K. Maag, 'The Huguenot Academies: Preparing for an Uncertain Future', in R.A. Mantzer and A. Spicer (eds), *Society and Culture in the Huguenot World, 1559–1685* (Cambridge, 2002), p. 139, at p. 148; Tucker, *Professeurs et régents écossais dans les académies protestantes en France*, p. 200.

lords of session not long afterwards to promote the foundation of a chair of law at the University of Edinburgh.[161] Their decision may in turn have had some bearing on the appointment of a 'civilist' and 'canonist' at King's College, Aberdeen, eight months later.[162] The 'professor of the civil law' appointed was the advocate Thomas Nicolson, who had been the last Scot to matriculate at Wittenberg before Murdison. Just as William Skene had held the chair of civil law at St Andrews while sitting as a judge in the commissary court there, so Nicolson held the chair in Aberdeen while also serving as the commissary there.[163] There is no evidence, however, that he offered even the elementary sort of teaching in law once made available by Skene at St Andrews.[164]

The foundation of a chair of law at Edinburgh had first been promoted by the lords of session thirty years earlier, when humanist reforms were belatedly introduced in the Scottish universities.[165] At that stage the suggestion was successfully resisted by the advocates, who felt obliged as graduates of St Andrews and Aberdeen to defend those 'universiteis and thair privilagis'.[166] Significance has been attached to the apparent lack of opposition to the revival of the suggestion in 1619, when law teaching had disappeared from the Scottish universities, though it still came to nothing.[167] By then a new form of scholasticism had come to dominate the teaching of philosophy and theology in Scotland as elsewhere, and even in 1589 concerns had been raised about how far the type

161 W. Fraser, *Memorials of the Earls of Haddington*, 2 vols (Edinburgh, 1889), vol. 1, p. 76, found evidence of the decision in 'an abridgement of the books of sederunt in the Haddington charter chest'. It is not mentioned in any known abridgement, though a related decision that new advocates must provide a copy of 'the works of any one of the doctors of lawes' is noted (*The Acts of Sederunt of the Lords of Council and Session*, ed. I. Campbell (Edinburgh, 1811), p. 75; NLS, Adv. MS 25.2.7, f. 56r).

162 D. Stevenson, *King's College, Aberdeen, 1560–1641: From Protestant Reformation to Covenanting Revolution* (Aberdeen, 1990), pp. 67–9.

163 *Fasti Aberdonenses: Selections from the Records of the University and King's College of Aberdeen, 1494–1584*, ed. C. Innes (Aberdeen, 1854), pp. 142 and 275–8; *Officers and Graduates of the University and King's College of Aberdeen*, ed. P.J. Anderson (Aberdeen, 1893), p. 31.

164 *Cf.* A.L.M. Wilson, 'Legal Practice and Legal Institutions in Seventeenth Century Aberdeen, as Witnessed in the Lives of Thomas Nicolson of Cockburnspath and His Associates', (2019) 9 *Journal of Irish and Scottish Studies* 93.

165 E.R. Holloway, *Andrew Melville and Humanism in Renaissance Scotland, 1545–1622* (Leiden, 2011); S.J. Reid, *Humanism and Calvinism: Andrew Melville and the Universities of Scotland, 1560–1625* (Farnham, 2011).

166 W.C. Dickinson, 'The Advocates' Protest against the Institution of a Chair of Law in the University of Edinburgh', (1925) 23 *Scottish Historical Review* 205, at pp. 209–11.

167 Cairns, *Law, Lawyers and Humanism*, pp. 67–87.

of teaching in law proposed would equip students for forensic practice.[168] One concern was that those who heard 'ane popular lessoun of ane soliter man without ony farder' would imagine they had heard everything there was to learn. It is not known what form any teaching offered at Aberdeen may have taken, but the course taught by Skene at St Andrews was certainly tailored to the needs of a 'popular' rather than a specialist audience. Its use of Cicero's *De legibus* as a basic text is indicative of an interest in Roman as opposed to civil law, which may also have been what Buchanan had in mind when he thought of assigning responsibility for law teaching to Skene in 1563, though given the reference in a similar scheme devised in 1560 to teaching 'in the municipall and Roman lawes', it could be that he wanted Scottish sources to be studied.[169] Instruction in the civil law was not a priority, but it was what the advocates believed was needed by prospective intrants to their profession. 'It sall fallow heirefter', they suspected, 'that ony man that hes hard thre lessonis of the new lawer sall theink himselff companyeone to Bartoll or Jason'.[170] A related concern was that the appointment of a single lecturer was inadequate for instruction in any subject, 'mekill less in the professioun of the law, the studie quharof is sa great and infinite that without plouralieter of techeris, emulacioun, als weill of professouris as auditouris, continuall disputacionis, and utheris scolastik exerceissis, na fruit can follow'.[171] The point was not simply that the subject was too large for one professor to cover adequately, or that the learning process needed to be active as well as passive, but was also that future advocates needed to serve an apprenticeship in the art of logical argumentation. As a matter of fact, the use of disputations had survived in the Lutheran universities and Calvinist academies, because it was seen as an effective way of consolidating knowledge and preparing ministers for engagement in controversies.[172] What was questioned

---

168 P.G. Ryken, 'Scottish Reformed Scholasticism', in Trueman and Clark, *Protestant Scholasticism*, p. 196; G. Gellera, 'Reformed Scholastic Philosophy in the Seventeenth-Century Scottish Universities', in Broadie (ed.), *Scottish Philosophy in the Seventeenth Century*, p. 94.

169 *The First Book of Discipline*, ed. J.K. Cameron (Edinburgh, 1972), pp. 137–41. In this scheme law teaching was to be associated with philosophy. Welwod, a friend of John Geddie, who served Buchanan as a scribe in the 1570s (S. Verweij, *The Literary Culture of Early-Modern Scotland: Manuscript Production and Transmission, 1560–1625* (Oxford, 2016), pp. 95–6), came closer to implementing Buchanan's vision when he taught law to theology students.

170 See n. 111 above.

171 As the phrase 'als weill of professouris as auditouris' reveals, the need was not only for disputation between students but also between teachers, the traditional means by which new ground had been broken at the frontiers of disciplines.

172 G. Astoul, 'Enseignement et pédagogie dans les académies protestantes au XVIIe siècle', (2018) 28 *Cahiers de Framespa* (https://doi.org/10.4000/framespa.4807), §§. 9–24;

there was the use of disputations as a means of extending knowledge beyond the scriptures or other authoritative texts, as if a consensus among the learned that opinions had become indisputable would make them too authoritative.[173] The advocates who had gone abroad to advance their studies clearly believed that participation in disputations had not only assisted them in mastering the law, but had also prepared them for participation in the style of argumentation encountered in the College of Justice. Some appear to have believed further in the possibility of extending knowledge of the law through academic or forensic disputation.

One of the signatories of the advocates' protest against the appointment of a professor of law at Edinburgh was Alexander King, who appears to have taken a degree *in utroque iure* at Angers in the late 1570s, after studying more briefly at Douai, Louvain and Paris.[174] It was as a Protestant alternative to the traditional University of Angers that the Academy of Saumur was established twenty-five miles up the Loire, and the other universities King attended were also Catholic institutions.[175] If his adherence to the old faith is the obvious explanation for his failure to follow the example of Balfour, Skene and Welwod by travelling to Wittenberg, it is equally obvious that the universities he did attend had not faced the epistemological problems thrown up by Luther's recognition of human depravity and rejection of human traditions. Of all King's teachers the one who had the greatest impact on his handling of maritime law was Pieter Peck, who taught a course on the *Liber sextus* and *Clementines* at Louvain while King was there.[176] In a dedicatory epistle printed with his *Ad regulas iuris canonici commentaria*, which had first appeared in 1564 and was reissued in 1573, when King left St Andrews, Peck took issue with the Protestants who, 'usurping the Christian name unto themselves', not only criticised the leaders of the established church but also 'scorned, held in derision, rejected and publicly

T.G. Van Raalte, *Antoine de Chandieu: The Silver Horn of Geneva's Reformed Triumvirate* (Oxford, 2018), pp. 248–52; R.J. Serina, 'A Debateable Theology: Medieval Disputation, the Wittenberg Reformation and Luther's Heidelberg Theses', (2019) 83 *Concordia Theological Quarterly* 85, at pp. 88–92.

173 A.J. Novikoff, *The Medieval Culture of Disputation: Pedagogy, Practice and Performance* (Philadelphia, PA, 2013); O. Weijers, *In Search of the Truth: A History of Disputation Techniques from Antiquity to Early Modern Times* (Turnhout, 2014).

174 Ford, 'Introduction', pp. xxxix–xlv. Graduation records have not survived from Angers, but King claimed to have a degree, and Angers comes last on the list of universities he claimed to have attended.

175 Calderwood, *History of the Kirk of Scotland*, vol. 4, p. 414, remembered King as a 'malicious papist'. He was certainly committed to Catholicism, and in his youth quite militantly.

176 King's debt to Peck is specified in the commentary attached to *Alexander King's Treatise on Maritime Law*.

burned on a fire the papal constitutions, decrees of most holy bishops, counsels of the fathers and the universal canon law'.[177] What they failed to appreciate was that by dismissing centuries of academic tradition they undermined their own endeavour to subject everything to 'secular judgments' governed by 'profane laws'. As Peck saw it, 'if they would promote human legislation and deny, contrary to the opinion of all the philosophers and ancient scholars, that law is a gift of God and promulgated through the mouths of rulers by divine inspiration, then it would also be necessary for them to get rid of the universal civil law and deprive secular rulers of the power of legislating, and to drive out all magistrates'.[178] The truth, he argued, was surely that God had inscribed 'the image of his justice within us, and wanted not only what is found in the gospel, the writings of the apostles and the old law to be observed, but also what the reason of discreet people approves'. Peck was pleased to observe that at Louvain students were fortified against the falsehoods spread elsewhere by being constantly reminded of the integral connection between the civil and canon laws, by the erudition of their professors, 'and by the exercise of frequent disputations'. It was the civil law that Peck had focused on in his *Commentaria in omnes pene iuris civilis titulos ad rem nauticam pertinentes*, which King relied on heavily in writing his book, but here too the aim had been to work within a learned tradition of enquiry.[179] In another dedicatory epistle Peck advised his readers not to dismiss the opinions of their predecessors, but to select and collect the best they could find, 'in handfuls, as if following after the gleanings of harvests, with the spoiled laid aside'.[180] This was what he had tried to do in composing his book, he explained, in which texts from relevant titles of the *Digest* and *Code* were brought together with material gleaned from an 'assiduous reading of the commentaries on the laws', all of which he had then 'related to daily usage, popular custom and court practice'. Ultimately the aim was to have maritime disputes resolved in the light of the learning gradually accumulated over many centuries through expert discussion of the significance of the texts studied in the law schools. His point was not just that use needed to be made of learned sources in developing the law, but was also that there needed

177 *Ad regulas iuris canonici commentaria* (Douai, 1573), sigg. A2–3.

178 Both here and earlier the word 'universum' is being translated as 'universal' because Peck was associating the loss of the civil and canon laws with rejection of the 'universum pontificatum, universum clerum, universa ecclesiastica et spiritualia iudicia'.

179 Again, the use of Peck's book is specified in the commentary attached to *Alexander King's Treatise on Maritime Law*.

180 *Commentaria in omnes pene iuris civilis titulos ad rem nauticam pertinentes* (Louvain, 1556), sigg. A6v-8.

to be full recognition of the intrinsic authority of the sources, which might be extended into new areas by lawyers who had mastered the sources and made use of them in the way they were taught to in the more traditional universities.

Apart from claiming in his treatise to have studied 'both the civil and canon laws at Douai, Louvain, Paris and Angers', and to have devoted further time after his return home to study of 'either the sacred canons or the civil laws of the Romans', King did not make any great effort to emphasise the traditional character of his education.[181] In remarking that he had come back from France intent on marrying (*coniungere*) his expertise in the learned laws with mastery of local sources, he made a conventional claim that might have been made by any advocate after returning from abroad, and was indeed made by Skene when he published his two editions of the old books.[182] Nevertheless, the treatise King wrote about maritime law was different from those written by Balfour and Welwod, as may be illustrated by a comparison of their handling of the contracts entered into by merchants and mariners to provide for the carriage of goods at sea. Balfour assembled under headings reading 'Anent frauchting of shippis', 'Anent laidning of shippis' and 'Anent making of sail' various acts of the parliaments of Scotland, several articles of the laws of Oleron and Wisby, a note of a decision of the lords of session, and an edict of a French king.[183] Anyone involved in a court action relating to the topics identified would have been assisted in finding sources that could be used in presenting effective arguments. Most of the same sources were cited in Welwod's treatise in a series of titles called 'Off frauchting of schippis', 'Off the maister of the schip, his power and dewtie thairanent', and 'Off the dewtie of the maister to the merchand and passinger, and of his priviledges'.[184] However, instead of reproducing his sources *in extenso*, Welwod summarised them in his own words in sentences formed into a connected outline of the subject, along with sentences summarising Roman law texts, comments on the texts by medieval jurists, articles of the *Nomos Rhodion nautikos* and legislation issued by a Danish king.[185] Mariners who read his treatise and recognised the rules they were accustomed to following would have found out where they had been written down, would have seen how consistent they were with other written rules, and might thus have been persuaded to follow the other rules as well. King dealt with the same

181 *Alexander King's Treatise on Maritime Law*, pp. 4–5.

182 *Regiam maiestatem: Scotiae veteres leges et constitutiones*, sig. A2v.

183 *Practicks of Sir James Balfour of Pittendreich*, vol. 2, pp. 618–22.

184 *Alexander King's Treatise on Maritime Law*, pp. 357–61.

185 His references to the *Nomos Rhodion nautikos* and the Danish legislation were omitted from his *Sea-Law of Scotland*, sigg. B2–5.

subject in a long chapter of his treatise entitled 'De locatione et conductione navium'.[186] Like Welwod, he wanted his readers to think of charter parties as a particular variant of the Roman contract of hire. While he appreciated that the Roman contract was complicated by procedural requirements of no practical significance in Scotland, he wrote primarily about Roman law, gradually easing into his discussion material drawn from the laws of Oleron and Wisby, together with a few more general observations on local usage.[187] In the form in which his text has survived, it is not clear whether it was originally accompanied by annotations identifying his sources, but it is clear that it was intended to leave readers with more than an impression of the consistentency of rules established at different times and in different places. Instead of summarising and juxtaposing rules, King brought together examples of arguments about the meaning of the Roman law texts he cited. In most chapters of his treatise he appropriated whole passages from Peck's commentary on the texts, or from other books written by continental jurists, including Wesenbeck's *Paratitla*.[188] If he too aimed to weave his sources together to form a tapestry, it would have bewildered Welwod's readers, for King's aim was to show his learned colleagues how the authoritive texts studied in the law schools, already exposed to novel interpretation in the disputations and commentaries of the doctors, could be put to further use in their discussion of the maritime law of Scotland. Whereas Balfour had offered his readers easy access to the sources they might wish to use in argument, and Welwod had encouraged his readers to enhance their appreciation of familiar rules of maritime law by recognising their origins and embracing related rules, King meant to show his readers how to engage in the kind of discussion that might gradually give rise to an expert consensus on how questions ought to be answered in the courts.[189]

To take another example, Balfour and Welwod dealt with the employment of mariners in much the same way as they handled contracts of affreightment.[190] King, however, did not handle the two subjects in quite the same way. Although he might, like Welwod, have treated employment contracts as another variant of the Roman contract of hire, a difficulty, as far as his approach to writing was

186 *Alexander King's Treatise on Maritime Law*, pp. 110–37.

187 In particular, there was no need to decide in Scotland who was the *locator* and who the *conductor*.

188 In fact, because Peck did not have a chapter on the contract of hire, less use was made of his commentary in dealing with this subject than others.

189 His particular concern, as will be explained in a moment, was with the central admiralty court.

190 *Practicks of Sir James Balfour of Pittendreich*, vol. 2, pp. 614–18; *Alexander King's Treatise on Maritime Law*, pp. 361–4; Welwod, *Sea-Law of Scotland*, sigg. B5v-7.

concerned, was that scarcely anything had been said about the employment of mariners in the Roman texts, and the subject had not therefore received much attention in the law schools.[191] But King was able to associate the subject with his academic learning in a different way. He was aware that the nautical vocabulary used in the Roman texts had been explored in several books written by humanists, which he had drawn upon in a preliminary chapter of his treatise devoted to elucidation of the words used to denote ships and their components, with the explanation that his later chapters would be difficult to follow without his terminology first being clarified.[192] He then added a similar chapter on the names applied to people found on ships, or in negotiations about ships, and it was in this connection that he wrote about the duties of masters and mariners, relying heavily on the laws of Oleron and Wisby (his understanding of the relationship between these laws is not entirely clear).[193] The importance of defining terms precisely, drawing accurate distinctions and distributing material in an orderly manner had been emphasised by the continental jurists who had revived Cicero's project of reducing the civil law to an art.[194] That the advice offered on these points by the Roman rhetoricians needed to be followed in teaching students was noted by Wesenbeck, who had himself been taught to study law in conjunction with the humanities by Gabriël van der Muyden (*praeceptor meus*, he called him) at Louvain, the university nearest to his home in Antwerp.[195] It may also have been there that King first learned the value of definition, division and methodical arrangement, yet he believed that to follow this approach was to handle the law 'crudely' or 'popularly', since it was – quite literally – to trivialise an advanced discipline by lowering it to the level of the most basic disciplines in the curriculum (once known as the *trivium*).[196] He took no apparent interest in the use of topics (either in

191 Welwod found it easier to get round this problem as he viewed the Rhodian sea law as part of Roman law.

192 *Alexander King's Treatise on Maritime Law*, pp. 44–59. It was thought that Lazare de Baïf, *Annotationes in l. ii, de captivis et postliminio reversis, in quibus tractatur de re navali* (Paris, 1549), had been written at Angers.

193 *Alexander King's Treatise on Maritime Law*, pp. 60–79. Welwod also devoted attention to the names given to 'persones ordinar in schippis', but in a chapter separated from his account of the employment of mariners by his account of contracts of affreightment. The chapter on nomenclature was omitted from his *Sea-Law of Scotland*.

194 I. Maclean, *Interpretation and Meaning in the Renaissance: The Case of Law* (Cambridge, 1992), pp. 103–14.

195 *Paratitla in Pandectas iuris civilis*, pp. 26 and 29.

196 *Alexander King's Treatise on Maritime Law*, pp. 2–3, 8–9 and 22–5. *Cf.* Jan Tack, *Oikonomia seu dispositio regularum utriusque iuris in locos communes* (Cologne, 1570), pp. 1–2, written by another professor teaching at Louvain during King's time there.

the Ciceronian or more Aristotelian sense of the term), nor in the comparative legal history taught by Baudouin, who had ended his teaching career at Angers not long before King studied there. Immersion in the traditional teaching of the civil and canon laws remained for King the key to gaining a sound understanding of the universal truths of justice. While he had paid attention in studying law to 'good studies' – Skene's 'bonae litterae', a standard alternative for 'litterae humaniores' – and incorporated into his treatise passages borrowed from jurists with humanist interests – Cujas was often followed in the chapter on the hiring of ships – his tendency was to work humanist insights into a treatment of maritime law that was in essence a continuation of the approach taken by the medieval doctors.[197]

By adopting this approach King hoped 'to leave to posterity, out of unwritten laws or vague custom, clearly defined laws to be read'.[198] Having returned home intent on 'marrying' his academic expertise with forensic practice, he had become dissatisfied as a judge presiding over debates in the central admiralty court with 'the inconstancy of the allegations of law, in which each party would produce his authorities from a variety of nautical customs, for some cited one custom, others another'. He was reminded of the need felt by the ancient Romans to escape from their early dependence on *incertum ius et consuetudo* by enacting *leges certa*, or to move away from reliance on *ius non scriptum* by establishing *ius scriptum*.[199] This was one concern King shared with the other writers on maritime law in the sixteenth century.[200] When Balfour fulfilled his instructions as a law reform commissioner by focusing on the law written down in the old books, the acts of parliament or the decisions of the session, he also fulfilled the expectations of humanists like Buchanan, who had learned the same lesson as King from their reading of Roman history.[201] Yet King did not believe that the solution to the problem of *incertum ius et consuetudo* lay in improving access to the laws set down in written sources in Scotland, but set out instead to write about maritime law as a learned author (*auctor*), a writer whose expert treatment of the texts studied in the schools would result in their being extended (*auctum*) to cover a new area.[202] Welwod

197 *Alexander King's Treatise on Maritime Law*, p. 350. For Skene see again n. 95 above.

198 *Alexander King's Treatise on Maritime Law*, pp. 6–9.

199 D.1.2.2.1–4.

200 With the possible exception of the author of the *Liber Kyntoris*.

201 Although court decisions may not sound like written laws, Skene included the 'decreetes given be the lords of the session and councell' in his list of 'the buikes conteinand the lawes of this realme' (n. 133 above).

202 A. Minnis, *Medieval Theory of Authorship: Scholastic Literary Attitudes in the Later Middle Ages* (Philadelphia, PA, 2009).

also aimed to connect the particular law of Scotland with the common law of Europe, but not in the same way. While his focus on written sources resulted to some extent from his adoption of Schard's plan to work on documents comparable to the *Nomos Rhodion nautikos*, he hoped to persuade mariners to place less reliance on their collective memory than on the texts in which, he believed, they would find the origins of their recollections. 'The debaitis of seafaireris', he remarked, 'aucht to be decydit accoirding to the receaved customes and statutes of the sea, quhilkis failzeand, then the voitis and opiniounis of honest men skillit in seafairing ar to be soucht and followit'.[203] It was the laws of Oleron that had been received into local usage, he maintained, and the opinions of expert mariners would be better informed if they not only became more familiar with the text of those laws but also appreciated their consistency with other written sources. King confirmed that when questions were raised before him in the admiralty court he did seek expert advice, but he talked of consulting *expertissimi fori togati et in re nautica versatissimi exercitores*, giving priority to educated advocates over experienced businessmen, and it was obviously the former for whom he had written his book, in a demanding style and a learned language.[204] Balfour and Welwod had both written in the vernacular, as had Skene in his dictionary, and although he was to publish an edition of the old books in Latin for the use of lawyers, when he published a vernacular translation at the same time he claimed that the use of Latin in the old books had resulted from a clerical conspiracy to 'continew and mentein kings and the people in ignorance'.[205] King's use of Latin to write his book was consistent with his conventional view that by writing about the law in a learned style he would help to define the law – that is, to make it more definite – in the minds of court practitioners.[206]

In conclusion, it first needs to be conceded that investigating the education of Scottish students at Wittenberg has shed little light on the disproportionate attention paid to maritime law in Scotland during the 1580s. Balfour gave the subject separate treatment because he came to realise that it could not be dealt with adequately within the body of his *Practicks*, Welwod was inspired to

203 *Alexander King's Treatise on Maritime Law*, p. 355. This chapter did not survive in the *Sea-Law of Scotland* either.

204 *Alexander King's Treatise on Maritime Law*, pp. 74–5.

205 *Regiam maiestatem: The Auld Lawes and Constitutions of Scotland*, sig. A3.

206 The law, in other words, was to be written in the minds of legal experts. While this was reminiscent to some extent of the conception of custom as law written in the minds of people rather than in books, the essential point for King was that the law was written in the minds of legal experts with authority derived from books of law. It was only because he was writing as an *auctor* that the thinking he encouraged could have *auctoritas*.

write about it by perusing Schard's edition of the Rhodian sea laws, and King was drawn to writing about it by his unsatisfactory experience as an admiralty court judge. To the extent that these three writers had a common concern it was with examining the exclusive jurisdiction over seafaring causes claimed by the admiral, which does not seem to have owed anything to their education.[207] Nevertheless, it has been suggested here that the way in which each writer handled the subject can be illuminated by consideration of his academic training. Balfour's compilation of written laws under topical headings may well have been influenced by the mode of instruction favoured at Wittenberg in the first half of the century, Welwod's juxtaposition of rules drawn from various times and places may in turn have been influenced by the later development of comparative legal history, as a way of recovering some sense of universality in the study of jurisprudence, and King's more traditional way of connecting the particular aspects of law with universal principles was more likely to have been pursued by a graduate of a Catholic university. This is not to argue that only a Catholic lawyer would have written in the way that King did, especially towards the close of the century, when Protestant institutions were reverting to a more scholastic mode of enquiry.[208] The relationship between law and the humanities, which was as uneasy as the relationship between the humanities and theology, while it did not end in divorce, lapsed into a loose form of cohabitation, dominated by the higher discipline.[209] The more enduring union was between the local and learned laws. There were similarities as well as differences between the ways in which Welwod and King wove Roman law texts together with material drawn from other sources. Both writers saw the laws of Oleron as part of the *ius antiquum* or *ius commune* of Scotland, which they sought to relate to the civil law as the *ius commune* of Europe.[210] They both aimed to draw their readers imperceptibly from familiar into unfamiliar territory. It may even be that Balfour would have welcomed the addition to his *Practicks* of Skene's *De verborum significatione*, with its use of learned sources to elucidate the meaning of local vocabulary. Yet what Balfour is most likely to have learned from Skene after his return from Wittenberg is how treating medieval texts as the foundations of a local tradition of written law could serve

207 This common concern is considered in Ford, 'Introduction', pp. lxxi–xc.

208 Just as a Catholic lawyer could write in much the same way as Balfour (n. 75 above), so a Protestant lawyer could write in much the same way as King. The obvious example is Thomas Craig of Riccarton.

209 For the relationship between the humanities and Lutheran theology see E. Rummel, *The Confessionalization of Humanism in Reformation Germany* (Oxford, 2000).

210 *Alexander King's Treatise on Maritime Law*, pp. 78–9 and 160–1.

as a defence against precipitate recourse to the learned laws, which needed in any case to form part of a broader recourse 'to foreign legislation and the usages of other nations'.[211] The contrasting styles of the treatises on maritime law written by Balfour, Welwod and King make it unlikely that they viewed the relationship between the local and learned laws in exactly the same way, and investigation of their education has shed some light on why this may have been so. However, something else they did have in common was an expectation that the law would be found primarily in written sources. The mentality of these learned lawyers was fundamentally at odds with the mentality of the merchants and mariners examined in the essays in the first part of this collection.[212]

211 *Regiam maiestatem: Scotiae veteres leges et constitutiones*, sig. A3r.

212 As a judge in the admiralty court, King was better placed than Balfour or Welwod to take account of the legal customs known to merchants and mariners, yet his training would have inclined him to recognise the validity of these customs only if they could be accommodated as customary laws within the knowledge common to learned lawyers. This point is dealt with more fully in the fourth essay in this collection.

PART 3

Legal Regimes

Communities of Interest in Maritime Commerce in Sixteenth-Century Scotland

'The medieval ship', Neville Williams observed, 'was essentially a community of interest'.[1] Mariners often owned shares of the ships they sailed in, as well as some of the goods loaded onto them, and during voyages decisions were often made collectively by masters, mariners and merchants, the whole enterprise being conducted in accordance with customary norms that were reckoned to have existed since time immemorial. By the end of the sixteenth century, in contrast, the English ship had become 'a floating department of the business-house'. Clearer distinctions had emerged between the roles, rights and responsibilities of shipowners, masters, various types of mariner, and merchants, and these were increasingly defined by the terms of the contracts parties entered into with each other at arm's length.[2] It was believed in England at the start of the seventeenth century that Scottish ships continued to operate along more conventional lines.[3] The aim of this essay is not to reconsider the change that is thought to have occurred in England, or to compare England with Scotland, but is to consider several ways in which people who participated in maritime commerce in Scotland may have formed communities of interest.[4] The first section looks at what happened if a ship was owned by more than one person, the second at what happened if a cargo was provided by more than one person, and the third at what happened when a ship loaded with a cargo finally departed under the control of a master and mariners.[5] Each section is divided

1 N.J. Williams, *The Maritime Trade of the East Anglian Ports, 1550–90* (Oxford, 1988), pp. 206–7.

2 To some extent, what was envisaged is an example of the transition from status to contract famously identified in H.S. Maine, *Ancient Law: Its Connection with the Early History of Society and Its Relations to Modern Ideas* (London, 1861), pp. 168–70.

3 S.G.E. Lythe, *The Economy of Scotland in Its European Setting, 1550–1625* (Edinburgh, 1960), pp. 207–8; B. Galloway, *The Union of England and Scotland, 1603–8* (Edinburgh, 1986), p. 100; B.P. Levack, *The Formation of the British State: England, Scotland and the Union, 1603–1707* (Oxford, 1987), p. 159.

4 Close engagement with the concept of a community of interest deployed by Williams is not the aim, since it is his broad idea that seems interesting for present purposes, rather than his account of the operation of a medieval ship, which (it is about to be remarked) may be rather misleading.

5 As will be explained later, the third section is not intended to be exhaustive in its coverage.

 | DOI:10.1163/9789004695009_009

into two parts, following an inexact distinction between practice and theory. The word 'practice' is being used here to signify no more than a focus on evidence found in the records of the coastal burghs, which happens to be where most information about how arrangements were made and disputes were settled can be found. The word 'theory' is being used to signify the thinking of the learned lawyers who represented litigants in the central courts or wrote treatises about maritime law.[6] These lawyers were learned in the sense that they knew about the law taught in the university schools of civil and canon law, and some attempt is made in the second part of each section to compare the practice described in the first part with this academic theory, especially as expounded by writers in Scotland. The boundary between practice and theory becomes more blurred when evidence of the involvement of learned lawyers in litigation is examined, and also when attention is turned to other written sources of law. When Williams talked about customary norms he actually had in mind those set down in writing in the *Rôles d'Oléron*, on the assumption that this code of maritime law was adhered to in practice.[7] Yet in earlier essays in this collection it has been seen in that merchants and mariners, at least in Scotland, showed no great interest in written codes of law, which tended to be examined closely only by learned lawyers, both in writing treatises and in presenting pleadings before the central courts.[8] It will be seen again here that when the customary norms adhered to by merchants and mariners resembled those set down in writing in the codes, it was probably because they had imitated the practices of merchants and mariners from other countries where the codes had a more direct influence.[9]

---

6 The first part of each section may thus be related to the essays in the first part of this collection, the second to the essays in the second part (though also to the second section of the fourth essay).

7 A similar assumption is made in R. Ward, *The World of the Medieval Shipmaster: Law, Business and the Sea, c. 1350–1450* (Woodbridge, 2009).

8 Williams supposed that his thesis was undermined to some extent by the interest shown in the laws of Oleron by 'Welwod and Malynes'. If the argument advanced in the sixth essay in this collection is correct, neither the publication of William Welwod, *An Abridgement of All Sea-Lawes* (London, 1613), nor its republication as 'A Collection of All Sea-Laws', in Gerard Malynes, *Consuetudo vel lex mercatoria* (London, 1686), pt 2, p. 43, is especially problematic, for the treatise was not designed to provide an account of English law.

9 This seems especially likely when the practices derived ultimately from the Mediterranean – a point returned to in the second parts of some sections below. As something similar to the transition identified by Williams had previously been identified – moving in the opposite direction – when ancient legal theory gave way to medieval practice in the Mediterranean (W. Ashburner, 'Introduction', in *The Rhodian Sea-Law* (Oxford, 1909), p. xliii, at pp. cxv–ccxciii), it may be wondered whether the lawyers who wrote about the civil law were inadvertently pushing practice in the English direction.

1 Joint Enterprise in Owning Ships

As was mentioned in the opening essay in this collection, ships became available in Scotland during the sixteenth century either by being seized as prizes from enemies in wartime, or by being bought from foreign owners, at home or abroad, or by being built under commission, again either at home or abroad.[10] However a ship came to be owned in Scotland, it might be acquired by a single person, but more often it was acquired by several people together.[11] This section is concerned with how people – women as well as men – came to own shares in ships, and with how the relationship between them was then understood.[12] Although ships were occasionally sold by 'roup', attention is focused in the first part of the section on records of contracts entered into between buyers and sellers, which were made in burghs throughout Scotland and throughout the sixteenth century.[13] Attention is also paid to records of litigation relating to joint ownership, which was believed to remain within the competence of the

10 When ships were acquired elsewhere any relevant records would normally have been kept elsewhere, but now and then these acquisitions were also mentioned in Scottish sources (ACA, CA1/1/30, pp. 254–6, and CA1/1/32, p. 100; DCA, BCMB, vol. 12, 13 January 1574; FCA, B/KDY/2/1/4, ff. 26v-7r; NRS, B19/1/2, 9 September 1573).

11 *Extracts from the Records of the Burgh of Edinburgh*, 1st ser., 5 vols, ed. J.D. Marwick (Edinburgh, 1869–92), vol. 1, p. 229; *Protocol Book of Gavin Ros, 1512–32*, ed. F.J. Grant (Edinburgh, 1908), p. 218; *Protocol Book of John Foular, 1500–34*, 4 vols, ed. W. MacLeod, M. Wood and J. Durkan (Edinburgh, 1930–85), vol. 3, pp. 232–3; ACA, CA1/1/12/2, p. 568, CA1/1/16, p. 777, CA1/1/23, pp. 222–3, CA1/1/25, pp. 495–7, CA1/1/27, pp. 128 and 786–7, CA1/1/28, pp. 6–7, CA1/1/32, p. 109, and CA2/2/1, ff. 22–3r; DCA, BCMB, vol. 12, 22 December 1572, vol. 14, 2 September 1577, and vol. 18, 27 May 1595; FCA, B/KDY/2/1/2, f. 40v; SAUL, B10/8/5, pp. 240 and 460–1; NRS, B6/1/1/1, ff. 491v-2, and B21/8/3, f. 15v.

12 In addition to the sources cited in the first part of the section, references to joint ownership can also be found in *Extracts from the Council Register of the Burgh of Aberdeen*, 2 vols, ed. J. Stuart (Aberdeen, 1844–8), vol. 1, pp. 331–3; *Protocol Book of Gavin Ros*, pp. 214 and 243; *Protocol Book of Mr Gilbert Grote, 1552–73*, ed. W. Angus (Edinburgh, 1914), p. 84; *The Compt Buik of David Wedderburne, Merchant of Dundee, 1587–1630*, ed. A.H. Millar (Edinburgh, 1898), p. 70; ACA, CA1/1/8, p. 857, CA1/1/16, pp. 195, 201 and 205, CA1/1/18, p. 595, CA1/1/21, pp. 641 and 658, CA1/1/22, p. 342, CA1/1/27, p. 638, CA1/1/34/1, pp. 405–6, and CA2/2/1, f. 165; DCA, BCMB, vol. 5, 18 May 1560, vol. 9, 1 June 1567, vol. 12, 23 April 1573, vol. 14, 22 February 1577 and 8 February 1578, vol. 19, 24 March 1597, and vol. 20, 28 March 1599, and PBD, vol. 11, ff. 62v-3r; FCA, B/KDY/2/1/3, f. 133; SAUL, B10/8/4, p. 373, and B65/8/1, f. 97v; NRS, B21/8/5, f. 123r.

13 DCA, BCMB, vol. 12, 31 June 1572, vol. 14, 4 November 1575, and vol. 20, 11 September 1598; FAC, B/KDY/2/1/1, p. 25; NRS, B37/12/1, p. 29.

burgh courts even after the admiralty courts asserted an exclusive jurisdiction over seafaring causes in the second half of the century.[14]

1.1 *Sharing Ships in Practice*

The obvious reason for believing that disputes relating to the sale of ships remained within the jurisdiction of the burgh courts was that burgesses had typically incurred debts to others.[15] Acknowledgements of obligations to pay for shares of ships 'sauld and disponit' to (or 'bocht and ressavit' from) parties often appear in court books, registers of obligations kept by courts or protocol books kept by notaries public.[16] In 1579, for instance, it was noted in the council register of Aberdeen that one burgess there had sold another 'the quartar pertenyng to him of ane boit of Abirdene callit the *Swallow*, presentlie being withtin this herberie, witht the graitht and ornamentis thairof belanging to the said quartar, for the soume of nyn scoir merkis usuall monee of Scotland', which the buyer promised to pay by a specified date, or sooner if he happened 'to returne hame fra his present veage furtht of Flanderis to Abirdene withtin twentie dais'.[17] In a few entries it is mentioned that 'arlis' or 'ane aril penne' had already been paid in earnest of the contract.[18] Equally often, instead of obligations to pay being acknowledged, the receipt of payments was acknowledged and buyers were discharged of further liability.[19] In 1573, for instance,

14 This was not only the case in Dundee, where the point was made explicitly in DCA, BCMB, vol. 3, 20–1 June 1552. The admiral's claim is dealt with in the first essay in this collection.

15 *Cf. The Practicks of Sir James Balfour of Pittendreich*, 2 vols, ed. P.G.B. McNeill (Edinburgh, 1962–3), vol. 2, p. 635.

16 'Notarial Note-Book of John Mason, Clerk of the Burgh of Ayr, 1582–1612', ed. J. Shedden-Dobie (1889) 6 *Archaeological and Historical Collections Relating to Ayrshire and Galloway* 209, at pp. 224–5; ACA, CA1/1/19, pp. 361–2, CA1/1/24, pp. 387 and 604, CA1/1/25, pp. 416–17, CA1/1/27, pp. 355 and 824–5, CA1/1/28, p. 471, CA1/1/29, pp. 91, 128–9 and 702, CA1/1/33/1, p. 347, and CA5/1/3, 15 May 1587; DCA, BCMB, vol. 13, 26 June 1575, vol. 14, 22 July 1578, vol. 15, 21 September 1581, and vol. 17, 6 and 10 March 1591, and PBD, vol. 1, f. 46v, and vol. 11, f. 183; FCA, B/KDY/2/1/2, ff. 44v and 97r; NRS, B19/1/4, 24 March 1583, B19/1/13, 24 September 1590, and B19/1/14, 18 December 1593.

17 ACA, CA1/1/29, p. 808. The 'boit' was presumably a small vessel used in coastal trade, but sometimes boats were mentioned along with other items of equipment sold with a ship (*Extracts from the Council Register of the Burgh of Aberdeen*, vol. 2, p. 6; ACA, CA1/1/21, p. 29, CA1/1/27, p. 679, CA1/1/32, p. 285, and CA1/1/37, pp. 12–13 and 234–5; DCA, BCMB, vol. 3, 15 March 1552).

18 *Burgh Records of the City of Glasgow, 1573–81*, ed. J. Smith (Edinburgh, 1832), p. 130; *The Records of Elgin, 1234–1800*, 2 vols, ed. W. Cramond (Aberdeen, 1903–8), vol. 1, pp. 88–9; ACA, CA1/1/23, p. 136, and CA1/1/24, pp. 158–9; EL, BCBE, vol. 1, p. 202.

19 ACA, CA1/1/21, p. 29, CA1/1/22, p. 56, CA1/1/23, pp. 226 and 238–9, CA1/1/24, p. 304, CA1/1/25, pp. 304 and 531–2, CA1/1/26, p. 352, CA1/1/27, pp. 377, 535–6, 703 and 738, CA1/1/29, pp. 165 and 201, CA1/1/30, p. 417, and CA1/1/31, pp. 294 and 688; DCA, BCMB, vol. 3, 11 April 1553,

payment was made in the presence of the bailies of Dundee for the 'half quarter of the schip callit the *Petir*', whereupon it was recorded that the seller 'exoneris, quytclames and discharges' the buyer of his debt under the contract they had made.[20] When payments were not made voluntarily, actions were raised against buyers in the standard form of actions for debt against burgesses.[21] On the other side of contracts, when buyers acknowledged their obligations to pay for ships or actually paid for them, sellers often undertook to maintain them in possession.[22] In 1597, for instance, the bailies of Kirkcaldy received an acknowledgment of payment for 'ane quarter of a gud schip callit the *Grace of God*', coupled with a promise 'to warrand the said schip' to the buyer 'in all menis handis quhatsumever'.[23] Both the undertakings buyers made to pay for ships, and the undertakings sellers made to maintain buyers in possession, can be found stated together in contracts that were put on record, 'to haif the strenth and effect of ane decreit of the provest and baillies'.[24] In some instances these contracts stated not only that a ship had been sold and disponed but also that it was being sold and disponed 'be thir presentis'.[25] In the last four decades of the century it was common for the same operative language to be used in records of appearances before courts.[26] In 1587, for instance, when two

and vol. 13, 16 September 1574 and 15 June 1575; FCA, B/KDY/2/1/2, f. 70r, and B/KDY/2/1/3, f. 154r.

20 DCA, BCMB, vol. 12, 13 August 1573. The form of the discharge in this and other cases was identical to the form used in many cases unrelated to the sale of ships. These were standard moves in debt recovery.

21 *Kirkcudbright Town Council Records, 1576–1658*, 3 vols, ed. M.B. Johnston, C.M. Armet and D. Stuart (Edinburgh, 1939), p. 22; ACA, CA1/1/16, pp. 106 and 205, CA1/1/22, pp. 472, 481–2, 485, 488–9 and 495, CA1/1/24, p. 287, CA1/1/31, p. 299, and CA1/1/38, pp. 501–2; DCA, BCMB, vol. 8, 24 October and 8 and 10 November 1563, vol. 12, 6 August 1572, vol. 13, 17 March 1574, vol. 14, 24 January 1580, vol. 18, 2 September 1594, and vol. 20, 18 December 1598; AA, B6/11/2, f. 498, and B6/12/2, p. 87; NRS, B6/1/1/1, f. 491, B9/1/2, f. 22r, B19/1/15, 21 May 1595, and B21/8/3, f. 24.

22 ACA, CA1/1/20, pp. 357–8, CA1/1/21, p. 661, CA1/1/23, p. 199, CA1/1/24, p. 12, CA1/1/26, pp. 627–8, CA1/1/27, pp. 190, 515, 723 and 847–9, CA1/1/29, pp. 772–3 and 839, CA1/1/36, p. 39, CA5/1/1, f. 17v, CA5/1/4, 23 November 1594 and 9 May 1595, and CA5/1/5, 27 May 1597; DCA, BCMB, vol. 3, 28 January 1552, and vol. 20, 15 July and 12 December 1597; NRS, B9/1/1, f. 8v, B19/1/3, 6 July 1576, and B51/1/1, pt 1, f. 48v.

23 FCA, B/KDY/2/1/4, f. 123r.

24 ACA, CA2/2/2, 29 August 1584; DCA, BCMB, vol. 13, 6 November 1574.

25 ACA, CA1/1/35, pp. 15–16, and CA2/2/2, 17 September 1576; DCA, PBD, vol. 7, f. 84, and vol. 11, f. 62v; NRS, RD1/68, ff. 367v-8r.

26 ACA, CA1/1/27, pp. 683–4, CA1/1/29, pp. 5–6, 549–50 and 697, CA1/1/30, pp. 79 and 201, CA1/1/31, p. 544, CA1/1/32, pp. 122–3, 279 and 633, CA1/1/33/1, pp. 513–14, CA1/1/33/2, p. 920, CA1/1/35, pp. 143 and 388–9, CA1/1/36, pp. 33, 292 and 614, CA1/1/37, pp. 144–5 and 655–7, CA1/1/38, p. 497, CA5/1/4, 26 August 1595, and CA5/1/5, 16 September and 20 October 1596, and 5

mariners appeared before the bailie court of Dysart, one 'grantit him be thir presentis to haif sauld and disponit, and be thir presentis sellis and dispones', to the other 'all and haill his half schippe callit the *Grace of God*, witht haill ornamentis and partinentis partening thairto', permitting the buyer 'to enter to the pecable possessione of hir as his awin proper geir', in return for which the buyer bound himself 'to thankfully content, pay and delyver' a specified sum of money to the seller within a specified period.[27] While buyers and sellers acknowledged obligations they had incurred and registered contracts they had made before the burgh courts throughout the sixteenth century, in its last four decades these courts became the venues in which buyers and sellers entered into binding contracts with each other.[28]

When a ship was believed to have passed into ownership in Scotland by being seized as a prize from enemies in wartime, it might be sold 'with all aventours as schow wes then lyand at the schoir', and without 'ony conditioun of warrandyse' against claims by its true owners.[29] In other cases, however, the usual expectation was that the ship would belong to the seller 'as his awin proper guds and geir', and that he would defend the buyer against 'all utheris pretendand ony rycht or tytill to hir'.[30] If a buyer had not already taken charge of a ship, the seller would promise that it would be 'deliverit' to him, or that he would receive 'full possessioune'.[31] Some entries describe a deliberate act of delivery. In the records of Aberdeen and Dundee there are references to the handing over of a token, 'as use is', as when the seller of one ship gave the buyer 'ane ring off gold in his hand, inputting off him in possessioun off the said schip', or when the seller of another ship put the buyer 'presentlie in

August 1597; DCA, BCMB, vol. 9, 6 January 1568, vol. 16, 29 May 1585, vol. 17, 6 March 1591, vol. 18, 31 October 1595, vol. 19, 10 February 1596, and vol. 20, 2 March 1599; SAUL, B10/8/5, pp. 434–5 and 651, and B65/8/1, 6 July 1591; NRS, B6/1/1/1, ff. 283v-4r, B21/8/3, f. 217, B21/8/5, f. 57v, and GD1/47/1/1.

27 NRS, B21/8/5, f. 92v.

28 It is of course possible that had more records survived from earlier in the century a different impression would have been given. The available records are reviewed in the first essay in this collection.

29 DCA, BCMB, vol. 5, 5 July 1558; NRS, B19/1/1, 3 October 1572. For further discussion of this point see J.D. Ford, *The Emergence of Privateering* (Leiden, 2023), pp. 60–1.

30 ACA, CA1/1/23, pp. 223–4, CA1/1/31, pp. 461 and 463, and CA2/2/3, ff. 20v-1; DCA, BCMB, vol. 13, 1 June 1575, and vol. 14, 6 and 7 March 1579, and PBD, vol. 11, f. 73v; NRS, B19/1/9, 11 September 1578.

31 ACA, CA1/1/13, p. 431, CA1/1/17, p. 139, CA1/1/20, p. 392, CA1/1/24, pp. 158–9, CA1/1/25, p. 570, CA1/1/27, p. 168, and CA5/1/5, 20 June 1597; DCA, BCMB, vol. 17, 18 August 1593; NRS, B6/1/1/1, ff. 444v-5r and 491v-3, and B19/12/1, 17 March 1590.

possessioun thairof be delyvering of ane ring of gold'.[32] In a protocol book written in Montrose it is recorded that the seller of a half share of a ship accompanied the buyer and a notary to the harbour 'and thair, reallie and witht effect, deliverit the said half schip' to the buyer 'be hir ankir and tow', and that on a similar occasion a buyer received possession of a ship by taking hold of 'ane cordell fast at ane ankar upone the schoir, and the tane end thairof fast withtin the schip'.[33] Other entries make reference to the production of 'ryts and evidentis', or of an 'instrument' showing that a buyer had 'enterit to the possessioun of the said schip'.[34] In 1595 an attempt to have a half share of a ship comprised for a debt owed by a burgess of Ayr was resisted on the ground that before the debt was incurred the ship had been sold and disponed to the debtor's brother, who had since been 'in reall possessioun of the said half schip continuallie'.[35] The argument that he had acquired the ship 'as his proper guidis be alienatioun and dispositioun' failed because he 'producit nathing in write for verefeing of the samin'. The point may merely have been that no record of the sale and disposition was produced, however, for despite the survival of a large number of protocol books written in coastal burghs, very little evidence has been found of notaries drafting instruments for use as proof of delivery. Once it was put on record that a seller had 'transferit his haill rycht and titil' in a ship to a buyer, the parties do not normally appear to have believed that anything further was required.[36] When the mariner of Dysart mentioned at the end of the last paragraph permitted the buyer of his share of a ship 'to enter to the pecable possessione of hir as his awin proper geir', the point does not appear to have been that the buyer should take possession in order to become the owner, but that he could take possession because he had already become the owner. Especially when ships were actively sold and disponed 'be thir presentis', the parties understood that they were doing something with their words, which

32 ACA, CA1/1/35, p. 365, and CA1/1/35, pp. 370–2; DCA, PBD, vol. 3, f. 127r; NRS, B19/1/11, 27 January and 2 February 1588, and B19/1/14, 19 June 1594.

33 NRS, B51/1/1, pt 1, f. 15v, and pt 2, f. 12r.

34 *Burgh Records of the City of Glasgow*, p. 130; ACA, CA1/1/37, p. 239, and CA2/2/3, ff. 169v-71r. In DCA, BCMB, vol. 5, 10 June, 19 July and 27 August 1560, a party is said to have 'producit his instrument off seasing of the half ferry boit', but what he had acquired was not a share of the ship so much as a share of the right to use a ship belonging to the burgh. No evidence has been found elsewhere of a party producing anything described as an instrument of sasine to prove entitlement to a share of a ship.

35 NRS, B6/1/1/1, ff. 477–80r and 481.

36 ACA, CA1/1/24, p. 458, and CA5/1/5, 2 April 1597.

seems to have extended beyond making a contract to conveying title to the ship.[37]

Whether a whole ship was sold to several people, 'equallie amangis thame', or a 'pairt' of a ship was sold by one person to another, the ship was understood to become the property of people known as 'pairtineris'.[38] In Dumfries four men who owned 'ane boit and nerrowschip amangis thame' agreed in the presence of a bailie to take turns in using it.[39] In Kirkcaldy two owners of a ship, 'for eschewing of cummer, anger and discentioun betwix thame in tymes cuming during thair pairtnerschip togidder', put formally on record their intention to submit any disputes that arose between them to the bailie court for settlement.[40] No other evidence of anything remotely resembling a partnership agreement between joint owners has been found. More typical was an agreement between the seller and buyer of a twelfth part of a ship that on its return to St Andrews from Bordeaux the buyer would be both bound 'to outred and furness the said pairt of the said schip in tyme cuming' and entitled to 'tak up his pairt of proffeitt as the uther awnaris dois'.[41] In Leith, Crail, Dundee, Aberdeen, Dumfries and Ayr (and probably in other burghs too) it was often recorded that when masters accounted to owners at the end of voyages, profits were to be distributed in proportion to each owner's share of the ship.[42] It

37 G. Yeo, 'Representing the Act: Records and Speech Act Theory', (2010) 31 *Journal of the Society of Archivists* 95; B. Smith, 'Document Acts', in A. Konzelmann-Ziv and H.B. Schmidt (eds), *Institutions, Emotions and Group Agents: Contributions to Social Ontology* (Dordrecht, 2014), p. 19; P. Henttonen, 'Looking at Archival Concepts and Practice in the Light of Speech Act Theory', in A.J. Gilliland, S. McKemmish and A.J. Lau (eds), *Research in the Archival Multiverse* (Clayton, 2017), p. 537.

38 *Records of Inverness*, 2 vols, ed. W. Mackay, H.C. Boyd and G.S. Laing (Aberdeen, 1911–24), vol. 1, p. 303; ACA, CA1/1/19, pp. 316–17, CA1/1/28, p. 291, CA1/1/36, p. 33, and CA1/1/37, pp. 369–70; DCA, BCMB, vol. 13, 5 March 1574 and 11 February 1575, and vol. 14, 7 June 1577; HAC, B1/1/2, f. 612r; GCA, C1/1/1, f. 104r, and C1/1/4, f. 160v; NRS, B9/11/2, f. 30v.

39 DAC, WC4/8, f. 94r.

40 FCA, B/KDY/2/1/3, ff. 103v-4r.

41 DCA, PBD, vol. 11, f. 42.

42 ACA, CA1/1/8, p. 590, CA1/1/12/1, pp. 20–2 and 74, CA1/1/12/2, pp. 526–7, CA1/1/15, p. 319, CA1/1/16, p. 618, CA1/1/24, pp. 24–5, 27, 54 and 62, CA1/1/25, p. 304, CA1/1/27, pp. 214 and 649, CA1/1/30, p. 692, CA1/1/32, pp. 198 and 520, and CA2/2/3, ff. 79–81r; DCA, BCMB, vol. 1, f. 113r, vol. 3, 14 March 1552, vol. 5, 24, 27 and 30 January 1559, and 18 May 1560, vol. 6, 26 January 1562, vol. 7, 23 April and 2, 5 and 11 July 1563, vol. 8, 6 December 1563, 17 and 19 January and 9 February 1564, and 2 March 1565, vol. 10, 26 August 1569, vol. 11, 17 October 1569, 8 February and 7 June 1570, and 18 July 1571, vol. 12, 16 November 1571, vol. 13, 25 August 1574 and 3 June 1575, vol. 14, 12 December 1575, vol. 15, 18 September 1581, vol. 18, 6, 11 and 13 September 1594, and 29 August 1595, vol. 19, 14 May 1596, and vol. 20, 5 October 1597 and 22 February 1598; SAUL, B10/8/4, p. 151; AA, B6/11/1/1, f. 151r, B6/11/2, ff. 501–2r, and B6/12/2, p. 75; DAC, WC4/9/2, f. 166r; NRS, NP1/17, f. 116.

was equally common for parties to have protestations or petitions drawn up to insist that the costs of voyages be met in proportion to the shares held in ships, of which evidence survives from Dysart, St Andrews, Dundee, Aberdeen, Inverness and Ayr.[43] When a quarter of a ship was sold in Aberdeen to a master from Middleburg who 'had na money to furness for his part quhill he come to Flanders', he had to borrow money since the obligation arose as soon as he became owner.[44] When the owner of a sixteenth of a ship was absent from Dundee, some of the other owners asked his wife to pay his part of the costs of a 'voage interprysed toward the Rochell', protesting when she refused that 'quhatsoever thai and the remanent awnaris sall deburse for outred of the said portioun, that the samin be reinbursat to thame witht sic profeitt as lent money gevis'.[45] When it became necessary in the course of a voyage for 'certan sailles and tackill' to be purchased, it was complained before the bailies of Inverness that one of the owners was refusing to pay his share of the costs, despite receiving 'proffeit and vantage of the lauboring of the saidis sailes and tackill'.[46] He had not been present when the sails and tackle were purchased, and in Dysart another owner protested that he should not be liable for costs after a ship was 'frauchtet by his consent'.[47] However, a similar protest made in Dundee met with the response that since the majority of the owners had consented, the protesting owner was also bound, 'according to the lawis'.[48] Other entries, in the records of Irvine as well as Dundee, indicate that 'pairtineris' were bound by majority decisions, and reference was made in these entries to 'the use of seyfaring' and 'the consuetude of the cuntrie uset amangis uther

43 *Protocol Book of Gavin Ros*, pp. 163–4; *Compt Buik of David Wedderburne*, pp. 53 and 132; ACA, CA1/1/8, p. 560, CA1/1/9, p. 301, CA1/1/19, p. 191, CA1/1/24, p. 174, CA1/1/27, pp. 41, 75, 77, 197 and 200, CA1/1/31, p. 546, CA1/1/32, p. 258, and CA/5/1/1, ff. 18v and 19v; DCA, BCMB, vol. 3, 29 January 1552 and 30 May 1553, vol. 5, 23 April 1560, vol. 10, 20 September 1569, vol. 11, 15 and 17 March, 12 April and 21 June1570, and 24 January and 16 March 1571, vol. 12, 15 December 1573, vol. 13, 20 August 1574 and 11 May and 1 June 1575, vol. 14, 28 February, 6 August and 19 September 1578, 8 April, 5, 7, 10 and 12 August and 4 December 1579, and 28 January, 26 February and 2 March 1580, vol. 18, 9, 11 and 13 September 1594, and 25 July and 4 and 15 December 1595, vol. 19, 19 March 1596 and 21 January 1597, vol. 20, 7 and 24 October and 2 and 13 November 1597, and vol. 21, 9 November 1599; SAUL, B65/8/1, f. 90r; HAC, B1/1/1, f. 47v; AA, B6/11/2, f. 155v; NRS, B6/1/1/1, ff. 426v-7r, and B21/1/1, f. 10v.

44 ACA, CA1/1/16, p. 794.

45 DCA, MBBC, vol. 2, p. 4.

46 HAC, B1/1/2, ff. 260r and 273.

47 *Gleanings from the Records of Dysart, from 1545 to 1796*, ed. W. Muir (Edinburgh, 1862), pp. 21–2; NRS, B21/1/2, f. 54v.

48 DCA, BCMB, vol. 17, 14 April 1591.

pertineris in uther schippis'.[49] In the Irvine record one owner intervened in the sale of another owner's share to make sure it was understood that the buyer 'sould be subject to do as the rest of the pertineris (being the maist pert) lyk in furneissing, and to mak sic ane veage as the rest pleises, and provyd for cost, skaytht and expenses just as they do'.[50] He presumably saw the need to intervene in the sale because it was not the normal practice for owners to enter into, let alone renew, partnership contracts with each other.

That joint owners were bound by majority decisions would help to explain two surprising cases in which owners complained about whole ships being sold without their consent, for they insisted on being paid their shares of the profits made before the dates of the sales but did not challenge the validity of the contracts or conveyances.[51] In the more common cases in which an owner sold his share of a ship, no mention tended to be made of the other owners. Indeed, one buyer does not appear to have known the identity of all the other owners at the time of the sale.[52] Once shares were acquired, however, owners often acted together in making contracts or pursuing actions.[53] In Aberdeen, for instance, two owners of a ship appeared before the bailie court to raise an action 'for thameselffis and remanent awnaris of the said schip', producing 'ane chartour pairtie for instructing thairof', which had been made by the master, 'one of the saids awnaris, witht consent of the remanent awnaris'.[54] The master was not one of those who raised the action, yet they were able to seek redress from a merchant who had failed to provide a promised cargo under a contract made with the master. In another case, in which a contract had been made by a merchant with one of the owners of a ship, 'takand the burdoun upoun him for himself and remanent awnaris of the same', it was argued that the master

49 DCA, BCMB, vol. 4, 28 January 1556 and 9 March 1558, and vol. 5, 19 June 1558; NRS, B37/12/1, pp. 29–30. The reference to 'the use of seyfaring' may have related to another aspect of the case, not to the ability of the majority to overrule the minority.

50 Slight liberties have been taken in the transcription of this record, which is not entirely legible but is clear at the important points.

51 ACA, CA1/1/12/2, pp. 480 and 570, and CA1/1/23, pp. 248–9, 266, 278–9 and 281.

52 *Records of Inverness*, vol. 1, pp. 222–3; HAC, B1/1/2, f. 232r.

53 *Extracts from the Records of the Burgh of Edinburgh*, 1st ser., vol. 3, pp. 129–30; ACA, CA1/1/27, pp. 609, 627 and 629; DCA, BCMB, vol. 3, 19 October 1552, vol. 12, 19 October 1571, vol. 14, 14 September 1579, vol. 15, 10 and 17 February and 6 September 1581, vol. 17, 23 April 1591 and 19 January 1592, vol. 18, 10 February, 1, 3 and 24 September, 10 October and 14 November 1595, and 19 and 12 March, 9 and 14 April and 23 June 1596, and vol. 20, 27 July and 14 November 1597, 4 August and 7 September 1598, and 12 January 1599; FCA, B/KDY/2/1/4, f. 6v; ECA, SL1/1/4, pp. 41, 45, 48–50 and 63–4; NRS, B9/11/1, f. 131v, B9/11/2, f. 24v, B19/1/1, 30 October 1571, and 2 February 1573, and B21/8/2, f. 31r.

54 ACA, CA1/1/34/1, pp. 239–40, 244–6, 254, 258–9 and 265.

could not raise an action since he had 'only subscrivit the chartor pairtie as witnes', yet it was found that he was 'ane sufficient persoun to persew', as one of the owners.[55] On a previous occasion the bailies of Aberdeen had rejected the argument that because the pursuer was 'bot awnar of ane part of the schip' he could not raise an action 'wythtout consent' of the other owner.[56] An even earlier case related to a ship that had been on its way from Dieppe to Aberdeen when its owner sold it to three merchants from Scotland.[57] It was found that the new owners could raise an action against a merchant whose goods had been carried in the ship under a contract made before the ship's departure with a master employed by the previous owner. In a later case two merchants who had bought a ship in Yarmouth sold shares to six others after they returned to Aberdeen.[58] It was acknowledged by one of the new owners that since the ship had not been paid for fully in Yarmouth, he now owed part of the original purchase price to the original seller. It would not be easy to reconcile either the case of the ship bought on its way from Dieppe or the case of the ship bought after arriving from Yarmouth with any notion of privity of contract. The rights and duties of the owners in these two cases cannot be explained by the making of the relevant contracts 'in thair name and behalf', and appear to owe something to a more flexible notion that people could sue or be sued on contracts if they had an interest in their performance. The same notion may have informed the understanding of recurring statements in the records that the joint owners of ships were bound 'conjunctlie and severallie', for this does not appear to have meant that they were liable for more than a share of any debt incurred, in proportion to the shares of the ships they owned.[59] The point appears to have been that any owner could be sued on a contract entered into with any other owner, and not necessarily when it had been explicitly made in the name of all the owners.

1.2 *Sharing Ships in Theory*

Although the burgh courts continued throughout the sixteenth century to deal with disputes relating to the sale of ships, there is evidence that disputes of the same type were also dealt with in the central admiralty court, sitting in

55 ACA, CA1/1/33/1, pp. 592–4.
56 ACA, CA1/1/16, pp. 606, 611–13 and 619.
57 ACA, CA1/1/12/1, pp. 157, 160, 164, 166–7, 169–70 and 173.
58 ACA, CA1/1/34/1, pp. 200–1.
59 ACA, CA1/1/14, p. 606, CA1/1/16, p. 316, and CA1/1/19, pp. 426–7 and 429; DCA, BCMB, vol. 19, 28 April 1596; HAC, B1/1/2, f. 190r; DAC, WC4/10/3, p. 779; NRS, B9/11/2, f. 117v, and B21/8/6, ff/ 105v-6r.

Edinburgh or Leith. Relevant entries can be found in the only surviving act book of that court, running from the late 1550s into the early 1560s, and one document registered with the burgh court of Dundee was an act passed by the central admiralty court in 1571.[60] In their style and vocabulary these acts resemble the entries found in the burgh court books, though the formal cancellation of the 'venditioun' of a ship is less familiar. In addition to these acts, a contract of sale was registered with the judges of the admiralty in 1557, and several other documents relating to the sale of ships were registered with the lords of council and session later in the century.[61] In their style and vocabulary these documents also resembled those found in the burgh court books, though the word 'venditioun' appears again in one of them. Some (and quite possibly all) of these documents, like those registered with the burgh courts, were written by notaries, as were many of the other documents reviewed in the first part of this section, and to some extent all of the evidence examined so far may probably be attributed to these lawyers, since the clerks who compiled the records of the courts were usually notaries. The involvement of these lawyers goes some way towards explaining the similarities of style and vocabulary found in records from burghs situated around the coasts of Scotland as well as from the central courts situated in Edinburgh. In his *Summa totius artis notariae*, Rolandinus de Passaggeriis had provided a style for a *venditio simplex*, stating that a thing was given, sold and delivered (*dedit, vendidit et tradidit*) in exchange for a specified price (*pretium*), that the buyer was authorised to take actual possession (*possessio corporalis*), and that the seller would defend him in any actions raised by others (*defendere, auctorizare et desbrigare*).[62] Essentially the same style had also been printed in several other handbooks, usually in relation to the sale of land, but sometimes in relation to the sale of moveable things.[63] In a treatise on notarial practice written during the sixteenth century, Jean Papon explained that the warranty sellers provided against 'eviction' of the buyer from the thing sold was an obligation derived from Roman law.[64] Because of its historical development, and complications

60 *Acta curiae admirallatus Scotiae, 6th Sept. 1557 – 11th March 1561–2*, ed. T.C. Wade (Edinburgh, 1937), pp. 13–14, 18, 24–5 and 246; DCA, BCMB, vol. 11, 16 February 1571.

61 *Acta curiae admirallatus Scotiae*, pp. 12–13; NRS, RD1/26, ff. 408v-9r, RD1/27, ff. 207–8, RD1/30, ff. 319–20, RD1/48, ff. 210v-11 and 310, RD1/49, pp. 313–17, and RD1/68, ff. 367v-8r.

62 Rolandinus de Passaggeriis, *Summa totius artis notariae* (Venice, 1546), ff. 8–12r.

63 *Artis notariatus, hoc est de officio exercitioque tabellionum, tomi duo* (Frankfurt, 1539), pt 2, f. 17; Stephanus Marcilletus, *Doctrinale florum artis notariae sive formularium instrumentorum* (Venice, 1518), ff. 19v-20; Leo Speluncanus, *Artis notariae tempestatis huius speculum* (Venice, 1574), ff. 3v-4 and 39–40.

64 Jean Papon, *Premier tome des trois notaires* (Lyons, 1568), p. 77.

that had affected the acquisition of property until the sixth century, the Roman law of sale did not require sellers to transfer title to buyers but merely required them to provide vacant possession of the thing sold, which might ripen into ownership by a form of prescriptive acquisition.[65] In the meantime the seller was usually required to guarantee the buyer against eviction, although it was possible to provide expressly that the risk of eviction would remain with the possessor.[66] Despite their peculiar origins, these rules had continued to be taught in the medieval universities as part of the civil law of *emptio venditio*, and even in the sixteenth century it was maintained that since the seller was not bound to provide anything more than vacant possession, yet the buyer was meant to become the owner, a warranty against eviction was a natural term in any contract of sale.[67] That the theory taught in the law schools ultimately lay behind the practice discussed in the first part of this section can hardly be doubted, even without the additional indications provided by the occasional references to *arra*.[68] It is obviously more doubtful that the parties to contracts for the sale of ships were aware of the theory behind the practice to which they conformed, and it may also be wondered whether notaries who merely copied out and adjusted styles had much awareness of the theory.

The lawyers who were educated at continental universities and wrote about maritime law after they returned to Scotland did not have much to say about the acquisition of ships. James Balfour referred in his collection of sea laws to two fifteenth-century acts of parliament that had encouraged the acquisition of 'schippis, busches and greit pinckboatis', but said nothing more about the subject.[69] In one chapter of his *Tractatus legum et consuetudinum navalium*

65 D.12.4.16, 18.1.25.1, 18.1.78.1, 18.1.80.3, 19.1.30.1, 21.2.55 and 21.2.56.3; F. De Zulueta, *The Roman Law of Sale: Introduction and Select Texts* (Oxford, 1945), pp. 35–7.

66 D.18.4.10, 19.1.11.2, 19.1.11.15–18, 19.4.1.pr., 21.2.34.2, 21.2.35, 21.2.46.pr., 21.2.62.2, 21.2.68.pr. and 45.1.38, and C.8.44.3, 8.44.6 and 8.44.8–9; R. Powell, 'Eviction in Roman and English Law', in D. Daube (ed.), *Studies in the Roman Law of Sale Dedicated to the Memory of Francis de Zulueta* (Oxford, 1959), p. 78.

67 Matthaeus Wesenbecius, *Paratitla in Pandectas iuris civilis* (Basel, 1566), p. 249; Charles Dumoulin (alias Gaspar Caballinus), *Tractatus de evictionibus* (Cologne, 1574), p. 13; Hubertus Giphanius, *Disputatio de actionibus empti et venditi in theses aliquot coniecta* (Ingolstadt, 1591), p. 10.

68 D.14.3.5.15, 18.3.6.2, 18.3.8 and 19.1.11.6, J.3.23.pr. and C.4.21.12 and 4.54.1; J.A.C. Thomas, '*Arra* in Sale in Justinian's Law', (1956) 24 *Tijdschrift voor Rechtsgeschiedenis* 253; A. Watson, '*Arra* in the Law of Justinian', (1956) 6 *RIDA* 385.

69 *Practicks of Sir James Balfour of Pittendreich*, vol. 2, p. 614; *The Acts of the Parliaments of Scotland*, 12 vols, ed. T. Thomson and C. Innes (Edinburgh, 1814–75), vol. 2, pp. 19 and 100; Records of the Parliaments of Scotland, ed. K.M. Brown (www.rps.ac.uk), 1429/10/4 and 1471/5/10.

Alexander King reviewed the vocabulary used to describe ships, their components and their equipment, adding towards the end that 'if anyone were to buy a ship' he would be entitled to receive the ship with all its equipment, since sails, ropes, anchors and so on were regarded as accessories of a ship and 'an accessory yields to the principal and follows its principal'.[70] In doing so he brought together the Roman law principle that *accessio cedat principali* and the civil law principle that *accessorium sequitur suum principale*.[71] These principles meant that it was not strictly necessary for contracts of sale to state explicitly that ships were sold together with their 'parts and pertinents', and in fact the draftsmen of the contracts tended to make use instead of the Germanic terms 'graith' and 'reidschip', which must have been picked up from intercourse with foreign merchants and mariners rather than from academic study.[72] 'But if anyone were to sell a ship', King went on, 'it should not be supposed in consequence that he sold its individual planks or the individual parts, so that he would be liable for eviction under the civil law if anything were repossessed'.[73] This statement was modelled on a text from the *Digest*, and King was following the civil law again when he added that the parties to a contract could agree different terms.[74] Reflecting further on the unity of the ship, he next observed that 'if several people were to be joint owners of a single ship, they would have a share not only in the entire ship, consisting of its combined parts, but also in its individual accessories, in proportion to their ownership'. At this point he said something about the practice followed in Scotland. 'Whether an entire ship or any part of it is sold', he remarked, 'the method of taking possession normally observed in our practice is that the buyer not only takes hold of the ship, consisting of its combined parts, with the seller or his agent (holding a special mandate) present and consenting, in the presence of a notary public, but also grasps with his hand the nautical ropes and other accessories'. It has been seen that this statement receives only limited support from the surviving records of practice.[75] Aware that ships were usually 'sold and disponed', and

---

70 *Alexander King's Treatise on Maritime Law*, ed. J.D. Ford (Edinburgh, 2018), pp. 54–5.

71 D.34.2.19.13; *Regulae iuris tam civilis quam pontificii*, 2 vols (Frankfurt, 1586), vol. 1, pp. 7–8.

72 W. Craigie, A.J. Aitken, J.A.C. Stevenson, H.D. Watson, and M.G. Dareau (eds), *A Dictionary of the Older Scottish Tongue from the Twelfth Century to the End of the Seventeenth*, 12 vols (Chicago, London and Aberdeen, 1931–2002), vol. 2, p. 688, vol. 5, pp. 459–60, and vol. 7, p. 167.

73 *Alexander King's Treatise on Maritime Law*, pp. 56–7.

74 D.21.2.36; see too D.2.14.27.8.

75 While it needs to be remembered that the records of the burghs are far from complete, it does seem significant that over a hundred protocol books written in coastal burghs have been examined, and only a few entries dealing with the delivery of ships have been found, none of which ties in exactly with King's statement.

that the sale and disposition of land was followed by its delivery into the hands of the buyer, King may have supposed that something like an 'instrument of sasine' was required to prove that ownership of a vessel had been acquired. His final remark that 'a ship is accounted among moveable things by Scots law, and is therefore subject to the same rules of our law as moveable things', while recognising that ships were not in the end like land, also provides some confirmation that he was mindful of the comparison.[76] More fundamentally, he was obviously mindful of the civilian principle that *traditionibus non nudis pactis dominia rerum transferuntur*.[77] He does not appear to have read Benvenuto Stracca's *De mercatura seu mercatore tractatus*, where it was pointed out that the medieval doctors of law had recognised not only that ships could be delivered in various ways, but also that once a buyer had effective control of a ship, 'ownership would be transferred without *traditio*'.[78] The same view was taken by the privy council of Scotland after a ship purchased in Norway was wrecked and the buyers claimed title to its remains.[79] The advocate John Russell argued that they could not do so as they had sailed away in the ship before it was formally delivered to them, but the court accepted the reply from the advocate Alexander King – the brother-in-law of the treatise writer – that being permitted to sail away was sufficient to transfer ownership. The nascent belief that selling a ship in court would automatically transfer title might have been related to the acquisition of property by *in iure cessio*, of which evidence had recently come to light, but King made nothing of this.[80]

Apart from remarking at the beginning of his abridgement of all sea laws that 'the awner is he to quhom the schip or ony pairt thairof belangs in

76 As one of the manuscripts of the treatise points out, he was probably alluding to a rule included in collections of the 'auld lawes' of Scotland (*The Ancient Laws and Customs of the Burghs of Scotland*, 2 vols, ed. C. Innes and R. Renwick (Edinburgh, 1868–1910), vol. 1, p. 171; *Acts of the Parliaments of Scotland*, vol. 1, pp. 254–5 and 724). On the origins of this rule see A.R.C. Simpson, '*Decretum fuit per burgenses*: A Fresh Perspective on Law Making in the Medieval Scottish Burghs', (2023) 74 *Innes Review* 1.

77 C.2.3.20.

78 Benvenuto Stracca, *De mercatura seu mercatore tractatus* (Venice, 1553), pp. 251–2.

79 *The Register of the Privy Council of Scotland*, 14 vols, ed. J.H. Burton and D. Masson (Edinburgh, 1877–98), vol. 4, pp. 79–80. Unfortunately, NRS, PC1/12, containing the original record of the case, was judged unfit for production when it was ordered.

80 Iacobus Cuiacius, *Opera quae de iure fecit*, 5 vols (Paris, 1584), vol. 1, pp. 76–7; P.F. Girard (ed.), *Textes de droit romain* (Paris, 1923), pp. 476–7. King did make use of the works of Cuiacius in writing his treatise, but if he knew about the *Ulpiani liber singularum regularum*, 19, he did not appreciate its relevance here. Nor did he explain how Roman partners came to own property in common, which remains a mystery, though some form of court process corresponding to the *actio communi dividundo* is a possibility.

proppertie', William Welwod omitted to deal with the acquisition of ships.[81] He did say more about joint owners, however, in a title of his book 'Off the outredderis of schippis, and of actionis bayth for and against thame, and of discordis amangis thameselfis'.[82] He observed there that, 'anent the awneris thameselfis, in cais thay cannot aggrie to remane in pairtnerschip, becaus it is a generall reull of law that no man sould be constrainit to keip societie or pairtnerschip, yit is thair many considderatiounis anent thair sundering fra pairtnerschip'.[83] In support of the 'generall reull of law' reference was made to a text from Justinian's *Code*, and more vaguely to texts on *societas* in the *Digest* and *Institutes*, which did indeed make it clear that Roman partnerships could have been ended by the *renuntiatio* of one of the partners.[84] Some of these texts also referred to considerations constraining renunciation, making it clear that partners were not to withdraw at times that would be awkward for their colleagues, but in support of the final clause in his opening statement Welwod went on to talk about two other sources. The first was an article from the code of maritime law enacted by Frederick II of Denmark in 1561, which was concerned with disagreements over whether a ship should embark on a new voyage.[85] To prevent ships from remaining idle in ports, it was provided that those who wished to sail should assume the risk of the ship being lost or damaged, and that only they should receive shares of the profits of the voyage. Welwod reworked the article to provide that when a ship was newly acquired, a voyage should be made 'befoir ony of thame be hard to quyt his pairt', adding that after the ship returned, 'gif thay cannot aggrie, he that desyres to be frie sould offer to the rest and sett his pairt on sic a pryce as he will ather hald or let'.[86] The second source was an article of the *Consolato del mare*, which provided that shares in ships should not be sold, nor should the sale of a whole ship be insisted on, until the end of a voyage.[87] Welwod again presented a rather creative reworking of the article, taking it to mean that if 'puir awneris' were

81 *Alexander King's Treatise on Maritime Law*, p. 352.

82 This passage was left out of the short treatise he published in 1590, but it was reinstated and expanded as a separate chapter in the treatise he published in 1613.

83 *Alexander King's Treatise on Maritime Law*, p. 365.

84 C.4.37.7, D.17.2.4, 17.2.65 and 17.2.17.2, and J.3.25.4. In his 1613 treatise Welwod added a more specific reference to D.17.2.14.

85 *Collection de lois maritimes antérieures au XVIIIe siècle*, 6 vols, ed. J.M. Pardessus (Paris, 1828–45), vol. 3, pp. 262–3.

86 In his 1613 treatise Welwod added that the provision was consistent with D.6.1.16.1, 6.1.62 and 7.1.12.1, and with *Digestum vetus* (Lyons, 1551), p. 558 (gl. 'Iure' ad D.6.1.62).

87 *Collection de lois maritimes antérieures au XVIIIe siècle*, vol. 2, p. 62; *Consulate of the Sea and Related Documents*, tr. S.S. Jados (University, AL, 1975), p. 29.

unable to buy shares from others at the prices they demanded, 'then ar they all bond to put the schip to rouping'.[88] Finally, he observed that 'gif nather that way can serve, as for scant of byaris and merchandis in that place, and that nather the richer can satisfie the wilfull puir pairtner, or that the puir pairtner cannot eschew the oppressioun of the riche and wealthie pairtner, then may the judge ordinar do and decerne in this caus and contraversie lyk as he may *in omnibus bonae fidei actionibus*'.[89] Reverting here to the *Digest*, Welwod drew attention to a text from the title on the contract of *depositum* in which it was explained that the good faith required by some contracts had to be understood in terms of *aequitas summa*, which meant that a judge should not adhere to *praecepta civilia et praetoria* but should turn to *ius naturale et gentium*.[90] More particularly, Welwod added, a judge 'sould considder all the circumstances of the persounis, thair motionis, the mater falling in or tuiching the debeat, with all the meritis thairof, and mak ane full decision of all togither, that ilk man may repoirt and obtene his dew rycht'. As well as encouraging flexible adjudication, Welwod was also tying his whole discussion together here, for comparison of laws from different times and places was a way of identifying *ius naturale et gentium*.[91] The articles of the Danish code and the *Consolato del mare* thus served to amplify the equitable principles embedded in Roman law, the source of the 'generall reull' under discussion.

If Welwod showed his treatise to the merchants in his family and their associates, as was suggested in the sixth essay in this collection, then they are likely to have raised doubts about the relevance of the passage discussed in the previous paragraph.[92] Quite apart from telling him that they had no knowledge of the written sources he relied on, they might well have told him how the owners of shares in ships dealt with each other in daily practice, which would have been difficult to reconcile with the Roman law of partnership. A *societas* was created by an agreement between several people to work together towards a shared objective, and was in origin and essence a kind of artificial family.[93] It was not only created by a mutual agreement between the partners but also remained in existence only as long as all the partners remained in agreement,

88 In a further addition in his 1613 treatise, Welwod made reference here to Macrobius, *Saturnalia*, 3 vols, tr. R.A. Kaster (Cambridge, MA, 2011), 2.6.2.

89 *Alexander King's Treatise on Maritime Law*, p. 366.

90 D.16.3.31.

91 Welwod's interest in comparative legal history, and its effect on the writing of his book, is discussed in the preceding essay in this collection.

92 This would of course help to explain why the passage was omitted from the treatise printed in 1590.

93 D.17.2.31-4; D. Daube, '*Societas* as Consensual Contract', (1938) 6 *Cambridge Law Journal* 391.

so that if one exercised his right of *renuntiatio*, the partnership would end, as it would if one of them died, or even if one of them resorted to litigation against another.[94] For a new partner to be brought into an enterprise, moreover, it was necessary for the existing partnership to be dissolved and a new agreement to be made among everyone involved.[95] These basic rules appear to have been taught at the University of Wittenberg when Welwod studied there, yet the evidence reviewed in the first part of this section shows that in Scotland the owner of a share of a ship was at liberty to transfer it to somebody else, who would take the seller's place as a partner of the other owners without any agreement being reached between them.[96] This practice was in fact quite widespread in Europe, and was reflected in the articles of the Danish code and *Consolato del mare* that Welwod had to rework before they could be connected with his Roman law sources.[97] For the practice to be reconciled with Roman law a better comparison would have been with the Roman understanding of the *communio* between people who happened to own something jointly, for they were also believed to be obliged to share profits and losses with each other, but *quasi ex contractu* rather than *ex contractu*.[98] A joint owner – provided he had not become a partner of the other owners – was at liberty to sell and transfer his share of the thing to another person, who then became answerable to the other owners for profits and losses.[99] In Roman law, however, a joint owner had a *ius prohibitionis* over the use of the thing, whereas in Scotland the majority appear to have been able to overrule the minority.[100] Furthermore, joint owners were regarded in Scotland as 'pairtineris', which seems to have affected their

94 D.17.2.52.9, 17.2.59.pr. and 17.2.63.10, and J.3.25.5; J.A.C. Thomas, '*Solutio societatis ex actione* and *Dissensus sociorum*', (1974) 48 *Tulane Law Review* 1103.

95 D.17.2.19-23 and 50.17.47.1.

96 Wesenbecius, *Paratitla in Pandectas iuris civilis*, pp. 245–6. Wesenbecius would have been taught the rules at Louvain, if Gabrielus Mudaeus, *Commentarii ad titulus Digestorum Pro socio, De contrahenda emptione et venditione, De actionibus empti et venditi, De pignoribus et hypothecis* (Louvain, 1563), pp. 15–16, 24–5, 41–2, 44 and 54–5, is any guide.

97 E.H. Byrne, *Genoese Shipping in the Twelfth and Thirteenth Centuries* (New York, 1970), pp. 12–21; U. Tucci, 'Venetian Shipowners in the XVIth Century', (1987) 16 *Journal of European Economic History* 277, at pp. 279–82; O. Gelderblom, *Cities of Commerce: The Institutional Foundations of International Trade in the Low Countries, 1250–1650* (Princeton, 2013), pp. 188–9.

98 D.10.3.4.3, 10.3.6.1, 10.3.11 and J.3.27.3; P. van Warmelo, 'Joint Ownership in Roman Law', (1957) 25 *Tijdschrift voor Rechtsgeschiedenis* 150.

99 D.10.3.14.3 and 10.3.24.1.

100 D.10.3.28. The Scottish evidence is far from conclusive, but it raises further doubts about the consistency of local practice with the articles of the Danish code and *Consolato del mare* that Welwod cited.

relations with those who dealt with the other owners. The partnership regime that operated in practice in Scotland seems to have been significantly different from the regime taught in the law schools, but to see just how different it will help to consider first the arrangements often made between merchants.

2 Joint Enterprise in Shipping Cargoes

When legislation was enacted in Scotland in the later fifteenth century requiring contracts of affreightment to be set down in writing in the form of charter parties, it seems to have been envisaged that merchants would consign goods to masters for transportation to other places and would accompany the goods on the voyages as passengers.[101] Ample evidence survives that this continued to happen in practice during the sixteenth century.[102] Ample evidence also survives of goods instead being consigned for delivery to somebody else at the end of a voyage.[103] The recipient was often a 'factour' residing abroad, who was expected to sell the goods on behalf of the consignor in a foreign market.[104] This section, however, does not deal with these situations but with what happened when a merchant who consigned (and possibly accompanied) goods took responsibility for his own and another merchant's goods, as it is consideration of this situation that may contribute to the task of assessing the extent to which the parties involved in voyages were seen as communities of interest rather than separate individuals. Evidence of this type of arrangement survives

101 *Acts of the Parliaments of Scotland*, vol. 2, p. 87; Records of the Parliaments of Scotland, 1567/1/4. This legislation and its effects are examined in the third essay in this collection.

102 ACA, CA1/1/10, p. 141, CA1/1/13, pp. 425 and 428, CA1/1/16, pp. 452, 457, 463–4, 467–8, 472, 474, 476, 482 and 486, and CA1/1/35, p. 303; DCA, BCMB, vol. 4, 4 August 1557, and vol. 13, 7 May 1574. Further examples are cited below.

103 ACA, CA1/1/8, pp. 552, 1006, 1018 and 1020, CA1/1/9, pp. 342 and 441–2, CA1/1/10, pp. 140, 166–7 and 169, CA1/1/12/1, pp. 102 and 307, CA1/1/12/2, pp. 596 and 877, CA1/1/13, pp. 68, 413 and 422, CA1/1/14, pp. 154, 536, 545, 557 and 560, CA1/1/15, pp. 54 and 588, CA1/1/16, p. 454, CA1/1/19, pp. 87, 90, 96, 141, 148 and 157, CA1/1/24, pp. 470 and 592, CA1/1/30, p. 623, CA1/1/31, pp. 328–9, CA1/1/33/1, pp. 596–7, CA5/1/2, 8 March 1582, and CA5/1/5, 4 September 1597; DCA, BCMB, vol. 3, 25 May 1552, vol. 4, 11 and 22 October and 15 December 1557, vol. 12, 8, 10 and 15 April 1573, vol. 14, 14 December 1575, vol. 17, 31 May 1592, vol. 18, 4 January 1595, and vol. 19, 21 and 31 January 1596; FCA, B/KDY/2/1/4, ff. 61v-2r, and B/CUL/1/1/1, p. 90; HAC, B1/1/2, ff. 391v and 470–1r (final paragraph printed in *Records of Inverness*, vol. 1, p. 267); ECA, SL234/1/5, 5 July 1599; NRS, B9/1/2, f. 15, and B51/10/2, f. 29. Sometimes too a master agreed to take money to someone overseas (ACA, CA1/1/24, pp. 39–40 and 109, CA1/1/26, pp. 404–5, 407 and 440, CA1/1/27, pp. 469 and 477, CA1/1/29, p. 786, and CA5/1/5, 15 October 1596).

104 *Cf.* T.S. Willan, *Studies in Elizabethan Foreign Trade* (Manchester, 1959), pp. 1–33.

in the records of the burgh courts – including some that were not situated on the coasts – since there was never any doubt that the burgh courts had jurisdiction over disputes between merchants. It was believed that disputes concerned with 'the calling and estait of merchandis traffiqueris' were best handled by other merchants, 'as men of best knawlege and experience in the said mater'.[105]

2.1 *Sharing Cargoes in Practice*

There are many entries in the burgh court books in which a merchant acknowledged that he had shipped goods 'for himself and tham for quhom he was merchand', or undertook to pay the freight 'of his awin gudis and of thame he is merchand to', or sought delivery of another person's wares, 'to the quhilkis guidis and geir I wes merchand for the tyme'.[106] Very often a merchant who accompanied someone else's goods overseas was responsible not only for their recovery from the ship but also for trading with them.[107] In 1587, for instance, in support of a 'clame of compt and rackining' made in the bailie court of Aberdeen, a merchant produced a 'merchand bill' he had given to someone else before he sailed to Dieppe, where he was to sell goods belonging to the pursuer and, 'the said geir being sauld, to wair the free money thairof on certane sortis of wairis nominat in the said merchand bill, conforme to the tennour of the same'.[108] The defender had bought some goods and brought them home, but the pursuer claimed to be lacking 'the soume of thre scoir thre frankis Frenche money, quhilk was nocht wairit on merchanrice according to the said bill'. The defender alleged that the pursuer had given him 'power to

---

105 ACA, CA5/1/5, 16 February 1597.

106 ACA, CA1/1/10, p. 142, CA1/1/15, pp. 31 and 33, CA1/1/16, p. 83, CA1/1/19, p. 406, CA1/1/20, p. 363, CA1/1/21, pp. 757–8, CA1/1/22, pp. 260–1 and 269, CA1/1/27, p. 486, CA1/1/33/1, pp. 466–7, and CA1/1/38, p. 272; DCA, BCMB, vol. 11, 10 March 1570, vol. 13, 20 October 1574, and vol. 19, 18 February 1597; FCA, B/KDY/2/1/3, f. 197r. See too *The Perth Guildry Book, 1452–1601*, ed. M.L. Stavert (Edinburgh, 1993), p. 346, and *Compt Buik of David Wedderburne*, pp. 71–2.

107 *Perth Guildry Book*, pp. 159–60, 189–90, 195, 206–7, 212–13 and 221–2; *Compt Buik of David Wedderburne*, pp. 53, 132 and 142–3; *The Gild Court Book of Dunfermline, 1433–1597*, ed. E.P.D. Torrie (Edinburgh, 1986), pp. 70–1, 82, 84 and 110; ACA, CA1/1/8, pp. 905–6, CA1/1/9, pp. 778 and 780, CA1/1/11, p. 636, CA1/1/12/1, p. 169, CA1/1/12/2, p. 489, CA1/1/13, pp. 96–7, CA1/1/14, p. 181, CA1/1/18, pp. 490–1, CA1/1/21, pp. 787–8, CA1/1/22, pp. 48–9, CA1/1/24, pp. 160–1, 168, 230 and 421, CA1/1/26, pp. 70–1, 145 and 218, CA1/1/27, pp. 20 and 489–90, CA1/1/28, pp. 312, 315–16, 335, 337–8, 397 and 534–5, CA1/1/32, pp. 533–4 and 575, CA1/1/33/1, p. 400, and CA1/1/38, pp. 315–16; DCA, BCMB, vol. 18, 17 September 1595, and PBD, vol. 11, f. 99r; EL, BCBE, vol. 2, p. 88; ECA, SL234/1/1, f. 27v; AA, B6/11/1/3, ff. 465v-6, B6/11/2, ff. 400–1r, and B6/12/2, p. 146; SCA, SBC37/1/2, 25 November 1546 and 20 May 1549; ELAC, B30/9/2, ff. 44r, 54r, 56v, 61v, 62r and 93r; NRS, B51/1/1, pt 1, f. 31r.

108 ACA, CA1/1/32, pp. 220–1, and CA5/1/3, 3 June 1587.

do witht his merchandreice and free money thairof as he did witht his awin', but it was accepted by the court that this phrase had been 'put in the said merchand bill interlynit' by the defender, without the pursuer's consent. In a similar case the pursuer admitted that he had authorised the defender to trade with his goods in the way he traded with his own, yet he also complained that the defender was failing to account for the proceeds, 'conform to the use of marchandis betwix marchand and marchand'.[109] If one way to avoid controversy over the contents of a merchant bill was to have it drafted in the form of an indenture, with 'the tane half' given to the travelling merchant and 'the toder half' kept at home, another might have been to have the bill recorded publicly.[110] However, when it was objected in another case raised before the bailies of Aberdeen that 'the wreting producit is nocht sufficient, bot ane messive bill, and aucht nocht to be admittit in respeck the same is nocht attentik', the pursuer insisted that 'ane missive bill betwix marcheand and marcheand is sufficient'.[111] In fact, examples of merchant bills have not been found either in protocol books or anywhere else in the burgh records.[112] It is beyond doubt, though, that they were widely used, albeit sometimes with the designation 'bills of factorie', since the travelling merchants were often referred to as 'factouris'.[113] For example, one entry that was made in a protocol book, written in Ayr, recorded the willingness of a merchant to make 'compt, rekning and payment' to another for the proceeds of trade with goods he had sent overseas, 'imployit according to his directioun and bill of factorie'.[114]

Some burgh authorities insisted that only burgesses with experience of buying and selling wares should be appointed as factors, not mariners, who were thought to 'have no perfection of knowledge to doe the same'.[115] Nevertheless,

---

109 ACA, CA1/1/20, pp. 142–3.

110 ACA, CA1/1/15, pp. 653–4.

111 ACA, CA1/1/27, p. 186. The objection was raised by a procurator with a university degree.

112 DCA, PBD, vol. 21, ff. 38v-9r, comes close, since a merchant was providing someone with goods to sell in foreign markets on his behalf, requiring him to account for his dealings there, but actually he was arranging for his son to acquire experience in business, not appointing a factor for a particular voyage.

113 ACA, CA1/1/8, p. 18, CA1/1/11, p. 636, CA1/1/15, pp. 655, 662 and 701–2, CA1/1/19, pp. 4–6, CA1/1/22, pp. 497–8, 608 and 654, CA1/1/24, pp. 26, 330 and 332, CA1/1/27, p. 323, CA1/1/30, p. 683, and CA1/1/38, p. 418; DCA, BCMB, vol. 5, 8 June 1560, vol. 8, 14 January 1564, vol. 10, 6 and 8 October 1568, vol. 13, 1 July 1575, and vol. 14, 26 February 1580; AA, B6/11/2, f. 221v; SCA, SBC37/1/2, 24 January 1547; ELAC, B30/9/2, f. 161r; PKCA, B59/12/4, ff. 31v, 116, 118–19, 121-4r, 125r, 127v-8, 129v, 134r, 135 and 141v-2r.

114 NRS, B6/1/1/1, f. 450r.

115 *Gild Court Book of Dunfermline*, pp. 70, 107, 111 and 145; *Burgh Laws of Dundee, with the History, Statutes and Proceedings of the Guild of Merchants and Fraternities of Craftsmen*,

many of the factors appointed were masters. In an action raised before the bailie court of St Andrews, for instance, a 'merchant bill' was produced to show that a master had been commissioned to take hides 'to Deip or Newhavin, and to have sauld the samyn thair conforme to the merkat for the tyme'.[116] In the normal way, the pursuer complained that the defender would make neither 'compt, rakning nor payment' of the proceeds of the sale of the goods 'without he be compellit'. In another case, in which the merchant bill showed that a factor had been commissioned to buy malt in Orkney and sell it in Bergen, he was ordered to pay the pursuer not the amount of profit he made but the amount he would have made had he done what was intended, 'conforme to his promeis and indentour foirsaid, and according to use of merchandreis'.[117] Other entries in the court books indicate more generally that a factor was expected to conduct business 'as merchand dois to merchandis', to fulfil 'his cuir and duety as factoure' or to manifest 'the diligense of ane just factour'.[118] If it was a factor's fault that goods or money were not brought home securely, he was expected to reimburse his principal, but it was the principal who bore 'the aventure of the sie'.[119] If loss was sustained through shipwreck, enemy action, piracy or confiscation, as long as it was not 'be ony occasioune, defect or negligence' of the factor, the principal had to bear the loss.[120] A case heard by the bailie court of Edinburgh was concerned with a commission given by one merchant to another, 'being boun to Flanders', to take goods with him, sell them on arrival and use the proceeds of the sale to buy other goods of specific types, 'as is contenit particularlie in his merchand bill, delyverit to him to that effect'.[121] When the pursuer did not receive goods the defender had bought in Flanders, he raised an action for 'compt, rakning and payment', but the court accepted the defender's explanation that he had sold the pursuer's goods 'according to the directioune gevin to him', had spent the money he was paid 'upon suamekle mercheandice as the

---

ed. A.J. Warden (London, 1872), pp. 118 and 121; DCA, MBBC, vol. 1, p. 3, and GBD, f. 11; NRS, B34/11/1, p. 1.

116 SAUL, B65/8/1, f. 28r.

117 DCA, BCMB, vol. 13, 19 March 1574.

118 ACA, CA1/1/10, pp. 211, 214, 221 and 226, and CA1/1/23, pp. 153 and 326; DCA, BCMB, vol. 5, 27 May 1560.

119 ACA, CA1/1/9, pp. 151, 154, 164, 171, 182, 230, 239, 249–50 and 597, CA1/1/29, p. 808, CA1/1/36, p. 267, and CA5/1/4, 26 July 1595; AA, B6/11/2, f. 69; NRS, B21/8/3, f. 256r. Cf. *Gild Court Book of Dunfermline*, p. 67, where any fault on the factor's part was unstated.

120 ACA, CA1/1/12/2, p. 507, CA1/1/25, p. 546, CA1/1/26, p. 52, and CA1/1/27, pp. 165, 172, 176, 179, 186, 188, 190, 194, 197 and 625–6; AA, B6/12/2, pp. 147 and 246. See too ACA, CA1/1/32, pp. 513–15, and CA1/1/33/1, pp. 237–8, 240–5, 248–52, 254–6 and 265.

121 ECA, SL234/1/3, pp. 795–8.

samyn wald extend to', had 'packit the samyn with his awin merchandreis', and had sent it home to Scotland, only to discover on his return that 'the schip was perischeit'. He had then made two journeys to England to visit the site of the wreck and search for the goods, all of which had disappeared, 'except ane small quantitie thairof, recoverit be his greit deligence and without ony fault to him'. The defender was now prepared to give the pursuer the part of the recovered goods 'pertening to him, he payand to him ane pairt of his expenssis in traveland twyse to Ingland for recovering of the samyn and careing of the samyn be land'. It was a common enough feature of the other actions of count, reckoning and payment considered here for the principal to be required to reimburse expenses reasonably incurred by the factor. There are also entries in the council register of Aberdeen in which reference is made to payment of a 'merchand fie' to a factor.[122] Although these entries are few and far between, and nothing comparable has been found in the records of any other burgh, it could be that merchants were willing to accept responsibility for each other's goods because they normally received a fee. Alternatively, the motivation could have been a belief that one good turn would be reciprocated with another, or that it was beneficial to acquire a reputation for amiability and reliability. No evidence whatsoever has been found of a factor being promised, let alone receiving, a share of the profits he made on someone else's behalf.

In a case heard by the bailie court of Inverness, in which one merchant claimed to have received money from another on the understanding that he would buy salt on his behalf and send it home to him on his 'awin ventour', the other merchant swore to the contrary that 'thai war pertenaris, pairt and pairt lyke, in winnyng and tynsall of the said salt', and that the accidental loss of some of the salt should therefore be shared between them.[123] An example of the type of 'pactioun or conditioun' the second merchant appears to have had in mind can be found in a protocol book written in Edinburgh, in which it was stated that one merchant, who was about to travel on a ship and had received money from another to purchase 'vitallis', was 'content to be partiner' with him, and that he would bring goods he purchased back to Leith 'apon baith the parties aventur and expens'.[124] Many other entries in the burgh records refer to merchants shipping goods that they had acquired 'amangis thame as partinaris'.[125] While the significance of the word 'partinaris' is not immediately

---

122 ACA, CA1/1/12/2, p. 866, CA1/1/19, pp. 45–6, CA1/1/20, pp. 63–4, CA1/1/27, pp. 264–5 and 699, CA1/1/36, pp. 478–9, and CA5/1/5, 16 February 1597.

123 HAC, B1/1/2, f. 443r.

124 *Protocol Book of John Foular*, vol. 3, pp. 231–2.

125 *Gild Court Book of Dunfermline*, p. 124; ACA, CA1/1/11, pp. 521 and 535, CA1/1/19, pp. 45–6, CA1/1/20, pp. 63–4, CA1/1/21, pp. 70–1 and 649, CA1/1/22, p. 573, CA1/1/23, p. 98, CA1/1/26,

apparent from every entry if read in isolation, when the entries are all read together it becomes quite clear that people who owned cargoes jointly were viewed in much the same way as people who owned ships jointly.[126] In essence they were 'pairtismen', as an alternative (though less common) label expressed it.[127] Another word found in the records with the same basic meaning is 'dailismen', which simply substituted the Germanic 'dail' for the Romance 'pairt'.[128] While the significance of the word is again not always obvious from individual entries, when taken together the entries show that 'dailismen' were people who chartered whole ships or parts of them.[129] Owners sometimes let their ships out in 'dailis' as opposed to 'hyris', a practice known as 'dailisfaring', the effect of which was to put the 'dailismen' in the position of the owners, with duties to cover the costs of voyages, and rights to profit from them, in proportion to their 'dailis'.[130] The 'partinaris' who shipped cargoes jointly, and the 'dailismen' who replaced joint owners of ships, were carefully distinguished from the people who loaded separately owned goods onto ships they had not chartered, who were referred to not only as 'merchandis' or 'frauchtismen', but sometimes as 'collegis' or 'complices'.[131] These words seem at times to have

pp. 701–2, CA1/1/27, pp. 209, 300 and 303, CA1/1/31, p. 598, CA1/1/35, pp. 394–5, CA1/1/36, p. 612, and CA5/1/5, 14 September 1596; DCA, BCMB, vol. 4, 21 May 1557, vol. 11, 10 October 1569, vol. 12, 16 July 1573, and vol. 14, 16 November 1575; DAC, WC4/10/2, p. 398; HAC, B1/1/2, f. 58r; AA, B6/11/3, f. 238; ECA, SL234/1/4, 25 March 1591; NRS, B9/1/1, f. 20v, and B19/1/1, 2 February 1573.

126 An important difference is that the partners who shipped cargoes together agreed with each other to do so. No evidence has been found of one partner selling his share in a cargo to someone else.

127 ACA, CA1/1/20, p. 75; DAC, WC4/8, f. 121v. See too ACA, CA1/1/20, pp. 368, 371, 374, 378–9, 407 and 410.

128 *Dictionary of the Older Scottish Tongue*, vol. 2, pp. 3–4 and 60.

129 *Court Book of the Regality of Broughton and the Burgh of the Canongate, 1569–73*, ed. M. Wood (Edinburgh, 1937), p. 195; ACA, CA1/1/18, p. 308, CA1/1/12/1, p. 167, ACA, CA1/1/13, pp. 428 and 441, CA1/1/14, p. 606, CA1/1/27, p. 582, and CA1/1/32, pp. 394–5; DCA, BCMB, vol. 3, 23 August 1553 and 13 July 1554, vol. 4, 29 July 1556 and 4 August 1557, vol. 6, 26 February, 2, 12–13 and 18–19 March 1562, vol. 7, 18 November 1562, vol. 9, 30 October 1566, vol. 10, 8 June 1569, vol. 11, 5 March 1571, vol. 12, 17 June 1572 and 17 June 1573, and vol. 13, 14 January 1575; SAUL, B10/8/6, pp. 526–7; NRS, B19/1/1, 30 October 1571, and B21/8/3, f. 36v.

130 ACA, CA1/1/19, p. 265, CA1/1/24, p. 469; DCA, BCMB, vol. 5, 24, 27 and 30 January and 4 August 1559, vol. 6, 26 January and 7 and 20 November 1562, vol. 11, 17 March 1570, vol. 12, 8 February 1572, vol. 14, 3 July 1579, vol. 15, 28 April 1581, vol. 16, 11 February 1583, and vol. 17, 19 January 1592; SAUL, B10/8/6, pp. 56–7; NRS, B21/8/2, f. 20r, B21/8/3, f. 36v, and B51/1/1, pt 1, f. 34r.

131 ACA, CA1/1/11, pp. 146–7 and 551–2, CA1/1/13, p. 215, CA1/1/20, pp. 446–7 and 450–1, CA1/1/21, pp. 469, 472–3, 619, 787–9, 793, 807, 812 and 826, CA1/1/24, pp. 181 and 341, CA1/1/29, pp. 462, 470, 481, 487–8, 491, 787 and 789, CA1/1/30, p. 165, CA1/1/32, pp. 497–8, CA1/1/34/

been used interchangeably, but the word 'complices' was also used more specifically to signify people on whose behalf goods were being brought home by factors.[132] In these terms, the question in the Inverness case outlined at the beginning of this paragraph was whether the merchant who had provided money for the purchase of salt was a 'complice' of the merchant who had travelled abroad or was his 'partinar'.[133] The question mattered because the risk of accidental loss of goods was evidently borne exclusively by a 'complice' but collectively by 'partinaris'.

The question may also have mattered in other ways. When a master claimed freight in Aberdeen from five merchants who had promised it would be paid 'be thame and thair complices', one of the merchants objected that the other four 'war nocht present, and he was bot ane, and mycht nocht, nor wald nocht, do na thing withtout his pertinaris'.[134] The five merchants do not appear to have been partners in the sense defined in the previous paragraph, and the word was never used again in ten further entries relating to the case. It may have been used in the first entry because partners were expected to consult each other when engaging in litigation and colleagues or complices were not. Certainly, while masters often raised actions against 'merchandis' or 'frauchtismen' as a group, or were pursued by one person 'in nayme and behalf of the merchands and frauchtismen', no evidence has come to light that merchants were expected to litigate in consultation with their 'collegis' or 'complices'.[135] On the other hand, no corroborating evidence that partners were required to do so has been found either. When merchants do appear to have shipped cargoes as 'partinaris', or to have chartered ships as 'dailismen', they were sometimes said to be bound 'conjunctly and severaly, ane as all and all as ane'.[136] In contrast, the 'collegis' who entered into charter parties with masters or owners

---

1, pp. 448 and 455–7, and CA5/1/2, 17 April 1581; DCA, BCMB, vol. 5, 27 August 1560, vol. 14, 9 December 1577, and vol. 15, 26 August 1580, and PBD, vol. 1, ff. 136v-7r; FCA, B/CUL/1/1/1, p. 161; NRS, B21/1/1, f. 51r.

132 The distinction is drawn fairly clearly, for example, in ACA, CA1/1/20, pp. 133–5, 139–41, 150–2 and 154–6. Efforts were made to restrict the number of colleagues involved in voyages (*Acts of the Parliaments of Scotland*, vol. 3, p. 42; Records of the Parliaments of Scotland, 1567/12/71; *Gild Court Book of Dunfermline*, p. 125; ACA, CA1/1/10, p. 32).

133 The same question was raised in AA, B6/12/2, pp. 243–4.

134 ACA, CA1/1/13, pp. 495–8, 502, 504–5, 508, 510 and 515, and CA1/1/14, p. 38.

135 ACA, CA1/1/12/1, pp. 407–8, CA1/1/13, pp. 417–18, CA1/1/20, pp. 88–9, and CA1/1/34/1, p. 448 and 455–7; DCA, BCMB, vol. 12, 13 January 1574. *Cf.* the entry mentioned at n. 56 above.

136 ACA, CA1/1/10, p. 323, and CA1/1/19, pp. 123–4 and 134; DCA, BCMB, vol. 11, 22 September 1570; DAC, WC4/9/2, f. 171r. The phrase 'all as ane and ane as all' also appears in ACA, CA1/1/12/2, pp. 480–1, but the nature of the relationship between the merchants is less clear there.

at the same time were only ever said to be liable 'ilk ane for thair awin pairt, corrispondand to thair guids that thai promyttit to lay in the said schip', or 'respective for thair awin partis'.[137] Less predictably, no entry has been found to impute joint and several liability to complices with the factors who shipped goods on their behalf. The normal practice was for a factor to pay freight to a master or owner before seeking 'relief' of his expenses from his complice, and he might also compensate his complice for loss of or damage to his goods before seeking relief from the master or owner.[138] When a master protested before the bailies of Aberdeen that the 'merchandis and frauchtismen' of his ship were slow in paying freight, one of the merchants protested in response that the master ought not to demand freight directly from his complices.[139] When it was proved before the bailies of Ayr that a master who had failed to carry goods as promised in a contract made with a merchant had reached a settlement with the merchant, an action raised by his complice was dismissed.[140] In another case heard in Aberdeen a procurator with a university degree argued that just as the skipper he was representing 'haid na place to persew na man for his fraucht bot his frauchtismen', so too 'na uther man suld have place to persew the said skipar for ony geir left out of his schip', yet the bailies did allow 'ane of the complices of the frauchting' to pursue an action.[141] The burgh courts did not insist that only the parties to contracts could pursue each other.[142] After a merchant complained that he had not received goods a factor was meant to buy 'witht the fre money of certane merchandreis quhilk he deliverat to him, conforme to the merchand bill', and the factor proved that he had 'coft the said weiris and schippit the same', the bailies of Aberdeen advised the principal that he would have 'to seik the awnars of the said schipe' for delivery of the goods.[143] It may have made a difference that the goods had been 'merkitt' with the symbol used by the principal rather than the agent.[144]

---

137 ACA, CA1/1/17, pp. 573–6 and 579–80, CA1/1/18, pp. 29 and 123, CA1/1/26, pp. 669, 692, 695–8 and 700, CA1/1/28, pp. 784 and 788–9, and CA1/1/32, p. 311; SAUL, B65/8/1, 3 December 1591.

138 ACA, CA1/1/10, pp. 345, 348–9 and 390, CA1/1/20, pp. 446–7 and 450–1, CA1/1/21, pp. 106 and 190, and CA1/1/27, pp. 141, 247 and 371.

139 ACA, CA1/1/15, pp. 17–18 and 52.

140 AA, B6/11/2, ff. 472v-3r, 494 and 497v-8r.

141 ACA, CA1/1/20, pp. 150–2 and 160. A threatened appeal to the lords of council does not appear to have been followed up.

142 ACA, CA1/1/9, pp. 721–4, 768–9, 771 and 775–7, CA1/1/13, pp. 303, 305–6 and 315, CA1/1/15, p. 44, CA1/1/16, pp. 707 and 710–12, CA1/1/28, p. 313, and CA1/1/34/1, p. 383; DCA, BCMB, vol. 3, 6 August 1551 and 26 March 1552; SAUL, B10/8/5, pp. 468–9.

143 ACA, CA1/1/26, pp. 218 and 222.

144 *Cf.* ACA, CA1/1/19, p. 104, and AA, B6/11/3, f. 44v.

In a case heard by the bailies of Kirkcaldy a merchant had appointed a mariner as his factor to sell 'salt att the markitt to his behuiff and resaive payment thairoff'.[145] Since he was not at liberty to leave the ship when it reached Holland, the mariner had asked one of the merchants on board to sell the salt for him, which he had done. The principal raised an action against the seller of the salt, who claimed to have acted within the authority given to the factor, 'quia potest quis per alium quod potest facere per se ipsum'. Although the principal was represented by a university graduate, he did not object that *delegatus non potest delegare*, and it was instead agreed that the seller would raise an action on the principal's behalf against the buyer of the salt. The emphasis in all these cases appears to have been on finding a workable solution to the problem encountered.[146]

2.2 *Sharing Cargoes in Theory*

A couple of cases in which one merchant had assumed responsibility for another's goods can also be found in the surviving act book of the central admiralty court. That the first was heard in an admiralty court is understandable enough as one of the owners of a ship was pursuing a merchant for the payment of freight.[147] The defender had 'schippit upoun his retinew in the said schip thre tun of wad' on behalf of another merchant, from whom he had received a sum of money to cover his share of the freight due, yet the defender was found liable to pay only his own share. Why he was not considered liable to pay the whole amount is not made clear in the record, nor is there any indication of what the pursuer was expected to do to recover the remainder. In the second case a merchant claimed 'compt, reknyng and payment' from the owner of a ship who had promised to buy wine in Bordeaux with money he was given, 'like as utheris merchandis quha past thair at that tyme warit thair money upoun wynis'.[148] The defender was ordered to pay the pursuer the amount of money given to him along with 'alsmekile proffett' as would have been made by 'gude faithfull factouris' with the same amount. It may have been hearing cases like these that led Alexander King to write briefly in his treatise on maritime law about the people known to the Roman lawyers as *institores*. In providing an introductory account of the people typically found on board ships he observed

---

145 FCA, B/KDY/2/1/2, ff. 6, 8r, 9r, 14v, 15v, 16v, 21v-2r, 24v-25 and 28v.

146 The procurators with university degrees referred to in this paragraph appear to have studied the liberal arts at Scottish universities, where they may possibly have acquired some basic knowledge of the civil law.

147 *Acta curiae admirallatus Scotiae*, pp. 212–13.

148 *Acta curiae admirallatus Scotiae*, pp. 33–5.

that 'passengers (*vectores*) are those who are on a ship at any time to be carried and transported, either alone or with their wares'.[149] The word *vectores* was used ambiguously in the Roman texts, sometimes to mean people who consigned goods for transportation, and sometimes to mean people who travelled on ships as passengers.[150] In noting that merchants who accompanied their wares on a voyage would be *vectores* in both senses King moved towards the subject of his next sentence, which stated that 'those persons are called managers (*institores*) who are put in charge of shipping', to which he added that 'nowadays we call them factors (*factores*)'. He may to some extent have been thinking of the factors living overseas to whom goods were sometimes sent, or who were sometimes instructed to buy goods and send them home.[151] The word *institores* had been used by the Roman lawyers with primary reference to people put in charge of running businesses, but its usage was fairly broad, and one text stated that if a shop keeper were to send a servant somewhere to buy goods and send them back, the servant would be *in loco institoris*.[152] In the language of Roman law, *vectores* who not only travelled with their wares but also shipped goods for other people, sold them and sent home other goods bought with the proceeds of the sale would at the very least have been *in loco institorum*, though whether this would have been of much interest to Scottish merchants is doubtful. Their practice of entrusting each other with goods or money to employ in foreign trade is less likely to have been influenced by familiarity with Roman law than by awareness of practice elsewhere. For several centuries use had been made in Mediterranean countries of a broadly similar arrangement known as *commenda*, which appears to have owed more to Islamic or Jewish than Roman influence.[153] By the sixteenth century variants of the same arrangement were in widespread use in northern Europe and must have been known to Scots involved in overseas commerce.[154] As reference is

149 *Alexander King's Treatise on Maritime Law*, pp. 70–1.

150 The former usage is found in the *Digest* title on the *lex Rhodia de iactu* (D.14.2), and the latter in the title on the edict *nautae, caupones, stabularii* (D.4.9).

151 *Cf.* M. Mollat, *Le commerce maritime normand a la fin du Moyen Age* (Paris, 1952), pp. 425–7.

152 D.14.3.3-5 and 14.3.18, and J.4.7.2; J.J. Aubert, *Business Managers in Ancient Rome: A Social and Economic Study of Institores, 200 BC – AD 250* (Leiden, 1994).

153 J.H. Pryor, 'The Origins of the *Commenda* Contract', (1977) 52 *Speculum* 5, and 'Mediterranean Commerce in the Middle Ages: A Voyage under Contract of *Commenda*', (1983) 14 *Viator* 133. See too Q. van Doosselaere, *Commercial Agreements and Social Dynamics in Medieval Genoa* (Cambridge, 2009), pp. 63–78.

154 S. Ogilvie, *Institutions and European Trade: Merchant Guilds, 1000–1800* (Cambridge, 2011), pp. 334–6; A. Amend-Traut, 'Legal Structure of Early Enterprises: From *Commenda*-like Arrangements to Chartered Joint-Stock Companies (Early-Modern Period)', in

made to the institution in the *Consolato del mare*, it is a little surprising that nothing was said about it in William Welwod's abridgement of all sea laws.[155]

When the university doctors of law sought to accommodate the *commenda* contract within the legal theory they taught, it tended to be treated as a species of partnership.[156] There were texts in which the Roman jurists had not only recognised the possibility of one partner to a valid contract contributing capital while another contributed labour, but had also mentioned the example of one partner investing capital in a voyage on which only another partner would be exposed to danger.[157] The theory extracted from these texts was easily reconcilable with contemporary practice because the parties to a *commenda* contract agreed both to contribute either capital or labour and to share between them any profits the travelling partner made, as the Roman jurists would have insisted. However, given that no evidence has come to light of the factors who took goods or money abroad from Scotland sharing in any profits they made, the influence of continental practice would appear to have been limited to the broad idea of entrusting a factor with the means to engage in overseas trade.[158] It may have been for this reason that King preferred to think of factors as *institores* rather than *socii*, perhaps believing that those who earned a fee had been appointed under contracts of hire, or (more plausibly) that they received *honoraria* under contracts of mandate.[159] If sharing in profits would have provided factors with an additional incentive to make as much money as possible, there were other motivations, and they were at least required by legal

D. De ruysscher, A. Cordes, S. Dauchy and H. Pihlajamäki (eds), *The Company in Law and Practice: Did Size Matter? (Middle Ages-Nineteenth Century)* (Leiden, 2017), p. 63, at pp. 65–70.

155 *Collection de lois maritimes antérieures au XVIIIe siècle*, vol. 2, pp. 200–1 and 311–14; *Consulate of the Sea and Related Documents*, pp. 122 and 197–9.

156 Cinus de Pistorio, *In Codicem et aliquot titulos primi Pandectarum tomi, id est Digesti veteris, doctissima commentaria* (Frankfurt, 1578), pt 1, f. 257v (ad C.4.37.1); Baldus de Ubaldis, *Consilia sive responsa*, 6 vols (Venice, 1580), vol. 3, f. 132r (n. 453, inc. 'Committere pecuniam alicui mercatori ad partem percipendam honesti lucri utrum est licitum et permissum'); Nicholas de Tudeschis (alias Panormitanus), *Commentaria in quartum et quintum Decretalium* (Lyons, 1527), f. 172v (ad X 5.19.19). These passages are examined in Pryor, 'Origins of the *Commenda* Contract', pp. 13–19.

157 D.17.2.5.1 and 17.2.29, J.3.25.2 and C.3.37.1.

158 As always, it needs to be remembered that the surviving records are incomplete, and that it remains possible that some factors did share in the profits they made. On the other hand, the evidence that principals bore the risk of accidental loss of purchased goods seems consistent with the exclusion of the factor from the profits, as does the distinction drawn between partners and complices.

159 A. Watson, *Contract of Mandate in Roman Law* (Oxford, 1961), pp. 102–11.

custom to come up to the standard of diligent factors.[160] Merchants regularly reminded each other of this, carefully reserving the language of partnership for their description of situations in which several people acquired a cargo or chartered a ship together. Here too there may have been some broad influence from continental practice, originating in the Mediterranean *compagnia* contract.[161] Although it was not always obvious whether a *commenda* or *compagnia* contract had been formed, the crucial difference was that the parties to the latter were reckoned to be liable jointly and severally for debts incurred by any of them in conducting partnership business.[162] As has been observed, it is only with reference to the merchants described as partners that joint and several liability is ever mentioned in the Scottish records.[163] These merchants included the joint owners of ships discussed in the first section of this essay, whose shares were freely transferable to others, but this was as close as practice in sixteenth-century Scotland came to the creation of joint-stock companies, which were already developing elsewhere.[164]

Although the joint and several liability of the partners in a medieval *compagnia* had made them very different from the partners in a Roman *societas*, the civil lawyers had gone some way towards reconciling commercial practice with the theory they taught.[165] Much had been made of a *Digest* text in

---

160 *Cf.* S. Talbott, *Conflict, Commerce and Franco-Scottish Relations, 1560–1713* (London, 2014), pp. 39–43. See too M.H.B. Sanderson, 'The Edinburgh Merchants in Society, 1570–1603: The Evidence of their Testaments', in I.B. Cowan and D. Shaw (eds), *The Renaissance and Reformation in Scotland: Essays in Honour of Gordon Donaldson* (Edinburgh, 1983), p. 183, at pp. 190–2.

161 M.M. Postan, *Medieval Trade and Finance* (Cambridge, 1973), pp. 68–74; R.S. Lopez, *The Commercial Revolution of the Middle Ages, 950–1350* (Cambridge, 1976), pp. 73–7. Examples can be found in R.S. Lopez and I.W. Raymond, *Medieval Trade in the Mediterranean World* (New York, 1955), pp. 185–211.

162 J. Puttevils, *Merchants and Trading in the Sixteenth Century: The Golden Age of Antwerp* (London, 2015), pp. 95–8; B. Van Hofstraeten, 'Historiographical Opportunities of Notarized Partnership Agreements Recorded in the Early-Modern Low Countries', in H. Pihlajamäki, A. Cordes, S. Dauchy and D. De ruysscher (eds), *Understanding the Sources of Early-Modern and Modern Commercial Law: Courts, Statutes, Contracts and Legal Scholarship* (Leiden, 2018), p. 119, at pp. 134–40.

163 As ever, it needs to be remembered that this could be an accident of survival rather than an aspect of practice.

164 Lythe, *Economy of Scotland in Its European Setting*, pp. 126–7; P. Spufford, *Power and Profit: The Merchant in Medieval Europe* (London, 2002), pp. 22–5; H. Hansmann, R. Kraakman and R. Squire, 'Law and the Rise of the Firm', (2006) 119 *Harvard Law Review* 1333, at pp. 1376–9.

165 P.G. Stein, 'The Mutual Agency of Partners in the Civil Law', (1958–9) 33 *Tulane Law Review* 595, remains a classic study and is of particular interest to students of Scottish legal history.

which it was observed that if several partners were to appoint a manager to run their business (*institorem praeposuerint*), and if their manager were to incur a debt, each one of the partners could be pursued for the whole debt incurred (*in solidum unumquemque conveniri posse*).[166] The appointment of the manager was important because the Roman courts had been prepared to allow people who dealt with an *institor* to pursue his principal, and a principal to pursue a third party who dealt with his *institor*, even though in principle only the *institor* and third party were bound by any contract they had entered into.[167] The doctors appear to have had this text in mind when they read two others in surprising ways. The first, which stated that a partner could not alienate more than his share of partnership property, was taken to mean that no one could do so fraudulently or without the consent of the others, on the assumption that partners in general mandated one another to trade with their common property (*alienationem invicem mandare videantur*).[168] In the interpretation of this text attention was also drawn to statements about the joint and several liability of Roman bankers (*argentarii*), and it was concluded that every partner was in effect the *institor* of the others.[169] In a humanist treatise published at the end of the sixteenth century it was pointed out that bankers had been treated as a special case in Roman law, that an exceptional rule had been mistakenly generalised, and that the general rule in Rome was that partners could not be pursued on each other's contracts.[170] The point was in fact made in relation to the other text that had been read in a surprising way by the medieval doctors, which stated that one partner was not liable for debts contracted by another unless they related to money put in a common chest (*in communem arcam*).[171] The first step was to interpret *communis arca* as a reference to 'common property' more broadly, and to infer more broadly still that one partner would be bound by another's debts as long as they were

166 D.14.3.13.2. On partnerships in Roman maritime commerce see A. Marzano, 'The Personal Infrastructure of Maritime Trade', in P. Candy and E. Mataix Ferrándiz (eds), *Roman Law and Maritime Commerce* (Edinburgh, 2022), p. 57.

167 A. Kirschenbaum, *Sons, Slaves and Freedmen in Roman Commerce* (Jerusalem, 1587), pp. 89–121.

168 *Digestum vetus*, p. 1156 (gl. 'Alienare' ad D.17.2.68.pr.).

169 D.2.14.25.pr., 2.14.27.pr., 4.8.34.pr. and 16.3.8, and N.136; Cinus de Pistorio, *In Codicem et aliquot titulos primi Pandectarum tomi, id est Digesti veteris, doctissima commentaria*, pt 1, f.193r (ad C.4.2.9); Baldus de Ubaldis, *Tomus secundus in Digestum vetus* (Lyons, 1541), f. 103r (ad D.17.2.68.pr.).

170 Iacobus Cuiacius, *In responsa Aemilii Papiniani recitationes* (Frankfurt, 1595), pp. 115–16, also citing *Ad Herennium*, tr. H. Caplan (Cambridge, MA, 1954), 2.13.19.

171 D.17.2.82.

incurred *in utilitatem communem*.[172] It was then concluded that one partner would be liable for another partner's debts as long as they were contracted *in communi nomine*, or *in nomine societatis*, and not *in proprio nomine*, for it was then that he would appear to have contracted under a mutual mandate.[173] Although it was correctly pointed out at the end of the sixteenth century that the text did not actually say that one partner would be liable to a third party for another's debts, and probably meant only that one would be liable to reimburse the other for debts he incurred in relation to shared funds, it had previously been accepted that in commercial practice one partner would oblige another 'when he contracts in the name of the partnership, although the law is different if he acts in his own name'.[174] It has been seen that the Scottish merchants who were designated partners did sometimes act 'in name and behalf of' each other, yet no evidence has been found of the adoption of partnership names, either by merchants who bought and shipped cargoes together, or by merchants who chartered ships, or for that matter by merchants who owned ships jointly.[175] Furthermore, merchants who were merely 'collegis', and who were never described as partners or as being jointly and severally liable, also acted 'in name and behalf of' each other.[176] The impression given is that merchants in Scotland had picked up certain patterns of speech while they were abroad but were unaware of the attempts that had been made to reconcile the practices to which they applied with the theory taught in the law schools.[177]

---

172 *Digestum vetus*, p. 1161 (gl. 'In communem' and gl. 'Arcam' ad D.17.2.82).

173 Baldus de Ubaldis, *Tomus secundus in Digestum vetus*, f.103v (ad D.17.2.82), and *Consilia sive responsa*, vol. 2, f. 36v (n. 120, inc. 'Quidam Antonius Zaninus et Francisus fratres steterunt'). On the significance of the words *nomen societatis* see too Baldus de Ubaldis, *Super Codicem commentaria*, 7 vols (Lyons, 1539), vol. 4, f. 101v (ad C.4.37 rub.).

174 Benvenuto Stracca, *De mercatura seu mercatore tractatus*, p. 139. Scottish notaries could have found styles for partnership contracts in the handbooks available (*Ars notariatus*, pt 2, f. 41v; Marcilletus, *Doctrinale florum artis notariae*, f. 59; Speluncanus, *Artis notariae tempestatis huius speculum*, f. 245), but neither there nor in the fuller treatises by Jean Papon (*Premier tome des trois notaires*, pp. 127–44, and *Trias judiciel du second notaire* (Lyons, 1575), pp. 262–7) would they have found a discussion of the liability of partners to third parties.

175 For an inexpert but interesting discussion of how far the Roman jurists moved in the direction of recognising artificial personality see G. Poitras and F. Willeboordse, 'The *Societas publicanorum* and Corporate Personality in Roman Private Law', (2021) 63 *Business History* 1055.

176 The Scots word clearly had nothing to do with the Roman term *collegiati*, meaning members of a *collegium*. See generally W. Broekaert, 'Partners in Business: Roman Merchants and the Potential Advantages of Being a *Collegiatus*', (2011) 41 *Ancient Society* 221.

177 Stein, 'Mutual Agency of Partners in the Civil Law', ends by discussing the reception of the civil law theory of partnership in Scotland from the later seventeenth century onwards, focusing in the familiar way on decisions of the lords of session and treatises written by

If the civil lawyers had provided some sort of explanation for the joint and several liability of merchants involved in *compagnia*-style arrangements, their belief that partners implicitly mandated each other to act as *institores* made it difficult to explain why merchants involved in *commenda*-style arrangements were not liable in the same way. After all, in arrangements of the latter type the travelling merchant received an explicit mandate to contract on behalf of the merchant who remained at home, and in Roman law, as King pointed out in his treatise, a third party who contracted with an *institor* could 'choose to sue the manager under the rule of the civil law or the principal instead under the equity of the praetor'.[178] King proceeded to draw attention to one situation in which the manager and principal might not both be liable to action, making reference to a decision of the *parlement* of Paris reported by Jean Papon.[179] A 'facteur' appointed to trade on behalf of a merchant had received goods 'pour et au nom dudit marchand', and had issued a written promise to pay for them within six months. Because he had promised payment *nomine proprio*, he was found to be liable to pay the seller himself, but Papon had wondered whether the decision was entirely consistent with views expressed by Bartolus de Sassoferrato and Paulus de Castro, both of whom had suggested that an agent might cease to be liable after he left office.[180] King remarked that this suggestion seemed 'aequissimum' to him, and agreed that only principals should be held liable after agents had settled their accounts.[181] This move towards a theory of 'direct agency' might have helped at least to distinguish temporary arrangements between merchants from continuing relationships between partners, but it would not have explained why only partners were said to be jointly and severally liable in the records of the burgh courts, which remains puzzling since it was not only partners who were permitted to sue or be sued on contracts made by other people.[182] To conclude that merchants

---

learned lawyers. Whether the development of the law in Scotland owed something to earlier commercial practice is not considered. See too L. Macgregor, 'Partnerships and Legal Personality: Cautionary Tales from Scotland', (2020) 20 *Journal of Corporate Law Studies* 237.

178 *Alexander King's Treatise on Maritime Law*, pp. 72–3.

179 *Recueil d'arrests notables des cours souveraines de France* (Paris, 1584), vol. 1, pp. 389–90.

180 Bartolus de Sassoferrato, *Opera omnia*, 5 vols (Lyons, 1523), vol. 1(2), ff. 93r (ad D.14.1.1.17), and 94v (ad D.14.3.20); Paulus de Castro, *Opera omnia*, 4 vols (Lyons, 1548), vol. 1(2), f. 107r (ad D.14.1.1.15).

181 *Alexander King's Treatise on Maritime Law*, pp. 72–3.

182 *Cf.* W.M. Gordon, *Roman Law, Scots Law and Legal History: Selected Essays* (Edinburgh, 2007), p. 54; and see too L. Macgregor, 'Empire, Trade and the Use of Agents in the 19th Century: The "Reception" of the Undisclosed Principal Rule in Louisiana Law and Scots Law', (2019) 79 *Louisiana Law Review* 985, at pp. 1028–36. It may again be wondered what

and mariners had adopted the expression 'joint and several liability' without understanding what it meant would fail to take account of its careful confinement in the context of overseas trade to partners alone, and would in itself be a misunderstanding of how the use of language develops.[183] The expression clearly signified something to its users, which seems to have been that the relatively loose relationships that existed between factors and complices or between colleagues, who had enough collective identity to be permitted to pursue or defend actions together, were different from the closer relationships that existed between various types of partners, who shared profits, expenses and risks with each other.[184] The allocation of risks between factors and complices was one other topic that came to the attention of the central courts. After goods belonging to a merchant in Edinburgh were seized by pirates before a merchant from Dysart could trade with them overseas, the sister of the Edinburgh merchant, who happened to be married to 'ane of the scrybis of counsall', raised an action as executrix of her deceased brother against the factor before the lords of council.[185] On her behalf, a report on 'the commoun custome of merchants' was obtained from the provost and bailies of Edinburgh, who maintained that a factor would be liable for any loss of goods unless he made it clear when he shipped them that he was doing so on someone else's 'aventure'. On the factor's behalf, a report was obtained from other merchants in Dysart, who maintained that it would make no difference whether he had shipped the lost goods 'in his awin name' or 'in that merchandis name', which seems more consistent with the evidence examined in the first part of this section.[186] As the advocates who appeared in the action – Henry Balfour, John

effect the practices of merchants may have had on the development of the law of agency in the College of Justice. The enquiry obviously needs to be broadened out beyond cases with a maritime dimension.

183 The expression was widely used in other contexts. When caution was provided for the payment of someone else's debt, for instance, the parties were clearly understood to be liable jointly and severally in the sense that either could be pursued for payment. In contrast, when more than one procurator was appointed to appear on someone else's behalf in court, they appear to have been liable jointly and severally only in the sense that they had a shared responsibility to their client. Both these usages are extremely common in the records of both the burgh and the central courts.

184 *Cf.* S.C. Yeazell, *From Medieval Group Litigation to the Modern Class Action* (New Haven, 1987).

185 NRS, CS4/4, CS7/114, f. 267v, and CS7/117, f. 301. Andrew Simpson kindly drew attention to the first item listed.

186 It is possible that a different practice was followed in Leith, from which records have not survived, although the suggestion made by the Edinburgh authorities that the custom they outlined 'aucht and sould be kepit be all' hints at a degree of innovation. The council register of Edinburgh unfortunately sheds no light on the matter.

Moncrieff and John Sharp – may have been aware, Benvenuto Stracca had referred in his treatise on commercial law to a *consilium* dealing with the question raised, in which one of his former teachers at Bologna had cited many civil law sources in support of the opinion that a principal would bear the risk of accidental loss of any goods shipped on his behalf, though he had added that much would depend on the *consuetudo mercatorum*, as Stracca himself emphasised.[187] As the Dysart merchant was permitted to prove his allegations of fact, it may be that his account of the relevant custom was accepted by the lords of council, but how the case was ultimately determined is not known.

3 Joint Enterprise in Making Voyages

When a ship was provided for a voyage, perhaps by joint owners, and a cargo was provided for transportation, perhaps by merchants acting on behalf of others, the remaining requirement before departure was the employment of a crew. In observing that the medieval ship was a 'community of interest', Neville Williams was thinking especially of the absence of exact distinctions between the roles, rights and responsibilities of merchants and mariners, all of whom might invest capital in a voyage (albeit to differing degrees), and all of whom might participate in the making of decisions relating to navigation.[188] It was seen in the fourth essay in this collection that mariners employed in Scotland continued throughout the sixteenth century to exercise rights of 'portage', shipping goods on their own account along with those provided by merchants, in accordance with legal customs established since time immemorial.[189] It was seen too that a novel attempt was made to involve mariners in the redistribution of losses sustained at sea by merchants or shipowners precisely because they were all involved in a joint enterprise. It is not the aim of this section to revisit the employment of mariners, or for that matter to investigate cases of general average, which is a subject of such importance that it deserves separate treatment in another essay.[190] Leaving that subject aside for the time being,

187 Stracca, *De mercatura seu mercatore tractatus*, p. 167; Petrus Parisius, *Consilia*, 4 vols (Venice, 1580), vol. 1, f. 105v (n. 47, inc. 'Intentio Dominorum Hyeronimi et Io. Baptis. de Piperariis satis et sufficienter probata').

188 *Maritime Trade of the East Anglian Ports*, pp. 206–7.

189 One way in which Scottish mariners may have participated in decision making was touched on at the end of the third essay.

190 In effect, this essay provides a broader setting for the enquiry conducted in the next essay into how issues of general average were dealt with in Scotland.

this section aims to consider some other ways in which relations between shipowners, merchants and mariners were affected by the law.[191] As disputes arising between these types of parties tended to fall within the category of 'seafaring causes' over which the admiralty courts claimed an exclusive jurisdiction in the second half of the century, when many of the cases discussed in the first part of the section were heard in the burgh courts, it is even more difficult than usual to know whether an accurate impression is being formed of how these disputes were generally handled.

3.1 *Sharing Voyages in Practice*

It has already been seen in passing in this essay that when disputes arose between shipowners and merchants, the connection between them was often formed by a master employed by the owners, who might himself own part of the ship.[192] One action raised in Dundee, for instance, related to a charter party formed between a master, 'witht the consent of his pertineris and awneris', and the defender, 'and utheris his collegis', before a voyage to Dieppe, where goods had been restored by the crew 'to thair merchands and factours'.[193] On another occasion, after a master sold some equipment from a ship, one of the owners appeared before the same court, 'for himself and the remanent awneris of the schip', and prohibited the master from acting in future 'by consent of his awneris', which suggests that he would otherwise have been able to make contracts without their express consent.[194] Many other entries in the burgh court books indicate that when contracts were made between masters and other people, whether or not the master owned a share of the ship or had obtained express consent from its owners, the owners were not only expected to relieve the master of any liabilities he incurred, but might also be pursued directly by the people with whom he had dealt.[195] To take two further examples from Dundee,

---

191 In 1542 a master appeared before the bailies of Aberdeen 'for him and his complices', meaning the members of his crew, in connection with an 'indentour' or 'chartir partye' that required coal to be delivered to 'smythtis' in the town (ACA, CA1/1/17, p. 220). It appears that the coal was being sold to the smiths, and attention focuses in this section on problems arising from contracts of affreightment, but it is of some interest that in this situation the master was effectively the crew's factor.

192 Ordinary mariners might also own shares of ships, although very little evidence of this has been found (DCA, BCMB, vol. 18, 10 October 1595).

193 DCA, BCMB, vol. 5, 16 September 1558.

194 DCA, BCMB, vol. 13, 13 May 1575.

195 ACA, CA1/1/30, p. 694, and CA1/1/38, pp. 530–1; DCA, BCMB, vol. 6, 12 and 31 August 1562, vol. 7, 2, 16, 18 and 20 November 1562, vol. 13, 6 September 1574, vol. 14, 8 April 1579, vol. 16, 12 April 1583, vol. 17, 23 July and 6 August 1593, vol. 18, 29 July and 5 August 1594, vol. 19, 15 January, 11 February and 20 October 1596, vol. 20, 11 October 1597 and 4 October 1598, and

the owners of a vessel acknowledged in one case that they were answerable to a merchant for goods their master had undertaken to transport there from another port.[196] Conversely, a merchant was ordered in another case to pay the owners of a ship in which his goods had been brought home from Norway the freight he had promised to their master.[197] Although it was the master who tended to enter into contracts with merchants, it was the clerk of the ship who tended to receive goods and freight from them, and to account to the owners at the end of the voyage.[198] When a clerk was pursued in Aberdeen by merchants who had not received goods after a ship arrived there, an inquest found that it was not his responsibility to make the cargo available, 'bot allanerlie compt and rakning quhat was doun witht it, nor yit na uther clerk of ane schip'.[199] Three years later, when a clerk offered an owner 'compt and raknyng' for a voyage, he claimed that any liability for damage to goods must 'ly to the skipperis charge', and that he must therefore be allowed to deduct in his accounts a sum he had been required to pay as compensation to a merchant by the court of the conservator in Veere.[200] In fact, he was then sued successfully in Aberdeen by other merchants, perhaps because he was identified as more than the clerk of the ship, 'beyng pertinar and clerk thairof, and having the haill cuyr and gyding under God of the samyn for the tyme', though another case has also been found in which someone described simply as 'the clark of the said schip' was pursued for failing to return goods.[201] Whether or not clerks were responsible as such for the safe delivery of goods, there were other cases in which they raised actions against merchants for the payment of freight promised to masters, and not always 'in name of the awnaris'.[202] In another case heard in

vol. 21, 14 and 21 December 1599, and PBD, vol. 16, ff. 33v-4r. It was different if a master had exceeded express directions (DCA, BCMB, vol. 15, 11 April 1581; AA, B6/11/1/2, ff. 266v and 280v-1r; NRS, B6/1/1/1, ff. 455v-7r).

196 DCA, BCMB, vol. 11, 13 and 17 March 1570.

197 DCA, BCMB, vol. 19, 15 September and 5 October 1596.

198 ACA, CA1/1/12/2, p. 494, CA1/1/14, p. 620, CA1/1/16, pp. 627–8, 637–8, 641, 644, 670, 741, 744, 750 and 880, and CA1/1/36, p. 198; DCA, BCMB, vol. 4, 21 May, 5 June and 18 September 1556, vol. 9, 20 February 1568, vol. 13, 17 November 1574, vol. 14, 20 February (in a sequence of entries misplaced after 5 February 1580) and 7 March 1579, and vol. 17, 11 and 21 June 1591, and PBD, vol. 1, f. 109r.

199 ACA, CA1/1/14, pp. 584–5 and 587–9, and CA1/1/15, p. 82.

200 ACA, CA1/1/15, pp. 660, 668. 682–4, 703–4, 710–11, 717, 719–20, 722–3 and 725, and CA1/1/16, pp. 51, 54, 61, 67, 71, 86, 90–1, 96, 122 and 453.

201 ACA, CA1/1/15, pp. 655, 662, 666, 669–70, 682, 685, 689–90, 692–4, 698–9, 701–2, 704 and 715, CA1/1/16, pp. 122, 124, 131, 136, 140, 157 and 172, CA1/1/32, pp. 533–4, and CA1/1/33/1, p. 528.

202 DCA, BCMB, vol. 4, 27 January and 5 February 1556, vol. 8, 6 October 1564, vol. 9, 19 March 1568, vol. 16, 6 February 1583, and vol. 17, 1 November 1591. Of course, freight could have

Aberdeen a clerk who had not only paid mariners the wages promised to them by the master, but had also paid them for use of their space in the hold of the ship, was found to have exceeded his authority and to be unable to include the expense in his accounts, but he was then permitted to pursue the mariners for reimbursement of the money they ought not to have received.[203]

In a case heard in Dundee near the end of the century the clerk of a ship was ordered, 'for himselff and in name of the remanent company and equipage of the said schipp the last vayage maid be hir fra Spane to this port', to compensate a merchant for the loss of wine, 'spilt in the said companeis defalt'.[204] In the third essay in this collection it was seen that when goods were damaged in transit it often was alleged to have been the fault of the crew, and that masters and owners were reckoned to be liable for damage only if fault was established.[205] In an unusual case heard in Aberdeen, in which a merchant complained about goods being damaged 'in the marenellis and skiparis defalt', the owners protested that 'quhat the merchandis of the said schip ouptenit one the said skipar and marenellis of the said schip suld cum one the said skipar and marenellis and nocht one the awnaris'.[206] It was replied that the owners should be held liable, 'becaus the said awnaris at the frauchtin of the same schip promittit to the merchandis and frauchtismen ane sufficient schip, sufficient skipar, steirsman and marenellis'. It was also seen in the third essay that it was typical for charter parties to contain such a promise but not to contain a clause providing separately for damage to goods, which was taken to be governed by customary norms.[207] As well as being accused of mishandling cargoes, mariners were also accused of committing other wrongs, including damage to or theft from other ships, and violence to or slander of other crews.[208] In some cases the members of a crew were found liable to compensate pursuers for losses inflicted on them, 'ilk ane of thame for thair awin pairtis'.[209] After a

been promised directly to the owners (ACA, CA1/1/8, p. 966, and CA1/1/37, p. 270). In one case a clerk chartered a ship (ACA, CA1/1/12/1, pp. 77 and 82–3), but no evidence has been found of clerks contracting with merchants on behalf of owners.

203 ACA, CA1/1/34/2, pp. 850–1, 863, 874, 876, 881, 883, 890 and 892.

204 DCA, BCMB, vol. 20, 8 July 1597.

205 See the penultimate paragraph of the essay especially.

206 ACA, CA1/1/12/2, p. 503.

207 See the opening sections of the essay especially.

208 *Extracts from the Council Register of Aberdeen*, vol. 2, pp. 132–3; ACA, CA1/1/8, p. 626, CA1/1/25, pp. 153–4 and 187, CA1/1/26, p. 94, CA1/1/27, p. 83, CA1/1/31, p. 134, CA1/1/36, pp. 389 and 535, and CA1/1/38, p. 923; DCA, BCMB, vol. 6, 14 January 1562; ECA, SL1/1/5, f. 30r; SAUL, B65/8/1, 8 December 1590 and 12 January 1591; NRS, B9/11/1, f. 93v.

209 ACA, CA1/1/34/1, p. 466; DCA, BCMB, vol. 17, 6 September 1592, and vol. 19, 10 September 1596; SAUL, B10/8/4, p. 159.

mariner was convicted in Aberdeen of theft from a ship, and a local woman of receiving the stolen goods, the merchants insisted that the master who had employed the mariner 'aucht to answer for his servandis deid', in response to which the master provided a guarantee that they would receive compensation for their loss.[210] There were several cases in which masters or owners who had compensated the victims of wrongs committed by mariners claimed relief from the guilty parties.[211] However, responsibility was not always accepted for the misconduct of mariners. In Dundee, after a master acknowledged that a gun on his ship had been removed from another vessel, the owners of the ship appeared and 'denyit expreslie that ever thai or ony of thame knew of the intromissioun of the said pece of ordinance, or yit gaf command or assistit to the taking thairof, and thairfor, be ressoun the samyn wes done by thair knawledge and command, thay allegit that thai suld nocht be bunde'.[212] The master agreed to pay the pursuer the value of the gun, and 'all the awnaris, sua mony as knew the away taking of the said pece', were ordered to relieve the master.[213] On the other hand, mariners were not found to be personally liable when they had committed a wrong at the master's command.[214]

It was not only the misconduct of mariners that could prevent a voyage from running according to plan. After the master of a Danish ship died during a voyage to Aberdeen, and its owners sent an agent there to recover the ship, the bailie court 'decernit all haveand entres to the said schip to compeir', requiring the agent when they did so to provide a guarantee that merchants who had made payments for the 'sustentatioune and furnesing' of the crew during the voyage, and for the 'reparatioune of the said schip and marenaris expenssis' after its arrival, would receive recompense.[215] On another occasion 'the merchandis that had gudis in Jakis schip' were required to contribute to the cost of a puncheon of wine that was taken from the hold for the crew's sustenance 'on the cost of Ingland quhen the lakit vittellis', each merchant paying a part 'corisponden to the quantite and avale of his gudis'.[216] In another

210 ACA, CA1/1/27, p. 174.

211 ACA, CA1/1/13, p. 493, and CA5/1/5, 23 May 1597; DCA, BCMB, vol. 4, 3 February 1557, vol. 5, 23 August 1560, vol. 13, 3 September 1574, and vol. 18, 27 May and 19 June 1594, and 17 March 1595; FCA, B/KDY/2/1/4, f. 14r; NRS, B9/11/2, f. 75.

212 DCA, BCMB, vol. 14, 6 July and 6, 13 and 25 September 1576. The word 'by' means 'without' here, as at n. 194 above.

213 For two similar findings see DCA, BCMB, vol. 11, 31 January 1571, and vol. 13, 22 March 1574.

214 ACA, CA1/1/20, pp. 304–5 and 315.

215 ACA, CA1/1/28, pp. 238, 248–9, 271 and 278–9.

216 ACA, CA1/1/14, p. 195. The record is not entirely clear, but it seems that the master had been 'adjugit afor' to pay for the wine.

case expenses incurred 'for the savite of the haile gudis' were similarly distributed among all the merchants who stood to benefit.[217] When perishable goods were returned to merchants at the end of a voyage, and it was then discovered that not enough had survived to provide them all with the amounts consigned, those who had already received the full amounts they expected were required to return some goods for redistribution among the others.[218] Similarly, when goods recovered from a shipwreck in England were sold there, the money received was distributed among the merchants in proportion to the amounts of cargo they owned.[219] Both merchants and the owners of a ship were required to contribute towards salvage costs after the ship ran aground in Orkney, the merchants in proportion to the quantities of cargo they had provided, the owners in proportion to their shares in the ship.[220] Merchants and owners also shared the expense of sending a representative abroad to seek redress for acts of piracy, and in one instance they invited mariners 'to be participant of his expenssis and laubouris as the rest, and gif thai refuis, that thai be nocht perticipant of ony thing that he recoveris'.[221] An exceptional case arose after a ship from Bristol was despoiled in Scotland and the English government intervened to ensure that compensation was paid.[222] The master who paid the compensation then tried to recover contributions from the 'dalismen' who had financed his voyage in Crail, but they objected that 'thair is na sic pracktique usit, nor na dalismen ather in Sanctandrois or the costsyd that payis ony sic contributioun'.[223] The master insisted that 'sic compositioun was payit nocht only in this burght, bot in all uthers places quhair ony maisters off schippis ar convictt for the said spoliatioun, and thairfor desyrit the defendars to be compellit to pay thair parte thairoff, conforme to thair dalis'. Not surprisingly, the bailies felt unable to reach a decision without further information.[224] Another case was raised after a ship was 'stayit and arrestit be the customer of

217 ACA, CA1/1/13, pp. 178–9. See too ACA, CA1/1/32, pp. 151 and 179, and DCA, BCMB, vol. 17, 12 August 1590.

218 ACA, CA1/1/8, pp. 1060–1, and ACA, CA1/1/9, pp. 282–3 and 291.

219 DCA, PBD, vol. 11, ff. 70v-1r.

220 DCA, BCMB, vol. 16, 18 February 1583.

221 ACA, CA1/1/25, pp. 372–3, and NRS, B51/10/2, f. 33r.

222 *Acts of the Privy Council of England*, 46 vols, ed. J.R. Dasent, E.G. Atkinson, J.V. Lyle, R.F. Monger and P.E. Penfold (London, 1890–1964), vol. 8, pp. 17, 150, 161–2, 185, 197, 208, 216 and 296; *Calendar of State Papers Relating to Scotland and Mary, Queen of Scots, 1547–1603*, 13 vols, ed. J. Bain, W.K. Boyd, H.W. Meikle, A.I. Cameron, M.S. Giuseppi and J.D. Mackie (Edinburgh, 1898–1969), vol. 4, pp. 640 and 683, and vol. 5, pp. 5, 27 and 58; *Extracts from the Records of the Burgh of Edinburgh*, 1st ser., vol. 4, pp. 18–20 and 40.

223 SAUL, B10/8/6, pp. 56–7.

224 SAUL, B10/8/6, p. 63.

the Pheir, to be escheytit for non payment in dew tyme of the said schippis custums'.[225] Because the customer 'wes extreyme in the persuit of the haill schipe and guids', and merely 'for eschewing of grytar inconvenientis and saiftie of the schipe and guids', an innocent merchant had paid the sum demanded, and the bailies of Aberdeen agreed after his return there that the other merchants, along with the owner, master and clerk of the ship, should make him 'recompensatioune and payment of the said soume of ressoune and guid consciens'. In most of these cases it seems to have been assumed by those involved that when losses were sustained or costs were incurred in the course of a voyage, it was appropriate for them to be redistributed among the participants, either to the extent that they had benefited, or in proportion to their investments in the enterprise.

Sometimes adjustments had to be made to the expectations of parties before ships reached their intended destinations. In another case heard in Aberdeen the master of a Stralsund ship, sailing from Danzig, reported that a steersman he had employed, 'eftir that he had guydit the schip withtin the havin, past away to Dundy as ane mercheand, withtout his knawlege or consent', adding that he had originally been 'myndit to haf had his said schip to Dundy witht the marcheandis guidis withtin the same'.[226] It was then agreed between the master and three 'burgessis of Dundy and Couper, frauchtismen off the said schip', that it should be unloaded 'withtin this hevin, and the saidis marcheandis to pay the skipper the fraucht of thair guidis withtin xv dayis eftir the dait of thir presentis'. When another burgess of Dundee claimed that one of the freightsmen was obliged to have goods he had shipped on his behalf carried on to Dundee, the freightsman swore under oath that 'he maid na promess nor wes nocht astrickit to fuir guidis and geir to Dundy, nor na uther speciall port in Scotland, bot quhar his awin come and wes lossit'.[227] While the master and merchants in this case may never actually have agreed to sail to Dundee, there are others in which an agreement reached during a voyage did change the terms of the contracts initially concluded.[228] In a case raised in Dundee a master reported that he had agreed to transport a cargo of fish to Dieppe, that despite his best

225 ACA, CA1/1/23, pp. 182–3. The location was also identified as 'the towne of Campheir in Zeland'.

226 ACA, CA1/1/22, p. 606.

227 ACA, CA1/1/22, p. 609.

228 ACA, CA1/1/26, pp. 650, 669, 692, 695–8, and 700, CA1/1/27, pp. 301, 305, 315, 318, 326, 328, 331–2, 335, 338, 340–1, 346–7, 351, 353, 355, 375, 378–9, 399, 414, 419, 422–3, 425, 428–9, 437, 443–4, 446–8, 450, 452–3, 458, 484, 494–5, 530, 549–51, 568–9, 650, 751–2, 756–7 and 762–4, and CA1/1/28, pp. 8–10, 12, 24, 91, 272 and 277–8; DCA, BCMB, vol. 5, 5 July 1560.

efforts he had been driven back repeatedly 'be contrary wyndis', and that most of the merchants, aware not only that 'the tyme and the merkat of the saidis fysches ar doin in the realme of Franche', but also that the outbreak of war with England meant there was a risk of 'invasioun of innemeis', had agreed with him that he should instead sail north to Königsberg.[229] Two merchants who were not party to the agreement were told by the bailies that they must either 'consent to the transporting of thair geir' to the new destination or else 'resaif the samyn at this port'. It was not always possible for an agreement to be reached even by a majority. After another ship put into Aberdeen on its way to Dundee, the master swore before the bailie court that 'he come in the havin allanerlie for the savite of the merchandis gudis and schip, and nocht for na prejudice nor hurt to thame, and was in purpose to loise the gudis for savite of tham, and mend his said schip, and thairefter to fuir the saidis guidis about to Dunde one his awin bodum after sche had bene mendit'.[230] The court decided that it would be better for the master to deliver the goods in Aberdeen and for the merchants to pay the freight promised to him there.[231] In another case heard in Aberdeen an inquest found that a master 'aucht nocht to pas with his schip and merchand gudis to the port of Sanctandrowis for the gret pestilance now ringand thar, albeit he was bundin to his merchandis be ane chartour party to the port of Sanctandrowis quhen the towne was clein without pest, for as thai understand, the law wald compell na man to pas wulfullie to his awin deid'.[232] There were other cases too in which courts made adjustments to contracts that had been 'frustrat' by unexpected events.[233]

3.2 *Sharing Voyages in Theory*

Both William Welwod and Alexander King suggested in their treatises on maritime law that the relations between shipowners, masters and merchants were best understood in terms of the relationship in Roman law between *exercitores* and *magistri navium*.[234] After defining the owner of a ship in the

229 DCA, BCMB, vol. 5, 18 March 1559.

230 ACA, CA1/1/12/1, pp. 258–9, 261–3 and 272.

231 For some similar rulings see ACA, CA1/1/18, pp. 235 and 245, CA1/1/21, pp. 70–1, 78 and 107; DCA, PBD, vol. 1, f. 94.

232 ACA, CA1/1/12/2, pp. 689–90, 697–701, 703, 705–6, 709–12 and 773. This ruling is noted in K. Jillings, *An Urban History of the Plague: Socio-Economic, Political and Medical Impacts in a Scottish Community, 1500–1650* (Abingdon, 2018), p. 83.

233 ACA, CA1/1/13, pp. 403–4 and 425, CA1/1/32, pp. 11–13, and CA1/1/38, pp. 625–6.

234 Although the strange collection of sea laws that James Balfour took to derive from the laws of Wisby had mentioned the *actio exercitoria* (*Habakkuk Bisset's Rolment of Courtis*, 3 vols, ed. P.J. Hamilton-Grierson (Edinburgh, 1920–6), vol. 2, p. 253), he chose to neglect this entry, though he did reproduce another that went beyond the rule that a hired ship

way mentioned previously, Welwod went on to say that 'the outredder is he to quhome, as dealsman for ane voyage or ane langer tyme during the setting of the schip, the proffeitis and commodities thairof chieflie redoundis, lyk as the maister is he to quhome the haill charge and cuir of the haill schip is committit'.[235] Welwod adopted here the definitions of 'exercitor' and 'magister navis' found in the opening text of the *Digest* title on the *actio exercitoria*, giving the impression that the 'outredder' was a 'dealsman' as opposed to an owner, though he used the same word to cover both owners and charterers in the title he later devoted to 'the outredderis of schippis'.[236] As King observed, the *exercitor* was defined in the text as 'the person to whom all the proceeds and profits accrue, whether he is the owner of the ship or has leased it from the owner'.[237] Both authors believed that the master ought to be the person on board a ship who was most expert in navigation, but they also knew that in practice this was not invariably the case, which was why the laws of Oleron and Wisby had required the master to take advice from the crew before making important decisions.[238] The crucial point was that in Roman law a merchant could choose between suing the master with whom he had contracted or the *exercitor*, even though the owner or charterer of the ship was not directly bound by the contract.[239] On the other hand, both authors observed that the *exercitor* could only sue the merchant if the master assigned his right of action to him, subject to an exception developed in relation to the suppliers of grain to the city of Rome, which had been generalised by the medieval doctors to cover any case in which a master had become insolvent.[240] Welwod originally

---

could be sublet (*The Black Book of the Admiralty*, 4 vols, ed. T. Twiss (London, 1871–6), vol. 4, p. 267; *Collection de lois maritimes antérieures au XVIIIe siècle*, vol. 1, p. 469) to say that 'the first hyrer' might sometimes have recourse against 'the secund hyrers gudis' (*Practicks of Sir James Balfour*, vol. 2, p. 627).

235 *Alexander King's Treatise on Maritime Law*, p. 352, preserved in his *Sea-Law of Scotland*, sig. B1.

236 D.14.1.1.1 and 15.

237 *Alexander King's Treatise on Maritime Law*, pp. 62–3.

238 *Alexander King's Treatise on Maritime Law*, pp. 64–5 and 354; E.B.I. Frankot, 'The Scottish Translations of the *Rôles d'Oléron*: Edition and Commentary', in A.M. Godfrey (ed.), *Stair Society Miscellany Eight* (Edinburgh, 2020), p. 13, at p. 28; *Black Book of the Admiralty*, vol. 4, pp. 268–9. Both authors hoped that the admiralty courts would raise standards, though Welwod dropped this point in his *Sea-Law of Scotland*, sig. B4r.

239 *Alexander King's Treatise on Maritime Law*, pp. 138–43 and 365, and *Sea-Law of Scotland*, sigg. 7v-8r; P. Huvelin, *Études d'histoire du droit commercial romain* (Paris, 1929), pp. 168–76.

240 *Alexander King's Treatise on Maritime Law*, pp. 140–1 and 365, and *Sea-Law of Scotland*, sigg. B8v-C1r; *Digestum vetus*, p. 972 (gl. 'Extra ordinem' ad D.14.1.1.18); A.J.B. Sirks, *Food for Rome: The Legal Structure of the Transportation and Processing of Supplies for the Imperial Distributions in Rome and Constantinople* (Amsterdam, 1991), pp. 121–2.

remarked at this point that 'heir thay observe to persew upon the maisteris contract, as thay wer contracteris principall', which was more consistent with the relaxed practice of the burgh courts, where parties were often permitted to sue on other people's contracts in which they had an interest.[241] King made a different reference to local conditions when he remarked that 'the practice of shipmasters today is to substitute others, whose responsibility it is to receive things brought and carried onto the ship, and to compile an inventory of these things and give an itemised account, for which reason they are known colloquially as clerks'.[242] To justify the practice he connected it with a *Digest* text stating that a master was 'not only a person an *exercitor* appointed, but also anyone a master appointed'.[243] When Welwod wrote about the person, 'of auld and now neidfull, callit the clerk of the schip', he drew attention to detailed regulations of the office in the *Consolato del mare*, but he was no doubt told that these regulations were not followed in Scotland, and the passage was omitted from his printed treatise.[244] In the act book of the central admiralty court there is a case in which two merchants pursued both the master and the clerk of a ship for recovery of money they had paid to a mariner 'for his meit, clething and uthir necessaris expenssis' during a voyage, at the end of which the mariner had absconded.[245]

Summarising a text from the *Digest*, Welwod observed in his treatise that 'a merchant contracting with ane mariner that is not a maister, he sall haif na action therfoir against the outredder, except for a falt done be the mariner'.[246] King explained that if 'someone appoints a master, he permits contracts to be made with him, whereas if he employs sailors, he does not permit contracts to be made with them, though he ought to take care that they avoid negligence and deliberate wrongdoing'.[247] In a title concerned with the duties owed by

241 No evidence has been found of burgh courts agonising over the status of parties as *exercitores, institores* or anything of the sort (*cf.* G. Minaud, *Les gens de commerce et le droit à Rome* (Aix-en-Provence, 2011), pp. 293–5 and 307). Where burgh court practice may have been more in line with civilian theory was when owners were not found to be liable on contracts made contrary to express directions (n. 195 above; *cf.* D. Johnston, 'Suing the *Paterfamilias*: Theory and Practice', in J.W. Cairns and P. du Plessis (eds), *Beyond Dogmatics: Law and Society in the Roman World* (Edinburgh, 2007), p. 173, at pp. 179–83).

242 *Alexander King's Treatise on Maritime Law*, pp. 64–5.

243 D.14.1.1.5.

244 *Alexander King's Treatise on Maritime Law*, p. 363; *Collection de lois maritimes antérieures au XVIIIe siècle*, vol. 4, p. 321; *Consulate of the Sea*, pp. 31–2.

245 *Acta curiae admirallatus Scotiae*, pp. 134–6.

246 *Alexander King's Treatise on Maritime Law*, p. 365, and *Sea-Law of Scotland*, sig. B8v; D.14.1.1.2.

247 *Alexander King's Treatise on Maritime Law*, pp. 70–1.

masters to merchants and passengers, Welwod wrote about the quasi-delictual liability of the Roman *nauta* for thefts of or damage to property committed by mariners he had employed.[248] In doing so he struggled to disentangle the texts dealing with this kind of liability from others dealing with the liability of the Roman *nauta* under the praetorian pact of *receptum*, which is scarcely surprising in view of their confused presentation in the *Digest*.[249] It was *receptum* liability that dominated King's treatment of the subject, much of which was borrowed from Petrus Peckius' commentary on the *Digest* title *Nautae caupones stabularii ut recepta restituant*.[250] As he had explained, when the safekeeping of goods was undertaken (*salvum fore receperint*), the *exercitor* – or any one *exercitor* if there were several – was liable for their return in good condition unless they were lost through shipwreck or piracy (known as the *exceptio Labeoniana*).[251] Following the standard civilian interpretation, both King and Welwod observed that the *exercitor* was liable for a failure of *exacta diligentia*, or for *culpa levissima*, meaning that he was liable for failing to prevent anything from happening that could have been prevented by 'a very diligent person'.[252] They added that this form of strict liability was imposed because masters were generally considered to be untrustworthy, and prone to employing unreliable mariners, yet there is no evidence in the records of the burghs that masters were viewed in this way in sixteenth-century Scotland. Even in the unusual case mentioned earlier in which owners were said to be responsible for damage to goods because they had promised merchants a sufficient crew, it was alleged that the goods had been damaged 'in the marenellis and skiparis defalt'.[253] The understanding in the burgh courts appears to have been that

---

248 *Alexander King's Treatise on Maritime Law*, pp. 360–1, and *Sea-Law of Scotland*, sigg. B4v-5, drawing especially on D.4.9.6.1, 44.7.5.6 and 47.5.1, and J.4.5.3.

249 J.A.C. Thomas, 'Carriage by Sea', (1960) 7 *Revue Internationale des Droits de l'Antiquité* 489, and 'Juridical Aspects of Carriage by Sea and Warehousing in Roman Law', (1974) 32 *Recueils de la société Jean Bodin pour l'histoire comparative des institutions* 117, at pp. 133–42 especially.

250 *Alexander King's Treatise on Maritime Law*, pp. 126–37; Petrus Peckius, *Commentaria in omnes pene iuris civilis titulos ad rem nauticam pertinentes* (Louvain, 1556), pp. 1–60; *Digest*, 4.9.

251 L.-R. Ménager, '*Naulum* et *Receptum rem salvam fore*: Contribution a l'étude de la responsabilité contactualle dans les transports maritimes en droit romain', (1960) 37 *Revue historique de droit français et étranger* 177 and 385; D.S. Bogen, 'Ignoring History: The Liability of Ships' Masters, Innkeepers and Stablekeepers under Roman Law', (1992) 36 *American Journal of Legal History* 326.

252 G. Rossi, 'The Liability of the Shipmaster in Early-Modern Law: Comparative (and Practice-Oriented) Remarks', (2017) 12 *Historia et ius* 1, at pp. 6–16. Scholars of Roman law today prefer to talk about *exactissima diligentia*.

253 ACA, CA1/1/12/2, p. 503.

liability for damage to or the loss of goods was contractual but not strict.[254] There is a case in the act book of the central admiralty court, however, in which a master sought to avoid liability for the loss of goods by insisting that he had done 'his exact diligence' and that they had been 'tane be the Inglismen' with whom the Scots were at war.[255] Twenty years later a master appeared before the bailie court in Dundee to register a promise he had made to merchants to show 'his exact diligence' in transporting their goods, pointing out that he would not be liable if they were 'tane awa be invasioun of pirattis or utherwayis be schipwrak'.[256] What the bailie present thought of the promise is not made clear, but it does suggest that practice may to some extent have been changing, perhaps because the admiralty courts were taking the approach encouraged in the treatises written by Welwod and King.

Further evidence is provided by a case raised before the lords of council in 1592.[257] A charter party had been entered into for the transportation of goods belonging to merchants from Abbeville in a ship from Burntisland to Calais, Boulogne or Dunkirk, at the choice of the merchants, but the voyage had been disrupted by maritime raiders sailing out of Dunkirk. When the merchants sought to recover the profit the goods might have yielded had they been sold at their intended destination, the advocate Thomas Wilson argued on behalf of the owners and master of the ship that they had done 'thair exact diligence', but were 'nocht able to accomplische the said veyage for danger of thair lyfeis, thair schip and guids', adding rather strangely that the law did not require masters to answer for *casus fortuitus* or *vis maior*, but only for *dolus* or *culpa lata*. On behalf of the merchants the advocate Thomas Craig, who was at the time an admiral depute, answered that masters were 'astrictit nocht to do diligence bot to deliver', adding that since other ships had managed to reach the ports in question, the presence of the raiders had not rendered the voyage impossible.[258] The lords of council found the answer relevant, and after it was proved that the voyage could indeed have been completed, they ordered the master and owner to compensate the merchants for the loss of the profit they might have made by selling their goods. Fifty years earlier a passenger on a ship had

254 *Cf.* A. Wijffels, 'Vicarious Liability for the Carrier by River', (2007) 75 *Tijdschrift voor Rechtsgeschiedenis* 333, at pp. 341–2.

255 *Acta curiae admirallatus Scotiae*, pp. 151, 153–4, 156, 158, 162–5 and 168–70. An attempt was made at one stage to have the case remitted to a burgh court, perhaps because a different approach was taken there.

256 DCA, BCMB, vol. 15, 28 September 1581.

257 NRS, CS7/139, ff. 341–2r, and CS7/143, ff. 151v-2r and 247v-9.

258 NRS, CS7/139, ff. 1–2.

raised an action before the same court against another passenger, who had allegedly stolen goods from him during a voyage.[259] According to Welwod, 'the maister is not onelie haldin for his awin deid, his servandis and ecquippage, bot also for the deid of the passingeris, in sic sort that quhatever want or lois cumis ather be chance, falt or negligence, quhilk mycht haif bene eschewit, as be stouth or fyre, albeit na fraucht sould haif bene payit for ather geir or for passage, yit sould he refound the same'.[260] King explained more fully that while it was less than clear from the *Digest* texts that a master was liable for the wrongdoing of passengers, it was clear that an *actio de recepto* could be raised.[261] Perhaps the passenger who raised the action before the lords of council simply preferred to sue the other passenger, but it could be that *receptum* liability had not been recognised as part of the law at that time, even in the central courts. One other case heard by a central court deserves attention here. In 1572 a ship returning with a cargo of wine from Bordeaux to Aberdeen was ordered by the admiral to put in at Leith.[262] The master feared that his heavily laden ship was at risk of destruction in the harbour 'gif ony storme succeidis', and he was willing to unload and sell wine transported on his own account without going further, but the merchant who had shipped most of the cargo was insistent on continuing to Aberdeen, not least because he had shipped wine on behalf of 'sindry utheris marchantis of Abirdene', who expected to receive it there. The privy council, conscious that Aberdeen was in the hands of 'oure soverane lordis declarit traitouris, rebellis and conspiratouris', and confident that if the wine were sold in Leith, 'als greit proffeit sall redound thairof to the saidis awnaris as gif the same wer usit and sauld be thame at thair pleasour', ordered the ship to be 'loist' immediately, declared the merchant immune from any action by 'his partinaris' other than for their shares of the proceeds of the sale, and directed the master 'to diffeis to the awnaris of the saidis wynis the soume of x s. money of this realme of the fraucht of every tun of the samyn'.

The 1572 case shows that the privy council at least was prepared to make adjustments to the responsibilities of parties when their intentions were frustrated. King attempted to provide some justification for this type of intervention by suggesting that if a voyage were interrupted by piracy or shipwreck, the amount of freight due should be reduced.[263] He was alluding here to texts

259 NRS, CS7/1/1, ff. 245v-6.

260 *Alexander King's Treatise on Maritime Law*, p. 360; *Sea-Law of Scotland*, sig. B5r, drawing on D.4.9.1.8, 4.9.5-6 and 18.6.12.

261 *Alexander King's Treatise on Maritime Law*, pp. 132–5.

262 *Register of the Privy Council of Scotland*, vol. 2, pp. 128–9.

263 *Alexander King's Treatise on Maritime Law*, pp. 116–18.

about *remissio mercedis*, all of which were concerned with the tenancy of land, but which were taken to provide for the making of equitable adjustments to the responsibilities of parties who dealt with each other in good faith.[264] King's argument brings to mind Welwod's discussion – reviewed in the first section of this essay – of the equitable approach required in the handling of disputes between shipowners.[265] Both authors expected equitable adjustments to be made in the light of the written sources to which they drew attention, although Welwod referred to a wider range of sources than King. Neither author suggested that every contract of hire contained an implied *clausula rebus sic stantibus*, or that when it became impossible for a contract to be performed, recourse could be taken to the *condictio causa data causa non secuta*.[266] It is possible that in believing a master could not be forced to sail to a town infested with plague, the inquest in Aberdeen mentioned earlier was drawing on the former notion.[267] The record of the case is exceptional in stating that 'as thai understand, the law wald compell na man to pas wulfullie to his awin deid, as thai belevit', which appears to emphasise that the inquest was drawing on something other than the maritime law it was expected to know about and rely on in reaching its decision. Its members may have known that moral theologians and canon lawyers, and to a lesser extent civil lawyers, had accepted the force of an argument put forward by Cicero and Seneca that 'if you are to hold me to the fulfilment of my promise, all the circumstances must remain the same as they were when I promised'.[268] Seneca had given the example: 'suppose I have promised that I will go abroad, but word is brought that the way is beset with robbers'. Any recollection of this argument is bound to have been coupled with appreciation that it derived from a literate culture that rarely had any bearing on the handling of disputes between merchants and mariners in the burgh courts. The lawyers who wrote treatises about maritime law

264 P.J. du Plessis, *A History of Remissio mercedis and Related Legal Institutions* (Dordrecht, 2003).

265 *Alexander King's Treatise on Maritime Law*, p. 365, at n. 83 above.

266 E.M. Meijers, *Etudes d'histoire du droit*, 4 vols, ed. R. Feenstra and H.F.W.D. Fischer (Leiden, 1956–73), vol. 4, pp. 27–51; R. Feenstra, '*Impossibilitas* and *Clausa rebus sic stantibus*: Some Aspects of Frustration of Contracts in Continental Legal History up to Grotius', in A. Watson (ed.), *Daube noster: Essays in Legal History for David Daube* (Edinburgh, 1974), p. 77; D.-E. Philippe and A.M. Reijnen, 'La genèse de la *clausula rebus sic stantibus*', in A. Ruelle and M. Berlingen (eds), *Le droit romain d'hier à aujourd'hui: Collationes et oblationes* (Brussels, 2009), p. 267.

267 ACA, CA1/1/12/2, pp. 689–90, 697–701, 703, 705–6, 709–12 and 773, at n. 232 above.

268 Cicero, *De officiis*, tr. W. Miller (Cambridge, MA, 1913), 3.25.94–5; Seneca, *De beneficiis*, tr. J.W. Basore (Cambridge, MA, 1935), 4.35.2-3.

or represented parties in the central courts hoped to avoid vagueness and to enrich the resources of argument by drawing on written sources of law. Since they ascribed authority to these sources, they believed that solutions to novel issues found in them would augment existing law, and would avoid the vagueness of competing assertions of acceptable behaviour.[269] If it seemed to the lawyers that the merchants and mariners who formed their own legal customs were trying to make bricks without straw, even when straw was available in sources they neglected to read, it has been seen that a sufficiently stable edifice had been constructed in the burgh courts to accommodate the sharing of ships, cargoes and voyages, and reconstructing the edifice in accordance with a more learned design would not necessarily have been to the advantage of the merchants and mariners engaged in overseas trade. Allowing anyone with an interest in the performance of a contract to raise or defend an action reflected the reality that the merchants and mariners involved in a voyage had shared interests in its success, and it is by no means certain that any clarity offered by the technical distinctions the lawyers preferred to draw would have resulted in more just or effective solutions being found to the issues raised. The adjustments the burgh courts made to the responsibilities of parties after their expectations were frustrated by events may have lacked the rigour the lawyers would have preferred to import from their studies, but they reflected a belief merchants and mariners shared with lawyers that in these situations recourse needed to be taken from law to equity.[270] It is again by no means certain that looking for answers in written sources would have produced more satisfactory results than relying on a broad sense of fairness.[271]

269 The case in which parties argued about whether dalismen should contribute to an award of compensation is an obvious example of competing assertions of custom (SAUL, B10/8/6, pp. 56–7, at n. 223 above). The aim in that case was to work towards a consensus on acceptable behaviour.

270 Lord Cooper of Culross, *Selected Papers, 1922–54* (Edinburgh, 1957), pp. 124–32, traced the roots of a belief in Scotland that equitable solutions were needed back to treatises written by learned lawyers and decisions of the central courts in the early-modern period. It has to be wondered again whether commercial practice and the legal customs developed in the burgh courts had any influence on this development.

271 This essay has been building up to an answer to a typically perceptive question asked by Penny Tucker at the British Legal History Conference in St Andrews in 2019.

9

General Average in Scotland during the Sixteenth Century

Although the expression 'general average' does not appear to have been used in Scotland during the sixteenth century, a significant amount of evidence survives of losses sustained at sea being distributed among people involved in maritime ventures.[1] The evidence is of two main types. First, there are entries in the surviving records of burghs situated on the coasts in which reference is made to the practice.[2] Secondly, there are treatises written towards the end of the century in which the law governing maritime trade is discussed. Bringing these two types of evidence together is not entirely straightforward, for they reflect the rather different perspectives of merchants and mariners on the one hand, who were recognised as experts in commercial practice, and of professional lawyers on the other hand, who were more expert in the legal theory of the universities. As the legal treatises were written towards the end of the century, and the relevant entries in the burgh records were mostly made in earlier decades, attention will focus to begin with on the thinking of merchants and mariners.[3] In the first of three sections a descriptive account of the material found in the burgh records will be presented. In the second section attention will shift to the legal treatises, and an attempt will be made to trace connections between the practice outlined in the first section and the theory known to the lawyers. If an obvious problem will be to understand how far the merchants and mariners involved in practice may have been influenced in their

1 Of course, that no use of the expression has so far been found in contemporary evidence does not mean that it was never used. The word 'average' was certainly used on its own, meaning a charge, cost or expense.

2 The survival of these records has inevitably been uneven, and generalisation from them is accordingly unwise. For many burghs, court books covering just a few years have survived, while for others, no books have survived at all. Moreover, of the surviving books, some are more detailed and informative than others. The most valuable records happen to be those in Aberdeen, which not only cover the entire century but are also more elaborate than most of those found elsewhere. See now the first essay in this collection.

3 A treatise on maritime law was apparently written around the middle of the century, and by a writer who had not been instructed in legal theory at a university, but unfortunately it has not survived, and what the writer may have said about general average is not made clear by the references to his treatise found in the others, which all appear to have been written in the 1580s or at the beginning of the 1590s.

 | DOI:10.1163/9789004695009_010

thinking by the theory with which the lawyers were familiar, understanding how far the lawyers may have been familiar with the practice outlined in the first section will also be problematic. The evidence examined there will be drawn mostly from the records of bailie courts operated by the coastal burghs, yet by the time the legal treatises were being written an exclusive jurisdiction over 'seafaring causes' had been claimed for admiralty courts sitting around the country, from which scarcely any records happen to have survived.[4] In the third section tangential evidence of the handling of general average cases in the admiralty courts will be considered, and the relationship between the practice of the burghs and the theory of the schools will be reassessed. In conclusion, it will be asked whether the Scottish experience may shed any light on the development of general average and insurance elsewhere.

1 Scotting and Lotting in the Practice of Maritime Communities

On 27 July 1527 Alexander Rutherford appeared before the bailie court of Aberdeen, in his own interest and on behalf of several other merchants whose goods had been put in the hold of Guillaume Roquette's vessel for a voyage to France.[5] He complained that 'for gret stowag' further goods were being put 'on the ourloft', protesting that if goods needed to be jettisoned from the ship during the voyage, 'the gudes under the ourloft sall nocht scot nor lot with the gudes abuf the ourloft that happinnis to be castin'. Similar protestations were entered on half a dozen other occasions, often prompting the master of the vessel to add a protestation of his own, warning merchants whose goods were 'aboun the ourloft' either to remove them or else 'tak the aventour thairof'.[6] It is clear both from these entries and from other records that the word 'ourloft', though sometimes written as 'overlope', did not have the same meaning as the English term 'orlop'.[7] It did not mean the deck forming the floor of the cargo

4 The only surviving record is from the central court sitting in Edinburgh or Leith, and has been printed as *Acta curiae admirallatus Scotiae, 1557–62*, ed. T.C. Wade (Edinburgh, 1937). Not all the entries in the burgh records related to court actions, and some actions were heard in the bailie courts even after the admiralty courts assumed their exclusive jurisdiction, especially (as will be seen) in Dundee. The relationship between the different courts is now examined in the first essay in this collection.

5 ACA, CA1/1/9, p. 732.

6 ACA, CA1/1/8, pp. 1029–30, CA1/1/12/1, pp. 407–8, CA1/1/12/2, p. 529, CA1/1/15, pp. 89–90, 94, 96, and 278, and CA1/1/16, p. 784.

7 *The Register of the Privy Council of Scotland*, 14 vols, ed. J.H. Burton and D. Masson (Edinburgh, 1877–98), vol. 1, p. 281; *Calendar of the State Papers Relating to Scotland and Mary, Queen of Scots, 1547–1603*, 13 vols, ed. J. Bain, W.K. Boyd, H.W. Meikle, A.I. Cameron,

hold but rather a deck above the cargo hold, on which goods were sometimes stowed beyond 'the sufficient laidinge of the schip'.[8] The word 'aventour' was used to signify a 'risk' or 'hazard', but also an unfortunate occurrence – as in the phrase 'gif ony aventour hapins to cum upoun ony gudis aboun the ourloft' – or a risky enterprise – ships were sometimes called the *Aventour* or the *Ventourer*.[9] The expression 'scot and lot' was widely used in the Scottish burghs, as well as some English boroughs.[10] Deriving from Old Norse or Old English words meaning 'tribute' or 'tax' (in the case of 'scot' – as in 'he got off scot free') and 'share' or 'part' (in the case of 'lot' – as in 'he tended his allotment'), the expression as a whole was used when members of a community were required to contribute towards common burdens.[11] Indeed, a willingness to 'scot and lot' was frequently identified as a condition of admission to burgh membership.[12] While the expression had the predominantly negative significance of an obligation to make payments, it had the more positive connotation of participation in a project of mutual benefit to those involved.[13] When used with reference to

M.S. Giuseppi and J.D. Mackie (Edinburgh, 1898–1969), vol. 10, pp. 352–4; *Extracts from the Council Register of the Burgh of Aberdeen*, 2 vols, ed. J. Stuart (Aberdeen, 1844–8), vol. 1, pp. 331–3; ACA, CA1/1/14, pp. 12–13; SAUL, B65/8/1, f. 116r.

8 ACA, CA1/1/22, pp. 261–2. *Cf.* P. Kemp (ed.), *The Oxford Companion to Ships and the Sea* (Oxford, 1976), p. 618.

9 W. Craigie, A.J. Aitken, J.A.C. Stevenson, H.D. Watson, and M.G. Dareau (eds), *A Dictionary of the Older Scottish Tongue, from the Twelfth Century to the End of the Seventeenth*, 12 vols (Chicago, London and Aberdeen, 1931–2002), vol. 1, pp. 149–50.

10 *Dictionary of the Older Scottish Tongue*, vol. 3, pp. 878–9; J.A. Simpson and E.S.C. Weiner (eds), *The Oxford English Dictionary*, 20 vols (Oxford. 1993), vol. 14, pp. 685–6.

11 *The Perth Guildry Book, 1452–1601*, ed. M.L. Stavert (Edinburgh, 1993), pp. 279–80, 288, 309, 314–17, 331, 337–41 and 366–7; *Records of Inverness*, 2 vols, ed. W. Mackay, H.C. Boyd and G.S. Laing (Aberdeen, 1911–24), vol. 1, pp. 189–91 and 273–4; *Extracts from the Council Register of the Burgh of Aberdeen*, vol. 1, pp. 87 and 252–3; ACA, CA1/1/9, p. 293, CA1/1/12/1, p. 310, CA1/1.24, pp. 512–13 and 518, CA1/1/33/1, pp. 135–6 and 443, CA/1/1/32, p. 469, and CA1/1/33/1, pp. 135–6; ELAC, B30/13/1, f. 4r. See too G. Gross, *The Gild Merchant: A Contribution to British Municipal History*, 2 vols (Oxford, 1890), vol. 1, pp. 53–60.

12 *Extracts from the Records of the Burgh of Edinburgh*, 1st ser., 5 vols, ed. J.D. Marwick (Edinburgh, 1869–92), vol. 1, pp. xxxiv and 172; *Extracts from the Records of the Royal Burgh of Lanark, 1150–1722*, ed. R. Renwick (Glasgow, 1893), p. 72; *Kirkcudbright Town Council Records, 1576–1604*, ed. M.B. Johnston and C.M. Armet (Edinburgh, 1939), pp. 94, 172–3, 181–2, 194–5, 212, 222–4, 232–3, 243, 253–4, 303–4, 317–20, 333, 336, 343–5, 358–9, 363 and 367–9; *The Records of Elgin, 1234–1800*, 2 vols, ed. W. Cramond (Aberdeen, 1903–8), vol. 1, p. 160; ACA, CA1/1/33/1, p. 350; SAUL, B10/8/7, p. 442; DAC, WC4/8, f. 146v, WC4/10/2, p. 431, WC4/11/1, pp. 154, 283–4, 289 and 296, WC4/11/2, p. 564, and WC4/11/3, pp. 626, 769, 822, 837 and 857; NRS, B21/8/2, f. 38v, and B72/5, ff. 63v, 78v and 89r.

13 As is observed at http://users.trytel.com/tristan/towns/glossary.html, the expression was not purely repetitive, though 'lot' no doubt did serve to some extent to reinforce 'scot'. On

merchants and mariners who embarked on a voyage together, the expectation was that they would share the burdens as well as the benefits of the enterprise, although the point of the recurring protestations found in Aberdeen was that this would not be the case if goods were placed above the overloft of a ship.[14]

There is only one known occasion on which merchants whose goods had been placed above the overloft, after their goods were 'cassin for saifety of the haill schip and guidis', claimed contributions from those whose goods were placed in the hold.[15] Five of those with goods in the hold of the ship complained that an agreement to contribute made by the others should 'hurt nocht thame, nor yit the commond lawis concerning se fair causis', since 'thai consentit nocht thairto'.[16] Nonetheless, the five merchants were required 'to scot and lott witht the remanent of the merchandis'.[17] The reasoning behind the court's ruling was not recorded, but it could be that those who participated in the voyage were taken to be bound by a majority agreement of the whole company. If so, it may be surmised that the outcome would have been different if the five merchants had protested against the placing of the goods on the overloft before the voyage.[18] In any case, implicit in the protestations made in preparation for a voyage was an acceptance that merchants whose goods were placed in the hold ought to scot and lot with each other if any of their goods had to be jettisoned. When the master of another ship sought contributions from merchants whose goods had been preserved by the jettison of goods taken from the hold, and one immediately declared his willingness to pay, a procurator appearing for the others insisted that 'his confessioun hurt nocht the said merchandis'.[19] Shortly afterwards, however, all the parties consented to the appointment of arbiters to decide whether 'the schip and guds suld lotte and pay thair part of the said kassin guds or nocht, and gif thai suld pay and lot,

---

the widespread use of 'binomials' in burgh discourse see J. Kopaczyk, *The Legal Language of Scottish Burghs: Standardization and Lexical Bundles, 1380–1560* (Oxford, 2013).

14 For an example of a maritime nature that does not relate to general average see ACA, CA1/1/19, pp. 216, 262, 267 and 410. For an example relating to fishing see ACA, CA1/1/28, pp. 367–8.

15 ACA, CA1/1/24, pp. 400 and 407.

16 ACA, CA1/1/24, pp. 404 and 417.

17 ACA, CA1/1/24, p. 476, and CA1/1/25, pp. 412, 431 and 568.

18 In other words, one purpose of entering protestations of the type considered in the last paragraph may have been to avoid being bound by agreements of the type made in this case.

19 ACA, CA1/1/17, pp. 128 and 132. If goods were 'castin in the sey' without any intention to preserve other goods, compensation was due only from those who committed the 'wrang' (ACA, CA1/1/8, pp. 797, 800, 810, 812–14, 817–18, 823–4, 861, 863, 866, 881, 940, 990, 994 and 1001).

to sett the said lott'. The arbiters' calculation of the contributions due was later recorded, and will be returned to below, but there is no sign that they saw any need to address directly the more basic question raised.[20] On another occasion goods were held in storage by the same master while he sought contributions from their owners.[21] 'The law of the see and use was', the master advised the court, 'that the haill guidis quhilks beand in ane schipe the tyme of cassing of any guidis, togidder witht the schipe or fraucht, suld scot and lott'. It was at once made clear that the merchants 'wer content to scot and lot, and to gif the inventour of thair guidis witht the availl thairof, for payment of the said scat'. It is notable that the inventories they submitted were referred to two university graduates, who presented the judges with their 'calculatioune' a month later, for graduates were rarely involved in the court's proceedings, and were scarcely ever involved as merchants and mariners.[22] As will be seen, the calculation of contributions could be a complicated business. Another master wanted merchants to pay 'thair part of the lote' after goods were jettisoned from his ship 'for savite of the self and the guds'.[23] A further action was raised against the 'frauchter' of a ship by three merchants whose goods had been 'castin furth of the said schip throw apperans of dangeir', but it failed after testimony was received from the master and a member of the crew that 'the merchands forsaid keist the saidis geir and guidis withtout consent or command of the skipper and marenaris being in the schip'.[24]

The records of other burghs confirm that 'scotting and lotting' in cases of jettison was not confined to Aberdeen. In the court books of Inverness a merchant undertook to reimburse someone who guaranteed performance of his obligation to contribute to a loss sustained when another merchant's goods

20 ACA, CA1/1/17, p. 163.

21 ACA, CA1/1/25, pp. 31 and 68.

22 The procurator who appeared for most of the merchants in the previous case was one of the rare exceptions. L. Febvre, *The Problem of Unbelief in the Sixteenth Century: The Religion of Rabelais*, tr. B. Gottlieb (Cambridge, MA, 1982), pp. 388–93, points out that arithmetic was not well understood in the sixteenth century, when people could marvel at a judge being able to calculate instantly that 50 x 100 = 5,000.

23 ACA, CA1/1/12/2, pp. 751–2.

24 ACA, CA1/1/25, pp. 302–3. A 'frauchter' was a person who 'put a ship out to fraucht' by inviting merchants to pay freight to have their goods carried in it. He might have been a shipowner, and was more often a master or clerk authorised to deal on the owner's behalf, but he could instead have been a merchant who had chartered a ship, which is what the unusual use of the word 'frauchter' here would seem to suggest, although elsewhere the word 'dailisman' tended to be used. See too ACA, CA1/1/24, pp. 605 and 667, CA1/1/25, pp. 52, 412, 431, 568 and 596, and CA1/1/34/2, pp. 589–90.

were 'cassin ower buyrd be occasioun of storme and weddir'.[25] In the court books of Dumfries mariners had it formally recorded that they had thrown goods out of a boat 'for saiffin of thair awin lyfis, and the bot and the layf of the guds beand in it for the tym'.[26] The obvious implication is that they would not be held liable for the loss of the goods jettisoned, but whether contributions to the loss were expected from the owners of either the boat or the goods preserved is not made clear. In the court books of Dundee, on the other hand, the master of a boat not only had it recorded that he, 'with consent of the rest of his equipage', had jettisoned goods during a storm 'for saftie of thair lyvis', but also arranged for arbiters to calculate the contributions due from everyone involved in the voyage.[27] Other entries in the same book reveal readiness on the part of both merchants and shipowners to 'scot and lot' when goods were 'cassine', the former in proportion to the value of the 'geir and guds' they had shipped, the latter in proportion to the value of either their 'schip' or the amount of the 'fraucht' payments due to them.[28] In the council register of Edinburgh 'personis appoyntet to sett the skat' for goods jettisoned from a boat were told that 'na guids quhilk payet nather fraucht nor custome suld skat or lott witht the rest, except the samyn had bene speciallie convenit upoun amangis the merchandis'.[29] Further entries in the court books of Dundee concern cases in which equipment was lost. In one case arbiters were appointed 'to set the scot and lot' of both goods and equipment jettisoned from a ship during a storm.[30] In another case the clerk of a ship raised an action for 'the scatt of ane ancker and tow tynt be the schip', alleging that merchants on board at the time had given their 'consent' to the cutting of the cable and had 'promittit the guds being in the said schip suld scatt thairanent'.[31] The court in Aberdeen similarly found that 'the haill geir and guidis' transported in a French ship 'suld scott and lott witht the schip or fraucht thairof' after several of its masts and sails were 'cuttit and tyntt for saifty of the schip and guidis'.[32]

---

25 *Records of Inverness*, vol. 1, pp. 267–8; HAC, B1/1/2, ff. 473v-4r.

26 DAC, WC4/8, f. 58r.

27 DCA, BCMB, vol. 11, 7 December 1569.

28 DCA, BCMB, vol. 3, 30 October 1550 and 16 December 1551, and vol. 11, 24 February 1570; see too MBBC, vol. 1, p. 90, and PBD, vol. 4, f. 15r.

29 ECA, SL1/1/8, f. 65v; see too SL1/1/4, p. 503.

30 DCA, BCMB, vol. 1, ff. 20, 22, 39v-40r, 77r, 79r and 116v. A brief account of this case can be found in A. Maxwell, *Old Dundee, Ecclesiastical, Burghal and Social, prior to the Reformation* (Edinburgh, 1891), p. 318.

31 DCA, BCMB, vol. 6, 14, 21 and 26 January 1562.

32 ACA, CA1/1/24, pp. 24–5 and 27. A brief account of this case can be found in W. Kennedy, *Annals of Aberdeen, from the Reign of King William the Lion, to the End of the Year 1818*, 2 vols (London, 1818), vol. 2, p. 486.

A third expedient, distinct from the casting of cargo or the ejection of equipment, lay behind protracted litigation in the bailie court of Aberdeen in 1532. A Flemish ship, carrying merchants and merchandise from Veere to Edinburgh and Aberdeen, had put in at Newcastle, where it had been arrested, apparently until custom duties unexpectedly imposed there were satisfied.[33] In order to secure the ship's release, goods were taken from its hold and sold. The master, who blamed the Edinburgh merchants for the arrest, then sailed directly to Aberdeen, without turning in at Leith (the port of Edinburgh). It was found by an assize of merchants and mariners that the master ought to remit part of the freight owed to him to pay for the transfer of goods to Leith, and that the merchants whose goods were still in the ship ought to contribute towards the loss of the goods sold in Newcastle.[34] Perhaps surprisingly, there was no dispute about the liability to contribute, or about the amount of the contributions that were calculated by arbiters, but four of the Aberdeen merchants, who had been travelling without merchandise, objected to a further finding of the assize that 'all kind of mony, baitht gold and silver, cunzeit and uncunzeit, and als rings, being in ane schip, suld lott and scott witht the uther guds of the said schip'.[35] They objected to the 'skait and lott' set by the arbiters on the procedural ground that they, 'nor nane of thame, consentit never thairto', and to the finding behind it on the substantive ground that their 'mony was never in nay dangar nor aventour of tinsall'. It was agreed that advice should be requested from the burgh council of Edinburgh, but one of the merchants instead procured royal letters there, directing the court in Aberdeen to proceed to its own decision.[36] A new assize found that there was indeed a problem with the 'decreit arbitrall', since it was not based on a 'compromit of the merchandis gangang afor', and since the Aberdeen merchants had not been summoned 'to heir and se the said decreit ratifiet or nocht'.[37] Nevertheless, they adhered to the finding that the Aberdeen merchants should contribute to the loss

33 ACA, CA1/1/13, pp. 403–4. Although it is far from clear what was going on in the case briefly noted at ACA, CA1/1/8, p. 321, it may have been something similar.

34 ACA, CA1/1/13, p. 410.

35 ACA, CA1/1/13, pp. 410–11, 422 and 508–9.

36 ACA, CA1/1/13, pp. 425, 465 and 506–7. Whether the Edinburgh council received or considered the request is unknown, because its register for this period has not survived. There is certainly no mention in the Aberdeen register of advice being returned, and no mention of the episode has been found in ECA, SL1/1/1, or NLS, Adv. MS 31.4.9, collections of notes on the business of the Edinburgh council composed at some stage during the late sixteenth century, before the loss of the register in question. It remains possible, however, that the writer of the notes passed over something significant.

37 ACA, CA1/1/13, pp. 511–13.

sustained in England, 'ilk man corispondene to the mone he fetchit hayme'. After the Edinburgh merchant who had procured the royal letters undertook to indemnify the master against any claims made against him by the merchants whose goods had been sold, he was allowed, in his capacity as 'ressaver of the skat and lott', to pursue the Aberdeen merchants who remained reluctant to contribute.[38]

A fourth expedient considered in Aberdeen was the surrender of goods from a ship to armed raiders, who then left the ship to proceed on its way with its remaining cargo. In 1515, after goods were taken from a ship by 'thair auld innimeis of Ingland', three local merchants whose goods had remained in the hold declared themselves willing to make any contributions due from them, 'gif it war sa fandin, other be law or pretik of siclik caisis obefor'.[39] No such finding was recorded, nor has any other instance come to light of contributions being made to merchants whose goods were seized by enemies in wartime.[40] A case raised in 1538 was concerned with a seizure made in peacetime. A vessel from Kinghorn was transporting goods from Flanders to Scotland when it was 'pilzeit be certane Frenschemen, se revars', and one of the merchants had a pack taken away.[41] He advised the court that 'the ald lovable use and consuetud of this nobill burght hes bene past memor of man, and yit is, that ony schip beying pilzeit in the streme be men of war or se revars, or ony gudds cassin be storme of wedder, the remanent of the gudds and money beying in the said schip for the tym, and als the sayd schip and profytt thairof, aucht to scot and lott witht the gudds pilzeit or cassin'.[42] In significantly different terms, an assize found that 'all the said gudds and money, togidder witht the sayd schip, or the haill fraucht of the same, at the wil of the merchands, aucht to skot and lott' for the goods taken, 'conforme to the ald lovabill consuetude of this burght'.[43] Arbiters were appointed to calculate the contributions due from the other merchants and the shipowner, who was to pay in proportion to either his 'schip or fraucht'.[44]

---

38 ACA, CA1/1/14, pp. 130, 175, 180, 360–1, 364 and 368.

39 ACA, CA1/1/9, pp. 391, 393, 396 and 399.

40 The burgh court in Dundee decided that contributions should be made after goods were seized during a civil war (DCA, BCMB, vol. 8, 17 January and 1 May 1564), but that was a different situation.

41 ACA, CA1/1/15, pp. 708 and 711–12.

42 If the mention of 'money' as well as 'gudds' suggests awareness of the decision made six years earlier, and if the mention of 'men of war' as well as 'se revars' suggests that contributions may after all have been paid when a seizure was made in wartime, it is hard to be certain on either count. In the quotation, a redundant use of 'that' before 'the remanent' has been left out.

43 ACA, CA1/1/15, p. 716.

44 ACA, CA1/1/15, pp. 717, 719–20, 723, 728 and 733.

In 1554 another merchant recounted that while a ship was beginning its voyage from Aberdeen towards Danzig, 'thair come ane Inglis schip upoun us, and pilleit and rubit our said schip'.[45] Several merchants whose goods had been left on board immediately 'promest to scat and lott thair haill gudis and geir', and they repeated their promise 'eftir that we come to Danskin'. There were other victims of the robbery 'witht quhome thai scottit and lottit and payt', but for some reason the defenders would not pay the pursuer, who had himself contributed to the losses sustained by the other victims, in proportion to the value of goods he had carried for someone else.[46] In 1574, after goods were pillaged on another Danzig voyage, merchants put it on record in the burgh court books of Dundee that they were ready to 'scott and lott' for the 'skaytht and loise' sustained by others, 'conforme to the lawis and daylie pretik'.[47] Brief entries in the council register of Edinburgh mention the appointment of merchants 'to sett the scatt of the schip callit the *Sie Catt*, quhairof Androw Ridpeth wes maister, quhilk wes laitley pilleit in hir voyage from Londoun'.[48]

More elaborate entries in the same council register shed light on how contributions were calculated. In 1580 a ship carrying wine and woad from Bordeaux to Leith 'wes pilleit and reft in the said vayage be certane Inglis pirats', who made off with some but not all of the cargo.[49] The master (who evidently owned the ship, and was carrying goods of his own), the merchants (who owned most of the wine and woad), and the crew (who also had goods in the hold) all lost part of their belongings. On reaching Scotland they declared themselves content that 'ane generall scatt and extent wer sett upoun the haill guids foirsaid and schip quhilks ar saif, for the releif of the guids pilleit'. Six merchants were appointed to make the calculation, but they found it challenging.[50] Two months later they asked whether the 'scatt suld be sett upoun the wairing onely, withtout respect of the fraucht and chairgis, or gif the said

45 ACA, CA1/1/21, pp. 733, 798–9, 803–4, 807 and 814.

46 ACA, CA1/1/22, pp. 438, 440, 444, 446, 509, 512, 516–17 and 556; see too CA1/1/28, pp. 38–9, 234–5 and 281.

47 DCA, BCMB, vol. 12, 27 January 1574, and vol. 13, 5 March 1574. The balancing of the phrases 'scott and lott' and 'skaytht and loise' seems to have been deliberate, and was reflected here and elsewhere in the Dundee records (vol. 14, 16 May 1576) in use of the word 'skaytht', meaning 'harm' or 'loss', as a synonym for 'scott'. For further piracy cases in the Dundee records see vol. 11, 15 April 1570, and vol. 21, 21 December 1599.

48 ECA, SL1/1/8, ff. 74v and 77v; *Extracts from the Records of the Burgh of Edinburgh*, vol. 4, pp. 486–7.

49 ECA, SL1/1/6, ff. 51v-2r. In the quotation, the word 'the' has been inserted before 'said vayage'.

50 ECA, SL1/1/6, ff. 53r and 64v.

fraucht and chairges suld be deduceit and comptit in the wayring'.[51] The court found that the costs of transportation should not be taken into account, adding that their ruling was to be 'observet in all uther scatts as ane perpetual law in all tymes hereafter'.[52] The merchants were still unable to complete the calculation, however, and eventually the court assumed the responsibility itself. After receiving evidence of the amounts spent on purchasing goods in France, of the exchange rate between French and Scottish currency at the time, of the quantities of goods lost, and of the value of the ship, the court calculated that the total value of the ship and goods at the start of the voyage had been just under £3,500, and that the total value of the goods despoiled had been just under £1,400.[53] It therefore concluded that every £100 of the original value ought to 'lose and tyne' £40, and proceeded to work out precisely how much each person ought to pay or be paid.[54] The same method of calculation was adopted two years later after mariners on a ship sailing from Dieppe to Leith were 'compellit throw storme of wedder, and for safetie of mennis lyfes, schip and guides, to cast ane pairt of hir laidyng of lychtning thairof'.[55] As in the earlier case – though this time those appointed to make the calculation managed to do so – the provost, bailies and council of Edinburgh ordained the 'scatt roll' to be 'registrat in thair buikis' and invested with 'thair authoritie', so that it could be executed like a court order.[56] In one of the Aberdeen cases mentioned earlier, a broadly similar method of calculation appears to have been adopted.[57] After working out the exchange rate between Flemish and Scottish currency, the arbiters appointed set the value of jettisoned goods ('at the first bying') against the value of the ship and goods to see how much loss needed to be borne for each unit of currency in the latter figure.

51 ECA, SL1/1/6, f. 69r.

52 As will become apparent in the third section of this essay, it is of some significance that the entries quoted were made in the council register of the burgh, not in the court books that were being kept separately. It seems clear that the burgh council of the capital city of Scotland was seeking to lay down the law on the calculation of contributions, even though the bailie court there did not normally have jurisdiction over seafaring causes.

53 ECA, SL1/1/6, ff. 71v and 86–7r.

54 The further complication arose that by this stage the six merchants appointed had managed to complete their calculation (ECA, SL1/1/6, ff. 89v and 92v-3r), but how they did so is not known.

55 ECA, SL1/1/6, ff. 195–7.

56 A lengthier account of the two cases can be found in D. Robertson and M. Wood, *Castle and Town: Chapters in the History of the Royal Burgh of Edinburgh* (Edinburgh, 1928), pp. 297–301.

57 ACA, CA1/1/17, p. 163. A complication with this case will be returned to later.

From the evidence examined so far it seems clear that merchants and mariners were expected in sixteenth-century Scotland to contribute to losses sustained when either cargo or equipment was jettisoned from a ship, when pirates were content to remove only some of the goods on a ship, perhaps also when enemies took part of a cargo, and when a penalty was paid to secure a ship's release from arrestment. In every instance, the expectation was expressed in terms of an obligation to 'scot and lot', which was indicative of an assumption that those involved in a common enterprise should share its burdens along with its benefits. If the records of three cases can be relied on, losses were distributed in proportion to the total value of the ship and goods at the beginning of the voyage, except that many records provide for the amount of freight payable being used in the calculation as an alternative to the value of the ship.[58] The evaluation of goods was based on what was paid for them before they were shipped, not on what they might have been sold for after arriving at their destination, and it was consistent with this emphasis on purchase price rather than potential profit that no account was taken of the costs of transportation.[59] That the shipowners, despite a suggestion made by one litigant, were not liable in proportion to both the value of the ship and the amount of freight payable was again consistent with an emphasis on the extent of each party's investment in the enterprise, instead of the benefit each party might have hoped to gain from it. The amount of freight payable was presumably treated as an alternative to the value of the ship because sometimes the 'frauchter' had hired the ship provided from its owner, who was not directly involved in the enterprise. Freight was usually owed by the merchants to the master, who in most cases was the key figure in the collection of contributions.[60] When merchants had contracted for transportation with the master, he was the obvious person for them to pursue if their goods were not delivered, and when shipowners had employed a master, he was the obvious person for them to pursue if the equipment of the ship was lost. The master thus had a special interest in ensuring that losses were distributed, although occasionally merchants seem to have made claims directly against one another, or to have agreed directly with each other that losses should be distributed. The consensual nature of the process

58 Although the method of calculation is elaborated on in the records of just three cases, no other record has been found to cast doubt on the reliability of these three.

59 To judge from the Aberdeen case, the ruling delivered in Edinburgh reflected existing practice.

60 Significantly, when freight was owed to the clerk of a ship, he became the key figure in the collection. For a further example, in which the clerk of a ship was ordered 'to set and mak the skat of this last Burdeaux veage', see DCA, BCMB, vol. 11, 5 March 1571.

is a recurring theme of the records, yet so too is a belief that it was governed in some sense by law. In what sense needs further consideration.

2 Marrying Practice with Theory in Books Composed by Lawyers

On 5 March 1575 the three estates assembled in the Scottish parliament, 'understanding the harme quhilk this commoune weill sustenis throw want of a perfyte writtin law, quhairupoun all jugeis may knaw how to proceid and decerne', charged nine commissioners with the task of examining 'the bukis of the law, actis of parliament and decisionis befoir the sessioun', forming out of them 'the body of oure lawis', and bringing this *corpus iuris* back to the estates for ratification, 'quhairthrow thair may be ane certain writtin law to all oure soverane lordis jugeis and ministeris of law to juge and decyde be'.[61] Although the burghs constituted one of the three estates, and three of the commissioners appointed were identified as burgh representatives, there was no suggestion that the 'pretik' or 'consuetude' followed in the bailie courts should be investigated. Indeed, although the 1575 act was one of a long series of measures introduced during the fifteenth, sixteenth and seventeenth centuries with a view to providing a written restatement of the law – prompting comparisons with the contemporary codification of customary laws in other countries, particularly in France, where Scots lawyers often went to study – at no point were the commissioners instructed to consult the recognised remembrancers of local customs.[62] The only way in which local customs might have been taken into account was if they had already been turned into customary laws by first being proved to exist before the lords of session, the judges of the supreme civil court of Scotland, and then being approved of as reasonable in one of the decisions delivered by those judges.[63] If the aim of the parliamentary commissions was to produce an authoritative restatement of the law, the law restated was to be found in statements already made by people who were regarded by

61 *The Acts of the Parliaments of Scotland*, 12 vols, ed. T. Thomson and C. Innes (Edinburgh, 1814–75), vol. 3, p. 89; Records of the Parliaments of Scotland, ed. K.M. Brown (http://www.rps.ac.uk), A1575/3/7.

62 J.W. Cairns, T.D. Fergus and H.L. MacQueen, 'Legal Humanism and the History of Scots Law: John Skene and Thomas Craig', in J. MacQueen (ed.), *Humanism in Renaissance Scotland* (Edinburgh, 1990), p. 48, at pp. 50–2.

63 The process of turning legal customs (*Rechtsgewohnheiten*) into customary laws (*Gewohnheitsrechten*) in the following century is briefly outlined in J.D. Ford, *Law and Opinion in Scotland during the Seventeenth Century* (Oxford, 2007), pp. 291–9. See now the fourth essay in this collection.

lawyers as having authority to issue declarations of the law. In fact, none of the commissions ever resulted in the enactment of a legislative code, but the 1575 act does appear to have resulted in the production of a survey of maritime law. A former lord of session, Sir James Balfour of Pittendreich, took up the instruction to examine the old books of law, the acts of parliament and the decisions of the session, and brought material found there together in a compilation that came to be called his 'practicks' (partly because the decisions of the session were known as 'practicks', and partly because the focus was on the law put into 'practick' as opposed to the 'theorick' taught in the schools).[64] At some stage Balfour extracted the material relating to maritime affairs from his general account of Scots law and dealt with it separately, in conjunction with material drawn from other sources.[65] Yet even at that stage he made no reference to the decisions of the bailie courts, with which he may not have had much acquaintance.[66] For their part, the bailies who presided over litigation in the coastal burghs may not have had much acquaintance with the written sources Balfour had consulted.[67] It cannot simply be presumed that the 'lawis and daylie pretik' referred to in the burgh records were the laws and decisions assembled in the survey of maritime law appended to Balfour's practicks.

The survey contained just three paragraphs concerned with general average.[68] The first reproduced in Scots translation an article from 'the sea lawis of Oleron', of which copies were often included in the manuscript collections of medieval texts referred to in 1575 as 'the bukis of the law'.[69] It provided that if a skipper felt the need to jettison cargo during a crisis (*la gettesone par*

64 A.L. Murray, 'Sinclair's Practicks', in A. Harding (ed.), *Law-Making and Law-Makers in British History* (London, 1980), p. 90, at pp. 90 and 102.

65 *Alexander King's Treatise on Maritime Law*, ed. J.D. Ford (Edinburgh, 2018), pp. lxxv–vii. See now the fifth essay in this collection, where an attempt is made to pin down the time at which the change was made.

66 As well as being a former lord of session – indeed the president of the court – Balfour had also been a judge in one of the commissary courts that took over some of the responsibilities of the courts of the Catholic church in Scotland – in which he had also served – after the Reformation in the early 1560s (T.M. Green, *The Spiritual Jurisdiction in Reformation Scotland: A Legal History* (Edinburgh, 2019), pp. 30, 62, 114–15 and 125). He may conceivably have appeared as a procurator before the bailies of Edinburgh or another burgh in his earlier years, but it was not usual for successful practitioners in the central courts to spend much time there.

67 See now the essays in the first part of this collection where a firmer line is taken on this point.

68 *The Practicks of Sir James Balfour of Pittendreich*, 2 vols, ed. P.G.B. McNeill (Edinburgh, 1962–3), vol. 2, pp. 622–3.

69 E.B.I. Frankot, 'The Scottish Translations of the *Rôles d'Oléron*: Edition and Commentary', in A.M. Godfrey (ed.), *Stair Society: Miscellany Eight* (Edinburgh, 2020), p. 13.

aventure) he should seek to secure the consent of any merchants present but could proceed anyway provided he and other members of the crew swore an oath on reaching land that their purpose had been to preserve their lives, the ship and other cargo (*pour sauver le corps, la nef, les denrees et les vins*).[70] In calculating contributions, the goods jettisoned were to be evaluated according to the prices obtained for those preserved after completion of the voyage (*ceulx qui seront gettes hors doivent estre aprisez aux feur de ceulx qui seront venuz a sauvete*), with the master contributing according to the value of the ship or the amount of freight owed to him, as he preferred (*la nef ou son frett, a son choys*). Another article in the same code, also reproduced in translation by Balfour, required a master to seek consent when he felt the need to cut a mast (*coupe son mast par force de tempeste*), and confirmed that merchants were to contribute when a master lost equipment in the same way as they would if cargo were lost (*comme get*).[71] The other relevant paragraph in Balfour's survey reproduced an article from 'the sea lawis of Wisbie', which he had not found in the old books of law. Here a distinction was drawn between the deliberate loss of equipment for the purpose of preserving a ship, its cargo and crew, and the accidental damage of equipment in a storm.[72] As Balfour's translation put it, merchants were not required 'to scat and lot' in the latter situation, although they were in the former.[73] If goods were jettisoned at the same time, the translation added, contributions were to be made 'like as the saidis gudis, be gude estimatioun, micht have gevin and thay had cum to the mercat', with the master contributing 'at the ships price, or the fraucht of the ship'. This choice, it has been seen, was often granted to masters in the bailie courts, but no evidence has been found of contributions from merchants being assessed in accordance with what jettisoned goods might have been sold for had they reached the markets for which they were intended.[74] Likewise, while two examples have been found of masters testifying after reaching land that they had only thrown cargo overboard as a means of saving other cargo, the ship and its crew, only two have been found, and on one occasion the master merely reported that he had the consent of his crew.[75] It does not seem to have been a standard

70 *The Black Book of the Admiralty*, 4 vols, ed. T. Twiss (London, 1871–6), vol. 1, pp. 96–9.
71 *Black Book of the Admiralty*, vol. 1, pp. 98–101.
72 *Black Book of the Admiralty*, vol. 4, p. 268.
73 The phrase 'scot and lot' was not used in the translation of the articles from the laws of Oleron, perhaps because the compilers of the old books had been unfamiliar with burgh practice.
74 DCA, BCMB, vol. 3, 30 October 1550 and 16 December 1551, and vol. 11, 24 February 1570.
75 DAC, WC4/8, f. 58r, and DCA, BCMB, vol. 11, 7 December 1569.

practice for groups of mariners to swear oaths after reaching land, nor does it seem to have been a strict requirement that merchants be consulted before goods or equipment were cast away. Although it was sometimes reported that consent had been given, no complaints have been found of lack of consent, whereas in one case it was complained that merchants had jettisoned goods without the consent of the mariners.[76]

The laws of Oleron and Wisby were consulted in the composition of another survey of maritime law later in the sixteenth century.[77] William Welwod may have heard about Simon Schard's unfulfilled promise to produce a compendium of sea laws while he was studying in Germany, before he returned to Scotland in 1577 to take up a teaching post at the University of St Andrews.[78] About a decade later he pulled the materials he had been gathering together in a compendium of his own, which survives in a single manuscript, but of which an abridged version was put into print in 1590.[79] Instead of methodically assembling extracts from his sources, as Balfour had done, Welwod summarised selected provisions in his own terms in chapters devoted to different topics, a series of which were concerned with general average. The printed version of his treatise differed from the manuscript version in two main respects. In the first place, whereas the manuscript version had been supportive of the admiral's claim to an exclusive jurisdiction over seafaring causes, the printed version was more supportive of the claims of the burghs, which made a concerted effort around 1590 to recover their former jurisdiction over disputes involving merchants and mariners.[80] In the second place, in revising his treatise for the press, Welwod excised a large number of references he had originally made to the *Nomos Rhodion nautikos* and the *Consolato del mare*. As he later revealed, when a longer version of his treatise was finally printed in 1613, he had been

---

76 ACA, CA1/1/25, pp. 302–3.

77 As is pointed out in the sixth essay in this collection, Welwod made use of provisions from the laws of Wisby as well as the laws of Oleron but believed for some reason that they all belonged to the laws of Oleron. Balfour cited these sources separately, although he may also have been confused about the relationship between them.

78 Schard, *De varia temporum in iure civili observatione, Eustathii olim Constantinopolitani antecessoris libellus; item, Leges Rhodiorum navales, militares et georgicae Iustiniani* (Basle, 1561), p. 271.

79 MCL, PL 2208; *The Sea-Law of Scotland* (Edinburgh, 1590).

80 *Records of the Convention of the Royal Burghs of Scotland*, 8 vols, ed. J.D. Marwick and T. Hunter (Edinburgh, 1870–1918), vol. 1, pp. 339–41; *Extracts from the Records of the Burgh of Edinburgh*, 1st ser., vol. 4, pp. 528 and 530–1; *Extracts from the Records of the Burgh of Edinburgh*, 2nd ser., 9 vols, ed. M. Wood and H. Armet (Edinburgh, 1927–67), vol. 1, p. 13; *Acts of the Parliaments of Scotland*, vol. 3, p. 580; Records of the Parliaments of Scotland, 1592/4/101.

frustrated to learn that merchants and mariners in Scotland were less familiar with the written sources he had been accumulating than he had anticipated.[81] In a preface attached to the 1590 version of his treatise he observed that maritime disputes were governed in part by 'the reulis of Olon receavit be our cuntrey men', but added that these provisions were only adhered to 'sa far as they are commonly knawin be peiple'.[82] It might therefore have been expected that in publishing his treatise 'for the reddy use of all seafairing men' he would not only have abandoned his references to the *Nomos Rhodion nautikos* and the *Consolato del mare*, but would also have made more selective use of the laws of Oleron and Wisby, concentrating on provisions that seemed consistent with the practice of the bailie courts. Yet he left the passages based on those sources largely as they had been written. He believed that 'all men be bound to ken the law, namely thair awne common lawe', and maintained that there was no excuse for ignorance of the sources copied in the manuscript collections of the books of law, to which he referred as 'wrets authorizit be our nation'. Aware that the laws of Oleron and Wisby were not followed closely in commercial practice, because they were not 'commonly knawin be peiple', he tried to encourage more exact use of the provisions incorporated into the books of law, because they had in this way been 'receavit be our cuntrey men'.

Welwod was inclined to go further. Although he believed people were only obliged to know their own common law – paradoxically, the *ius commune proprium* of Scotland – he also believed he should use his expertise as a teacher of the civil law – the *ius commune* of Europe – in expounding the law of the sea.[83] He associated the first of the two articles reproduced by Balfour from the laws of Oleron with the opening texts of the *Digest* title on the *lex Rhodia de iactu* (which he associated further in the manuscript version of his treatise with the *Nomos Rhodion nautikos*).[84] It seemed to him that if the general practice of scotting and lotting for jettisoned goods could be connected with an article in the laws of Oleron, that article could in turn be connected with a general principle enunciated in the *Digest* that when 'wares are jettisoned for the sake of lightening a ship, what is given up for everyone ought to be made up by the contribution of everyone'.[85] By the same token, he believed that the other article

81 *An Abridgement of All Sea-Lawes* (London, 1613), p. 7. The treatise was repackaged for a British audience, but was substantially the same as most of the original manuscript version.

82 *Sea-Law of Scotland*, sig. A3.

83 On Welwod's competing conceptions of common law see *Alexander King's Treatise on Maritime Law*, pp. ci–ii.

84 *Sea-Law of Scotland*, sig. C1; *Alexander King's Treatise on Maritime Law*, p. 366.

85 D.14.2.1. Welwod used the phrase 'skatt and lott' in summarising these sources in Scots.

reproduced by Balfour could be connected with a principle twice enunciated in the *Digest* that when 'a mast or other equipment of a ship is cast out for the sake of removing a shared danger, contribution ought to happen'.[86] Welwod pointed out that the Roman jurists had not only distinguished this situation from the accidental damage of equipment in a storm, but had also explained why contributions were not required in the latter situation.[87] If a smith were paid to work on something, they had remarked, and his hammer were broken during the process, the customer would hardly have been expected to pay for a new hammer.[88] Drawing these connections enabled Welwod to bring into his discussion questions that do not appear to have been raised in practice, but to which the Roman jurists had provided answers, such as what would happen if goods transferred to a lighter to enable a ship to enter a shallow harbour were then lost, or if some goods were harmed while others were being jettisoned.[89] It was not possible, however, to reconcile everything found in the laws of Oleron and Wisby with the texts in the *Digest*. The Roman jurists, for example, had maintained that while jettisoned goods should be evaluated according to their purchase price before a ship began its voyage, preserved goods should be evaluated according to their sale price after it reached its destination.[90]

Further engagement with the civil law can be found in a third survey of maritime law written around the same time, in which Alexander King, an advocate before the lords of session as well as a judge of the central admiralty court, which also sat in Edinburgh, combined occasional references to the laws of Oleron and Wisby with more extensive use of civil law sources.[91] In dedicating his treatise to the admiral of Scotland, King recalled that when he had returned from several years of legal study at universities in France and the Netherlands, he had been eager to marry (*coniungere*) the academic theory he had mastered there with the forensic practice in which he was immersing himself.[92] He had decided to write a treatise on maritime law after presiding over disputes in the admiralty court, where he found discussions of the law between litigants to be

86 D.14.2.3 and 14.2.5.1.

87 *Sea-Law of Scotland*, sigg. C1v-2r; *Alexander King's Treatise on Maritime Law*, p. 367.

88 D.14.2.2.1 and 14.2.6.

89 *Sea-Law of Scotland*, sigg. C2v-3r; *Alexander King's Treatise on Maritime Law*, pp. 367–8.

90 D.14.2.2.4.

91 *Alexander King's Treatise on Maritime Law*, pp. 78–9 and 160–1. It is far from clear how King understood the relationship between the laws of Oleron and Wisby, for his treatise, at least in the form in which it has survived, does not contain explicit citations from these sources. It does seem clear, however, that both sources were used.

92 *Alexander King's Treatise on Maritime Law*, pp. 4–5.

constantly confused, 'for some cited one custom, others another'.[93] The solution might have been to assume the role of a commissioner appointed to codify the local customs referred to, and he did claim to have sought advice when writing his treatise from experts in maritime affairs (*in re nautica versatissimos exercitores*), as he had done when hearing cases in court.[94] He also claimed, however, to have consulted expert lawyers (*expertissimos fori togatos*), as both a writer and a judge. His professed aim had been to combine the customs and legislation followed around Scotland (*consuetudines et statuta locorum*) with the learned laws in a *iuris marini concordia*. As he put it in a preface addressed to his readers, his aim had been to use his learning to reduce 'the admiral's laws, which the statute or custom of the land had introduced', into a volume that might serve in effect as a complete body (*quasi perfectum corpus*).[95] He would thus have produced something like 'the body of oure lawis' envisaged by the estates in 1575, although in a different way. He believed that by establishing his credentials as a learned author, using his learned authority in writing about the law, and generating a consensus among his learned colleagues, he could 'leave to posterity, out of unwritten laws or vague custom, clearly defined laws to be read'.[96] If the legal customs known to mariners and merchants (*inveteratae patriae consuetudines*) were appraised in the light of the expertise acquired at continental universities by lawyers like him (*doctiorum prudentia*), there was some prospect of a coherent and concordant understanding of the law being established.[97]

King's *iuris marini concordia* would have been easier to achieve if the 'law of the see' referred to by mariners and merchants had actually been founded on the legal theory studied by advocates. It would of course be facile to surmise from similarities between the practice of general average and the writings of the Roman jurists that the former must have been based on the latter, but nor can it safely be supposed that similar thinking was bound to emerge whenever a maritime community confronted the legal issues arising from crises in

93 *Alexander King's Treatise on Maritime Law*, pp. 6–9.

94 *Alexander King's Treatise on Maritime Law*, pp. 74–5.

95 *Alexander King's Treatise on Maritime Law*, pp. 20–1 (*cf.* pp. 154–5).

96 For a fuller discussion of this point see *Alexander King's Treatise on Maritime Law*, pp. xc–ciii. This process of marrying theory with practice was widespread at the time, and is what Welwod was also engaged in, albeit in a rather different way. The difference, and Balfour's reasons for eschewing reference to learned sources, receive further consideration in the essays in the second part of this collection and are returned to in the final essay.

97 *Alexander King's Treatise on Maritime Law*, pp. 20–1.

navigation.[98] For instance, it is by no means obvious that the loss sustained by a master when his ship was damaged in a storm should not be distributed among the participants in the venture. If merchants were expected to share the risk of equipment being deliberately cast away, then why not the risk of equipment being accidentally damaged through the same eventuality? It seemed to the Roman jurists that contributions should only be made when losses were sustained in order to preserve persons or property, but was it inevitable that anyone who thought about the problem would see it in this way? Surely not, yet it is a feature of the cases recorded in the burgh court books that when merchants were required to scot and lot for equipment lost at sea, the equipment was said to have been lost 'for saifty of the schip and guidis'.[99] In contrast, while it was recorded in another case that a ship seeking shelter from a storm in a harbour 'wantit ankers, cabillis and towis and uthers necessars quhilkis war lost and tynt be ressoun of the said storme', it was not suggested that the merchants whose goods were being carried ought to scot and lot with the master.[100] Similarly, while goods were often salvaged from wrecked ships, there was never any suggestion that those whose property was recovered ought to contribute towards the losses suffered by others.[101] Salvors expected to be reimbursed for their services, and the use of salvaged goods to meet their expectations was customary, but the language of scotting and lotting was never used in the court books when relations between the victims of shipwreck were dealt with.[102] Was it a coincidence that the Roman jurists had explicitly ruled out the making of contributions not only when ships were damaged but also when they were destroyed in storms?[103] There are admittedly entries in the court books that mention scotting and lotting without identifying the type of crisis to which it was a response, but the fact remains that scotting and lotting is not mentioned in the entries in which the damage or destruction of a ship was identified as a problem in need of a response.[104]

98 Compare R. Zimmermann, *The Law of Obligations: Roman Foundations of the Civilian Tradition* (Cape Town, 1990), pp. 411–12, with O.R. Constable, 'The Problem of Jettison in Medieval Mediterranean Maritime Law', (1994) 20 *Journal of Medieval History* 207, at p. 220.

99 ACA, CA1/1/24, pp. 24–5, 27, 54 and 62.

100 ACA, CA1/1/21, p. 71.

101 The evidence is discussed in the next essay in this collection.

102 *Cf.* A.R.C. Simpson, 'Spuilzie and Shipwreck in the Burgh Records', (2018) 9 *Journal of Irish and Scottish Studies* 70, at pp. 87–8.

103 D. 14.2.4.1 and 14.2.7.

104 ACA, CA1/1/10, p. 123; DCA, BCMB, vol. 3, 9 October 1550, vol. 6, 2 March 1562, vol. 10, 20 September and 8 and 22 October 1568, vol. 11, 24 January, 1 June and 13 July 1571, vol. 12, 17

Another question that ought to be asked is why those who benefited from the loss of property in a storm were required to contribute in proportion to the value of the property that was preserved. As a recurring justification for the deliberate loss of property was a desire to preserve the lives of persons on board ships, why were those persons not required to contribute something for the preservation of their lives? No doubt the focus on property in the *Digest* texts reflected the Roman aversion to evaluating free people, which would have been to treat them as if they were slaves, but why was property focused on in places where slaves were not owned?[105] In fact, the Roman jurists had qualified the point by accepting that even passengers who were carrying nothing but items too light to weigh down a ship ought to contribute to the extent that they had anything of value with them, such as jewels and pearls (*gemmas et margaritas*) or clothes and rings (*vestimenta et anuli*).[106] This last example may seem familiar. When the question was raised in Aberdeen whether merchants who were only carrying money should contribute to a loss, the answer initially provided was that 'all kind of mony, baitht gold and silver, cunzeit and uncunzeit, and als rings, being in ane schip, suld lott and scott witht the uther guds of the said schip'.[107] No further mention was made of rings, nor is there any indication anywhere in the extensive records of the case that anything other than money was at stake. It is possible that the Edinburgh merchants involved had spoken at some time to lawyers familiar with the *Digest*, or even that someone who had studied the civil law had been found in Aberdeen. It is considerably less likely that the mariners and merchants who formed the assize responsible for the ruling were directly acquainted with the text, or for that matter minded to adhere to the reasoning of the jurists. After all, their ruling was that merchants with money alone should contribute towards the payment of a penalty, which was not one of the situations in which the jurists had written about contributions being made. The jurists had not explicitly denied that contributions should be made if penalties were imposed, and the opinions they did express do seem to have informed other aspects of the handling of general average cases in the bailie courts, but at a considerable distance.[108]

June and 5 November 1572, vol. 14, 19 March and 16 May 1576, and vol. 20, 25 October 1598 and 12 February 1599.

105 E. Chevreau, 'La *Lex Rhodia de iactu*: Un exemple de la réception d'une institution étrangère dans le droit romain', (2005) 73 *Tijdschrift voor Rechtsgeschiedenis* 67, at p. 75.

106 D.14.2.2.2.

107 ACA, CA1/1/13, p. 410.

108 Another, very tentative, step towards extending general average beyond the situations envisaged in the *Digest* (the only situations discussed by Welwod and King) can be found in DCA, BCMB, vol. 12, 9 January 1572; see too ACA, CA1/1/20, p. 166.

Neither the *Digest* nor the laws of Oleron and Wisby were ever mentioned in the entries examined here.[109] In one of the protestations against the loading of goods on the overloft of a ship it was pointed out that scotting and lotting when goods placed there were jettisoned had been ruled out by two acts of parliament, but in only one protestation among many, and the legislation did not prevent scotting and lotting from taking place on the only known occasion on which it became an issue.[110] It may be concluded that while the written sources consulted by the lawyers had a distant influence on the practice of the bailie courts, it was 'pretik' itself – the customary way of doing things, whether or not consistent with a written source – that was regarded in these courts as the law of the sea.

3 Reconfiguring Maritime Practice in the Courts of the Admiral

It would be a mistake to conclude further that the burghs attached no importance to legislation. On 27 January 1576 their own representatives, meeting in Edinburgh, passed 'ane generale law to be keipit in all tymes cuming'.[111] They declared that 'incais ony schippis be pilleitt, the gudes saiff sall contribute scatt and loitt for the relief of the personis dampnefeit, bayth schip and gudes according to thair wairing', then added that in each case a 'scatt' was to be set and put to execution by 'the magistratis of the poirtis within this realme quhair the saidis schippis sall happin to aryve', and that 'the samyn ordour' was to be observed 'anent the gudes casten for saiftie of lyfe and gudes upoun commoun consent'. Four years later representatives of the burghs meeting in Stirling declared that the act passed in 1576 should be 'observit inviolablie in all tyme cuming', with the further additions that contributions were not to be made for

109 On the use of written sources like the laws of Oleron in the fifteenth century see E.B.I. Frankot, 'Maritime Law and Practice in Late Medieval Aberdeen', (2010) 89 *Scottish Historical Review* 136, and *'Of Laws of Ships and Shipmen': Medieval Maritime Law and Its Practice in Urban Northern Europe* (Edinburgh, 2012).

110 ACA, CA1/1/16, p. 784; *Acts of the Parliaments of Scotland*, vol. 2, pp. 87 and 178; Records of the Parliaments of Scotland, 1467/1/4 and 1487/10/19. Legislation on the point was also enacted by both the king's council (NRS, CS5/19, f. 170) and the burgh council of Aberdeen (ACA, CA1/1/9, p. 398).

111 *Records of the Convention of the Royal Burghs of Scotland*, vol. 1, pp. 44–5, and vol. 2, p. 494; ECA, SL1/1/5, f. 65v; *cf.* NRS, CS7/53, f. 294. In the year in which the second act of parliament touching on scotting and lotting was passed, another act was passed authorising the burghs to assemble and legislate on the affairs of merchants (*Acts of the Parliaments of Scotland*, vol. 2, p. 179; Records of the Parliaments of Scotland, 1487/10/21).

any 'cloithis nor uther geir' kept in 'sey kistis', nor for 'gudis imput in the schip' anywhere apart from its 'ladinning port'.[112] The 'scatt' set in Edinburgh later in 1580 was drawn up explicitly 'according to the acts of burrowes'.[113] In the following year representatives from Dundee tried unsuccessfully to have further additions 'eikit to the acts of burrowes maid anent the scatting and lotting for pilleit and cassin guids', and a year after that the proposed additions were given effect in an act passed in Dundee to govern its own procedures.[114] The reason for this repeated resort to legislation begins to appear from two complaints made to the privy council in 1580.[115] In the first the admiral protested that the assertion in the act just passed by the burghs of a responsibility for the distribution of losses should not be allowed to 'prejudge him in his office and jurisdictioun'. The burghs were seeking to recover control of a process over which they had lost jurisdiction, although they were not yet seeking to recover their lost jurisdiction generally, as they would do ten years later. The second complaint was made by a number of shipowners, skippers and sailors, who questioned the authority of the burghs to pass legislation on general average, believing the legislation passed to be unduly favourable to the merchants with whom they contracted.[116] A division was thus emerging between the maritime and mercantile communities, apparently because the admiralty courts were handling general average cases in a way that seemed satisfactory to mariners but not to merchants. The admiralty courts seem to have adopted an approach to the distribution of losses that differed from the approach taken in the bailie courts, which is what the burgh authorities were seeking to revive with their legislation. So how did the practice of the admiralty courts differ?

Sadly, the surviving records of the admiralty courts shed scarcely any light on the subject. One case was noted in which a merchant was required to pay freight for the transportation of wine from Bordeaux to Leith, notwithstanding the loss of several barrels of fish on the outward voyage, 'sen the samyn wer

112 *Records of the Convention of the Royal Burghs of Scotland*, vol. 1, pp. 99–100.

113 ECA, SL1/1/6, ff. 52r, 64v, 69r and 71v. This is the only other case in which legislation was cited.

114 *Records of the Convention of the Royal Burghs of Scotland*, vol. 1, pp. 117–18; DCA, BCMB, vol. 2, p. 72, and GBD, ff. 11 and 18v; A.J. Warden, *Burgh Laws of Dundee, with the History, Statutes and Proceedings of the Guild of Merchants and Fraternities of Craftsmen* (London, 1872), p. 121. The 1576 act may conceivably have been inspired by the handling of a piracy case in Dundee in 1574 (n. 47 above). The admiral's claim to jurisdiction over contribution cases had actually been resisted in another case heard there (n. 31 above).

115 *Register of the Privy Council of Scotland*, vol. 3, pp. 308–9.

116 See too DCA, PBD, vol. 11, ff. 139v-40r; *Acts of the Parliaments of Scotland*, vol. 3, p. 214; Records of the Parliaments of Scotland, 1581/10/28.

cassin for sauftie of lyve and gudis'.[117] Although the point was not discussed, the other participants in the voyage were probably expected to contribute towards the loss, for the record of a case brought before the lords of session confirms that the admiralty courts did hear actions 'for contributioun, skatting and loitting'.[118] Part of a cargo of wine had been confiscated in Bordeaux before a ship returned to Leith, where the master claimed before an admiralty court that mariners in his employment, who had been permitted to carry goods of their own (a right known as 'portage'), should help to defray the loss.[119] The mariners objected that 'the lyk wes nevir hard within this realme nor na uther land of befor', and argued that any such imposition would be unjust, 'seing the merchand be his traffik reporits greit gaine and commoditie be the aventour of his guids, and the mariner ressavis na thing, bot his simple fie and hyre, and hes na libertie to imput ony forder in the schip except the pure fie and wareing therof in portage allanerlie'. The mariners might have cited in support of their objection several articles of the *Consolato del mare*, but there is no indication in the record that they did so.[120] For his part, the master might have cited an article of the laws of Oleron, though again there is no indication that he did so.[121] Whatever was actually argued in the admiralty court, judgment was given in the master's favour. The mariners then sought to have the action 'advocated' before the lords of session, 'quha hes onelie power to juge and decyde in the said like maters of novelitie as this is, to the effect the same may remane as ane commoun practike fra thynce furth to all inferiour jugis'. The lords of session, however, instructed the judges of the admiralty court to reconsider the question themselves, in conjunction with four advocates experienced in maritime causes, and how the issue was ultimately resolved is not known.[122] A record of the court's deliberations would of course be interesting, but whether it would explain why mariners found the handling of disputes over general average in the admiralty courts preferable to their handling in the bailie courts is doubtful. It has been seen that a bailie court in Aberdeen had required contributions to be made after goods were removed to secure a ship's release in Newcastle, and that a court in Edinburgh had required mariners to contribute to a loss

---

117 *Acta curiae admirallatus Scotiae*, pp. 129–30 and 132–3.

118 NRS, CS7/139, ff. 1–2.

119 Rights of 'portage' are considered further in the fourth essay in this collection.

120 *Collection de lois maritimes antérieures au XVIIIe siècle*, 6 vols, ed. J.M. Pardessus (Paris, 1828–45), vol. 2, pp. 71–3; *Consulate of the Sea and Related Documents*, tr. S.S. Jados (University, AL, 1975), pp. 125–8.

121 *Black Book of the Admiralty*, vol. 1, pp. 98–9.

122 One of the advocates was Alexander King, who had ceased to sit as a judge of the central admiralty court in the previous year.

when some of the goods left on a ship belonged to them.[123] There is no reason to think that a decision delivered in a bailie court would have been different from the one originally delivered in the admiralty court, which in any case favoured the merchants involved more than the mariners.

However, a possible difference between the handling of disputes over general average in the admiralty and bailie courts is suggested by the stress placed in the legislation passed by the burghs on the need for scotting and lotting whenever 'ony schippis be pilleitt'.[124] The Roman jurists had considered it appropriate for contributions to be made when a ship was redeemed from pirates (*a piratis redempta sit*), but they had distinguished the situation where the property of some merchants was carried off by brigands (*praedones abstulcrint*).[125] Their reasoning was accepted by King, who observed in his treatise that in the latter situation there was not usually any 'intention on the part of the person confronting the danger to yield reluctantly to the brigands for the sake of the common benefit', although he did concede that it would be different if brigands were 'content with the wares of one of the shippers, which they professed to seize for the common liberation'.[126] King had appropriated this part of his treatise from an earlier treatise on maritime law written by Petrus Peckius, a professor at one of the universities he had attended in the Netherlands, and Peckius had in turn followed the example of a commentary on the *Digest* by the fifteenth-century jurist Raphael Fulgosius.[127] It could be, however, that King's aim at this point was not so much to move the practice of the admiralty courts into line with civilian thinking as to support a move that was already under way. Welwod also rehearsed the civilian thinking in his treatise, observing that if a ship were redeemed, 'contributioun salbe maid for all, becaus the redemptioun is for the saiftie of all', whereas if only some of the cargo were removed, 'then na skat salbe maid thairfoir, becaus it cannot be allegit in this cais that the rest of the geir is saif thairby'.[128] As a member of a family of merchants in a coastal burgh, he appreciated that this thinking was inconsistent with local practice, adding immediately that 'nowadayes, becaus that this chance is found to be common to the rest, thairfoir it is aggriet that

123 ACA, CA1/1/13, pp. 403–4 and 410; ECA, SL1/1/6, ff. 195–7.

124 *Records of the Convention of the Royal Burghs of Scotland*, vol. 1, pp. 44 and 99.

125 D.14.2.2.3.

126 *Alexander King's Treatise on Maritime Law*, pp. 174–7.

127 Peckius, *Commentaria in omnes pene iuris civilis titulos ad rem nauticam pertinentes* (Louvain, 1556), pp. 179–80; Fulgosius, *In primam Pandectarum partem commentariorum libri duo*, 2 vols (Lyons, 1554), vol. 2, f. 95r (ad D.14.2.2.3).

128 *Alexander King's Treatise on Maritime Law*, p. 367.

the upsett be also commoun to all to quhome the chance is come'.[129] In revising his treatise for the press he deleted this sentence, remarking that losses of this kind could not be attributed to 'any common necessity, for oftentimes pirats takis nothing'.[130] Given that Welwod tended at this stage to favour the claims of the burghs, the alteration he made may seem surprising, but it could be that he had only just become aware of a different approach being taken in the admiralty courts, and that as a teacher of the civil law he found it congenial. It would certainly help to explain the legislative intervention of the burghs, and the support the admiral received from shipowners, skippers and sailors, if the admiralty courts were restricting general average to cases in which ships were redeemed from pirates. As contracts for the carriage of goods were not understood to transfer the 'aventour' of 'invasioun of pirattis' from merchants to mariners, it would have suited mariners if the admiralty courts had moved away from distributing all losses inflicted by pirates among everyone involved in a maritime enterprise.[131]

If Welwod was correct about merchants and mariners expecting contributions to be made in all cases of piracy because 'this chance is found to be common', and not only where losses were found to have been sustained for what King called 'the common benefit', then their thinking would have been consistent with the approach taken in the bailie courts to the calculation of contributions, for it has been seen that scotting and lotting was arranged there in proportion to the investment each participant risked in an enterprise. In a chapter of his treatise devoted to the calculation of contributions Welwod started by summarising an article of the *Consolato del mare*, according to which goods jettisoned in the first half of a voyage were to be evaluated on the basis of what they had cost before departure, whereas goods jettisoned in the second half were to be evaluated on the basis of what they could be sold for on arrival.[132] When he removed his references to the Mediterranean laws in revising his treatise for the press, Welwod could have reverted to the articles of the laws of Oleron and Wisby requiring all evaluations to be based on prices after arrival, or he could have turned instead to the practice followed in the bailie courts of basing all evaluations on prices before departure.[133] Instead,

129 J.W. Cairns, 'Academic Feud, Bloodfeud, and William Welwod: Legal Education in St Andrews', (1998) 2 *Edinburgh Law Review* 158 and 255.

130 *Sea-Law of Scotland*, sig. C2.

131 *Alexander King's Treatise on Maritime Law*, p. 290.

132 *Alexander King's Treatise on Maritime Law*, pp. 368–9; *Collection de lois maritimes*, vol. 2, p. 102; *Consulate of the Sea*, p. 55.

133 An example of the sort of error that can easily be made if the burgh records are viewed through a civilian lens will be found in *Alexander King's Treatise on Maritime Law*, p. 305.

he adhered to the *Digest* text requiring jettisoned goods to be evaluated on the basis of their purchase price and preserved goods on the basis of their resale value.[134] King also took the Roman line that the profit jettisoned goods might have yielded was irrelevant, since what needed to be distributed was the loss sustained, while the profit actually made on preserved goods was relevant, since payments were due to the extent that other merchants and mariners had benefited from the jettison.[135] He mentioned too that the person who owned or chartered the ship could contribute on the basis of either the value of the ship or the amount of freight due to him.[136] While support for this point could have been drawn from the laws of Oleron and Wisby, King actually attributed it to local custom (*consuetudine nostra nauta introductum est*). He clearly had no difficulty with local usage, or with treating it as such (*nostris moribus obtinet*), provided it was compatible with legal theory.[137]

To suppose that the lawyers simply found some aspects of practice inconsistent with theory but not others would be to miss something important. In the law schools, the Roman texts on general average were taken to reflect a broader principle that *damnum pro communi utilitate acceptum, commune esse debeat*.[138] Those who suffered losses at sea for the benefit of others, it was explained, deserved to be reimbursed by the others, just as when buildings were demolished to prevent the spread of fire.[139] Peckius, for example, with reference again to the commentary on the *Digest* by Fulgosius, observed that a more obvious remedy for a merchant whose goods were jettisoned to use was the *actio negotiorum gestorum*.[140] The civilian doctors accepted that the contractual arrangements entered into when mariners and merchants engaged in an enterprise provided a convenient mechanism for the recovery

---

In making the calculation detailed in ACA, CA1/1/17, p. 163, the arbiters based their evaluations on the cost of goods in Flanders. Though they did also ask about sale prices in Scotland, they did so as a means of working out the exchange rate between the currencies of the two countries.

134 *Sea-Law of Scotland*, sig. C4v; D.14.2.2.4.

135 *Alexander King's Treatise on Maritime Law*, pp. 165–7.

136 *Alexander King's Treatise on Maritime Law*, pp. 182–5.

137 The view might have been taken that freight payments were the gain the master might make, but the jurists had not actually said as much.

138 *Digestum vetus* (Paris, 1559), col. 1460 (gl. 'Aequissimum' ad D.14.2.2.pr.).

139 B. Zalewski, 'Creative Interpretation of *Lex Rhodia de iactu* in the Legal Doctrine of *Ius commune*', (2016) 8 *Krytyka Prawa* 173.

140 Peckius, *Commentaria in omnes pene iuris civilis titulos ad rem nauticam pertinentes*, pp. 166–7; Fulgosius, *In primam Pandectarum partem commentariorum libri duo*, vol. 2, f. 94v (ad D.14.2.2.3). It was being assumed, of course, that the merchants were not present to give their consent.

of contributions, but the obligation to contribute was itself viewed in more quasi-contractual terms. Essentially, losses were distributed because and to the extent that benefits were gained from them. In the bailie courts, in contrast, losses were distributed to the extent that risks materialised, not to the extent that benefits were gained. Anyone engaged in an enterprise risked losing whatever he had invested in it. If it was a joint enterprise, as voyages typically were, then the risks undertaken by all those involved were understood to be shared between them in proportion to their investments. It was in keeping with this notion of risk sharing that those whose goods were placed 'aboun the ourloft' of a ship were taken to bear their own 'aventour', along with those who 'payet nather fraucht nor custome', and those whose goods were 'imput in the schip at ony uther port uther nor at hir ladinning port'.[141] It was only those who embarked on an enterprise together who were taken to underwrite each other's risks. The mariners and merchants who regulated their own affairs in the bailie courts did expect losses to be distributed among them, and their thinking does appear to have been influenced in some respects (albeit at a deep and distant level) by the theory of the civil law, which also provided for the distribution of losses, but the practice of the bailie courts differed from the theory of the law schools not only in certain details but in its fundamental rationale. Behind the distribution of losses in the bailie courts was an assumption that risks had already been shared, and it may be that this assumption did not underpin the handling of general average cases in the admiralty courts. It may be that practitioners in the admiralty courts, some of whom were learned lawyers like King, had adopted the vocabulary of scotting and lotting but not the presuppositions behind its original usage.

As well as helping to explain the legislative intervention of the burghs in the last quarter of the sixteenth century, a move away from risk sharing in the admiralty courts would also help to explain a different development that seems to have taken place around the same time. In 1574 it was placed on record in the burgh court books of Dundee that a sum of money was to be paid following the return of a ship and crew from abroad, with an additional sum if the voyage was extended, and that the creditors were 'to beir the aventour of the saids money quhill the saids schippis or persones arriving in Scotland'.[142] In 1580 it

141 ECA, SL1/1/8, f. 65v; *Records of the Convention of Royal Burghs*, vol. 1, p. 100. Ironically, the thinking of merchants and mariners was more consistent with the reasoning behind the *Nomos Rhodion nautikos*, of which they professed ignorance (N. Bogojevic-Gluscevic, 'The Law and Practice of Average in Medieval Towns of the Eastern Adriatic', (2005) 36 *Journal of Maritime Law and Commerce* 21, at pp. 28–9).

142 DCA, BCMB, vol. 13, 3 April 1574.

was placed on record in the burgh court books of Aberdeen that a merchant, 'purposand to saill to France', had borrowed a sum of money and promised to repay it with interest on his return, with the creditor again 'bering the aventour thairof be the see and piracy'.[143] Nearly twenty years later the actual terms of a contract were registered in Dundee.[144] A master from Anstruther promised to pay a French creditor 'the soume of twelf hundretht punds money usuall of Scotland, witht twentie punds money as for the profeit of ilk hundreth thairof', as soon as his ship returned safely from the Canary Islands, taking care to explain that the creditor had lent him the principal sum 'upon his adventour, sa that he salbe ane warrand of the samin fra schipwrak and pirat, the quhilk God avoid, untill the said schippis arryvall and returning fra the saids iles'.[145] In the longer version of his treatise Welwod remarked that there were important differences 'twixt that money quhilk is lent amangis men to uses on land and that quhilk is lent for the sea'.[146] One difference was that money was lent for use on land 'upone the perrell of the borrower', whereas it was lent for use at sea 'upon the hazard of the lender'. Another was that charging interest on a loan for use on land was 'odiouslie callit *usura* in generall', whereas charging interest on a loan for use at sea was 'callit *usura maritima* or *foenus nauticum*, and is the pryce not of the len bot of the hazard and danger quhilk the lender takkis upon him duiring the len'.[147] Both distinctions were backed up in Welwod's treatise with references to *Digest* texts.[148] Whether the borrowers who recorded their obligations in the burgh court books were familiar with these texts may be doubtful, but the notary public who drafted the document registered in 1599 may have known them, or have followed an exemplar drafted by someone else who knew them, and there may also have been notarised documents behind the earlier entries. It seems fairly likely that other loans of the same type were made of which no trace has been found, and it is entirely possible that some were made before the mid 1570s, yet it would make sense for this type of loan to have come into vogue only then. If general average cases were not being handled in the admiralty courts on the basis of the assumptions once made in the bailie courts about risk sharing among the participants

143 ACA, CA1/1/30, p. 219.

144 DCA, BCMB, vol. 20, 5 March 1599.

145 The word 'pirat' is not clearly written, but it is not easy to see what else could have been intended.

146 *Alexander King's Treatise on Maritime Law*, p. 364. Neither King nor Balfour dealt with the topic.

147 *Cf. Register of the Privy Council of Scotland*, vol. 2, pp. 329–30.

148 D.22.2.1 and 5.

in maritime ventures, then those embarking on such ventures would have had reason to look for ways of shifting the risks involved onto other people.

The evidence of maritime loans from the closing decades of the century is the only evidence that has come to light of anything remotely resembling marine insurance being used in the period under review.[149] It is possible that mariners and merchants from Scotland were paying premiums to insurers overseas in exchange for promises to indemnify them against specified risks.[150] Although no trace of any such contract has been found in the sources examined here, the adoption of a civilian approach to general average, whether it was already under way in the admiralty courts or was merely being recommended by lawyers, would have increased the attraction of any available form of risk shifting.[151] Conversely, as long as general average continued to be conceived of as a form of risk sharing, the attraction of insurance contracts would have been reduced, for the obvious reason that general average would have been a more efficient mechanism. When a loss is generalised among the participants in a venture, only the loss has to be covered, whereas people who are persuaded to bear the risk of a venture in which they have no personal interest will normally require to be paid for their trouble, through interest on loans, insurance premiums or something of the sort. The extra payment might always have seemed worthwhile when situations were envisaged in which it was not considered appropriate to talk about scotting and lotting, such as the damage or destruction of a ship in a storm, and perhaps the seizure of a ship or cargo by enemies in wartime.[152] The extra payment might also have started to seem worthwhile when piracy was envisaged, if it came to be considered appropriate to talk about scotting and lotting only in the exceptional circumstances specified by the Roman jurists. The extra payment may again have started to seem more worthwhile if contributions came to be calculated on the basis of

149 *Cf.* A.D.M. Forte, 'Marine Insurance and Risk Distribution in Scotland before 1800', (1987) 6 *Law and History Review* 393.

150 The original move from maritime loans to marine insurance is outlined in L. Piccinno, 'Genoa, 1340–1620: Early Development of Marine Insurance', in A.B. Leonard (ed.), *Marine Insurance: Origins and Institutions, 1300–1850* (Basingstoke, 2016), p. 25, at pp. 27–35. The recourse taken to maritime loans in Scotland suggests that more developed forms of marine insurance were not readily available there.

151 *Cf.* S.C. Styles, 'Scottish Marine Insurance before the Mid-Eighteenth Century', in A.R.C. Simpson, S.C. Styles, E. West and A.L.M. Wilson (eds), *Continuity, Change and Pragmatism in the Law: Essays in Memory of Professor Angelo Forte* (Aberdeen, 2016), p. 237.

152 It should be stressed again that while there are extensive records on prize taking, some of which are discussed J.D. Ford, *The Emergence of Privateering* (Leiden, 2023), pp. 8–101, scotting and lotting is not often mentioned. Insurance is never mentioned, either in these records or in those on shipwreck.

the benefits merchants gained when their goods were preserved. Quite apart from any incentive to insure against their own losses, merchants might have found the payment of premiums preferable to the generalising of everyone's losses in accordance with the gains they might make rather than the sums they invested. In these ways, what might be termed the increasing Romanisation of general average may have driven mariners and merchants in Scotland towards the use of insurance, when it became available. It may be wondered whether a change in the understanding of general average played a similar part in the rise of insurance elsewhere.

10

The Law and Economy of Shipwreck in Scotland during the Sixteenth Century

The title above specifies the spatial as well as the temporal limitations of this essay, which examines evidence of shipwrecks in Scotland during the sixteenth century alone.[1] During this period many ships sailing out of Scottish ports were wrecked in other countries, including Norway, and these disasters sometimes had repercussions at home.[2] The concern here, however, is with the legal and

1 On the fifteenth century see E.B.I. Frankot, 'Maritime Law and Practice in Late Medieval Aberdeen', (2010) 89 *Scottish Historical Review* 136, at pp. 145–8, and *'Of Laws of Ships and Shipmen': Medieval Maritime Law and Its Practice in Urban Northern Europe* (Edinburgh, 2012), pp. 175–6.

2 *Acts of the Lords of Council in Public Affairs, 1501–54*, ed. R.K. Hannay (Edinburgh, 1932), pp. 77, 285 and 489; *Register of the Privy Council of Scotland*, 14 vols, ed. J.H. Burton and D. Masson (Edinburgh, 1877–98), vol. 2, pp. 584–5, and vol. 14, pp. 201–2 and 246; *Acta curiae admirallatus Scotiae, 1557–62*, ed. T.C. Wade (Edinburgh, 1937), pp. 7, 10, 12, 29, 37–8 and 72; *The Letters of James the Fourth, 1505–13*, ed. R.L. Mackie (Edinburgh, 1953), p. 147; *The Letters of James V*, ed. R.K. Hannay and D. Hay (Edinburgh, 1954), pp. 7, 155, 189 and 369; *Bronnen tot de Geschiedenis van der Handel met Engeland, Schotland en Ierland*, 2nd ser., 2 vols, ed. H.J. Smit (The Hague, 1942–50), vol. 1, p. 535; *Letters and Papers, Foreign and Domestic, of the Reign of Henry VIII, 1509–47*, 21 vols, ed. J.S. Brewer, J. Gairdner and R.H. Brodie (London, 1862–1910), vol. 7, pp. 414–15; *The State Papers and Letters of Sir Ralph Sadler*, 2 vols, ed. A. Clifford (Edinburgh, 1809), vol. 1, pp. 582–3; *Calendar of the State Papers Relating to Scotland and Mary Queen of Scots, 1547–1603*, 13 vols, ed. J. Bain, W.K. Boyd, H.W. Meikle, A.I. Cameron, M.S. Giuseppi and J.D. Mackie (Edinburgh, 1898–1969), vol. 1, pp. 264 and 502, and vol. 10, pp. 272, 318, 393, 461, 475–6, 515–17 and 525–8; *Calendar of State Papers, Foreign Series, of the Reign of Elizabeth*, 23 vols, ed. J. Stevenson, A.J. Crosby, A.J. Butler, S.C. Lomas, A.B. Hinds and R.B. Wernham (London, 1863–1950), vol. 2, pp. 107, 113–14, 116, 131 and 256, vol. 4, pp. 114, 346 and 376–7, vol. 5, p. 148, and vol. 6, pp. 122, 421 and 550; *The Border Papers: Calendar of Letters and Papers Relating to the Affairs of the Borders of England and Scotland*, 2 vols, ed. J. Bain (Edinburgh, 1894–96), vol. 2, pp. 819–20, and vol. 9, p. 670; *Acts of the Privy Council of England*, 46 vols, ed. J.R. Dasent, E.G. Atkinson, J.V. Lyle, R.F. Monger and P.E. Penfold (London, 1890–1964), vol. 17, pp. 41–2, 77–9, 81, 86, 106, 156, 179–82 and 350–1; *Extracts from the Council Register of the Burgh of Aberdeen*, 2 vols, ed. J. Stuart (Aberdeen, 1844–8), vol. 1, pp. 331–3; *Aberdeen Council Letters*, 6 vols, ed. L.B. Taylor (London, 1942–61), vol. 1, p. 4; *Extracts from the Records of the Burgh of Edinburgh*, 1st ser., 5 vols, ed. J.D. Marwick (Edinburgh, 1869–92), vol. 4, p. 545; *Protocol Book of Mr Gilbert Grote, 1552–73*, ed. W. Angus (Edinburgh, 1914), p. 84; ACA, CA1/1/20, pp. 561, 564–6 and 572, CA1/1/21, pp. 23, 94–6 and 100, CA1/1/24, pp. 79 and 402, CA1/1/25, pp. 546, 568 and 586, CA1/1/26, pp. 52, 56, 60, 64, 76, 78–9, 84, 107, 110–11, 144, 151 and 154, CA1/1/27, p. 197, and CA1/1/29, pp. 20–1; DCA, BCMB, vol. 19, 14 January 1596, and PBD, vol. 11, ff. 70v-1r.

 | DOI:10.1163/9789004695009_011

(to a lesser extent) the economic consequences of the shipwrecks that often occurred on the coasts of Scotland.[3] More precisely, the concern is with the rights and duties people were believed to have when they were involved in recovering the remains of ships – including their equipment and cargoes – after they were destroyed while sailing near Scotland. Two main types of evidence are considered, both of which must be handled cautiously. In the first place, access to the subject is eased by the existence of several treatises touching on the legal aspects of shipwreck, written by lawyers during the last quarter of the century.[4] The caveat requiring to be attached to this material is that its writers tended to draw their information from other books, and may not have provided an accurate account of how wrecks were dealt with in practice. In the second place, records survive of litigation relating to the subject, sometimes in burgh courts sitting in coastal towns, sometimes in central courts sitting in Edinburgh. The caveat requiring to be attached to this material is that for much of the century the expectation was that litigation relating to navigation would be dealt with in specialised admiralty courts, from which scarcely any records have survived.[5] Since the treatise writers usually wrote about the law applicable in the admiralty courts, they may be taken to compensate to some extent for the absence of these records, just as the availability of records from other courts may be taken to compensate to some extent for the theoretical tendencies of the treatise writers. If viewed from the different perspectives provided by these two bodies of material, the consequences of shipwrecks in Scotland during the sixteenth century may come into view fairly clearly, but it needs to be remembered that there is a significant gap in the evidence available.

1 The Right to 'Wrak' and the 'Auld Lawes'

The earliest account of the relevant law is found in a compilation of sources known as the 'practicks' of Sir James Balfour of Pittendreich, who seems to have followed instructions issued by a Scottish parliament in 1575 to a commission

3 The essay is based on a paper that formed one of a pair, the other (delivered by Jørn Sunde) dealing with the law and economy of shipwreck in Norway.

4 Not all the treatises referred to were completed, let alone published, before the end of the century.

5 *Register of the Privy Council of Scotland*, vol. 3, pp. 242–3; *Calendar of the State Papers Relating to Scotland and Mary Queen of Scots*, vol. 4, p. 300; A. Maxwell, *Old Dundee, Ecclesiastical, Burghal and Social, prior to the Reformation* (Edinburgh, 1891), pp. 318–19; DCA, BCMB, vol. 1, ff. 119v-20r and 139v; NRS, PS1/71, f. 148. The only surviving court book, covering a period of less than five years, is cited in n. 2 above.

set up to compare, condense and consolidate 'the bukis of the law, actis of parliament and decisionis befoir the sessioun'.[6] In dealing with the consequences of shipwrecks, Balfour drew attention to one item from each of these categories. According to the first, it had been 'statute and ordanit' that if a ship was wrecked and any creature 'cum living and quick to the land', the ship should not be treated as 'wrak', but rather all 'gudis and geir' washed ashore should be gathered and preserved by the local authorities, in order to be restored to anyone who appeared within a year and a day and established title to them.[7] It was added that if no one claimed salvaged property within the prescribed period, it would 'pertene to the king', unless 'wrak' had already been granted to someone else. Both in the compilation known as Balfour's 'practicks' and in two surveys of 'the bukis of the law' used in its production, these provisions were ascribed to a collection of regulations called the *Leges forestarum*.[8] It may be wondered what they had to do with the regulation of activities in forests, and they are indeed absent from modern editions of the collection, which are limited to provisions on the hunting of game, the straying of livestock, the gathering of wood and similar matters.[9] Yet the provisions on shipwreck do appear in a longer version of the *Leges forestarum* found in many manuscripts containing the medieval texts known as the 'bukis of the law' or 'auld lawes'.[10] Perhaps the confusion resulted from the widespread association of the word 'wrak' with the word 'waith', which seems to have come from the Old Norse term 'veiðr', meaning hunting or fishing, and to have been wrongly identified with the English term 'waif', more suggestive of straying.[11] In any case, it was from the

6 *The Acts of the Parliaments of Scotland*, 12 vols, ed. T. Thomson and C. Innes (Edinburgh, 1814–75), vol. 3, p. 89; Records of the Parliaments of Scotland, ed. K.M. Brown (http://www.rps.ac.uk), A1575/3/7.

7 *The Practicks of Sir James Balfour of Pittendreich*, 2 vols, ed. P.G.B. McNeill (Edinburgh, 1962–3), vol. 2, pp. 623–4 (here and in other quotations from primary sources, the punctuation and capitalisation of the original are sometimes adjusted, but not the orthography). On the compilation of Balfour's work see now the fifth essay in this collection.

8 NLS, Adv. MS 25.4.11, f. 33v (in Latin), and NRS, GD112/71/5, f. 41r (in Scots).

9 *Acts of the Parliaments of Scotland*, vol. 1, pp. 687–92; M.L. Anderson, *A History of Scottish Forestry*, 2 vols (London, 1967), vol. 1, pp. 150–4; J.M. Gilbert, *Hunting and Hunting Reserves in Medieval Scotland* (Edinburgh, 1979), pp. 291–307.

10 For instance, NRS, PA5/3, f. 116; NLS, Adv. MS 7.1.9, f. 406v, Adv. MS 25.4.12, ff. 250v-1r, Adv. MS 25.5.6, ff. 233v-4r, and MS 16497, ff. 127v-8r; SAUL, msKF51.R4, ff. 124v-5r.

11 W. Craigie, A.J. Aitken, J.A.C. Stevenson, H.D. Watson and M.G. Dareau (eds), *A Dictionary of the Older Scottish Tongue from the Twelfth Century to the End of the Seventeenth*, 12 vols (Chicago, London and Aberdeen, 1931–2002), vol. 11, pp. 619–20, and vol. 12, pp. 320–3. Brian Smith has kindly drawn attention to an illuminating account of the derivation of 'waith' in his *Toons and Tenants: Settlement and Society in Shetland, 1299–1899* (Lerwick, 2000), pp. 58–63.

longer version of the *Leges forestarum* that Balfour (or one of his assistants) had extracted these provisions.

Towards the end of the century they were ascribed to the *Leges forestarum* again by Sir John Skene of Curriehill, who may have been familiar with the surveys of 'the bukis of the law' used by Balfour.[12] In a dictionary of the technical and archaic terms encountered in the old laws Skene explained that the word 'wrek' meant the 'power, libertie and prerogative competent to the king, or to ony person to quhome the samin is granted be him, be infeftment or ony uther disposition, to intromet and up-take sik guds and geare as are schip-broken'.[13] After adding that the right enjoyed by a landowner 'infeft with wreck' would be as extensive as the right enjoyed by 'the king himself, giver theirof', Skene made reference to '*L. forest.* c. *Inter antiqua* 56'. It may be significant that unlike Balfour, who cited the relevant article by its number alone, Skene also drew attention to its opening phrase, which indicated that the provisions on shipwreck had been 'found written among old royal statutes'.[14] He moved on at once to rehearse the terms of a statute attributed to the English king Edward I, and it was not until this point that he took his readers through the provisions Balfour had reproduced from the *Leges forestarum*. As a matter of fact, the terms of the fourth chapter of the first Statute of Westminster, enacted in 1275, were almost identical to the terms of the article cited from the *Leges forestarum*, differing mostly in the order of their presentation.[15] In the English statute the aim had been to codify the law of shipwreck emerging from previous legislation and the thinking of lawyers.[16] Skene went on to close his discussion by mentioning the statute *De praerogativa regis*, supposedly enacted during

12 J. Buchanan, 'The MSS of *Regiam Maiestatem*: An Experiment', (1937) 49 *Juridical Review* 217, at pp. 220–1; J.W. Cairns, T.D. Fergus and H.L. MacQueen, 'Legal Humanism and the History of Scots Law: John Skene and Thomas Craig', in J. MacQueen (ed.), *Humanism in Renaissance Scotland* (Edinburgh, 1990), p. 48, at p. 51. Skene may have assisted in compiling the surveys, and working on them may have led him to compose his dictionary, which was first circulated as an appendix to Balfour's practicks. These connections are now explored in the fifth and seventh essays in this collection.

13 *De verborum significatione* (Edinburgh, 1597), sigg. S4v-5r (the word 'are' has been inserted at the end of this quotation, where it surely belongs).

14 As the numbering of the articles in the manuscripts is variable, and sometimes differs even internally between tables of contents and the articles themselves, this suggestion must be made with some hesitation.

15 *The Statutes of the Realm*, 11 vols (London, 1810–28), vol. 1, p. 28.

16 *The Annals of Roger de Hoveden*, 2 vols, ed. H.T. Riley (London, 1853), vol. 2, pp. 170–1; *Calendar of the Charter Rolls Preserved in the Public Record Office*, 6 vols, ed. H.C. Maxwell Lyte and C.G. Grump (London, 1903–27), vol. 1, p. 220; *Bracton on the Laws and Customs of England*, 4 vols, ed. S.E. Thorne (Cambridge, MA, 1968–70), vol. 3, pp. 339–40.

the reign of Edward II, which extended 'wreck of the sea' to encompass 'whales and great sturgeons taken in the sea or elsewhere within the realm, except in certain places privileged by the king'.[17] If Skene suspected, and may have been trying to suggest to his readers, that the 'old royal statutes' among which the provisions on shipwreck had been 'found written' by the compilers of the *Leges forestarum* were actually acts passed in the parliaments of England, he did not make his thinking explicit. He was forced to admit that in Scotland too 'wrek' was 'ane worde specified in the lawes and sindrie infeftments'.[18] Quite apart from being found in many copies of the *Leges forestarum*, the word continued to appear throughout the sixteenth century in feudal charters.[19]

Whatever Skene may have been thinking when he wrote his dictionary, he changed his mind shortly after it was printed in 1597. The provisions on shipwreck were omitted from a draft edition of the old laws he produced, in which a short version of the *Leges forestarum* was included.[20] Then, in revising his draft for the press, he reintroduced the provisions, but as part of another medieval text, called the *Statuta regis Alexandri*.[21] Now presented as an act passed by a Scottish king during the first half of the thirteenth century, they appeared without the statement that they had been found *inter antiqua statuta regia*, and in the slightly different order recorded in the Statute of Westminster,

17 *Statutes of the Realm*, vol. 1, p. 226.

18 *De verborum significatione*, sig. S4v.

19 *Acts of the Parliaments of Scotland*, vol. 2, pp. 271–3 and 562–5, and vol. 3, pp. 154–7, 254–6, 263–7, 323–5, 510–16, 629–36, 645–8 and 650–6; Records of the Parliaments of Scotland, A1504/3/147, 1567/4/14, 1579/10/57, 1581/10/90 and 94, 1584/5/54, 1587/7/144, 1592/4/196, 1592/4/203 and 1592/4/209; *Shetland Documents*, 3 vols, ed. J.H. Ballantyne and B. Smith (Lerwick, 1999–2016), vol. 1, pp. 98, 147, 165, 171, 181 and 238; *Registrum magni sigilli regum Scotorum: The Register of the Great Seal of Scotland*, 11 vols, ed. J. Balfour Paul, J.M. Thomson, J.H. Stevenson and W.K. Dickson (Edinburgh, 1984), vol. 4, pp. 727–8, and vol. 5, pp. 263–4, 467–8, 516, 565 and 590.

20 NLS, Adv. MS 7.1.10, ff. 164r-6v. Skene claimed to have transcribed at least some of the twenty-two articles he listed from an 'antiquus codex' belonging to Sir David Lindsay of Edzell, adding that they were said there to date from the reign of William I (1165–1214). Gilbert, *Hunting and Hunting Reserves in Medieval Scotland*, pp. 272–3, has identified NLS, Adv. MS 25.9.7(1), ff. 30–5, as Lindsay's copy, though why is not entirely clear. Someone had written on it in pencil that it came from the 'Edzell Charter Chest', and it does contain twenty-two articles. However, they are not identical with Skene's articles, they are manifestly not from an old transcription, since the last two are based on sixteenth-century legislation, and there is no indication at any point that the rest date from the reign of William I.

21 NLS, Adv. MS 25.5.8, f. 197; *Regiam maiestatem: Scotiae veteres leges et constitutiones* (Edinburgh, 1609), pt 2, f. 28; *Regiam maiestatem: The Auld Lawes and Constitutions of Scotland* (Edinburgh, 1609), pt 2, f. 19r.

although in substance they remained the same.[22] In a marginal annotation to his Latin edition of the old laws Skene claimed to have found these provisions in a manuscript he labelled the *liber Perthensis*, but what this signified is hard to tell.[23] There is no known manuscript in which the shipwreck provisions appear in the *Statuta regis Alexandri*. There is one in which they are separated from the *Leges forestarum*, but they are not attached there to any other medieval text, nor is the manuscript connected in any discernible way with Perth.[24] Alice Taylor, who has recently published a reliable edition of the *Statuta regis Alexandri* from which these provisions are absent, has plausibly proposed that awareness of the presence in the longer version of the *Leges forestarum* of other articles that did actually derive from Alexander II's legislation may have encouraged the belief that these provisions came from the same source.[25] For a patriotic Scot, determined to defend the authenticity of the old laws, the belief would have been attractive.[26] As Habakkuk Bisset, who assisted both Balfour and Skene in the late sixteenth century, was to point out in the early seventeenth century, it implied that it was an English king who had copied a Scottish legislator, not vice versa.[27]

Skene may possibly have known that the shipwreck provisions had already been attributed to Alexander II by another author, for that author had been appointed to the chair of civil law at the University of St Andrews previously held by his brother.[28] In a treatise on maritime law apparently written around

22 The king to whom the act was attributed was Alexander II, the immediate successor of William I.

23 A. Taylor, *The Laws of Medieval Scotland: Legal Compilations from the Thirteenth and Fourteenth Centuries* (Edinburgh, 2019), pp. 13–14. Although NLS, Adv. MS 25.5.10, originated in the priory of Chartreux at Perth, it was certainly not Skene's source (*Laws of Medieval Scotland*, pp. 393–402).

24 NLS, Adv. MS 25.4.15, ff. 198v-9r.

25 *Cf.* Taylor, *Laws of Medieval Scotland*, pp. 127 and 350–1.

26 H.L. MacQueen, '*Glanvill* Resarcinate: Sir John Skene and *Regiam maiestatem*', in A.A. MacDonald, M. Lynch and I.B. Cowan (eds), *The Renaissance in Scotland: Studies in Literature, Religion, History and Culture Offered to John Durkan* (Leiden, 1994), p. 385, at p. 385, and '*Regiam maiestatem*, Scots Law and National Identity', (1995) 74 *Scottish Historical Review* 1, at pp. 16–17.

27 *Habakkuk Bisset's Rolment of Courtis*, 3 vols, ed. P.J. Hamilton-Grierson (Edinburgh, 1920–6), vol. 2, pp. 214–16.

28 It was from his elder brother William that Skene had received the copy of the old laws now known as the Bute manuscript, but it does not have the shipwreck provisions among either the *Leges forestarum* or the *Statuta regis Alexandri* (Taylor, *Laws of Medieval Scotland*, pp. 52–3). Whether there was any personal contact between John Skene and William Welwod is unclear, but it could be significant that they had both been encouraged to study at the University of Wittenberg, an unusual destination for Scottish students at this time, as is now investigated in the seventh essay in this collection.

1587 (of which an abbreviated version was printed three years later without the attribution), William Welwod had also compared the laws of Scotland and England, although he had not confined his comparison to those laws, and had been intent on making a different point.[29] In the year of his appointment to the St Andrews chair, the earl of Bothwell had received a new charter as admiral of Scotland, in which the officials who staffed his courts had been instructed to follow the example of the maritime laws of 'France, Spain, England, Denmark or other foreign nations'.[30] With this perhaps in mind, Welwod cited a document entitled *De officio admiralitatis Angliae*, along with 'statut. Alexa. 2', in support of the proposition that 'quhair admiralities ar constitut and allowit', if a ship was sunk without survivors and no one appeared within a year and a day to claim salvaged goods, 'the half belangis to the admirall, the rest to the finder'.[31] The English document, unlike the provisions contained in the first Statute of Westminster or attributed to Alexander II, did mention this division into two parts, but it was another distribution that had been adopted in Scotland. 'And agane in uther countries', Welwod continued, 'a third to the king, a thrid to the admiral, and a thrid to the finder, as in France'. He cited in support of this proposition a French edict issued by Henry III in 1584, which had renewed an edict issued by Francis I in 1544, subject to the qualification that the king's share had sometimes been transferred to the owners of land where goods were recovered.[32] The Scottish admiral's new charter assigned him two thirds of '*wrak* et *weth gudis*', with the other third assigned to the finders.[33] Welwod surmised that 'in Scotland the prince hes quatt his thrid to the admirall', but neglected to consider what would happen if the king's share had been

29 *Alexander King's Treatise on Maritime Law*, ed. J.D. Ford (Edinburgh, 2018), p. 371. For an examination of the relationship between the manuscript and printed versions see the sixth essay in this collection.

30 *Registrum magni sigilli regum Scotorum*, vol. 5, pp. 449–50; NRS, PS1/55, ff. 190v-3.

31 *The Black Book of the Admiralty*, 4 vols, ed. T. Twiss (London, 1871–6), vol. 1, p. 241.

32 *Collection de lois maritimes antérieures au XVIIIe siècle*, 6 vols, ed. J.M. Pardessus (Paris, 1828–45), vol. 4, p. 300; *Recueil général des anciennes lois françaises*, 29 vols, ed. F.-A. Isambert, M. Jourdan and M. Decrusy (Paris, 1822–33), vol. 12, p. 854, and vol. 14, p. 561. On the origins of the distribution see J. Darsel, *L'Amirauté en Bretagne: Des origines à la fin du XVIIIe siècle*, ed. G. Le Bouëdec (Rennes, 2012), p. 160, and F. Trivellato, 'Amphibious Power: The Law of Wreck, Maritime Customs and Sovereignty in Richelieu's France', (2015) 33 *Law and History Review* 915, at pp. 931–2.

33 The myth that the distribution in thirds of whales driven ashore in the Northern Isles derived from 'udal law' has been exploded in B. Smith, 'Pilot Whales, Udal Law and Custom in Shetland: Legal Red Herrings', (2003) 23 *Northern Scotland* 85. The response recorded in R.A. Houston, 'Custom in Context: Medieval and Early-Modern Scotland and England', (2011) 211 *Past and Present* 35, at p. 44, is simply bizarre.

transferred to a landowner. With reference to provisions added to some French copies of the *Rôles d'Oléron*, a compilation dating from the thirteenth century, he had already limited the rights of landowners to items 'found without flude-mark', and had hinted at an adjustment to the 'custome' underpinning their rights when admiralties were constituted across Europe.[34]

2 The Confiscation of Wrecks and the Civil Law

According to the 1587 charter, '*wrak* et *weth gudis*' were 'bona eiecta et pro derelictis habita' – that is, items washed ashore from a wreck were 'regarded as' abandoned things. In the theory of the civil law taught by Welwod, had they been genuinely abandoned things (*res derelicta*) they would have been ownerless (*res nullius*) and open to acquisition by the finders who took possession of them (*occupatio*), whereas merely regarding them as abandoned things served to justify a different mode of acquisition.[35] In a treatise dealing with the 'droit de varech' or 'droit de bris' recognised in France, Christophle du Bois-Gelin explained how this worked by drawing attention to three texts from the books of the civil law.[36] In the first, an extract from the juristic writings of ancient Rome, which had been preserved in the *Digest* compiled at the behest of the emperor Justinian, it was observed that unclaimed goods (*bona vacantia*) were assigned in certain circumstances to the imperial treasury (*fiscus*) in order to prevent things from remaining without an owner for a long time.[37] In the second, a passage from the twelfth century compilation known as the *Libri feudorum*, which had been incorporated into the books studied in the schools of civil law, *bona vacantia* were listed among the peculiar privileges of the ruler (*inter regalia*).[38] In the third text, again from Justinian's *Digest*, things open to acquisition by the ruler were described quite literally as goods deserving of assignment to the treasury (*bona confiscanda*).[39] In England, similarly,

34 *Collection de lois maritimes*, vol. 1, pp. 348–9 and 351–4. Although the *Rôles d'Oléron* were often included in copies of the old laws of Scotland, and were consequently regarded by Welwod as part of the 'common law' of the land, these particular provisions were not among those transcribed.

35 D.41.1.9.8 and J.2.1.47. How much teaching Welwod did at St Andrews, where students were not admitted to read for law degrees, is unclear.

36 *Traité des droits royaux de bris et de brefs* (Dinan, 1595), pp. 44–5.

37 D.38.9.1.pr. The circumstances envisaged were not the recovering of goods from wrecks.

38 *Volumen legum quod parvum vocant* (Lyons, 1604), cols 117–18 ('Libri feudorum', 2.56); K. Lehmann, *Das Langobardische Lehnrecht* (Gottingen, 1896), p. 182.

39 D.48.21.3.7.

Christopher St German remarked that 'the lawe must nedes reduce the propertye of all goodes to some man'.[40] If goods retrieved from a shipwreck were not claimed, he explained, 'it shold not be knowen who ought to take them, and so might they be distroyed and no profite com of theym'. It was therefore 'resonable' for the law to 'appoynt who ought to have them', and it was 'not unreasonable' for them to be 'forfet to the kyng', since he incurred 'great charge' in clearing the sea of 'pyrates'. In Scotland the same line of argument was rehearsed by Thomas Craig of Riccarton, who commented that the king had 'granted the greatest part of the goods known as wrack to the admiral, so that he may keep navigation safe for his people'.[41] Craig was unsure how consistent the custom (*consuetudo*) that had grown up around this grant was with the grants often made to coastal landowners.

The charter granted to the Scottish admiral in 1587 was unusually precise in its terms, but there is some evidence that the 'privileges' or 'profits' vaguely referred to elsewhere were taken in practice to encompass a customary right to the remains of wrecked vessels.[42] In 1549 the admiral rewarded someone with a gift of a pinnace wrecked at St Monans, 'now pertening to us be resoun of eschete throw rycht and privilege of admiralite grantit to us and our predecessouris'.[43] It was clearly expected that the recipient of the gift would obtain items recovered from the wreck by certain named individuals, who remained in possession of them, but whether it was expected that those individuals would retain a portion is unclear. In 1581 a landowner who was ordered by the privy council to surrender ordnance recovered from a wreck at Scoughall was prepared to do so only on receiving a discharge of liability to the admiral, without which she would have been 'in danger to be persewit for the samin'.[44] In 1596 landowners on the coast of Fife were summoned before an admiralty court to answer for timber, tackle and other things they had recovered from a wreck there.[45] When the case was transferred to the College of Justice, the highest

40 *St German's Doctor and Student*, ed. T.F.T. Plucknett and J.L. Barton (London, 1974), pp. 291–2.

41 *Jus feudale tribus libris comprehensum, Book I*, tr. L. Dodd (Edinburgh, 2017), pp. 496–7. It was under the rubric 'Escheit' that the provisions on 'wrak', as found in the *Leges forestarum*, were cited in David Chalmers of Ormond, *Compendium of the Laws of Scotland*, ed. W. Coutts, J. Goodare and A.R.C. Simpson (Edinburgh, 2023), pp. 410–12.

42 *Acts of the Parliaments of Scotland*, vol. 3, pp. 256–9; Records of the Parliaments of Scotland, 1581/10/91; NRS, GD150/2278; B. Seton, 'The Vice Admiral and the Quest of the "Golden Pennie"', (1923) 20 *Scottish Historical Review* 122, at p. 123.

43 *Memorials of the Family of Wemyss of Wemyss*, 3 vols, ed. W. Fraser (Edinburgh, 1888), vol. 2, pp. 177–8.

44 *Register of the Privy Council of Scotland*, vol. 3, pp. 367–8; NRS, PC1/10, p. 547.

45 NRS, CS7/159, ff. 193v-4r and 283v-4.

civil court in the country, one of the defenders objected that his family had been infeft in their lands 'as ane frie barone, with privilege of wrak, wathe and wier guidis arryving within the boundis of the said baronie', and long before 'ony infeftment grantit to the said admerall and his predicessouris in the said office of admeralitie'.[46] Advocates appearing on behalf of the admiral resisted this objection on the two grounds adumbrated in the manuscript version of Welwod's treatise, to which they may conceivably have had access, although there is no evidence that it had been put into circulation. In the first place, they argued that the objects at issue had been found 'within the sie merk be the said defender, to the quhilk the privilegis contenit in his said infeftment can na wayes be extendit'. Any claim founded on ownership of land, they reasoned, would have to depend on items from a wreck being washed by the waves onto the land granted, beyond the foreshore retained by the crown. In the second place, they argued that no infeftment in land could possibly 'derogat the richt, privileges, commoditeis and casualiteis of the said admeralitie, without the said admerall or his predicessours haid gevin thair express consent and assent to the said infeftment'. Despite the 'allegit anteraitie' of the grant of the land, they insisted, it could not undermine the right exercised by the admirals of Scotland 'past memorie of man'. The lords of council and session, as the judges of the court were known, dismissed the landowner's objection 'in respect of the said answer and replye', but whether both arguments were considered equally convincing is not revealed by the records of the case.[47]

The admiral whose interests were defended in the 1596 case was presumably unaware that one of the lawyers selected to represent him had written critically about his immediate predecessor's grant of '*wrak* et *weth gudis*' in another unpublished treatise.[48] Alexander King, a judge in the central admiralty court sitting in Edinburgh as well as an advocate in the College of Justice, had drawn attention to civil law texts in which the Roman emperors had refused to take advantage of the misfortunes of others by claiming wrecked goods for their treasury, and had similarly denied coastal landowners the right to benefit

46 It is a source of some uncertainty that the word 'wrak', like the word 'wair', with which it was associated in many charters and other documents, could instead signify a right to gather seaweed for use as manure on land (*Dictionary of the Older Scottish Tongue*, vol. 11, pp. 613–14).

47 NRS, CS7/159, ff. 356r and 385. Although the significance of the brief entry in DCA, BCMB, vol. 8, 5 March 1565, is obscure, it may be that a landowner had claimed title to a 'wrak schip that brak' on his property.

48 The second duke of Lennox had replaced the fifth earl of Bothwell as admiral in 1591, and had immediately removed the author of the treatise from office as an admiral depute.

from maritime disasters.[49] Both a medieval emperor and a pope, it was further pointed out, had threatened those who plundered wrecks with condign punishment.[50] King had devoted much of his chapter 'De naufragiis' to discussion of various procedures provided by the civil law for the protection of the victims of shipwrecks, conscious that they did not form part of the law of Scotland, yet eager for them to exert some influence on the handling of shipwrecks in the admiralty courts.[51] In particular, he had argued that while 'the letter of the law' conferred on the admiral a share of unclaimed goods retrieved from wrecks, 'equity' required him to abstain from exploiting such a 'corrupt custom'. Although Welwod had been less dismissive of the admiral's privilege, he had drawn attention to other civil law sources suggesting that unclaimed goods should be donated to the poor or the church.[52] Furthermore, he had prefaced his account of 'wrak' with an account of the civil law procedures protecting the victims of shipwrecks, and it was only this part of his discussion that survived in the printed version of his treatise, from which several passages defending the admiral's privileges were omitted.[53] Skene too drew attention to some of the civil law sources in annotating the provisions he had come to attribute to Alexander II, beginning with the axiom that *fiscus ex naufragio et aliena calamitate compendium sectari non debet*.[54] He left his readers to draw their own conclusions from comparison of these sources with the Statute of

---

49 C.11.6.1; D.47.9.7.

50 *Codex Iustiniani* (Paris, 1559), col. 1192 (authentic 'Navigia', between C.6.2.18 and 19); Monumenta Germaniae historica, *Constitutiones et acta publica imperatorum et regum*, 11 vols, ed. L. Weiland, W. Stürner, I. Schwalm, R. Bork, W. Eggert, K. Zeumer, R. Salomon, M. Kühn and W.D. Fritz (Hanover, 1893–2003), vol. 2, p. 109; X 5.17.3; *Sacrorum conciliorum nova et amplissimo collectio*, 56 vols, ed. G.D. Mansi, P. Labbe, G. Cossart and N. Coleti (Florence, Venice and Paris, 1759–1927), vol. 22, cols 230–1. These threats were echoed in the provisions from the *Rôles d'Oléron* in which Welwod had found evidence of the demands typically made by 'the men quha hes the superioritie on the coistis' (n. 34 above).

51 *Alexander King's Treatise on Maritime Law*, pp. 186–207.

52 Ioannes Faber, *Commentaria super Institutis* (Lyons, 1527), f. 25v (ad J.2.1.47); *Codex Iustiniani*, col. 1485 (authentic 'Omnes peregrini', between C.6.59.10 and 11).

53 *Alexander King's Treatise on Maritime Law*, pp. 370–1; *The Sea-Law of Scotland* (Edinburgh, 1590), sigg. C5-6r.

54 The axiom put into a more pithy and emphatic form the sentiment expressed as a rhetorical question in C.11.6.1: 'what right has the treasury in another's calamity, in order to seek profit from so lamentable an affair?' The other sources to which Skene drew attention at this point were D.47.9.1.pr.-1, and the gloss 'Criminibus' on that text, in *Digestum novum* (Lyons, 1569), col. 1358.

Westminster, to which he referred in the margins of his Latin edition of the old laws, alongside the *Statuta regis Alexandri*.[55]

Welwod and Skene both referred further to an act passed by the Scottish parliament in 1430, which was another of the three sources gathered together by Balfour in his treatment of the law of shipwreck.[56] The act opened by confirming that when wrecks occurred in Scotland, 'the schip and the gude salbe eschete to the king gif thai be of tha cuntreis the quhilkis oysis and kepis the samyn law of brokyn schippis'.[57] It was well known, for instance, that Scottish ships destroyed on the coasts of England would be treated as 'just wrack' unless claims were promptly made for the return of anything salvaged from them.[58] Accordingly, since the same law of shipwreck was used and kept in England as in Scotland, English vessels destroyed on the coasts of Scotland would be treated in the same way there. However, the act proceeded to provide that if ships broken in Scotland came from 'ony lande that kepis nocht that law, thai sal hafe the sammyn favor her as thai kep to schippis of this lande brokyn with thaim'. There were other countries where the civil and canon laws had been more influential, and where no rights to 'wrak' had been either asserted by rulers or granted to landowners.[59] The innovation in the 1430 act was to exempt vessels from these countries from the law of 'wrak'. King did not mention the act in his treatise, but nor did he refer directly to the provisions found in the *Leges forestarum* or added to the *Statuta regis Alexandri*. He reasoned instead, on the strength of his civilian learning, that the privilege introduced by 'corrupta nostra aliorumque consuetudo' should be allowed to fall into disuse.[60] Balfour and Skene merely made reference to the act, which was accessible in print elsewhere, while reproducing the provisions from the old laws in their

55 *Regiam maiestatem: Scotiae veteres leges et constitutiones*, pt 2, f. 28.

56 *Practicks of Sir James Balfour*, vol. 2, p. 624. Chalmers, *Compendium of the Laws of Scotland*, p. 504, cited the act as well, under the rubric 'Scheippis'.

57 *Acts of the Parliaments of Scotland*, vol. 2, p. 19; Records of the Parliaments of Scotland, 1430/19.

58 *Letters and Papers of the Reign of Henry VIII*, vol. 17, p. 95; *Calendar of the State Papers Relating to Scotland and Mary Queen of Scots*, vol. 2, p. 272, and vol. 9, p. 547; M.M. Meikle, *A British Frontier? Lairds and Gentlemen in the Eastern Borders, 1540–1603* (East Linton, 2004), p. 255.

59 R.A. Melikan, 'Shippers, Salvors and Sovereigns: Competing Interests in the Medieval Law of Shipwreck', (1990) 11 *Journal of Legal History* 163; *cf.* A.H. Krappe, 'Le droit de bris', (1943) 5 *University of Toronto Law Journal* 113.

60 *Alexander King's Treatise on Maritime Law*, pp. 206–7.

entirety.[61] Welwod, on the other hand, began his whole discussion of the law of shipwreck not only by summarising the terms of the act, but also by turning them back to front. 'Strangeris incurring schipwrak in Scotland', he wrote, 'suld have the same favour of us that our peopill usses in sic caisses to receave of thame on thair coistis, sua that na confiscatioun sould be maid thairof, except thay use to da sa to us'.[62] On this basis, he was able to maintain that the law of Scotland prohibited the plundering of wrecks and encouraged the salvaging of goods for the benefit of their current owners. It helped, of course, that the provisions from the old laws themselves required goods to be 'saisit and keipt at the sicht of the schiref or coroner or of the kingis baillies or officiaris', and to be retained for a year and a day 'in the handis of the indwellaris of the town quhair thay wer fund'.[63] As Welwod pointed out, even the period of time prescribed was consistent with the civil law procedures designed to assist the victims of shipwrecks.[64]

3 The Salvaging of Wrecks and Forensic Custom

The third source referred to by Balfour was a note summarising a decision delivered by the lords of council and session in the later 1520s.[65] The court had ruled that when a vessel was driven ashore by a storm in Scotland, 'not beand just wrak be the lawis of this realme', everything recovered from it was to be restored to the owners or their representatives as soon as they provided the salvors with a guarantee against liability for 'intromissioun thairwith, at all handis havand or pretendand to have interes thairto'.[66] Records relating to the case

61 *The Actis and Constitutiounis of the Realm of Scotland* (Edinburgh, 1566), was available by the time Balfour was writing – indeed, he had been personally involved in its editing – and Skene had himself edited *The Lawes and Actes of Parliament* (Edinburgh, 1597).

62 *Alexander King's Treatise on Maritime Law*, p. 370; *Sea-Law of Scotland*, sig. C5r.

63 *Practicks of Sir James Balfour*, vol. 2, p. 624; *Regiam maiestatem: Scotiae veteres leges et constitutiones*, pt 2, f. 28; *Regiam maiestatem: The Auld Lawes and Constitutions of Scotland*, pt 2, f. 19r.

64 C.11.6.2. On the originally limited scope of the procedures referred to here see A.J.B. Sirks, *Food for Rome: The Legal Structure of the Transportation and Processing of Supplies for the Imperial Distributions in Rome and Constantinople* (Amsterdam, 1991), pp. 213–17.

65 *Practicks of Sir James Balfour*, vol. 2, pp. 623–4 (the precise date provided here is misleading). On the origins of Balfour's notes summarising decisions of the lords of session see W.M. Gordon, *Roman Law, Scots Law and Legal History: Selected Essays* (Edinburgh, 2007), pp. 283–96.

66 Nothing in the surviving records of the case supports the first phrase quoted, which may have been added to the note by Balfour in order to emphasise the difference between the ground covered by this entry and by his previous extract from the *Leges forestarum*.

reveal in more detail that 'ane greit schip' belonging to the king of Denmark, Norway and Sweden, called the *Peter de Hulle* or *Peter van Hulle*, had been wrecked near Aberdeen, where various local dignitaries and others had taken possession of a considerable quantity of equipment and wares.[67] An ambassador sent from Denmark had raised an action against them for 'the wranguis, violent and maisterfull spoliatioune, away taking, intrometting and withhalding' of the things obtained, they had been ordered to restore the things to the ambassador, and he had been required to provide 'sufficient cautioun to keip all the intromettours witht the saids guds recoverit, and all uthers our soverane lords liegis, harmless and skaithless thairof as law will'.[68] In another case heard around the same time the lords of session had confirmed that the appropriate course of action for victims of shipwreck to take in Scotland was to 'rais summondis apoun the spulzearis and intromettouris'.[69] Complaints of 'spuilzie', which were linked in the minds of learned lawyers with the *actio spolii* of the canon law, were widely used in Scotland as a means of recovering possession of property.[70] In 1530, after 'ane schip of Danskin' called the *Jhesus* was wrecked near Aberdeen, dignitaries and others there were warned by the central authorities that if they did not restore everything they had salvaged from the ship to its owners, 'thai suld be accusit as intromettors and spulzears of the haile guds'.[71] Eventually, several summonses for spuilzie were raised before the session in the case.[72] Fifty years later it was the turn of some shipowners from Aberdeen to raise a summons for 'spoliatioun' after timber and tackle from a

67 *Acts of the Lords of Council in Public Affairs*, pp. 254–5, 264, 272 and 314–15; NRS, CS5/36, ff. 154r, 157v and 159, CS5/37, f. 229r, CS5/38, ff. 46v-7r, and CS5/40, f. 98v; *Acts of the Parliaments of Scotland*, vol. 2, p. 302; Records of the Parliaments of Scotland, 1526/6/13 and 1526/6/15; *Letters of James V*, pp. 130, 134, 151 and 198; *Diplomatarium Norvegicum*, 23 vols, ed. C.A. Lange, C.R. Unger, H.J. Huitfeldt-Kaas and G. Storm (Oslo, 1847–1992), vol. 8 (2), pp. 562–3, vol. 9, pp. 550–3, and vol. 18, pp. 585–6.

68 The particular decreet summarised in Balfour's book is recorded at NRS, CS5/38, ff. 46v-7r.

69 *Acts of the Lords of Council in Public Affairs*, pp. 296, 308 and 352; NRS, CS5/40, ff. 8v-9r and 139, and CS5/42, f. 122; *Registrum secreti sigilli regum Scotorum: The Register of the Privy Seal of Scotland*, 7 vols, ed. M. Livingston, G. Donaldson, J. Beveridge and D.H. Fleming (Edinburgh, 1908–66), vol. 2, pp. xx and 47.

70 A.M. Godfrey, *Civil Justice in Renaissance Scotland: The Origins of a Central Court* (Leiden. 2009), pp. 239–47.

71 *Acts of the Lords of Council in Public Affairs*, p. 356; NRS, CS5/42, ff. 181v-2r; ACA, CA1/1/13, pp. 15–23, 70, 103, 105–7, 113–17, 134–9 and 141–4. At an early stage in the affair, the owner of the land on which the ship was driven aground claimed that they were 'on his land as wrak', but this was clearly a misunderstanding (*Acts of the Lords of Council in Public Affairs*, p. 345; CS5/41, f. 150v).

72 This episode is examined in some detail in A.R.C. Simpson, 'Spuilzie and Shipwreck in the Burgh Records', (2018) 9 *Journal of Irish and Scottish Studies* 70.

ship destroyed at North Berwick was found in the possession of people living all across East Lothian.[73] At the end of the century a shipowner from Bergen – a burges of the town, but with the Scottish surname Dewar – was pursuing various inhabitants of Easter Ross before the privy council to satisfy 'ane decreit obtenit be him befoir his hienes admirall aganis thame for spoliatioun of ane schip'.[74] It seems likely that traces of other actions for spuilzie raised before the admiral have been lost along with the records of his courts.

The language of 'wranguis, violent and maisterfull spoliatioune' may be misleading. For example, there is no evidence anywhere in the records of the *Peter de Hulle* case that the parties pursued intended to retain the goods they had 'wone or recoverit within the say, sand or uther placis', still less that they had resorted to violence and force in taking them.[75] On the contrary, the dignitaries summoned had been appointed agents by the king's ambassador 'to ressave and intromett witht the saids gudis to his behuf', and they had 'intromettit witht' (or taken possession of) the remains of the ship at his direction.[76] The problem was that while the ambassador represented Christian II, a claim to the items recovered was also being made by representatives of Frederick I.[77] Understandably, the 'spulzearis and withhaldaris of the gudis and stuff' were reluctant to surrender them to one claimant to the throne of Denmark, Norway and Sweden unless they received effective protection against an action by the other claimant. Similarly, at least some of the defenders in the *Jhesus*

73 NRS, CS7/97, f. 358, CS7/98(1), ff. 328v and 331v, and CS7/98(2), f. 245v.

74 *Register of the Privy Council*, vol. 5, pp. 643–4, and vol. 6, pp. 48–9, 54, 120 and 175; NRS, PC1/17, pp. 170–1, 183–4 and 326–7, and PS1/71, f. 148; *The Calendar of Fearn: Text and Additions, 1471–1667*, ed. R.J. Adam (Edinburgh, 1991), p. 184; *Old Ross-Shire and Scotland, as Seen in the Tain and Balnagown Documents*, 2 vols, ed. W. MacGill (Inverness, 1909–11), vol. 1, p. 269; T. Brochard, 'The Socio-Economic Relations between Scotland's Northern Territories and Scandinavia and the Baltic in the Sixteenth and Seventeenth Centuries', (2014) 26 *International Journal of Maritime History* 210, at pp. 223–4.

75 *Acts of the Parliaments of Scotland*, vol. 2, p. 302; Records of the Parliaments of Scotland, 1526/6/15.

76 NRS, CS5/38, ff. 46v-7r. As Skene's definition of 'wrek' (quoted at n. 13 above) shows, the word 'intromet' could be used in a neutral or even positive sense.

77 *Acts of the Lords of Council in Public Affairs*, pp. 254–5 and 272; NRS, CS5/36, f. 159, and CS5/38, ff. 46v-7r. Having already lost power in Sweden, Christian had been deposed by the Danish nobility in favour of his uncle in 1523 (P.D. Lockhart, *Denmark, 1513–1660: The Rise and Decline of a Renaissance Monarchy* (Oxford, 2007), pp. 18–20). His ambassador reported that the Scots were relying on Frederick's claim as an 'excuse' for not returning the equipment and wares, but this comment in a defensive letter to his principal is as close as any source comes to suggesting that the Scots meant to retain the goods (*Letters of James V*, p. 151; *Diplomatarium Norvegicum*, vol. 18, pp. 585–6). That they never were returned to Christian, who never recovered his throne, is scarcely surprising.

case seem to have been quite innocent. The master of the ship had asked for assistance from the local dignitaries, 'promittand thame faithfully the thrid of the haile gudis that hapint to be wone, kepand the twa part to thame that has just tytill thairto'.[78] Both the master and the Hanseatic merchants whose cloth the ship was carrying had appointed the dignitaries as their agents to 'resave and ouptak all maner of claithtis and gudis' preserved in Aberdeen.[79] One local man insisted that 'he, at the marinaris command, had intromettit and wone ane part of thair gudis', another maintained that he had become involved at the request of one of the local dignitaries, who had promised 'to reward him for his labouris', while a third professed himself willing to hand over cloth as soon as he was paid 'for his labouris, coistis and expensis he maid in the first wynyng of the said claith'.[80] An assise was left to decide whether the third man had been promised 'ony maner of thing for his laboris in the wyning of the said claitht, or gif he aucht to have ony thing thairfor'.[81] There is no doubt that some people in Aberdeen took advantage of the misadventure of the *Jhesus*, but others took part in a consensual salvage operation, and retained possession of goods only to ensure that they received the recompense to which they believed they were entitled for the efforts they had made.[82]

Salvage agreements are mentioned in other records of cases heard in the burgh courts. The language of spuilzie is absent from these cases, in which there was no intervention by the central authorities.[83] Sometimes reference was made to an agreement, but not always. In 1528, for example, the master of a German ship wrecked at Aberdeen promised a local man fifteen pounds Scots, 'or thane samekle gudis of the said schip as will corespond to the said xv *lib.* money forsaid, and that for the savite of himself and his childer, and bringing

78 ACA, CA1/1/13, p. 16.

79 ACA, CA1/1/13, pp. 113–14 and 134–5.

80 ACA, CA1/1/13, pp. 19, 106–7 and 116.

81 ACA, CA1/1/13, pp. 136–7 and 143.

82 Details of a salvage contract requiring mariners from Anstruther to use their boats and cables to recover goods belonging to merchants of Edinburgh from a ship 'sunkyn and drownit' off Port Seton, in exchange for payment of an agreed sum of money, can be found in NRS, CS6/3, f. 121v.

83 The language of spuilzie is lacking from the records of a case initially handled by a burgh court in Ayr after a ship was wrecked at Dunure, even though it ended up being handled by the lords of council and session (*Acts of the Lords of Council in Public Affairs*, p. 487; NRS, CS6/12, ff. 157v-8r). Presumably the tone had already been set before the case was drawn to the attention of the central court. Although the word 'intromissioun' sometimes appears, the word 'spuilzie' is also absent from ACA, CA1/1/9, p. 328, CA1/1/10, p. 286, CA1/1/11, p. 675, and CA1/1/21, pp. 25, 28–9, 79, 83, 88, 99, 117, 123, 126, 182–3, 187–8, 194, 200–1 and 228; AA, B6/11/2, f. 312; SAUL, B10/8/4, pp. 419–20; NRS, NP1/36, f. 39v.

tham, the said schip and the merchandis gudis to ane havin'.[84] Similarly, in 1565 the master of a French ship run aground at Balmedie promised to pay some local people 'for thair labouris taikynd in, saifeing and winning of the said schipe and the geir being in hir and pertening to hir'.[85] In 1554, on the other hand, when two men appeared before the bailies of Dundee and admitted that the master of a wrecked ship to whom they had restored tackle had 'contentit us for oure saiffing of the said gudis', no mention was made of a prior agreement.[86] In 1583 the same court found that the master and owners of a ship wrecked at Orkney were obliged to reward a mariner 'for his gryt laboris, travellis and expensis maid in the saiftie of thair schipis geir and mercheandis geir', as well as for 'aventering of his lyff in saiftie thairof'.[87] Again, no mention was made of a prior agreement, though the mariner could have been a member of the crew. An article of the *Rôles d'Oléron* obliged the mariners of a wrecked vessel 'to save as much as they can of the vessel and goods', and obliged the master to give those who fulfilled their responsibility 'as much as will get them home', if necessary by using the salvaged goods to raise funds.[88] Some versions of the code added advice to judges that if 'the master and merchants should promise folk who helped them to save the said goods and vessel a third part or a half of the vessel and wares', it would be misguided to pay strict attention to the agreement when the emphasis ought to be on ensuring that the salvors' labours were adequately recompensed.[89] Unlike the articles cited by Welwod to illustrate the avarice of landowners, the first of these provisions was included in a version the *Rôles d'Oléron* found in some copies of the old laws of Scotland.[90] While the people who appeared as litigants or served as judges and jurors in the burgh courts may not have had much familiarity with these or any other written sources, a vague awareness of the provisions they contained may nonetheless have informed a popular belief that rewards ought to be paid to salvors, and that things recovered from wrecks might be used to provide the rewards.[91]

84 ACA, CA1/1/12/1, p. 317.

85 ACA, CA1/1/25, pp. 531–2 and 570.

86 DCA, BCMB, vol. 3, 3 September 1554.

87 DCA, BCMB, vol. 16, 18 February 1583.

88 *Black Book of the Admiralty*, vol. 1, pp. 90–1.

89 *Collection de lois maritimes*, vol. 1, pp. 325–6.

90 E.B.I. Frankot, 'The Scottish Translations of the *Rôles d'Oléron*: Edition and Commentary', in A.M. Godfrey (ed.), *Stair Society: Miscellany Eight* (Edinburgh, 2020), p. 13, at pp. 29–30.

91 Masters, mariners and merchants in Scotland were probably not familiar with the *Nomos Rhodion nautikos*, which Welwod took to be fundamental to the rights of salvors (*Alexander King's Treatise on Maritime Law*, p. 371; *The Rhodian Sea-Law*, tr. W. Ashburner (Oxford, 1909), pp. 37–8 and 117–19).

Although it was stipulated in the *Rôles d'Oléron* that a master must not sell equipment recovered from a wreck without the express permission of the shipowners, the remains of the German ship wrecked at Aberdeen in 1528 were sold there by its master without the apparent involvement of its owners.[92] In fact, there are many examples in the burgh records of masters selling the remains of ships as well as goods to local purchasers, and in no case is it specified that the master had been authorised to do so by the owners.[93] In 1526, for instance, the master of a ship from Stralsund was content to record in the council register of Aberdeen that he had been paid by two local men for 'all and haill the wrak of the said schip, witht maistis, takillis, cabillis, ankoris and all and sindry uthir thingis pertenend to hir'.[94] The purchase of equipment from wrecks must have benefited the maritime economy of Scotland, where it was not always easy to find essential items, yet it would be rash to presume that masters were forced to sell at discounted prices.[95] In a later case entered in the Aberdeen council register, after a Dutch ship was 'cassin be storme off wedder on the sandis of this burgh', the master, 'thinking thairby that scho suld have wrackit', sold his 'boit' to a local man.[96] When it transpired that the ship could be refloated, the purchaser promptly agreed to let the master buy the boat back for 'the same price as he sauld hir'. The parties ended up in dispute, but the local man had not tried to take advantage of the master's predicament by driving a hard bargain. Another Dutch master, whose ship actually was 'wrackit on the sandis' at Aberdeen, professed himself 'thankfullie receavit and interteneit be the provest, bailleis, consall and inhabitantis of the said burgh', in particular through 'bying, selling, dettis and utheris contractit be the said burgh or ony off the inhabitantis thairoff, be ressone off the said schip'.[97]

92 *Black Book of the Admiralty*, vol. 1, pp. 90–1; ACA, CA1/1/12/1, p. 323. The remains of the ship run aground at Balmedie in 1565 were also sold, but with the consent of the mariners, who were understood to be the owners of the ship.

93 *Extracts from the Council Register of the Burgh of Aberdeen*, vol. 1, p. 428; ACA, CA1/1/8, pp. 86–7, CA1/1/12/1, p. 358, CA1/1/16, pp. 316 and 538, CA1/1/27, p. 738, CA1/1/32, p. 496, CA1/1/35, p. 341, CA1/1/36, pp. 17–18, CA5/1/1, f. 156r, and CA5/1/2, 25 August 1582; AA, B6/11/1/3, f. 465v, and B6/11/2, f. 498; SAUL, B10/8/6, pp. 526–7.

94 ACA, CA1/1/12/1, p. 66.

95 In 1538, for example, the master of a damaged ship who was forced to put into Aberdeen found that 'thair was nether takill nor sails to be gottin within this burgh' (ACA, CA1/1/16, pp. 104–5). For the benefit derived from even modest findings from wrecks see T. Johnson, 'Medieval Law and Materiality: Shipwrecks, Finders and Property on the Suffolk Coast, ca. 1380–1410', (2015) 120 *American Historical Review* 406, and 'The Economics of Shipwreck in Late Medieval Suffolk', in J.P. Bowen and A.T. Brown (eds), *Custom and Commercialisation in English Rural Society: Revisiting Tawney and Postan* (Hatfield, 2016), p. 121.

96 ACA, CA1/1/34/2, p. 602.

97 ACA, CA1/1/34/2, p. 532. See too *Letters of James the Fourth*, pp. 103–4.

Someone representing the crew of a third Dutch ship wrecked at Aberdeen simply thanked the local inhabitants for 'the greit humanite doune to tham', while the same people were urged by the bailies of Dundee, after a ship from that burgh was wrecked near Aberdeen, to provide assistance 'as ye wald that we did siclik to your nychtbours, and ony utheris, for mericy and zeal of justice'.[98] When shipwrecked sailors were found to be destitute, with nothing they could sell to raise funds for their passage home, subventions were made to them from burgh funds, 'for making thair chairges hamewart, and for thair present support'.[99] It was indeed suspected that the burghs were in danger of being taken advantage of by 'maisterfull and ydle beggaris' who pretended to be 'schipbrokin'.[100]

4 The Plundering of Wrecks and Popular Custom

It should not be imagined, however, that the victims of shipwreck invariably received charitable treatment in Scotland. If the master of the *Jhesus* was grateful to the authorities and people of Aberdeen for the recovery of goods from his vessel, 'confessand him richt honestlie and humanlye tretit amangis thame', it is not without significance that the provost of the town had felt the need to contact the most powerful nobleman in the area and urge him 'to cum to defend and caus the saids guds be keipit fra violance and spulze, quhilk he dred of gentilmen of the cuntretht'.[101] The language of spuilzie was sometimes used quite aptly. When the lords of council and session advised that spuilzie was the appropriate form of action for the victims of shipwreck to employ in Scotland, they were dealing with a case in which the pursuers were able to

98 ACA, CA1/1/11, p. 155, and CA1/1/18, pp. 316–17.

99 *Extracts from the Council Register of the Burgh of Aberdeen*, vol. 2, pp. 115–16 and 176; *Extracts from the Records of the Burgh of Edinburgh*, vol. 4, pp. 338, 531–2, 542 and 546; *Extracts from the Records of the Burgh of Edinburgh*, 2nd ser., 9 vols, ed. M. Wood and H. Armet (Edinburgh, 1927–67), vol. 1, pp. 35–6, 48, 74, 133, 176 and 199; *Ayr Burgh Accounts, 1534–1624*, ed. G.S. Pryde (Edinburgh, 1937), p. 161; *Calendar of the State Papers Relating to Scotland and Mary Queen of Scots*, vol. 9, p. 624; *Calendar of Letters and State Papers Relating to English Affairs, Preserved in or Originally Belonging to the Archives of Simancas*, 4 vols, ed. M.A.S. Hume (London, 1899), vol. 4, pp. 547–8; ACA, CA1/1/36, p. 302, CA1/1/37, pp. 749–50, and CA1/1/38, p. 281; ECA, SL1/1/5, f. 172v, SL1/1/7, f. 161v, SL1/1/8, f. 114r, SL1/1/9, p. 293, and SL1/1/10, f. 186; C. Sáenz-Cambra, *Scotland and Philip II, 1580–98* (Sevenoaks, 2005), pp. 124–9.

100 *Acts of the Parliaments of Scotland*, vol. 3, pp. 86–9 and 139–42; Records of the Parliaments of Scotland, 1575/3/5 and 1579/10/27.

101 ACA, CA1/1/13, pp. 18 and 115.

allege 'the spoliatioun, down breking, distructioun, away taking and withthalding' of their ship and goods by the defenders.[102] Likewise, the Aberdonian shipowners who appeared before the same judges to recover their property from inhabitants of East Lothian were able to allege 'the dimolesching and cutting downe of the said schip', after it was driven in a tempest onto 'the sands of North Berwick', from which it could perhaps have been refloated.[103] A pursuer in an admiralty court used the equally robust language of 'brekking and distroying', while another case apparently heard there concerned a 'shipe hewed asunder with axis and other weapons, whiche otherwise might have bene made mony of'.[104] In diplomatic correspondence and contemporary histories, complaints were made about 'rude and ravenous people' in Buchan who 'rifled, spoyled and caried away' everything left of a ship driven onto the rugged coastline there, about the burning of a vessel run aground at Mull 'by treacherie of the Irishe, and almost all the men within it consumed with fire', and about the 'spoliatioun' at an unspecified location of a 'schip and gudis, and murthour of the personis for the maist pairt being in the same schip, committit be certane Scottismen'.[105] Another well documented case of 'wrangous, violent and maisterfull spoliatioun and awaytaking' related to a vessel that was stripped of its equipment and torn apart after its whole crew went ashore in Shetland to search for provisions.[106] No clearer example of the destroying of a ship by 'wreckers', as opposed to the plundering of ships wrecked by storms, has been found.[107]

---

102 NRS, CS5/40. f. 139.

103 NRS, CS7/98(1), ff. 328v and 331v.

104 *Acta curiae admirallatus Scotiae*, p. 172; *Calendar of the State Papers Relating to Scotland and Mary Queen of Scots*, vol. 4, pp. 159, 178, 258, 293–4, 300 and 303; NAK, SP52/23/1, f. 42.

105 *Register of the Privy Council*, vol. 1, pp. 251–2; *The Warrender Papers*, 2 vols, ed. A.I. Dunlop (Edinburgh, 1931–2), vol. 1, pp. 30–2; *Calendar of the State Papers Relating to Scotland and Mary Queen of Scots*, vol. 9, p. 635; *Acts of the Privy Council of England*, vol. 6, pp. 27, 51–2, 54 and 56–7; Robert Lindesay of Pitscottie, *The Historie and Cronicles of Scotland*, 3 vols, ed. A.J.G. Mackay (Edinburgh, 1899–1911), vol. 2, p. 117; John Leslie, *De origine, moribus, et rebus gestis Scotorum libri decem* (Rome, 1578), pp. 528–9, and *The Historie of Scotland*, tr. James Dalrymple, 2 vols, ed. E.G. Cody (Edinburgh, 1888–95), vol. 2, p. 367; Richard Hakluyt, *The Principal Navigations, Voyages, Traffiques and Discoveries of the Englis Nation*, 16 vols, ed. E. Goldsmid (Edinburgh, 1885–90), vol. 3, pp. 141–51; NAK, SP52/42, f. 119.

106 *Register of the Privy Council*, vol. 5, pp. 153 and 195–7; *Ancient Criminal Trials in Scotland*, 3 vols, ed. R. Pitcairn (Edinburgh, 1833), vol. 1(2), p. 336; *Shetland Documents*, vol. 2, pp. 95–6 and 102–3; *Memorials of the Family of Skene of Skene*, ed. W.F. Skene (Aberdeen, 1887), pp. 164–5; NRS, RH9/5/21, and PC1/15, p. 308; D.M. Ferguson, *Shipwrecks of Orkney, Shetland and the Pentland Firth* (Newton Abbot, 1988), pp. 29–30.

107 No example has been found of ships being lured to their destruction with false lights, which according to H. Henningsen, 'Legends about "Wreckers"', (1985) 71 *Mariner's Mirror*

Given that rewards could be earned by people living on the coasts if they participated in salvage operations, that in lieu of payment salvors were sometimes permitted to retain part of the goods they recovered, that goods recovered from wrecks could often be purchased, and that if goods recovered from a ship lost with all hands remained unclaimed after a year and a day, the finders may have been able to claim a share, it may be suspected that the people who plundered wrecks believed they were acting within their rights. Popular investigations of 'wrecking' in the western and northern isles of Scotland during the twentieth century have revealed that the people involved were inclined to resent any imputation of wrongoing.[108] Their attitude was that the sea, to which they were in danger of losing their lives or livelihoods, occasionally included among the rich bounty it returned the remains of other people's property.[109] A scholarly study of wrecking in England in the eighteenth century has brought to light a great deal of evidence of similar attitudes at that place and time.[110] The author discovered that people residing in coastal communities did not draw a clear distinction between legal 'salvage' and illegal 'wrecking', but believed they were entitled to appropriate anything retrieved from the sea. He found more instructive the historian Edward Thompson's distinction between the 'political economy' of the wealthy, which was supported by the laws written down in books, and the 'moral economy' of the poor, which was sustained by popular usages and customs.[111] Comparison might be made with Eric Hobsbawm's use of the phrase 'social criminality' to describe behaviour that is condemned by an 'official' system, favoured by the rich and powerful, yet sanctioned by an 'unofficial' system, favoured by the poor and vulnerable.[112] The evidence available from England in the eighteenth century

---

215, was a mythical activity existing only in the minds of people who read written sources like the *Digest* uncritically, assuming that legislators only dealt with abuses that actually existed.

108 R. Hutchinson, *Polly: The True Story behind Whisky Galore* (Edinburgh, 1990), pp. 53 and 94; B. Bathurst, *The Wreckers: A Story of Killing Seas, False Lights and Plundered Ships* (London, 2005), pp. 61–101. It seems more than a little outrageous for the latter author, after pointing out that the northern isles are closer to Norway than England, to attribute the wrecking activities of their inhabitants to 'the fishy stink of their Viking past'.

109 *Cf.* A.M. Richmond, '"The Broken Schippus He Ther Fonde": Shipwrecks and the Human Costs of Investment Capital in Middle English Romance', (2015) 99 *Neophilologus* 315, at pp. 315–16.

110 J.G. Rule, 'Wrecking and Coastal Plunder', in D. Hay, P. Linebaugh, J.G. Rule, E.P. Thompson and C. Winslow, *Albion's Fatal Tree: Crime and Society in Eighteenth-Century England* (London, 1975), p. 167.

111 E.P. Thompson, *Customs in Common* (London, 1991), pp. 271 and 336–40 especially.

112 E.J. Hobsbawm, 'Social Criminality', (1972) 25 *Bulletin of the Society for the Study of Labour History* 5, at pp. 5–6 especially.

reveals not only that ordinary people who plundered wrecks did not think they were really doing anything wrong, but also that they adhered to certain norms governing the plundering process, such as respect for each other's acquisitions when made in particular ways.[113] No such evidence has come to light from Scotland in the sixteenth century. All the evidence discussed so far suggests that a distinction was recognised between legal salvage and illegal wrecking.[114] The people who were accurately described as 'violent and maisterfull spuilzearis' appear to have accepted that they were wrongdoers. Yet this evidence is derived almost entirely from books written by lawyers or records compiled by the clerks of various courts. It may be wondered what chance there is of the moral economy of the poor ever being represented in sources of these types, and whether an unofficial system of norms could possibly have found its way into the repositories of an official system.

An answer begins to emerge if attention is finally paid to two exceptional cases noted in the council register of Aberdeen, in which ordinary people did assert rights to things salvaged from wrecks. In the first case, heard in 1548, several local men proved that they were present 'at the wynninge of the geir of the Ingliss schip quhilk brak laitly in the raid', and were consequently awarded as much of the things retrieved 'as the laif of the wynnars of the same gat'.[115] In the second case, heard two years later after equipment was salvaged from an 'Inglis schip that brak one the bar', an anchor and cables were claimed by two local men who sought to prove that they were 'the princypall laborars and wynnars thairof'.[116] What sets these cases apart from all the other salvage disputes encountered in the records of the burgh courts is that the masters of the wrecked ships were not present, nor any other Englishmen for that matter. Instead of claiming rewards for their labours from the master, mariners, merchants or owners of the ships wrecked, the pursuers were demanding appropriate shares of the things recovered from the other parties involved in their recovery. They were claiming to be entitled to things salvaged from wrecks, which were to be distributed evenly among everyone who took part in the salvage operation, and were not to be returned, even in part, to their original owners. The explanation cannot be that the ships had been lost without survivors, because a year and a day had not elapsed since they were wrecked, after which claims would have been expected from the admiral or landowners.[117] Yet the

113 *Cf.* M. Rediker, *Between the Devil and the Deep Blue Sea: Merchant Seamen, Pirates and the Anglo-American Maritime World, 1700–50* (Cambridge, 1987), p. 285.

114 In the case of the *Jhesus*, for instance, it was this distinction that was being applied.

115 ACA, CA1/1/20, pp. 9, 13, 15 and 18.

116 ACA, CA1/1/20, pp. 368, 371, 374, 378–9, 407 and 410.

117 It may be recalled that a landowner did register an interest in the *Jhesus* case (n. 71 above).

explanation cannot be that salvors were generally reckoned to be entitled to keep what they took either, for then all the other records of salvage disputes (as well as the spuilzie cases and the legal treatises) would make little sense. The crucial point about these two cases would appear to be that they were heard at a time when Scotland was at war with England.[118] According to the theory taught in universities throughout Europe, things pertaining to enemies (*res hostium*) were not only to be regarded as, but were equated with, things that had no owner (*res nullius*), and therefore became the property of anyone who took effective possession of them (*occupatio*).[119] It was this theory that underpinned the litigation over prize acquisition that is often encountered in the records of the burgh and other courts in sixteenth-century Scotland.[120] It is important to note, however, that no express mention was made in either of these cases of the theory of the law schools, with which the parties present are unlikely to have had much acquaintance.[121] Instead, the parties seem to have shared a belief that in practice things taken from enemies became the property of the takers, without necessarily knowing where the belief originated.

In fact, no express mention of the learned laws, or of written sources generally, has been found in any of the entries from the burgh court records cited in this essay, in which the connections occasionally drawn between theory and practice have necessarily been vague and imprecise. The claims made in practice to 'wrak' did not fit neatly with the written sources referred to by the lawyers in their treatises, although the practice may ultimately have been founded on those sources, just as the claims made by salvors to rewards, and the use of salvaged property to provide rewards, may ultimately have been founded on provisions of the *Rôles d'Oléron*, although the terms of the provisions in question were not adhered to exactly. The sources referred to by the lawyers may have come to influence the practice of the courts sitting in coastal towns, but it was practice itself, or the accepted way of doing things, that was considered obligatory by the people who litigated there.[122] When his account of the moral economy of the poor was reprinted, Edward Thompson remarked that custom lies at the interface between law and practice.[123] His remark is instructive,

118 G. Phillips, *The Anglo-Scots Wars, 1513–50* (Woodbridge, 1999), pp. 201–55.

119 D.41.1.5.7, 41.2.1.1 and 41.2.3.21, and J.2.1.17.

120 Some of this material is discussed in J.D. Ford, *The Emergence of Privateering* (Leiden, 2023), pp. 8–39.

121 The same might be said in relation to the prize cases.

122 See now the essays in the first part of this collection.

123 *Customs in Common*, p. 97.

provided it is properly understood.[124] For one thing, it indicates that when law takes the form of custom it may look rather different when viewed from the perspectives of authors expert in the law and of lay people engaged in practice.[125] The authors in sixteenth-century Scotland who dealt with the law of shipwreck in their treatises tried not only to connect the practice of the courts with the books they had been reading, but also to use their reading as a basis for reappraising, and sometimes reforming, practice.[126] To Thomas Craig, for example, it seemed that the 'custom' of assigning wrak to the admiral was defensible in the light of the feudal law, which was in keeping with certain civil law texts, whereas to Alexander King the same 'custom' seemed indefensible when compared with other civil law texts, which were more consistent with the canon law. Both King and Welwod wanted actions of spuilzie and disputes over salvage to be handled in Scotland in accordance with the written sources they studied.[127] Their attempts to marry theory with practice are interesting, but their treatises cannot simply be read as reliable accounts of the law applied in practice.

For lay people – the ordinary people whose voices can in fact be heard in the records of the burgh courts – practice became law when it was established as custom, regardless of how closely it might have accorded with the law written down in books. In the burgh courts lay people claimed things to which they believed they had customary rights, not things to which lawyers told them they had rights in accordance with written sources of law.[128] The other thing Thompson's remark about custom indicates, however, is that just as written law need not be reflected perfectly in the customs it informs, so practice need not pass through custom into law.[129] The efforts made by central authorities

124 R.J. Blakemore, 'The Legal World of English Sailors, c. 1575–1729', in M. Fusaro, B. Allaire, R. Blakemore and T. Vanneste (eds), *Law, Labour and Empire: Comparative Perspectives on Seafarers, c. 1500–1800*, (Basingstoke, 2015), p. 100, at pp. 101–3.

125 Legal historians typically make this point by distinguishing between the legal customs of communities and the customary laws into which they were often turned by lawyers. See now the fourth essay in this collection.

126 There is a difference, of course, between the practice or 'practick' of the courts, developed especially in the minds of the lawyers who represented litigants there, and the practice or settled behaviour of those litigants. In the burgh courts parties were sometimes represented by university graduates, who made clever procedural moves on their behalf, but it was the practices of the parties themselves that were often treated as customs.

127 The broad aims of these authors are examined more fully in *Alexander King's Treatise on Maritime Law*, pp. xc–xcvii; and see now the essays in the second part of this collection.

128 When they were represented by university graduates, the discussion of procedure typically became more technical, but not the discussion of the substantive law applied.

129 See too M. Weber, *Economy and Society: An Outline of Interpretive Sociology*, 2 vols, ed. G. Roth and C. Wittich (Berkeley, 1978), vol. 1, pp. 319–25.

and local dignitaries to prevent the plundering of wrecks are suggestive of a popular practice of plunder, which might even have extended at times to deliberate wrecking. Yet even if it had been normal for people to help themselves to whatever could be recovered from wrecks, and even if the practice had been in some sense normative – even if people had believed they had some sort of right to the things they recovered – it would only follow that the practice was considered legal if the relevant norms were regarded as the kind of customs that counted as laws. People were not slow to assert their rights before the courts when they considered them to be legal, and to do so they made use of the language of custom or usage. We hear the voices of lay people asserting rights to things taken from enemy ships, as well as to rewards for salvaging things from other ships, and we hear them insisting that these rights were customary. But we do not hear them asserting rights to keep things taken from wrecks more generally. If there was an unofficial and unrecorded system of plunder, it appears to have been regarded neither by lawyers nor by lay people as a system of legal norms. The moral economy of shipwreck, if there was one in sixteenth-century Scotland, must have been of a different nature.[130]

130 For further examples of shipwrecks in Scotland not touched on above see *Acta curiae admirallatus Scotiae*, pp. 8–9, 39–40, 44 and 46; *Records of Inverness*, 2 vols, ed. W. Mackay, H.C. Boyd and G.S. Laing (Aberdeen, 1911–24), vol. 1, pp. 126 and 209; *Shetland Documents*, vol. 1, pp. 249–50; *Bronnen tot de Geschiedenis van der Handel met Engeland, Schotland en Ireland*, 1st ser., vol. 1, p. 160; *Calendar of the State Papers Relating to Scotland and Mary Queen of Scots*, vol. 2, p. 395, vol. 4, p. 54, and vol. 8, p. 354; *A Diurnal of Remarkable Occurrents that Have Passed within the Country of Scotland since the Death of King James the Fourth till the Year 1575*, ed. T. Thomson (Edinburgh, 1833), pp. 122–3; Sir James Melville of Halhill, *Memoirs of His Own Life* (Edinburgh, 1827), pp. 186 and 369–70; ACA, CA1/1/8, p. 132, CA1/1/18, pp. 308, 582 and 595, CA1/1/22, pp. 448 and 455, and CA1/1/27, pp. 303, 473–4 and 517; DCA, BCMB, vol. 12, 23 April 1573, and vol. 14, 14 September 1579, and PBD, vol. 1, ff. 188v and 209v; SAUL, B10/8/4, pp. 419–20; DAC, WC4/8, f. 184v; AA, B6/11/2, f. 498; HAC, B1/1/1, f. 310v, and B1/1/2, f. 182v; NRS, PS1/56, f. 25r, and GD106/135; D.M. Ferguson, *Shipwrecks of North East Scotland, 1444–1990* (Aberdeen, 1991), p. 1; P.D. Anderson, *Robert Stewart, Earl of Orkney, Lord of Shetland, 1533–93* (Edinburgh, 1982), pp. 55, 72 and 120, and *Black Patie: The Life and Times of Patrick Stewart, Earl of Orkney, Lord of Shetland* (Edinburgh, 1992), pp. 40 and 45; C. Martin, *Scotland's Historic Shipwrecks* (London, 1998), pp. 11–45; T.M.Y. Manson, 'The Fair Isle Spanish Armada Shipwreck', in G.W.S. Barrow (ed.), *The Scottish Tradition: Essays in Honour of Ronald Gordon Cant* (Edinburgh, 1974), p. 121.

Conclusion

Concepts of Maritime Law in Sixteenth-Century Scotland

The first essay in this collection started by recalling the expectation expressed in some of the written sources of Scots law that disputes arising from navigation would be submitted for resolution to the courts of the coastal burghs, before going on to show that these courts were still dealing with maritime disputes in the early sixteenth century, and to some extent even after the mid 1540s, when the admiral began to assert an exclusive jurisdiction for his courts over 'seafaring causes'.[1] Essays in the first and third parts of the collection have shown that the burgh courts were expected to resolve disputes in accordance with law that was described as the 'commond prattik and use of this burght', the 'auld lovabill consuetude of this burght' or the 'lovable actis, use or consuetud of this burght'.[2] Indeed, as well as the parties to an action before a bailie court 'renunciand thair awin jurisdictioun' and submitting themselves 'onlie to the jurisdictioun of the bailzeis of this burght', they might also renounce all other 'lawis' and submit themselves to the 'burrow lawis'.[3] Each burgh was expected to have its own law and to apply its own law to the cases raised before its courts. Yet it has also been seen, in essays in the second and third parts of the collection, that a treatise was printed in 1590 under the title *The Sea-Law of Scotland*, as if its concern was with a body of law common to the whole realm.[4] It has been argued, moreover, that the treatise printed in 1590 was an abbreviated version of a longer 'abridgement of all sea laws', and was written at about the same time as a book described as 'a treatise on the maritime laws and customs that are observed in practice by almost all nations', which suggests that the treatise writers were concerned with a body of law common to the whole of Europe.[5] As the writers were university graduates, it may be wondered whether they were

1 *The Acts of the Parliaments of Scotland*, 12 vols, ed. T. Thomson and C. Innes (Edinbrugh, 1814–75), vol. 1, p. 337, and vol. 2, p. 87; Records of the Parliaments of Scotland, ed. K.M. Brown (www.rps.ac.uk), 1467/1/4 and 1487/10/19; *The Ancient Laws and Customs of the Burghs of Scotland*, 2 vols, ed. C. Innes and R. Renwick (Edinburgh, 1868–1910), vol. 1, p. 13.

2 ACA, CA1/1/15, p. 716, and CA1/1/20, p. 137; DCA, BCMB, vol. 12, 13 October 1573.

3 SAUL, B10/8/5, pp. 460–1; DAC, WC4/10/3, p. 779.

4 William Welwod, *The Sea-Law of Scotland, Shortly Gathered and Plainly Dressit for the Reddy Use of All Seafairingmen* (Edinburgh, 1590), sig. A1r.

5 *Alexander King's Treatise on Maritime Law*, ed. J.D. Ford (Edinburgh, 2018), pp. 2–3.

 | DOI:10.1163/9789004695009_012

interested in examining the maritime law applied in the burgh courts from an academic perspective, or were intent on promoting a different understanding of maritime law. As the writers of the 'abridgment' and 'treatise' (though not the printed treatise) appear to have been interested especially in the practice of the admiralty courts, it may be wondered whether the maritime law applied there differed from the law applied in the burgh courts. These questions have been addressed from time to time in the preceding essays in this collection, but no attempt has so far been made to answer them conclusively. The aim of this final essay is to draw together some strands of thought running through the collection as a whole and to find out whether they can be wound together into a fibre that does not snap under the slightest strain. Has it been possible after all to write about the history of maritime law in sixteenth-century Scotland? If so, what was the essential character of that law? Is it instead necessary to think in terms of different laws applied in different courts or written about in different books? Attention focuses in the opening section of the essay on the burgh courts, then turns in two further sections towards the thinking of the writers and their reflections on the practice of the admiralty courts.

1 The Common Law of the Sea

The view persists among modern scholars of international trade law that disputes between merchants were settled throughout medieval Europe in accordance with a uniform body of norms known as the *lex mercatoria*, which was distinct from the laws ordinarily applied in each place.[6] As historians have repeatedly pointed out, however, beyond a shared expectation that mercantile disputes would be settled expeditiously and flexibly, freed from the subtelties of particular procedural norms, there was no commercial law common to all the nations of Europe.[7] Disputes tended to be settled in accordance with legal customs, which by their nature were formed in local linguistic communities, for there were no written codes of mercantile law, comparable to the *Consolato*

6 O. Volckart and A. Mangels, 'Are the Roots of the Modern *Lex mercatoria* Really Medieval?', (1999) 65 *Southern Economic Journal* 427.

7 The persistence of the myth has generated a huge literature. See, for example, A. Cordes, 'The Search for a Medieval *Lex mercatoria*', in V. Piergiovanni (ed.), *From Lex Mercatoria to Commercial Law* (Berlin, 2004), p. 53; S.E. Sachs, 'From St Ives to Cyberspace: The Modern Distortion of the Medieval "Law Merchant"', (2006) 21 *American University International Law Review* 685; E. Kadens, 'The Myth of the Customary Law Merchant', (2012) 90 *Texas Law Review* 1153.

del mare in the south or the *Rôles d'Oléron* in the north. The existence of codes of maritime law has led some historians to concede that disputes arising from the transportation of goods by sea may conceivably have been handled differently.[8] Yet even this tentative concession has been withdrawn by others.[9] Coastal towns throughout Europe drew up their own regulations to govern maritime disputes, and often borrowed rules from elsewhere in doing so, yet the rules were usually modified in the process.[10] Furthermore, maritime disputes were often settled in accordance with local customs too.[11] A rigorous study of the handling of maritime litigation in five northern towns (including Aberdeen) in the fifteenth century has shown that even when reference was made to written codes of maritime law, different codes were used in different places, the versions of the codes used were not consistent, and the solutions provided to problems varied considerably.[12] In Aberdeen in particular, relatively little reference was made to written sources of law, and the decisions delivered in the burgh court are not easily reconciled with the precise terms of the provisions found in any of the codes.[13] Medieval maritime law thus appears to have been broadly similar in character to the rest of medieval commercial law. However widespread the expectation may have been that the departure of ships would not be delayed by protracted litigation, the substantive law relied on for the resolution of disputes was the law of the places in which the disputes were raised.

The entries from the records of the coastal burghs of Scotland examined in previous essays in this collection suggest that maritime law was understood there during the sixteenth century in much the same way as it had

8 See, for example, C. Donahue, 'Benvento Stracca's *De mercatura*: Was There a *Lex mercatoria* in the Sixteenth Century?', in Piergiovanni (ed.), *From Lex Mercatoria to Commercial Law*, p. 69, at pp. 74–6.

9 A. Cordes, '*Lex maritima*? Local, Regional and Universal Maritime Law in the Middle Ages', in W. Blockmans, M. Krom and J. Wubs-Mrozewicz (eds), *The Routledge Handbook of Maritime Trade around Europe, 1300–1600* (Abingdon, 2017), p. 69.

10 O. Gelderblom, *Cities of Commerce: The Institutional Foundations of International Trade in the Low Countries, 1250–1650* (Princeton, 2013), pp. 102–40.

11 M. Fusaro, 'The Invasion of Northern Litigants: English and Dutch Seamen in Mediterranean Courts of Law', in M. Fusaro, B. Allaire, R. Blakemore and T. Vanneste (eds), *Law, Labour and Empire: Comparative Perspectives on Seafarers, c. 1500–1800* (Basingstoke, 2015), p. 21, at pp. 33–5.

12 E.B.I. Frankot, *'Of Laws of Ships and Shipmen': Medieval Maritime Law and Its Practice in Urban Northern Europe* (Edinburgh, 2012).

13 E.B.I. Frankot, 'Maritime Law and Practice in Late Medieval Aberdeen', (2010) 89 *Scottish Historical Review* 136, at pp. 141–2.

been in fifteenth-century Aberdeen.[14] Only two explicit references to written codes have been found.[15] The first appears in connection with a case discussed briefly at the end of the third essay, in which a merchant produced 'the *Seyricht*' in support of his claim against a master for damage to his goods.[16] As was explained in that essay, what exactly was referred to, and what effect the reference had, is not clear from any of the entries concerned with the dispute.[17] The other reference was in a source mentioned in several earlier essays. In 1570 it was decided by the burgh authorities in Dundee that 'all and sindrie lawes, actis and statutis contained in the majestie, actis of parliament and statutis of this brugh concerning merchandis, thaire freedome, libertie and priviledge, and the mainteining thairof', should be collected together in a book kept to inform the dean of guild and his council.[18] A new 'guildry book' was duly opened, beginning with extracts taken from parliamentary and burgh legislation, royal correspondence, and the *Leges burgorum*, a component of the 'auld lawes' of Scotland (often called 'the majestie'), though no extracts were included from the 'Schiplawis' (as the *Rôles d'Oléron* were known when copied into collections of the same laws).[19] Ten years later the dean of guild and his council decided to repeat the exercise, but with the addition of material taken from the 'lawes of the sea'.[20] In the record of their decision this new source was listed separately from 'the majestie', and only two provisions were reproduced from it, under a note stating that it was 'the watter richt of the sea that the skippers and merchandis and steirman and boatsman sall hald, and it is the oldest watter richt', which suggests that use was made of the code printed under the title *Dyt ys dat högeste unde öldeste water recht, dat de gemene copman und schippers geordinert unde gemaket hebben tho Wissby*, though both of

14 A different impression might have been formed if the records had been more complete. In particular, it could be that the *Rôles d'Oléron* were better known in Edinburgh.

15 There is also a reference to 'the law of Oleron' in a contract registered at DCA, BCMB, vol. 12, 13 January 1574, but the contract was written in England. It may be that when William Welwod later claimed that this code was typically incorporated into charter parties he was thinking of English practice.

16 ACA, CA1/1/21, pp. 313–117, 323, 323A and 355.

17 Although the use of the word *Seyricht* suggests that a copy of the laws of Wisby had been produced, even that is not entirely certain.

18 DCA, GBD, f. 5r.

19 E.B.I. Frankot, 'The Scottish Translations of the *Rôles d'Oléron*: Edition and Commentary', in A.M. Godfrey (ed.), *Stair Society Miscellany Eight* (Edinburgh, 2020), p. 13.

20 DCA, GBD, f. 11r. In the new collection the extracts from the *Leges burgorum* were given the heading: 'The actis following are drawen furth of the buik of the law called *Regiam majestatem*'.

the provisions included derived ultimately from the *Rôles d'Oléron*.[21] In fact, no evidence has been found that their inclusion in the guildry book made the slightest difference to the handling of maritime litigation in Dundee. There, as well as in other burghs, questions were often raised to which the written codes provided answers, yet in no case other than the one already mentioned were the codes ever cited by (or on behalf of) litigants. Moreover, it has been found repeatedly in previous essays that while remarks recorded in the court books can be broadly reminiscent of provisions in the codes, exact correlation is almost always lacking. The impression is given that merchants and mariners in Scotland were familiar with practices consistent with provisions of the codes – and possibly dictated by those provisions elsewhere – but were not familiar with, or especially interested in, the precise prescriptions of the codes. Although reference to the laws of Wisby was a novelty in the sixteenth century, if anything even less attention appears to have been paid to the written codes then than in the fifteenth century.

A vaguer reference to the written codes had been made by the burgh authorities in Dundee as early as 1560, when an act had been passed to provide that if any ship 'chancis to doe uther ship, crear or boat any manner of harme or skaith, the skaith and damnag sall be mad and requirit upon the expens of baith the parties that does the skaith and sustains the skaithes equally, conform to the sea lawes'.[22] The laws of Oleron and Wisby provided that if one ship collided with another lying at anchor, and the master and crew of the first ship swore an oath that they had not caused the collision deliberately, any damage to the ships or their cargoes should be divided equally between their owners.[23] The next article provided that if two ships were moored beside each other in a harbour, the master of one could require the master of the other to move an anchor if its line was likely to cause damage to the first ship, adding that the master of the second ship would not be responsible for any

21 DCA, GBD, f. 16v; Frankot, 'Scottish Translations of the *Rôles d'Oléron*', pp. 35–6 and 40–1; *The Black Book of the Admiralty*, 4 vols, ed. T. Twiss (London, 1871–6), vol. 4, pp. 74–7 and 80–3. Since the laws of Wisby – the title quoted here is taken from the third edition, published at Lübeck in 1537 – replaced a reference in the second provision to Bordeaux with a reference to Sluis, yet the guildry book reads 'Bourdeous', it is not entirely certain which source was used.

22 *Burgh Laws of Dundee, with the History, Statutes and Proceedings of the Guild of Merchants and Fraternities of Craftsmen*, ed. A.J. Warden (London, 1872), pp. 21–2; DCA, BCMB, vol. 2, pp. 14–17. Entries in the records relating to collisions are dealt with in this paragraph partly because the topic has so far been neglected.

23 Frankot, 'Scottish Translations of the *Rôles d'Oléron*', pp. 45–6; *Black Book of the Admiralty*, vol. 4, pp. 86–9.

damage if he had affixed a buoy to his anchor, as was generally expected.[24] The second article may have had some influence on legislation enacted repeatedly by the burgh authorities of Ayr during the 1590s, in which masters were forbidden from casting 'ankeris in the wattir withtout ane buy, under the pane of x *lib.*, besyd satisfactioun of the pairtie of the skaytht sustenit be the ankir nocht having ane buy'.[25] In 1582 the master of a ship had already been ordered by the bailies of Ayr to compensate the master of another for the loss of an 'ankir and cabill' he had run across while the second ship was moored 'in the raid'.[26] No mention was made of the attachment of a buoy, however, and it was instead emphasised that the defender had run across the line 'withtout licence or command had thairto'. In 1592 it was complained before the same court that a 'flie boit' had caused harm to a 'bark' while it was 'rydand in the loche of Lochryane at the thrid stanes'.[27] It is possible that the crew of the first vessel had the provisions of the codes in mind when they 'deponit and maid faith upoun thair consciences that thai wer na awneris of the said flie boit, bot onelie hyrit marineris to serve for thair hyris', and that they had not laid 'thair cabill across the said barkis cabill', yet the reason the claim was dismissed was that they also 'deponit be thair greit bodelie aithis that thair said flie boit nevir dampnifeit nor hurt the said bark in hir how, cabillis, ornamentis or geir quhatsumevir na maner of way'. In 1570 the bailies of Dundee had ordered the owners of one ship to pay the owners of another 'the half price' of a yard it had broken, 'conforme to the lawe of the see'.[28] No explicit mention was made of the written codes, maybe because the collision had occurred on the open sea, 'betwix this and Burdeaux', though no mention was made of the act passed in 1560 either, which was not restricted in its terms to collisions with moored ships. In a case heard in Aberdeen in 1517 goods in one ship appear to have been damaged when another ship collided with it in the harbour, but again no mention was made of the written codes, and the court required the master and merchants of the second ship to pay compensation for 'the thrid part of the scaitht done', not half.[29] As in the examples discussed more fully in earlier essays, the impression given by the relatively few entries found in the burgh

24 Frankot, 'Scottish Translations of the *Rôles d'Oléron*', pp. 46–7; *Black Book of the Admiralty*, vol. 4, pp. 88–91.

25 AA, B6/11/3, ff. 151v-2r, 226, 277v and 279r.

26 AA, B6/11/1/1, f. 96r.

27 AA, B6/11/2, f. 215.

28 DCA, BCMB, vol. 11, 24 May 1570.

29 ACA, CA1/1/9, pp. 728–9 and 732–3. Another case from Aberdeen, discussed in the fourth essay, in which a master complained about the streersman and crew of his ship leaving it at risk of harm from the anchor lines of another vessel in the harbour (ACA, CA1/1/31,

records relating to collisions between ships is that while the practices referred to may have been influenced in their development by the written codes, the terms of the codes were not adhered to closely.[30]

The 1560 act on collisions at sea was not among those extracted from the burgh legislation of Dundee in the guildry book, perhaps because interest focused there on the behaviour of merchants more than mariners.[31] That it was not cited in the 1570 case is less surprising, given that only a single reference to the legislation of the burgh has been found in all the records of litigation reviewed in earlier essays.[32] The provenance of the act that was referred to was doubtful, and it was suggested at the end of the third essay that the most revealing aspect of its citation was the added comment that 'the said act hes tane effect in the maist pairt of schippis arryving at this port'. In Dundee as elsewhere, burgh legislation, like the written codes of maritime law, appears to have been considered relevant only to the extent that it was adhered to in practice, and it was practice that appears to have been considered important, not any written laws that had influenced its development.[33] Parliamentary legislation appears to have been regarded in much the same way in the burghs. As was observed in the third essay, the acts of parliament requiring contracts of affreightment to be written in the form of charter parties were referred to only once in about two hundred protestations relating to these contracts, and not even once in almost six hundred and sixty cases to which they gave rise, many of which were recorded in multiple entries in the court books. Furthermore, it was seen in the same essay that the acts of parliament had little discernible effect on the drafting of charter parties, the terms of which appear to have owed more to the example of previous contracts. Parties complained that the terms of contracts had not been fulfilled, not that the provisions of the acts of parliament were being neglected. When they needed assistance with the interpretation of their contracts, they did not turn to the acts of parliament but to 'use and wount', the 'use and custom observit in all tyme bygane' or 'the auld

pp. 465–6), may have owed something to the general idea that ships must be properly moored, but it was clearly a case of a different type.

30 The relative paucity of these entries may itself provide evidence of the distant influence of the codes. If loss was to be shared after a collision caused by negligence, there was less incentive to seek compensation than there would have been if the negligent party had been held fully liable, as in Roman law (referred to in n. 117 below).

31 DCA, GBD, ff. 1 and 15v-17r.

32 DCA, BCMB, vol. 15, 10 February 1581.

33 A different view may have obtained in Edinburgh, where the exceptional cases on general average recorded in the council register were certainly designed to implement burgh legislation.

use observit withtin this guid towne past memour of man'.[34] If a problem arose that had not been foreseen and provided for when a contract was made, it was typically argued that something should be done 'as use is amang merchandis', 'conforme to the use of marenellis' or 'as use and wont is amang marinaris'.[35] Indeed, when merchants and mariners spoke about the law applicable to their disputes they generally described it in language of this type, and if necessary the courts took advice from 'men usit in seefair materis', 'marenaris or men of knawlege of sey' or 'the body of the mercheandis'.[36] If less frequent references to the 'lovable actis, use or consuetud of this burght' also drew attention to legislation, it was only considered relevant to the extent that it had informed the knowledge and understanding of merchants and mariners with expertise in overseas trade.[37]

Over a hundred years ago Émile Durkheim observed that 'custom does not exist only in a state of immanence in the successive actions which it determines, but, by a privilege without example in the biological kingdom, expresses itself once and for all in a formula repeated by word of mouth'.[38] The approach adopted in this collection of essays has been to view custom as something that was not only capable of description in language but was created and kept in existence by its description in language.[39] Behaviour mattered because it provided the practical contexts in which it was possible for people to reach agreements about both the correctness of descriptions of

34 ACA, CA1/1/9, pp. 344 and 399, CA1/1/12/2, p. 643, CA1/1/13, pp. 157–8, 452 and 502, CA1/1/15, p. 716, CA1/1/20, pp. 160, 162 and 167–8, CA1/1/21, pp. 313–14 and 462–3, CA1/1/22, pp. 497–8, CA1/1/24, pp. 158–9, CA1/1/25, p. 31, CA1/1/27, pp. 473–4, CA1/1/34/1, pp. 480–1 and 492–3, CA1/1/36, p. 512, and CA1/1/37, p. 37; DCA, BCMB, vol. 4, 19 March, 5 June and 29 July 1556, and 10 February, 12 March and 4 August 1557, vol. 5, 27 August and 13 September 1560, vol. 6, 13–14 and 23 January 1562, vol. 8, 14 January 1564, vol. 12, 27 January 1574, vol. 13, 1 July 1575, and vol. 19, 10 September 1596; SAUL, B13/10/1, 22 October 1550, and B65/8/1, f. 123; NRS, B72/5, ff. 244r and 272r.

35 ACA, CA1/1/9, p. 4, CA1/1/12/2, pp. 672–3, CA1/1/15, pp. 48, 230 and 711–12, CA1/1/16, p. 205, CA1/1/19, pp. 45–6, 63–4 and 401, CA1/1/20, pp. 24 and 142–3, CA1/1/21, pp. 707–8, and CA1/1/28, p. 623; DCA, BCMB, vol. 4, 27–8 January 1556, vol. 13, 19 March 1574, vol. 15, 22 September 1581, vol. 19, 15 and 29 April 1597, and vol. 20, 11 October 1597; NRS, B19/1/3, 30 July 1576, and B48/7/1, f. 277r.

36 ACA, CA1/1/8, p. 978, CA1/1/14, p. 413, CA1/1/19, pp. 290–1, CA1/1/21, pp. 448–9, CA1/1/27, p. 655, and CA1/1/28, p. 623; DCA, BCMB, vol. 3, 30 May 1553, vol. 5, 4 August 1559, vol. 6, 16 and 21 June 1562, and vol. 15, 15 September 1581.

37 DCA, BCMB, vol. 12, 13 October 1573.

38 *The Rules of Sociological Method*, tr. W.D. Halls (Houndsmills, 2013), p. 24.

39 For a classic account of the view that custom simply emerged from behaviour see M. Weber, *Economy and Society*, 2 vols, tr. G. Roth and C. Wittich (New York, 1968), vol. 1, pp. 319–25.

usage and the correctness of any usage described. More often, as Wittgenstein was eager to emphasise, people agree not so much 'about' the correctness of descriptions as 'in' their descriptions, forming an implicit consensus in their consistent use of words. When people use language to describe behaviour as correct and agree that it may be so described, they place constraints on the actions of those who wish their behaviour to be considered correct by the society to which they belong. As J.R. Searle has explained, it is by this means that 'social reality' is brought into existence, and it is by the same means that it is maintained in existence, through the constant reiteration of descriptions of correct behaviour.[40] Crucially, Searle has also explained that it is by agreeing at one level that agreements reached at another level should be regarded as creating legal norms that these norms are brought into and kept in existence. While the boundary between one type of norms and another may be rather porous, so that moral norms may give way only gradually to legal norms, it remains possible for the boundary to be clearly defined.[41] It was seen in the tenth essay in this collection, for example, that if there was a 'moral economy' of shipwreck in sixteenth-century Scotland, it did not give rise to assertions of legal rights to goods recovered from wrecks. In contrast, in other essays it has been seen that merchants and mariners constantly asserted legal rights to the safe delivery of goods, the payment of freight or wages, the provision of services and such like. There were cases, typically involving a new problem in need of a solution, in which litigants endeavoured to reach agreements about their entitlements, but the best evidence of established entitlements can actually be found in the recurrence of uncontentious descriptions of customary behaviour. That the behaviour described was thought to be legally obligatory is confirmed by the further recurrence of statements that behaviour was generally governed by customs, which served to keep in existence the agreement made at one level that the norms recognised at another level were legal norms. That advice on these norms was sometimes sought from the merchants and mariners who were considered to be most expert in them confirmed that it was merchants and mariners who constituted the linguistic community in which the maritime law applied to their disputes took shape.[42] Since language use is

40 This understanding of custom is outlined especially in the third and fifth sections of the third essay.

41 *Cf.* R.G. Court, '*Honore et utile*: The Approaches and Practice of Sixteenth-Century Genoese Merchant Custom', in H. Pihlajamäki, A. Cordes, S. Dauchy and D. De ruysscher (eds), *Understanding the Sources of Early-Modern and Modern Commercial Law: Courts, Statutes, Contracts and Legal Scholarship* (Leiden, 2018), p. 55.

42 The bailies and members of assizes who determined disputes, it needs to be remembered, were themselves the people who appeared as litigants on other occasions.

fluid and flexible, any law created and preserved merely by the use of language is also bound to be dynamic and to defy precise definition, yet it does seem possible to form an impression of how maritime commerce was regulated in the burgh courts of sixteenth-century Scotland.[43]

As was mentioned in the second essay, the need for custom to be fashioned by a linguistic community led Clifford Geertz to identify it as a species of 'local knowledge'.[44] It was seen in the same essay that when mariners from Danzig objected to a custom alleged in Aberdeen that it was 'nocht the use of thair cuntra', the court adhered to 'the auld use observit withtin this guid towne past memour of man'.[45] This case also illustrates the contact that Scottish merchants and mariners inevitably had with merchants and mariners from other countries, and it was not only in dealing with the French notaries public mentioned in the third essay that language barriers had to be overcome.[46] It has been noted in several essays that merchants and mariners made use of words of varied origins to describe their activities, as in distinguishing between the 'pairtinaris' who owned ships jointly and the 'dailismen' who sometimes chartered ships together.[47] To take another example, whereas at the close of the fifteenth century use was still being made of the words 'schipmen' or 'barnyis' to distinguish crew members from masters or skippers, new terminology was developed during the sixteenth century.[48] In the first sixty years the word commonly used was 'childer', which like 'barnyis' was a word of northern origin commonly used to designate offspring.[49] In the last forty years 'childer' was

43 The problem remains, though, that records have not survived evenly across the country or the century, so that caution has to be exercised in drawing conclusions about the law in sixteenth-century Scotland as a whole.

44 Geertz's cultural anthropology, deeply influenced by linguistic philosophy, was discussed at the end of that essay.

45 ACA, CA1/1/15, pp. 167–8. The same court appears to have rejected the argument advanced in another case that it ought to decide 'according to the consuetude of the contrie quhaire the bargane was maid', which would anyway have been to adopt a local rule on the conflict of laws (ACA, CA1/1/33/1, p. 435).

46 ACA, CA1/1/13, p. 236, CA1/1/22, pp. 497–8, and CA1/1/24, pp. 186–7.

47 A. Nesse, 'Trade and Language: How Did Traders Communicate across Language Borders?', in Blockmans, Krom and Wubs-Mrozewicz (eds), *Routledge Handbook of Maritime Trade around Europe*, p. 86. See too M. Lorvik, 'North Sea Timber Trade Terminology in the Early-Modern Period: The Cargo Inventory for the *White Lamb* Revisited', in M. Stenroos, M. Mäkinen and I. Saerheim (eds), *Language Contact and Development around the North Sea* (Amsterdam, 2012), p. 207.

48 ACA, CA1/1/6, pp. 279, 519 and 718, and CA1/1/8, pp. 116, 604 and 624.

49 W. Craigie, A.J. Aitken, J.A.C. Stevenson, H.D. Watson and M.G. Dareau (eds), *A Dictionary of the Older Scottish Tongue from the Twelfth Century to the End of the Seventeenth*, 12 vols (Chicago, London and Aberdeen, 1931–2002), vol. 1, pp. 191 and 517–19.

rarely used, giving way to the word 'equippage' or 'kippage'.[50] The reasons for the change are not obvious, but the French origins of the new terminology are.[51] It has been suggested that the 'micro regions' in which language, and the institutions it was used to fashion, could develop were also components of looser 'macro regions', brought together by international trade.[52] It has been further suggested that in borrowing terminology from each other people involved in international trade also borrowed institutions fashioned by the use of language.[53] Attention has been drawn to a number of examples of this phenomenon in previous essays, where it has been suggested that when norms recognised in Scotland bore a rough resemblance to those stated in the written codes of maritime law, the explanation is less likely to have been that the codes were read and their provisions consciously modified than that merchants and mariners were familiar with practices elsewhere which had been influenced in some way by the codes.[54] It may have been their awareness that some of their customs were similar to practices in other countries that led merchants and mariners to talk at times about 'the law of the sey' or 'the prattik and use of the sea', and about 'the commoune practik in seafer causis' or 'the commond lawis concerning sefair causes'.[55] While the law applied to maritime cases in the burgh courts was the law of each burgh, it was a particular part of that

50 Over forty examples of use of the word 'childer' have been found in records dated before 1560, but only six afterwards. In sharp contrast, forty examples of use of the word 'equippage' or 'kippage' have been found in records dated after 1560, and only two before then.

51 Paradoxically, the diplomatic realignment that followed the Reformation may possibly have made the French word more attractive as Scots became more familiar with the standard use of the English word 'children', but a simpler explanation would be a growing realisation that the French word could be applied more specifically to the crews of ships.

52 L. Heerma van Voss, 'North Sea Culture, 1500–1800', in J. Roding and L. Heerma van Voss (eds), *The North Sea and Culture, 1550–1800: Proceedings of the International Conference Held at Leiden, 21–22 April 1995* (Hilversum, 1996), p. 21.

53 S. Gialdroni, A. Cordes, S. Dauchy, D. De ruysscher and H. Pihlajamäki (eds), *Migrating Words, Migrating Merchants, Migrating Law: Trading Routes and the Development of Commercial Law* (Leiden, 2020).

54 All the same, there were limits to how far merchants and mariners in Scotland were prepared to go in adopting foreign models. Their failure to make use of bills of lading, noted in the third essay, remains surprising, and see too what was said at the end of the ninth essay about their limited use of insurance. If the maritime law applied in the burgh courts consisted of custom, it did not consist of whatever was customary in northern Europe.

55 ACA, CA1/1/12/2, p. 675, CA1/1/14, p. 413, CA1/1/20, p. 120, CA1/1/21, pp. 314–15, CA1/1/24, p. 417, CA1/1/29, p. 105, CA1/1/30, p. 79, and CA1/1/33/1, pp. 249–52 and 245–6; DCA, BCMB, vol. 4, 28 January 1556.

law, formed by agreements reached among people who were conscious of also belonging to a wider seafaring community.[56]

2 The Common Law of Scotland

As was pointed out in the fourth essay in this collection, when reference was made in actions brought before the central admiralty court to 'the law of the sey' or 'the use and prettik of the seyfair', litigants also 'repetit the dispositioun of the buk of Olrinis' or 'repetit the law of the buik of Olouris, safer as thai ar ressavit in this realme'.[57] In the fifth essay it was pointed out that when material was gathered together from the 'auld lawes' of Scotland to form the basis of the compendium that came to be known as Balfour's *Practicks*, it included extracts not only from the *Leges burgorum*, but also from the *Leges navium* or 'Schiplawis'. From the beginning of his work on the compendium, James Balfour was assisted by the advocate John Skene, who had recently returned from several years of study at the University of Wittenberg, where he appears to have become familiar – as was observed in the seventh essay – with the idea that medieval texts could form the foundations of local common laws. The same idea was revived when William Welwod, a contemporary of Skene's at Wittenberg, had the abbreviated version of his abridgement of all sea laws printed as *The Sea-Law of Scotland*. Declaring that 'all men be bound to ken the law, namely, thair awne common lawe', he argued – as was observed in the sixth and seventh essays – that 'the reulis of Olon' were part of the common law of Scotland, partly because they tended to be 'fellowit in our quarter of the Ocean', and partly because they were included in 'the wrets authorizit be our nation'.[58] Skene had come to doubt the authenticity of the 'Schiplawis' as a component of the *veteres leges Scotiae*, and the discovery of their French origins may also be part of the reason for Balfour's decision to deal with maritime law in a separate appendix to his *Practicks*, not in the body of the book as originally intended.[59] Alexander King, on the other hand, shared Welwod's belief

56 Attention was drawn in the ninth essay to an argument that something 'wes nevir hard within this realme nor na uther land of befor' (NRS, CS7/139, ff. 1–2). This was an argument advanced by an advocate before a central court, but it could have reflected observations made to him by the mariners he represented.

57 *Acta curiae admirallatus Scotiae, 1557–62*, ed. T.C. Wade (Edinburgh, 1937), pp. 31, 164–5 and 168–70.

58 *Sea-Law of Scotland*, sig. A3.

59 No evidence has been found of any awareness in Scotland that the *Rôles d'Oléron* had been composed while Aquitaine was ruled by the same kings as England.

that the 'Schiplawis' were part of 'the ancient law that we call *ius regium*'.[60] Although King claimed that the maritime law he was writing about was 'observed in practice by almost all nations', in rehearsing a provision of the 'Schiplawis' at one point in his treatise he remarked that the duty it imposed arose 'ex iuris communis dispositione', by which he appears to have meant the common law of Scotland rather than the common law of the sea.[61] Although the contents of the sea law of Scotland were understood to be shared to a certain extent with other nations, it was believed by some lawyers at least that 'the reulis of Olon receavit be our cuntrey men' formed part of 'thair awne common lawe'.[62]

It is impossible to confront the idea that the Scots had a common law of their own without being reminded of the thesis, defended by Lord Cooper of Culross in a lecture he delivered in 1951, that there was a 'dark age of Scottish legal history' in the later Middle Ages.[63] Though he harboured reservations about the aptness of the expression 'dark age', coined by one of his judicial colleagues, Lord Cooper maintained that despite a 'false start' made in the twelfth and thirteenth centuries, the Scots had lacked the institutions required for a sophisticated common law to be developed until they established a new College of Justice in 1532. 'For it has never yet proved possible to construct a first-class system of common law', he explained, 'without a first-class system of judicial organisation and a skilled body of lawyers to work it'.[64] He was comparing Scotland with England, where the administration of justice had been centralised at a remarkably early stage in the hands of royal justices, before whom parties were represented by lawyers with a specialised training in the practice of courts sitting alongside each other in Westminster Hall.[65] These lawyers were not only familiar with 'writs' used to initiate the actions heard in these courts, but also acquired detailed knowledge of what the terms of the writs were taken to entail by the royal justices, which eventually developed into the 'common erudition' of their profession.[66] Following English examples, royal justices called sheriffs and justiciars were appointed in Scotland, and 'brieves' modelled on English writs were available to initiate actions before

60 *Alexander King's Treatise on Maritime Law*, pp. 78–9 and 160–1.

61 *Alexander King's Treatise on Maritime Law*, pp. 2–3 and 76–7.

62 Welwod, *Sea-Law of Scotland*, sig. A3.

63 *Selected Papers, 1922–55* (Edinburgh, 1957), pp. 219–36.

64 The use of the phrase 'first-class' provided some room for manoeuvre, and allowed his thesis to be defended despite the references to common law that can be found in medieval sources.

65 P.A. Brand, *The Origins of the English Legal Profession* (Oxford, 1992).

66 J.H. Baker, 'English Law and the Renaissance', (1985) 44 *Cambridge Law Journal* 295.

them, providing what Lord Cooper referred to as 'the indispensable skeleton to be clothed with the flesh and blood of legal doctrine'.[67] But because the sheriffs and justiciars sat in courts scattered around the country, not in central courts attended by a special group of experts, legal doctrine was unable to develop in Scotland in the same way as in England. For this reason, Lord Cooper concluded, 'a first-class system of common law' was not developed in Scotland during the fourteenth and fifteenth centuries. In response to this line of argument, Lord Cooper's belief that the brieves fell into disuse has been challenged, and the correctness of the response has in turn been called into question, yet this debate is largely beside the point as far as the 'dark age' thesis is concerned.[68] Lord Cooper's central claim was that even if the brieves had remained in use, a body of legal doctrine comparable to the English common law could not have been fleshed out around them without centralised courts being established in which discussion of their significance could give rise to a coherent body of expert opinion.[69] Although, as he put it, 'there was plenty of law in Scotland and plenty of lawyers to apply it', these lawyers were unable to develop a shared understanding of the law to any significant extent.

Although the creation of the College of Justice is now viewed as a consolidation of earlier developments, Lord Cooper was certainly correct that the Scottish brieves were not meant to be used to initiate proceedings subject to adjudication in central courts.[70] Nevertheless, despite the absence of a forum in which focused discussion of law applicable to the whole country could have taken place, historians have argued that a common law was still formed in the minds of lawyers in late-medieval Scotland.[71] In the fifth essay in this collection

---

67 Alice Taylor, *The Shape of the State in Medieval Scotland, 1124–1290* (Oxford, 2016), pp. 266–348.

68 H.L. MacQueen, *Common Law and Feudal Society in Medieval Scotland* (Edinburgh, 1993); D.A. Carpenter, 'Scottish Royal Government in the Thirteenth Century from an English Perspective', in M. Hammond (ed.), *New Perspectives on Medieval Scotland, 1093–1286* (Woodbridge, 2013), p. 117; A. Taylor, 'Law and Administrative Change in Scotland, Twelfth-Fourteenth Centuries', in A.R.C. Simpson and J.Ø. Sunde (eds), *Comparative Perspectives in Scottish and Norwegian Legal History, Trade and Seafaring, 1200–1800* (Edinburgh, 2023), p. 122.

69 W.C. Dickinson, 'The Administration of Justice in Medieval Scotland', (1952) 34 *Aberdeen University Review* 338, at p. 351, expressed the point clearly – albeit at the cost of oversimplification – by saying that the problem was 'Scotland's failure to develop her own inns of court'.

70 A.M. Godfrey, *Civil Justice in Renaissance Scotland: The Origins of a Central Court* (Leiden, 2009). Lord Cooper would presumably have been prepared today to modify at least the dating of his thesis.

71 For a survey that may prove to be the owl of Minerva's view of this lawyers' law thesis see A.R.C. Simpson, 'The Scottish Common Law: Origins and Development, c. 1124-c. 1500', in

reference was made to an act of parliament passed in 1473 in which uneasiness was expressed about 'the gret diverseite now fundin in diverse bukis put in be diverse persones that ar callit men of law'.[72] The men of law who were producing books before the courts were presumably procurators hired by clients on the strength of their perceived expertise in some sort of law.[73] That they knew how to conduct court proceedings can scarcely be doubted, but it has also been suggested that in proceedings initiated by brieves they must also have teased out the more substantive significance of some of the language used in the documents, and that legal doctrine could thus have emerged from the handling of cases in the courts.[74] Even if this supposition could be substantiated, however, it would still have to be shown how the same legal doctrine could have been generated throughout the country.[75] It is far from obvious how this could have happened, for it seems more likely that (if substantive law did emerge from discussion of the brieves) each court would have developed its own law, and that law would have been common only in the sense that justice was being administered throughout the country by royal officials.[76] Admittedly, the 'men of law' mentioned in the 1473 act did have 'bukis' to produce before the courts. It has indeed been found that the collections of the 'auld lawes' in circulation contained not more or less accurate copies of *Regiam maiestatem* and associated texts but variants of the texts that were being actively modified to take account of more recent legislation and other sources of law.[77] Legal doctrine was thus being generated in the composition of the collections, yet among distinct scribal communities, which goes some way towards explaining why

H. Pihlajamäki, M.D. Dubber and A.M. Godfrey (eds), *The Oxford Handbook of European Legal History* (Oxford, 2018), p. 450.

72 *Acts of the Parliaments of Scotland*, vol. 2, p. 105; Records of the Parliaments of Scotland, 1473/7/17.

73 The question here is to what extent a secular profession, with common knowledge of law followed in secular courts, took shape. That there were ecclesiastical lawyers, appearing before ecclesiastical courts and presumably offering their services more widely too, is not especially interesting for present purposes. The type of common law with which they were familiar is considered in the final section of this essay.

74 H.L. MacQueen, 'Pleadable Brieves, Pleading and the Development of Scots law', (1986) 4 *Law and History Review* 403.

75 Of course, the point is that the lawyers who developed the common law of England met each other every day in the courts, inns or streets. There was no medieval equivalent of a WhatsApp group or Teams meeting.

76 D. Broun, 'The Treaty of Perth: Union of the Realm and the Laws of the Kingdom', in Simpson and Sunde (eds), *Comparative Perspectives in Scottish and Norwegian Legal History, Trade and Seafaring*, p. 63.

77 A. Taylor, 'Introduction', in *Regiam maiestatem: The Earliest Known Version*, ed. J. Reuben Davies and A. Taylor (Edinburgh, 2022), p. 1.

the diversity of the collections had become a problem. Even when passages of text remained fairly constant across different collections, it need not follow that the legal knowledge shared was knowledge of law in actual practice. It has been argued that *Regiam maiestatem* itself was not composed as a straightforward summary of the law in force in Scotland, but was an amalgamation of sources in need of adjustment to reflect Scottish practice.[78] Some passages never were adjusted, and before the book could be read as a reliable account of the law in force its original design had first to be forgotten.[79]

The sixteenth-century authors who searched for the common law of Scotland in the 'auld lawes' do appear to have read these books as authoritative texts. Welwod maintained that the 'reulis of Olon' had been 'receavit' as binding law in Scotland 'sa far as they are commonly knawin be peiple', yet he complained that he had found familiarity with them 'to be very litle in this cuntry', chiding merchants and mariners for ignorance of 'thair awne common lawe'.[80] His complaint is borne out by the evidence reviewed in the first section of this essay. Quite apart from the scarcity of references to the written codes of maritime law in the burgh records, the composition of the guildry book of Dundee suggests that the 'Schiplawis' in particular were not regarded as a component of 'the majestie'. Some procurators appeared before the burgh courts with such regularity that they probably would have been regarded as 'men of law', and actions in which they appeared were typically prolonged by technical arguments about court procedure.[81] Although points of procedure were sometimes referred to as the 'prattick of this burght' or the 'prattik and styill of this court', they were also referred to as the 'commoun law and practik of this realm' or the 'pratik and consuetude of this realme'.[82] The procedural law known to the men of law was to some extent seen as a common law, and it does appear that a broadly similar 'form of process' was in use throughout the country. If the expert procurators knew about this common procedural law, however, they relied on their clients for knowledge of the substantive law of

78 A. Taylor, 'What Does *Regiam maiestatem* Actually Say (and What Does It Mean)?', in W. Eves, J. Hudson, I. Ivarsen and S. White (eds), *Common Law, Civil Law and Colonial Law: Essays in Comparative Legal History from the Twelfth to the Twentieth Centuries* (Cambridge, 2021), p. 47. Understanding of this subject is likely to be transformed by a book the same author is working on at the moment.

79 S. Marshall, *Illegitimacy in Medieval Scotland, 1100–1500* (Woodbridge, 2021), pp. 29–53.

80 *Sea-Law of Scotland*, sig. A3. What he meant by the last phrase is returned to in the next paragraph.

81 An example can be found at ACA, CA1/1/33/1, pp. 237–8, 240–5, 248–52, 254–6 and 265.

82 ACA, CA1/1/8, p. 830, and CA1/1/24, p. 434; DCA, BCMB, vol. 3, 24 February 1552, and vol. 14, 17 October 1575; NRS, B20/10/2, f. 87r.

the sea. While that law too was referred to as the law of each burgh, it could be that when reference was made to 'the commoune practik in seafer causis', or 'the commond lawis concerning sefair causes', what was envisaged was not so much law common to all seafaring people as law common to the whole realm. Perhaps Scotland was understood to have its own common law of the sea, for in one case a party was said to have 'tane to preif be the cognicion of maisteris that ane schip, beand in dalefaring, be use and practik of this realm, aucht to pay hir part of steremanfe'.[83] If so, however, the common law consisted of customs that may have been influenced by the written codes of maritime law, not of rules the lawyers found written down in the 'auld lawes'. Moreover, although the treatise writers may perhaps have managed to move the practice of the admiralty courts towards closer engagement with the text of the 'Schiplawis' in particular, it would be rash for historians to conclude from the evidence available that it ever became a reliable statement of the law in force in Scotland. To put this another way, while some maritime customs may have been recognised throughout the country, they can only have formed a common law in a descriptive, rather than a prescriptive, sense. Indeed, while maritime law may have been exceptional, it has to be wondered whether the common law of Scotland may not more broadly have been common only in this sense.[84] As Scotland had much closer connections in the later Middle Ages with France than England, it is of some interest that common law in a descriptive sense was identified there by medieval authors.[85] Each region subject to the jurisdiction of the French crown had its own courts and customs, yet historians agree that

83 DCA, BCMB, vol. 3, 30 May 1553. In another case, mentioned in the eighth essay, reference was made to the 'consuetude of the cuntrie uset amangis uther pertineris in uther schippis' (NRS, B37/12/1, pp. 29–30), and after an argument about the 'pracktique usit' arose in another case mentioned there, the parties based their allegations on what was done 'in all uthers places' (SAUL, B10/8/6, pp. 56–7). In the same essay again it was noted that the burgh authorities in Edinburgh provided the lords of council and session with advice on 'the commoun custome of merchants' (NRS, CS4/4). There is also a case in which payment of custom duties was demanded 'conforme to use and prattik of the burrowis of this realme' (ACA, CA1/1/19, pp. 341–2), but it was not really a 'seafaring cause'.

84 The likelihood that maritime law was exceptional is diminished by the argument advanced in the first section that overseas trade was not governed by a written law common to all seafaring people. Any common law of the sea was again common only in a descriptive sense. Each burgh had its own set of legal customs, but some were known to be similar to those recognised in other countries, and some to those recognised in other burghs.

85 P. Petot, 'Le droit commun en France selon les coutumiers', (1960) 38 *Revue historique de droit français et étranger* 412.

the medieval authors had good reason to identify a 'droit commun de France'.[86] The evidence of continuity in the formation of Scots law, which has been used to refute Lord Cooper's claim that Scottish legal history consisted of a series of 'false starts and rejected experiments', should perhaps be attributed to the survival of popular customs rather than the emergence of expert jurisprudence.[87]

In investigating law that was common to the whole realm, French legal historians have the advantage over their Scottish counterparts that their local customs were officially redacted in the fifteenth and sixteenth centuries.[88] They do still have to overcome one obstacle, however, for the redacted customs, however faithfully they may have recorded existing practice, were changed in character by being fixed in written form.[89] Although the legal customs of Scotland were not turned into customary laws in the same way, the law reform commissions appointed in the fifteenth and sixteenth centuries – examined briefly in the first section of the fifth essay – were intended to change the character of the 'auld lawes'.[90] If the 'diverseite' of the books produced in the courts by men of law had resulted partly from their active revision in distinct scribal communities, and if the purpose of producing an authorised version was to standardise knowledge among lawyers throughout the country, a further consequence

86 A Castaldo, 'Pouvoir royal, droit savant et droit commun coutumier dans la France du Moyen Âge: À propos de vues nouvelles', (2007) 46 *Droits* 117, and (2008) 47 *Droits* 173.

87 W.D.H. Sellar, 'The Common Law of Scotland and the Common Law of England', in R.R. Davies (ed.), *The British Isles, 1100–1500: Comparisons, Contrasts and Connections* (Edinburgh, 1988), p. 82, and 'A Historical Perspective', in Lord Cooper, *The Scottish Legal Tradition: New Enlarged Edition*, ed. S.C. Styles (Edinburgh, 1991), p. 29. See further C.J. Neville, *Land, Law and People in Medieval Scotland* (Edinburgh, 2010), where the survival of 'Gaelic custom' is found to be inconsistent with the impression given by the 'auld lawes'. Historians of the 'whaur's yer Harrie Bracton noo?' variety may actually find it liberating to be relieved of their craving to demonstrate that whatever was done well in England was also done in Scotland.

88 R. Filhol, 'The Codification of Customary Law in France in the Fifteenth and Sixteenth Centuries', in H.J. Cohn (ed.), *Government in Reformation Europe, 1520–60* (London, 1971), p. 265.

89 The interventionist thesis expounded in J. Krynen, 'Entre science juridique et dirigisme: Le glas medieval de la coutume', (2000) 7 *Cahiers de recherches médiévales* 170, has been shown in the essay cited at n. 86 above to exaggerate the extent to which lawyers and other officials took the opportunity to 'correct' the customs they redacted, yet the written texts still need to be read with caution.

90 Although the resources available to Scottish legal historians are limited, they would become less limited if it were accepted that the common law existed in the minds of lay people rather than lawyers. The works of poets and historians, for instance, which are at most assumed to contain frustratingly unreliable reflections of the law known to lawyers, could be read as meaningful contributions to the spread of popular knowledge.

would have been to impede future development of legal knowledge in scribal communities. Skene tried to address this problem when he prepared an edition of the 'auld lawes' for publication at the end of the sixteenth century. A scribe he instructed to make a polished copy of a volume containing both Latin and Scots texts placed annotations after some passages and left blank pages after others.[91] Since the annotations were attached to passages near the start of the volume, the expectation may have been that Skene would provide more to be added later, yet it may instead have been the intention that blank pages would appear in a printed edition, on which readers would have been encouraged to follow Skene's example by adding comments of their own.[92] It was seen in the seventh essay that he did later encourage scholarly interaction with the texts in a preface attached to a printed edition composed entirely in Latin.[93] Some of the annotations included in the manuscript volume were preserved in the printed edition, where more were also added, but no pages were left blank, and fixing the texts in print obviously limited the possibilities of critical correction.[94] No annotations were included in a vernacular edition printed at the same time, in which lay people were encouraged to read the texts in a different way. After drawing attention to the repeated recognition in acts of parliament that 'all the statuts and constitutions written in these bukes were authentick and publick lawes', Skene warned his readers that they could have no further excuse for 'ignorance of the lawes', urging them to 'seik the knawledge and understanding thereof and give obedience conforme to the samine'.[95] He did not include the 'Schiplawis' in his editions, but it was essentially the same line of argument that Welwod advanced when he exhorted merchants and mariners to become more familiar with 'the wrets authorizit be our nation'.[96]

---

91 NLS, Adv. MS 7.1.10. See too G. Dolezalek, *Scotland under Jus Commune: Census of Manuscripts of Legal Literature in Scotland, Mainly between 1500 and 1660*, 3 vols (Edinburgh, 2010), vol. 2, p. 128. It is clear from dates added at the end of each section of material copied that the passages of text were written in 1601, and the annotations in 1602.

92 The rebinding of the volume in the nineteenth century makes it difficult to be sure how it was put together.

93 *Regiam maiestatem: Scotiae veteres leges et constitutiones*, ed. Sir John Skene of Curriehill (Edinburgh, 1609), sigg. A2–3.

94 An example of the kind of critical engagement Skene may still have hoped for is provided in the tenth essay. The English legislation with which he compared one provision from the 'auld lawes' has been discussed since that essay was written in D. Cressy, *Shipwrecks and the Bounty of the Sea* (Oxford, 2022), pp. 54–70.

95 *Regiam maiestatem: The Auld Lawes and Constitutions of Scotland*, ed. Sir John Skene of Curriehill (Edinburgh, 1609), sigg. A3v-5r.

96 *Sea-Law of Scotland*, sig. 3.

In presenting the 'auld lawes' to his lay readers Skene expressed the optimistic hope that 'albeit some of them are abrogat be posterior lawes, or be desuetude are obscured', the effect of their publication under royal licence might be to restore them to 'use and practick for good administration of justice and quyetnes of the realme'.[97] A kinsman of George Buchanan later recalled that his response to the problem of acts of parliament falling into desuetude had been to say that 'it would be good if one act were set in place by which the other acts were ordered to be observed'.[98] It was pointed out in the fifth essay that in 1578 Buchanan had in fact been appointed to a parliamentary commission instructed to assemble references to neglected acts in a new act that would serve to 'estableis the same as perpetuall lawes'.[99] Ineffective though it was, the commission reinforces the impression formed in that essay and elsewhere that the reform movement was connected with the lesson learned from ancient sources by Buchanan and other humanists that *consuetudines vagae* needed to be replaced with *leges certae*.[100] As both the reform movement in Scotland and the codification movement in France began in the fifteenth century, this humanist ideology offers a better explanation for the desire to replace customs with statutes than the interest university scholars started to take in local customs in the later sixteenth century.[101] Furthermore, the absence of any attempt to have local customs redacted in Scotland is also better explained by opposition to, as opposed to interest in, legal customs.[102] By the time the

97 *Regiam maiestatem: The Auld Lawes and Constitutions of Scotland*, sig. A5r.

98 Thomas Craig of Riccarton, *Jus feudale tribus libris comprehensum: Book 1*, ed. L. Dodd (Edinburgh, 2017), p. lxxxvii.

99 *Acts of the Parliaments of Scotland*, vol. 3, p. 105; Records of the Parliaments of Scotland, 1578/7/18.

100 J.D. Ford, 'Conciliar Authority and Equitable Jurisdiction in Early-Modern Scotland', in Godfrey, *Law and Authority in British Legal History*, p. 140, at pp. 141–50.

101 In R.A. Mason, *Kingship and the Commonweal: Political Thought in Renaissance and Reformation Scotland* (East Linton, 1998), pp. 104–38, the reform movement is connected with the rise of a secular legal profession in Scotland, and the humanism of these lawyers is contrasted with the scholasticism of clerics. If the argument that using the slogan *rex est imperator in regno suo* to justify James III's assumption of authority to appoint notaries probably carried connotations of legislative authority, given that it had that significance when used in England, seems in itself less than compelling, the slogan did also have similar significance elsewhere (A. Bossuat, 'The Maxim "The King is Emperor in His Kingdom": Its Use in the Fifteenth Century before the *Parlement* of Paris', in P.S. Lewis and G.F. Martin (eds), *The Recovery of France in the Fifteenth Century* (London, 1971), p. 185).

102 At the time of the Reformation, opposition to custom may have strengthened among lawyers familiar with a statement in the *Decretum* that 'in these matters in which nothing certain has been established by holy scripture, the custom of God's people and the practices of the majority are regarded as law' (D. 11 c. 7).

reform movement was revitalised in the later sixteenth century a different way of turning legal customs into customary laws had emerged. It has been seen in several earlier essays that court decisions were regarded in the burghs as contributions to the recognition of legal customs, notwithstanding that precedents were never cited in arguments there, whereas the fourth essay showed that in Edinburgh court decisions were regarded as a means of having customs both proved as fact and approved as law.[103] The terms of the reform commission of 1575 appear to have led Balfour and Skene to regard the decisions of the lords of session as a species of written law, and if customs were included in Balfour's *Practicks*, it can only have been in the form of rulings made by those judges after customs were alleged in arguments before them. In 1592, when Umphra Blindseil argued that the lords of session had the authority to lay down rules to be followed in lower courts, Balfour's book was starting to circulate among lawyers, who could also have been familiar with Jean Bodin's *Six livres de la république*.[104] In arguing that laws could only derive authority from a sovereign legislator, Bodin had observed that judges might be authorised to make laws, had insisted that customs could only be laws if they were approved or tolerated by a sovereign, and had added that if laws fell into desuetude they could always be revived by a sovereign.[105] As Skene was found in the seventh essay to have had an interest in the comparative legal history exemplified by Bodin's book, it is possible that he had it in mind when he addressed his lay readers.[106] If so, he was far from believing that common law emerged from ordinary people reaching agreements with each other throughout the country that certain modes of behaviour were customary, and that customs counted as

103 A different view appears to have been held in the burgh courts, as well as the central courts, in Edinburgh. It was seen in the ninth essay that the burgh council there tried to use its decisions to establish rules about general average. In the late 1570s entries were collected from the council register under the heading: 'Certane practiques or exampillis of punisment of all crymes withtin burght, conforme to the auld use and consuetude thairof, that it may be knawin quhow ilk cryme of law or consuetude aucht and suld now be punist, according to the wecht and gravity thairof. This may be ane instructioun be experience and ane warrand to follow heirafter' (NLS, Adv. MS 31.4.9, f. 169r).

104 Blindseil's argument was discussed at the end of the fourth essay and touched on again in the ninth essay.

105 *Les six livres de la Republique* (Paris, 1577), pp. 162–3; *The Six Bookes of a Commonweale*, tr. Richard Knolles (London, 1606), pp. 160–1.

106 The point is of course that Skene responded to the problem of desuetude in the same way as Bodin. It was not an especially effective response. If legislators could reenact statutes, as they often did in Scotland, what was to prevent the new acts from also being left in desuetude, as they often were in Scotland?

laws.[107] Even if the common law of medieval Scotland had consisted of popular customs more than professional expertise, the lawyers who wrote about it towards the end of the sixteenth century were only prepared to look for it in the books they read.

3 The Common Law of Europe

The concept of law that may have been beginning to acquire adherents in Scotland at the end of the sixteenth century is likely to appeal to lawyers today since it is readily recognisable.[108] Students are now taught to search for the law of Scotland in acts of parliament, failing which in decisions of the highest courts, failing which in a selection of old books accorded the same kind of binding authority.[109] Law can be discovered in these sources since there is agreement – constantly reaffirmed in their use – that the rules they state count as laws.[110] One challenge facing historians of modern Scots law is to explain how, when and why this agreement or set of agreements came into existence.[111] If it is correct, as has been argued here, that the law of the sea was found by

107 It is shown in K. Bowie, *Public Opinion in Early Modern Scotland, c. 1560–1707* (Cambridge, 2020) that the legal device of making a protestation was turned into a political device used to influence legislators. Perhaps this became necessary because law making had moved away from the localities in which protestations had originally been made – not so much the creation of a 'public sphere' as the replacement of one with another. It may matter that protestations have mostly been found in the burgh records from the earlier decades of the sixteenth century.

108 The distant echo here of H.L.A. Hart, *The Concept of Law* (Oxford, 1961), is deliberate, for the broad notion that law arises from a union of primary and secondary rules, including secondary rules of recognition, has been found instructive in attempting to make sense of early-modern Scots law. For a different view see D.J. Ibbetson, 'What Is Legal History a History of?', in A.D.E. Lewis and M. Lobban (eds), *Law and History* (Oxford, 2004), p. 33, at pp. 34–5.

109 M.H. Dewart, *The Scottish Legal System* (Haywards Heath, 2019), pp. 153–74.

110 The structural similarity between Hart's theory of law and Searle's theory of society may not be accidental, given that both these philosophers were closely associated with J.L. Austin (*cf.* N. Lacey, *A Life of H.L.A. Hart: The Nightmare and the Noble Dream* (Oxford, 2004), pp. 132–6).

111 Modern theorists of sovereignty tend to simplify the enquiry by identifying law with rules enforced by courts and concluding that only the views of the officials who staff the courts matter (J. Goldsworthy, *The Sovereignty of Parliament: History and Philosophy* (Oxford, 1999), pp. 9–16). But looking at law in this way itself needs to be investigated historically. There is of course a difference between viewing the application of rules by courts as evidence that they were regarded as laws, and thinking that rules could only have been laws if they were applied by courts.

the burgh courts of sixteenth-century Scotland in legal customs known to merchants and mariners, and if the common law of medieval Scotland may possibly have enjoyed the same character more generally, it will need to be explained how agreement that customs counted as laws came to be replaced with agreement that all law must derive from the exercise of sovereign authority.[112] The challenge is increased by the existence in early-modern Scotland of a third way of looking at the law.[113] When Skene told his lay readers that the authority of the 'auld lawes' was evident from many acts of parliament, his obvious point was that they had been clothed with legislative authority by the sovereign rulers of Scotland, yet his point may instead have been that parliaments had repeatedly recognised authority that the 'auld lawes' had already acquired, not from approval in sovereign legislation, nor from acceptance in popular custom, but from appreciation in the minds of experts of their learned authority.[114] As was seen in the seventh essay, in addressing his fellow lawyers Skene urged them to study the texts of medieval Scots law in the way they had learned to study the texts of ancient Roman law.[115] Although the relationship between the Scottish texts and legal practice seems to be as problematic as the relationship between the treatises on maritime law and the hearing of cases in the courts, both the texts and the treatises provide evidence of a view held in some quarters that law could take shape in the minds of lawyers.[116] Lord

112 Even if parliamentary sovereignty is recognised as the doctrine that holds today's legal system together, that doctrine must itself be dependent on an agreement made at a different level from the enactment of legislation or anything else of the kind. Writing the agreement down would not remove the need for an agreement either.

113 This view is examined in its later forms in J.D. Ford, *Law and Opinion in Scotland during the Seventeenth Century* (Oxford, 2007).

114 Skene certainly held the view that law could derive from sovereign legislation – no student of the civil law could have failed to believe as much. What is less clear is whether he or any of his colleagues accepted Bodin's novel claim that law could only ever derive from the exercise of sovereignty.

115 There was clearly some tension between the views Skene expressed to his lay and expert readers, or between the reform movement he was drawn into in Scotland and the learned method he had been taught in Germany. If the reading of the reform commissions proposed here is correct then the irony is that the endeavour to replace a customary common law with a body of written texts, capable of close study and exact application, had the effect of turning the texts into a different type of law as well. In other words, connecting the common law with the old texts obstructed the further development of both custom and learning. As Alice Taylor has remarked, Skene may have been consciously seeking to revive a medieval tradition of enquiry.

116 It is perfectly possible that when the men of law cited their diverse books in court it was not only in relation to the procedural 'practick' in which they were considered to be especially expert. While references to the 'auld lawes' have not been found in sixteenth-century

Cooper maintained that it did eventually become possible for Scots lawyers to fashion 'a first-class system of common law' after the creation of the College of Justice enabled them to devote their concentrated expertise to the solution of issues raised throughout the country. Skene's concern was that the law his colleagues in the College of Justice were fashioning was at risk of being slavishly dependent on the *ius commune* taught in the continental law schools.

In fact, in Skene's Latin edition of the 'auld lawes', and also in the collections of medieval texts he made use of in its compilation, the Scottish texts often were connected with the texts studied in the law schools.[117] How extensive knowledge of the learned laws had been is hard to tell. An act of parliament passed in 1496 required the heirs of landowners to 'remane at the grammer sculis quhill thai be competentlie foundit and have perfite Latyne, and thaireftir to remane thre yeris at the sculis of art and jure', so that they would have enough 'knawlege and understanding of the lawis' to administer justice correctly when they took over the running of their father's estates.[118] The aim of the act was to prevent the king's 'principale auditouris' – the forerunners of the judges who sat in the College of Justice – from being troubled with 'ilk small injure', and it was clearly believed both that the knowledge currently available in local courts was inadequate, and that it would not need to be raised to a significantly higher level to become adequate. The intention was not that students would master the liberal arts at Scottish universities before proceeding to learn the civil and canon laws at continental universities, as became fashionable among prospective advocates in the sixteenth century, but was that students of the arts at Scottish universities would in the course of a three year degree programme learn something about the law.[119] As was seen in the seventh essay, the association of a limited amount of instruction in law with study of the arts continued to appeal in the following century to humanist scholars, including Buchanan. The grandfather of Thomas Nicolson, the 'civilist' of the University of Aberdeen mentioned in that essay, was a notary public and a clerk of the bailie court there in the early sixteenth century, and was

---

cases concerned with seafaring, they have been noted in passing in the records of other cases. This need further investigation.

117 An example of particular interest for present purposes is the inclusion in some copies of the *Leges navium* or *Leges burgorum* of a provision about the collision of ships that appears to have been derived from D.9.2.29.2–5 (*Acts of the Parliaments of Scotland*, vol. 1, p. 753).

118 *Acts of the Parliaments of Scotland*, vol. 2, p. 238; Records of the Parliaments of Scotland, 1496/6/4.

119 *Cf.* L.J. Macfarlane, *William Elphinstone and the Kingdom of Scotland, 1431–1514: The Struggle for Order* (Aberdeen, 1995), pp. 312–13.

also described as an 'artium professor scribaeque communis vicecomitatus de Abirden'.[120] He may have had the combination of learning 'in art and jure' desired of officials in local courts, as may his son, also a notary public, who owned a copy of Lanfrancus de Oriano's *Practica iudiciaria*, together with other books on the civil and canon laws.[121] The technical points raised about court procedure by professional procurators in the burgh courts often owed something to the learned laws.[122] Indeed, it was in relation to court procedure that the only explicit reference to a text of the civil and canon laws encountered in the burgh records examined in the first and third parts of this collection was made.[123] A university graduate objected on behalf of some merchants he was representing that the pursuer could not renounce his action after it had gone to proof without the consent of the defenders, 'as is wretin in *C. lege postquam lite, de probationibus*'.[124] The reference makes no sense, though a different text could instead have been cited.[125] It has been observed in more than one essay that when notaries public drafted documents for merchants or mariners they sometimes relied on styles that were informed by the civil law, even though the extent of their knowledge of that law is doubtful. They referred, for example, to 'conductores (*or frauchtismen*)', but do not appear to have had much understanding of the use of the terms *conductor* and *locator* in the Roman law texts.[126] How much the merchants and mariners who received assistance from notaries and procurators knew about the learned laws is even more doubtful. While learned influence can be traced behind some of the legal customs they alleged, that influence appears to have been at least as distant as the influence of the written codes of maritime law. For example, though the idea that

120 *Records of the Sheriff Court of Aberdeenshire*, 3 vols, ed. D. Littlejohn (Aberdeen, 1904–7), vol. 1, pp. 464–8; *Illustrations of the Topography and Antiquities of the Shires of Aberdeen and Banff*, 4 vols, ed. J. Robertson (Aberdeen, 1847–69), vol. 4, p. 469; *Registrum episcopatus Aberdonensis*, 2 vols, ed. C. Innes (Edinburgh, 1845), vol. 2, pp. 112 and 323.

121 ACA, CA1/1/25, p. 332. The identity of the other books is less clear, but he may also have owned a copy of Baldus de Ubaldis' *Practica iudiciaria*. He owned treatises on moral theology as well.

122 In an argument about the admissability of 'weimen witnesses', reference was explicitly made to 'the lawis municipall, civill and canon', from which relevant texts were 'producit in judgment' (DCA, BCMB, vol. 12, 5 March 1572). This was not a 'seafaring cause', however.

123 ACA, CA1/1/27, p. 348.

124 Although the record does not say so, the procurator may have been a notary public.

125 Reference is more likely to have been made to N.112.3. It could have been the clerk of the court rather than the procurator who was confused, but he fell into the same category of educated men who were meant to know some law.

126 As Scottish notaries spent far more of their time dealing with transactions relating to land tenure, it could be that they had a better grasp of Roman property law.

certain types of loss sustained at sea should be distributed among the owners of ships and goods may ultimately have derived from Roman law, it was seen in the ninth essay that distributing losses had a fundamentally different purpose for merchants and mariners, on the one hand, and for learned lawyers, on the other.[127]

It has been suggested recently that in seeking to make sense of how lay people understood the law in late-medieval Scotland, it helps to consider the presence of what sociologists mean when they talk about 'legal consciousness'.[128] It does not help historians that the expression means different things to different sociologists.[129] If it has a core meaning it seems to be that social behaviour cannot be properly explained unless account is taken of the various ways in which people act in relation to law, which is regarded by ordinary people as something that is made elsewhere and better understood by other people. Seen in this way, the idea of legal consciousness does help to make sense of at least some of the ways in which lay people continued to behave in the sixteenth century.[130] It has been argued elsewhere, for instance, that the violent seizure of ships and goods at sea was understood by lawyers to be governed by national laws formed within a framework of legitimacy provided by the laws studied in universities everywhere in Europe.[131] The records of the burgh courts reveal that lay people had some awareness of the prize law developed in Scotland and behaved in accordance with that awareness, even if they did not know much about the theory of the schools, and they also show that those courts were sometimes reluctant to deal with issues that were known to be dealt with in the central courts, in accordance with law that was better

127 While in one case an allusion may have been made to a *Digest* text stating that passengers carrying nothing more than rings or money should contribute to losses, the text was not cited, and may have been brought to the attention of the court by advocates consulted by the Edinburgh merchants involved in the case.

128 A.R. Borthwick and H.L. MacQueen, *Law, Lordship and Tenure: The Fall of the Black Douglases* (St Andrews, 2022), pp. 5–9.

129 *Cf.* L.J. Chua and D.M. Engel, 'Legal Consciousness Reconsidered', (2019) 15 *Annual Review of Law and Social Science* 335.

130 A striking example may seem to be the case considered in the eighth essay in which an inquest declared that the law would not force a master to visit a port infected with the plague, 'as thai understand' or 'as thai belevit' (ACA, CA1/1/12/2, pp. 689–90). Reference was clearly being made to some other law than the legal customs in which the inquest was expected to be expert, but what may have been remembered were the writings of Cicero and Seneca that were influencing the development of canonist doctrine rather than canon law itself.

131 J.D. Ford, *The Emergence of Privateering* (Leiden, 2023), pp. 8–101.

understood there.[132] Another example of this kind of legal consciousness may have been the recovery of goods from ships wrecked in Scotland – examined in the tenth essay – since lay people asserted rights as salvors in the burgh courts, but also acted in the knowledge that actions of 'spuilzie' might be raised before the lords of council and session. To a take a more pervasive example, whenever merchants and mariners employed notaries or other procurators to represent them in the courts, their reason for doing so may partly have been the need to comply with procedural standards with which these 'men of law' were more familiar. Similarly, when they employed notaries to prepare documents for them, they may have understood that the documents needed to satisfy legal niceties of which they were only dimly aware themselves. In the eighth essay, for example, it was seen that bills drawn up throughout Scotland for the sale of ships contained clauses that could have been explained by university graduates in law but would almost certainly have puzzled merchants and mariners, though possibly also the average notary. On the other hand, it was also seen in the same essay that the law governing the effects of the sale of ships on the rights and responsibilities of their owners was reckoned to be best known to merchants and mariners themselves, as indeed was most of the maritime law applied to seafaring causes in the burgh courts.[133] In the broad sense understood here, legal consciousness does not help to elucidate this kind of law, which, it has been suggested above, may have been more broadly characteristic of the common law of Scotland before the sixteenth century.[134] While merchants and mariners did have some awareness that written laws made elsewhere, and better known to other people, were designed to have some bearing on their activities, it was their own customs that they regarded as laws, and because they regarded them as laws.[135]

132 *Extracts from the Council Register of the Burgh of Aberdeen*, 2 vols, ed. J. Stuart (Aberdeen, 1844–8), vol. 1, pp. 304–6; ACA, CA1/1/9, p. 348, CA1/1/18, pp. 241, 243, 247–8 and 251–2, and CA1/1/22, p. 590–2 and 596.

133 The fact that some merchants and mariners were believed to be more expert than others does not prevent the law of the sea from being essentially what all merchants and mariners agreed that it was. Some lawyers are more expert than others, but this does not stop the others from being expert in law.

134 It is not entirely helpful either to associate the notion with the 'common knowledge' discussed in C. Hawes, 'Reassessing the Political Community: Politics and the Public Domain in Fifteenth-Century Scotland', about to appear in the next Stair Society miscellany volume, which appears to be a broader notion capable of embracing legal customs.

135 It follows that traces of influence from written laws cannot be used as a pretext for reconstructing legal customs in the light of those laws. *Cf.* M.I. Finley, *The Use and Abuse of History* (London, 1975), pp. 134–52.

When it was said in 1591 that lay people were expected 'to knowe onely the comon lawes of this realme', because 'knowledge of the civill lawe appertayneth to the lords of the session and such like', a distinction was being drawn not simply between two different bodies of law but also between two different modes of legal enquiry.[136] Whereas lay people focused on the customs they described to each other, paying scarcely any attention to the written sources that may have influenced their development, learned lawyers focused on written sources, ignoring customs unless they were brought to their attention by lay people.[137] As Sir John Baker put it in relation to the common law of England, customs can only form part of the law found in the minds of lawyers to the extent that they come within the contemplation and understanding of those lawyers.[138] Skene recognised that this might happen in reminding his fellow advocates of the basic civilian precept that 'in each state and realm written law should be followed first, second place ought to be assigned to usage and inveterate custom, and recourse should lastly be taken to foreign laws and the usage of alien nations'.[139] He was alluding quite obviously to the *Digest* text, mentioned in the fourth essay, in which it was observed that in the absence of *leges scriptae* the law ought to be searched for in *mores et consuetudo*, failing which in *quod proximum et consequens ei est*, failing which in *ius, quo urbs Roma utitur*.[140] The expression 'what is closest and following from it' was usually taken to invite reasoning by analogy, and the expression 'the law that the city of Rome uses' to invite recourse to the civil law, but both were sometimes taken together to invite recourse to the example of laws used in neighbouring and other nations.[141] Skene aimed to reduce the need for recourse to either usage and custom or foreign laws by publishing editions of the written laws of

136 This statement, touched on in previous essays, appears in *Calendar of State Papers Relating to Scotland and Mary, Queen of Scots, 1547–1603*, 13 vols, ed. J. Bain, W.K. Boyd, H.W. Meikle, A.I. Cameron, M.S. Giuseppi and J.D. Mackie (Edinburgh, 1898–1969), vol. 10, p. 525. It may well have been intended that the first mode of enquiry would be modified to take greater account of acts of parliament and other written sources of Scots law.

137 *Cf.* R.C. Van Caenegem, *Law, History, the Low Countries and Europe*, ed. L. Milis, D. Lambrecht, H. De Ridder-Symoens and M. Vleeschouwers-Van Melkebeek (London, 1994), pp. 119–33.

138 J.H. Baker, *The Law's Two Bodies: Some Evidential Problems in English Legal History* (Oxford, 2001), pp. 2 and 60–3, mentioned at the beginning of the fourth essay.

139 *Regiam maiestatem: Scotiae veteres leges et constitutiones*, sig. A3r.

140 D.1.3.32.

141 A strikingly similar interpretation to Skene's can be found in David Chalmers of Ormond, *Compendium of the Laws of Scotland*, ed. W. Coutts, J. Goodare and A.R.C. Simpson (Edinburgh, 2023), p. 191, in a dedicatory epistle attached to another book that may have been connected with the law reform movement.

Scotland and promoting the view (implicit in most of the law reform commissions) that the common law of Scotland was to be found in the 'auld lawes'.[142] In assuring his lay readers that statutes were merely 'obscured' when they fell into desuetude, he was again prioritising written over unwritten laws. He was also departing from the *Digest* text, which had gone on to allow for desuetude, and opposing the tendency of learned lawyers to accept that statutes could be deprived of force by popular disapproval, which might serve – along with their strict interpretation – to increase the need for recourse to the civil law.[143] Although the effect of desuetude could have been to replace statutes with customs, because customs that had not yet been reduced to writing needed to be both proved and approved in courts before they could be known to lawyers, the tendency of more learned lawyers was to move directly from the discovery that no legislation was available to discussion of the civil law.[144] As was seen in the fourth essay, even if customs were proved to exist, their approval often depended on appraisal of their consistency with the civil law, to see whether they could be reconciled with the theoretical expectations that lawyers formed during their university studies. To revert to England, it has been found that the customs of merchants were gradually absorbed there into the common law of the realm by a similar process of both proof and approval, though subject to appraisal of their consistency with the shared erudition of the legal profession.[145] The early centralisation of the administration of justice in England had enabled local customs more generally to be drawn into the common law by the sixteenth century.[146] In contrast, though the development of Scots law was more continuous than Lord Cooper realised, the customs of merchants and mariners had certainly not been absorbed into the law known to practitioners in the central courts of Scotland by the same time. It is indeed hard to see how

142 As was seen in the seventh essay, Skene was also keen to compare local statutes and customs not with the civil law so much as foreign laws more generally.

143 *Regiam maiestatem: The Auld Lawes and Constitutions of Scotland*, sig. A5r.

144 Compare L. Warner, 'Customary Law? Roman Law? Sixteenth-Century Lawyers' Pleadings before the *Parlement de Paris*', in A. Bauer and K.H.L. Welker (eds), *Europa und seine Regionen: 2000 Jahre Rechtsgeschichte* (Cologne, 2007), p. 253, with D. De ruysscher, 'From Usages of Merchants to Default Rules: Practices of Trade, *Ius commune* and Urban Law in Early-Modern Antwerp', (2012) 33 *Journal of Legal History* 3.

145 J.H. Baker, 'The Law Merchant and the Common Law before 1700', (1979) 38 *Cambridge Law Journal* 295.

146 P. Tucker, *Law Courts and Lawyers in the City of London, 1300–1550* (Cambridge, 2007) points out, though, that the extent to which local custom simply gave way to the common law can be exaggerated.

custom could possibly have formed part of the collective expertise of a unified profession before the foundation of the College of Justice.[147]

It has been argued that continental treatise writers sought to accommodate commercial law within the *ius commune* taught in the universities in much the same way as court practitioners in England absorbed it into their common erudition.[148] Bartolus de Sassoferrato had observed, when commenting on the *Digest* text paraphrased by Skene, that customs could be reduced to writing either officially, in which case the *auctoritas superioris* directing the redaction would render them necessarily binding, or unofficially, in which case they could acquire the force of probability from *auctoritas excellentis doctoris*.[149] It was suggested in the seventh essay that it was this second sort of authority that Alexander King hoped to exercise in writing a treatise that would 'leave to posterity, out of unwritten laws or vague custom, clearly defined laws to be read'.[150] He had apparently consulted learned advocates along with business experts when writing, as he also did when presiding over hearings in the central admiralty court, and it was for his learned colleagues in particular that he provided in his treatise the means to appraise customs alleged in the court against the standards of the *ius commune*. His aim was not to stabilise legal customs by setting them down in writing, but to have them turned into another type of written law by clothing them with learned authority. While his laws would still be like customs in taking their force from agreement, he was relying on a consensus reached among learned lawyers at one level that any consensus they reached at another level would count as law. His laws would also resemble legislation in being legible, though their authority would come from their being written by an author capable of augmenting a textual tradition. King's understanding of maritime law was thus fundamentally different from the understanding both of the merchants and mariners who believed that customs counted as law, and of the lawyers and others who were beginning to believe that only rules imposed by sovereign legislators or judges could count as law. How far his understanding was shared by the other treatise writers is impossible to tell since they addressed a different audience. By the time Balfour put

147 The suggestion in R.A. Houston, 'Custom in Context: Medieval and Early-Modern Scotland and England', (2011) 211 *Past and Present* 35, that custom contributed less to the development of the law in Scotland than in England may be the opposite of the truth. Custom was undoubtedly more important in Scotland than it is made to appear in that essay.

148 C. Donahue, 'Medieval and Early-Modern *Lex mercatoria*: An Attempt at the *Probatio diabolica*', (2004) 5 *Chicago Journal of International Law* 21.

149 *Opera quae nunc extant omnia*, 10 vols (Basel, 1588–9), vol. 1, pp. 67–8 (ad D.1.3.32.1).

150 *Alexander King's Treatise on Maritime Law*, pp. 6–9.

his separate appendix on sea law together he had decided that his task in writing must be to make the law 'mair familiar and the bettar knawin to all oure soverane lordis liegis and pepill off his realme'.[151] He may have adhered to the assumption behind the law reform commission of 1575 that a comprehensive restatement of Scots law could be provided without recourse to the learned laws, or he may have agreed with his assistant Skene that lay readers needed to be addressed in different terms from professional readers.[152] Skene urged his fellow lawyers to study their native sources in the way they had learned to study the civil law, enhancing their appreciation of those sources by comparing them with foreign laws, yet without reading them restrictively if they conflicted with the civil law.[153] His interest in comparative legal history was shared by Welwod, who considered it appropriate to draw the attention of 'all seafairing men' not only to the written texts that lay behind their own common law, but also to the written texts of the civil law, together with those of other foreign laws, from which the intrinsic reason and equity of provisions could be identified.[154] Although none of the writers on maritime law believed that the civil law was itself part of the law of Scotland, as a body of rules immediately applicable in the absence of rules found in local sources, at least two did believe that the law applied in practice could be developed further in the light of the theory taught in the law schools.[155]

151 NRS, GD112/71/5, f. 5r.

152 On the one hand, Balfour gave a firm impression that the 'practicks' of the session were authoritative simply as decisions of the court, not manifestations of any authority residing in other sources. On the other hand, since he concentrated on questions about which decisions had already been delivered, the possibility remains that he may have expected novel questions to be answered through recourse to the learned laws, about which lay people were not expected to be knowledgeable. On balance, the authority attributed to the decisions does seem to make it more likely that he regarded the learned laws as nothing more than examples that the judges might choose to follow or not, but it is difficult to be certain. See too the argument advanced in the seventh essay.

153 A.R.C. Simpson, 'The Authority of the Laws of Scotland in Chalmers' *Compendium*', in *Compendium of the Laws of Scotland*, p. 61, argues that the reference to foreign laws instead of the civil law in the passage cited at n. 141 above was already meant to limit use of the learned laws, before the rise of comparative legal history.

154 *Sea-Law of Scotland*, sig. A1r.

155 A view more consistent with the *mos Italicus* was held during the first two or three decades of the existence of the College of Justice (G. Dolezalek, 'The Court of Session as a *Ius commune* Court', in H.L. MacQueen (ed.), *Stair Society: Miscellany Four* (Edinburgh, 2002), p. 51; A.L. Murray and G. Dolezalek, 'Legal Argumentation and Citation of *Ius commune* Sources in Pleadings in the Court of Session, 1549/50', in Godfrey (ed.), *Stair Society: Miscellany Eight*, p. 113). How one view gave way to the other will be investigated by Andrew Simpson in a book anticipated in (for example) 'Legislation and Authority in Early-Modern Scotland', in Godfrey (ed.), *Law and Authority in British Legal History*, p. 85.

Given that these writers were trying to steer further development of the law in a particular direction, their treatises cannot be read as straightforward summaries of the maritime law in force in sixteenth-century Scotland.[156] Indications have been found in a couple of essays that the practice of the admiralty courts may have been moving in the direction the treatise writers desired, but with only a fragment of the records of these courts to work from, it is impossible to proceed far beyond speculation.[157] More information is available about the practice of the burgh courts. Significant gaps in the surviving records, along with the fluid nature of the legal customs they disclose, mean that considerable caution is also required in drawing conclusions about the law applied in those courts.[158] Nevertheless, it has proved possible in several essays to form an impression of rules that were in force at certain times and certain places, or even at various times and various places. Although it cannot be known how representative these rules would have seemed had fuller records been available, they do obviously need to be taken into account in any attempt to reconstruct the history of the law governing maritime commerce in sixteenth-century Scotland. Indeed, if a general conclusion may be drawn from this collection of essays, it has to be that the history of maritime law, and of commercial law more broadly – and perhaps even of private law more broadly still – cannot be written unless the records that do survive from the burgh courts are thoroughly examined.[159] Although the admiralty courts assumed responsibility at one stage for the handling of all seafaring causes, the burgh courts continued to hear actions between merchants into the seventeenth century.[160]

156 Still less can Welwod's *Abridgement of all Sea-Lawes* (London, 1613) be read as a straightforward account of the law in force in seventeenth-century England, as has often been done (*e.g.* W.S. Holdsworth, *A History of English Law*, 16 vols (London, 1922–66), vol. 8, pp. 245–73).

157 As has been pointed out, the records that do survive from the central court may give a misleading impression of how cases were handled in the other courts. Whereas King was addressing the advocates who appeared in the central court, Welwod was addressing the merchants and mariners who may have continued to play a prominent part in the proceedings of the other admiralty courts as well as the burgh courts.

158 *Cf.* A. Wood, *The Memory of the People: Custom and Popular Senses of the Past in Early Modern England* (Cambridge, 2013), p. 141.

159 The same is probably true of the records of other local courts in relation to other branches of the law. In each case it has first to be asked where disputes were being raised for determination, though also (of course) whether other types of source may be instructive. It is unfortunate that no evidence has been found to show how masters maintained order on board ships.

160 Whether the burgh courts regained jurisdiction over seafaring causes is itself in need of further investigation.

It needs to be discovered whether legal customs developed in the burgh courts were in fact incorporated as customary laws into the learned jurisprudence developed in the College of Justice, and if so, what impact they had on that jurisprudence. It also needs to be discovered whether it came to be accepted in the burgh courts that binding rules could be imposed by acts of parliament and decisions of the session, and if so, when exactly this happened. If another general conclusion may be drawn from this collection, it is that to enquire into the law in force in the past without also enquiring into where it was looked for is a recipe for misunderstanding.[161] When lawyers decide to try their hands at writing history they tend to search for the origins of today's laws in sources of types they are familiar with – legislation, court decisions, old books – and to read these sources in the ways they usually do. Of course, at some stage it must have been agreed that only rules found in certain written sources were to count as laws, and that they should be interpreted in ways learned by lawyers, but this was itself an event in the history of the legal system.[162] The lawyers eventually won the argument about where and how the law should be found, and everyone knows that 'history is written by the winners', yet the point of this saying is that the winners cannot be trusted to write history accurately.[163]

---

161 In Hart's terms, primary rules cannot be investigated in isolation from secondary rules (allowing for the lax use that needs to be made here of the word rules, which is best understood in terms of Wittgenstein's account of rule following).

162 The view that was only starting to take shape in the minds of lawyers at the end of the sixteenth century must somehow have prevailed over the view held by lay people, like the merchants and mariners studied here, and the view more widely held by lawyers. This was a competition not between sources of law – legislation, custom and learning – but between views of how all the sources should be related to each other. For some reflections on the seventeenth century see J.D. Ford, 'Paradigms of Authority in the College of Justice in Scotland', in G. Rossi (ed.), *Authorities in Early-Modern Courts* (Edinburgh, 2021), p. 29.

163 It would clearly be a mistake to presume that a movement from the legal customs of merchants and mariners to the jurisprudence of learned lawyers was an improvement. Viewing commercial practice through the lens of the civil law created complications in the minds of lawyers that they struggled to overcome. It never crossed the minds of merchants and mariners, for instance, that *ex nudo pacto non oritur actio*. See now S. Bogle, *Contract before the Enlightenment: The Ideas of James Dalrymple, Viscount Stair, 1619–95* (Oxford, 2023).

Index

www.ingramcontent.com/pod-product-compliance
Lightning Source LLC
LaVergne TN
LVHW010541300926
849162LV00002B/202

* 9 7 8 9 0 0 4 6 9 4 9 9 6 *